To the loving memory of my mother Laura and to my father Giuliano.

This book would not exist, were it not for the unwavering support and terrific help of my wife Silvia. This work is as much hers as mine.

I'm older now,
but still runnin' against the wind

Bob Seger, *Against the Wind*

About the Book Cover

The cover and title of this book are tributes to Joe Kaufman's *What Makes It Go?, Work?, Fly?, Float?*, which inspired my childhood with the love for technology.

It is not an exaggeration to say that if I had not read Mr. Kaufman's book around age seven, I would not have written this one forty years later.

The book cover is by Paolina Brando.

Paolina has her own unique style, but was kind enough to imitate Mr. Kaufman's illustrations at my request.

Discover more about Paolina's creations at *www.paolinabrando.com*.

What Makes It Page?

The Windows 7 (x64) Virtual Memory Manager

Downloadable Code

Much of the material for this book has been obtained by means of experiments performed with test programs. These experiments are described in detail, so that readers can reproduce the results, if they choose to do so. The test programs can be downloaded at

http://www.opening-windows.com/wmip/testcode/testcode.htm

The download package includes all the source code.

Important Note

These programs include test kernel mode drivers which call undocumented functions to demonstrate some of the concepts. These drivers must be considered *experimental software*, as they are likely to cause instability and system crashes. Also, they work only on Windows 7 x64 RTM (i.e. without service packs) and are almost guaranteed to crash any other version of Windows. The download package includes source code for all the programs, including the drivers, so readers can adapt them to different Windows versions.

More details are provided in the description of each experiment.

Analyzed Kernel Build

The analysis presented in this book has been conducted on the kernel included in Windows 7 x64 RTM, without service pack 1 and with no updates installed. All the excerpts from debugging sessions were obtained for this particular build. The following report, extracted with the `lm v` command of WinDbg provides full details about the analyzed kernel image:

```
0: kd> lm v m nt
start             end               module name
fffff800`02808000 fffff800`02de5000   nt         (pdb symbols)
c:\apps\pw7hp\devpgm\symw7x64retail\ntkrnlmp.pdb\F8E2A8B5C9B74BF4A6E4A48F180099942\ntkr
nlmp.pdb
    Loaded symbol image file: ntkrnlmp.exe
    Image path: ntkrnlmp.exe
    Image name: ntkrnlmp.exe
    Timestamp:        Tue Jul 14 01:40:48 2009 (4A5BC600)
    CheckSum:         0054B487
    ImageSize:        005DD000
    File version:     6.1.7600.16385
    Product version:  6.1.7600.16385
    File flags:       0 (Mask 3F)
    File OS:          40004 NT Win32
    File type:        1.0 App
    File date:        00000000.00000000
    Translations:     0409.04b0
    CompanyName:      Microsoft Corporation
```

```
ProductName:        Microsoft® Windows® Operating System
InternalName:       ntkrnlmp.exe
OriginalFilename:   ntkrnlmp.exe
ProductVersion:     6.1.7600.16385
FileVersion:        6.1.7600.16385 (win7_rtm.090713-1255)
FileDescription:    NT Kernel & System
LegalCopyright:     © Microsoft Corporation. All rights reserved.
```

Table of Contents

Part I Intel Architecture Basics

1 Introduction

The aim of Part I is to give just the minimum amount of information about the Intel architecture needed to fully understand the rest of this book. Nothing Windows-related is presented here, so readers who are already familiar with how the processor works can safely skip to part II.

This introduction is by no means a complete description of the processor. Full details can be found in the Software's Developer Manual, freely available from the Intel website.

Also, this introduction explains how the processor works when it is set up *like Windows do*es. Several statements made in the following sections are true only when a number of data structures that the processor uses for itself are set up int the way Windows sees fit. As an example, we will state later that an interrupt changes the privilege level at which the processor executes. This is not set in neither in stone, nor in silicon, but stems from how Windows sets up a data structure called Interrupt Descriptor Table. This approach has been adopted to keep things simple, considering this is, after all, a book on Windows.

2 Privilege Levels

2.1 Definition of Privilege Level

The processor maintains an internal state called the *current privilege level* (CPL), which is used to determine whether certain operations can be executed or not.

Four privilege levels are defined, identified by numerical values ranging from 0 to 3, with 0 being the most privileged one.

Windows configures the processor to use only privilege 0 and 3, so we will restrict our analysis to these two levels from now on.

At any given time, the processor is executing at one of the possible levels and its effect is to restrict what can be done:

- Certain instructions can be executed only at CPL 0

- Certain memory regions can be configured to be accessible only at CPL 0

- I/O ports can be configured to be accessible only at CPL 0

Consider now a program being executed while the CPL is 3. What does it happen if the program attempts one of these forbidden operations? The processor generates what is called an exception, which will be explained in greater detail in sec. 4.2 on p. 13. For now, we will only say that the processor jumps to the address of a function which is part of the operating system and has the job to deal with the situation. The forbidden operation is not executed, e.g. an attempt to write to a protected memory location leaves the memory content untouched.

2.2   Code Privilege Level

According to the definition given in the previous section, the CPL is a state of the processor. We can also define a privilege level for code, as the CPL of the processor while it executes a given section of code.

Conceptually, this definition does not assign a single privilege level to a given piece of code in memory: the same block of instructions could be executed while the processor is at CPL 0 or 3.

In Windows, however this never happen: certain parts of code are always executed at CPL 0, others at CPL 3. For code that resides in memory accessible only at CPL 0, this is actually enforced by the processor: an attempt to execute this code generates an exception. Code residing in memory accessible at CPL 3 *could* be executed while the CPL is 0, but Windows is not designed to do so.

Normally, application code and parts of the operating system are executed at CPL 3, while CPL 0 is used only for operating system code (and third party OS extensions lik device drivers).

2.3   Definition of Rings

It is common to represent the four privilege levels with the diagram below:

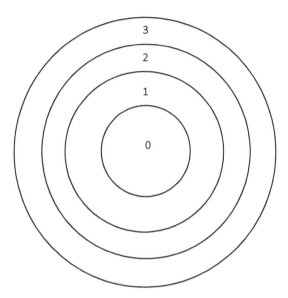

Figure 1 - Privilege Rings

which shows that level 0 is the most protected and level 3 the least protected. This diagram led to the use of the term *ring* as a substitute for privilege level, so when we say that the processor is at ring 0 we actually mean that the CPL is 0.

We will use the terms *ring 0 code* and *ring 3 code* with similar meaning.

2.4   Privilege Level Transitions

Now that we know that the processor can be at different privilege levels, we must ask ourselves how the CPL is changed. This will be the subject of the next sections.

2.4.1 Instructions for Privilege Control

There are specific instructions for changing the CPL. Examples are `syscall`, which goes from CPL 3 to CPL 0 and `sysret`, which reverts back to CPL 3. These instructions couple the CPL change with a jump to a new address, which must be loaded into a processor register before executing them. Normally, these instructions are used to call ring 0 code part of the operating system, so it makes sense to change the CPL and transfer control to somewhere else at the same time.

The register storing the address to which `syscall` jumps can be modified only when the CPL is 0, so ring 3 code cannot change it. This means that application code cannot change the entry point into operating system code.

`syscall` saves the current instruction pointer (`rip`) in the `rcx` register, so the destination code can save it somewhere in memory and use it later to return to the calling code with `sysret`.

2.4.2 Hardware Interrupts

An hardware interrupt occurring while the processor is executing ring 3 code causes it to jump to a different address and to set the CPL to 0 (again, this is how things work in Windows). We will describe interrupts in more detail in sec. 4.1 on p. 8, but we need to mention them here, because, as we said, they can cause a CPL change.

When an interrupt occurs, the address at which the processor was executing (that is, the value of `rip`) and the CPL (held in the `CS` processor register) are saved on the stack (more details on stack handling in Chapter 3 on p. 7), so they can later be used to resume the code that was interrupted. The `iret` instruction, which is meant for this, loads `rip` and `CS` with values from the stack, so this instruction can change the CPL from 0 to 3. By design, the CPL loaded from the stack by `iret` can either be the same as the current one (this happens if the interrupt occurred at ring 0) or be a numerically higher, i.e. less privileged, value. In simple terms, `iret` can go from ring 0 to ring 3, but cannot go from ring 3 to ring 0.

2.4.3 Processor Exceptions

Processor exceptions are similar to interrupts in the sense that they too result in the processor jumping to a different address and setting the CPL to 0, if it is currently 3. However, exceptions are generated by the processor itself and caused by the instruction being executed. An example is a `div` (unsigned division) instruction attempting to divide by 0. Since this operation is undefined, the processor generates an exception and transfer control to its handler. Exceptions will be described in more detail in sec. 4.2 on p. 13, so, for now, we will just say that, when the processor generates them, it saves the current `rip` and `CS` on the stack, then jumps to ring 0 code, just like it does for hardware interrupts. If the exception occurred at ring 3 this result in a privilege level transition.

`iret` can also be used to resume code interrupted by exceptions, eventually transitioning from ring 0 to ring 3.

3 The Stack

3.1 Basic Concept

The stack is an address range used implicitly by several processor instructions and by other processor mechanisms, like interrupt handling. When the processor accesses the stack implicitly, it does so through the `rsp` register.

As an example, we can consider the `call` instruction, used to call a function. When executing a `call`, the processor performs these steps:

- Decrements `rsp` by 8 bytes.

- Saves the address of the instruction after the `call` at the memory address pointed by `rsp`.

- Loads `rip` with the destination address, specified as part of the instruction.

The end result is that the processor has jumped to a new address, but has saved the address it was at on the stack. The companion `ret` instruction can later be used to return to the point of the call. `ret` performs the following steps:

- Loads `rip` with the value found at the address pointed by `rsp`.

- Increments `rsp` by 8.

There are a couple of things worth noting about this example.

First, `rsp`, which is called the *stack pointer* is decremented when a new value is written to the stack. In other words, `rsp` is initialized, e.g. by the OS when a process is started, to a suitable value and the region *below* the initial value is used. This is usually expressed saying that the stack *grows downward*.

The second, more subtle point concerns the return address. For a programmer used to high level languages, returning from a function means returning to the statement after the function call. In a C function, the `return` statement is used to go to whatever is written after the function invocation.

8   What Makes It Page?

At the processor level, there is *no relationship* between a `ret` and the instructions executed before. `ret` always performs the same, elementary actions: loads whatever is pointed by `rsp` into `rip`, then moves `rsp` up by 8 bytes.

Thus, a `ret` could be used to tansfer control to an entirely different address from the one saved by the preceding `call`.

But it does not stop here: a `ret` could be used even *without* a preceding `call`. The processor does not keep track of `call`s internally and does not attempt to match a `ret` with some internally preserved state representing the fact that a `call` was executed earlier. It simply performs the steps we described: load `rip`, move `rsp` and on we go, wherever it may be.

The stack is also used implicitly by other processor instructions like `push` and `pop`, which store and load, respectively, data to/from it and update `rsp` automatically.

Another example of stack usage is the handling of interrupt and exceptions, described in the next chapter.

3.2   Ring 0 Stack vs Ring 3 Stack

The processor uses different stacks, i.e. different values of `rsp` for CPL 0 and CPL 3.

`rsp` is loaded with the address of the right stack when a privilege change occurs. For interrupt and exceptions, this is done automatically by the processor. For `syscall` and `sysret`, it is done by OS code.

In general, this is useful to separate application state and variables from OS state. For this reason, the OS usually sets up the address range used at ring 0 as inaccessible from ring 3.

We will return on the importance of this separation in the upcoming section about interrupts and exceptions.

4 Interrupts and Exceptions

4.1   Interrupts

4.1.1 Handling an Interrupt

Interrupts are caused by devices sending electric signals to the chipset and processor, to cause the latter to execute some code which interacts with the devices themselves. An example could be a disk controller sending an interrupt to signal that it has finished transferring data to memory. We will refer to the actions the processor takes in response to an interrupt as *handling* or *servicing* the interrupt.

Each hardware interrupt is associated with a number called the *interrupt vector*, which is supplied to the processor when the interrupt is requested. The processor uses the vector as an index into a data structure called *Interrupt Descriptor Table* (IDT). Each entry of this table store a data structure, called a *gate*, which contains the address to which execution must be transferred and other control information. In summary, each hardware interrupt causes the processor to jump to the address specified in its associated IDT entry.

If an hardware interrupt occurs while the processor is at ring 3, the CPL is changed to 0 (at least, this is how things work when the IDT is set up like Windows does). If the processor is already at ring 0, the CPL does not change.

The IDT can be modified only at CPL 0. This is the same approach adopted for the destination address of `syscall`: application code cannot change the destination address of a mechanism that switches to CPL 0.

Normally, the code at the address found in the IDT is part of the operating system and is called an *interrupt handler routine*. During boot, the OS loads its interrupt handlers in memory and initializes the IDT to point to them.

When the processor receives an interrupt, it executes the following steps:

- Completes executing the current instruction. Interrupts are always serviced at instruction boundaries. E.g., if an instruction updates the content of a processor register and of a memory location, both updates are carried out before the interrupt is serviced.

- Saves the current stack pointer (`rsp`) and another stack-related register (`SS`) on the stack. The first saved register (which is actually `SS`) is not saved at the address pointed by `rsp`, but, rather, at the next lower multiple of 16. Afterwards, each register will be saved 8 bytes below the previous one. Aligning the saved values this way improves performances.

- Saves a register called `rflags`, which contains status information about the processor on the stack.

- Saves the `CS` register, storing the CPL along with other control information, on the stack

- Saves the address of the next instruction (after the last one completed before servicing the interrupt) on the stack. It is usual to refer to this address as the value of `rip`.

- Sets the CPL to 0, if it was 3

- Begins executing the instruction at the address found in the IDT

The stack layout resulting from the steps above is called an *interrupt frame*. It contains all the data required to be able to resume the code that was suspended as if no interrupt occurred. The following figure shows the format of an interrupt frame.

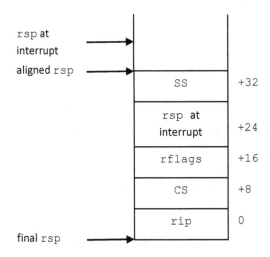

Figure 2 - Interrupt Frame

`rsp` itself must be saved on the stack because the frame is built at an aligned address. When execution of the interrupted code will resume, `rsp` will have to be restored to the value it had before the interrupt. Without alignment, this would simply be the value above the saved `ss`, i.e. it could be computed from the value of `rsp` at the beginning of the interrupt handler. However, aligning the frame decreases `rsp` of an unknown quantity between 0 and 15 depending on its initial value, so the syack pointer must be saved.

4.1.2 Returning from an Interrupt

Resuming the interrupted code is accomplished with the `iret` instruction, which reloads all the saved registers from the stack, thus resuming execution at the saved `rip` value, with the other registers restored. Note that the intterrupt/`iret` mechanism saves and restores only the registers shown in Figure 2 on p. 10. Any processor register not saved in the interrupt frame must be saved by the interrupt handler and restored to its original value before executing the `iret`.

In sec. 3.1 (p. 7), we saw how a `ret` instruction performs certains steps regardless of whether a `call` instruction had actually been executed before. The same concept applies to `iret`, which simply loads the registers shown in Figure 2 (p. 10) with the values found at the current `rsp`. No state is maintained by the processor on whether an interrupt occurred or not before the `iret`.

`iret` can change the CPL from 0 to 3. The processor dects this from the value at `rsp` + 8, i.e. the one to be loaded into CS, so that if the interrupt occurred at ring 3 the CPL is restored.

By design, the CPL loaded from the stack by `iret` can either be the same as the current one (this happens if the interrupt occurred at ring 0) or a numerically higher, i.e. less privileged, value. In simple terms, `iret` can go from ring 0 to ring 3, but cannot go from ring 3 to ring 0.

4.1.3 Stack Switch on Privilege Level Change

As we anticipated in sec. 3.2 on p. 8, when an interrupt occurs at ring 3 and the CPL changes from 3 to 0, `rsp` is loaded with an address pointing to the ring 0 stack. This is done *before* building the stack frame visible in Figure 2 on p. 10, so that the interrupt frame is built on the ring 0 stack.

This is a very important feature, because, as we are about to see shortly, the same handling scheme is used for exceptions, which are generated when the processor detects that the next instruction cannot be executed. One possible cause of exception is an invalid stack: if an instruction attempts to use `rsp` while it is pointing to an invalid address, an exception is generated. This, in turn, requires that the processor has a working stack to save the processor state in the interupt frame. By using a different stack for the interrupt handler, this can be accomplished, at least for exceptions occurring at ring 3. Since the interrupt frame itself is built on the ring 0 stack, the ring 3 `rsp` is saved in the frame, but not used at all, so it does not matter where it is pointing.

This approach cannot help us if we have an invalid stack at ring 0. This is a serious error condition and we are not going to analyze it here. A little more information will be provided in sec. 47.1 on p. 521.

It may not be immediately clear how the address stored into `rsp` can be invalid and thus cause an exception. After all, an address is just a number, so any value could be good. There are two main reasons why an address may be not valid.

The first one is that the address may not be in canonical form, which is defined later in sec. 5.2.2 on p. 17. For now, it is enough to say that not every numerical value in the range 0 - 0xFFFFFFFF`FFFFFFFF is a valid address.

The second one is that the address may not correspond to physical memory. This will be explained in Chapter 5 (p. 16), so a little more patience is required.

In general, since ring 0 code is usually the core of an OS, stack switching ensures that this code is executed with a known good stack.

Now that we know that a different stack is used at ring 0 and why this is important, we must ask ourselves *were* is the rsp value loaded from. The processor uses a data structure called *Task Status Segment* (TSS) to store certain data about its configuration. The TSS has a slot reserved for the ring 0 `rsp`, so, when the CPL changes from 3 to 0, rsp is loaded with the value found there. Note that this does not happen when an interrupt occurs at ring 0 and the CPL does not change. In this scenario, the current `rsp` is used and the interrupt frame is built at the next lower 16 bytes aligned address, as explained in sec. 4.1.1 on p. 8.

The TSS is initialized and updated by operating system code, which stores a proper value for the ring 0 `rsp` before executing ring 3 code. This way, whenever an interrupt occurs in application code, the OS code can count on having `rsp` pointing to its own, reserved stack. Furthermore, the OS usually places this stack in memory inaccessible at ring 3, so that application code cannot touch it.

When an `iret` is executed, `rsp` is always loaded with the value at +24 from the interrupt frame (see Figure 2 on p. 10), so the `rsp` at the time of interrupt is restored. If the interrupt occurred at ring 3, the stack for that privilege level will be again available for use to application code.

Normally, the OS creates a separate TSS for each processor.

4.2   Exceptions

4.2.1 Basic Concept

Exceptions are similar to interrupts, but are generated by the processor when an instruction cannot be executed (or a serious malfunctioning is detected). This occurs, for instance, when a division by 0 is attempted.

When an exception is generated, the processor behaves much in the way it does when it receives an interrupt.

We know that, when an interrupt is requested, a vector must be supplied to the processor by the hardware, so that the processor knows which IDT entry must be consulted to find the address of the interrupt handler (see sec. 4.1.1 on p. 8). Since exceptions are generated by the processor itself, each exception is, by design, associated with a vector number. Note that interrupts and exceptions use the same number range for their vectors, so hardware designers must be careful not to assign to an hardware interrupt the same vector of a processor-defined exception. For this reason, the Intel documentation states that vectors 0-31 are reserved for the architecture.

When the processor generates an exception, it builds an interrupt frame much like the one we saw in Figure 2 on p. 10. Some exceptions (but not all of them) write an additional 8 bytes error code with further information about its cause below `rip`. Since each exception uses a different IDT entry, each one has its own specific handler, which can be written according to whether the interrupt frame contains the error code or not.

Given the similarity between exceptions and interrupts, it should not surprise us that `iret` is the instruction to be used to return from an exception. If the specific exception pushed an error code on the stack, the exception handler must move `rsp` up by 8 bytes before executing `iret`.

4.2.2 Processor Exceptions vs Windows Exceptions

It is important not to confuse the term *exception* as defined by the Intel architecture with Windows exceptions. The latter are events generated by system code which can divert execution of a program to some other piece of code, most of the times because the program did something wrong. Windows exceptions are implemented by OS code and represented by OS-defined data structures. Processor exceptions are interrupt-like events generated by the processor in response to invalid instructions. Of course, a processor generated exception may be at the root of a Windows exception. The oh-so-familiar 0xC0000005 access violation exception is almost always Windows way to handle the exception that the processor generates when an invalid address is referenced. This means that the exception handler that windows installs for this processor exception does not resume execution at ring 3 at the instruction which caused the (processor) exception itself. Rather, execution is resumed inside Windows code which implements the Windows exception mechanism. For readers familiar with Windows Structured Exception Handling, this will be the code looking for a (structured) exception handler and, eventually, terminating the process if none is found. This is an example of an `iret` which is not used simply to reload the state saved in the interrupt frame. Rather, the saved state is updated by ring 0 code so that, when the `iret` is executed, Ring 3 processing magically resume somewhere else.

4.2.3 Exceptions Classification

The Intel architecture classifies exceptions in the following three categories.

4.2.3.1   Faults

Faults are exceptions generated before an instruction having something wrong is executed. Given this, the interrupt frame created on the stack holds, in the `rip` slot, the address of the instruction causing the fault (called the *faulting instruction*), which has not been executed. If the exception handler is able to remove the cause of the fault, executing `iret` will direct the processor to re-execute the faulting instruction which, by now, might succeed.

Among the various faults Intel defines is the *page fault*, which is generated when invalid memory is referenced. In some sense, most of this book is devoted to explain how Windows handles this fault. This is a good example of a fault which can be resolved, so that it makes sense to re-execute the faulting instruction: when a program attempts to reference memory content which has been moved to the paging file, a page fault is generated. The job of the VMM is to retrieve the content and re-execute the faulting instruction.

4.2.3.2   Traps

Traps are exceptions generated after the "trapped" instruction has been executed. The saved `rip` points to the instruction *following* the trapped one. The most common example is the debug trap: the processor can be configured to generate it on every instruction it executes, to implement single stepping with a debugger. When an instruction of the debuggee must be executed, the debugger code executes an `iret`, which transfers control to the next instruction of the debuggee. After this instruction is executed, a new trap is generated, with the saved `rip` pointing at the next instruction, etc.

Note: [1] defines, on p. 85, a trap in abstract terms, not directly related to the Intel architecture. That definition is not equivalent to the one given here.

4.2.3.3   Aborts

Aborts are generated when severe error conditions are detected and don't guarantee that the interrupted code can be resumed, because the saved `rip` may not point at the exact instruction which caused the exception. The exception handler for an abort should normally try to terminate the process as gracefully as possible.

4.3   Interruptions

The terms interrupt, exception, fault, trap and abort are defined by the Intel architecture. In this book the term *interruption* will be used to refer generically to an event belonging to one of these categories, when the specific type it is not relevant.

4.4   Software Interrupts

4.4.1 Basic Concept

The Intel architecture also defines software interrupts, which are not actual interruptions of program execution.

The `int` *n* instruction causes the processor to invoke the handler pointed by entry *n* in the IDT. This instruction is similar to an interrupt in the sense that it invokes an handler. However, this invocation is explicitly coded in the program itself, because the `int` instruction is part of the code being executed.

This instruction is actually a form of indirect call to another portion of code. Instead of providing the address to be called, the index of an IDT entry is given. The destination address will be retrieved from the IDT.

With `int`, the vector to be used is explicitly specified as part of the instruction.

The processor treats `int` as an interrupt in the sense that it creates an interrupt frame on the stack. Since the instruction explicitly specifies the vector to be used, it is possible to call handlers of processor exceptions. The result is not exactly the same we have when the actual exception occurs, because `int` *n* never pushes an error code on the stack. Thus, if it is used with the vector of an exception that does push an error code, the interrupt frame is not the same one created by the actual exception. Since there is no easy way to communicate to the handler whether the error code is present or not, the handler itself is normally written under the assumption that the error code must be on the stack, so it will malfunction when called with `int`.

`int` does not provide a means for ring 3 code to call into handlers at will, because most IDT entries are configured to be accessible only by an (eventual) `int` instruction executed at ring 0. Attempting an `int` for a protected entry while at ring 3 will generate a *general protection exception*, resulting in the execution of the related handler which will punish the misbehaving code, usually by terminating the process.

4.4.2 Processor Software Interrupts vs. Windows Software Interrupts

Windows define its own concept of software interrupt, which we are going to examine later, and is completely different from the processor defined one. It is very important not to confuse them, since they have nothing in common even though they, quite unfortunately, share the same name.

5 Paging

5.1   Paging Overview

Paging is the set of functionalities offered by the processor memory management unit which allow to implement virtual memory. With paging, it is possible to mark a given address as not valid, i.e. not pointing to actual memory and to have the processor generate an exception when an instruction attempts to access the address. The exception handler can then make the address valid and resume the faulting instruction, which will then be executed as if memory had always been there.

5.2   Address Translation

5.2.1 Address Translation Overview

Paging is based on the concept of *address translation*. *Every* address used in the code being executed is translated into a different one before actually referencing memory. This does not simply include the addresses of instruction operands: the address stored in the stack pointer (`rsp`) is translated too, so any reference to the stack, including implicit ones due to calls and interrupts go through translation before making it to memory; addresses of instructions are translated as well. Instruction addresses are found in the instruction pointer (`rip`) and as operands of instructions that transfer execution to another point in code (jumps and calls, which, ultimately, load the destination address into `rip`).

In short, *any* reference to memory is translated. There is no processor instruction which allows to specify an address to be used "as is" to access memory.

Paging can, however, be disabled altogether, which means that *all* the address values used in code are the actual ones used to reference memory. This is done during system initialization to set up processor data structures, including those used by paging itself. Actually, after a reset or power on, the processor is initialized with paging disabled. However, when Windows is up and running, paging is always enabled.

Given this, we can define two distinct types of address.

The *virtual address* is the address before translation and used in processor instructions, either explicitly or implicitly (`rsp`, `rip`, etc.).

The *physical address* is the one resulting from the translation and actually used to refer to memory. Physical and virtual addresses can be completely different and this allows to have virtual addresses much higher than the amount of memory on the system. Windows normally uses addresses above 0xFFFF8000`00000000 or 16,777,088TB for system code and data, regardless of the amount memory installed.

5.2.2 Canonical Address Form

Before explaining how a virtual address is translated into a physical one, we must understand that the processor imposes a limitation on virtual addresses.

A 64 bit value can address 2^{64} bytes of memory, i.e. 16 Exabytes or 16 Gigabytes of GigaBytes. This is an enormous address space, much greater than what is needed in real systems so far. This size comes with a cost: since virtual addresses must be translated, the memory management unit must deal with every address bit, so its complexity increases with the address size.

Given this, current x64 processors actually limit the number of usable bits to 48, but do so in a clever way.

Simply disallowing the use of bits 48-63 would result in limiting virtual addresses below 256TB, which would complicate operating system design. As an example, in 32 bit Windows, were the full 32 bits of virtual addresses are available, system code and data are placed in the upper half of the virtual address space, i.e. above 2GB, giving a clean separation between application and system code. This would not be possible in x64 if addresses were limited to 256TB, well below the half size mark at 8EB.

The solution comes with realizing that forcing bits 48-63 to be clear is not the only way to make them unimportant. A better way is to require that they be equal to bit 47. This means that we have two valid address ranges:

- 0 - 0x7FFF`FFFFFFFF, where bit 47 is 0 and so are bits 48-63.

- 0xFFFF8000`00000000 - FFFFFFFF`FFFFFFFF, where bits 47-63 are all set.

We can picture this as an invalid range in the middle of the valid ones as in the following figure:

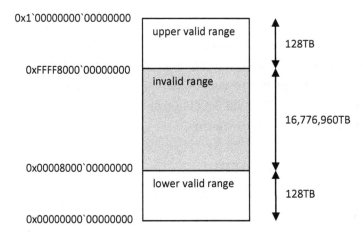

Figure 3 - Canonical Address Ranges

This way, the memory management unit can be simplified, because bits 48-63 are not used in the translation but, at the same time, the higher portion of the virtual range can be used. Also, future processors will have the possibility to use more bits of the virtual address, narrowing the gap between the two valid ranges.

A virtual address is said to be *canonical* if it has bits 47-63 either all set or clear.

All addresses used in x64 code must be canonical. Attempting to use a non canonical address causes a Page Fault exception.

5.2.3 Virtual to Physical Translation

5.2.3.1   Valid and Invalid Addresses

The processor uses tables stored in memory to translate addresses. These tables can either specify a translation for an address or mark it as *invalid*, which means that it cannot be translated to a physical address. A virtual address for which a translation exists is called *valid*.

5.2.3.2   Access to Invalid Addresses

Any attempt to reference an invalid address generates a Page Fault exception, so an interrupt frame is pushed on the stack, with the saved `rip` pointing to the instruction attempting the memory reference. This particular exception also pushes an error code with additional information about the type of access attempted: read, write or instruction fetch. Furthermore, the CR2 register is set to the address that the code was attempting to access.

The exception handler for the Page Fault has all the information needed to resolve the fault. It can, for instance, set up a valid translation and reissue the faulting instruction, or determine that the attempted access is not allowed and transfer control to operating system code which terminates the offending process.

5.2.3.3   Translation of Valid Addresses

The processor uses a set of tables in memory to determine the physical address corresponding to a virtual one as depicted in Figure 4 on p. 20. Translation is performed as follows:

- Register CR3 of the processor stores the *physical* address of the first level table, which is called Page Map Level 4 (PML4). The PML4 is 4kB in size and contains 8-bytes entries called PML4Es. The other tables we are about to see have the same size and structure.

- Bits 39-47 of the virtual address are used as an index into the PML4 to select a PML4E. Since each PML4E is 8 bytes long, its offset from the beginning of the table is index * 8, or the index shifted left by 3 positions.

- The selected PML4E stores the *physical* address of the next level table, called Page Directory Pointer Table (PDPT), which has the same structure of the PML4.

- Bits 30-38 of the virtual address are used to select a PDPT entry (PDPTE), storing the physical address of the next level table, called the Page Directory (PD).

- Bits 21-29 select a PDE, which has the physical address of the last level table, the Page Table (PT).

- Bits 12-20 selects a PTE which stores yet another physical address. This will be the base for the computation of the final physical address.

- Bits 0-11 are added to the physical address obtained in the previous step, i.e. they are an offset from that address. The result is the final memory address which is actually accessed.

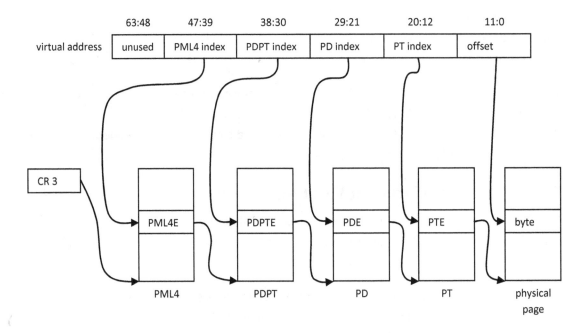

Figure 4 - Virtual to Physical Translation

We will use the term *paging structure* (PS) to refer to any of the tables used in the translation and the acronym PxE to refer to a generic entry from any of them. As we said, paging structures are 4kB in size and each entry is 8 byte long, so a PS can store up to 512 entries and thus 9 bits from the virtual address are used to index into it.

By design, the starting address of a paging structure must be a multiple of 4kB. Such an address has bits 0-11 set to 0 and this fact is exploited in the paging structure entries, where these bits are used for control information about the translation. The same requirement applies to the physical address stored in the PTE, were similar control bits are used.

We saw that 12 bits of the virtual address are used as an offset from the physical address found in the PTE. This means that the same virtual to physical translation applies to an address range where bits 12-63 have the same values. Such a range is 2^{12}, i.e. 4kB long.

So, to summarize, this translation scheme uses bits 12-47 of the virtual address to retrieve a 4kB aligned physical address and uses bits 0-11 as an offset from this address, covering a range of 4kB.

The memory range addressed by a translation is therefore 4kB aligned and 4kB long. We will call such a memory block a *physical page*. The starting address of a physical page divided by 4k is called the *physical page number* (PFN). Since physical pages are 4kB aligned, PFNs are integer values: the first physical page has PFN 0, the second has PFN 1 and so on. Another way of looking at this is that the PFN is the physical address shifted right by 12 positions, which discards the zeored bits.

A paging structure, given its alignment and size requirements, occupies exactly one physical page. This allows an operating system to manage memory allocation in a consistent way, regardless of whether a page is used to store program code and data or a paging structure.

Dividing the virtual address by 4k and rounding down the result to the nearest integer we obtain what is called the *virtual page number* (VPN). The VPN includes all the bits used to retrieve the PFN for the translation, so an address range where the VPN does not change translates to the same physical page. Such a range is itself 4kB aligned and 4kB in size and is called a *virtual page*. All the addresses inside a virtual page are translated into the same physical page. The virtual page is said to be *mapped* to the physical one.

From now on we will use the term *virtual memory* to refer to a range of virtual addresses and the associated content mapped to it, including eventually, invalid addresses for which content is undefined. We will use the term *physical memory*, to refer to the actual memory of the system.

5.2.3.4   The Demise of the Physical Address

It's interesting to observe that the Intel documentation used to define the physical address as the address that "appeared at the address pins" of the processor, after all the translation work had been done. Contemporary processors incorporate the memory controller, so they interact with memory chips using signals completely different from an address bus and there is not a set of pins where the physical address can actually be observed as a sequence of high and low voltage levels. In this sense, the physical address does not exist anymore. Nevertheless, even on contemporary systems memory is arranged in byte locations uniquely identified by a number, i.e. an address, which the processor must use to access them, no matter how the hardware is designed. The value found in paging structure entries is the one used to this end and it is still called physical address.

5.2.3.5   Multiple Address Spaces

If we load the CR3 register with the physical address of a different PML4, we establish a completely different translation. The PML4Es will point to different PDPTs, whose entries will point to different child structures and so on, up to the physical pages storing the memory content. In short, what is mapped to any virtual address can be completely different from what was visible with the earlier CR3 value.

Thus, changing this single register establishes a new *address space*: the memory content changes completely, because different physical pages are mapped to the same virtual ones. This is the mechanism used to implement a separate address space for every process.

5.2.3.6   Range Mapped by a PxE

The PML4 entry mapping an address is selected by bits 39-47, therefore each entry maps an address range where these bits remain constant. This correspond to a range where the rightmost 39 bits range from all zeroes to al ones, i.e. a range of 2^{39} bytes or 512GB.

By the same token, a PDPT entry maps a range with size 2^{30}, i.e. 1GB.

A PD entry maps a range with size 2^{21}, i.e. 2MB.

A PT entry maps a range of 2^{12} bytes or 4kB.

5.2.3.7   Structure of a valid PxE

A valid PxE stores the address of a physical page, either for a child paging structure or for the physical page mapped to the virtual one. Bit 0 of the PxE determines whether it is valid or not: when this bit is set, the PxE is valid.

A valid PxE has the following layout:

63	62:52	51:12	11	10	9	8	7	6	5	4	3	2	1	0
XD	i	PFN	i	i	i	G	PAT	D	A	PCD	PWT	U/S	R/W	P

Figure 5 - Valid PxE

The meaning of the PxE fields is as follows:

P: When this bit is set, the PxE is valid and contains the physical address of either the next PS in the hierarchy or the mapped physical page. When this bit is clear, the PxE is invalid, so the meaning of all the other bits changes as we will see in sec. 5.2.3.9 on p. 27.

R/W: When this bit is set, writes to the virtual range mapped by this entry are allowed; when it is clear, writes cause a Page Fault exception.

For a PTE, the effect of the bit applies to the physical page mapped by the translation.

For PxEs of higher level, the protection applies to all the range mapped by the entry, e.g. 512GB for a PML4E, 1GB for a PDPTE, etc.

Another control bit (in register CR0) allows to configure the processor to allow writes when CPL < 3, even if R/W is clear. Windows configures this bit so that read only protection is enforced at CPL < 3 as well.

U/S: When this bit is set, addresses in the range mapped by the entry can be accessed at CPL 3. When it is clear, accesses are allowed only at CPL < 3. As for the R/W bit, this applies to the whole range mapped by the PxE, depending on its level in the hierarchy.

The primary use of this bit is to configure part of the virtual address space to be accessible only at ring 0, to protect system code and data from application code.

Attempting to access at ring 3 a virtual range protected by this bit causes a Page Fault exception.

PWT: Controls how memory is cached and will be discussed in Chapter 6 (p. 32)

PCD: Controls how memory is cached and will be discussed in Chapter 6 (p. 32)

A: Set by the processor when an instruction accesses memory and causes this entry to be used. It provides a mechanism for code to know if the virtual range mapped by the entry has ever been accessed. This bit is "sticky": once set at the first access, it remains set until code clears it by explicitly updating the PxE.

D: Set by the processor when an instruction writes to an address mapped by the entry. It provides a means for code to know when a physical page has been written to, i.e. when it is "dirty". This bit is "sticky": the processor sets it but does not clear it. Software can clear it by updating the PxE, perhaps after having saved the page into the paging file.

        The processor sets this bit only for PxEs at the bottom of the PS hierarchy, like PTEs and PDEs mapping large pages, which will be discussed in sec. 5.2.3.8 on p. 25. It is ignored for higher level entries.

PAT: In PTEs, controls how the memory is cached and will be discussed in Chapter 6 (p. 32). In higher level PxEs, controls the page size. In a PML4E is reserved and must be set to 0; in a PDPTE can be set to 1, but we are not going to analyze this, since Windows does not use this feature; in a PDE can be set to 1 and this changes how the virtual to physical translation is done, which will be discussed in sec. 5.2.3.8 on p. 25. The translation we have described so far takes place when this bit is set to 0 in the PDPTE and PDE.

G: Controls how this entry is cached in the TLB. This will be discussed in sec. 5.2.4 on p. 31. This bit is only used for the last level of the PS hierarchy, i.e. PTEs and PDEs for large pages. In higher level PxEs is ignored.

i: All the bit fields marked as i are ignored by the processor and available to software.

PFN: These bits store the PFN of the physical page pointed by the entry. For PTEs and large page PDEs (discussed later in sec. 5.2.3.8 on p. 25) points to the physical page mapping the virtual one. For higher level PxEs points to the physical page storing the child PS. Note that this field stores a PFN, i.e. a physical address shifted right by 12 positions. Since the field begins at bit 12, if we take bits 0-51 of the PxE value and clear bits 0-11, we have the physical address of the page.

Since bits 51 is the highest possible bit of the physical address, the latter is 52 bits long and can address up to 2 Petabytes of memory, which is the current limit of the architecture.

For simplicity, Figure 5 shows bit 12-51 as being all used for the PFN, however the Intel documentation specifies that a particular processor model can restrict the physical address length to less than 52 bits. When this happens, the unused bits becomes *reserved* and must be set to 0.

XD: When this bit is set, instruction fetching is not allowed in the range mapped by the entry. Like R/W and U/S, it applies to the entire mapped range, whose size depends on the level of the entry in the PS hierarchy. Forbidding instruction fetching means disallowing the execution of instructions in the affected address range. This is a security feature designed to block an attempt to execute code injected in memory areas used for data, e.g. code injected on the stack through buffer overrun attacks.

If a control transfer instruction like a call or a jump loads `rip` with an address inside a range protected by this bit, the processor attempts to execute whatever is found at the address in `rip` and this causes a page fault exception.

5.2.3.8   Valid PDE for a Large Page

Setting bit 7 in a PDE changes the way the processor performs the translation. The PDE is used to map the virtual page directly and the PT is removed from the translation hierarchy. So, bits 21-47 of the virtual address select a PML4E, a PDPTE and a PDE, and the physical address stored in the PDE becomes the starting address of the translation. Bits 0-20 are used as an offset from this starting address, so the range mapped by this translation has size equal to 2^{21} bytes, i.e. 2MB. The physical address stored in the PDE must, by design, be aligned on a 2MB boundary, so the PDE is mapping a range which is 2MB aligned and 2MB in size, which we call a *large page*. The following figure shows the translation process for a large page:

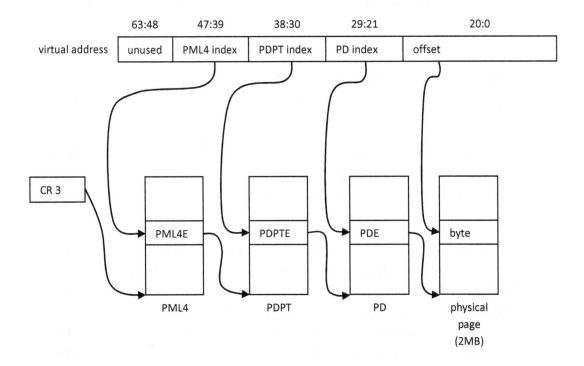

Figure 6 - Virtual to Physical Translation for a Large Page

Since a 2MB aligned address has bits 0-20 set to 0, these bits are used for control information or reserved. The following figure shows the format of a large page PDE

63	62:52	51:21	20:13	12	11	10	9	8	7	6	5	4	3	2	1	0
XD	i	PFN	res	PAT	i	i	i	G	1	D	A	PCD	PWT	U/S	R/W	P

Figure 7 - Valid PDE Mapping a Large Page

The format is very similar to the PxE in Figure 5 on p. 23, with the following differences:

bit 7:   This bit is set, because this is what causes the PDE to map a large page. When this bit is clear, the PDE refers to a PT.

PAT: This bit is the same as the PAT bit for a PTE. It controls how memory is cached and will be discussed in Chapter 6 (p. 32).

The PAT bit is relevant only for PxEs which are at the bottom of the translation, i.e. those who refer to the physical page being mapped to the virtual one. As far as Windows is concerned, this means either a PTE or a large page PDE.

For a PTE, the PAT bit is bit 7.

For a PDE, bit 7 is used to distinguish between a PDE for a large page and one for a small page. The latter has bit 7 clear and does not have a PAT bit, since it is not at the bottom of the translation hierarchy (it has a child PTE).

A large page PDE must have bit 7 set to 1, but also needs a PAT bit, which is therefore moved to bit 12. Note that, for a small page PDE, bit 12 is not available, since it is part of the PFN of the PT. However, in a large page PDE, bits 12-20 can be used because the page must be 2MB aligned, so the PAT bit is moved to bit 12 (and bits 13-20 are defined as reserved, thus they must be 0).

PFN: For such a PDE the PFN only uses bits 21-51, since the page must be 2BM aligned.

5.2.3.9   Invalid PxEs

Any level in the hierarchy, not just PTEs can be set up as an invalid entry, making all the virtual range encompassed by it invalid.

For instance, a PML4E can be invalid, which means it does not refer to a PDPT. When this happens all the 512GB region mapped by the entry is invalid, i.e. has no translation from virtual to physical. The same applies to PDPTEs (invalid region size is 1GB) and PDEs (invalid region size is 2MB).

A PxE is invalid when bit 0 is clear. For such a PxE the processor ignores all the remaining bits, so its format is simply:

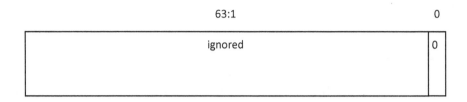

Figure 8 - Invalid PxE

Bits 1-63 are available to software, e.g. to store the location of the content the PxE should point to in the paging file.

5.2.3.10   Why All These Paging Structures

We can understand by now that that address translation does three fundamental things needed to implement virtual memory:

- It allows to map a virtual address to a completely different physical one, allowing the use of address ranges that don't exist in actual system memory (e.g. 0xFFFF8000`00000000 - 0xFFFFFFFF`FFFFFFFF).

- It allows to map the *same* virtual address to *different* physical pages by changing CR3, thus providing a simple way to switch from an address space to another.

- It allows to set an address as invalid, thereby allowing the page fault handler to take control and decide whether to map the address (set up a valid translation) or complain in a suitable way.

We could observe that none of these functionalities requires the multilevel scheme we saw. If all we need is a data structure associating (that is, mapping) a virtual address with a physical one, we could use a simple array indexed by virtual address, where each entry stores the address of a physical page. Going even further, we can ask ourselves why have memory pages at all, i.e. why not have an entry of our hypothetical array just store a physical address anywhere in memory.

If we were to do such a one-to-one mapping, we would need an array entry for each mapped virtual address, which would mean we would occupy 8 bytes, the size of an entry, to map a single virtual byte, an obviously excessive overhead. Instead, by using pages, an 8 byte entry maps 4kB of virtual memory, which is much better. Also, this opens up the possibility of using the lower 12 bits of the entry for some useful control information simply by requiring that the page starting address must be aligned on a multiple of the page size.

We could still think of using a single array of 8-bytes entries mapping virtual addresses to pages and index into it with bits 12-63 of the virtual address.

With this approach, to map the lower valid region of canonical addresses we would need an array with size equal to: the size of the range divided by the size of a page and multiplied by the size of an array entry:

$$0x8000`00000000 / 0x1000 * 8 = 0x40`00000000 = 256GB$$

We would also need another array of the same size for the upper valid range and we would need this pair of arrays for every existing address space, all of them stored in *physical* memory. Most of this memory would be wasted, because the majority of entries would map virtual ranges that have never been allocated in the address space, so they would simply represent somehow that the translation is invalid (e.g. P bit clear). They would not store useful information as is the case when the translation has been valid sometime in the past and the mapped content has been moved to the paging file. In short, the biggest shortcoming of this approach is that we have to set up an entry for every possible virtual page, including those the process will never use.

On the other hand, with the translation scheme we saw, a small 4kB paging structure maps all the 256TB of virtual address space of the two canonical ranges. This makes it necessary to have other intermediate level paging structures, since there are only 512 entries in the PML4, thus a single one maps

$$256TB / 512 = 512GB$$

By adding other level of tables, the range mapped by a single entry is divided by 512 - the number of entries in a child table - at each level, until we arrive at the PT entries, which map 4kB pages.

This allows to map an address space with "holes" of invalid regions without wasting too many unused entries, as in the following figure:

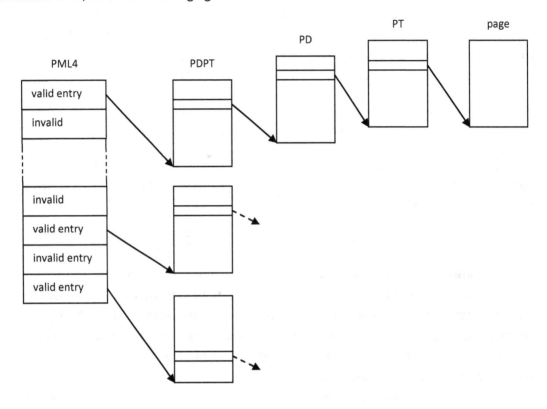

Figure 9 - Sparse Virtual Address Space

The invalid entries don't point to physical memory, so only the paging structures needed to map valid ones are allocated.

Finally, this scheme allows to *share* paging structures among different address spaces. Suppose a second address space sets its highest valid PML4 entry to point to the same PDPT of Figure 9. This fact alone materializes the same content in the corresponding 512GB region of the two address spaces, sharing all the levels of the paging structures hierarchy. We will see that this is the way Windows shares the system address range among all processes.

5.2.4 Overview of TLB and Paging Structures Caches

To translate a virtual address into a physical one, the processor has to perform 4 memory accesses, one for each PS in the hierarchy. Since memory latency is much longer than instruction execution time, this slows down the processor considerably. To avoid this, translations are cached in two types of caches: the translation lookaside buffer (TLB) and the paging structures caches.

The TLB caches complete translations from a virtual address to a physical one, together with all the control information, i.e. whether the page is read/write or read-only, whether it is accessible at ring 3, etc. If the translation for a virtual address is found in the TLB, no access to the paging structures in memory is required.

The paging structures caches store partial translations. The PML4E cache stores the content of PML4Es, allowing to retrieve the PFNs of PDPTs without accessing the PML4 in memory. An entry in this cache is selected by bits 39-47 of the virtual address, like a PML4E in memory.

The PDPTE cache stores a translation up to the PDPTE content, i.e. up to the PFN of the PD. This means that an entry in this cache is selected by bits 30-47 of the VA, i.e. the bits selecting the PML4E *and* the PDPTE. The entry also stores the control information coming from the PDPTE and the PML4E. Such an entry can be used to perform the remaining part of the translation by accessing only the PD and the PT.

The PDE cache is similar to the PDPTE cache and stores partial translations up to the PT address.

All these caches come with a significant price: they must be explicitly invalidated by software. If code modifies a PxE in memory, the processor does not detect the update and does not flush cached translations. The code must explicitly invalidate the TLB and paging structures caches when it modifies PxEs. This is a complex task, because, on a multiprocessor system, all the processors must have their caches invalidated, which requires an inter-processor interrupt and synchronization logic among all the processors. Such an operation cannot be performed too often, otherwise performances would suffer too much, so even more complex logic must be implemented, to perform invalidation in batches of translations.

The processor automatically invalidates the caches when a value is loaded into CR3, since this operation changes the PML4 address, thus switching to a different address space. It would not make sense to retain cached translations referring to a different set of paging structures.

However, a system may have a range of memory shared by all the address spaces (Windows does), so it would be a waste to invalidate its cached translations on every context switch.

This is what the G bit of PTEs and large pages PDEs is for: when this bit is set, the TLB entry for the translation (if it exists) is not invalidated when CR3 is loaded. Thus, shared addresses are retained in the TLB. Note that the paging structures caches are always invalidated, because the G bit is ignored in intermediate level PxEs.

6 Cache Control

6.1   How Memory Caching Is Controlled

The Intel architecture defines caching in terms of memory types and cache control registers and bits.

A memory type specifies if memory is cached at all, i.e. if a copy of it is brought into the processor cache hierarchy, and how updates are written to main memory when an instruction writes to an address.

Control registers and bits specify the memory type for a given physical or virtual address range.

6.2   Memory Types

The following memory types are relevant for the rest of this book.

6.2.1 Writeback Memory (WB)

This is the "most cached" type, which keeps traffic on the memory interface at a minimum. Memory content is copied into the processor cache on read, if it is not already present. Subsequent reads will not access main memory and will retrieve the value from the cache instead. Writes will update the cached copy of the value, without being propagated to main memory.

A system has more than one processor (typically) and can also have other devices which read from and write to system memory, like a DMA controller. Collectively, all the components which access main memory are called bus agents.

With multiple bus agents, care must be taken to ensure that each of them has a consistent view of the memory content. For instance, if a processor updates the copy of a memory location in its cache without updating main memory (as it is normal with WB memory), other agents could see a stale copy of the location.

This is avoided through *snooping*: bus agents exchange signals which allow each of them to snoop updates made by other agents to their cached data. If an agent updates a value in its cache and another agent has a copy of the same value, the second agent throws away its copy. The next time the second agent will need that particular piece of data, will load it from memory.

This is not enough however, since the main memory copy is also stale, as long as the updated value is kept in the cache of the agent which modified it. To solve this problem, each agent snoops accesses to main memory made by the others. When it detects that another agent wants a piece of data which has been modified in the cache, the two agents cooperate so that the one needing the data gets the up-to-date copy from the one that was caching it.

With this type of memory, when a processor writes to an address which is not in the cache, the memory content is first copied into the cache, then updated there. In other words, both reads and writes fill the cache.

Cached memory is read and written in entire cache lines (typically 64 bytes blocks aligned on 64 bytes boundaries), which are handled most efficiently by the memory interface. This means that reading or writing a single byte not found in the cache causes an entire cache line to be copied to it.

6.2.2 Write Combining Memory (WC)

This memory type is suitable for video buffers, which have a few peculiarities.

Writes to a video buffer must be propagated outside the processor in a timely fashion, to update the video content, so writeback memory cannot be used. However, writes need not occur in program order, so the processor is allowed to combine them in an intermediate internal buffer, to use the most efficient transfer cycle to send the data out.

Memory writes don't cause the cache line containing the data to be loaded into the cache. If this were to happen, the cache would be filled with video buffer data, mostly useless. Memory reads are not cached either.

The processor does not guarantee memory coherency for WC memory, because accesses to it are not snooped, so there is a window of time in which other agents see stale content. Again, this makes sense for a video buffer, which is seldom read and not used to store shared data structures. If code needs to be sure that WC memory is up to date, there are instructions to explicitly flush the intermediate buffers.

6.2.3 Uncached Memory (UC)

This memory type is not cached, so reads and writes are always propagated to the interface bus. It is mostly indicated for memory mapped devices were reading or writing an address causes an interaction with the device. Usually, devices are sensitive to the order in which their memory mapped registers are read and written, i.e. changing the order of read and writes can produce different effects on the device. In WB memory, the processor does not execute read an writes exactly in program order:

- A read can be executed ahead of a write which comes before it in program order, if they cover different memory locations.

- The processor can perform reads written, in code, after a conditional jump. It attempts to predict the outcome of the condition, i.e. whether the jump will be taken or not and can execute reads which are part of the block of code that would be executed if the prediction was correct. The data read is stored in intermediate buffers and is later used for actual code execution if the prediction turns out to be correct, or discarded. If the processor predicts the wrong path, it ends up reading addresses that should not have been read according to the program logic and state. This is harmless for memory, but can cause undesired effects with devices.

In UC memory, only reads and writes resulting from actual code execution are performed and exactly in program order.

Access to UC memory downgrades overall system performance because:

- Each processor have to wait for reads and writes to be completely carried out before executing other memory accesses.

- Traffic on the memory interface shared by all bus agents is increased, since every access is propagated to memory. This increments the probability of bus contention, which further delays memory accesses.

6.3   Memory Type Range Registers (MTRR)

MTRRs are registers that specify one of the possible memory types for a given range of physical addresses. Generally, Windows programs the MTRRs so that all actual memory (as opposed to mapped devices) has type WB.

6.4   Page Attribute Table (PAT)

While the MTRRs specify memory types for physical address ranges, the PAT allows to specify the same information in terms of virtual addresses. Thus, a given VA will have a type specified by the PAT and will be translated to a physical address with a, potentially different, type specified by an MTRR. The final type results from the combination of the two, as we will see.

The PAT is a 64 bit special register (what the Intel documentation calls a Model-Specific Register) divided in 8 entries of 8 bits each. Each entry can be set to a value corresponding to a memory type, according to the following table:

PAT Field Value	Memory Type
0x00	UC
0x01	WC
0x06	WB
0x07	UC-

Table 1 - Memory Types Encoding in the PAT

The Intel architecture defines more memory types than the ones shown in Table 1, but Windows programs the PAT using only these. The UC- type will be defined shortly.

Entry 0 of the pat corresponds to bits 0-7, entry 1 to bits 8-15, etc.

The bottom level of the virtual-to-physical translation (either the PTE or a PDE for a large page) selects a PAT entry and thus a memory type for the page through its PWT, PCD and PAT bits, which are shown in Figure 5 (p. 23) and Figure 7 (p. 26). The three bits select a PAT entry according to the following table:

PAT	PCD	PWT	PAT Entry
0	0	0	0
0	0	1	1
0	1	0	2

PAT	PCD	PWT	PAT Entry
0	1	1	3
1	0	0	4
1	0	1	5
1	1	0	6
1	1	1	7

Table 2 - PAT Entry Selected by PxE Control Bits

A given virtual page has a memory type specified by the selected PAT entry and is mapped to a physical address, which has a memory type specified by an MTRR. The intel documentation defines the resulting memory type for the possible combinations (see [11], Vol. 3A, p. 11-22, Table 11-7). For our purpose, it is enough to say that when the MTRR specifies WB, the resulting type is the one selected by the PAT.

The UC- type in Table 1 on p. 35 is equivalent to UC, when the MTRR specify WB and they both result in UC memory.

 UC- differs from UC when the MTRR specifies a memory type other than WB. For instance, when the MTRR specifies WC type (usually for a video buffer), selecting UC- in the PAT results in the final type being WC, while selecting UC gives UC memory. UC- specifies uncached memory but can be overridden by WC in the MTRR. UC in the PAT overrides WC in the MTRR.

What we have seen so far concerns the caching of a physical page mapping a virtual one. Physical pages storing paging structures have a memory type as well, which is determined in the same way. The only difference is that, as we saw in sec. 5.2.3.8 on p. 25, PxEs pointing to child paging structures don't have a PAT bit, so the processor behaves as if PAT is 0, and selects a PAT entry based on PCD and PWT.

It is worth noting a difference between the cache control bits of a PxE and other control bits like R/W, U/S and XD. The cache control bits control the memory type of the page pointed by the entry. If the entry is not the bottom level one, e.g. is a PDPTE, these bits specify the memory type of the next level paging structure, the PD in our example. Only the cache control bit of the last level entry have effect on the caching policy of the physical page resulting from the translation. Conversely, the other control bits always act on the result of the translation. For example, a PDE with R/W clear protects as read only the entire range mapped by the PD, but does not specify that the PT it points to is read-only.

7 Model-Specific Registers (MSR)

The architecture defines several registers which configure how the processor works. These registers are identified by a number called the *register address* and there are specific instructions for reading and writing to them.

It's possible to examine the content of an MSR with WinDbg by issuing the `rdmsr` command followed by the register address. For instance, the PAT has address 0x277 and can be dumped as follows:

```
lkd> rdmsr 277
msr[277] = 00070106`00070106
```

Appendix B of [11], Vol. 3B lists the MSRs addresses.

Part II - Windows Kernel Basics

8 Introduction

Part II explains a few concepts concerning the Windows kernel which can be of help in understanding the rest of this book.

We will describe the concepts of IRQL, interrupt processing and synchronization.

9 User Mode and Kernel Mode

The terms *user mode* and *kernel mode* are equivalent to CPL 3 and CPL 0, respectively. User mode code includes executables and DLLs, including ones that are part of Windows itself. Kernel mode code includes the kernel, the hal and kernel mode drivers, either part of the OS or installed by third party software.

Application code is executed in user mode and the processor switches to kernel mode when:

- An hardware interrupt is requested.

- The processor generates an exception.

- A mode-switching instruction (usually `syscall`) is executed as part of the implementation of a system API. Some APIs are implemented entirely in user mode, while others need to call the kernel or the executive, so they switch to kernel mode. As an example, a call to a waiting function like *WaitForSingleObject* must suspend the executing thread until the wait is satisfied. To accomplish this, it must call the thread dispatcher, which saves the thread status on the stack and resumes some other thread. The thread dispatcher, in turn, is made of kernel mode code.

The processor switches from kernel to user mode when:

- An `iret` instruction is executed to return from an interrupt or exception handler.

- A mode-switching instruction (usually `sysret`) is executed, to return from the kernel mode part of an API implementation.

10   IRQL

10.1 Definition of IRQL

Windows defines the concept of IRQL (Interrupt Request Level) to specify the rules governing how a block of code can be interrupted and a thread preempted by a context switch.

The IRQL is a numerical value which determines which interrupts are enabled on a processor. At any given time, each processor in the system has its own current IRQL value and different processors can be at different IRQLs.

Each hardware interrupt is assigned an IRQL value. The IRQL range is 0-15, so the same value can be assigned to different devices.

When the processor is not responding to an interrupt, its current IRQL is usually set to PASSIVE, i.e. 0. When an hardware interrupt is serviced by a processor, the handler raises the IRQL of the executing processor to the value assigned to the interrupt. Before executing the `iret` which will resume the interrupted code, the handler restores the IRQL to the value it had when the interrupt occurred.

When the current IRQL of a particular processor has been raised to i, all the interrupts with IRQL <= i are masked on that processor, i.e. they cannot interrupt the executing code. If such an interrupt is requested, it is noted as pending and will be serviced when the current IRQL value will drop below the one of the interrupt. However, interrupts with IRQL <= i can still interrupt code executing on other processors, when the IRQL of these processors is < i.

If a pending interrupt becomes visible when the IRQL is lowered, its handler is called and the process is repeated, setting the IRQL to the value for the new interrupt.

The current IRQL is stored in register CR8 and causes the processor to ignore hardware interrupts with a priority equal or below its value. Interrupt priorities are established by programming the interrupt controller, something that Windows does during its initialization. Thus, the masking of hardware interrupts with IRQL equal or less the current one is performed in hardware, by the processor itself.

At the hardware level, this scheme is designed to guarantee that less important interrupts cannot delay the execution of handlers of more important ones. However, this scheme has also logical implications on how the code of interrupt handlers is executed, and this will be the subject of the next section.

10.2 IRQL Implications on Code Execution

10.2.1   Introduction

In the next sections, we are going to analyze how masking interrupts by means of the IRQL has implications on the way interrupt handlers code is executed. While doing this, we will consider IRQL values in general, with no distinctions among them.

We will see later, though, that IRQLs 1 and 2 have a special meaning and are used in a special way. However, before going into these details, it is useful to examine the effects of interrupt masking on code execution in general.

It is also useful to keep in mind that an interrupt handler is composed of different parts: the first level code pointed by the IDT usually calls into other parts of the kernel, which, in turn, may call code which is part of drivers installed in the system. Drivers must be allowed to install their own interrupt service routines, which must be called when an interrupt occurs. This allows a driver, to interact with its device.

10.2.2   Code vs. Processor Implications

The interrupt masking outlined in the previous section imposes some constraints on when a particular processor can execute certain parts of code.

Consider the code of an interrupt handler, which is being executed by processor p at IRQL i, i.e. after the IRQL has been raised and before it is restored to its previous value.

This code can be written assuming that the same interrupt is masked on processor p, so p cannot be interrupted in the middle of the code and reenter it. It may be interrupted by *other* interrupts and execute *other* handlers, but it will never reenter the same handler, until the IRQL is restored.

This code can, eventually, keep state information in per-processor data structures, like the Processor Control Region (_KPCR) and the Processor Control Block (_KPRCB) and assume that access to them is serialized. Only when the handler returns and the IRQL is lowered, the handler code can be executed again by processor p. Even if the same code is concurrently executed by other processors, it will access *different instances* of the state variables, if the data structures are per-processor ones.

There is an exception to this rule, which will be examined in sec. 10.2.4 on p. 45.

Note that code of third party drivers does not usually access the _KPCR or the _KPRCB, which are not even documented. However, in this analysis, we are considering how kernel mode code works in general, regardless of where it came from. It's possible that internal kernel functions take advantage of this implication. Also, driver code can, conceivably, call the documented DDI *KeGetCurrentProcessorNumber*, which does what its name says, and store per-processor information, e.g. in an array indexed by processor number.

10.2.3   Code vs. Thread Implications

10.2.3.1   Interrupts with IRQL 2 or Above

The IRQL also has implications on the relationship between code and the thread executing it.

We can begin our analysis by observing that an interrupt always occurs in the context of a thread. The processor receiving the interrupt is executing thread t and it is diverted to execute the handler code while t is the current thread. Thus, when the handler raises the IRQL, it does so in the context of t.

We will see in greater detail later that, when the IRQL of a processor is greater or equal than 2, that processor is prevented from executing the thread scheduler code which performs context switches, i.e. which suspends the current thread and resumes another one. For now, we will just say that this is how the scheduler is implemented. The thread scheduler is also called the thread dispatcher, so these two terms are equivalent.

It follows that, when an interrupt at IRQL 2 or above occurs while t is the current thread running on processor p, this processor will continue to run thread t at least until the IRQL is lowered below 2.

This implies that the handler code can be written under the assumption that it will not be reentered in the context of t. The same handler can only be executed concurrently by other processors, which, in turn, can only execute *other threads*, since t is stuck with p, because of the IRQL.

This opens the door to assumptions on where the handler code can store state information. If the code stores values in per-thread data structures, access to these variables will be implicitly serialized. The same code, when executed in a different thread context, will access different instances of these variables.

10.2.3.2   Interrupts with IRQL 1

Now, suppose that thread t running on p is interrupted by an interrupt at IRQL = 1. A processor running at this IRQL can execute the thread scheduler and resume a different thread, so the thread can be preempted while in the middle of the handler. However, the IRQL is saved and restored together with the rest of the thread context, so, when t will eventually be resumed by a processor (either p or another one), the current IRQL will be set to 1, before resuming execution of the handler code. From this follows that execution of the handler in the context of t cannot be interrupted by the same interrupt either. While it's true that *t* can be moved across processors by thread scheduling, it brings along its own IRQL, so the interrupt masking remains in effect.

Thus, access to per-thread variables is serialized for interrupts at IRQL 1 as well.

10.2.4   Code vs. Processor - Reprise for IRQL 1

We saw in the previous section that a processor may switch thread context while the IRQL is 1 and that, when a different thread is resumed, the IRQL is restored to the value it had when that thread was preempted. This implies that the following can happen:

- Processor *p*, executing thread *t* services an IRQL 1 interrupt, transferring control to the handler. The handler sets the current IRQL to 1.

- While the handler execution is in progress, a thread switch occurs and thread *t* is preempted.

- Thread *s* is resumed by processor *p* and, since *s* was running at PASSIVE when it was preempted, the IRQL is set to PASSIVE.

- The same IRQL 1 interrupt (we will see there is actually only one such interrupt) is serviced again by processor *p*. This interrupt is not masked, because now the IRQL is PASSIVE.

- The handler of the IRQL 1 interrupt is reentered, with *p* being the executing processor.

In this scenario, if the interrupt handler had state saved in per-processor variables, these variables would have been partially updated by the first call to the handler, which has been frozen midway by the thread switch. The second call to the handler would then update the same variables, because the executing processor is the same, corrupting the execution of the first call, which will eventually go on, when thread *t* will be resumed.

Thus, for IRQL 1 only, access to per-processor variable is not serialized and the handlers of interrupts at this IRQL (again, there is actually just one such handler, as we will see) must be written accounting for this.

This concerns only the IRQL 1 interrupt, because, as we said, when a processor is at IRQL 2 or above, it does not switch thread context.

In the scenario above, however, it is still true that an interrupt at IRQL 1 cannot interrupt thread *t* in the middle of an IRQL 1 handler. When *t* is executing the handler, no matter on which processor, the processor IRQL is set to 1 and interrupts at this IRQL are masked. Thus, the logic of an IRQL 1 handler can safely store state information in per-thread variables and assume that they will be accessed serially.

10.2.5   User Mode Code

User mode code is always executed at IRQL = PASSIVE and there are no APIs available to change the current IRQL. Since PASSIVE is the lowest IRQL, user mode code can always be interrupted and thread context switches are always possible. Normally, user mode code is not disturbed by interrupts, because no part of it is called by interrupt handlers, so the code can't be re-entered in the context of the same thread because of an interrupt. Thus, as we will see shortly, user mode code only needs to synchronize execution among different threads.

10.2.6   The Golden Rule for Code Called by Interrupt Handlers

In the previous sections, we saw the assumptions that can be made when writing handlers code, thanks to the combined effects of masking interrupts and disabling thread switching at IRQLs greater than or equal to 2. The price to be paid for this is an important rule, that all interrupt handlers code must follow.

An handler code must *never* lower the IRQL, except in its very final stage, when it's about to return from the interrupt. When this happens, the handler *must* restore the IRQL that was in effect before its interrupt occurred. In particular, it must not set the IRQL to a value lower than the pre-interrupt one.

Consider for instance a block of code which is part of an handler of an interrupt with IRQL= 5, interrupting another handler for an interrupt with IRQL = 4. Suppose that the code at IRQL 5 changes the IRQL to 3, violating the rule we just stated. A new pending interrupt at IRQL 4 can be serviced before resuming the originally interrupted code, that was itself running at IRQL 4. The latter has been de facto interrupted by code at the same IRQL, which should never happen. Suppose now that the new IRQL 4 interrupt is from the same source which caused the original IRQL 4 one. The same handler will be reentered while the previous call to it has not completed yet, because it was interrupted by the IRQL 5 interrupt. This can completely disrupt the result of the handler execution.

Every piece of handler code can be written under the assumption that the conditions detailed in sections 10.2.2 to 10.2.4 (pp. 43 - 46) apply, but this is true only if it cannot be interrupted, on the same processor, by code with IRQL less or equal than its own. This, in turn, can be guaranteed only if the IRQL is lowered only when the handler is about to return and is restored to its previous value (in our example, 4).

It is true that decreasing the IRQL by a single unit could be seen as a particular case: this would at most cause the handler which lowered the IRQL to be reentered. If all of the handler code could be written accounting for this, no problem should occur. However, code executed by an interrupt handler is not a monolithic and immutable block. It is composed by a first layer which is part of the kernel and calls code which is part of other components, often including third party drivers. It is therefore a practical impossibility to be sure that all the code making up the handler can survive reentrancy caused by lowering the IRQL, thus this operation is forbidden altogether.

The problem would be even worse if, in the previous example, the handler at IRQL 5 were to set the IRQL to 0 or 1. Doing this would enable thread switching, so the poor handler running at IRQL 4 could even be preempted by a thread switch and have to wait until the thread is resumed, before being allowed to go on. The code for that handler has not been written accounting for this possibility, because, at IRQL 4, thread switching is disabled.

10.2.7   I Raised It Myself, Can I Lower It Now?

A block of code can explicitly *raise* the IRQL above the current level, to disable higher IRQL interrupts. This can be done both in handlers and in code which is not part of any handler. We will see later, in Chapter 14 (p. 52) how this is used to synchronize execution. When this is done, the IRQL can, of course, be later lowered to its previous level. So it would not be correct to say that an handler can never lower the IRQL. Rather, it cannot set it to a value lower than the one assigned to its interrupt, except when returning.

11   Software Interrupts

11.1 Basic Concept

Windows defines its own concept of software interrupt, which must not be confused with software interrupts as defined by the Intel architecture (these were described in section 4.4 on p. 15). These are entirely different concepts even though they share the same name.

Windows software interrupts are implemented in kernel code. A per-processor variable can be set to request such an interrupt. Kernel code checks this variable at various stages during its operation and, if the flag for an interrupt is set, it calls the associated handler.

Currently, only two software interrupts are defined: APC and DPC. They have an associated IRQL level: 1 for the APC interrupt and 2 (called DPC/dispatch) for the DPC one. When the code that checks for software interrupts founds that one is pending, it calls the handler only if the current IRQL is less than the interrupt IRQL, mimicking what the processor does for hardware interrupts.

All hardware interrupts have IRQL greater than DPC/dispatch, so software interrupts are always masked inside an hardware interrupt handler (but they are masked *only* on the processor executing the handler; other processors may be at any IRQL).

One of the stages when the kernel checks for software interrupts is when it is restoring the IRQL before exiting an handler. For instance, the following sequence of events may take place:

- Code executing at PASSIVE is interrupted by an hardware interrupt.

- The handler code requests a software DPC interrupt. The current IRQL is greater than DPC/dispatch, because it has been raised at the beginning of the handler logic, so the DPC interrupt is kept pending.

- The handler code returns, restoring the IRQL to PASSIVE.

- The code lowering the IRQL checks for pending software interrupts and finds the DPC one. Since the IRQL is being set to PASSIVE, the interrupt can be serviced. The IRQL is set to DPC/dispatch and the handler for the DPC interrupt is called.

- When the handler returns, the IRQL is again restored to PASSIVE. This time no further interrupts are pending and the interrupted code is resumed.

We can see that software interrupts can indeed be seen as asynchronous events by the interrupted code running at PASSIVE, even though they actually "piggyback" on hardware interrupts.

11.2 The APC Interrupt

The APC (Asynchronous Procedure Call) interrupt is used to request execution of a routine, usually called a *callback routine*. When the interrupt is serviced, the routine is called and, when the callback returns, the interrupt handler returns to the interrupted code. It is actually a peculiar kind of interrupt, because it is used to cause the callback to be executed in the context of a particular thread, specified when requesting the interrupt. Normally, interrupts break into the currently executing thread, whichever it may be, so this one is handled in a peculiar way by the kernel. More details on APCs can be found in [22].

As we saw in sec. 10.2.4 on p. 45, the handler of the APC interrupt must account for the fact that it can be reentered on the same processor in the context of another thread. This is due to thread dispatching being enabled at this IRQL and applies to any callback invoked through this interrupt.

The first layer of the APC handler is part of the kernel and, presumably, accounts for the peculiarities of this interrupt. This code even does the unthinkable: it lowers the IRQL to PASSIVE, *in the middle of its logic*, because there are three kinds of APC callbacks and one of them must be executed at PASSIVE IRQL. This breaks the rule we saw in sec. 10.2.6 on p. 46, but it can be done for the following reasons:

- The handler code is written accounting for the possibility of being reentered, even by the same thread.

- There are no IRQL levels between APC and PASSIVE: APC is 1 and PASSIVE is 0. No handlers of other interrupts can have been interrupted by the APC one and be in progress, when the IRQL is lowered.

In short, the APC handler only causes troubles to itself by doing this, and it knows how to clean its own mess.

APCs are used internally by the kernel and are not available to driver developers, because the functions implementing them are undocumented.

11.3 The DPC Interrupt

The DPC (Deferred Procedure Call) interrupt is also used to request asynchronous execution of a callback, but is different from an APC interrupt because:

- It is a "real" interrupt, which is executed in an arbitrary thread context as soon as the IRQL allows it to be serviced.

- It has a higher IRQL, so it is handled ahead of an APC interrupt.

There are DDIs to request a DPC interrupt specifying the callback routine to be called. Normally, kernel mode drivers use DPCs to keep the amount of processing done in their ISRs at a minimum. An ISR is called by the interrupt handler and is executed at the IRQL assigned to the hardware interrupt. As such, it blocks other interrupts with lower IRQL (and all software interrupts). Given this, the ISR should return as soon as possible, deferring time consuming work to be performed at a lower IRQL. This is usually done by requesting a DPC for a driver-defined callback which will complete the interrupt handling. The ISR can thus perform the minimum amount of work needed, request the DPC interrupt and return.

The Windows component responsible for scheduling threads, called the thread dispatcher, is itself executed by means of a DPC interrupt. This interrupt is requested by various kernel functions. For instance, the handler for the clock interrupt checks to see whether the currently executing thread has run for its allotted time (called its *quantum*) and, if so, requests a DPC interrupt for the dispatcher. When the IRQL is about to drop below DPC (i.e. when the clock and other pending hardware interrupts have all been serviced), the DPC interrupt is serviced and the dispatcher is called, preempting the current thread and resuming another one.

We are now ready to understand why setting the IRQL at 2, i.e. DPC/dispatch or above, inhibits thread context switches on a processor: the thread dispatcher is not invoked by that processor, because DPC interrupts are masked.

12   Restrictions for Code Executed at DPC/dispatch or Above

Both kernel mode and user mode code can voluntarily call the thread dispatcher to be suspended until a certain logical condition is met. This is usually implemented by means of a data structure provided by an API or DDI on which the code can wait. For instance, two threads can synchronize among themselves by using an event object: thread t waits for the event to be "signaled" and thread s "signals" the event when the logical condition t is waiting for is true. What thread t does is called *entering a wait state*. As an example, application code can call *WaitOnSingleObject* to accomplish this. When this happens, the thread is suspended and another thread is resumed.

Code executing at DPC/dispatch or above cannot enter a wait state.

Doing this would mean that the processor should suspend the current thread and resume another one. This, in turn, implies that the IRQL of the processor should be lowered below DPC/dispatch.

Suppose, for the sake of argument, that a thread could actually suspend itself while at DPC/dispatch or above. Other threads may have blocked themselves or have been preempted at a lower IRQL, e.g. PASSIVE or APC. When the dispatcher picks one such thread to run, it must restore the IRQL it was running at, thus bringing it down from the current level.

Also, if the executing thread blocks, the processor which is executing it should resume the normal thread scheduling process, switching among threads. This can occur only if the DPC interrupt invoking the dispatcher can be serviced on the processor, something possible only when the IRQL is less than DPC/dispatch.

So, code executed in this IRQL range could block only if the IRQL could be set to a lower value, but this *cannot* happen inside the code of an handler, as we saw in sec. 10.2.6 on p. 46, which, in the end, means this kind of code can't block.

Consider, for instance, a DPC callback routine, executing at DPC/dispatch. This code is called by the DPC interrupt handler, which is written under the assumption that interrupts at DPC/dispatch or below cannot be serviced on the same processor while it is running. A DPC callback lowering the IRQL would cause unexpected reentrancy of the handler on the same processor, disrupting its work.

The same consideration applies to code executed at higher IRQL, in the context of an hardware interrupt handler: lowering the IRQL below DPC/dispatch would cause all sorts of lower IRQL interrupts to be serviced, reentering other handlers that may have been interrupted in the middle of something. Furthermore, it makes little sense to enter a wait state inside an hardware interrupt handler, which should quickly interact with its device and return.

So, in general, code executed at DPC/dispatch or above cannot wait on synchronization objects like events, mutexes, etc. We will see shortly how synchronization is implemented in this code.

An implication of this constraint is that code running at DPC/dispatch or above cannot cause a page fault. To resolve such a fault, an I/O operation on a file may be required. This would cause the thread to enter a wait state, because, after the I/O has been issued to the storage device, the thread must wait for an interrupt signaling that data is available. Since waiting is not acceptable, neither are I/O operations. Therefore, one of the first things the page fault handler does is checking the current IRQL. If it is DPC/dispatch or higher, the handler crashes the system.

Crashing the whole system may seem extreme, however a page fault occurring at IRQL >= DPC/dispatch can only be caused by kernel mode code (because user mode means PASSIVE). As such, it is a serious error and it is better to bring everything to an halt.

13   Historical Note: IRQL and Software Interrupts in the VAX/VMS

It is a known fact that the Windows architecture has its roots in the Digital VAX/VMS system. In the world of computer urban legends, someone went so far to notice that the acronym WNT can be obtained by substituting each letter in VMS with the next alphabet letter.

It is interesting to note that the concept of IRQL and software interrupts is also present in VAX/VMS and even implemented in hardware. The PSL CPU register records the processor status and includes a field called IPL (interrupt priority level), which is equivalent to the IRQL and masks all interrupts with priority less than or equal to its value.

Software interrupts are requested by writing to a processor register and, when the IPL is lowered, the processor checks if any software interrupt is pending that can be serviced, i.e. with priority greater than the new IPL value. This is exactly the same logic implemented by Windows, but supported by the CPU itself.

Another interesting point is that the x64 architecture has taken a step toward the venerable VAX/VMS one, with the introduction of register CR8 (available only in 64 bit code) where the IRQL is stored. CR8 acts like the VAX PSL, masking interrupts. Before x64, e.g. in 32 bit Windows, the IRQL was implemented in software. Windows kept the current IRQL in a per-processor variable and programmed the interrupt controller to mask interrupts when the IRQL changed, mimicking what the VAX/VMS CPU did. This, by the way, is the reason why x64 Windows has 16 IRQL levels while the x86 version has 32: CR8 only allows 16 priority values. In 32 bit windows, the IRQL is implemented in software and not constrained by the processor.

14   Synchronization

14.1 The Problem

It is often needed to write a block of logic that reads and updates a set of variables as a whole. Consider for instance code managing a linked list. To add a node at the head of the list, the variable pointing to the first node must be read and copied into the *next* field of the new node, then the list head pointer must be updated with the address of the new node.

Such a block of logic is written under the assumption that the list head pointer is not changed by other events during its execution. However, in a multithreaded operating system, two threads could be executing this block of code simultaneously and corrupt the list.

To solve this problem, the system must provide code with a mechanism to ensure that only one thread at a time can execute such a block of code, i.e. to *synchronize* its execution.

Also, the thread executing such a block of code can be diverted by an interrupt while it is in the middle of the read/update sequence. If the code executed by the interrupt handler updates the same variables, we have the same problem, even though we are still in the same thread. Again, the system must provide some mechanism to deal with the problem.

Access to device registers is a similar problem: normally, a device expects its registers to be accessed according to a set of rules concerning the order of accesses and the data written to the registers themselves. If a block of code performing these accesses is preempted by another thread or suspended by an interrupt and the new thread or interrupt handler begins a new access to the same device, the latter is subjected to inconsistent actions on its registers.

We can therefore say that, in general, there is a *resource*, like the variables and registers of our examples, that must be protected by serializing access to it.

In Windows, we can identify three different scenarios for these problems, depending on the IRQL:

- The resource is accessed only in code paths which are not part of handlers of any interrupts, either hardware or software. As such, these code paths are executed at PASSIVE IRQL. Note that there is a kind of APC callback which is executed at PASSIVE, so this IRQL level does not mean, by itself, that the code is not part of *any* handler. Thus, we explicitly define this scenario as one where the code paths are not part of any handler and this, in turn, implies they are executed at PASSIVE. We will call this scenario *passive synchronization*.

- The resource is accessed both in code paths which are not part of any handler and in code paths invoked by the APC interrupt handler, executed either at PASSIVE or APC. We will call this scenario *APC synchronization*.

- The resource is accessed in at least one code path which is part of the handler for an interrupt with IRQL >= DPC. This code path could be a DPC callback called by the DPC interrupt handler or an interrupt service routine for a device. In this scenario, the resource may also be accessed by code not part of an handler, executed at PASSIVE, and by code called by the APC handler, executed either at PASSIVE or APC. We will call this scenario *high IRQL synchronization*.

We will now analyze how synchronization is achieved in these three scenarios, with one restriction: we will only consider resources accessed either by kernel mode code or by user mode code, but not by a mix of the two. Such a mix, if at all possible, is of little practical interest for the following reasons:

- Device registers are usually protected from access by user mode code.

- All the data structures that kernel mode code allocates for its own logic are in memory ranges inaccessible to user mode code (protected by the U/S bit of the PxEs).

- Kernel mode code could, conceivably, access a data structure in user mode memory, but it would need to be sure that the particular address space of the process which allocated the data structure is the one currently mapped.

Under this limitation, the only scenario which applies to user mode is passive synchronization, since the other two imply that at least one code path must be executed in kernel mode, to be part of an handler. There is a kind of APC called *user mode APC*, which executes a user mode callback, but it does not interrupt user mode code asynchronously. The callback is executed when the code calls certain APIs of its own accord, so we are not going to analyze this case.

14.2 Passive Synchronization

This scenario applies to user mode, but kernel mode code can perform passive synchronization too if the shared resource is never accessed inside an handler. Under this assumption, we know by design that we don't have to worry about interrupts, but only about concurrent threads trying to access the same resource.

Since the IRQL is PASSIVE, the thread can enter a wait state, so the resource is protected by using Windows APIs or DDIs which serialize execution by suspending threads. For instance, in user mode code, we can create a *mutex*, which is an object managed by Windows that can be in one of two states: owned by a thread or free. The *WaitForSingleObject* API can be used to ask ownership of the mutex. If the mutex is free when the call occurs, it becomes owned by the thread and execution is allowed to go on. If the mutex is owned by another thread, the one attempting to acquire it is suspended. From the code perspective, the thread is suspended inside the call to *WaitForSingleObject*. When the thread currently owning the mutex releases it, Windows notices that another thread is waiting for it and gives ownership of the mutex to the waiting thread, which is inserted in the list of threads ready to run. The code logic can be written on the assumption that, when the call to *WaitForSingleObject* returns, the thread owns the mutex and any other thread attempting to acquire it will be blocked. To serialize access to the resource it is thus enough that all the code paths that access it perform a call to *WaitForSingleObject* for the same mutex before doing so, and release the mutex only after their access to the resource is complete.

The Windows API offers various other synchronization objects with different behaviors but, all, ultimately, result in suspending one or more threads until a certain condition is satisfied.

There are similar synchronization objects and DDIs for kernel mode code.

14.3 APC Synchronization

We will consider this scenario mostly for the sake of completeness. It may also be the case that no resource in the kernel is actually accessed this way, but since the APC interrupt exists, we will examine how execution could be synchronized, if this scenario were to take place.

This kind of synchronization can still serialize execution of concurrent thread by means of objects like mutexes. Even the code invoked by the APC interrupt handler can block itself in a waiting state, because the IRQL is less than DISPATCH. In other words, we can, as in the previous scenario, be sure that only one thread is accessing the resource. However, the following could happen:

- The thread acquires the mutex protecting the resource on the code path which is not triggered by the APC interrupt and begins accessing the resource.

- The APC interrupt occurs, diverting the thread to another code path which attempts to access the same resource.

- The code on this path attempts acquisition of the mutex and *succeeds*, because such an object can be acquired multiple times by the same thread.

- Execution passes the mutex acquisition and accesses the resource, corrupting its state.

We can see how the mutex, by itself does not protect the resource. A couple of additional considerations are in order.

First, acquisition of a mutex disables delivery of *certain* APCs, which cannot interrupt the first code path in the example above. However, other APCs (called special kernel mode APCs) are still delivered.

Second, the possibility, for a mutex, to be acquired multiple times by the same thread is a necessity, otherwise a thread attempting to acquire the same mutex twice would block forever, waiting for itself to release it.

So, how can synchronization be achieved in this scenario? The code not part of the APC path can disable APCs completely by raising the IRQL to APC, or by calling a DDI called *KeEnterGuardedRegion* and acquire the mutex afterward. When both steps have been performed, only the code that follows can touch the resource and cannot be executed concurrently by multiple threads.

The code on the APC path does not have to worry about the no-handler code. It must only protect itself from concurrent execution by multiple threads and can do so by acquiring the mutex before accessing the resource. It's worth repeating that the code on the APC path can block, because its IRQL is less than DPC/dispatch, otherwise it could not.

14.4 High IRQL Synchronization

In this scenario, one or more code paths touching the resource are part of handlers and executed at IRQL >= DISPATCH. In order not to be too restrictive, we can consider multiple handlers executed at different IRQLs, including APC callbacks, all accessing the resource, together with code paths non part of an handler.

It is not possible to serialize execution of the handlers at DPC/dispatch IRQL or above by suspending competing threads, because the IRQL does not allow to call wait functions, as explained in Chapter 12 on p. 50.

Furthermore, all the code paths must account for the possibility of being interrupted by code accessing the resource. This can happen to the non-handler code, but also to an handler, which can be frozen by an interrupt at a higher IRQL. In other words, we have to solve two problems:

- Find a way to ensure only a single thread at a time can enter any of the code paths.

- Find a way for this thread to "synchronize with itself", with respect to interrupts.

The first step to solve these problems is to have all the code paths that access the resource raise the IRQL. Consider for instance a resource accessed by non-handler code and by a DPC callback. The highest possible IRQL at which the resource is accessed is DPC/dispatch. The code executing at PASSIVE, raises the IRQL to DPC/dispatch before accessing the resource.

If the resource is also accessed by an interrupt handler executed at IRQL 4, both the non-handler path and the DPC callback raise the IRQL to 4 before accessing it. In short, all code paths touch the resource at the highest possible IRQL value.

Let's focus first on what this means for interrupts, in the example above. The non-handler code raises the IRQL to 4, so it cannot be interrupted neither by a DPC, nor by the hardware interrupt. As long as the IRQL remains 4, only this code path will access the resource (we will consider other threads later).

The DPC code raises the IRQL too, so it cannot be interrupted by the hardware interrupt. The non-handler code is, by definition, not executed as part of an interrupt, so the DPC code will be the only one accessing the resource (again, let's forget other threads, for now) as long as the IRQL is 4.

Finally, the code of the handler for the hardware interrupt cannot be interrupted by a DPC which has a lower IRQL, so, when it runs, with the IRQL already set to 4 at the beginning of the interrupt handling, it is the only possible code path accessing the resource.

If, for the sake of completeness, we imagine the resource is also accessed by code invoked by the APC interrupt handler, the same reasoning applies: raising the IRQL to 4 on the other code paths inhibits the APC interrupt as well and the APC-invoked code can protect itself by raising the IRQL, like everybody else is doing.

Now let's turn our attention toward other threads. Suppose a processor is executing one of the three code paths of our example. After the IRQL has been raised to 4, thread switching is inhibited on that processor, because it requires a DPC interrupt. This is always true in the High IRQL Synchronization scenario, because the resource access occurs at least at DPC/dispatch IRQL. If there was only one processor in the system, we would not have to worry about other threads, simply thanks to having raised the IRQL. Actually, in older releases of Windows where there was a build of the kernel specialized for single processor systems, this was how this kind of synchronization worked in that build.

With more than one processor, now the norm, raising the IRQL is not enough. Other processors execute threads which may enter any of the three code paths of our example. It is therefore still necessary to place on each code path some logic that ensures that only one thread at a time can enter the block of code accessing the resource. However, since at least two code paths are executed at IRQL >= DPC/dispatch, they cannot enter a wait state.

The only solution left is to have the code test if another thread is executing the protected block and, if so, spin in a loop until the other thread has completed its job. To accomplish this, the kernel uses a data structure called a *spinlock*, which is similar to a mutex in the sense that is has two states: free and acquired. To acquire a spinlock, code uses a processor instruction capable of testing its state and changing it in the same uninterruptible access. This ensures that only one processor at a time can find the spinlock free and acquire it. Afterwards, all the code blocks attempting to acquire the spinlock cause the executing processor to spin in a loop until it becomes free again.

In our example, all the code paths acquire the same spinlock after having raised the IRQL and release it when access to the protected resource is concluded and before lowering the IRQL. This ensures that only one processor at a time can execute the code accessing the protected resource and solves the remaining part of the synchronization problem.

Every code path accessing the protected resource must perform two operations: raising the IRQL and acquiring the spinlock, so it is natural to wonder in what order they should be performed.

The correct sequence is to raise the IRQL first and acquire the spinlock later. This is required because a spinlock cannot be acquired multiple times by the same processor. In other words, after a processor has successfully acquired the spinlock, it cannot execute code that attempts to acquire the same spinlock again. This code would see the spinlock as acquired and spin in an infinite loop. There is no information associated with the spinlock status which records the fact that it is being requested by the same processor which acquired it previously. The spinlock is simply acquired, so the code spins. In this regard, spinlocks are different from mutexes.

Now, suppose the PASSIVE code path of our example performs the wrong sequence: acquire the spinlock first, raise the IRQL later. After having acquired the spinlock, the processor can service the interrupt at IRQL 4 which enters the handler code path. This, in turn, will try to acquire the same spinlock, causing an infinite loop.

Instead, raising the IRQL first, ensures that, when the spinlock acquisition is attempted, the related interrupt is *already* masked. After acquiring the spinlock, the executing processor can go on undisturbed until the point where it releases it, without being waylaid by an interrupt.

The correct order of operations is so important that kernel DDIs for spinlocks raise and restore the IRQL internally, as part of their operation, to ensure that everything occurs in the correct sequence. For instance, *KeAcquireSpinlock*, which is used when the highest IRQL of the various code paths is DPC/dispatch, raises the IRQL internally, *then* acquires the spinlock.

With this overall logic, all the code paths which acquire a given spinlock do so at the same IRQL level (4, in our example). Thus, a spinlock is always associated with an IRQL value, the level at which it is acquired.

When code which acquires a spinlock, like *KeAcquireSpinlock*, finds it already acquired, spins in a loop, thereby stalling a processor. It is thus important that spinlocks are held for the shortest possible time (the Windows WDK recommends a maximum of 25 microseconds). It would therefore be a disaster if a thread switch could occur after having acquired a spinlock, suspending the thread before it reaches the point where the spinlock is released. This cannot happen, however, because the spinlock is always acquired after raising the IRQL to DPC/dispatch or above.

Part III - Memory Management Fundamentals

15   Virtual Address Space Fundamentals

15.1 Basic Regions

The virtual address space can be divided into these four fundamentals region:

- The user mode range, from 0 to 0x7FF`FFFFFFFF, which is 8 TB in size and is the address range for the user mode part of the process, i.e. executables, DLLs and their working memory, like the stack and the heap.

- An unused address range from 0x800`00000000 to 0x00007FFF`FFFFFFFF. Since Windows limits the user mode address range to 8 TB, this range is not used.

- An invalid address range, due to the processor requirement that addresses be in canonical form, from 0x00008000`00000000 to 0xFFFF7FFF`FFFFFFFF. The addresses in this range break the canonical address rule: bits 47-63 must be either all 0 or all 1.

- The range from 0xFFFF8000`00000000 to 0xFFFFFFFF`FFFFFFFF which is the allowed range for canonical addresses with bit 47 set to 1. Windows uses regions inside this range for the kernel code and data structures, which will be analyzed in more detail later. For now, we will refer generically to these regions as system ones.

Each process has a private copy of the user mode range, which means virtual addresses (VAs) in these range are mapped to different physical pages. Given the necessary privileges and access rights, there are APIs to access the user range of a process from another one, however the basic VMM behavior is to create each process with its own private user range.

The system regions are, for the most part, shared among all processes, i.e. the VAs inside them map to the same physical pages. There are exceptions to this rule and we will examine them in more detail later.

15.2 Paging Structures Region

Given what the VMM must accomplish, it must be able to modify the processor paging structures. This, however, brings us to an interesting problem: processor instructions can only use virtual addresses, i.e. there is no way to update the content of a memory location by directly specifying its physical address. So, the only way to access the PML4, PDPT, etc is to map them to virtual addresses as well, which, at first sight, seems to lead us back to where we started.

15.2.1   The PML4 Auto-entry

The solution to this problem, which is simpler than it seems and is quite interesting, is to use a single PML4 entry in a very special way: the entry at index 0x1ed stores the PFN of the PML4 itself. We will call this entry the *PML4 auto-entry* and we are now going to see that it has some intriguing implications.

Let's start by recalling that a PML4 entry maps 512GB of VA space, so there will be such a range reserved for this special purpose (but with 256TB of VA space we can afford to be generous). To determine the address range corresponding to this PML4 entry, we must remember that the PML4 index is stored into bits 39-47 of the VA; when this index is set to 0x1ed, the corresponding virtual address range is as follows:

0x1ed = 1 1110 1101b

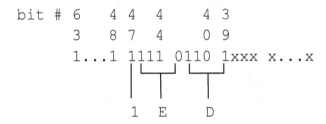

Figure 10 - VA with PML4 Index = 0x1ed

Figure 10 shows a VA with bits 39-47 set to 0x1ed. Since bit 47 = 1, bits 48-63 must be 1 as well. Bits 0 − 38 can range from 0...0 to 1...1. The resulting VA range is:

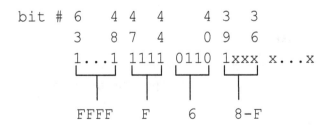

Figure 11 - Paging Structures VA Range

The hex digit comprising bits 36-39 range from 8 to 0xf, as its rightmost "x" bits range from 000 to 111. Thus, the resulting address range is:

0xFFFFF680`00000000 – 0xFFFFF6FF`FFFFFFFF

Let's focus now on what happens when the processor translates a VA inside this range: it uses index 0x1ed to select the PML4 entry and uses the entry PFN to locate the PDPT. But, wait! The PFN of this entry points to the PML4 itself, so this table is used as PDPT as well. This means that:

- The PDPT index from the VA (bits 30-38) selects an entry from the PML4, which is acting as PDPT; this entry points to a PDPT, because it is actually a PML4 entry. Note the "shift" in the index usage: the PDPT index is applied to the PML4.

- The PD index (bits 21-29) selects an entry from the table retrieved in the step above, i.e from the PDPT. Again we have a shift in the index usage: the PD index is applied to the PDPT, so it selects a PD.

- The PT index is applied to the table from the previous step, i.e. the PD and selects a PT. This becomes the physical page to which the VA maps, because it is the one selected by the PT index field of the VA. In other words, what we "see" at this VA is the content of a page table.

For instance, at address 0xFFFFF680`00000000 we see the first byte of a PTE for some virtual address. PTEs are 8 bytes in size, so the next PTE will be at 0xFFFFF680`00000008 and so on.

15.2.2 Relationship Between a VA and the Address of Its PTE

While it is nice to know that the PTE for a given VA is somewhere inside a 512GB region, it would be better to narrow its actual location down a little. It turns out there's a very simple relationship between a VA and the address of its PTE. Below we see a VA broken down into its components:

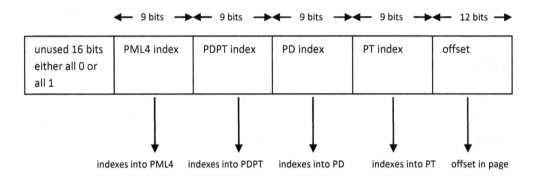

Figure 12 - Virtual Address Components

Let's see what happens when we do the following:

- Shift the VA 9 bits to the right

- Set the leftmost 16 bits (48-63) to 1

- Replace the PML4 index with the auto-entry index

- Set bits 0-2 to 0

We end up with the following:

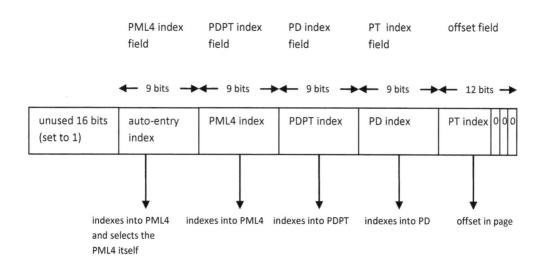

Figure 13 - PTE VA

As we saw before, the auto-entry index "shifts" the meaning of the remaining indexes: the PDPT index is applied to the PML4 and so on. But here we have also shifted to the right the VA content by 9 bits, i.e. by one "index slot", so the field for the PDPT index is now set to the original PML4 index and so on.

This way, the original PML4 index is still indexing into the PML4 (from the PDPT index field of the new value) and selecting the PDPT for the original VA; the PDPT index is still indexing into the PDPT and selecting the PD for the original VA and so on, until the PT which maps the original VA is mapped as the physical page. In other words, given a VA, this transformation gives us another VA, at which we "see" the PT used to map the VA we began with.

Finally, the offset in page is PT index followed by three bits set to 0, which gives

    (PT index) x 8

and since PTEs are 8 bytes in size, this is the offset, inside the PT, of the PTE for the original VA.

The end result is that the VA resulting from the steps above is the VA of the PTE.

Also, we had to set bits 0-2 to 0 because, after the shift, the offset field which is 12 bits wide contains the PT index in bits 3-11 and bits 0-2 retain what is left of the original offset field, i.e. its three leftmost bits, which are meaningless: they just give a random offset from the PTE starting address. We also had to set bits 48-63 to 1 because, when we set bits 39-47 to the auto-entry index, bit 47 is set to 1.

Now suppose to update the PTE address we just computed as follows:

- Shift it left by 9 positions

- Set bits 48-63 according to the value of bit 47 after the shift

This is what we get:

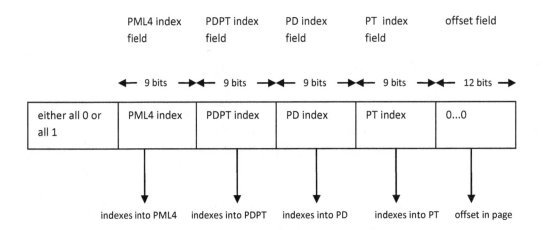

Figure 14 - VA from PTE VA

We have the original VA, with the offset component set to zero. In other words, given a PTE address, this operation obtains the address of the first byte of the virtual page mapped by the PTE.

15.2.3   Virtual Addresses for PDEs, PDPTEs, PML4Es

Being able to access PTEs is nice, but what about the other kind of tables (PML4, PDPT, etc.)? Windows must have a way to access their content as well. It turns out that the PML4 auto-entry solves this problem as well.

Consider a VA like the following one:

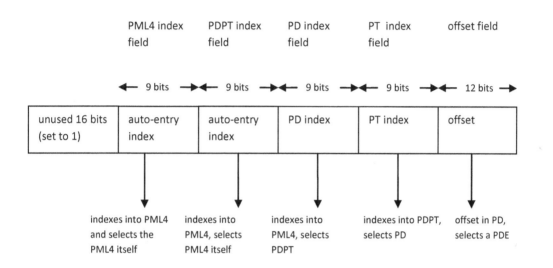

Figure 15 - PDE Virtual Address

This time we have set both the PML4 index and the PDPT index to the auto-entry index, so that the PD index selects a PDPT and the PT index selects a PD. An address of this kind maps a page directory into the virtual address space and we "see" PDEs at the addresses inside this virtual page.

We can compute the starting and ending address of the PDE range as follows:

starting address:

>   bits 63-48 = 1

>   bits 39-47 = 1ed (i.e. auto-entry index)

>   bits 30-38 = 1ed

>   bits 0-29 = 0

ending address: same as above, but with bits 0-29 = 1.

The results are:

> PDE range starting address = 0xFFFFF6FB`40000000

> PDE range ending address = 0xFFFFF6FB`80000000

Note here and in the following, we will use the term ending address for the first byte after the range, e.g 0xFFFFF6FB`80000000 instead of 0xFFFFF6FB`7FFFFFFF.

This range is inside the PTE range computed previously, so now we see that it splits the actual PTE range into two regions, with a range in between were PDEs rather than PTEs are mapped.

The same logic we used for PTE addresses shows the relationship between a VA and its PDE address: the latter is obtained from the former by shifting it right by 18 positions (i.e. 2 "index slots") and replacing the indexes for PML4 and PDPT with the auto-entry index (and by making it canonical).

By reversing the process (left-shift eighteen times and set address in canonical form), we get back the starting address of the region mapped by the PDE. Of course this region is not a single page anymore: it's encompassed by a single PDE, which maps 512 PTEs, therefore it covers 512 pages i.e. 2MB.

Similar results apply for PDPTEs: their addresses have the three leftmost indexes set to the auto-entry index. This results in the following range:

> PDPTE range starting address = 0xFFFFF6FB`7DA00000

> PDPTE range ending address = 0xFFFFF6FB`7DC00000

To get the PDPTE address for a VA, we have to shift it right 9 x 3 = 27 times and set the auto-index in the PML4, PDPT and PD slot.

Finally, an address with all four indexes set to the auto-index maps the PML4 itself in the following 4 kB range.

> PML4E range starting address = 0xFFFFF6FB`7DBED000

> PML4E range ending address = 0xFFFFF6FB`7DBEE000

The auto-entry has index 0x1ed, i.e. offset 0x1ed x 8 = 0xf68 into this page, so it's VA is:

0XFFFFF6FB`7DBEDF68

The following figure depicts the various paging structures regions:

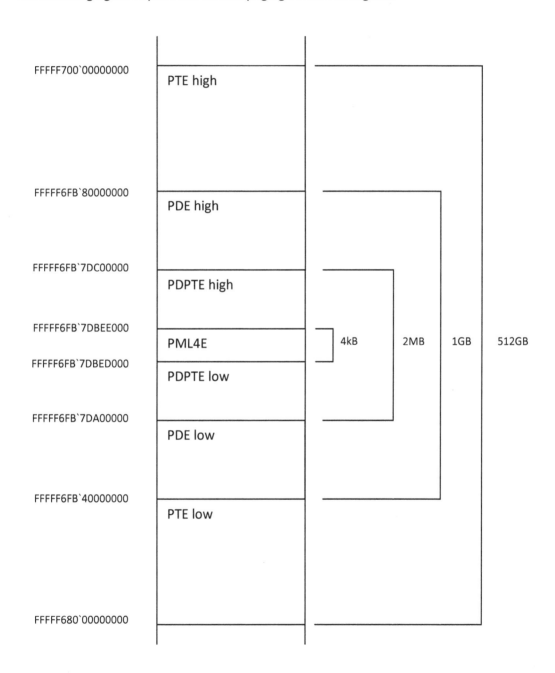

Figure 16 - Paging Structures Region

WinDbg comes with the handy !pte extension which computes the VAs of the paging structure entries mapping a virtual address, so we don't have to do it by hand: just enter !pte followed by the virtual address.

15.2.4   Paging Structures Region Protection

The paging structures region must, of course, be accessible from kernel mode code only (i.e. code executed at CPL = 0). How this is accomplished is somewhat interesting. Let's start with the output of !pte for a valid user mode address:

```
0: kd> !pte 1c0000
                                             VA 00000000001c0000
PXE at FFFFF6FB7DBED000   PPE at FFFFF6FB7DA00000   PDE at FFFFF6FB40000000   PTE at FFFFF68000000E00
contains 00C0000031C17867  contains 0100000036F1A867  contains 011000002A19B867  contains 9F40000034CAB867
pfn 31c17    ---DA--UWEV  pfn 36f1a    ---DA--UWEV  pfn 2a19b    ---DA--UWEV  pfn 34cab    ---DA--UW-V
```

The shaded "U"s represent the fact that each PxE sets the protection of the virtual range it maps to user mode. In other words, the PML4E, PDPTE, PDE, PTE all have the U/S bit set. U/S is bit 2 of a PxE and the output above shows that the rightmost byte of each PxE is 7, so bit 2 is set.

We can compare this with the output for the first page of the kernel:

```
0: kd> !pte fffff800`02857000
                                             VA fffff80002857000
PXE at FFFFF6FB7DBEDF80   PPE at FFFFF6FB7DBF0000   PDE at FFFFF6FB7E0000A0   PTE at FFFFF6FC000142B8
contains 0000000000199063  contains 0000000000198063  contains 00000000001DA063  contains 8000000002857963
pfn 199      ---DA--KWEV  pfn 198      ---DA--KWEV  pfn 1da      ---DA--KWEV  pfn 2857     -G-DA--KW-V
```

The shaded "K"s and the values ending with 3, tell us that the VA protection is kernel mode, as it should be.

Now, let's see the protection of a VA at which a PTE is visible. We are going to look at the address of the PTE mapping the user mode address 0x1c0000 above. We see from the previous !pte output, that the PTE address is 0xFFFFF680`00000E00, so let's see how the page enclosing it is mapped:

```
                                             VA fffff68000000000
PXE at FFFFF6FB7DBEDF68   PPE at FFFFF6FB7DBED000   PDE at FFFFF6FB7DA00000   PTE at FFFFF6FB40000000
contains 000000001AB3D863  contains 00C0000031C17867  contains 0100000036F1A867  contains 011000002A19B867
pfn 1ab3d    ---DA--KWEV  pfn 31c17    ---DA--UWEV  pfn 36f1a    ---DA--UWEV  pfn 2a19b    ---DA--UWEV
```

The output above shows that the PTE for the address is at 0xFFFFF6FB`40000000 and is set to 0x011000002A19B867. If we look at the output for the first !pte command, we see that the same address and value were reported for the PDE. This comes from the way the PTE address is computed: we must shift the VA right by 9 bits and replace the PML4 index with the auto entry index, so all the original indexes are shifted into the next hierarchy level, i.e. the PML4 index becomes the PDPT index, etc.

So, the PTE for the page at 0xFFFFF680`00000000, is the PDE of our original address. Now, since the original address was a user mode one, its PDE has the U bit *set*, so we see from the output above that the PTE for this *system* page ends with 7 and "U" is reported by the debugger.

The same applies to the PDE and the PDPTE: they are the same used to map the original user mode address, so they all have the U/S bit set. This can be seen in the output of the last !pte command above and is quite different from the result for address 0xFFFFF800`02857000.

Does this mean that the PTE is accessible from user mode? Can user mode code corrupt PTEs simply by using a stray pointer? No, because, for a virtual address to be accessible in user mode, *all* the PxEs of the hierarchy must have U/S set, and the !pte output above shows that this bit is clear in the PML4E. *This* is what actually protects the PTE address and ensures that all the paging structures region is protected.

Having the PxEs for a VA with different protection is not usual: normally, the U/S bits are either all set or all clear, depending on the address range, but this can't be avoided in the paging structures region, due to the "overloaded" used of PxEs, e.g. the fact that a PDE for a user range address, becomes the PTE for a system range one.

15.2.5   A Note on !pte Usage

Let's take another look at the !pte output for our original address:

```
0: kd> !pte 1c0000
                                         VA 00000000001c0000
PXE at FFFFF6FB7DBED000   PPE at FFFFF6FB7DA00000   PDE at FFFFF6FB40000000   PTE at FFFFF68000000E00
contains 00C0000031C17867  contains 0100000036F1A867  contains 011000002A19B867  contains 9F40000034CAB867
pfn 31c17    ---DA--UWEV  pfn 36f1a    ---DA--UWEV  pfn 2a19b    ---DA--UWEV  pfn 34cab    ---DA--UW-V
```

It's PTE is at 0xFFFFF680`00000E00, so, to see its mapping we feed this address to !pte. Here is what we get:

```
0: kd> !pte FFFFF68000000E00
                                         VA 00000000001c0000
PXE at FFFFF6FB7DBED000   PPE at FFFFF6FB7DA00000   PDE at FFFFF6FB40000000   PTE at FFFFF68000000E00
contains 00C0000031C17867  contains 0100000036F1A867  contains 011000002A19B867  contains 9F40000034CAB867
pfn 31c17    ---DA--UWEV  pfn 36f1a    ---DA--UWEV  pfn 2a19b    ---DA--UWEV  pfn 34cab    ---DA--UW-V
```

Not quite what we were expecting: we are still seeing the mapping for 0x1c0000. As it turns out, when !pte is given an address in the paging structures region, it assumes what we really want to see is the address mapped by it and this is what we get.

We can work around this behavior by moving up one level in the paging structures hierarchy: use !pte with the *PDE* address. This will show us the PxEs for the address *mapped by* the PDE, which happens to be the *page table*:

```
0: kd> !pte FFFFF6FB40000000
                                          VA fffff68000000000
PXE at FFFFF6FB7DBEDF68    PPE at FFFFF6FB7DBED000    PDE at FFFFF6FB7DA00000    PTE at FFFFF6FB40000000
contains 000000001AB3D863  contains 00C0000031C17867  contains 0100000036F1A867  contains 011000002A19B867
pfn 1ab3d    ---DA--KWEV  pfn 31c17    ---DA--UWEV  pfn 36f1a    ---DA--UWEV  pfn 2a19b    ---DA--UWEV
```

We are finally seeing the mapping of the page table address. This can be confusing at times, but is enough to remember that, in the paging structures region, we must use !pte with the address of the next upper hierarchy level.

15.3 System Address Range

This section is an introduction to the virtual range reserved for the kernel. We will only define some fundamental concepts here, saving all the details for part V of this book.

15.3.1   Where Does the System Address Range Begins?

The starting address of the system address range was an easy concept with 32 bits Windows: it was simply 0x8000000, or 0xC0000000 when using the /3GB boot option. In other words, the system address range was simply the upper half of the 4GB virtual range or the upper 1GB, if /3GB was used to leave more breathing room for user mode code.

With x64 things have become more complex.

First of all, canonical addressing with 48 bits means the higher region of the virtual address space lays between 0xFFFF8000`00000000 and 0xFFFFFFFF`FFFFFFFF, which corresponds to the upper 128TB of the virtual range, with the top of the range at 16 Exabytes – 1 (we will refer to this region as the *high range* in the following).

This does not mean, however, that Windows places the beginning of the system address region at the high range start. The lowest used region in the high range is the paging structures one, starting at 0xFFFFF680`00000000. This means that a huge portion of the high region (0xFFFF8000`00000000 – 0xFFFFF67F`FFFFFFFF or 118.5TB) is not used.

In the remainder of this book we will use the term *system range* to refer to the used portion of the high range.

Certain data structures cannot be stored at addresses below 8TB from the top of the system range. This will be explained in detail in sec. 44.1 on p. 414. For now, we are just going to point out that the part of the system range below the 8TB limit is not available for all purposes and, for this reason, there are various sources stating that the system range is 8TB in size. This is not correct, however: 8TB from the top of the range gives address 0xFFFFF800`00000000, but Windows uses an extra 1.5TB in the range 0xFFFFF680`00000000 – 0xFFFFF7FF`FFFFFFFF, so the total system range is 9.5TB in size.

15.3.2   Main System Regions

With this in mind, we can further break down the system address range by looking with WinDbg at the PML4 content for the high range, whose PML4Es start at 0xFFFFF6FB`7DBED800 and end at 0xFFFFF6FB`7DBEDFF8. We can see that:

- PML4Es for VAs from 0xFFFF8000`00000000 to 0xFFFFF680`00000000 (excluded) are unused (set to 0).

  As we anticipated, this address range is unused by Windows, a fact which is also stated in [2].

- The PML4E for the range 0xFFFFF680`00000000 – 0xFFFFF700`00000000 is the auto-entry.

- Other PML4Es above the auto-entry are used and thus map various 512GB regions.

The figure below depicts the high range mapped by a typical PML4. We will examine in more detail the various regions introduced here in part V of this book.

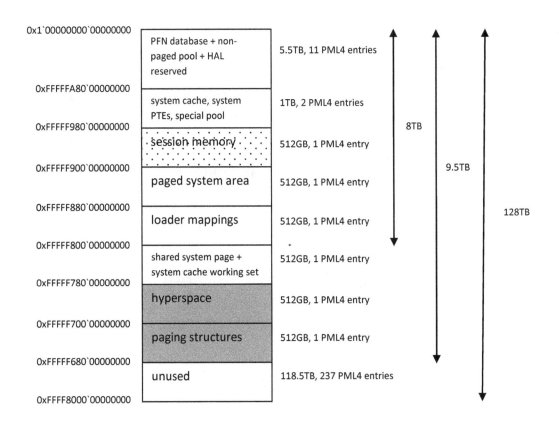

Figure 17 - High Range Regions

For now, we are not going to worry about the exact meaning of these regions. However, simply by looking at PML4s of different processes, we observe two very significant facts.

First of all, the shaded regions, which correspond to 1 PML4E each, store *different* values for different processes. This means each process has *its own private copy* of these regions, even though they are in the system address range. The first region is hardly a surprise: it's the paging structures region. Obviously, each process maps *its own* paging structures or, in other words the PML4E stores the PFN of the PML4 for that particular process.

The second region is more mysterious and we will return to it, to see how Windows uses it. For now, let's just note that this too is process-private.

The second interesting fact is that the content of the PML4E for the dotted region is the same for all the processes belonging to the same session, but it's different among sessions. This region of memory is therefore shared among the processes of a session, but each session has its own private copy of it.

Let's concentrate now on the other PML4Es: their content is the same for every process, so each address space maps the same physical pages in the corresponding regions. It is not strictly necessary to have identical PML4Es to achieve this: each process could have different PML4Es pointing to different PDPTs, PDs and PTs. The only requirement is that the PT entries must ultimately point to the same physical pages. By setting the PML4Es to the same values in each address space, Windows reuses the PDPTs and, thus, the whole hierarchy of paging structures for each address space, instead of duplicating it. This gives us two benefits. The more obvious one is that we save physical memory; the more subtle, but perhaps more important, is that when we map or unmap a physical page in these ranges, we only have to update one PT entry. If we were to have multiple page tables pointing to the same physical page, we would have to update them all, to make a shared system page present or not present. To do this, we would have to walk the paging structures for all the running processes, which would be a huge waste of time. Add to this that the same applies to PTs, PDs and PDPTs, which can be added to and removed from the whole hierarchy as well, and we see how important it is to share the latter among all address spaces.

We can also guess that the PML4s structure does not change during a Windows session: entries set to 0 are never used and entries for shared regions always point to the same PDPT; otherwise we would be back at having to update all PML4s for all the address spaces, which is unlikely.

There are a couple more interesting things worth mentioning.

The high range is 128TB wide and is mapped by the upper half of the PML4, consisting of 256 PML4Es. Only a handful of these entries, 19, are used by Windows, corresponding to the upper 9.5TB of the address space, so there is a lot of unused virtual address space.

Finally, inside the kernel, is a static variable named MmSystemAddressStart whose name appears to be self-explaining. However, this variable stores the following value:

    0xFFFF0800`00000000

which is not even a canonical address: bits 48-63 are set to 1 and bit 47 is set to 0. As of 32 bit Windows 2000, this variable used to store the actual system range start (0x80000000 or 0xC0000000, [3], p. 427), but now it appears to be useless.

16   Introduction to NUMA Systems

16.1 What NUMA Systems Are

The acronym NUMA stands for Non Uniform Memory Access and indicates a system were a processor accesses different ranges of memory in different ways.

Consider for instance a system with two processors, P0 and P1, each including an on-chip memory controller. Each processor will be tightly connected to a number of RAM chips through its controller. If P0 wants to access memory connected to P1, it must use the interprocessor bus while, for memory connected to its own controller, the access path is much shorter. The memory latency changes depending on *where* the memory is, with respect to the processor.

On contemporary processors, it is common to have multiple cores on a single chip which includes the memory controller. These cores are actually independent processors and they all have the same access path to memory, with faster access to RAM connected to the on-chip controller and slower access to other memory. Such a set of processors and the memory closest to them is called a *node*.

System memory is still organized as a single address space accessible to all processors so, functionally, a NUMA system works like a Simmetric Multiprocessing (SMP) one. This means that a certain physical address will give access to a byte belonging to node 0, while another address will reference memory on node 1. Normally, a physical page belong entirely to a single node.

A system with more than two nodes can have different access latencies across different nodes. For example, node 0 can access memory belonging to node 1 faster than memory belonging to node 2, etc., depending on how the interprocessor bus works.

NUMA must be kept in mind to improve system performances. For example, it is better to schedule a process preferably on processors belonging on a single node and to map its virtual addresses with pages of the same node. If there are no available pages on the preferred node and access time changes across nodes, it is better to attempt to allocate memory from the node with shorter access time, also called the nearest node.

16.2 Numa Support in Windows

We will see, while analyzing some details of memory management, how NUMA is supported throughout the VMM. It is therefore useful to introduce now a few basic concepts about NUMA support in Windows.

When the VMM initializes, it executes a function named *MiComputeNumaCosts* ([1], p. 791) which determines the distribution of physical pages among nodes in the system, so that the VMM "knows" which pages belong to which nodes. It also determines the distance between nodes, building a logical representation of the system. This way, when the VMM needs to allocate a page from a particular node, it knows which pages belong to it and whether some of them are available. If there are no available pages on that node, it tries the nearest one, and so on until it finds an available page. In short, the VMM attempts to allocate the nearest available page.

The Windows scheduler assigns each thread an ideal processor and tries to run each thread on this processor for most of the time; when the VMM allocates a physical page on behalf of a thread, it extracts from the _KTHREAD of the thread the ideal processor index, which it uses to access the processor _KPRCB structure; from there, it can find the list of physical pages for the node the processor belongs to and perform the allocation sequence outlined above.

Thus, the VMM and the thread dispatcher cooperate in trying to keep a thread running on a given node and allocating physical pages belonging to the same node.

A thread can run on a processor other than its ideal one if the latter is busy and there are other idle processors ([1], p.443). This makes sense because it means Windows prefers to make use of an idle processor rather than keep the thread waiting. When this happens, and the VMM must provide a physical page to the thread, it still looks for available pages in the order described earlier, starting with the node for the ideal processor. The fact that a thread is temporarily running on some non-ideal processor does not mean its physical pages are allocated from the node of this particular processor. The thread dispatcher will return the thread to its ideal processor as soon as it can, so it is better to always take memory pages from the ideal node (the node of the ideal processor).

17   Cache and Page Color

Before going on examining the VMM internals, we need to define the concept of page color. To explain it, we need to understand how the processor cache works.

17.1 Cache Fundamentals

To make a practical example, we will consider the L2 cache found on the Intel Core2 Duo Mobile processor, which has the following characteristics (which will be explained shortly):

size:	4MB
ways:	16
cache line:	64 bytes

Now suppose the processor wants to access the following physical address:

```
bit #         3333 3322 2222 2222 1111 1111 11
              5432 1098 7654 3210 9876 5432 1098 7654 3210
0x781f423 =   0000 0000 0111 1000 0001 1111 0100 0010 0011
```

We represent the address as a 36 bits binary number, because this particular processor limits the address size to 36 bits. We are now going to see how the processor looks for this address into the cache.

First of all, data is loaded from memory into the cache in fixed-size blocks of contiguous bytes called *cache lines*. The first byte of a cache line must have an address which is a multiple of the cache line size. When the processor needs to load into the cache one or more bytes at an arbitrary address, it loads the entire cache line (or lines) which include the desired bytes. More than one line can be loaded if the byte block being accessed straddles a cache line boundary.

Obviously, the cache must be organized in a way that allows to know the address from which a cached byte has been loaded. However, since bytes in a line are contiguous, the cache organization only keeps track of the address of the first byte in the line, which we will call the *line address*. Addresses of other bytes are simply computed from the line address and the byte offset into the line.

In the following, we will also use the term *memory line* to indicate a line-size-long block of bytes in memory beginning at a multiple of the line size, i.e. a memory block which can be loaded into a single cache line and completely fill it.

For the processor we are considering (and for almost all x64 processors today) the cache line size is 64 bytes. Since a line address is a multiple of 64, bits 0-5 which range from 0 to 63 are always 0 for such an address. For a generic address, they give the offset into the line, if the latter is found in the cache; they are not used to locate the line containing the desired data into the cache.

Given this, the processors uses the next 12 bits, i.e. bits 6-17, to look for the desired line into a group of arrays of cache memory blocks. Each array is called a *way* and in our example we have 16 of them. The processor uses bits 6-17 as an index into the ways and locates 16 data blocks, one for each way. Collectively, these 16 data blocks are called the *set* for the particular index value extracted from bits 6-17.

Each data block in the set holds the content of a cache line which *might* be the one the processor is looking for, because it is a line with address bits 6-17 equal to 01 1111 0100 00; it could therefore refer to the desired line or to another one with the same values for these bits. This means we need some more data to know if our address is cached and into which of the data blocks. To solve this problem, the processor stores bits 18-35 of the line address in the data block, together which the cache line content (remember, on this particular processor the physical address is limited to 36 bits, so we are not interested in bits higher than bit 35). This group of bits is called the *tag*. Suppose the content of our address is indeed cached into one of the cache ways. We can represent the way content as in the following figure:

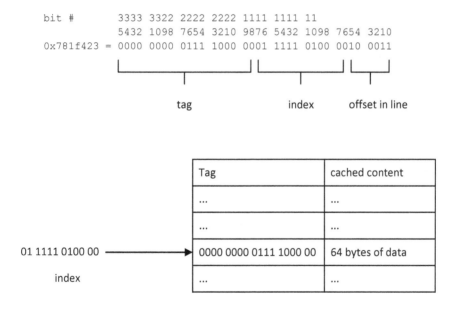

way containing cached content of
0x781f423

Figure 18 - Logical Scheme of a Cache Way

The other data blocks in the set will store content from different addresses and will have different tags. It is also interesting to note that the processor can simultaneously compare all the tags stored in the 16 data blocks with the tag from our address, without iterating over the blocks, thus the cache can be very fast.

But why having more than one way, i.e. why having *sets* of data blocks? Because, with a single way, two memory lines having the same index, i.e. the same value for bits 6-17 of the line address, could never fit in the cache at the same time: there would be only one "slot" for this particular index and a new line pointing to this slot would evict the previous one from the cache. With 16 ways the processor can store up to 16 lines with the same index and, eventually, evict the least recently used (LRU), when all the ways are in use.

It is not always the case that all entries in the cache contain valid memory data. A particular way entry could simply never have been used, because less than 16 addresses with its index have been cached, or its content could have been invalidated. Invalidation of a cache line usually occurs when the processor detects that another processor is writing to the address of the cached data. This means that the copy in the cache is not up to date anymore, so the detecting processor marks its data block as invalid (a processor does not reload the cache line until the code it is executing tries to actually access the same physical address).

A cache with this architecture is called a *set associative* cache, while a cache with only one way would be a *direct mapped* cache.

The ideal cache would be a *fully associative* cache, i.e. one allowing a cache line to be stored anywhere, without using part of the address as an index. With such a cache, the processor would need to evict a line only when the whole cache would become full, instead of when the 16 possible blocks for its index are all in use and the evicted line could be the LRU one of the whole cache, not just of the 16 blocks. The problem is that realizing a fully associative cache becomes more complex as the cache size grows and it is not practically possible with sizes of the order of megabytes, which are found in today's L2 caches. The processor does have a fully associative cache, named *translation lookaside buffer*, which we will discuss later in this book, but is used only for a specialized purpose and is very small (less than 100 entries).

The number of bits used to index into the ways can be computed from the cache size, the cache line size and the number of ways. In our example:

cache size =4 MB

total number of lines in the cache = 4 MB / 64 Bytes = 65,536

number of lines per way = 65536 / 16 = 4,096

Each way has 4,096 entries, therefore we need 12 bits to index over it.

17.2 Page Color

The *color* of a physical memory page is a number which identifies the sets into which addresses from the page can be cached. Pages with the same color are cached in the same sets and therefore compete with each other to find room in the 16 ways of the cache.

The starting address of a page is aligned on a 4kB boundary and therefore has bits 0-11 set to 0. For instance, the page containing the address considered in the previous section (0x781f423) begins at 0x781f000; the set index for the first line in the page is the value of bits 6-17 of this address:

Figure 19 - Components of the Starting Address of a Page

In the following, we will call the set index of the first page line the *page set index.* Our page set index is therefore 01 1111 0000 00.

With 4kB pages and 64 bytes per cache line, a page spans 64 adjacent lines or 64 consecutive index values beginning from the page set index.

Every page with the same page set index will be cached in the same 64 sets used for this one, therefore we could define the page color as the page set index. However, since the first line is page-aligned, it has bits 0-11 set to 0, so the lower 6 bits of the page set index are always 0:

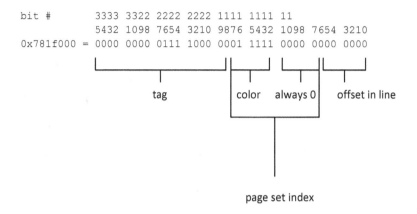

```
bit #          3333 3322 2222 2222 1111 1111 11
               5432 1098 7654 3210 9876 5432 1098 7654 3210
0x781f000 =    0000 0000 0111 1000 0001 1111 0000 0000 0000
```

tag   color   always 0   offset in line

page set index

Figure 20 - Page Set Index

Thus, we define the page color as the 6 leftmost bits of the page set index, or bits 12-17 of the page starting address. Our page has color = 0y011111 = 0x1f and all the pages with this color will be cached in the same cache sets with indexes ranging from 0y011111000000 to 0y011111111111.

But why is the page color important? Because two addresses inside two different pages with the same color *can* end up in the same cache set, i.e. have the same cache index, while, on the other hand, addresses from pages with different colors are *guaranteed* to occupy different cache sets. When the VMM allocates physical pages, it keeps this in mind. For instance, when a new physical page is allocated for the address space of a process, the VMM tries to locate an available physical page with color equal to the color of the last page assigned to the same process plus one. A per address space color counter is updated on each allocation to track the color of the last allocated page. This way, the VMM minimizes the chance that physical pages of a single address space compete with each other for cache sets, possibly bumping each other out of the cache while that address space is current.

True, since the cache has 16 ways, it can store up to 16 pages with the same color, but with today's memory sizes a process can allocate *hundreds of thousands* of physical pages, so distributing them evenly over all the possible colors is important to improve performance.

Which address bits are actually included in the page color depends on the cache characteristics (the examples we saw so far were for an Intel Core 2 Duo mobile processor). The cache line size alone determines the least significant bit of the set index, e. g. bit 6 for 64 bytes lines. The line size, cache size, and number of ways determine how many entries each way has and therefore the number of bits in the set index. The color bits begin at bit 12, because pages are 4kB in size and extend up to the most significant bit of the set index.

For instance, an Intel Core i7 Q720 mobile processor has an L3 cache with the following characteristics:

size: 6MB
ways: 12
cache line: 64 bytes

This yields a 13 bits set index:

total number of lines in the cache = 6 MB / 64 Bytes = 98,304

number of lines per way = 98.304 / 12 = 8,192

13 bits are therefore needed to index into 8,192 entries. The set index will be made up of bits 6-18 of the address and the page color bits will be bits 12-18, with the color number being 7 bits in size.

Windows uses a bitmask stored into the `_KPRCB.SecondaryColorMask` member to filter the page color bits. To compute the color of a page, the VMM ANDs the PFN with the mask.

It can be observed that, with a Core 2 Duo processor, the mask is set to 0x3f, which filters the 6 rightmost bits of the PFN, i.e. bits 12-17 of the physical address (recall that PFN = physical address >> 12).

Consistently, on the Core i7 processor the mask is set to 0x7f, accounting for the extra bit in the set index.

17.3 Page Color vs. Other Caches

So far we have been considering the L2 cache of the Core 2 Duo processor and the L3 cache of the Core i7, but what about the other caches?

In general, caches nearer to the processor, like the L1 cache or, in the case of the Core i7, the L2, are smaller than the last level cache. As long as all the caches have the same line size, as it usually is the case, allocating pages with consecutive colors for the largest cache gives the same benefit for the smaller ones. Consider for instance the Core i7 L2 cache:

size: 256kB
ways: 8
cache line: 64 bytes

total number of lines in the cache = 256 kB / 64 Bytes = 4,096
number of lines per way = 4,096 / 8 = 512
set index size: 9 bits
set index bits: 6-14

The page color bits with respect to this cache are therefore bits 12-14.

We already saw that the VMM computes the page color as the value of bits 12-18 for this processor, which is consistent with the characteristics of the larger L3 cache. We also know that the VMM tries to optimize the page placement in the cache by choosing pages with consecutive colors. This means the physical address bits for the pages of an address space will be as in the following table:

L3 Cache Color Bits							L2 Cache Color Value	L3 Cache Color Value
				L2 Cache Color Bits				
18	17	16	15	14	13	12		
0	0	0	0	0	0	0	0	0
0	0	0	0	0	0	1	1	1
0	0	0	0	0	1	0	2	2
0	0	0	0	0	1	1	3	3
0	0	0	0	1	0	0	4	4
0	0	0	0	1	0	1	5	5
0	0	0	0	1	1	0	6	6
0	0	0	0	1	1	1	7	7

The L2 color wraps around with the next allocation								
0	0	0	1	0	0	0	0	8
0	0	0	1	0	0	1	1	9
...	...	...	...	...	...	...	...	...

The table lists the pages in order of allocation, assuming the first color value used is 0, but this is not important. We can see that the color has consecutive values for both the L2 and the L3 cache, thanks to the fact that the L2 color is a subset of the L3 one and the least significant bit is the same. Of course, the color of the smaller L2 wraps around first, so it takes less pages before this cache begins to have lines with the same set index and to rely on associativity (i.e. having more than one way) to make them fit. This is simply due to the fact that the cache is smaller and it can't be helped.

In summary, we can generalize our reasoning and say that with a cache hierarchy consisting of an arbitrary number of levels, choosing the page color in this way optimizes the placement of pages in all the caches, as long as they have the same line size, so that the least significant color bit is the same for all levels.

17.4 L1 Caches

A final note concerns the L1 cache. The physical address of the working set pages has no effect on the placement of the memory content in this cache, because of a surprising detail. This cache is not indexed using bits from the physical address, but, rather, from the *virtual* one, while the tag bits still come from the physical address.

This may seem surprising, because virtual addresses are mapped to physical ones depending on where CR3 is pointing and the content of the paging structures, thus an entry associated with a virtual address is correct only as long as the mappings don't change.

Consider the following scenario: virtual address VA1 is mapped to physical address PA1 and the content of PA1 is cached in the L1. Afterwards, the virtual to physical mapping is changed, so that VA1 now maps to PA2. If we index into the L1 ways using VA1, we find the data block caching PA1, but we really need the memory content for PA2. How do we detect that the cache content is for the wrong physical address?

If the size of the L1 cache is small enough, this problem is actually a false one. Consider for instance, the L1 data cache of the Core 2 Duo Mobile and the Core i7 Mobile, with the following characteristics:

size: 32kB
ways: 8
cache line: 64 bytes

total number of lines in the cache = 32 kB / 64 Bytes = 512
number of lines per way = 512 / 8 = 64
set index size: 6 bits
set index bits: 6-11

The set index bits are completely contained into the page offset bits. The value of these bits is the same in both the physical and virtual address, because the virtual to physical mapping only translates bits 12-48. Bits 0-11 are the offset into the page and are unchanged by address translation, therefore the set index is unchanged and it makes no difference if we extract it from the virtual or physical address.

Another way of looking at this is that the size of a cache way is less or equal the size of a page; in this example:

size: 32kB
ways: 8
way size: 4kB

Thus, each way stores one memory page and the set index does not extend to the portion of the virtual address which is translated.

There are however L1 caches with ways bigger than a single page, for instance the Core i7 L1 instruction cache:

size: 32kB
ways: 4
way size: 8kB
cache line: 64 bytes

total number of lines in the cache = 32 kB / 64 Bytes = 512
number of lines per way = 512 / 4 = 128
set index size: 7 bits
set index bits: 6-12

This cache has only 4 ways, so the way size is 8kB, spanning two memory pages. The set index includes bit 12, which can change between the virtual and physical address. This means indexing through the virtual address does not guarantee to select a set for the desired physical address (if the virtual to physical mapping has changed after the data has been cached).

One possible solution to this problem is to include in the tag all the bits of the PFN, i.e. bits 12-36. This way, when a tag matches the physical address, we are sure the cache data block stores data from the correct memory page; also, the selected set corresponds to the offset in page for the desired physical address, because, as we said, the offset does not change with the virtual to physical mapping. Putting it all together, the data block found refers to the correct page and the correct offset, thus is for the desired physical address.

An alternate solution would be to have the processor flush the L1 cache when CR3 changes and flush L1 entries when paging structure entries change. Remember that when software modifies a paging structure entry, it must inform the processor by invalidating the corresponding TLB entry, so the processor has a way to know that the virtual to physical mapping has changed. Since the L1 is small and fast, flushing it can be acceptable ([9], p. 30).

But why go through all this trouble to use virtual addresses? Because the physical address is known only *after* the processor has translated the virtual one, thus, if the former is used, the cache lookup cannot start until the translation is complete. This implies an higher cache latency, unacceptable for the L1 cache which must be very fast. By using the virtual address for the index, the processor can select the cache set in parallel with address translation; true, the physical address is ultimately needed to compare the tags, but translation and set selection can now take place at the same time. On the other hand, bigger, slower caches like the L2 in the Core 2 Duo and the L3 in the Core i7 can have higher latencies and are involved later in instruction execution, when the physical address is already available. These caches can thus be physically indexed.

A cache like the L1 one is described as *virtually indexed, physically tagged*; caches of the other kind are said to be *physically indexed, physically tagged*.

Part IV - User Range Memory Management

18 User Range Content

Basically, the user range of a running process stores the following content:

- Executable for the process

- DLLs

- Process heap(s)

- Thread stacks

This content is stored in regions of the VA range chosen by the VMM and the addresses outside these regions are invalid, which means that if code tries to access them in any way, an access violation is generated. If a program wants to use a given region, it must first call VMM APIs to make it valid. In the next sections we are going to examine what this APIs do and this will help us understand the inner working of the VMM. For now, we will focus on user range memory allocated through these APIs. Later, we will examine how the VMM manages the loading of executable code, the stacks and the heaps.

19 User Range Memory Allocation

In the user range, allocation of a region of memory is done in two steps: first, a range of virtual addresses is *reserved*, i.e. taken from the available (that is, unallocated) VAs of the process and set aside. This does not make the range usable: if the process tries to touch an address inside this range, it still gets an access violation, i.e. the same exception it would get for a completely invalid address. The second step is *committing* the range, which makes it usable. When a range is committed, we can say (simplifying things a little) that it is either in physical memory or in the paging file and Windows is prepared to map it into the address space when it is needed, so code can freely touch the range. *VirtualAllocEx* is one of the APIs which can be used for reserving and committing memory.

But why splitting memory allocation in two steps? The main reason is the way Windows keeps track of how much virtual memory can be allocated. The system computes a value called *commit limit*, which can be retrieved as a performance counter (Memory\Commit Limit). It's value is somehow less than the amount of physical RAM plus the size of the paging files and it's the number of bytes that can be kept either in memory or swapped out. Since a page of data must be kept somewhere, either on disk or in memory, this value represents the maximum number of pages the system can handle.

As processes allocate memory, Windows keeps track of how many pages of data they are using in the counter named Memory\Committed Bytes. This value, which is also called the *commit charge* can't be greater than the commit limit, because these data pages must be stored somewhere.

Thus, when a process attempts to increase the commit charge, the operation can fail if it would exceed the commit limit. Actually, the commit limit can grow, because the paging files themselves can grow, up to a specified maximum size. As long as the paging files are below their maximum, Windows is forgiving enough to allow the operation to succeed. If we go on allocating memory, however, we are bound to be stopped by the commit limit, when it can't grow anymore.

Now suppose we need to write a piece of code which must allocate a very large range of contiguous memory for a data structure, even though we are not sure how much of this range we are actually going to use. If allocating memory meant committing pages, we would consume a large portion of the commit limit (which is system-wide) and perhaps only use a fraction of it.

Instead, reserving a range of memory allows us to set aside a contiguous range of addresses, without consuming commit limit. A reserved range can later be committed in separate smaller chunks, thus increasing the commit charge only when needed.

Besides the system-wide commit limit, Windows allows to impose a per-process limit on how much memory a process can commit. Although this feature is disabled by default (see [1], p. 162), it can be turned on and it is therefore another good reason for committing memory only when needed.

It is however true that committing virtual memory does not necessarily mean creating the paging structures to map physical pages to it: when possible, Windows waits until the memory is actually referenced to do it, so that this becomes the job of the page fault handler. We are going to discuss shortly one scenario in which Windows cannot avoid creating the paging structures at commit time.

Based on this allocation scheme, a virtual address in the user range can be in one of three allocation states: invalid, reserved or committed. The page storing a committed address is not necessarily present: before an access to the page is actually made, the VMM does not actually map the VPN to a physical page; even when the mapping has been done, the page can be moved to the paging file afterwards. The point is, once a virtual page is committed, the VMM is ready to make it valid, eventually retrieving its content from the paging file.

There are memory allocation APIs which take a NUMA node number among their input parameters, so that we can specify a preferred node for the allocation. This overrides the default VMM behavior of allocating pages from the ideal node. As an example, *VirtualAllocEx* reserves and commits pages according to the default VMM behavior, while *VirtualAllocExNuma* allows to specify the preferred node. The node is only considered preferred, because physical pages are not actually allocated when memory is reserved or committed, but rather when it is accessed. If, when this happens, there are no available pages on the specified node, the VMM will use physical pages from the nearest one.

20   VMM Data Structures

20.1 Virtual Address Descriptor (VAD)

VADs are used to keep track of reserved and committed addresses in the user mode range. For every range which is either reserved or committed, a VAD stores the addresses delimiting it, whether it's only reserved or committed and it's protection, i.e. the type of access allowed to the range.

VADs are organized in a tree structure where each node is a VAD instance and can have up to two children. The left children, if present, is a VAD for an address range below the one covered by the parent; the right children is for a range above it:

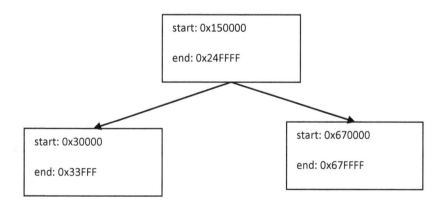

Figure 21 - VAD Tree

There are three data types defined for VADs among the Windows symbols: _MMVAD_SHORT,
_MMVAD and _MMVAD_LONG, where each structure is a superset of the preceding one. The
VMM logic examined here only concerns the members of _MMVAD_SHORT, for which WinDbg
shows us the following definition:

```
struct _MMVAD_SHORT, 8 elements, 0x40 bytes


   +0x000 u1                 : <unnamed-tag>
      +0x000 Balance : Pos 0, 2 Bits
      +0x000 Parent : Ptr64 _MMVAD
   +0x008 LeftChild          : Ptr64 _MMVAD
   +0x010 RightChild         : Ptr64 _MMVAD
   +0x018 StartingVpn        : Uint8B
   +0x020 EndingVpn          : Uint8B
   +0x028 u                  : <unnamed-tag>
      +0x000 LongFlags : Uint8B
      +0x000 VadFlags : _MMVAD_FLAGS
         +0x000 CommitCharge : Pos 0, 51 Bits
         +0x000 NoChange     : Pos 51, 1 Bit
         +0x000 VadType      : Pos 52, 3 Bits
         +0x000 MemCommit    : Pos 55, 1 Bit
         +0x000 Protection   : Pos 56, 5 Bits
         +0x000 Spare        : Pos 61, 2 Bits
         +0x000 PrivateMemory : Pos 63, 1 Bit
   +0x030 PushLock           : _EX_PUSH_LOCK
   +0x038 u5                 : <unnamed-tag>
      +0x000 VadFlags3    :
         +0x000 PreferredNode : Pos 0, 6 Bits
         +0x000 Teb          : Pos 6, 1 Bit
         +0x000 Spare        : Pos 7, 1 Bit
         +0x000 SequentialAccess : Pos 8, 1 Bit
         +0x000 LastSequentialTrim : Pos 9, 15 Bits
         +0x000 Spare2       : Pos 24, 8 Bits
         +0x000 LargePageCreating : Pos 32, 1 Bit
         +0x000 Spare3       : Pos 33, 31 Bits
```

It is also interesting to note that _MMVAD_SHORT is itself based on _MMADDRESS_NODE,
another smaller structure which has the same layout up to the pointer at +0x20 and stores
the essential information to build the VAD tree. The tree itself is named an AVL self-balancing
tree after its inventors: Adelson-Velskii and Landis. Below is the layout of
_MMADDRESS_NODE.

```
struct _MMADDRESS_NODE, 5 elements, 0x28 bytes

   +0x000 u1                 : <unnamed-tag>
      +0x000 Balance : Pos 0, 2 Bits
      +0x000 Parent : Ptr64 _MMADDRESS_NODE
```

```
+0x008 LeftChild        : Ptr64 _MMADDRESS_NODE
+0x010 RightChild       : Ptr64 _MMADDRESS_NODE
+0x018 StartingVpn      : Uint8B
+0x020 EndingVpn        : Uint8B
```

We can look at the VADs for a process with WinDbg. In the following example, a test allocation program called MemTests.exe is used: first, the !process extension gives us the address of the VAD root; afterwards, the !vad command prints out information on the process VADs:

```
0: kd> !process 0 1 memtests.exe
PROCESS ffffffa80011e7b30
    SessionId: 1  Cid: 098c    Peb: 7fffffdf000  ParentCid: 02bc
    DirBase: 3311c000  ObjectTable: fffff8a001ea9c00  HandleCount:   6.
    Image: MemTests.EXE
    VadRoot ffffffa8000fdf160 Vads 21 Clone 0 Private 131. Modified 0. Locked 0.
    ...
```

```
0: kd> !vad ffffffa8000fdf160
VAD            level    start     end    commit
ffffffa8000e997a0 ( 3)      10      1f        0 Mapped      READWRITE
ffffffa8002e48290 ( 4)      20      2f        0 Mapped      READWRITE
ffffffa8000f45c70 ( 2)      30      33        0 Mapped      READONLY
ffffffa8002f6d0b0 ( 4)      40      40        1 Private     READWRITE
ffffffa8001004010 ( 3)      50      b6        0 Mapped      READONLY
ffffffa8002b92220 ( 4)      c0     1bf       32 Private     READWRITE
ffffffa8002bc3720 ( 1)     1e0     2df        7 Private     READWRITE
ffffffa8002b607a0 ( 3)     410     50f       41 Private     READWRITE
ffffffa8000e295d0 ( 2)     660     66f       10 Private     READWRITE
ffffffa8000f7fe10 ( 4)     670     a6f     1024 Private     EXECUTE
ffffffa8002f47640 ( 3)   77020   7713e        4 Mapped  Exe EXECUTE_WRITECOPY
ffffffa8000fdf160 ( 0)   77140   772ea       12 Mapped  Exe EXECUTE_WRITECOPY
ffffffa8002fc6980 ( 3)    7efe0   7f0df        0 Mapped      READONLY
ffffffa8000f71ec0 ( 2)    7f0e0   7ffdf        0 Private     READONLY
ffffffa80010454a0 ( 1)    7ffe0   7ffef       -1 Private     READONLY
ffffffa8002c0f1d0 ( 4)   13f540  13f5b8        5 Mapped  Exe EXECUTE_WRITECOPY
ffffffa8002d093b0 ( 3) 7fefd190 7fefd1fa        3 Mapped  Exe EXECUTE_WRITECOPY
ffffffa8000e27e50 ( 4) 7feff460 7feff460        0 Mapped  Exe EXECUTE_WRITECOPY
ffffffa8000fd9360 ( 2) 7fffffb0 7fffffd2        0 Mapped      READONLY
ffffffa8002ea52b0 ( 4) 7fffffdd 7fffffde        2 Private     READWRITE
ffffffa8002ea4b80 ( 3) 7fffffdf 7fffffdf        1 Private     READWRITE
```

Actually the "VadRoot address" printed by !process can also be retrieved as follows: given the address of the _EPROCESS for the process, the VadRoot is given by

```
_EPROCESS.VadRoot.BalancedRoot.RightChild
```

The meaning of the output columns is as follows:

- VAD affress, i.e. the address of the VAD data structure

- Level in the VAD tree. The example shows that the VAD at level 0 has the same address obtained from !process and supplied to !vad, i.e. this node is the tree root.

- Starting and ending address of the range, expressed as *virtual page numbers* (VPN), i.e. the address value divided by the page size (4kB), which is also the address value shifted right by three hexadecimal digits. Thus, for instance, the first row defines a range starting at address 0x10000 and ending at address 0x1ffff. Note how the ending address is the VPN of the last page, so the address of the last byte is 0x1F000 + 0xFFF.

- The # of committed pages in the range. We must remember that we can reserve a range and then commit only part of it, so this number tells us how many pages in the range are actually committed. This brings us to an interesting question: how can the VMM know *which* pages are committed? We are going to answer in a short while.

- The type of allocation. For now, we are going to examine memory which is private to a process, which, imagine that, is marked as "Private"

- The type of access allowed on the page. We will expand on this subject later.

20.1.1   Partially Committed Ranges

After having reserved a range, we can commit as many subranges of it as we like, which can lay anywhere inside the containing range, with the only limitation that each subrange must start on a page boundary and must consist of whole pages. This is, after all, the point of reserving and committing memory in separate steps and it implies we can build memory ranges with uncommitted "holes" in them. The VMM must therefore be able to record which individual pages in a range are committed. A VAD cannot store this level of detail, so the VMM uses the PTEs to do the job. This does not mean, however, that the VMM always initializes PTEs when a range is committed. Rather, it does so when a range is *partially* committed and therefore the PTEs are needed.

For instance, it is possible to reserve and commit an address range in a single step, thereby committing the whole range. When this happens, the VMM does not initialize the PTEs for the range and if we examine them we find they are set to 0 (PTEs can also be absent, but we will see this later). PTEs are also set to 0 for a range which is reserved but not committed, as well as for an invalid one, so they don't help the VMM in knowing that the range in our example is committed. However, this information is stored in the VAD, because the range is wholly committed. By performing a few experiments on memory allocation, it is possible to observe that the member named `_MMVAD_SHORT.u.VadFlags.MemCommit` is set to 1 for a range that has been reserved and wholly committed at the same time. For such a range, the VMM updates a PTE only when we access an address inside the range. In this scenario, the PTE has not been set up at commit time, but at memory access time and the final PTE value points to a physical page and has the control bits set according to the protection assigned to the range.

Now consider a different situation, where we reserve a range without committing it. If we observe the PTEs for the range, they are set to 0, like in the previous case, but this time `_MMVAD_SHORT.u.VadFlags.MemCommit` is also 0. When we commit a portion of this range, the VMM has no choice but to record this fact in the PTEs mapping this subrange, which are set to nonzero values. However, since we have not actually accessed addresses inside the range, the PTEs are not yet fully set up to translate virtual addresses: they don't include a physical address, because physical pages have not yet been assigned to map the virtual range. At this stage, these PTEs contain an abstract representation of the protection of the page they map, which we will examine better in a short while and, of course, they still have the present bit clear. This will change when we will finally access the memory mapped by these PTEs.

Until now, we have assumed PTEs always existed, however we must remember the hierarchical nature of the paging structures:

- When a PML4 entry has the present bit clear, no PDPTs, PDs or PTs exist for the corresponding VA range. There is no physical page storing the PDPT for this range, there are no pages storing the PDs, etc.

- Likewise, a PML4 entry can point to an existing PDPT, but a PDPT entry can have its present bit clear, so no PDs or PTs exist for this particular range.

When it comes to tracking reserved and committed memory, this means that it's possible to have committed memory ranges for which the PTEs don't even exist. This happens when the VMM does not need to use PTEs to track partial commitments. Thus, in the previous examples, when we said that the PTEs were set to 0, it is more accurate to say that they can be 0 or they can be missing.

On the other hand, if the VMM is forced to create a page table, to set up some PTEs for a partial commitment, it will set all other PTEs in the page to 0, to record that those other ranges are not committed.

The behavior explained so far can be observed running a test program which calls VirtualAllocEx and observing the VADs and PTEs state at various stages. Let's wrap it all up with a practical example: we use a test program called MemTests which reserves 128MB of VA, without committing it. We use a large range, to have a better chance of observing not present PTEs: while the PTs for the beginning of the range may be present because they have already been used by the VMM for other allocations, the ones at the end of the range have a good chance of not having been allocated when we call the function.

When we reserve the range, we have the following situation:

Starting address = 0x00000000`00530000

Ending address   = 0x00000000`0852FFFF

The starting address has been chosen by VirtualAllocEx, because we did not request a particular address, just a range size of 128MB, i.e. 0x80000000.

The !vad command output shows our range with no committed pages:

```
VAD                 level       start     end     commit
fffffa8001452140 ( 4)             530      852f          0 Private        READWRITE
```

Thanks to the known relationship between a VA and the VA of its PTE, we can compute the addresses of the PTEs for the first and last page of the range which are as follows:

first page PTE: 0xFFFFF680`00002980
last page PTE: 0XFFFFF680`00042978

We can now look at the content of these 2 PTES:

```
0: kd> dq 0XFFFFF68000002980
fffff680`00002980   00000000`00000000 00000000`00000000
fffff680`00002990   00000000`00000000 00000000`00000000
fffff680`000029a0   00000000`00000000 00000000`00000000
fffff680`000029b0   00000000`00000000 00000000`00000000
fffff680`000029c0   00000000`00000000 00000000`00000000
fffff680`000029d0   00000000`00000000 00000000`00000000
fffff680`000029e0   00000000`00000000 00000000`00000000
fffff680`000029f0   00000000`00000000 00000000`00000000

0: kd> dq 0XFFFFF68000042978
fffff680`00042978   ????????`???????? ????????`????????
```

This tells us that the PTEs for the first pages of the range are present, so the VMM has already created the page table for some reason. However, the PTEs are all set to 0, consistently with the fact that we have not committed anything yet.

The last PTE is even more interesting, because it does not exist.

As a side note, when we want to look at PTEs, we must remember that the VAs at which they are visible map to the PTEs for the *current* process. We cannot simply break into the debugger with Ctrl-C and look at the PTEs for MemTests, because when the debugger takes control the current process is System. One way to solve this problem is use the .process metacommand with the /i option, which allows to resume execution and break again with the desired process being the current one. .process requires the address of the _EPROCESS instance for the process, which can be obtained with

        !process 0 0 MemTests.exe

Our test program goes on by committing the first and last page of the range and the !vad output changes accordingly:

```
VAD                 level      start    end    commit
fffffa8001452140 ( 4)           530    852f         2 Private       READWRITE
```

The PTEs status is also different:

```
0: kd> dq 0XFFFFF68000002980
fffff680`00002980  00000000`00000080 00000000`00000000
fffff680`00002990  00000000`00000000 00000000`00000000
fffff680`000029a0  00000000`00000000 00000000`00000000
fffff680`000029b0  00000000`00000000 00000000`00000000
fffff680`000029c0  00000000`00000000 00000000`00000000
fffff680`000029d0  00000000`00000000 00000000`00000000
fffff680`000029e0  00000000`00000000 00000000`00000000
fffff680`000029f0  00000000`00000000 00000000`00000000


0: kd> dq 0XFFFFF68000042978
fffff680`00042978  00000000`00000080 00000000`00000000
```

The first PTE is now set to 0x80 which represents the page protection in a way we are going to discuss later. This nonzero PTE tells the VMM the page is committed, therefore an access to this page will not cause an access violation.

The same is true for the last PTE, with the addition that now this PTE exists, while, before the commit, there was not even a physical page to store it.

Both PTEs have the present bit clear and the PFN set to 0, so no physical memory has yet been used to map the virtual addresses inside these two pages of our range.

Finally, we see that the PTEs for pages beyond the first one are still set to 0 and this tells the memory manager that they have not been committed. If we were to touch an address inside these pages we would crash and burn with an access violation.

The last thing our program does is touch the first byte of both pages. Since MemTests did his homework well and committed those pages it's not slapped with an access violation and the PTEs change like this:

```
0: kd> dq 0XFFFFF68000002980
fffff680`00002980  97a00000`1bf22867 00000000`00000000
fffff680`00002990  00000000`00000000 00000000`00000000
fffff680`000029a0  00000000`00000000 00000000`00000000
fffff680`000029b0  00000000`00000000 00000000`00000000
fffff680`000029c0  00000000`00000000 00000000`00000000
fffff680`000029d0  00000000`00000000 00000000`00000000
fffff680`000029e0  00000000`00000000 00000000`00000000
fffff680`000029f0  00000000`00000000 00000000`00000000

0: kd> dq 0XFFFFF68000042978
fffff680`00042978  97b00000`308e3867 00000000`00000000
```

Which clearly shows PTEs now mapping physical pages (a little trick: they are odd numbers and this fact alone tells us the present bit is 1). The other bits in the three rightmost digits are set according to the protection and caching attributes we specified in the call to VirtualAllocEx (there will be more on this later). Bit 63, the execute disable bit, is set, so code can't be executed from these pages, which also stems from the protection we requested in the first place. Bits 52-62, which are ignored by the processor, are used by the VMM and we will return on them (they store the truncated working set index of the page). Finally, bits 12-51 store the PFN. The two physical pages used for these mappings have PFN:

0x1bf22 (first page)

0x308e3 (last page)

A final note: the theoretical limit of x64 physical addresses is 51 bits, however the VMM code appears to always truncate them to 48 bits, so it can presently handle "only" 256 Terabyte of physical memory.

20.1.2   Decomitted Subranges

We can decommit a portion of a reserved range with the VirtualFreeEx API, leaving it in the reserved state. When this happens, the corresponding PTEs are set to 0x00000000`00000200, which WinDbg interprets as follows:

```
0: kd> !pte c0000
                                        VA 00000000000c0000

PXE at FFFFF6FB7DBED000   PPE at FFFFF6FB7DA00000   PDE at FFFFF6FB40000000   PTE at FFFFF68000000600
contains 02A000000E8F2867   contains 02E00000141F5867   contains 02F0000009736867   contains 0000000000000200
pfn e8f2    ---DA--UWEV   pfn 141f5    ---DA--UWEV   pfn 9736    ---DA--UWEV   not valid
                                                                           PageFile:  0
                                                                           Offset: 0
                                                                           Protect: 10 - Decommitted
```

For a range reserved and committed in one step, where _MMVAD_SHORT.u.VadFlags.MemCommit = 1, the VMM must record inside the PTE the information that it has been decommitted, because the VAD flag marks the range as wholly committed. For such a range, the VAD flag is left set to 1 and decommitted PTEs are set as explained.

For a range with _MMVAD_SHORT.u.VadFlags.MemCommit = 0, the VMM could conceivably set the PTE to 0: the range is not marked as committed in the VAD, so a PTE set to 0 represent an uncommitted page. However, what actually happens is that the PTE is set to 0x00000000`00000200 like in the previous case.

20.1.3   VAD and Memory Protection

When we call *VirtualAllocEx* to allocate a range of memory, we can specify how this memory can be accessed, i.e. its protection, and how it must be cached, through the flProtect parameter.

Possible values for flProtect include:

PAGE_READONLY: the range cannot be written to and code cannot be executed from it (instruction fetches cause exceptions)

PAGE_READWRITE: reads and writes are allowed; code execution is not.

PAGE_EXECUTE_READ, PAGE_EXECUTE_READWRITE: similar to the values above, but instruction fetches are allowed.

A protection value of particular interest is PAGE_EXECUTE, which should make the range usable only to execute code, disallowing read and write accesses. This kind of protection is not supported in hardware by x64 processors and does not appear to be actually working on the x64 version of Windows. A simple test program can allocate a PAGE_EXECUTE range and then read it's content (although for a newly allocated range it's just zeroes). It is true, however, that such a range is not writable and we get an access violation if we try to modify its content.

The value of the `flProtect` parameter passed to VirtualAllocEx determines the value of the `_MMVAD_SHORT.u.VadFlags.Protection` member. This can be observed by calling *VirtualAllocEx* and dumping the resulting VAD in the debugger; `Protection` is not set to the value of `flProtect` itself, but is derived from it. This VAD member is particularly interesting, because its value ends up in a PTE when it is initialized like we saw in the previous section, to track memory commitment. We will examine PTEs in greater detail later, however bits 5-9 of a PTE like the one we saw earlier store the value of the `Protection` member from the VAD. We must keep in mind that these are still PTEs with the present bit clear, therefore all other bits are completely ignored by the processor and the VMM is free to use them. We will see how the VMM uses this value to compute the actual control bits of the PTE when finally mapping a physical page.

The table below shows the resulting `Protection` for some of the possible values of `flProtect`:

flProtect	Allowed Access	Caching Policy	Protection
PAGE_EXECUTE_READWRITE	read, write, execute	normal	6
PAGE_EXECUTE_READ	read, execute	normal	3
PAGE_READWRITE	read, write	normal	4
PAGE_READONLY	read	normal	1
PAGE_READWRITE | PAGE_NOCACHE	read, write	no caching[1]	0xc
PAGE_READWRITE | PAGE_WRITECOMBINE	read, write	write combining[1,2]	0x1c

Table 3 - Win32 Protection vs. VAD and PTE Protection

Notes

1. We will analyze the various caching policies later, when we will see how the final PTE is computed when memory is accessed

2. The term write combining comes from the MSDN documentation for *VirtualAllocEx*. We will see how this protection corresponds to WC memory as defined by the Intel documentation in sec. 26.6.3 on p. 167.

The example of the previous section showed that PTEs initialized to track a committed page were set to 0x80. The test was performed calling *VirtualAllocEx* with `flProtect` set to PAGE_READWRITE, which sets `_MMVAD_SHORT.u.VadFlags.Protection` = 4. By mapping 4 into bits 5-9 of the PTE we have:

```
        6      00 0000 0000
bit # 3        98 7654 3210
PTE = 0... 0000 1000 0000 = 0x80
                 |    |
               +-+--+
                 |
                 4
```

We can see in the previous example that the PTEs were actually set to 0x80.

As a final note we can ask ourselves: since we are talking about memory management, where does the memory for the VADs come from, or, in other words, how is itself managed? It comes from a memory pool maintained by the VMM for kernel components, named the *nonpaged pool*, which we will analyze later. For now, it is better to focus on how the VMM provides virtual memory to the user address range.

20.1.4   NUMA Support in VADs

The `_MMVAD_SHORT` structure has a 6 bits member called `u5.VadFlags3.PreferredNode`, which is used when a preferred node is explicitly specified, e. g. through the *VirtualAllocExNuma* function. For instance, calling *VirtualAllocEx* results in `PreferredNode` being set to 0; calling *VirtualAllocExNuma* with `nndPreferred` (the node number) set to 0 creates a VAD with `PreferredNode` = 1. We will see in sec. 26.4.2 on p. 150 how this field is checked in the page fault handler when choosing the node from which the physical page is allocated. For now, we can anticipate that, when `PreferredNode` is set to zero, the fault handler allocates physical pages from the ideal node as outlined in sec. 16.2 on p. 79; on the other hand, a nonzero value is decremented and then used as the node number for the allocation. This explains why `PreferredNode` is set to `nndPreferred` + 1: the value zero has the special meaning of "no node specified", so the value passed to the API, whose range starts at zero, is incremented to avoid ambiguity.

 [6] also states, on p. 18, that the preferred node can be specified at VAD level with *VirtualAllocExNuma* or *MapViewOfFileExNuma*.

20.2 Virtual Address Space Bitmaps

20.2.1   The User Mode Address Space Bitmap

Part of the information stored in VADs is replicated in data structures which we will call *User Mode Address Space Bitmaps* (UMAB).

Bitmaps are blocks of bytes where each bit is used to track the status of some resource. The bitmap bytes are usually pointed by an instance of `_RTL_BITMAP` with the following layout:

```
+0x000 SizeOfBitMap      : Uint4B
+0x008 Buffer            : Ptr64 Uint4B
```

For UMABs, each bit is associated with a 64 kB range in the user mode virtual address range. Thus, when bit 0 of byte 0 of the bitmap is set, it means the range 0 - 0xFFFF is allocated (reserved or reserved and committed), bit 1 represents the range 0x10000 - 0x1FFFF, etc.

The VMM maintains an UMAB for each process with the buffer (*not* the `_RTL_BITMAP`) starting at address 0xFFFFF700`00000000. If we look at the memory map in Figure 17 (p. 76), we can see that this is the starting address of the Hyperspace region, which is process-private, so each process has its private UMAB. The UMAB must be long enough to have a bit for each 64k portion of the user mode range (which is 8 TB), so the number of bits needed is:

   0x800`00000000 / 0x10000 = 0x8000000

with each byte storing 8 bits, the UMAB length in bytes is therefore

   0x8000000 / 8 = 0x1000000 = 16 MB

Thus, in each address space, the region 0xFFFFF700`00000000 0xFFFFF700`00FFFFFF is used for the UMAB.

But why track virtual addresses both in VADs and in the UMAB? One possible explanation is that the UMAB is faster when it comes to find a free virtual range.

VADs are very handy to check whether a given virtual address falls in a range that has been properly reserved and committed. This is exactly what the page fault handler does when it must decide whether it has been invoked for an invalid address or for an address that is unmapped for a legitimate reason (e.g. a page of memory moved to the paging file). The problem the fault handler has to solve is: "I have this faulting address, is there an allocated region which encloses it?" The VAD tree can be quickly searched to answer this question.

However, when it comes to allocating a new virtual region the problem is different: unless the code attempting the allocation asks for a specific starting address, the problem becomes "Where can I find a free range *n* bytes long?". It is probably more efficient to look into a bitmap for the answer, because it amounts to search for a long enough sequence of bits set to 0, so this is what *VirtualAllocEx* does.

The presence of the UMAB explains why functions like *VirtualAllocEx* reserve regions whose starting address must be aligned on a 64kB boundary. VADs and page tables could manage allocations aligned on page boundaries, but the UMAB cannot. Possibly, the VMM designers chose to map 64kB for each bit to reduce the UMAB size.

The length of a memory region allocated with *VirtualAllocEx* does not have to be a multiple of 64kB, because this would be a waste of committed, and, ultimately, physical memory. However, given a 1 page region whose starting address is *n* * 64k, the next virtual region must begin at (*n* + 1) * 64k, so the tail of the virtual range is unused.

Although the VMM reserves a virtual range of 16MB for the whole UMAB, it appears that in most processes it uses a single physical page, so that only the range 0xFFFFF700`00000000 - 0xFFFFF700`00000FFF is actually valid. This results in 0x8000 bitmap entries, mapping up to the following address:

> 0x8000 x 0x10000 - 1 = 0x80000000 − 1, i.e. 2GB - 1

This is true even if the process has valid VA ranges above 2GB (several system DLLs are usually mapped in the range 7-8TB) and therefore means that the VMM is able to manage the range above 2GB using the VADs only. Possibly, the reasoning behind all this is that allocations in the lower 2GB of the VA are more frequent and the UMAB is meant to speed them up, but consuming the 16MB required by the whole UMAB for every process would be too expensive.

Among the members of _MMWSL we find LastVadBit which is usually set to 0x7FFF and is used to record the last valid bit index in the UMAB (one page stores 0x8000 bits). We will return on this in sec. 20.2.3.1 on p. 108).

108   What Makes It Page?

20.2.2   The User Mode Page Tables Bitmap

Immediately following the UMAB is another bitmap, which we are going to call the *User Mode Page Tables Bitmap* (UMPB). Each bit corresponds to a page table mapping the user mode range and, when set, means the page table exists, i.e. the corresponding PDE is valid (which implies the PML4E and PDPTE for addresses mapped by that page table are valid as well).

A single PT maps 512 pages or 2 MB, so, in order to map 8 TB of user mode addresses we need

   0x800`00000000 / 0x200000= 0x400000

PTs, i.e. bits in the bitmap, which gives a size for the bitmap buffer of

   0x400000 / 8= 0x80000 = 512 kB.

Thus, the UMPB lies in the range 0xFFFFF700`01000000 - 0xFFFFF700`0107FFFF. We will see shortly that the process working set list immediately follows the UMPB, beginning at 0xFFFF70001080000.

Unlike the UMAB, the UMPB appears to be used for the whole user mode range and can actually consume up to 512kB of physical memory. This overhead is not fixed, though, because the VMM maps UMPB pages only when needed, so its virtual range has holes in it, where no entries are in use.

20.2.3   Verifying the Presence of Virtual Address Space Bitmaps

This section shows evidence of the existence of the UMAB and the UMPB.

20.2.3.1   UMAB

We can start with an experiment where the MemTests program (included in the download package and explained in greater detail later) allocates a range of virtual addresses. Right before the call to *VirtualAllocEx*, we break into the debugger and set a breakpoint on access to the starting address of the UMAB for the thread of MemTests only. When we resume execution, the breakpoint is hit with the following call stack:

```
0: kd> !thread @$thread
THREAD fffffa8002076760  Cid 0a0c.0a10  Teb: 000007fffffde000 Win32Thread:
0000000000000000 RUNNING on processor 0
Not impersonating
DeviceMap               fffff8a001c8f840
```

```
Owning Process                 fffffa80011d7380      Image:       MemTests.EXE
Attached Process              N/A          Image:        N/A
Wait Start TickCount          38323        Ticks: 1 (0:00:00.015)
Context Switch Count          491
UserTime                      00:00:00.031
KernelTime                    00:00:00.093
Win32 Start Address MemTests!wmainCRTStartup (0x000000013f997270)
Stack Init fffff8800230edb0 Current fffff8800230e690
Base fffff8800230f000 Limit fffff88002309000 Call 0
Priority 9 BasePriority 8 UnusualBoost 0 ForegroundBoost 0 IoPriority 2 PagePriority 5
Child-SP          RetAddr          : Args to Child
: Call Site
fffff880`0230e990 fffff800`02bbe474 : ffffffff`ffffffff ffffffff`ffffffff
fffff880`0230eca0 00000000`00003000 : nt!MiFindEmptyAddressRange+0xca

fffff880`0230ea00 fffff800`028be153 : ffffffff`ffffffff 00000000`002ffb98
00000000`00000010 00000000`002ffba0 : nt!NtAllocateVirtualMemory+0x724

fffff880`0230ebb0 00000000`7775003a : 000007fe`fd822a96 00000000`00000000
00000001`3f997832 00000000`00000000 : nt!KiSystemServiceCopyEnd+0x13 (TrapFrame @
fffff880`0230ec20)

00000000`002ffb48 000007fe`fd822a96 : 00000000`00000000 00000001`3f997832
00000000`00000000 00000001`3f996588 : ntdll!ZwAllocateVirtualMemory+0xa

00000000`002ffb50 000007fe`fd822ad6 : 00000001`00000003 00000000`00000000
00000000`00010000 00000001`00000030 : KERNELBASE!VirtualAllocExNuma+0x66

00000000`002ffb90 00000000`7762c101 : 00000001`3f9f1b20 00000001`3fa082c0
00000000`00000000 00000000`00000000 : KERNELBASE!VirtualAllocEx+0x16

00000000`002ffbd0 00000001`3f995b19 : 00000001`3f9f5680 00000001`3fa082c0
00000000`00000000 00000000`00000000 : kernel32!VirtualAllocExStub+0x11

00000000`002ffc10 00000001`3f9f5680 : 00000001`3fa082c0 00000000`00000000
00000000`00000000 00000001`00000004 : MemTests!VirtAllocTest+0x159
[b:\programm\memtests\memtests\main.cpp @ 4175]

00000000`002ffc18 00000001`3fa082c0 : 00000000`00000000 00000000`00000000
00000001`00000004 00000000`002ffcc4 : MemTests!__xt_z+0x41c0

00000000`002ffc20 00000000`00000000 : 00000000`00000000 00000001`00000004
00000000`002ffcc4 00000000`002ffc78 : MemTests!_iob+0x30
```

The call stack above shows that VirtualAllocEx transitions to kernel mode and ultimately calls *MiFindEmptyAddressRange* where the breakpoint is hit. The breaking instruction can be examined with the `ub` (unassemble backwards) command, because the breakpoint is a fault and `rip` points to the address *after* the faulting instruction:

```
1: kd> ub
nt!MiFindEmptyAddressRange+0xa0:
fffff800`02bd12c0 4c89442438      mov     qword ptr [rsp+38h],r8
fffff800`02bd12c5 89542430        mov     dword ptr [rsp+30h],edx
fffff800`02bd12c9 8bc8            mov     ecx,eax
```

```
fffff800`02bd12cb 83ff01              cmp      edi,1
fffff800`02bd12ce 0f8585000000        jne      nt!MiFindEmptyAddressRange+0x139
(fffff800`02bd1359)
fffff800`02bd12d4 4881fe00000100      cmp      rsi,10000h
fffff800`02bd12db 0f8557d10100        jne      nt! ?? ::NNGAKEGL::`string'+0x9628
(fffff800`02bee438)
fffff800`02bd12e1 a10000000000f7ffff  mov      eax,dword ptr [FFFFF70000000000h]
```

If we step with the debugger for a few instructions, we see the function calls *RtlFindClearBits* (documented in the WDK), which takes a pointer to an RTL_BITMAP as its first parameter. Since such a parameter is passed into rcx, the processor registers tell us where, in memory, the RTL_BITMAP is:

```
rax=000000003fffff9f rbx=000000003fffff9e rcx=fffff8800230e9c0
rdx=0000000000000001 rsi=0000000000010000 rdi=0000000000000001
rip=fffff80002bd1302 rsp=fffff8800230e990 rbp=000007fffffdffff
 r8=0000000000000005  r9=fffff70001080040 r10=8000000000000000
r11=fffffa80011d7380 r12=fffff8800230ea58 r13=0000000000010000
r14=fffffa80011d7380 r15=fffff70001080034
iopl=0         nv up ei pl nz na po nc
cs=0010  ss=0018  ds=002b  es=002b  fs=0053  gs=002b          efl=00000206
nt!MiFindEmptyAddressRange+0xe2:
fffff800`02bd1302 e81906d1ff        call    nt!RtlFindClearBits (fffff800`028e1920)
```

We see that rcx points a little above the current rsp, so we have an RTL_BITMAP on the stack which we can dump:

```
0: kd> ?? ((nt!_RTL_BITMAP *) @rcx)
struct _RTL_BITMAP * 0xfffff880`0230e9c0
   +0x000 SizeOfBitMap     : 0x8000
   +0x008 Buffer           : 0xfffff700`00000000  -> 0x3fffff9f
```

So we are passing to *RtlFindClearBits* an RTL_BITMAP which points to the UMAB. The value of _RTL_BITMAP.SizeOfBitmap, which is set to 0x8000, require some additional explanation. First of all, if we look at *RtlInitializeBitmap*, which is also documented in the WDK, we discover that SizefOfBitmap stores the size *in bits* of the bitmap. *RtlInitializeBitmap* takes this size as its 3rd parameter and copies it into SizeOfBitmap. So our bitmap il 0x8000 bits or 0x1000 bytes long.

MiFindEmptyAddressRange computes this value by loading _MMWSL.LastVadBit at offset +0x89 and adding 1 to it, so this member contains the index of the last valid bits of the UMAB (usually 0x7FFF, as we saw earlier).

It is also interesting to compare the allocated address space ranges as resulting from the VADs with the bitmap content. Below is an excerpt from the !vad output for the explorer.exe process:

```
1: kd> !vad fffffa8000e6ce50
```

```
VAD                level       start      end     commit
fffffa8000f57410 ( 6)            10       1f           0 Mapped      READWRITE
[...]
fffffa8000fa8c20 ( 6)          4040     4087          72 Private     READWRITE
fffffa8001032250 ( 9)          40c0     40c0           1 Mapped      WRITECOPY
fffffa800105e290 ( 8)          40d0     40d0           1 Private     READWRITE
fffffa8000eb2b50 ( 9)          40e0     40e0           1 Private     READWRITE
[...]
```

This shows that:

- the range 0x4040000 - 0x4087FFF is allocated

- the range 0x4088000 - 0x40BFFFF is free

- beginning from 0x40C0000, a number of contiguous ranges are in use.

We are now going to compare this with the UMAB content. The offset of the byte for the range 0x4040000 is:

0x4040000 / 0x10000 / 8 = 0x80

Notice how we divided the address by 64k, because each bit tracks a range of this size. The index of the bit inside the byte is the remainder of the division by 8:

0x4040000 / 0x10000 % 8 = 4

The size of the first allocated range, in 64k blocks is

(0x4088000 - 0x4040000 + 0xFFFF) / 0x10000 = 5

We have added 0xFFFF to the range size in bytes to round the result up to the nearest multiple of 64k. Notice how the actual end address 0x4088000 is not a multiple of 64k, but since the allocation granularity of *VirtualAllocEx* is 64k, the range 0x4088000 - 0x408FFFF will simply be unused. In bitmap terms, a single bit tracks the whole 0x4080000 - 0x408FFFF range.

So, we expect to find 5 bits set beginning at bit 4 of byte +0x80 inside the UMAB. Here is the UMAB content:

```
1: kd> db 0xfffff70000000000 + 80 l2

fffff700`00000080  f0 f1
                   ..
```

The byte at +0x80 is 0xf0, which means it has bits 4,5,6,7 set. These are the first 4 bits of our range. The fifth bit is bit 0 of the next byte (+0x81), which contains 0xf1, so bit 0 is set, as expected.

The next bit, i.e. bit 1 of the byte at +0x81, corresponds to the range 0x4090000 - 0X409FFFF, which we know from the VADs to be free, together with the following 64k slots up to address 0x40BFFFF. This means that we expect, beginning from bit 1, a number of bits set to 0 given by:

$$(0x40C0000 - 0x4090000 + 0xFFFF) / 0x10000 = 3$$

that is, bits 1, 2, 3 must be clear, which is consistent with byte 0x81 being set to 0xF1. Furthermore, 0xF1 has bits 4, 5, 6, 7 set, which is consistent with the addresses from 0x40C0000 on being in use.

In summary, this shows that the bitmap content mirrors the virtual address space allocation stored in the VADs.

20.2.3.2   UMPB

Evidence of the UMPB can be found in the code of *MmAccessFault*, which is called by the page fault handler. This function examines an address range starting at 0xFFFFF700`01000000, and extending for _MMWSL.MaximumUserPageTablePages / 8 bytes. MaximumUserPageTablePages is a member of the working set list (explained in the next section) and it is usually set to 0x400000. As we saw in sec. 20.2.2 on p. 108 this value is the number of page tables needed to map 8TB (as the member name name implies). This tells us that at 0xFFFFF700`01000000 begins a data structure whose size is equal to the number of user mode page tables divided by 8 (incidentally, the division is rounded up to the nearest multiple of 8), i.e. a data structure with a number of *bits* equal to the number of page tables.

We can also compare the content of this region with the address space allocation reported by the VADs. Below is another excerpt of the VADs for explorer.exe:

```
0: kd> !vad fffffa8000e6ce50
VAD             level    start    end     commit
[...]
fffffa8000e6ce50 ( 0)    7ffe0    7ffef      -1 Private    READONLY
fffffa8000fb1c10 ( 8)    ff500    ff7be       6 Mapped  Exe EXECUTE_WRITECOPY
\Windows\explorer.exe
[...]
```

This shows a free VA range from 0x7FFF0000 to 0xFF4FFFFF. Now we want to find the PT for the last in-use page, which is at address 0x7FFEF000. This PT will be in use, while the next one will be free. Since each PT maps 2MB of address space, the 0-based index of the PT for 0x7FFEF000 is:

   0x7FFEF000 / 0x200000 = 0x3FF

The index of the PT for the first in-use page after the free range is:

   0xFF500000 / 0X200000 = 0x7FA

Thus, we expect the bit with index 0x3FF to be set, the ones in the range 0x400 - 0x7F9 to be clear and bit 0x7FA to be set. The corresponding bitmap offsets are:

   0x3FF / 8 = 0x7F

with the index within the byte given by

   0x3FF % 8 = 7

and for the end of the free range:

0x7FA / 8 = 0xFF

0x7FA % 8 = 2

Now let's see the UMPB content:

```
0: kd> db 0xfffff70001000000 + 0x7F 0xfffff70001000000 + 0xFF
fffff700`0100007f  ff 00 00 00 00 00 00 00-00 00 00 00 00 00 00 00   ................
fffff700`0100008f  00 00 00 00 00 00 00 00-00 00 00 00 00 00 00 00   ................
fffff700`0100009f  00 00 00 00 00 00 00 00-00 00 00 00 00 00 00 00   ................
fffff700`010000af  00 00 00 00 00 00 00 00-00 00 00 00 00 00 00 00   ................
fffff700`010000bf  00 00 00 00 00 00 00 00-00 00 00 00 00 00 00 00   ................
fffff700`010000cf  00 00 00 00 00 00 00 00-00 00 00 00 00 00 00 00   ................
fffff700`010000df  00 00 00 00 00 00 00 00-00 00 00 00 00 00 00 00   ................
fffff700`010000ef  00 00 00 00 00 00 00 00-00 00 00 00 00 00 00 00   ................
fffff700`010000ff  0c                                               .
```

Which shows that bit 7 of byte +0x7F is set, then all bits are clear up to byte +0xFF, where bits 0 and 1 are clear and bits 2, 3 are set. This is entirely consistent with the virtual address space state.

20.3 Process Working Set Data Structures

This section will cover another fundamental set of VMM data structures, used to keep track of the working set of a process.

The *working set* (WS) of a process is a *subset* of the physical memory pages used by that process. We define it as a subset, because it does not include:

- Pages in the system range, which, however, are part of the process address space, i.e. mapped into it. This includes pages used for: kernel mode images, kernel memory pools, kernel stacks, etc. Some system subranges are an exception and we will cover them later.

- Large pages, which are inherently non-pageable (see Chapter 40 – p. 392). The working set is used to decide whether to unmap physical pages used by the process to increase the amount of free memory, so it accounts for pageable pages only.

On the other hand, the WS includes the pageable pages in the user range, i.e.:

- Pageable private pages.

- Pageable shared pages (we will see later how shared memory works).

The VMM keeps track of the size of the WS and keeps a list of VAs currently mapped by physical pages, which we will call the *working set list* (WSL).

One question that could come to mind is: why should we want the WSL? After all, that's what paging structures are for: to track which VAs have physical pages mapped to them. While this is true, having the WSL helps the VMM doing its job.

For one thing, there are situations when the VMM needs to round-up all the physical pages used by a process, e.g. when a process is terminating and its memory must be released. Collecting this information from the paging structures would mean scanning the PML4 for existing PDPTs, then scanning each PDPT for existing PDs and so on, which could be quite expensive. Thus, having a quick list of mapped VAs comes in handy. For non-pageable pages like large pages, this information is presumably collected from other data structures, like the VADs.

Also, the WSL stores some additional information for each pageable VA, which the VMM uses. For instance, it records for how long a page has not been accessed, which helps the VMM decide whether to move the page content to the paging file.

20.3.1   Working Set Size

The WS size can be found as follows: the _EPROCESS structure has a member called Vm of type _MMSUPPORT:

```
_EPROCESS:

   +0x000 Pcb              : _KPROCESS
   . . .
   +0x398 Vm               : _MMSUPPORT
```

_MMSUPPORT stores all kind of information about the process address space, including the following:

_MMSUPPORT.WorkingSetSize gives the current WS size in pages.

_MMSUPPORT.PeakWorkingSetSize gives the maximum value reached by WorkingSetSize in this _MMSUPPORT lifetime.

20.3.2   Virtual Address Range of the WSL

The address of the WSL is stored in the Vm member as well, in the VmWorkingSetList field of _MMSUPPORT:

```
_MMSUPPORT:

   +0x000 WorkingSetMutex  : _EX_PUSH_LOCK
   . . .
   +0x068 VmWorkingSetList : Ptr64 _MMWSL
```

VmWorkingSetList stores the address of the WSL, which is of type _MMWSL. Here is an example with our favorite lab rat, MemTests:

```
0: kd> !process 0 0 memtests.exe
PROCESS fffffa80012eeb30
    SessionId: 1  Cid: 0a54    Peb: 7fffffd5000  ParentCid: 0ad0
    DirBase: 1396c000  ObjectTable: fffff8a002aabc10  HandleCount:    6.
    Image: MemTests.EXE

0: kd> dt nt!_eprocess fffffa80012eeb30 Vm.VmWorkingSetList
   +0x398 Vm                   :
      +0x068 VmWorkingSetList   : 0xfffff700`01080000 _MMWSL
```

If we perform the same test for other processes in the system, we discover something interesting; here is the result for an instance of notepad.exe:

```
0: kd> !process 0 0 notepad.exe
```

```
PROCESS fffffa8001391b30
    SessionId: 1  Cid: 0b5c    Peb: 7fffffdc000  ParentCid: 0ad0
    DirBase: 34c67000  ObjectTable: fffff8a0027695f0  HandleCount:  77.
    Image: notepad.exe

0: kd> dt nt!_eprocess fffffa8001391b30 Vm.VmWorkingSetList
    +0x398 Vm                    :
      +0x068 VmWorkingSetList     : 0xfffff700`01080000 _MMWSL
```

let's try one of the fundamental Windows processes, lsass:

```
0: kd> !process 0 0 lsass.exe
PROCESS fffffa80028d94c0
    SessionId: 0  Cid: 021c    Peb: 7fffffdd000  ParentCid: 0194
    DirBase: 1bca3000  ObjectTable: fffff8a005b50520  HandleCount: 588.
    Image: lsass.exe

0: kd> dt nt!_eprocess fffffa80028d94c0 Vm.VmWorkingSetList
    +0x398 Vm                    :
      +0x068 VmWorkingSetList     : 0xfffff700`01080000 _MMWSL
```

The address of the list is always the same. Does this mean that there is a single WSL? Not at all, if we look at the memory map in Figure 17 (p. 76), we see this address is inside the shaded region called Hyperspace. Recall that each process has a private copy of these shaded regions, because it has its own PML4 entry for it. Thus, at address 0xFFFFF700`01080000 is usually found the WSL for the address space currently active on a given processor.

20.3.3   WSL Entries

_MMWSL has a member called Wsle which point to an array of _MMWSLE structures:

```
0: kd> dt nt!_MMWSL Wsle
    +0x010 Wsle : Ptr64 _MMWSLE
```

An _MMWSLE is 8 bytes long and can store a virtual address along with some control bits, because they store VPNs which are 4 kB aligned, so the lower 12 bits are available.

Working set list entries (WSLE) in the array can be in-use, which means they store a VA of the process which is mapped to a physical page, or they can be free, with a value which has no relationship with VAs of the process. This is reflected in the definition for _MMWSLE:

```
struct _MMWSLE, 1 elements, 0x8 bytes
    +0x000 u1                    : union <unnamed-tag>, 4 elements, 0x8 bytes
```

```
+0x000 VirtualAddress : Ptr64 Void
+0x000 Long : Uint8B
+0x000 e1  : _MMWSLENTRY
   +0x000 Valid   : Pos 0, 1 Bit
   +0x000 Spare   : Pos 1, 1 Bit
   +0x000 Hashed  : Pos 2, 1 Bit
   +0x000 Direct  : Pos 3, 1 Bit
   +0x000 Protection : Pos 4, 5 Bits
   +0x000 Age     : Pos 9, 3 Bits
   +0x000 VirtualPageNumber : Pos 12, 52 Bits
+0x000 e2  : _MMWSLE_FREE_ENTRY
   +0x000 MustBeZero : Pos 0, 1 Bit
   +0x000 PreviousFree : Pos 1, 31 Bits
   +0x000 NextFree : Pos 32, 32 Bits
```

_MMWSLENTRY defines the layout of an in-use entry while _MMWSLE_FREE_ENTRY is for a free one.

The array is a mix of in-use and free entries, i.e. the two types are not grouped into contiguous blocks. This happens for a number of reasons. For instance, the VMM can decide to unmap a virtual page of a process to free a physical page, so the WSLE which was storing that VPN becomes free, while others around it may still be in use. Also, a process can deallocate a range of virtual addresses at a time when they were physically mapped and were using WSLE entries, which become free.

The values of in-use WSLEs don't appear to be ordered, which suggests the VMM uses the first free WSLE when it needs one, regardless of the VA it is mapping.

20.3.3.1   In-use WSLEs

In-use WSLEs store instances of _MMWSLENTRY, with the VPN in bits 12-63. Their Valid bit is set to 1, while for free entries the same bit is clear, so that all in-use entries have odd values and free entries have even ones. The Hashed and Direct bits will be discussed in sec. 37.14 on p. 331, together with shared memory.

Here is an example of a WSLE array with some in-use entries:

```
1: kd> dt nt!_mmwsl 0xfffff700`01080000
   +0x000 FirstFree       : 0x179
   +0x004 FirstDynamic    : 5
   +0x008 LastEntry       : 0x259
   +0x00c NextSlot        : 5
   +0x010 Wsle            : 0xfffff700`01080488 _MMWSLE
   ...
1: kd> dq 0xfffff700`01080488
fffff700`01080488  fffff6fb`7dbed009 fffff6fb`7dbee009
```

```
fffff700`01080498   fffff6fb`7dc00049 fffff6fb`80008409
fffff700`010804a8   fffff700`01080009 fffff700`00000c09
fffff700`010804b8   fffff700`01000c09 fffff700`0107f009
fffff700`010804c8   fffff6fb`7da0f009 fffff6fb`41fff009
fffff700`010804d8   fffff683`fffff009 000007ff`fffb1c15
fffff700`010804e8   000007ff`fffb2c15 000007ff`fffb3015
fffff700`010804f8   000007ff`fffb4c15 000007ff`fffb5c15
```

The odd numbers are all in-use entries; below is the content of the first one:

```
1: kd> dt nt!_mmwslentry fffff700`01080488
   +0x000 Valid              : 0y1
   +0x000 Spare              : 0y0
   +0x000 Hashed             : 0y0
   +0x000 Direct             : 0y1
   +0x000 Protection         : 0y00000 (0)
   +0x000 Age                : 0y000
   +0x000 VirtualPageNumber  : 0y1111111111111111111110110111110110111101101111101101
(0xfffff6fb7dbed)
```

Here we see there are WSLEs for system addresses, which may seem curious at first: a system VA should either be mapped or invalid for all the processes, so why track its status into the process working set? However, these addresses are inside two of the shaded regions of the memory map in Figure 17 on p. 76, which are process-private, so the WSL also tracks these regions besides the user mode range.

The Age member of _MMWSLENTRY is particularly important, because it is used by the VMM to decide whether the page should be removed from the working set, because it is "aged" i.e. it has not been accessed for a while ([5], p. 2). This will be explained in greater detail in the section on working set trimming (sec. 28.2.4 on p. 185).

20.3.3.1.1   The First Five WSL Entries

The first five WSL entries appear to be the same for all the processes and deserve a closer inspection:

```
1: kd> dq 0xfffff700`01080488
fffff700`01080488  fffff6fb`7dbed009 fffff6fb`7dbee009
fffff700`01080498  fffff6fb`7dc00049 fffff6fb`80008409
fffff700`010804a8  fffff700`01080009 fffff700`00000c09
```

The first four entries are all in the paging structures region described on p. 63, so we must ask ourselves what their meaning is. On one hand, a WSL entry stores the starting address of a virtual page which is mapped to physical memory. On the other hand, an address in the paging structures region is the VA of, say, a PTE, or a PDE, etc. Thus, finding such an address in the WSL means the paging structure (PT, PD, ...) storing that entry is in physical memory. For instance, the address of a PDPTE in the WSL means a whole PDPT is in memory, i.e. it means that the PML4E pointing to it is valid. These WSL entries store page-aligned addresses as well: such an address corresponds to the 1st entry in the paging structure (e.g. the 1st PTE) and the meaning of the entry is that the whole paging structure (e. g. the whole PT), is in physical memory. Note that this does not mean that the entries are valid: the paging structure could contain all zeroes. The WSL entry merely tells us that particular paging structure instance exists in physical memory.

Entry 0, 0xFFFFF6FB`7DBED009, is the VA of the PML4 (remember we must ignore the rightmost three digits, because entries store page-aligned addresses). This means the VMM tracks in the WSL the fact that this VA is mapped, as with any other VA.

Entry 1, 0xFFFFF6FB`7DBEE009 is in the PDPTE range, as we can see from Figure 16 on p. 71. This entry means the PDPT visible at 0xFFFFF6FB`7DBEE000 is mapped to a physical page, i.e. the PML4 entry selecting it is valid (present bit set). A PDPT maps a 512GB range and we can compute the starting address of the mapped range as explained in section 15.2.3 on p. 69, which turns out to be 0xFFFFF700`00000000. The meaning of this WSL entry is therefore that the PDPT mapping the range 0xFFFFF700`00000000 - 0xFFFFF780`00000000 is in physical memory. This is the hyperspace range (see Figure 17 on p. 76), where the WSL itself lives. In other words, this entry records that the PDPT needed to map the whole hyperspace is in physical memory. Again, this does not mean that the PDPTEs inside of it are valid, only that the PDPT exists in physical memory.

Entry 2, 0xFFFFF6FB`7DC00049 is in the PDE range, so it means a PD is in physical memory. The 2GB range mapped by this PD is 0xFFFFF700`00000000 - 0xFFFFF700`80000000, i.e. the first 2GB of hyperspace, where the WSL itself is stored.

Entry 3, 0xFFFFF6FB`80008409 is in the PTE range and tells us the PT mapping the 2MB range 0xFFFFF700` 01000000 – 0xFFFFF700`01200000 is present. This range too is inside hyperspace and it comprises the WSL itself.

Following these four entries is entry 4, 0xFFFFF700`01080009, which is not for a paging structure address, but, rather, it is the address of the page storing the WSL itself.

So, the overall meaning of these 5 entries is that the whole paging structure hierarchy needed to map the WSL itself is in place. Apparently, the VMM records the use of these pages in the WSL, just like it does for every other page used by the address space. Also, this brings to our attention that physical pages storing paging structures are accounted for in the process working set, just as "regular" pages storing data (using the term "data" in a broad sense, which means whatever is stored in memory, as opposed to the paging structures which are used by the processor to do its job). This is consistent with the fact that both data pages and paging structures can be unmapped from the virtual address space. The working set of a process includes both its resident virtual pages *and* the paging structures needed to map them to their physical pages. Addresses in the paging structure and hyperspace ranges are exceptions to our previous statement about the WSL not accounting for system range addresses. This is consistent with the fact that these virtual address ranges are process-private.

The `_MMWSL` structure has a member named `FirstDynamic` which appears to be always set to 5. We can guess that this member stores the index of the first entry in the WSLE array available for "normal" usage. Entries 0 – 4 are "fixed" and therefore "not dynamic", because they refer to the pages needed to bring the WSL itself into existence, entries from #5 on are free game. This hypothesis is supported by analysis of VMM code, e.g. the *MiUpdateWsle* function, which seems to regard an index less than FirstDynamic as not valid.

20.3.3.2   Free Entries

A free WSLE store an instance of `_MMWSLE_FREE_ENTRY`:

```
_MMWSLE_FREE_ENTRY
    +0x000 MustBeZero : Pos 0, 1 Bit
    +0x000 PreviousFree : Pos 1, 31 Bits
    +0x000 NextFree : Pos 32, 32 Bits
```

As implied by its name, bit 0 of a free WSLE must be 0.

PreviousFree and NextFree link the instances into a list of free entries for quick access. Besides their name, this can be confirmed by analyzing the VMM routine named *MiRemoveWsleFromFreeList*. The function logic also shows that the first entry of the chain has PreviousFree = 0x7FFFFFFF, while the last one has NextFree = 0xFFFFFFFF. The values stored in these fields are not addresses, but rather indexes into the array pointed by `_MMWSL.Wsle`. It's also interesting to note that this function does consistency checks on these values when it scans the list of free entries and bugchecks if it finds they are not valid.

20.3.4   Other _MMWSL Members

We are now going to see a few other significant members of the `_MMWSL` structure.

```
+0x000 FirstFree        : Uint4B
```

Points to the head of the list of free _MMWSLE in the array pointed by the `Wsle` member. Can be observed in: *MiRemoveWsleFromFreeList*.

```
+0x008 LastEntry         : Uint4B
```

It seems to store the highest value among the indexes of in-use entries. In other words, all existing entries with index greater than `LastEntry` are free. Can be observed in: *MiRemoveWsleFromFreeList, MiUpdateWsle*.

```
+0x010 Wsle              : Ptr64 _MMWSLE
```

Points to the beginning of the WSLE array. It is worth noting that it appears to have always the same value, with the array beginning right after the _MMWSL structure. _MMWSL is at 0xFFFFF700`01080000 and is 0x488 bytes in size, thus `Wsle` is usually set to 0xFFFFF700`01080488.

```
+0x020 LastInitializedWsle : Uint4B
```

Address of the last WSLE. It appears that the VMM maps a variable number of virtual pages for the WSLE array, probably extending it whenever it becomes full. The array begins at the address stored into the `Wsle` member and extends to the end of the last mapped page. This member stores the index of the last valid entry, which usually is in the last 8 bytes of the last mapped page. We can verify this with an instance of notepad.exe:

```
0: kd> !process 0 0 notepad.exe
PROCESS fffffa8001391b30
    SessionId: 1  Cid: 0b5c    Peb: 7fffffdc000  ParentCid: 0ad0
    DirBase: 34c67000  ObjectTable: fffff8a0027695f0  HandleCount:  77.
    Image: notepad.exe
```

The following command is to switch to the memory context of notepad.exe. We must remember to do this, because the WSL is in process-private memory.

```
0: kd> .process /i fffffa8001391b30
You need to continue execution (press 'g' <enter>) for the context
to be switched. When the debugger breaks in again, you will be in
the new process context.
0: kd> g
Break instruction exception - code 80000003 (first chance)
nt!DbgBreakPointWithStatus:
fffff800`028bbf60 cc              int     3
```

Now let's dump the address of the WSL. We know it normally is 0xFFFFF700`01080000, but we are not taking any chances:

```
0: kd> dt nt!_eprocess Vm.VmWorkingSetList @$proc
   +0x398 Vm                 :
      +0x068 VmWorkingSetList    : 0xfffff700`01080000 _MMWSL
```

The content of _MMWSL:

```
0: kd> dt nt!_mmwsl 0xfffff700`01080000
   +0x000 FirstFree          : 0x87
   +0x004 FirstDynamic       : 5
   +0x008 LastEntry          : 0x6e2
   +0x00c NextSlot           : 5
   +0x010 Wsle               : 0xfffff700`01080488 _MMWSLE
   +0x018 LowestPagableAddress : (null)
   +0x020 LastInitializedWsle : 0x76e
   ...
```

The address of the last initialized entry is given by the value of `Wsle` (the array start address) added to `LastInitializedWsle` multiplied by 8, the size of an entry. Here are the address and its content:

```
0: kd> dq 0xfffff700`01080488 + 0x76e*8
fffff700`01083ff8  ffffffff`00000eda ????????`????????
fffff700`01084008  ????????`???????? ????????`????????
fffff700`01084018  ????????`???????? ????????`????????
fffff700`01084028  ????????`???????? ????????`????????
fffff700`01084038  ????????`???????? ????????`????????
fffff700`01084048  ????????`???????? ????????`????????
fffff700`01084058  ????????`???????? ????????`????????
fffff700`01084068  ????????`???????? ????????`????????
```

This address is indeed eight bytes before the end of a page and the next page is not mapped. The address content is a free entry, because it's even and has

_MMWSLE_FREE_ENTRY.NextFree (i.e. bits 32-63) set to 0xFFFFFFFF, so it is the last in the free entries list.

```
+0x048 NonDirectHash      : Ptr64 _MMWSLE_NONDIRECT_HASH
```

```
+0x050 HashTableStart     : Ptr64 _MMWSLE_HASH
```

We are only going to mention these two members briefly here and we will analyze them later, together with shared memory (see sec. 37.14 on p. 331). Consider a memory page shared by two processes. Each process has its own WSLE storing the VA mapped to the page, but the index of the entry can be different in the two WSLs, i.e. the VA can be stored at different entries in different WSLs. When this happens these hash tables are used to associate VAs and indexes.

20.3.5   The !wsle Debugger Extension

Armed with the knowledge we gained so far, we can better understand the output of the `!wsle` debugger extension. Here is a sample output when the command is used without arguments:

```
1: kd> !wsle

Working Set @ fffff70001080000
    FirstFree      11c  FirstDynamic       5
    LastEntry      60e  NextSlot           5  LastInitialized    76e
    NonDirect        3  HashTable          0  HashTableSize        0
```

We can see that the usual WSL address is used and some of the members we discussed earlier are shown.

NonDirect, HashTable and HashTableSize will be explained in the section on shared memory (see sec. 37.14 on p. 331).

20.3.6   Getting from the Virtual Address to the WSLE

We will see, in the discussion on how memory content is written to the paging file, that the VMM uses the WSL to decide which physical pages to remove from a process working set, when it needs to increase the number of available pages. In this logic, the VMM uses the WSL as its starting point. Once a particular WSLE has been elected to be removed from the WS, the VMM knows the VA it refers to, because it's stored in the WSLE itself. From the VA, the VMM can easily compute the address of the PTE used for the mapping and get to the PFN of the physical page. In short, the VMM can get to all the data structures it needs to update (we will analyze this process at length in later sections).

However, there are situations where the VMM only knows a VA and needs to get to the WSLE for it. Consider, for instance, what happens when a process releases a range of virtual memory by calling *VirtualFreeEx*. This function takes a virtual address as input and must release a virtual range. This, of course, implies freeing any physical pages currently mapped to the range and free any WSLEs for mapped VAs.

As we saw earlier, in-use WSLEs are not kept in any particular order, so finding the one for a given VA would mean scanning the entire WSL, which would be inefficient.

It appears instead that the VMM has a better way of solving this problem. As we are going to see shortly, the VMM maintains an array of data structures for each physical page in the system, called PFN database. Each array element stores information on the current state of a particular physical page. When a physical page is in-use and is mapping a VA included in a working set, a member of this structure stores the index of the WSLE for the VA. In other words, the VMM can get from VA to WSLE doing the following:

- compute the PTE address from the VA

- extract the PFN from the PTE

- compute the address of the PFN database element from the PFN

- extract the WSLE index from the PFN database

- access the WSLE

We can corroborate this hypothesis with an experiment. As many other experiments in this book, this one requires that the system is attached to a kernel debugger.

We use the MemTests program included in the download package to allocate and touch a region of memory. Allocation is performed by selecting the *VirtualAllocExTest()* option on the main menu. MemTests prompts for a set of parameters, which can be set as follows:

lpAddress:	0, to let the allocation function choose the starting address
dwSize:	0x1000, i.e. 64kB
flAllocationType:	0x3000, to reserve and commit memory
flProtect:	4, for read/write memory
specify NUMA node:	n

When the program returns to the main menu, it has allocated the region. We need to take note of the region starting address, displayed above the menu (in the following it will be 0xC0000). We then must write into the region to ensure physical pages are actually mapped to it. We can do this by selecting the *Access region* option, then *Private memory region* and *Write memory*; we leave the start and end address to their default values, so the whole region is written to.

Afterwards, we choose *Release private region* on the main menu to deallocate the region. At the next prompt we choose to break into the debugger. When the debugger takes control, we are in the context of the thread about to free the memory region by calling *VirtualFreeEx*.

Now we have to anticipate a few things about the PFN database. We are going to place a breakpoint on accesses to the PFN db entry where the working set index is stored and one on the WSLE itself. This will allow us to confirm that *VirtualFreeEx* uses this information to do the job.

First, we use the `!pte` extension to find the physical address of the first page of the region. We need the virtual address we noted before here:

```
0: kd> !pte c0000
                                  VA 00000000000c0000

PXE at FFFFF6FB7DBED000   PPE at FFFFF6FB7DA00000   PDE at FFFFF6FB40000000   PTE at FFFFF68000000600
contains 02A0000028768867 contains 02E000003916B867 contains 02F0000036F6C867 contains A0500000196A9847
pfn 28768    ---DA--UWEV  pfn 3916b    ---DA--UWEV  pfn 36f6c    ---DA--UWEV  pfn 196a9    ---D---UW-V
```

This tells us that the PFN is 0x196a9 (i.e. the physical address is 0x196a9000). When we feed it to the !pfn extension, we get information on the PFN database entry for the page:

```
0: kd> !pfn 196a9
    PFN 000196A9 at address FFFFFA80004C3FB0
    flink       00000205 blink / share count 00000001  pteaddress FFFFF68000000600
    reference count 0001     used entry count  0000       Cached     color 0    Priority 5
    restore pte 00000080  containing page      036F6C  Active     M
    Modified
```

We are not going to examine the PFN entry in detail now. For this experiment, it is enough to know that the number 205 after `flink` is the WSLE index (in hexadecimal) and that its address is at the very beginning of the PFN entry, i.e. at the address 0xFFFFFA80`004C3FB0 shown above. We can place a breakpoint on reads at this address with the following debugger command:

```
ba r 8 /t @$thread FFFFFA80004C3FB0
```

This will cause the processor to break into the debugger whenever a byte in the 8 bytes range beginning at 0xFFFFFA80`004C3FB0 is read. The `/t @$thread` option tells the debugger to actually stop execution only when the breakpoint is hit in the context of the thread that is now current. This last condition is very important since kernel data structures like the PFN database are accessed by many system threads and the breakpoint would capture all sorts of system functions without it.

The following command sets a breakpoint for the current thread on write accesses to entry 0x205 of the WSLE:

```
ba w 8 /t @$thread @@( &(((nt!_mmwsl *) 0xfffff70001080000)->Wsle[0x205]) )
```

With this, we are about to see what happens when VirtualFreeEx is called. If we resume
execution we see breakpoint 0 being hit at *MiDeleteVirtualAddresses*+0x484. Note that data
breakpoints stop the processor at the instruction *after* the one accessing the memory
address on which the breakpoint is set, so the latter is at offset +0x47a inside the function.
The call stack shows we are inside the call to *VirtualFreeEx*:

```
0: kd> k
Child-SP          RetAddr           Call Site
fffff880`04877970 fffff800`028c6c4a nt!MiDeleteVirtualAddresses+0x484
fffff880`04877b30 fffff800`02884153 nt!NtFreeVirtualMemory+0x5ca
fffff880`04877c20 00000000`770e009a nt!KiSystemServiceCopyEnd+0x13
00000000`002df978 000007fe`fd1129c1 ntdll!NtFreeVirtualMemory+0xa
00000000`002df980 00000001`3fa73973 KERNELBASE!VirtualFreeEx+0x41
00000000`002df9b0 00000000`00000000 MemTests!ReleasePrivateRegion+0x83
[b:\programm\memtests\memtests\main.cpp @ 3432]
```

We can also have a look at WSLE 0x205 and confirm that it is still in use and tracking VA
0xc0000:

```
0: kd> ?? ((nt!_mmwsl *) 0xfffff70001080000)->Wsle[0x205].u1
union <unnamed-tag>
   +0x000 VirtualAddress   : 0x00000000`000c0009 Void
   +0x000 Long             : 0xc0009
   +0x000 e1               : _MMWSLENTRY
   +0x000 e2               : _MMWSLE_FREE_ENTRY
```

When we resume execution, we are stopped by breakpoint 1 at
MiDeleteVirtualAddresses+0x541. This means the WSLE has been updated, so it's better to
have a look at it again:

```
0: kd> ?? ((nt!_mmwsl *) 0xfffff70001080000)->Wsle[0x205].u1
union <unnamed-tag>
   +0x000 VirtualAddress   : 0x00000000`000c0008 Void
   +0x000 Long             : 0xc0008
   +0x000 e1               : _MMWSLENTRY
   +0x000 e2               : _MMWSLE_FREE_ENTRY
```

The entry value is now an even number, so the entry is not in use anymore. This is the call
stack at this time:

```
0: kd> k
Child-SP          RetAddr           Call Site
fffff880`04877970 fffff800`028c6c4a nt!MiDeleteVirtualAddresses+0x541
fffff880`04877b30 fffff800`02884153 nt!NtFreeVirtualMemory+0x5ca
fffff880`04877c20 00000000`770e009a nt!KiSystemServiceCopyEnd+0x13
00000000`002df978 000007fe`fd1129c1 ntdll!NtFreeVirtualMemory+0xa
00000000`002df980 00000001`3fa73973 KERNELBASE!VirtualFreeEx+0x41
00000000`002df9b0 00000000`00000000 MemTests!ReleasePrivateRegion+0x83
[b:\programm\memtests\memtests\main.cpp @ 3432]
```

We are still in the middle of *VirtualFreeEx*.

If we go on, we see the WSLE is updated again at *MiDeleteVirtualAddresses*+0x5bd:

```
0: kd> ?? ((nt!_mmwsl *) 0xfffff70001080000)->Wsle[0x205].u1
union <unnamed-tag>
   +0x000 VirtualAddress    : 0x00010289`fffffffe Void
   +0x000 Long              : 0x10289`fffffffe
   +0x000 e1                : _MMWSLENTRY
   +0x000 e2                : _MMWSLE_FREE_ENTRY

0: kd> k
Child-SP          RetAddr           Call Site
fffff880`04877970 fffff800`028c6c4a nt!MiDeleteVirtualAddresses+0x5bd
fffff880`04877b30 fffff800`02884153 nt!NtFreeVirtualMemory+0x5ca
fffff880`04877c20 00000000`770e009a nt!KiSystemServiceCopyEnd+0x13
00000000`002df978 000007fe`fd1129c1 ntdll!NtFreeVirtualMemory+0xa
00000000`002df980 00000001`3fa73973 KERNELBASE!VirtualFreeEx+0x41
00000000`002df9b0 00000000`00000000 MemTests!ReleasePrivateRegion+0x83
[b:\programm\memtests\memtests\main.cpp @ 3432]
```

It's interesting to note how the WSLE now appears to be chained in the free list. After some more hit on breakpoint 1, we hit again the one on the PFN entry inside a function with the telltale name *MiInsertPageInFreeOrZeroedList*, while still inside *VirtualFreeEx*:

```
Breakpoint 0 hit
nt!MiInsertPageInFreeOrZeroedList+0x280:
fffff800`0289d890 488bda          mov     rbx,rdx
0: kd> k
Child-SP          RetAddr           Call Site
fffff880`048776c0 fffff800`028b688f nt!MiInsertPageInFreeOrZeroedList+0x280
fffff880`048777c0 fffff800`028b5b51 nt!MiDeletePteRun+0x49f
fffff880`04877970 fffff800`028c6c4a nt!MiDeleteVirtualAddresses+0x408
fffff880`04877b30 fffff800`02884153 nt!NtFreeVirtualMemory+0x5ca
fffff880`04877c20 00000000`770e009a nt!KiSystemServiceCopyEnd+0x13
00000000`002df978 000007fe`fd1129c1 ntdll!NtFreeVirtualMemory+0xa
00000000`002df980 00000001`3fa73973 KERNELBASE!VirtualFreeEx+0x41
00000000`002df9b0 00000000`00000000 MemTests!ReleasePrivateRegion+0x83
[b:\programm\memtests\memtests\main.cpp @ 3432]
```

We can then remove all the breakpoints with `bc*` and resume execution.

In summary, this experiment shows us that *VirtualFreeEx* performs the following steps:

- Accesses the WSLE index inside the PFN database

- Accesses the WSLE, releasing it

These steps are consistent with our initial hypothesis.

There is still one remaining problem with this approach. As we will see further on, the VMM allows different processes to share a section of physical memory. It may not always be possible to use the same WSLE in all the sharing processes: a process can have a shared physical page mapped to a VA tracked by entry *x* of the WSL and another process can use entry *y* in its own WSL to do the job. This can happen because the WSL is filled depending on the order in which each process touches virtual addresses according to its own logic.

However, the PFN database for the physical page can accommodate a *single* WSL index, which cannot be good for all the sharing processes. We will see when discussing shared memory that the VMM uses two hash tables which are part of the WSL to solve this problem (see sec. 37.14 on p. 331). This is where `_MMWSL.NonDirectHash` and `_MMWSL.HashTableStart` which we encountered in sec. 20.3.4 on p. 120 come into play.

20.4 Page Frame Number Database

The Page Frame Number Database (PFNDB) is another fundamental VMM data structure.

The PFNDB is used to manage each page of physical memory. It is an array of `_MMPFN` structures with a size equal to the number of physical pages. It is located at address 0xFFFFFA80`00000000 (see [1], p. 748) and it is indexed by PFN, i.e. the array element for the page with physical address 0x12345000 is the one with index 0x12345.

A physical page can be in one of several different *states*: it can be mapping a virtual page of some process; it can be in the process of being written out to or read from disk; it can be unused. The content of an `_MMPFN` instance changes depending on the state of the page. To keep an `_MMPFN` as small as possible, several members are overloaded with different meanings depending on the current state of the page.

Keeping `_MMPFN` small is important, because the PFNDB imposes a fixed overhead directly proportional to the amount of physical memory: if a system has *x* pages of physical memory, it also has *x* `_MMPFN` instances, which are themselves stored in physical memory. Furthermore, the PFNDB is not pageable, so it uses a fixed amount of physical memory and of virtual address space.

In the next section, we are going to examine the different page states.

21   Physical Page States

The state of a page is stored in its PFN database occurrence, in the `_MMPFN.u3.e1.PageLocation` member and the possible values are defined by the `_MMLISTS` enumeration. The following sections describe each page state and whether a PTE referring to the page exists for any of the possible states. What follows is merely a generic introduction on page states. We will return on several of them as we go on detailing the VMM architecture.

The VMM allows to map the content of a file in memory, something we will cover in detail in Chapter 38 (p. 338). When this happens, the page content is read from and written to the mapped file, as opposed to the paging file. For this reason, the following sections use the term *external storage* to refer to where the page content can be found. We will see later how paging actually works in both cases.

21.1 Active

A page is active when it is mapping a virtual address and one or more PTEs point to it. This state also applies to pages storing paging structures. Examples of active pages are:

- Pages in a process WS, mapping user mode VAs.

- Pages storing paging structures; we already saw these too are accounted for in the WS.

The PTE which points to the page has the P bit set, so the remainder of its content is as defined by the Intel x64 architecture.

We will see later when analyzing system range memory, that, for certain virtual ranges, the VMM does not use working sets. It maps virtual to physical translations, but the mapped VA is not accounted for in any working set list. Usually, this is done for non-pageable system regions like the nonpaged pool. For a physical page used in such a mapping, `_MMPFN.u3.e1.PageLocation` is still set to Active, so it would not be one hundred percent correct to state that an Active page is part of a working set. Rather, such a page is used in a translation (or more than one, if it is shared).

21.2 Modified

The page belonged to a working set, but was removed from it. The content of the page has not yet been saved to external storage, so the page itself cannot be reused until this happens.

The PTE which pointed to this page has the P bit clear, so its content is ignored by the processor, however, most of the remainder of the PTE is still set as it was when P was set, i.e. the PFN is in bits 12-48, etc. If some code tries to touch this page, the VMM restores it into the working set. Since this does not involve a disk access, this kind of page fault is usually called a *soft* fault. Actually, some of the PTE control bits are changed when the page is brought into this state, but the VMM is able to revert them to their values when a soft fault occurs. Soft faults are analyzed in detail in Chapter 31 (p. 236).

A page enters this state when the memory manager decides to remove it from the WS, to reduce the WS size. We will see in sec. 38.2.7 on p. 354 that pages used for mapped files can also enter this state for different reasons.

21.3 Standby

This state is similar to the modified one, except for the fact that the page content has been written to external storage, so the page can be reused, if the VMM needs it. However, as long as the page is in this state, its content is still valid and the PTE still points to it, like in the modified case. If a thread touches the page, the latter is restored into the working set and becomes active again, as in the modified case (i.e. soft fault).

21.4 Transition

There is an I/O in progress on the page, i.e. its content is either being read from or written to external storage. For instance, a page in the modified state enters the transition state while it is being written to storage and the standby state afterwards.

A page arriving from the modified state still has a PTE pointing to it, as explained before. We will discuss the PTE for a page being read when we will analyze in-paging in Chapter 34 (p. 249).

21.5 Free

The page has unspecified dirty data in it. No PTE points to it and it can be reused. When the VMM reuses a Free page, it cannot simply map it "as is" to a new virtual address. This would allow the old page content to be visible at the new address. For instance, a process could read data left in the page by another one. To avoid this, the VMM fills such a page with zeroes before mapping it.

21.6 Zeroed

The page is free for use, no PTE points to it and it is also already initialized with zeroes.

21.7 Rom

The physical address corresponds to read-only memory.

21.8 Bad

The page has generated hardware errors and cannot be used. This state is also used internally to handle transitions from one state to another ([1], p. 804).

21.9 Modified no-write

This state is similar to the modified one, but, as long as a page is in this state, it cannot be written to external storage. This state is not used for paging of user mode range virtual addresses, so we will not examine it for now, but we will return on it in sec 49.4 on p. 546, while examining the Cache Manager.

22   Page Lists

For some of the possible states, physical pages are kept in a list, so that the VMM can quickly retrieve a page of that type. There are lists for: Standby, Modified, Free, Zeroed, Modified no-write and ROM pages ([1], p. 805).

To keep things simple, for now we can think in terms of these lists, even though we will see later how some of them are actually divided into sub-lists.

These lists are made of _MMPFN instances linked together through some of their members and each instance represent a physical page in the list (the one with PFN equal to the instance index into the _MMPFN array).

23   Allocation of a New Physical Page

When a newly allocated address is first referenced, a page fault occurs, because the VMM does not allocate physical pages until the first actual access. This is called a *demand-zero* fault, because it must be resolved by mapping the VA to a zero initialized page. The VMM attempts to handle such a fault by taking a page from the Zeroed list. If the Zeroed list is empty, it takes a Free page and zeroes it. If the Free list is empty, it takes a Standby page and zeroes it.

The last possibility, leads us to an interesting question: we know that a Standby page has a PTE pointing to it, which still holds the page PFN and is ready to be used for an eventual soft fault. If the page is reused, this PTE must be updated, so that an eventual fault involving it will be handled as a "hard" one, requiring to read the content back from external storage. But we also know that PTEs are mapped in a per-process region: when the VMM is looking for a page to be given to a process, the address space of that process is the current one, which means the PTEs *of that process* are mapped in the mapping structures region.

However, if we want to grab a page from the Standby list, it could belong to *another* process and we must have a way to update the PTE belonging to it. We will see how this is done - stay tuned.

It is a little hard to find out what happens if even the Standby list is empty, because most of the existing literature does not consider this case.

It is stated, in [7], that a page is taken from the Modified list after its content has been saved to disk and the page has been moved to the Standby list. It is not further detailed how the faulting thread is kept waiting while the write is in progress and, anyway, this sounds more like triggering the replenishing of the Standby list and then taking the page from there.

We will present in sec. 26.4.3.4.3 on p. 158 a detailed analysis of allocation from the Standby list, albeit limited to demand-zero faults.

Finally, [7] states that if the Modified list is empty, a page is removed from the working set. It is not stated explicitly *which* working set, however a reasonable hypothesis is that the page is taken from the WS of the process which incurred the fault. Possibly, the VMM could look at pages whose content is already written to external storage first and at unsaved pages later.

When the Standby and Modified lists are empty, the system is seriously running low on physical memory, because the VMM tries to avoid this, by trimming working sets.

24   Overview of State Transitions

A page goes from one state to another while the VMM does its job, so this section outlines the state transitions involved. This is not an exhaustive description of all the possible transitions, in order not to impose too much complexity on the reader at this stage. For instance, transitions related to file mapping are not mentioned here, because we will cover this subject later. We will refer to the diagram in Figure 22 on p. 135 to better understand state transitions.

We can begin our description considering a page which is part of a WS. Such a page can be removed from the WS as the VMM attempts to keep physical memory available. This can happen, for instance, because memory is becoming scarce and the page has not been accessed for a while. Whatever the reason, the page goes to the Standby list if a copy of its content exists in the paging file, or to the Modified list if it has unsaved content.

From the Modified list the page can be restored into the original WS if the process accesses it. Since the process incurs a page fault, this operation is also called *faulting back* the page and the fault is a soft fault (no disk access).

A VMM thread named Modified Page Writer is dedicated to writing the content of a modified page to the paging file. When this happens, the modified page goes into the Transition state while the write is in progress, then enters the Standby state. We are simplifying things a little here, because while the write is in progress the process could try to access the page, but we will analyze this kind of event later. In the remainder of this book, we will use the term *outpaged* to mean that a page has been written to the paging file, i.e. a *copy* of it exists in the paging file.

We are now ready to introduce a *key point* of the VMM architecture. A page is not outpaged when it is reused, e.g. for another process. In other words, memory content is not written to the paging file when the VMM wants to reuse a physical page for something else. Rather, a page is outpaged *in background* by the modified page writer, and, afterwards, it can remain for an undetermined amount of time on the Standby list. The actual *reuse* of a page takes place at a later stage and this can happen a long time after the page has been outpaged, if there is enough physical memory.

From the Standby state, a page can be faulted back into the original WS to map the same VA or it can be *reused* by the VMM when a page fault needs to be satisfied and the free and zero lists are empty. When the latter happens, the PTE which was pointing at the Standby page is updated so that, when the related process will access the corresponding VA again, it will incur an hard fault. If the page is reused to satisfy a demand-zero fault, it is zeroed before being made Active into the new WS. If it is reused to read content back from the paging file, it goes into the Transition state while the read is in progress.

In the remainder of this book, we will use the term *repurpose* to indicate page reuse. We can now understand that outpaging and repurposing are two distinct actions taken by the VMM at different moments: it outpages memory to make standby pages available and it *repurposes* pages when it needs to give physical memory to a process. We will also use the term *swapped out* to refer to content of a physical page which has been repurposed, so that the content itself is only available in the paging file. Thus, memory content becomes swapped out after the physical page storing it has both been outpaged *and* repurposed.

Active, Standby and Modified pages go to the Free list when they are released, for instance when the process exits.

From the Windows literature examined by the author, it seems that Standby pages are not moved into the Free list until released. [8] states that they are, but all the other sources that were reviewed don't mention anything about it. It's likely that the VMM leaves Standby pages untouched until it actually needs a physical page to satisfy a fault and the Zero and

Free list are empty. This way, Standby pages remain available and can be faulted back until physical memory is actually needed.

Pages in the Free list are zeroed and moved to the Zeroed list by the zero page thread, which is part of the VMM and has priority 0, therefore it runs when the CPU would otherwise be idle.

Also, pages in the Free list are used when the VMM must bring back into the WS a page from the paging file. The VMM needs to read the content back into the physical page, so it can use a Free one, because its content will be overwritten with the paging file data.

Pages in the Free list can be filled with zeroes and used to resolve a demand-zero fault if the Zeroed list is empty.

From the Zeroed list, pages can be taken to satisfy faults for newly allocated virtual addresses and go into a working set. Zeroed pages can also be used to read content back from the paging file, if the Free list is empty.

The following diagram depicts the state transitions covered so far:

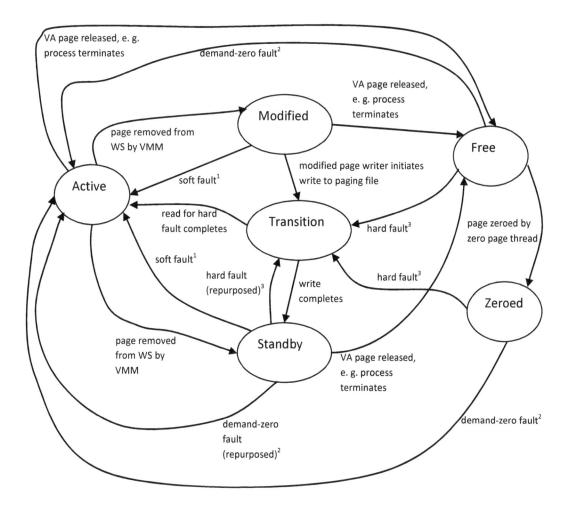

Figure 22 - Page State Diagram

Notes

1. A page on the Modified or Standby list can be faulted back into the WS which owned it when it was active, if the process touches it. This is the soft fault.

2. A demand-zero fault is resolved taking a page from the Zeroed list, however, if the list is empty, a Free page is taken and zeroed. If both lists are empty, a page from the Standby list is taken. This means the page is reused and given to a WS which is *not*

the one from which it was previously removed. The page is filled with zeroes before being added to the new WS. The PTE of the WS which previously owned the page is updated, so that it records where the page content is in the paging file. When the corresponding process will try to reference this page, it will incur an hard page fault.

3. To resolve a hard fault a physical page is allocated and a read operation is initiated, so that the page enters the transition state. When possible a Free page is used; if the Free list is empty, a Zeroed page is used; if both lists are empty, a Standby page is used; see also note 2.

In the next sections, we are going to follow one of the possible life cycles of a physical page, from when it is first assigned to an address space to when it is repurposed and, later, its content is eventually brought back. While doing this, we will be able to explain several details of the VMM. Before going on with this analysis, though, we will spend a few words on how synchronization is handled in the VMM.

25   Synchronization in the VMM

25.1 Working Set Pushlock

When the VMM needs to update the paging structures of an address space, it acquires the WS pushlock. If more than one thread attempt to update the paging structures, they can do so in a serialized fashion, so that the structures are left in a consistent state.

The pushlock used is stored in the `WorkingSetMutex` member of `_MMSUPPORT` and each address space has its own `_MMSUPPORT` instance (in spite of its name, this variable is of type `_EX_PUSH_LOCK`).

We will see, for instance, in sec. 26.1 on p. 139 how `WorkingSetMutex` is acquired at the beginning of a page fault handling and released after the PTE has been updated (sec. 26.8, p. 172). APIs which need to update the paging structures such *VirtualAllocEx* and *VirtualFreeEx* try to acquire `WorkingSetMutex`, so that a thread calling them is kept waiting while a page fault for the same address space is being handled.

A pushlock can be acquired either in exclusive or shared fashion according to the following rules:

-   An attempt to acquire the pushlock in shared fashion succeeds if the pushlock is free or already acquired in shared fashion by another thread

-   A shared acquisition attempt blocks if the pushlock is already exclusively acquired

- An attempt to exclusively acquire the pushlock succeeds only if the pushlock is free and blocks otherwise (i.e. a previous shared acquisition blocks an exclusive acquisition)

Both the page fault handler and the VMM APIs mentioned above acquire the pushlock exclusively, serializing their execution among themselves. This also means that different threads causing a page fault in the same address space will also be serialized by the pushlock.

Most of the handling of a PF takes place without raising the IRQL, so that VMM code can be interrupted and even preempted by another thread. Instead of taking exclusive control of the system, the VMM uses synchronization primitives like the working set pushlock to protect shared data, and allows normal thread scheduling to go on.

When a thread blocks waiting for a pushlock the scheduler puts it into a waiting state, so it does not consume CPU cycles until it eventually acquires the pushlock and is resumed.

25.2 _MMPFN Lock

Bit 0 of _MMPFN.PteAddress is used as a lock to synchronize updates to an _MMPFN instance. Before the update, the IRQL is raised to DISPATCH and the bit tested; if the bit is set, the thread spins in a loop until it becomes clear; if the bit is clear it is set, blocking updates from other threads (the test and set operations are part of a single atomic instruction). In summary, this bit is used as a spinlock acquired at DPC level.

Other existing Windows sources mention a "PFN database spinlock", however, at least in the Windows 7 code there does not seem to be a single lock for the whole database, but, rather, this per-instance lock. This makes a lot of sense, because each instance can be locked independently of all the others. The demise of the PFN spinlock seems confirmed by the output of the !qlocks extension:

```
1: kd> !qlocks
Key: O = Owner, 1-n = Wait order, blank = not owned/waiting, C = Corrupt

                        Processor Number
    Lock Name           0   1

KE   - Unused Spare
MM   - Expansion
MM   - Unused Spare
MM   - System Space
CC   - Vacb
CC   - Master
EX   - NonPagedPool
IO   - Cancel
EX   - WorkQueue
```

```
IO    - Vpb
IO    - Database
IO    - Completion
NTFS  - Struct
AFD   - WorkQueue
CC    - Bcb
MM    - NonPagedPool
```

This command shows the state of the system global queued spinlock. According to [1], p. 176, this list used to include (at least until Windows Vista) a spinlock named MM - PFN, which is now absent.

Note that bit 0 of `_MMPFN.PteAddress` can be reused, because PTE addresses are aligned on 8 bytes boundaries.

The `_MMPFN` lock is only acquired in short sections of code, since it keeps other threads waiting for the lock spinning inside a busy-wait loop. This contrasts with the WS pushlock, which is often exclusively acquired throughout many VMM functions.

26   First Access to a Private Address

In this section we are going to describe what happens when the first access is made to an address inside private process memory. Limiting the analysis to this particular case will help us reduce the complexity of the description, while still allowing us to understand a number of details on how a VA is mapped to a physical page.

First, we must remember that the address must be inside a region of the VA which has been reserved and committed, otherwise it can't be accessed. This is explained in detail in Chapters 19 (p. 93) and 20 (p. 95).

When the first access happens, there are a few possible situations:

- The page table entry (PTE) for the address is set to 0. This happens when the VA range has been reserved and committed as a whole (see section 20.1.1, p. 98).

- The PTE can be set to a nonzero value, which stores the protection for the page in bits 5-9, which happens when a reserved range has been only partially committed (see section 20.1.2, p. 103).

- One or more of the paging structures mapping the address may not have been allocated yet. For instance, the page table (PT) may be missing, which means the page directory entry (PDE) is set to 0. Or it could happen that both the page directory (PD) and the PT are missing, so that the page directory pointer table entry (PDPTE) is set to 0. Finally, the page directory pointer table (PDPT) can be missing too, meaning only the page map level 4 entry (PML4E) for the VA exists and is set to 0. The page map level 4 (PML4) always exists, because it is created when the process is initialized.

- Likewise, one or more of the paging structures could have been swapped out, so, even if the PxE of the parent table is not set to 0, because it stores enough information to retrieve the swapped out content, it still has the P (present) bit clear. We are not going to analyze this case now, because we will examine the paging of paging structures themselves in Chapter 36 (p. 288).

All the scenarios above result in a page fault (PF), so the processor diverts execution to the PF handler. By looking at the IDT, we can see that this handler is a function named *KiPageFault*, which saves the current execution status on the stack, building an instance of a _KTRAP_FRAME structure and then calls *MmAccessFault*. The latter is the main VMM PF handling code, whose job is to either *resolve* the fault by mapping the virtual address, or return an appropriate NTSTATUS value representing an invalid memory access.

In the next sections, we are going to describe the steps *MmAccessFault* takes to handle the fault. It's worth stating once more that this analysis is limited to a particular case: the first access to a user mode VA.

26.1 Initial Checks and Synchronization

First of all, *MmAccessFault* checks whether the address causing the fault is in canonical form and returns STATUS_ACCESS_VIOLATION if this is not the case.

Afterwards, it ensures that the current IRQL is less than DPC/dispatch. Again, if this check fails an error NTSTATUS is returned; since the IRQL implies that the fault occurred in kernel mode, the caller of *MmAccessFault* will probably bugcheck. For PF generated by user mode code, the current IRQL is always PASSIVE.

Next, the functions checks if any of the following flags is set in the _ETHREAD for the current thread:

- OwnsProcessWorkingSetExclusive

- OwnsProcessWorkingSetShared

- OwnsSystemCacheWorkingSetExclusive

- OwnsSystemCacheWorkingSetShared

- OwnsSessionWorkingSetExclusive

- OwnsSessionWorkingSetShared

- OwnsPagedPoolWorkingSetExclusive

- OwnsPagedPoolWorkingSetShared

- OwnsSystemPtesWorkingSetExclusive

- OwnsSystemPtesWorkingSetShared

If one or more of these flags are set, the function bugchecks with code 0x1a (MEMORY_MANAGEMENT). From the flag names, the logic appears to be to crash the system if a thread which already owns (that is has a lock on) a working set incurs a page fault.

If the previous check does not end up in a disaster, the function disables APC delivery for the thread and acquires the process working set pushlock, which is stored in _MMSUPPORT.WorkingSetMutex (in spite of its name, the variable is of type _EX_PUSH_LOCK). The pointer to _MMSUPPORT is obtained from the current thread. When the pushlock has been successfully acquired, the function sets _ETHREAD.OwnsProcessWorkingSetExclusive, one of the flags checked before.

The working set pushlock has been introduced in Chapter 25 on p. 136.

26.2 Checking the Memory Access and Setting up the PTE Protection

The next steps taken by the VMM check whether the attempted memory access is valid and, if so, set the PTE to an intermediate value which will be used in the rest of the process.

26.2.1   When the PTE Is Found To Be Zero

If the PT for the VA exists and the corresponding PTE is set to 0, the VMM must check whether the VA has been correctly reserved and committed. It does so inside the *MiCheckVirtualAddress* function, which looks for a VAD for the VA. If a VAD is not found, *MmAccessFault* returns STATUS_ACCESS_VIOLATION, because the VA has not been neither reserved nor committed.

If the VAD is found, the value of _MMVAD_SHORT.u.VadFlags.Protection is copied to bits 5-9 of the PTE.

The code which accesses PTEs is consistent with the layout of the `_MMPTE` structure found among the Windows symbols. This structure is a union of several others, used for the different states of a PTE, e. g. when a PTE has the P bit set, its layout is dictated by the processor and is consistent with the `_MMPTE_HARDWARE` structure. `_MMPTE` has a member named `_MMPTE.u.Hard`, of type `_MMPTE_HARDWARE`.

During this part of the process, the PTE is treated in a way consistent with the `_MMPTE.u.Soft` member, which is of type `_MMPTE_SOFTWARE` and has a member named `Protection`, covering bits 5-9.

Using the data types above, we can state that the protection from the VAD is copied into the PTE as follows:

```
_MMPTE.u.Soft.Protection = _MMVAD_SHORT.u.VadFlags.Protection
```

After setting up the PTE this way, the VMM goes on mapping the VA according to the protection found in the VAD, without checking whether the memory access causing the fault is allowed by the page protection. This means a physical page will be mapped into the process address space and the faulting instruction attempted again. If this instruction is performing an access not allowed by the page protection, a new PF will occur and control will return again to *MmAccessFault*, which, discovering that the VA is already mapped, will take a different course of actions and thus will detect the protection violation and return STATUS_ACCESS_VIOLATION.

26.2.1.1   Experiment: Seeing the Double Page Fault in Action

The behavior outlined at the end of the previous section is peculiar, so it is worth observing it with an experiment. Readers willing to take what has been said for granted may want to skip this section.

We will use again our MemTests program, which will reserve and commit one page, with read-only protection, then attempt to write into the page. Note: the MemTests code visible in this experiment is different from the final release included in the download package, because MemTests grew more complex as this book progressed. However, the downloadable version can be used to perform this test and reproduce its result.

Here is the output from MemTests after having allocated the page and before trying to write to it:

```
Size            = 0x1000
flAllocationType = 0x3000
flProtect       = 0x2
enter key for VirtualAlloc...
```

```
Starting address = 0X00000000000C0000
Ending address  = 0X00000000000C0FFF
PDPTE - first: 0XFFFFF6FB7DA00000, last: 0XFFFFF6FB7DA00000
PDE   - first: 0XFFFFF6FB40000000, last: 0XFFFFF6FB40000000
PTE   - first: 0XFFFFF68000000600, last: 0XFFFFF68000000600
enter key...
Enter key to write memory
```

Now let's use WinDbg to examine the PTE:

```
1: kd> dq 0XFFFFF68000000600 l1

fffff680`00000600  00000000`00000000
```

The PT exists and the PTE is set to 0, so we are on the right path. We then put a breakpoint at *MmAccessFault* + 0x22E: this is where *MiCheckVirtualAddress* is called for the PTE = 0 case. We use the /p option of the bp command to set the breakpoint only for MemTests.exe, otherwise we would continuously hit the breakpoint while the VMM does its job for the rest of the system. With the breakpoint in place, we let MemTests go on, so that the breakpoint is hit.

We can now examine the call stack and see that our memory access triggered the fault:

```
Breakpoint 0 hit
rax=0000000000000000 rbx=0000000000000000 rcx=00000000000c0000
rdx=fffff88004fd5ba8 rsi=0000000000000000 rdi=ffffffffffffffff
rip=fffff800028dde0e rsp=fffff88004fd5ac0 rbp=fffff88004fd5b40
 r8=fffff88004fd5ba0  r9=fffff6fb40000000 r10=fffff68000000600
r11=fffff6fb40000000 r12=fffffa8002a94b60 r13=00000000000c0000
r14=0000000000000000 r15=fffffa8001c08a38
iopl=0         nv up ei pl zr na po nc
cs=0010  ss=0000  ds=002b  es=002b  fs=0053  gs=002b         efl=00000246
nt!MmAccessFault+0x22e:
fffff800`028dde0e e82d2a0000     call    nt!MiCheckVirtualAddress (fffff800`028e0840)
1: kd> k
Child-SP          RetAddr           Call Site
fffff880`04fd5ac0 fffff800`028c1fee nt!MmAccessFault+0x22e
fffff880`04fd5c20 00000001`3f8216af nt!KiPageFault+0x16e
00000000`002dfa00 00000001`3f87dd80 MemTests!VirtAllocTest+0x20f
[d:\dati\bob\programm\memtests\memtests\main.cpp @ 480]
00000000`002dfa08 00000000`00000000 MemTests!__xt_z+0x9a0
1: kd> lsa MemTests!VirtAllocTest+0x20f
   476:                    case 2:
   477:                            wprintf(L"\nEnter key to write memory");
   478:                            key = _getwch();
   479:                            wprintf(L"\nWriting byte 0...");
>  480:                            *lpMem = 1;
   481:                            bVal = *lpMem;
   482:                            wprintf(L"\nByte 0 = 0x%x", bVal);
   483:                            break;
   484:                    }
   485:            }
```

```
1: kd> kn
 # Child-SP          RetAddr           Call Site
00 fffff880`04fd5ac0 fffff800`028c1fee nt!MmAccessFault+0x22e
01 fffff880`04fd5c20 00000001`3f8216af nt!KiPageFault+0x16e
02 00000000`002dfa00 00000001`3f87dd80 MemTests!VirtAllocTest+0x20f
[d:\dati\bob\programm\memtests\memtests\main.cpp @ 480]
03 00000000`002dfa08 00000000`00000000 MemTests!__xt_z+0x9a0
1: kd> .frame 2
02 00000000`002dfa00 00000001`3f87dd80 MemTests!VirtAllocTest+0x20f
[d:\dati\bob\programm\memtests\memtests\main.cpp @ 480]
1: kd> ?? lpMem
unsigned char * 0x00000000`000c0000
"--- memory read error at address 0x00000000`000c0000 ---"
```

The highlighted source line comes from MemTests.exe and it is where the program tries to set the first byte inside the page to 1. The .frame 2 command sets the debugger stack context into MemTests, so that we can examine the value of lpMem with the "??" command, which shows us we are indeed trying to write to 0xC0000, i.e. our page. Finally, the line complaining about a memory read error tells us the debugger is trying to dereference lpMem and failing, which does not surprise us, since the VA is not mapped.

The call to *MiCheckVirtualAddress* we are examining passes the pointers to two local variables to the function: one is located at `rbp` + 0x60 and *MiCheckVirtualAddress* will return the pointer to the _MMVAD_SHORT instance for the address into it. The second variable is at `rbp` + 0x68 and it is where _MMVAD_SHORT.u.VadFlags.Protection will be copied. We can examine the value of these two variables before and after the call:

```
1: kd> dq @rbp + 60 l1
fffff880`04fd5ba0  00000000`00000000

1: kd> db @rbp + 68 l1
fffff880`04fd5ba8  00

1: kd> r
rax=0000000000000000 rbx=0000000000000000 rcx=00000000000c0000
rdx=fffff88004fd5ba8 rsi=0000000000000000 rdi=ffffffffffffffff
rip=fffff800028dde0e rsp=fffff88004fd5ac0 rbp=fffff88004fd5b40
 r8=fffff88004fd5ba0  r9=fffff6fb40000000 r10=fffff68000000600
r11=fffff6fb40000000 r12=fffffa8002a94b60 r13=00000000000c0000
r14=0000000000000000 r15=fffffa8001c08a38
iopl=0         nv up ei pl zr na po nc
cs=0010  ss=0000  ds=002b  es=002b  fs=0053  gs=002b             efl=00000246
nt!MmAccessFault+0x22e:
fffff800`028dde0e e82d2a0000      call    nt!MiCheckVirtualAddress (fffff800`028e0840)

1: kd> p
rax=0000000000000000 rbx=0000000000000000 rcx=0000000000000000
rdx=0000000000000001 rsi=0000000000000000 rdi=ffffffffffffffff
rip=fffff800028dde13 rsp=fffff88004fd5ac0 rbp=fffff88004fd5b40
 r8=fffff88004fd5ba0  r9=fffff6fb40000000 r10=fffff68000000600
r11=fffff6fb40000000 r12=fffffa8002a94b60 r13=00000000000c0000
```

```
r14=0000000000000000 r15=fffffa8001c08a38
iopl=0           nv up ei ng nz na pe nc
cs=0010  ss=0018  ds=002b  es=002b  fs=0053  gs=002b           efl=00000282
nt!MmAccessFault+0x233:
fffff800`028dde13 448b7568        mov     r14d,dword ptr [rbp+68h]
ss:0018:fffff880`04fd5ba8=00000001


1: kd> dq @rbp + 60 l1
fffff880`04fd5ba0  fffffa80`01584220


1: kd> db @rbp + 68 l1
fffff880`04fd5ba8  01
```

The p command allowed us to step execution over the function and regain control upon returning from it. Before the call the locals were both set to 0. After the call, the one at `rbp + 0x68` is set to 1. Let's look at the content of the VAD pointed by the one at `rbp + 0x60`:

```
1: kd> dt nt!_MMVAD_SHORT fffffa80`01584220
   +0x000 u1           : <unnamed-tag>
   +0x008 LeftChild    : (null)
   +0x010 RightChild   : (null)
   +0x018 StartingVpn  : 0xc0
   +0x020 EndingVpn    : 0xc0
   +0x028 u            : <unnamed-tag>
   +0x030 PushLock     : _EX_PUSH_LOCK
   +0x038 u5           : <unnamed-tag>

1: kd> dt nt!_MMVAD_SHORT u.VadFlags. fffffa80`01584220
   +0x000 u1           :
   +0x028 u            :
      +0x000 VadFlags     :
         +0x000 CommitCharge : 0y00000000000000000000000000000000000000000000000000000000000000001
(0x1)
         +0x000 NoChange     : 0y0
         +0x000 VadType      : 0y000
         +0x000 MemCommit    : 0y1
         +0x000 Protection   : 0y00001 (0x1)
         +0x000 Spare        : 0y00
         +0x000 PrivateMemory : 0y1
```

We can see from the values of `StartingVpn` and `EndingVpn` that the VAD covers our page at 0xC0000 and that `u.VadFlags.Protection` is set to 1, i.e. the value copied into the local variable at `rbp + 0x68`. Table 3 on p. 104 shows that 1 is actually the value for a page with PAGE_READONLY protection.

So far, the PTE for our address has not yet been updated:

```
1: kd> dq 0XFFFFF68000000600 l1
fffff680`00000600  00000000`00000000
```

Now we let execution go on until we exit MmAccessFault with the `g @$ra` command which stops when we return from the current function:

```
1: kd> g @$ra
rax=0000000000000111 rbx=0000000000000000 rcx=0000000000000001
rdx=0000000000000111 rsi=0000000000000000 rdi=0000000000000000
rip=fffff800028c1fee rsp=fffff88004fd5c20 rbp=fffff88004fd5ca0
 r8=0000000000000111  r9=0000000000029418 r10=fffffa8000c015e0
r11=fffff70001080488 r12=0000000000000000 r13=0000000000000000
r14=0000000000000000 r15=0000000000000000
iopl=0         nv up ei ng nz na pe nc
cs=0010  ss=0018  ds=002b  es=002b  fs=0053  gs=002b             efl=00000282
nt!KiPageFault+0x16e:
fffff800`028c1fee 85c0            test    eax,eax
```

We see that we are inside *KiPageFault* and the return value, stored in `rax` is 0x111. A look at the ntstatus.h Windows header tells us that this value corresponds to STATUS_PAGE_FAULT_DEMAND_ZERO. Let's take a look at our PTE:

```
1: kd> dq 0XFFFFF68000000600 l1
fffff680`00000600  97700000`00d5e025
```

It has the P bit set and a PFN for physical address 0xd5e000, so our VA is now mapped. Thus, even though we are trying to write to a read-only page, we got a virtual to physical mapping.

MemTests is still waiting to complete its write into the page, so we set another breakpoint for it at the beginning of *MmAccessFault* and let things go on. The `bp /p @$proc` command sets a breakpoint valid for the current process only, i.e. MemTests:

```
1: kd> bp /p @$proc nt!MmAccessFault
1: kd> g
Breakpoint 1 hit
rax=0000000000000001 rbx=0000000000000000 rcx=0000000000000001
rdx=00000000000c0000 rsi=0000000000000000 rdi=0000000000000000
rip=fffff800028ddbe0 rsp=fffff88004fd5c18 rbp=fffff88004fd5ca0
 r8=0000000000000001  r9=fffff88004fd5c20 r10=fffffa8002a94b60
r11=00000000000c0000 r12=0000000000000000 r13=0000000000000000
r14=0000000000000000 r15=0000000000000000
iopl=0         nv up ei pl nz na pe nc
cs=0010  ss=0000  ds=002b  es=002b  fs=0053  gs=002b             efl=00000202
nt!MmAccessFault:
fffff800`028ddbe0 48895c2410      mov     qword ptr [rsp+10h],rbx
ss:fffff880`04fd5c28=0000000000000000
```

Let's see what MemTests was up to:

```
1: kd> k
Child-SP          RetAddr           Call Site
fffff880`04fd5c18 fffff800`028c1fee nt!MmAccessFault
fffff880`04fd5c20 00000001`3f8216af nt!KiPageFault+0x16e
00000000`002dfa00 00000001`3f87dd80 MemTests!VirtAllocTest+0x20f
[d:\dati\bob\programm\memtests\memtests\main.cpp @ 480]
00000000`002dfa08 00000000`00000000 MemTests!__xt_z+0x9a0
1: kd> lsa MemTests!VirtAllocTest+0x20f
   476:                            case 2:
```

```
477:                                    wprintf(L"\nEnter key to write memory");
478:                                    key = _getwch();
479:                                    wprintf(L"\nWriting byte 0...");
> 480:                                  *lpMem = 1;
481:                                    bVal = *lpMem;
482:                                    wprintf(L"\nByte 0 = 0x%x", bVal);
483:                                    break;
484:                    }
485:            }
1: kd> .frame 2
02 00000000`002dfa00 00000001`3f87dd80 MemTests!VirtAllocTest+0x20f
[d:\dati\bob\programm\memtests\memtests\main.cpp @ 480]
1: kd> ?? lpMem
unsigned char * 0x00000000`000c0000
 ""
```

MemTests is still stuck at the same point, trying to write to 0xC000: it has incurred the
second page fault before it could make any progress. Note the difference from the first PF:
the debugger now succeeds in dereferencing lpMem, i.e. there is no memory read error
message.

Now we let once again execution go on until we return from *MmAccessFault*:

```
1: kd> g @$ra
rax=00000000c0000005 rbx=0000000000000000 rcx=0000000000000002
rdx=00000000c0000005 rsi=0000000000000000 rdi=0000000000000000
rip=fffff800028c1fee rsp=fffff88004fd5c20 rbp=fffff88004fd5ca0
 r8=00000000c0000005  r9=0000000000029418 r10=fffff68000000600
r11=fffff88004fd5c20 r12=0000000000000000 r13=0000000000000000
r14=0000000000000000 r15=0000000000000000
iopl=0         nv up ei ng nz na pe nc
cs=0010  ss=0018  ds=002b  es=002b  fs=0053  gs=002b              efl=00000282
nt!KiPageFault+0x16e:
fffff800`028c1fee 85c0            test    eax,eax
```

We are back inside *KiPageFault*, but take a look at the return value into `rax`: now it is
0xC0000005, i.e. the infamous STATUS_ACCESS_VIOLATION. If we let execution go, we get
the usual complaint from the system:

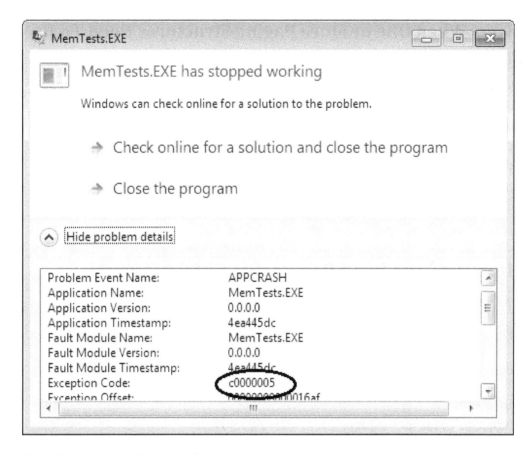

Figure 23 - Access Violation

26.2.2   When the PTE Is Not Zero

This situation occurs when the protection has already been written into the PTE, to keep track of a partially committed range (see section 20.1.1, p. 98). When this happens, the VMM performs some additional checks on the attempted memory access, inside a function named *MiAccessCheck*. For instance, an attempt to write to read-only memory is caught here and causes an access violation before the VA is mapped.

Not every protection condition is checked though. For instance, *MiAccessCheck* does not check whether an attempt is being made to execute code inside a page where instruction fetches are not allowed (e.g. a page with PAGE_READWRITE protection). This violation will be caught by a second page fault as explained in the previous section.

If the access is allowed, the PF handling will go on as explained after the end of section 26.2.

26.2.3   When One or More Paging Structures Need To Be Allocated

We will analyze this scenario later (sec. 36.2 on p. 289), when we will describe how paging structures are themselves paged. For now, we are just going to say that the VMM calls *MiCheckVirtualAddress* to ensure that the attempted access is to committed memory and returns STATUS_ACCESS_VIOLATION if the check fails. If the address is valid, it builds the paging structures hierarchy up to the PT. As an example, if the entire hierarchy is missing because the PML4E is set to 0, the VMM allocates pages for the PDPT, PD and PT and builds the three missing levels of paging structures. Afterwards, our address has a zeroed PTE and the PF handling goes on as outlined in section 26.2.1 on p. 140.

26.3 Updating the Used Page Table Entries Count

So far, we have seen how the VMM manages to:

- Perform fundamentals check on the nature of the PF and on the state of the thread.

- Ensure that the paging structures hierarchy is such that a PTE for the address exists.

- Ensure that the PTE for the address has `_MMPTE.u.Soft.Protection` set to the protection mask for the page.

Having accomplished this, the VMM locates the `_MMPFN` instance for the physical page storing the page table. It is more common to think of `_MMPFN` instances as referring to pages backing virtual memory, however PTs and all the other paging structures are themselves stored in physical pages. Since there is exactly one `_MMPFN` instance for every physical page, there will be instances referring to paging structures. To obtain the address of the PT `_MMPFN`, the VMM computes the VA of the PDE for the faulting address and reads the PFN inside the PDE, which refers to the PT. It then uses the PFN as an index in the PFN database to get to the `_MMPFN` instance. This is done to increment the `_MMPFN.UsedPageTableEntries` member. We will return on the meaning of this member later, in sec. 36.2 on p. 289.

26.4 Allocating a Physical Page With the Right Color (and from the Right Node)

The VMM computes the color of the new page to optimize cache utilization and, while doing this, also accounts for the NUMA nodes topology.

At this stage, there are two possibilities: either the page has been allocated explicitly requesting a NUMA node, or the default node selection logic is going to make the choice.

26.4.1   Color Computation for the Default NUMA Node

First of all, `_MMSUPPORT.NextPageColor` is a counter incremented each time a new physical page is assigned to the address space associated with the `_MMSUPPORT` instance (see section 17.2, p. 83).

Then, the VMM accesses the `_KPRCB` instance for the thread ideal processor. To achieve this, it uses the `IdealProcessor` member of the `_KTHREAD` instance for the current thread, which stores a number identifying the processor chosen to be the ideal one when the thread was initialized. The VMM uses this number to index into a pointers array named KiProcessorBlock. Each array item points to an instance of `_KPRCB`, therefore:

```
KiProcessorBlock[_KTHREAD.IdealProcessor]
```

gives the address of the ideal processor `_KPRCB`.

The VMM ANDs the incremented NextPageColor with _KPRCB.SecondaryColorMask, which masks the higher bits of the counter to give the actual color value, as explained in section 17.2.

Now it's time to see some NUMA related work. The VMM ORs the color value obtained so far with the `NodeShiftedColor` member of the ideal processor `_KPRCB`. This value sets bits zeroed by the previous AND with `SecondaryColorMask` to a number identifying the NUMA node. For instance, for a Core 2 Duo Mobile processor with SecondaryColorMask = 0x3F, NodeShiftedColor will use bits from 6 on. This final value will be used to index into an array of lists of physical pages. Each index corresponds to a NUMA node and a color and selects a list of pages having the desired color and belonging to the desired node. We will call this index the *color-NUMA index.*

To summarize, the color-NUMA index is computed as follows:

- retrieve the ideal processor `_KPRCB`

- increment `_MMSUPPORT.NextPageColor`

- AND the result with `_KPRCB.SecondaryColorMask`

- OR the result with `_KPRCB.NodeShiftedColor`

26.4.2   Color Computation for an Explicit Node

It is possible to allocate memory specifying that the physical pages must come from a specific node with a number of APIs, for instance *VirtualAllocExNuma*. This function takes the same parameters of *VirtualAllocEx* plus a node number, which is stored in the VAD, into `_MMVAD_SHORT.u5.VadFlags3.PreferredNode`; this member is otherwise set to zero for allocations which don't specify a node.

If the VMM finds a nonzero `PreferredNode` in the VAD for the faulting address, the color-NUMA index is computed in a different way:

- the base for the computation is still the incremented _MMSUPPORT.NextPageColor

- `SecondaryColorMask` is read from the `_KPRCB` of the current processor, not the ideal one

- the incremented `NextPageColor` is ANDed with `SecondaryColorMask` as in the previous section

- `PreferredNode` is decremented and shifted left MmSecondaryColorNodeShift times

- the result is ORed with `NextPageColor` from the previous steps

The main difference from the default node case is that the node number component of the color-NUMA index is not equal to `_KPRCB.NodeShiftedColor`, but rather to the specified node number decremented by one, which means we get the chance to explicitly set the node component of the index. MmSecondaryColorNodeShift contains the shift count needed to position the node number to the left of the color bits, while in the previous case `_KPRCB.NodeShiftedColor` was already positioned in the correct bits for the sake of efficiency. Here we have a node number coming from an API call, so we must shift it as we go.

The fact that `SecondaryColorMask` comes from the current processor is probably a performance optimization: all the processors in the system have the same color mask and it's easier to get to the current processor than to the ideal one. In the previous case we had to access the ideal processor data to get `NodeShiftedColor`, so it made sense to take `SecondaryColorMask` from the same `_KPRCB` instance.

26.4.2.1   Explicit Node and Nonzero PTEs

In section 26.2.2 (p. 147) we saw that when the PTE for the address is not equal to zero, the VAD is not retrieved, because the page protection is already in the PTE. This is not completely correct, when the page was allocated from an explicit node. This particular case is handled inside a function named *MiResolveDemandZeroFault*, which extracts `_KTHREAD.Tcb.ApcState.Process` from the current thread. This is a pointer to the `_EPROCESS` of the process whose address space is currently mapped. The function then checks the `_EPROCESS.NumaAware` flag and, if it is set, calls *MiLocateAddress* to locate the VAD for the faulting address, from which `u5.VadFlags3.PreferredNode` is extracted and used as explained in the previous section.

Thus the logic is: if `NumaAware` is clear, we skip a search into the VAD tree and use the default node selection logic; otherwise, we check in the VAD for this particular address whether a node was specified for it. We can conclude that `NumaAware` is probably set if the process has called one of the NUMA aware APIs at least once.

26.4.3   Physical Page Lists Used for Allocation

Once the VMM has computed the color-NUMA index, the latter is used to select a list of physical pages with the required attributes (i.e. color and node). Each list links together `_MMPFN` instances for pages having the same attributes and the lists heads are organized in arrays indexed by color-NUMA index.

There are two different kinds of `_MMPFN` lists: *singly linked* and *PFN linked*.

26.4.3.1   Singly Linked _MMPFN Lists

The first type of list is linked to an instance of _SLIST_HEADER, which stores the list head and is a union defining alternate memory layouts for its content. By examining the code of *MmAccessFault* (see for instance the code fragment at +0xB1C) we can see that the static MiZeroPageSlist stores the address of an array of `_SLIST_HEADER`s. The code indexes into this array by color-NUMA index and gets to the head of a list of pages having the desired attributes. If we examine the content of the `_SLIST_HEADER` occurrences, we discover that it is consistent with the `HeaderX64` member of `_SLIST_HEADER` and `HeaderX64.Depth` is the count of list elements. `HeaderX64.NextEntry` stores the address of an `_MMPFN` instance inside the PFN database address range. Actually, `NextEntry` is only 60 bits wide, so it stores the address shifted right by 4 positions, i.e. divided by 16, as explained on page 751 in [1]. This is not a problem, because the size of `_MMPFN` is 0x30 bytes and instances in the PFN database have addresses which are multiples of this size, so the rightmost digit is always 0.

In turn, _MMPFN.u1.Flink stores the address of the next list element and is set to zero for the last node.

Interestingly, _MMPFN.u3.e1.PageLocation is set to 5. The PageLocation member content is consistent with the values defined in the _MMLISTS enumeration:

```
0: kd> dt nt!_MMLISTS
   ZeroedPageList = 0n0
   FreePageList = 0n1
   StandbyPageList = 0n2
   ModifiedPageList = 0n3
   ModifiedNoWritePageList = 0n4
   BadPageList = 0n5
   ActiveAndValid = 0n6
   TransitionPage = 0n7
```

We see that 5 stands for bad page. This is an example of how the VMM uses the bad page value for pages set aside for particular purposes.

Looking at how *MmAccessFault* accesses this list, we can conclude that this is actually a list of zeroed pages grouped by color-NUMA index, so they are not actually bad pages.

With a little bit of guesswork on symbol names, we find the MiFreePageSlist symbol which appears to be the starting point of the singly linked list of free pages. It points to an array of _SLIST_HEADERs, each pointing to a list of _MMPFNs having color-NUMA index equal to the array index. For instance, this command shows that element [0] of the array is a list with 3 nodes:

```
1: kd> ?? ((nt!_SLIST_HEADER *) @@(poi nt!MiFreePageSlist))->HeaderX64.Depth
unsigned int64 3
```

The following expression gives the PFN of the 1st node:

```
1: kd> ?? (((unsigned int64) ((((nt!_SLIST_HEADER *) @@(poi nt!MiFreePageSlist)
)->HeaderX64.NextEntry) << 4)) - 0xfffffa8000000000) / 0x30

unsigned int64 0x24900
```

To compute the PFN, we first extract _SLIST_HEADER.HeaderX64.NextEntry and shift it left by 4 positions, which gives the actual address of the _MMPFN instance. The corresponding PFN is given by

(_MMPFN *address* – PFN db start) / _MMPFN *size*

with

PFN db start = 0xFFFFFA80`00000000

_MMPFN *size* = 0x30

The resulting PFN has color 0, because this particular machine has a color mask equal to 0x3f, so the color is in bits 0-5 of the PFN.

We can also examine the next node in the list. First, we use the !pfn extension to look at the content of the u1.Flink member, which stores the address of the next node:

```
1: kd> !pfn 24900
    PFN 00024900 at address FFFFFA80006DB000
    flink       FFFFFA80009BAC00  blink / share count 00000000  pteaddress
FFFFF6FC4001AED2
    reference count 0000    used entry count  0000      Cached     color 0   Priority 0
    restore pte 000003E0  containing page        02C9D9  Bad
```

then, we compute the PFN for the next node:

```
1: kd> ?? (0xFFFFFA80`009BAC00 - 0xFFFFFA80`00000000) / 0x30

unsigned int64 0x33e40
```

which also has color 0.

The lists at indexes 1 and 2 give the following results:

```
1: kd> ?? ((nt!_SLIST_HEADER *) @@(poi nt!MiFreePageSlist) + 1)->HeaderX64.Depth
unsigned int64 3

1: kd> ?? (((unsigned int64) ((((nt!_SLIST_HEADER *) @@(poi nt!MiFreePageSlist) + 1)-
>HeaderX64.NextEntry) << 4)) - 0xfffffa8000000000) / 0x30

unsigned int64 0x2a581
1: kd> ?? ((nt!_SLIST_HEADER *) @@(poi nt!MiFreePageSlist) + 2)->HeaderX64.Depth
unsigned int64 3
1: kd> ?? (((unsigned int64) ((((nt!_SLIST_HEADER *) @@(poi nt!MiFreePageSlist) + 2)-
>HeaderX64.NextEntry) << 4)) - 0xfffffa8000000000) / 0x30

unsigned int64 0x2a442
```

The results show the colors are consistent with the array indexes.

Finally, it is interesting to look at the page content with the !db extension, which dumps memory at a given *physical* address. We can see that these pages are indeed dirty, i.e. not zeroed:

```
1: kd> !db 2a442000
#2a442000 25 00 5c 00 73 00 79 00-73 00 74 00 65 00 6d 00 %.\.s.y.s.t.e.m.
#2a442010 33 00 32 00 5c 00 73 00-76 00 63 00 68 00 6f 00 3.2.\.s.v.c.h.o.
#2a442020 73 00 74 00 2e 00 65 00-78 00 65 00 00 00 49 00 s.t...e.x.e...I.
#2a442030 4b 00 45 00 45 00 58 00-54 00 00 00 00 00 00 00 K.E.E.X.T.......
```

```
#2a442040 00 00 00 00 00 00 00 00-b1 ed 55 55 c7 00 00 80 ..........UU....
#2a442050 02 00 78 74 01 00 00 00-90 92 f7 00 00 00 00 00 ..xt............
#2a442060 00 00 00 00 00 00 00 00-1f 10 00 00 00 00 00 00 ................
#2a442070 78 10 b4 01 00 00 00 00-98 10 b4 01 00 00 00 00 x...............
```

The same test on the Zeroed list shows a page filled with zeroes:

```
1: kd> ?? ((nt!_SLIST_HEADER *) @@(poi nt!MiZeroPageSlist ))->HeaderX64.Depth

unsigned int64 3

1: kd> ?? (((unsigned int64) ((((nt!_SLIST_HEADER *) @@(poi
nt!MiZeroPageSlist))->HeaderX64.NextEntry) << 4)) - 0xfffffa8000000000) / 0x30

unsigned int64 0x30040

1: kd> !db 30040000
#30040000 00 00 00 00 00 00 00 00-00 00 00 00 00 00 00 00 ................
#30040010 00 00 00 00 00 00 00 00-00 00 00 00 00 00 00 00 ................
#30040020 00 00 00 00 00 00 00 00-00 00 00 00 00 00 00 00 ................
#30040030 00 00 00 00 00 00 00 00-00 00 00 00 00 00 00 00 ................
#30040040 00 00 00 00 00 00 00 00-00 00 00 00 00 00 00 00 ................
#30040050 00 00 00 00 00 00 00 00-00 00 00 00 00 00 00 00 ................
#30040060 00 00 00 00 00 00 00 00-00 00 00 00 00 00 00 00 ................
#30040070 00 00 00 00 00 00 00 00-00 00 00 00 00 00 00 00 ................
```

26.4.3.2   PFN Linked _MMPFN Lists

These lists are indexed by color-NUMA index, as the ones of the previous kind, but the _MMPFN instances are linked together through their index in the PFN database. It's useful to remember that, by design, this index is equal to the PFN of the physical page associated with the _MMPFN instance.

The static MmFreePagesByColor is the starting point to access the PFN linked lists. It is an array of two pointers: the first points to the lists of zeroed pages and the second to the lists of free pages. Given the _MMLISTS enumeration of the previous section, we can formally express this as:

MmFreePagesByColor[ZeroedPageList] = pointer to the zeroed lists

MmFreePagesByColor[FreePageList] = pointer to the free lists

Each of these pointers is the address of an array of _MMPFNLIST indexed by color-NUMA. _MMPFNLIST.Flink holds the index of the first _MMPFN in the list. This will be an instance associated with a zeroed or free page (depending on the pointer we are using) with the specified color-NUMA index. In turn, _MMPFN.u1.Flink will contain the index of the next instance in the list and, for the last node, will be set to 0xFFFFFFFFFFFFFFFF. Note that this is the same member which stored the *address* of the next node in the singly linked list. The list is doubly linked: `_MMPFNLIST.Blink` stores the index of the last list element and each node has `_MMPFN.u2.Blink` set to the index of the previous one; for the first element, this member is 0xFFFFFFFFFFFFFFFF.

`_MMPFN.u3.e1.PageLocation` is set to the value corresponding to the list the page is in: `_MMLISTS.ZeroedPageList` (i.e. 0) or `_MMLISTS.FreePageList` (i.e. 1). This contrasts with the singly linked lists of the previous section, where it was set to `_MMLISTS.BadPageList`.

We will detail in sec 44.13 on p. 497 where, in the system address range, both kinds of lists are stored.

26.4.3.3   Comparison Between List Types

Since the elements of singly linked lists are linked through their addresses, the VMM can quickly grab a list node to allocate the page. On the other hand, access to the PFN linked lists should be a little slower, because the `_MMPFN` address must be computed from the index.

The singly linked lists appear to be quite small (it's common to find only 3 elements for each list), so they look like a "cache" of sorts of quickly available `_MMPFN` instances. When *MmAccessFault* needs to allocate a zeroed page, it looks at the singly linked list first and goes to the PFN linked one only when the former is empty.

26.4.3.4   Page Lookup Order

To resolve a PF like the one we are considering, the VMM needs a zeroed page, so it first looks into the list for this state. If the zeroed list is empty, the VMM looks at the free list and, if the latter is empty as well, it goes to the standby list.

26.4.3.4.1   Page Allocation from the Zeroed List

If an already zeroed page is found, the VMM moves on to map it into the address space; the actions involved will be analyzed in the next sections. We can represent the page state transition in the diagram introduced in Figure 22 on p. 135 and reproduced below, with our particular transition highlighted by means of a thicker arrow:

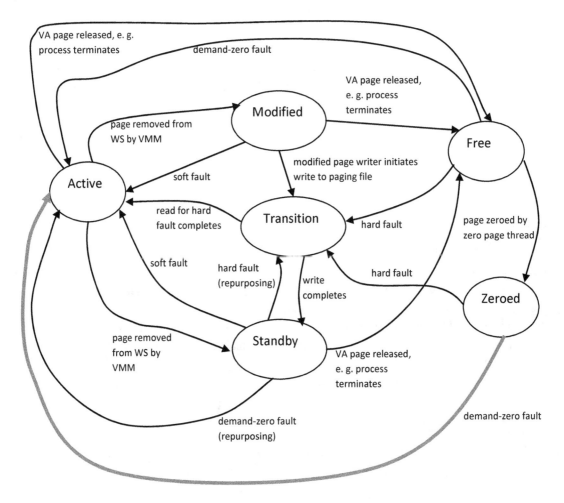

Figure 24 - Page Allocation from the Zeroed List

26.4.3.4.2   Page Allocation from the Free List

A page in the free list is available for use, but is "dirty" and must be zeroed before being mapped into the address space. This does not seem a big deal: writing 0 into all the bytes of a page should be straightforward enough. The problem is that instructions that write to memory (as well as ones that read from it) use *virtual* addresses. There is no way to write a piece of code which means "write 0 at *physical* address 0x1234", so the page must be mapped somewhere in memory in order to be zeroed. On the other hand, a page from the free list is not mapped to any virtual address by design: this is what makes it ready to be used. The VMM must therefore map it at a temporary virtual address and then fill it with zeroes.

Much of the existing Windows literature states that the VMM maps the page into the Hyperspace region to accomplish this, however this is not actually correct in x64 Windows 7.

A look at the code shows that *MmAccessFault* calls *MiZeroPhysicalPage* to get the job done and this function, in turn, maps the page in the System PTE range (0xFFFFF880`00000000 – 0xFFFFF900`00000000), which will be analyzed in detail later in sec. 44.8 on p. 440. For now, we will just say that, if we look at the PML4E for this range in different processes, we see that it points to the same PDPT, hence this range is shared across all address spaces and is not process private, like the real Hyperspace, which is the range 0xFFFFF700`00000000 - 0xFFFFF780`00000000.

Since this behavior is not mentioned in the existing literature, it has probably been introduced with Windows 7.

At any rate, it is not so important whether the page is mapped in a process-private region like Hyperspace or in a shared one: the mapping is temporary and is done only for the purpose of zeroing it.

One question worth asking is why going through all the trouble of mapping the page to a temporary VA, when we are going to map it into the process address space anyway. The VMM could conceivably map it at the faulting address, where it is bound to end up, and fill it with zeroes before returning from the fault.

The problem with this approach is that as soon as the page is mapped at its final user mode VA, other threads in the process which incurred the fault have access to it. There would therefore be a window of time in which the page dirty content would be visible to these threads.

This is unacceptable: by design Windows must ensure that a process cannot get a page with data left from another process in order to meet C2 security requirements. This is the reason why our fault is resolved by mapping a zero-filled page and not just a dirty one and the VMM makes sure that the page has already been zeroed before making it visible to the process, hence the need for a temporary system VA.

This kind of state transition for a free page is highlighted in the diagram below:

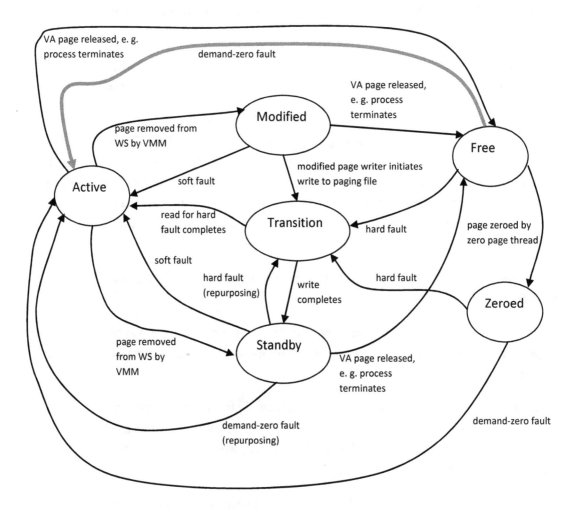

Figure 25 - Page Allocation from the Free List

26.4.3.4.3   Page Allocation from the Standby List

26.4.3.4.3.1 Updating the PTE Pointing to the Page

A page on the Standby list has already been removed from some working set and the PTE pointing to it has the P bit clear. The page is still storing valid content for the address space it was removed from, so it must be filled with zeroes, like in the previous case.

In this scenario, however, there is one more twist to consider: the PTE which was mapping the page is still pointing to it (it stores the page's PFN) and is set up so that when a PF for this page occurs, the VMM knows it must recover the page from the standby list (see the definition of the Standby state in section 21.3 on p. 130). Before reusing the page, the VMM must clearly update this PTE, so that, from now on, a reference to it will be treated as an *hard* fault, reloading its content from the paging file (remember that a standby page, by design, has already been written to the paging file).

Here is the rub: in general, this PTE may belong to *any* of the existing address spaces, not necessarily the active one, for which the VMM is resolving the fault. The paging structures region, where the VMM can access PTEs, is mapping those of the *active* address space and there is no guarantee that the one we want to update is among them. It's worth remembering that the PML4 entry for the paging structures region is one of those which are different for every address space (it points to the PML4 itself).

So the VMM is facing a familiar problem: it needs to have the PTE mapped at some virtual address, in order to update it, but this time it can't rely on the paging structures region. The solution is to map *the physical page storing the page table* into a work virtual address. Some sources (e. g. [10]) state that the page is mapped into Hyperspace, however, this is not completely correct for x64 Windows, where the behavior is similar to the one found when zeroing free pages. The VMM calls *MiMapPageInHyperSpaceWorker*, which maps the page in the 0xFFFFF880`00000000 - 0xFFFFF900`00000000 region instead of Hyperspace. At any rate, what matters is that the PT is made visible at a work virtual address. Below is a typical call stack for this situation, with a page fault occurring in the test program and *MiMapPageInHyperSpaceWorker* being called:

```
0: kd> kn
 # Child-SP          RetAddr           Call Site
00 fffff880`04c5d9d8 fffff800`02836566 nt!MiMapPageInHyperSpaceWorker
01 fffff880`04c5d9e0 fffff800`0293223d nt!MiRestoreTransitionPte+0x86
02 fffff880`04c5da40 fffff800`0281e398 nt!MiRemoveLowestPriorityStandbyPage+0x2ad
03 fffff880`04c5dac0 fffff800`02870fee nt! ?? ::FNODOBFM::`string'+0x43555
04 fffff880`04c5dc20 00000001`3fac131d nt!KiPageFault+0x16e
05 00000000`001efd40 00000001`3fb1d748 MemTests!PrvAllocTouchLoop+0x12d
[d:\dati\bob\programm\memtests\memtests\main.cpp @ 244]
06 00000000`001efd48 00000000`00000000 MemTests!__xt_z+0x370
```

But how can the VMM find the PT physical page? The answer is that _MMPFN.u4.PteFrame stores the PFN of the PT page. It's worth focusing our attention on the fact that we have two physical pages involved here: the standby page we want to reuse and the page storing the PT. The _MMPFN instance *of the standby page* has its u4.PteFrame set to the PFN of the PT.

With this information, the VMM can make the PT temporarily visible at a work VA, but then it must get to the specific PTE, which is somewhere in the 4 kB range of the page. Another field of the standby page's `_MMPFN` comes to the rescue: `_MMPFN.PteAddress`, which stores the *virtual* address of the PTE mapping the page.

True, this VA is valid only when the address space owning the PTE is current, i.e. when the PT is mapped in the paging structures region, but the VMM only needs the VA offset inside the page, which is the same in both mappings.

This enables the VMM to update the PTE and store into it enough information to be able to retrieve the page content from the paging file, when it will be needed. Thus, the VMM must know, at this stage, the location in the paging file of the page content, and it does, because it is recorded into `_MMPFN.OriginalPte`. Actually (see [1], p. 815) this member stores the whole PTE content to be written to the PTE in memory when the page is reused, so this is what happens at this point. This can actually be observed at *MiRestoreTransitionPte*+0x99: `_MMPFN.OriginalPte` is loaded into `rax` and stored at the PTE address, which is held into `rcx`.

With the steps above, the VMM has made the page available for reuse, can fill it we zeroes and use it to resolve the present fault.

This transition of a Standby page is represented by the thick arrow in the next diagram. Note the difference with the dotted arrow, which represents the transition occurring when the Standby page is returned to the address space from which it had been previously removed. This kind of transition is a soft fault where the page content is still valid and it is simply returned to the working set. The transition we just analyzed is for a page which is being *reused*. In summary, the two are completely different transitions, even though, as far as page states are concerned, they follow the same path.

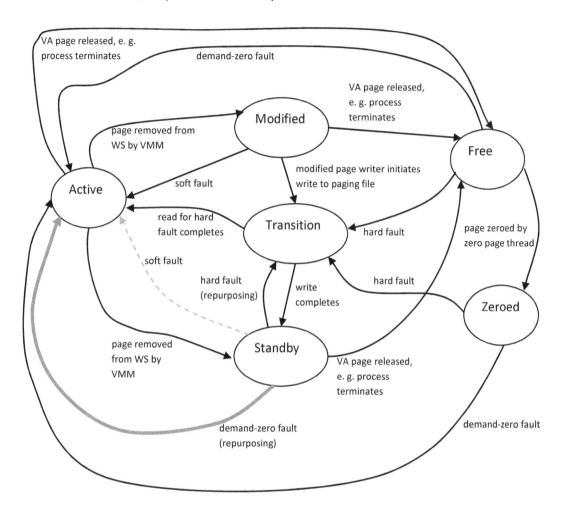

Figure 26 - Page Allocation from the Standby List

We use the term *repurposing* to indicate this transition.

26.4.3.4.3.2 Page Priority

So far, we have pretended that there is a single standby list, but this is not the case. There are actually eight of them, each grouping pages with different *page priorities*. The priority of a page is a number ranging from 0 to 7 assigned to it; there is a standby list of pages with priority 0, another of pages with priority 1, etc.

The priority is used in deciding which pages to remove first from the standby lists: the VMM looks first at the list with priority 0, then, if the list is empty at the one with priority 1 and so forth, so that pages with higher priorities are reused last. Not surprisingly, the priority is stored in the _MMPFN into _MMPFN.u3.e1.Priority.

But how are priority values assigned to pages? Each thread has a page priority attribute, so when it incurs a page fault and a physical page is allocated on its behalf, the page priority is set to the thread's page priority. A thread's page priority is stored into _ETHREAD.ThreadPagePriority and its value comes from the process page priority. Thus, assigning a process a higher memory priority has the effect of increasing the chance that its address space pages will be retained in physical memory: even though its working set may be trimmed, as long as the pages remain on the standby list, the process will only incur a soft fault when accessing them.

Processes are normally created with their page priority set to 5 and, as of Windows 7, there are no documented APIs to change it, so it is a feature used by the system only. However, at the time of writing, the online version of the MSDN lists two new APIs with this capability: *SetProcessInformation* and *SetThreadInformation*; they are available in what is currently termed "Windows Developer Preview", a preview version of Windows 8.

26.5 Updating the Page _MMPFN

After obtaining a physical page to resolve the fault, the VMM updates various members of the corresponding _MMPFN. Most of the work is done inside a function named *MiInitializePfn*. Below is a list of the most relevant members.

OriginalPte: set to the current content of the PTE. At this stage, the PTE stores the protection from the VAD, so this is what is copied into OriginalPte. E. g. for a read/write page, OriginalPte is set to 0x80.

u2.ShareCount: set to 1. This is the count of address spaces sharing the page, so for private pages it is simply set to 1. If the page is later removed from the working set (e. g. because of trimming), this counter is decremented.

u3.ReferenceCount: set to 1. This counter is used by the VMM to track when a page can be moved to the Modified or Standby list and we will return on it later.

u4.PteFrame: set to the PFN of the page table containing the PTE which will map this page. We saw in section 26.4.3.4.3 on p.158 why this must be done.

`PteAddress`: set to the virtual address of the PTE which is going to map this page. This address is inside the paging structures region and is valid only when the current address space is active.

`u3.e1.PageLocation`: set to `_MMLISTS.ActiveAndValid` (i.e. 6)

`u3.e1.Priority`: set to `_ETHREAD.ThreadPagePriority` for the current thread. See sec. 26.4.3.4.3.2 on p. 161.

`u3.e1.Modified`: set to 1. We will return on this bit in section 26.6.2 on p. 164.

At this stage, the VMM also sets `_MMPFN.u3.e1.CacheAttribute` to a value computed from the protection stored in the PTE (`_MMPTE.u.Soft.Protection`), but we are going to analyze this later (sec. 26.7 on p. 169), after we will have examined the PTE cache control bits.

At this stage, the VMM also increments `_MMPFN.u2.ShareCount` in the instance corresponding to the page table for the page. We will see in sec. 36.3 on p. 292 that the share count of a page table is the number of valid PTEs it contains plus one and, as long as this count is greater than zero, the page table is not moved to the Modified or Standby list.

26.6 Setting up the PFN and the Control Bits in the PTE

With the `_MMPFN` ready to go the VMM turns to the PTE. At this stage, the PTE has `_MMPTE.u.Soft.Protection` set to the value resulting from the protection specified when the memory was reserved and committed, while the other PTE bits are still set to 0.

The PTE is being set up as a valid one, i.e. with the P bit set, so we will now refer to its content in terms of the `_MMPTE.u.Hard` layout, which is consistent with the processor one.

26.6.1   Basic PTE Setup

`_MMPTE.u.Hard.PageFrameNumber` is set to the PFN of the physical page. It is interesting to observe that this field is 36 bits wide. Currently, the x64 architecture defines the maximum width of the PFN as 40 bit. Since the PFN is the physical address shifted right by 12 positions, this allows for physical addresses of up to 52 bits, spanning bits 0-51 and giving a maximum of 2 Petabyte of physical memory. However, as of Windows 7, the VMM code limits the PFN to 36 bits only, resulting in a theoretical maximum of 48 bits or 256 Terabyte of memory.

Bits 0-11 of the PTE control the page protection (read only, read/write, etc.) and its caching policy. They are initially set to a value read from a static array named MmProtectToPteMask, whose items are 8 bytes values. *MmAccessFault* uses the current

`_MMPTE.u.Soft.Protection` as an index into the array and copies the selected item into a working variable which will become the final PTE. This array maps the logical protection to the corresponding bit values for the actual processor architecture.

If we name the work variable as NewPagePte, having type `_MMPTE`, we can formally express the steps above as:

```
NewPagePte = (_MMPTE) nt!MmProtectToPteMask[protection];
NewPagePte.u.Hard.PageFrameNumber = PFN;
```

Afterwards, NewPagePte is further updated as follows:

```
NewPagePte.u.Hard.Valid = 1; // P = 1   - makes this a valid PTE
NewPagePte.u.Hard.Owner = 1; // U/S = 1 - allows ring 3 access
NewPagePte.u.Hard.Accessed = 1;
```

26.6.2   Setting the Page as Writable

The VMM does a little extra work for writable pages. Consider the protection value 0x4 which corresponds to a read/write page. The corresponding MmProtectToPteMask element is:

```
1: kd> dq nt!MmProtectToPteMask + 4*8 l1
fffff800`02b0c5d0   80000000`00000800
```

This mask has bit 1 set to 0 and the processor looks at this bit to decide whether the page is writable or not. A value of 0 means the page is read only. However, this mask has bit 11 set to 1. This is one of the few bits of a valid PTE ignored by the processor and available to the operating system. It appears that the VMM uses this bit to record the fact that a page is writable. *MmAccessFault* checks this bit and, when it is set, updates NewPagePte as follows:

- Sets `NewPagePte.u.Hard.Dirty1` = 1. Dirty1 is actually bit 1, i.e. the processor defined writable bit and is the one that actually makes the page writable.

- Sets `NewPagePte.u.Hard.Dirty` = 1. This is bit 6, the processor dirty bit

But why does the VMM go through all this trouble instead of simply using the processor bit? It has to do with how the VMM allocates space into the paging file; we will be able to understand the reason when we will examine pages whose content has been written to the paging file, so we will return on this point later.

For now, it is interesting to note that the PTE for a writable page is made valid with the processor dirty bit already set. Regardless of whether the page has been written to or not, the VMM considers it a dirty page. This makes sense if we think that, from the VMM standpoint, a page is dirty when it is different from its copy into the paging file or when *no copy of it exists in the paging file*. Our new page falls in the latter case.

Suppose the VMM will decide to reuse this physical page at some point. It will have to save its content into the paging file, even if the page has never been written to and is still full of zeroes. This way, when the virtual page will be accessed again, it will be read back into memory and the address space will have its page of zeroes back. So, as far the VMM is concerned, a page is "clean" when it can be reused without bothering to save its content to the paging file, i.e. when an identical copy of it already exists in the file. If this is not the case, the VMM sets the Dirty bit, to track that it has not yet saved the page content.

We saw earlier in sec. 26.5 on p. 162 that `_MMPFN.u3.e1.Modified` is also set. This bit appears to track into the `_MMPFN` that the page is dirty, which may seem redundant at first. However, we must remember that only the PTEs of the currently active address space are mapped in the paging structures region. This additional bit allows the VMM to know whether a page is dirty by looking at its `_MMPFN`, which is always accessible.

26.6.2.1   An Interesting Behavior

This section details an exception which can be observed with regard to the logic outlined in the previous one. It is actually an implementation detail, so it may be of interest only for the more curious readers.

From observed behavior, it appears that there are instances when the VMM actually avoids paging out a page which is entirely filled with zeroes.

This can be observed with a test program which performs the following actions:

- reserves and commits a good sized chunk of memory (300 MB)

- reads the first byte of every page, thus causing the VAs to be mapped to physical pages

- calls

```
SetProcessWorkingSetSize(GetCurrentProcess(), (SIZE_T) -1, (SIZE_T) -1 );
```

This call tells the memory manager that the process is willing to release all its working set. After the call, the VA range is still reserved and committed, but the VAs are not mapped to physical pages anymore: the physical pages have been moved to a different state and the PTEs have the P bit clear.

According to the logic outlined in the previous sections, when the physical pages for the allocated range are released they are marked as dirty. They should therefore go to the Modified list from where, eventually, their content (which is nothing but 4096 zeroes) will be written to the paging file.

However, when performing this experiment, we observe a different behavior: the initial part of the range (1,306,624 bytes - i.e. 0x13f000 - in one particular run) is actually treated this way: the pages go into the Modified state and the PTEs, albeit invalid still "point" to them.

Below is the output of the !pte command for the first page of the range:

```
1: kd> !pte 5b0000
                              VA 00000000005b0000

PXE at FFFFF6FB7DBED000   PPE at FFFFF6FB7DA00000   PDE at FFFFF6FB40000010   PTE at FFFFF68000002D80
contains 00C0000018BB0867   contains 012000000D233867   contains 006000002862767   contains 9710000020515886
pfn 18bb0     ---DA--UWEV   pfn d233     ---DA--UWEV   pfn 28627    ---DA--UWEV   not valid
                                                                                 Transition: 2051e
                                                                                 Protect: 4 - ReadWrite
```

The shaded "Transition" description means that the PTE points to a page which is either on the modified or standby list (which are collectively called transition lists). 0x2051E is the physical page PFN, which is also visible in the raw PTE content (shaded). We can look at the physical page state with the !pfn extension command, which takes the PFN as its input (see: Appendix A on p.565 for more details on this extension).

```
1: kd> !pfn 2051e
    PFN 0002051E at address FFFFFA800060F5A0
    flink        00011B71   blink / share count 0001FA9F   pteaddress FFFFF68000002D80
    reference count 0000     used entry count    0000       Cached     color 0     Priority 5
    restore pte 00000080     containing page        028627   Modified   M
    Modified
```

The output clearly shows that the page is in the Modified state. We can also see that the PTE VA, listed as "pteaddress", matches with the one from the !pte command. Also the number listed as "containing page" is the PFN of the page table containing the PTE, as we saw in section 26.4.3.4.3 on p. 158. A look at the PDE data from the !pte command confirms this: the PFN inside the PDE is equal to containing page.

So far, so good: the page is in the modified state and order reigns in the universe. However, the PTE for the byte at + 0x13f000 is another story:

```
1: kd> !pte 5b0000 + 13f000
                              VA 00000000006ef000

PXE at FFFFF6FB7DBED000   PPE at FFFFF6FB7DA00000   PDE at FFFFF6FB40000018   PTE at FFFFF68000003778
contains 00C0000018BB0867   contains 012000000D233867   contains 005000000C2EE867   contains 0000000000000080
pfn 18bb0     ---DA--UWEV   pfn d233     ---DA--UWEV   pfn c2ee    ---DA--UWEV   not valid
                                                                                 DemandZero
                                                                                 Protect: 4 - ReadWrite
```

The PTE is simply set to 0x80, i.e. the usual protection mask for a never-touched-before read/write page. This means the VMM actually released the physical page instead of treating it as a modified one. This is likely a performance optimization: instead of saving a page of zeroes in the paging file, the PTE is simply set up so that the next access to its VA range will trigger a fault, which will be resolved with a brand new zeroed page. It appears that all the remaining memory range is handled this way.

If we were to perform the same test with a much smaller range (e. g. 1 MB) we would see that all the pages in the range are actually freed.

What is interesting, is that, in order to accomplish this, the VMM *must* examine the page content to find out that it's filled with zeroes. There is *no way* the VMM can "know" whether the page has been modified or not. This is corroborated by the following facts:

- When the page is touched for the first time, the PTE is set up for read/write access, with the dirty bit set. There is simply no other processor feature which tracks whether the page has been written to or not - that would have been the job of the Dirty bit.

- If we change the test program so that it writes into all the pages of the memory range rather than reading from them, we discover that:

  o When we write nonzero values, the physical pages become modified; this is a must or we would lose the written data.

  o When we write zeroes, the behavior is the same as when we read from memory: most of the pages are freed.

- If we perform the read test again and, before releasing the working set, we modify a byte in a page with the kernel debugger, that page becomes modified, when the working set is shrunk.

From these facts we can conclude that the VMM bases its decision to free the pages on their actual content.

26.6.3   Cache Control Bits

The cache control bits of a PTE (PAT, PCD, PWT) are set to the value read from MmProtectToPteMask. To fully understand their setting, we must examine how the PAT is programmed by Windows.

The PAT is MSR 0x277 and can be dumped in the debugger with WinDbg's `rdmsr` command, which gives a value of 0x0007010600070106. The following table shows the resulting memory types for each PAT entry

PAT entry	Value	Memory type
0	06	WB
1	01	WC
2	07	UC-
3	00	UC
4	06	WB
5	01	WC
6	07	UC-
7	00	UC

Note: you cannot see the actual PAT in a virtual machine, at least with VmWare player where it appears to be set to 0. Instead, a local kernel debugging session can be used, which requires to boot Windows with kernel debugging support enabled.

If we dump the MmProtectToPteMask values for all the 32 possible values of `_MMPTE.u.Soft.Protection`, we notice that PAT, PCD and PWT are controlled by bit 3,4 of Protection, according to the following table

Protection Bits		PTE Bits			Selected PAT Entry	Memory Type
4	3	PAT	PCD	PWT		
0	0	0	0	0	0	WB
0	1	0	1	0	2	UC-
1	0	0	0	0	0	WB

1	1	0	0	1	1	WC

Note that protection values with bits 4:3 set to 00 and 10 have the same cache setting; we will see why when we will discuss guard pages in sec. 26.9 on p. 173.

When we reserve/commit memory with *VirtualAllocEx*, we can OR the `flProtect` parameter with the value PAGE_NOCACHE (0x200) to specify uncached memory. If we look at the resulting Protection, we can see this has the effect of setting bit 4:3 to 0y01, which, from the table above, result in the UC- memory type. The PAGE_WRITECOMBINE value sets them to 0y11 when OR-ed with `flProtect`, which gives WC memory. If we don't specify either of these two values, bit 4:3 are set to 0y00 giving WB memory.

The resulting Protection is also used by *MiInitializePfn* to compute the value of `_MMPFN.u3.e1.CacheAttribute`, as explained shortly (sec. 26.7 on p. 169).

26.6.4   Final Considerations for the PTE

The PTE value computed so far is *not* written to the actual PTE used by the processor at this stage. It is kept in a work variable, while the PTE is still set as "not present". When the PTE is made valid, the physical page can be accessed at any moment by other threads of the process, so the VMM has no control left over the page. For this reason, updating the PTE is performed as the very last step and, right now, we still have some work to do.

26.7 Cache Control Bits in the _MMPFN and TLB Flush Considerations

This section is actually a reprise of section 26.5 on p. 162, because it concerns the page _MMPFN.

The VMM records the caching policy of the physical page inside the `_MMPFN`, specifically in the `u3.e1.CacheAttribute` member.

When the VMM updates the `_MMPFN` of a page about to be mapped, *MiInitializePfn* computes the new value of `CacheAttribute` from bits 3-4 of `Protection`. The table below shows the relationship between these `Protection` bits, the resulting PTE bits, the memory type and the value of `_MMPFN.u3.e1.CacheAttribute`.

Protection Bits		PTE Bits			Selected PAT Entry	Memory Type	CacheAttribute
4	3	PAT	PCD	PWT			
0	0	0	0	0	0	WB	01
0	1	0	1	0	2	UC-	00
1	0	0	0	0	0	WB	01
1	1	0	0	1	1	WC	10

`CacheAttribute` is used in functions which temporarily map a physical page to a work virtual address like *MiZeroPhysicalPage* and *MiMapPageInHyperSpaceWorker*. They are called when a physical page which is not currently mapped must be made visible at some virtual address, to access its content. This happens, for instance, when a page must be zeroed or when a PTE of a non-current address space must be updated (see section 26.4.3.4.3 on p. 158). Under these circumstances, the VMM does not have a PTE specifying the caching policy, so it sets PAT,PCD and PWT of the PTE for the work VA according to the current value of `_MMPFN.u3.e1.CacheAttribute`. This is probably done to ensure that the page is mapped with the same caching policy used for other possible existing mappings. This is actually an Intel recommendation: multiple mappings with different caching policies for the same physical page should be avoided ([11], vol. 3A, sec. 11.12.4 *Programming the PAT*, p. 11-51) and is further confirmed in the WDK documentation that states:

" Processor translation buffers cache virtual to physical address translations. These translation buffers allow many virtual addresses to map a single physical address. However, only one caching behavior is allowed for any given physical address translation. Therefore, if a driver maps two different virtual address ranges to the same physical address, it must ensure that it specifies the same caching behavior for both. Otherwise, the processor behavior is undefined with unpredictable system results." ([16], from the page for MEMORY_CACHING_TYPE)

But, wait: we are talking about pages which have *no* mapping here, so why should we bother? The fact is, there is evidence that the VMM may leave around stale TLB entries mapping the page.

This evidence comes from an analysis of *MiInitializePfn* (see sec. 26.5 on p. 162), which, having computed the value of `_MMPFN.u3.e1.CacheAttribute` from the PTE Protection, compares it with the previous value stored in the `_MMPFN`. If the two values are different, it calls a function named *KeFlushTb* with input parameters specifying to *flush all TLB entries on all processors in the system.*

This is evidence of the fact that the VMM uses some form of lazy TLB invalidation.

First of all, the very fact that TLBs are invalidated implies that, at this stage, there could be cached paging structures entries pointing to this page. However, the page is not presently mapped in any address space, because it comes from either the Zeroed, Free or Standby list (*MiInitializePfn* is called to initialize pages taken from one of these lists). This is corroborated by the fact that no PTEs are updated at this time; only the TLBs are flushed, so there are no PTEs pointing to the page, but there might still be cached TLB entries.

Probably, the TLB must be flushed because of the Intel recommendation we already mentioned. Here the VMM is detecting that the value of `CacheAttribute` is changing, so it knows it is about to map the page with values for the cache control bits (PAT, PCD, PWT) different from the ones that were used the last time the page was mapped. An eventual stale TLB entry with the previous values for PAT, PCD, PWT would violate Intel's recommendation, so the TLB is flushed.

Delaying TLB invalidation has a few implications, however we are not going to discuss them now, in order to keep focusing on the page fault resolution. We will return on this subject in Chapter 27 on p. 176.

Before moving on with the page fault analysis, it is interesting to observe that the value of `_MMPFN.u3.e1.CacheAttribute` and the resulting caching policy perfectly match the declaration of `MEMORY_CACHING_TYPE` in [16]. The table below shows the symbolic names defined by `MEMORY_CACHING_TYPE` applied to the values of `CacheAttribute` and the resulting caching policy:

Protection Bits		PTE Bits			Selected PAT Entry	Memory Type	Cache-Attribute	MEMORY_CACHING_TYPE
4	3	PAT	PCD	PWT				
0	0	0	0	0	0	WB	01	MmCached

0	1	0	1	0	2	UC-	00	MmNonCached
1	0	0	0	0	0	WB	01	MmCached
1	1	0	0	1	1	WC	10	MmWriteCombined

26.8 Updating the Working Set and the PTE

So far we have seen how the VMM finds a physical page to resolve the fault and how it updates the _MMPFN and a *working copy* of the PTE content. The final steps in resolving the fault are: updating the working set data structures (working sets were introduced in section 20.3 on p. 114) and updating the PTE in memory.

To update the working set, the VMM calls *MiAllocateWsle*, which obtains a free WSL entry and stores the Virtual Page Number being mapped into _MMWSLE.u1.e1.VirtualPageNumber. It also sets _MMWSLE.u1.e1.Valid = 1, to mark the entry as in use. For private memory, _MMWSLE.u1.e1.Direct is set to 1.

At this stage, the _MMPFN of the physical page is further updated, setting _MMPFN.u1.WsIndex to the index of the WSL entry, making it possible to get to the entry from the _MMPFN, but there is one thing we should not forget about: the WSL region is in Hyperspace, which is a process-private space region. The particular entry pointed by _MMPFN.u1.WsIndex will be accessible only when the address space using the page is the current one. The PFN database is a system shared region, accessible from every address space, thus WsIndex is always there for us to look at, but the *right* WSL must be mapped. This is similar to what happens when the VMM needs to update a PTE as explained in sec. 26.4.3.4.3.1 on p. 158.

Having the WSL entry index in the _MMPFN allows to get from a mapped VA to its WSL entry, as we saw in sec. 20.3.6 on p. 123.

It is actually *MiAllocateWsle* which updates the PTE and "turns on" the virtual to physical mapping. The working copy of the PTE computed in the previous steps is first updated by setting _MMPTE.u.Hard.SoftwareWsIndex to bits 0-10 of the WSL entry index (these bits are ignored by the processor) and then copied into the PTE. Thus, the PTE stores a partial (i.e. truncated) back-reference to its working set entry, but it is not the full index, which is 32 bits wide.

Finally, the pushlock at _MMSUPPORT.WorkingSetMutex is released, *MmAccessFault* returns to *KiPageFault*, which restores the thread execution context from the _KTRAP_FRAME on the stack and resumes execution of the faulting instruction.

26.9 Guard Pages

26.9.1   Concept

Guard Pages are allocated with a special protection mask and act as a one shot alarm for a region of virtual memory. When an address inside a guard page is touched for the first time, the VMM raises an exception with code STATUS_GUARD_PAGE_VIOLATION. The code touching the page can handle the exception with a try/except block and continue its execution. Subsequent accesses to the same guard page don't cause the exception anymore and are treated as accesses to regular pages, that is they succeed if they are consistent with the regular protection of the page.

Guard pages are meant to give the code the chance to take a different course of action when they are touched for the first time. A typical application is expanding a region of committed memory for a data area which grows dynamically. In this scenario, the code reserves a range of memory corresponding to the maximum size of the data area. Remember that reserved virtual memory has little impact, because it is not accounted for in the global committed memory count (see sec. 19 on p. 93). Afterwards, it commits as little pages as possible (perhaps just one) at the beginning of the range and marks the next page as a guard one. When the regular committed region is exhausted and the data area reaches the guard page, the code is notified by means of the exception and has the chance to extend the accessible region and set up a new guard page for the next extension.

A guard page is allocated by setting the flProtect parameter of *VirtualAllocEx* (or other similar functions) to the desired protection (e. g. PAGE_READWRITE) OR-ed with PAGE_GUARD. The first access to the page will raise the one-time exception and, for any access after that, the specified protection will be in effect.

A page must still be committed in order to act as a guard one: if the page is only reserved, the VMM raises a STATUS_ACCESS_VIOLATION exception when an access is attempted and the page remains invalid (that is, if the exception is caught and the access reattempted, the same exception will be raised again).

26.9.2   Implementation

Guard Pages handling is implemented inside *MiAccessCheck*, which is called by *MmAccessFault*. The VMM sets bits 4:3 of `_MMPTE.u.Soft.Protection` = 0y10 for these pages. *MiAccessCheck* detects this, clears bit 4 and returns STATUS_GUARD_PAGE_VIOLATION, which causes the exception to be raised in user mode code. Since *MiAccessCheck* clears bit 4, the next access to the page will succeed.

In sec. 26.6.3 on p. 167 we saw that bits 4:3 of `Protection` are also used to encode the caching policy for the page. More to the point, the relationship between `Protection(4:3)` and the memory type is:

Protection Bits		PTE Bits			Selected PAT Entry	Memory Type
4	3	PAT	PCD	PWT		
0	0	0	0	0	0	WB
0	1	0	1	0	2	UC-
1	0	0	0	0	0	WB
1	1	0	0	1	1	WC

This implies that a guard page can have WB type only: when bit 4 is cleared, `Protection(4:3)` becomes 0y00 and the page is a "regular" WB page.

This can be confirmed by calling *VirtualAllocEx* with `flProtect` specifying PAGE_GUARD together with PAGE_NOCACHE or PAGE_WRITECOMBINE: the function fails the allocation with ERROR_INVALID_PARAMETER.

26.9.3   Special Handling for User Mode Stacks

Windows uses guard pages to dynamically commit memory for user mode stacks. Instead of committing all the stack at once, it makes a portion of it accessible and places a guard page at the end of it.

This requires some special treatment from the VMM, because otherwise user mode code would see a STATUS_GUARD_PAGE_VIOLATION exception materialize when `rsp` reaches the guard page, e. g. when calling a function. It can be observed that when *MiAccessCheck*

returns STATUS_GUARD_PAGE_VIOLATION to *MmAccessFault*, the latter calls
MiCheckForUserStackOverflow, which, when the faulting access is into the thread's user
mode stack, establishes a new guard page and change the return code to
STATUS_PAGE_FAULT_GUARD_PAGE. This becomes the value returned from *MmAccessFault*
to *KiPageFault*.

STATUS_PAGE_FAULT_GUARD_PAGE has a numerical value of 0x113, which means it does
not represent an error (NTSTATUS for errors have bit 31 set, so are >= 0x80000000). On the
other hand, STATUS_GUARD_PAGE_VIOLATION, i.e. the value returned for the non-stack
case, is 0x80000001, representing an error condition.

For the non-stack case, the error value causes an exception to be raised in user mode code,
with the exception code set to the error code.

For the stack case, the success code from *MmAccessFault* has the effect of directing
KiPageFault to reattempt the faulting instruction, i.e. the one accessing the stack. At this
stage, the PTE for the stack page has been updated so that `Protection(4:3) = 0y00`, i.e.
the guard status has been turned off. This is done by the VMM before calling
MiCheckForUserStackOverflow. Thus, the resumed instruction causes a new page fault,
because the PTE is still invalid, but now `Protection` is set to read/write, so this is resolved
as a normal demand-zero fault, mapping a new physical page for the stack. The faulting
instruction is resumed yet once more and this time it succeeds.

26.10   Conclusion and Next Steps

We have seen how a user mode demand-zero fault is resolved by mapping a page into the
address space. The VMM first ensures that the memory access is a valid one, then selects a
physical page, updates its data structures (PFN db and working set) and finally maps the
page.

From now on, the page is available to the process code, which can freely read and write from
it. Also, the page is considered dirty as soon as it is mapped, because no copy of it exists in
the paging file. This means that the next logical state in the life of the page is the Modified
one: when the VMM decides to shrink the working set, the page is moved to the modified list
so that its content is saved in the paging file. This process will be analyzed shortly.

There are other possible transitions besides the one just mentioned: the page could be
released by the process or the process could terminate freeing it. We are going to analyze
the transition to the Modified state, because it is more interesting: it is the path taken when

the VMM does its magic and pages out a portion of the address space "behind the back" of the process.

Before doing this, however, the next chapter will analyze some implications related to the delayed TLB invalidation mentioned in sec. 26.7 on p. 169.

27   Implications of Delayed TLB Invalidation

27.1 Why Delay Invalidation and What Problems Could Arise

TLB invalidation negatively affects performances, because it must occur on all processors. This means the VMM must send an inter-processor interrupt to all processors, directing them to invalidate the outdated entries. The VMM code must rely on some form of inter-processor synchronization to ensure that all of them have completed the invalidation. This process slows everything else down, so it makes sense, when possible, to wait until there are a certain number of outdated entries and then invalidate all of them.

However, leaving around stale TLB entries means that one or more processors can still be using the outdated PTE content to map virtual addresses. Consider the case where the VMM removes a page from a working set and places it on the Standby list. The TLB entry for this page must be invalidated as part of this process, because, otherwise, a processor could still be accessing the page, even though, from the Standby list, the page can be grabbed and reused for another working set.

Also, if a process frees some virtual memory, the VMM should immediately invalidate the corresponding entries, because there is no guarantee that the process code will not try to access the freed range due to bugs in its logic. Suppose the VMM does not invalidate the TLB in this scenario and reuses the freed physical pages for another process. The first process could be writing into pages of the second one through a stale entry.

In general, it is likely that entries for user mode addresses are immediately invalidated, because the system has no control over what user-mode code does, so this is the only way to ensure that each virtual user mode range is truly isolated from the others.

27.2 Delayed Invalidation for System Temporary Mappings

Apparently, the VMM delays invalidation for kernel mode virtual addresses it uses for internal purposes, e. g. for the PTEs used by *MiMapPageInHyperSpaceWorker* and *MiUnmapPageInHyperSpaceWorker*.

These functions map and unmap pages in the range 0xFFFFF880`00000000 - 0xFFFFF900`00000000, which is not actually the Hyperspace, but the System PTE range (analyzed in detail in sec. 44.8 on p. 440).

MiMapPageInHyperSpaceWorker uses a *single* work PTE to map a physical page, meaning that, if we call it twice for two different pages, it uses the *same* PTE both times. We cannot call it to map different physical pages at the same time; instead, we can use it to map at most one page at its working VA.

Furthermore, *MiMapPageInHyperSpaceWorker* does not invalidate the TLB entry for its working VA, so, if we were to call it twice to map two different pages, accesses to the work VA after the second call could still be mapped to the first physical page, because of a stale TLB entry.

Here is where *MiUnmapPageInHyperSpaceWorker* comes into play: when called, it sets the PTE for the VA to 0 and then increments a counter, which *MiMapPageInHyperSpaceWorker* uses to determine the work VA for the mapping. The next time the mapping function is called, it will not use the last used VA, for which there are stale TLB entries, but will use the address of the next virtual page. In summary, after having called the mapping function once, we must call the unmapping function before calling the mapping one again. Note however that the used VAs can have stale TLB entries, because the unmapping function does not invalidate the TLB each time it is called.

MiUnmapPageInHyperSpaceWorker does not blindly go on incrementing the counter and leaving stale TLB entries around indefinitely. When 64 virtual pages have been used, it invalidates all their TLB entries and resets the counter, so that the next mapping will reuse the first work VA in the range.

If a thread which called the mapping function were to be preempted before calling the unmapping one, another thread could call the mapping function and mess things up. For one thing, the new mapping might not work because of the stale TLB entry and also, when the preempted thread would eventually be resumed, it would not have the physical page it was working on mapped anymore.

For this reason, the mapping function internally raises the IRQL to DISPATCH and returns leaving it at this value. This ensures that the thread cannot be preempted before calling the unmapping function. The previous IRQL is saved in a buffer, which the caller to the mapping function must supply and is later passed to the unmapping function, which, in turn, restores the original IRQL.

In a multiprocessor system, however, this is not enough: one processor could be between the mapping and the unmapping, e. g. busy zeroing the mapped page, while another one calls *MiMapPageInHyperSpaceWorker* and changes the virtual to physical mapping, resulting in a disaster. The classic solution would be to use a spinlock to protect the mapping, but this would create a significant bottleneck, so the VMM employs a more clever trick.

The work VA and the counter are stored in the `HyperPte` member of `_KPRCB`, and there is a `_KPRCB` instance for each processor. Furthermore, each processor uses a different VA range, so one processor can freely map at its current working VA without disturbing the other ones.

This trick couples nicely with the fact that, while the mapping is in effect, the thread cannot be preempted: the thread using the current work VA of a processor will never be executed on another one, because, in order for this to happen, the thread itself should be preempted and resumed by another processor. This means that the 64 work virtual pages of a processor will be referenced only by code executed by that processor and there will be TLB entries for them only in the TLB of that particular processor. Thus, when the unmapping function invalidates the TLB, it does so only for the processor which is executing the function and does not send costly inter-processor interrupts to the other ones.

The format of _KPRCB.HyperPte is as follows: bits 63:12 contain the VPN of the first page of the range and bits 11:00 contain the counter. The mapping function maps the physical page at the address given by:

(HyperPte & 0xFFFFFFFFFFFFF000) + (HyperPte & 0xFFF) * 4096

Note how the counter in bits 11:0 shifts the VA in page size increments.

27.3 Final Considerations

The logic explained in the previous section is based on the following principle: the VMM can delay invalidation, because it keeps track of which VAs have outdated TLB entries and avoids using them. However, this approach has one weakness: a buggy kernel mode component using a stray pointer could, conceivably, use one of these VAs and cause unpredictable effects by writing to a physical memory page through a stale TLB entry. Possibly, the reasoning behind this approach is that a kernel mode component which uses stray pointers can do so much damage that stale TLB entries don't matter anymore: it can corrupt kernel variables; it can corrupt the content of the user mode range for whatever address space is current; it can cause memory mapped devices to malfunction by referencing their addresses; etc.

Since worrying about software vulnerabilities has become the fashionable thing to do, it is worth to point out that stale TLB entries are not very useful to malicious software. These entries map *system* addresses, which can be accessed only by code running in kernel mode. If we want to worry about malicious code exploting them, we are, implicitly, considering malicious kernel mode code that has somehow managed to be executed. This scenario is a total disaster by itself, because kernel mode code can do whatever it wants. Such a piece of code does not need to rely on something as whimsical as stale TLB entries, which may or may not be retained inside a processor. Kernel mode code can simply access *any* address it wants, as well as attach to the address space of any process to access a particular user mode space. In summary, if kernel mode malware is being executed on the system, we are in serious trouble and stale TLB entries are the least of our problems.

There is one more twist worth mentioning. Conceivably, it would be possible to leave around stale TLB entries with no adverse effects, by avoiding reuse of the physical pages that these entries are referencing. This way, buggy code using an invalid pointer would, at most, access a physical page no one else is using. However, it appears that this is not what happens inside the VMM. One scenario where *MiMapPageInHyperSpaceWorker* and *MiUnmapPageInHyperspaceWorker* are called is inside *MiInitializePfn*, when a physical page about to be mapped into an address space needs to be flushed from the cache (the memory cache, not the TLB). Since cache-flushing instructions operate on virtual addresses, the page is temporarily mapped and flushed, then it is unmapped. As explained before, this leaves behind a stale TLB entry for the VA; this entry, in turn, points to a physical page which is very much in use: it is about to be mapped into an address space. This scenario does not occur for every page mapping, but, rather, only when the caching policy of the physical page changes in such a way that it is necessary to evict it from the cache.

In summary, these two functions are used, *to prepare physical pages for use*, so the pages mapped through them are inevitably going to be used afterwards. Possibly, the VMM designers concluded that the performance gain resulting from delaying invalidation is worth the risk of leaving stale entries accessible through stray pointers, because these kind of bugs result in unpredictable effects anyway, even without delayed invalidation.

28   Working Set Trimming

In section 26, we described how a physical page is allocated to resolve a demand-zero fault and becomes part of a working set. To be able to follow the lifecycle of such a page across its various states, we must analyze how a page can be *removed* from a working set. The term *trimming* is used to refer to the act of removing pages from a working set.

28.1 Working Set Size Limit

The VMM sets the maximum WS size of a process to 345 pages ([1], p. 828), but this limit is normally ignored, meaning that, if there is enough available memory, the VMM allows working sets to grow beyond this value.

A process can set a real upper limit to its working set size by calling *SetProcessWorkingSetSizeEx* specifying the QUOTA_LIMITS_HARDWS_MAX_ENABLE flag, which has the effect of setting `_EPROCESS.Vm.Flags.MaximumWorkingSetHard` = 1 (without this call, the flag is set to 0).

This flag is evaluated by *MiDoReplacement*, which is called by *MiAllocateWsle*, the function which allocates the WSL entry for a new page, as described in sec. 26.8 on p. 172. When the flag is set to 1 and the current WS size is greater or equal to `_EPROCESS.Vm.MaximumWorkingSetSize`, *MiReplaceWorkingSetEntry* is called, which results in a WSL entry being released before allocating the new one.

The normal scenario, however is to have `MaximumWorkingSetHard` = 0, so that the WS can grow as long as there is enough available memory and is trimmed later, when the VMM determines that the time has come to free some memory. This job is performed by a VMM component named *Working Set Manager* (WSM) and implemented in the function *MmWorkingSetManager*, which is the subject of the next section.

28.2 The Working Set Manager

28.2.1   The Balance Set Manager Thread

MmWorkingSetManager is executed by a dedicated system thread (i.e. a thread belonging to the system process) named *Balance Set Manager* (BSM), which spins inside a function named *KeBalanceSetManager* whose job is to perform a number of housekeeping chores, among which is the call to *MmWorkingSetManager*.

The BSM waits on two events: one is periodically signaled once per second, the other is signaled by other VMM functions when they determine that working set trimming should be performed.

28.2.2   Memory Context Activation

The WSM examines working sets to determine which pages to remove and updates the PTEs mapping the page being removed. Both the working set list and the PTEs are mapped into private virtual regions, that is, regions whose content changes from one address space to another. Remember that the PML4 entries for Hyperspace (where the WSL is found) and for the Paging Structures Region point to different physical pages for different address spaces. Thus, the WSM faces a fundamental problem: how to access the WSL and paging structures of every address space in the system.

The solution lays in a kernel feature which allows a thread to "attach" itself to the memory context of another process. At any given time, a thread *belongs* to a process, the one that created it, but may be *attached* to another process, i.e. the memory context of the latter is mapped while the thread is executing. Normally, a thread sees the memory context of its own process, but the kernel has facilities to allow a thread to attach to a different one.

As an example, below is the output of the !thread debugger extension command for a thread belonging to explorer.exe:

```
1: kd> !thread fffffa8000d98060
THREAD fffffa8000d98060  Cid 04e8.070c  Teb: 000007fffffde000 Win32Thread:
fffff900c01952e0 WAIT: (WrUserRequest) UserMode Non-Alertable
    fffffa8000dfdb40  SynchronizationEvent
Not impersonating
DeviceMap                    fffff8a0020fe120
Owning Process               fffffa8000e197f0       Image:          explorer.exe
Attached Process             N/A          Image:          N/A
Wait Start TickCount         5404093         Ticks: 51068 (0:00:13:17.937)
Context Switch Count         6213                   LargeStack
UserTime                     00:00:00.546
KernelTime                   00:00:01.046
Win32 Start Address 0x00000000ff4cc178
Stack Init fffff88002b81db0 Current fffff88002b81870
Base fffff88002b82000 Limit fffff88002b7b000 Call 0
Priority 12 BasePriority 8 UnusualBoost 0 ForegroundBoost 2 IoPriority 2 PagePriority 5
```

The shaded entries show the owning process and the attached one, or N/A when the thread is not attached to a different process.

The WSM uses this facility to attach to each running process in order to access its WSL and PTEs. This can be observed by setting a breakpoint on *MiTrimWorkingSet*, the function invoked to reduce a WS, and by running a test program which increases its working set up to the point when the VMM decides to step in and remove pages from it.

The first interesting thing we see is that, on an idle system with enough memory (e. g. a Windows 7 box with 1 GB of RAM), the breakpoint is only seldom hit, which means that the VMM does not aggressively trim working sets when there is no reason to do it.

This is what we find when we eat so much memory that the VMM decides to take action and the breakpoint is finally hit:

```
Breakpoint 0 hit
rax=0000000000000002 rbx=0000000000000000 rcx=0000000000000f11
rdx=fffffa8001977ec8 rsi=fffff88003139ba0 rdi=fffffa8001977ec8
rip=fffff800029a15e0 rsp=fffff88003139ad8 rbp=0000000000000001
 r8=0000000000000006  r9=0000000000000f11 r10=0000000000018786
r11=0000000000000f11 r12=0000000000001e22 r13=0000000000000000
r14=0000000000000000 r15=fffff80003c68000
iopl=0         nv up ei pl zr na po nc
cs=0010  ss=0018  ds=002b  es=002b  fs=0053  gs=002b             efl=00000246
nt!MiTrimWorkingSet:
fffff800`029a15e0 48895c2420      mov     qword ptr [rsp+20h],rbx
ss:0018:fffff880`03139af8=fffff88003139ba0

0: kd> !thread @$thread

THREAD fffffa800095f1a0  Cid 0004.0064  Teb: 0000000000000000 Win32Thread:
0000000000000000 RUNNING on processor 0
Not impersonating
DeviceMap                fffff8a0020fe120
Owning Process           fffffa80008da990      Image:        System
Attached Process         fffffa8001977b30      Image:        MemTests.EXE
Wait Start TickCount     5504576         Ticks: 64 (0:00:00:01.000)
Context Switch Count     133389
UserTime                 00:00:00.000
KernelTime               00:02:13.375
Win32 Start Address nt!KeBalanceSetManager (0xfffff800028e57ac)
Stack Init fffff88003139db0 Current fffff88003139710
Base fffff8800313a000 Limit fffff88003134000 Call 0
Priority 16 BasePriority 8 UnusualBoost 0 ForegroundBoost 0 IoPriority 2 PagePriority 5
```

The shaded entries show that the thread hitting the breakpoint belongs to System and is *attached* to MemTests.exe.

The thread call stack shows it is inside *MmWorkingSetManager*:

```
Child-SP          RetAddr         : Args to Child
: Call Site

fffff880`03139ad8 fffff800`029519c3 : 00000000`00000000 fffffa80`01977ec8
00000000`00000001 fffff880`03139ba0 : nt!MiTrimWorkingSet
```

```
fffff880`03139ae0 fffff800`028e56e2 : 00000000`00005028 00000000`00000000
00000000`00000000 00000000`00000000 : nt! ?? ::FNODOBFM::`string'+0x498d1

fffff880`03139b80 fffff800`028e596f : 00000000`00000008 fffff880`03139c10
00000000`00000001 fffffa80`00000000 : nt!MmWorkingSetManager+0x6e

fffff880`03139bd0 fffff800`02b74166 : fffffa80`0095f1a0 00000000`00000080
fffffa80`008da990 00000000`00000001 : nt!KeBalanceSetManager+0x1c3

fffff880`03139d40 fffff800`028af486 : fffff800`02a49e80 fffffa80`0095f1a0
fffff800`02a57c40 00000000`00000000 : nt!PspSystemThreadStartup+0x5a

fffff880`03139d80 00000000`00000000 : fffff880`0313a000 00000000`00000000
00000000`00000000 00000000`00000000 : nt!KxStartSystemThread+0x16
```

We can confirm that the address space currently active is the one of MemTests.exe in a couple of ways. First, the `@$proc` debugger pseudo-register points to the `_EPROCESS` instance for MemTests, as can be seen with the `!process` extension command:

```
0: kd> !process @$proc 0
PROCESS fffffa8001977b30
    SessionId: 1  Cid: 09e4    Peb: 7fffffd5000  ParentCid: 0b8c
    DirBase: 05f94000  ObjectTable: fffff8a002b54e80  HandleCount:   6.
    Image: MemTests.EXE
```

Second, we can disassemble the code of MemTests.exe in the user mode region:

```
0: kd> u memtests!wmain
MemTests!wmain [l:\pers\tosave\vmmcache\memtests\memtests\main.cpp @ 74]:
00000001`3f5c1000 4889542410    mov     qword ptr [rsp+10h],rdx
00000001`3f5c1005 894c2408      mov     dword ptr [rsp+8],ecx
00000001`3f5c1009 4883ec38      sub     rsp,38h
00000001`3f5c100d 488b542448    mov     rdx,qword ptr [rsp+48h]
00000001`3f5c1012 8b4c2440      mov     ecx,dword ptr [rsp+40h]
00000001`3f5c1016 e8e5090000    call    MemTests!XtractParams (00000001`3f5c1a00)
00000001`3f5c101b 85c0          test    eax,eax
00000001`3f5c101d 750b          jne     MemTests!wmain+0x2a (00000001`3f5c102a)
```

This clearly shows that, in the user mode region, the address space of MemTests is visible.

It is also interesting to observe the results of the call to *MiTrimWorkingSet*: below are the counts of available and modified pages when the breakpoint is hit:

```
0: kd> dd nt!MmAvailablePages l1
fffff800`02a5bdc0  000048f2
0: kd> dt nt!_mmpfnlist Total @@masm(nt!MmModifiedPageListHead)
   +0x000 Total : 0x68
```

Thus, we have 0x4F82 available memory pages and 0x68 modified ones. Now we let execution go on until we exit from *MiTrimWorkingSet* and examine the counters again:

```
0: kd> g @$ra
```

```
rax=0000000000000f11 rbx=0000000000000000 rcx=0000000000000077
rdx=0000000000000008 rsi=fffff88003139ba0 rdi=fffffa8001977ec8
rip=fffff800029519c3 rsp=fffff88003139ae0 rbp=0000000000000001
 r8=0000000000000077  r9=fffff80002a49e80 r10=0000000000000080
r11=0000000000000008 r12=0000000000001e22 r13=0000000000000000
r14=0000000000000000 r15=fffff80003c68000
iopl=0         nv up ei ng nz na po nc
cs=0010  ss=0018  ds=002b  es=002b  fs=0053  gs=002b          efl=00000286
nt! ?? ::FNODOBFM::`string'+0x498d1:
fffff800`029519c3 8b4618          mov     eax,dword ptr [rsi+18h]
ds:002b:fffff880`03139bb8=00003bf6

0: kd> dd nt!MmAvailablePages l1
fffff800`02a5bdc0  000049d1

0: kd> dt nt!_mmpfnlist Total @@masm(nt!MmModifiedPageListHead)
   +0x000 Total : 0xea0
```

We now have 0x49D1 available pages and 0xEA0 modified ones, with the extra pages having been removed from the working set of MemTests.

28.2.3   Process Trimming Criteria

The WSM takes into account various factors to decide which working sets to trim, attempting to favor processes actually needing physical memory. For instance, a process with a large working set which has been idle for a long time will be trimmed more aggressively than a more active one with a smaller working set; the process running the foreground application is considered last, and so on. The WSM goes on trimming working sets until a minimum number of available pages is reached, then stops. It is stated, on p. 829 of [1], that the WSM stops trimming when enough "free pages" are available on the system. Possibly, the term "free" is used in a generic fashion and not to actually refer to pages on the Free list. In general, the VMM keeps trimmed pages on the Standby list until they are actually repurposed to resolve a fault and the available memory is usually computed as the sum of the Zeroed, Free and Standby lists sizes. Pages on the Standby list are ready for reuse, because the paging file stores a copy of their content, so are considered available memory. At the same time, until they are actually reused, they are left in Standby, so that eventual faults involving them do not require a disk access.

The overall logic is to free memory when the system is running low on available pages, without imposing hard limits on how much a process can consume. After all, there is no point in limiting how much memory a process can use when there is an abundance of Free and Zeroed (and hence *unused*) memory.

28.2.4   Working Set List Entries Age

When the WSM decides to trim a working set, it must also choose *which* pages to remove from it. To do this effectively, the WSM keeps track of how recently a page has been accessed, so that it can remove the least recently used ones.

This is accomplished by exploiting the accessed bit of a PTE: when a page is first mapped, the accessed bit is set, as described in section 26.6.1 on p. 163. When the WSM examines a working set, it clears the accessed bit. If the bit is found to be clear when the same working set is examined again, this means the page has not been accessed between the two passes, so the WSM increments a counter stored into `_MMWSLE.e1.Age`. The counter value is thus equal to the number of times the WSL examined the page and found it had not been accessed. If, on the other hand, the accessed bit is found set, the counter is reset and the bit cleared again. The WSL removes pages with higher Age values first, because they are the least recently used.

It is interesting to point out how the age is not actually an attribute of the physical page, but is related to the working set entry instead. Although we have not discussed shared memory yet, it is a well known fact that physical pages for common DLLs are shared among processes. Such a page can be unaccessed and thus aged in a particular process and accessed in another one. This is why the age information is kept in the WSL entry, which is specific to each process, rather than in the `_MMPFN`, which describes the global physical page.

The age of WSL entries can be examined with the `!wsle` command extension. Since the WSL is a process-private region, the desired process must be made current with the `.process /P` or `.process /i` command before using `!wsle`.

28.3 Trimming While Resolving a Fault

So far, we described two situations where pages are removed:

- When the working set size limit is in effect, a page can be removed to make room for another one.

- When the WSL performs global trimming to reclaim memory.

The VMM can also choose to trim a working set as part of the handling of a page fault the process encountered. This is similar, but not identical to the first scenario above, because instead of removing a single page from the working set, *MiTrimWorkingSet* is called, which suggests that multiple pages can actually be removed. This can be observed in at least two stages of the processing of a fault.

One is towards the end of the fault resolution, after the VA has been mapped:
MmAccessFault calls *MiCheckAging* at +0x3BB and this function, in turn, under certain
conditions, calls *MiForcedTrim*, which calls *MiTrimWorkingSet*, i.e. the same function invoked
by the WSM. Below is the status of a thread performing these calls:

```
THREAD ffffffa8000b897f0  Cid 0570.0a90  Teb: 000007fffffde000 Win32Thread:
0000000000000000 RUNNING on processor 1
Not impersonating
DeviceMap                fffff8a0020fe120
Owning Process           fffffa8000ae04f0         Image:         MemTests.EXE
Attached Process         N/A             Image:          N/A
Wait Start TickCount     9441866         Ticks: 2 (0:00:00:00.031)
Context Switch Count     297
UserTime                 00:00:00.359
KernelTime               00:00:05.718
Win32 Start Address 0x000000013fa32ea0
Stack Init fffff880027a5db0 Current fffff880027a5730
Base fffff880027a6000 Limit fffff880027a0000 Call 0
Priority 8 BasePriority 8 UnusualBoost 0 ForegroundBoost 0 IoPriority 2 PagePriority 5
Child-SP          RetAddr           : Args to Child
: Call Site
fffff880`027a59e8 fffff800`029a1a5d : fffffa80`00278700 00000000`00000080
00000000`00000000 fffff800`02b092c0 : nt!MiTrimWorkingSet

fffff880`027a59f0 fffff800`02939787 : 00000000`00000001 fffff800`029096e2
00000000`00000000 00000000`0002df7e : nt!MiForcedTrim+0x11d

fffff880`027a5a60 fffff800`028eafa0 : 00000000`00000000 00000000`1eee3000
fffff700`01080000 ffffffff`ffffffff : nt! ?? ::FNODOBFM::`string'+0x21e23

fffff880`027a5ac0 fffff800`028cefee : 00000000`00000001 00000000`00000000
fffffa80`014dc401 00000000`00000000 : nt!MmAccessFault+0x3c0

fffff880`027a5c20 00000001`3fa3131d : 00000001`3fa8d748 00000000`00000000
00000000`002dfb48 00000000`00000000 : nt!KiPageFault+0x16e (TrapFrame @
fffff880`027a5c20)

00000000`002dfcf0 00000001`3fa8d748 : 00000000`00000000 00000000`002dfb48
00000000`00000000 00000000`004c0000 : 0x1`3fa3131d

00000000`002dfcf8 00000000`00000000 : 00000000`002dfb48 00000000`00000000
00000000`004c0000 00000000`25800000 : 0x1`3fa8d748
```

We can see that the thread belongs to MemTests.exe, so *MiTrimWorkingSet* is not being
called by the WSM, but, rather, the faulting thread is trimming its own working set. This *is*
the faulting thread, because we see *KiPageFault* and *MmAccessFault* on the stack.

The call stack entry "nt! ?? ::FNODOBFM::`string'+0x21e23" is actually part of *MiCheckAging*,
but is displayed this way because the instruction is in a block of code apart from the main
function code. This is a common occurrence in 64 bit Windows code.

Another stage where this happens is inside *MiDoReplacement* (which is called by *MiAllocateWsle*, described in sec. 26.8 on p. 172), which may choose to call *MiForcedTrim* under certain conditions.

MiDoReplacement checks three conditions to decide whether to call *MiForcedTrim*:

1. Computes the value:

   _MMSUPPORT.WorkingSetSize - _MMSUPPORT.FirstDynamic

   which should represent the number of pageable entries in the working set (see sec. 20.3.3.1.1 on p. 118 for more details on `FirstDynamic`).

   The result must be greater than 75% of the total count of physical pages, for the call to occur.

   This condition means that the working set is big, compared to the amount of physical memory.

2. Checks whether Standby pages have been used to satisfy memory requests since the last time the BSM ran (which happens at least once per second). If no Standby pages have been reused, *MiForcedTrim* is not called.

   This condition means that the system is taking pages from the Standby list, presumably because there are no Free or Zeroed pages available, and this will cause other working sets to incur hard faults when they will need their pages back.

3. The sum of the counts of Free, Zeroed and Standby pages must be less than 0x40000, i.e. less than 1 GB.

   This condition means that the Standby list is below 1 GB. We will see later that the system uses Standby pages to cache prefetched memory pages, so the Standby list can grow because the system proactively loads pages from the paging file (and from open files as well), even though they have not actually been accessed. Thus, condition #2 does not mean by itself that the system is stealing pages being actively used by some processes. However, when coupled with this other condition it is more likely that the pages being taken from the Standby list are actually needed ones.

This policy is always in effect, even when the working set limit is not (as is usually the case).

Below is the status of the thread which performed this call:

```
THREAD ffffffa800112bb60  Cid 0470.0ae0  Teb: 000007fffffdd000 Win32Thread:
0000000000000000 RUNNING on processor 1
Not impersonating
DeviceMap               fffff8a0020fe120
Owning Process          ffffffa80026f91e0      Image:        MemTests.EXE
Attached Process        N/A          Image:        N/A
Wait Start TickCount    8910141        Ticks: 38 (0:00:00.593)
Context Switch Count    375
UserTime                00:00:00.453
KernelTime              00:00:06.921
Win32 Start Address 0x000000013f422ea0
Stack Init fffff880044f8db0 Current fffff880044f86c0
Base fffff880044f9000 Limit fffff880044f3000 Call 0
Priority 8 BasePriority 8 UnusualBoost 0 ForegroundBoost 0 IoPriority 2 PagePriority 5
Child-SP          RetAddr        : Args to Child
: Call Site
fffff880`044f89c8 fffff800`029a1a5d : 00000000`00000000 fffff800`0292fc67
ffffffa80`0036be50 00000000`00000001 : nt!MiTrimWorkingSet

fffff880`044f89d0 fffff800`02939485 : ffffffa80`026f9578 fffff800`028a268a
00000000`00000000 00000000`00000001 : nt!MiForcedTrim+0x11d

fffff880`044f8a40 fffff800`029095e7 : fffff680`000f1a80 fffff680`000f1a80
ffffffa80`026f9578 00000000`00000000 : nt! ?? ::FNODOBFM::`string'+0x21b13

fffff880`044f8a70 fffff800`028eb82c : fffff680`000f1a80 fffff880`044f8b40
00000000`00000000 ffffffff`ffffffff : nt!MiAllocateWsle+0x3f

fffff880`044f8ac0 fffff800`028cefee : 00000000`00000001 00000000`00000000
00000000`00000001 00000000`00000000 : nt!MmAccessFault+0xc4c

fffff880`044f8c20 00000001`3f42131d : 00000001`3f47d748 00000000`00000000
00000000`0012fb78 00000000`00000000 : nt!KiPageFault+0x16e (TrapFrame @
fffff880`044f8c20)

00000000`0012fd20 00000001`3f47d748 : 00000000`00000000 00000000`0012fb78
00000000`00000000 00000000`00500000 : 0x1`3f42131d

00000000`0012fd28 00000000`00000000 : 00000000`0012fb78 00000000`00000000
00000000`00500000 00000000`25800000 : 0x1`3f47d748
```

Again, we can see the thread which incurred the page fault calling *MiTrimWorkingSet*.

nt! ?? ::FNODOBFM::`string'+0x21b13 is actually part of *MiDoReplacement*.

28.3.1   How the VMM Tracks the Reuse of Standby Pages

In this section we are going to see in greater detail how condition #2 is verified. This section is for the more curious readers and can eventually be skipped.

MmGetStandbyRepurposed is a function returning the count of standby pages that have been reused, presumably since the system started. It computes its return value as the sum of an array of counters named MiStandbyRepurposedByPriority, which appear to track a separate count for each page priority.

It can be observed that *MiRestoreTransitionPte* increments these counters and this function, in turn, is called by *MiRemoveLowestPriorityStandbyPage*, which is used to take a page from the Standby lists in order to reuse it (or "repurpose" it, as the counter name implies). In other words, when a Standby page is reused, the counter for its priority is updated; *MmGetStandbyRepurposed* returns the sum of the current values of the per-priority counters.

The *MiComputeSystemTrimCriteria* function is executed by the WSM and calls *MmGetStandbyRepurposed*, with the call instruction being at +0x2F. A little later, at +0x44, it copies the returned count to a variable named MiLastStandbyRePurposed. In other words, at least once every second the value returned from *MmGetStandbyRepurposed* is sampled and stored into MiLastStandbyRePurposed.

By placing a breakpoint at *MiComputeSystemTrimCriteria* +0x44 we can see that it is hit shortly, usually inside the WSM. Below is an example of a hit with a call stack:

```
0: kd> bp0 nt!MiComputeSystemTrimCriteria+0x44
breakpoint 0 exists, redefining
0: kd> g
Breakpoint 0 hit
nt!MiComputeSystemTrimCriteria+0x44:
fffff800`028e5a4c 8905f6721b00    mov     dword ptr [nt!MiLastStandbyRePurposed
(fffff800`02a9cd48)],eax
0: kd> k
Child-SP          RetAddr           Call Site
fffff880`03139b50 fffff800`028e56c8 nt!MiComputeSystemTrimCriteria+0x44
fffff880`03139b80 fffff800`028e596f nt!MmWorkingSetManager+0x54
fffff880`03139bd0 fffff800`02b74166 nt!KeBalanceSetManager+0x1c3
fffff880`03139d40 fffff800`028af486 nt!PspSystemThreadStartup+0x5a
fffff880`03139d80 00000000`00000000 nt!KxStartSystemThread+0x16
```

The mov at +0x44 stores into MiLastStandbyRePurposed the value returned from *MmGetStandbyRepurposed*, which is held into `eax`, so, by breaking here, we can see both the old and new value of the variable. With Windbg, we are able to set a breakpoint which automatically executes a series of command when it is hit, so we can have the debugger execute the `r` command, which shows the registers content and the variable value before the mov (since the mov references the memory variable, Windbg displays its content as part of the output of `r`). Afterwards, we can have Windbg execute the `g` command, which resumes execution, so that the breakpoint does not actually stop the system, but, rather, displays the counter's old and new values and automatically resumes. Such a breakpoint is set with the following debugger command:

```
1: kd> bp nt!MiComputeSystemTrimCriteria+0x44 "r;g"
```

We can then see the breakpoint being hit once per second (when the WSM awakens) showing us the counter new value in `eax` and the old value in the variable. On every hit we get the following output:

```
rax=00000000002185b1 rbx=0000000000000000 rcx=00000000000072fc
rdx=fffff80002a86820 rsi=0000000000000000 rdi=000000000001c28c
rip=fffff800028e5a4c rsp=fffff88003139b50 rbp=0000000000000001
 r8=0000000000000000  r9=0000000000000100 r10=0000000000000000
r11=0000000000000000 r12=fffff88003139ba0 r13=fffff80002b07900
r14=0000000000000000 r15=fffff80003c68080
iopl=0         nv up ei pl zr na po nc
cs=0010  ss=0018  ds=002b  es=002b  fs=0053  gs=002b             efl=00000246
nt!MiComputeSystemTrimCriteria+0x44:
fffff800`028e5a4c 8905f6721b00    mov     dword ptr [nt!MiLastStandbyRePurposed
(fffff800`02a9cd48)],eax ds:002b:fffff800`02a9cd48=002185b1
```

The first thing we can observe is that, as long as there is ample available memory in the system, the counter value does not change, even over extended periods of time.

If we launch a program that requires a lot of memory, we see the counter increasing, and the breakpoint being hit more often, albeit with iregular frequency, as the WSM is awakened by the VMM which is trying to reclaim memory from processes. Below is an excerpt of the output while MemTests touches all the pages of a 700 MB range on a machine with 1 GB:

```
rax=000000000022fade rbx=0000000000000000 rcx=000000000022c9ab
rdx=fffff80002a86820 rsi=0000000000003133 rdi=0000000000000005
rip=fffff800028e5a4c rsp=fffff88003139b50 rbp=0000000000000001
 r8=0000000000000000  r9=0000000000000100 r10=0000000000000000
r11=0000000000000000 r12=fffff88003139ba0 r13=fffff80002b07900
r14=0000000000000000 r15=fffff80003c68080
iopl=0         nv up ei pl nz na po nc
cs=0010  ss=0000  ds=002b  es=002b  fs=0053  gs=002b             efl=00000206
nt!MiComputeSystemTrimCriteria+0x44:
fffff800`028e5a4c 8905f6721b00    mov     dword ptr [nt!MiLastStandbyRePurposed
(fffff800`02a9cd48)],eax ds:002b:fffff800`02a9cd48=0022c9ab

rax=000000000022fcb8 rbx=0000000000000000 rcx=000000000022fade
rdx=fffff80002a86820 rsi=00000000000001da rdi=00000000000001eb
rip=fffff800028e5a4c rsp=fffff88003139b50 rbp=0000000000000001
 r8=0000000000000000  r9=0000000000000100 r10=0000000000000000
r11=0000000000000000 r12=fffff88003139ba0 r13=fffff80002b07900
r14=0000000000000000 r15=fffff80003c68080
iopl=0         nv up ei pl nz ac pe nc
cs=0010  ss=0000  ds=002b  es=002b  fs=0053  gs=002b             efl=00000212
nt!MiComputeSystemTrimCriteria+0x44:
fffff800`028e5a4c 8905f6721b00    mov     dword ptr [nt!MiLastStandbyRePurposed
(fffff800`02a9cd48)],eax ds:002b:fffff800`02a9cd48=0022fade

rax=000000000022fe0a rbx=0000000000000000 rcx=000000000022fcb8
rdx=fffff80002a86820 rsi=0000000000000152 rdi=000000000000049e
```

```
rip=fffff800028e5a4c rsp=fffff88003139b50 rbp=0000000000000001
 r8=0000000000000000  r9=0000000000000100 r10=0000000000000000
r11=0000000000000000 r12=fffff88003139ba0 r13=fffff80002b07900
r14=0000000000000000 r15=fffff80003c68080
iopl=0         nv up ei pl nz na pe nc
cs=0010  ss=0000  ds=002b  es=002b  fs=0053  gs=002b          efl=00000202
nt!MiComputeSystemTrimCriteria+0x44:
fffff800`028e5a4c 8905f6721b00    mov     dword ptr [nt!MiLastStandbyRePurposed
(fffff800`02a9cd48)],eax ds:002b:fffff800`02a9cd48=0022fcb8
```

It is interesting to notice how the value of the variable appears to always be equal to the value found in `eax` on the previous breakpoint hit. This suggests that MiLastStandbyRePurposed is updated only by this instruction.

MiLastStandbyRePurposed appears to be a running count of all the times a Standby page has been repurposed, which never decreases. It has nothing to do with how much memory is currently available, a fact confirmed when the test program terminates freeing its memory: the counter does not decrease, but it merely stabilizes to a constant value again, because the system does not need to repurpose Standby pages anymore.

Turning back our attention to condition #2 of the previous section, *MiDoReplacement* calls *MmGetStandbyRepurposed* and compares the return value with the current value of MiLastStandbyRePurposed; if the values are equal, it does not call *MiForcedTrim*.

When the two values are different, it means that between the last time *MiComputeSystemTrimCriteria* updated MiLastStandbyRePurposed and the time of the page fault being resolved, Standby pages have been repurposed, so *MiForcedTrim* is called, providing that conditions #1 and #3 are met as well.

28.4 Effect of Trimming on the Page Share Count and Reference Count

When a page is removed from a working set for any of the reasons explained earlier, its share count, stored in `_MMPFN.u2.ShareCount` is decremented. The share count is incremented each time a page is added to a working set. For private pages, the share count can be at most one, but for shared memory, which will be analyzed later, can also be greater than one.

 When the share count is decremented and drops to 0, the page reference count (`_MMPFN.u3.ReferenceCount`) is decremented as well and, if this counter too reaches to zero, the page is moved to the Modified or Standby list.

28.5 Locking a Page in Memory

Kernel mode components like device drivers can lock a page in memory preventing it from being repurposed, regardless of whether it is part of a user mode WS. This is accomplished by incrementing `ReferenceCount` through kernel mode runtime functions meant to lock a page. When this happens, `ReferenceCount` remains greater than 0 even when `ShareCount` drops to 0, so the VMM leaves the page in the Active state. To be one hundred percent accurate, *MiPfnShareCountIsZero*, which is called when the share count drops to zero, decrements the reference count and, if it is still greater than 0, changes the page state to Modified or Standby, but avoids linking the page to the relevant list. So the state of the page is not strictly Active, but since the page itself is not on any list it will not be repurposed. The goal of locking is to ensure that the physical page is left available to whoever locked it. When all the components who had previously locked the page unlock it, `ReferenceCount` drops to 0 and the page is moved into one of the lists ([1], p. 814). For the sake of simplicity, we will say that a locked page remains Active.

With this logic, a page cannot be brought out of the Active state as long as its reference count is not zero. All the working sets including the page (there can be more than one for shared pages) contribute with a single unit of increment to the reference count. Each lock established by other components contribute with a unit as well.

29   Dirty Page Removal and Outpaging

Now that we know how pages are removed from working sets, we can go back to following a page through its lifecycle. In section 26 we saw how a new physical page is faulted in as modified or dirty. The next logical step is to see what happens when a modified page is removed from the working set.

29.1 From the Working Set to the Modified List

29.1.1   What the Modified List Is for

When the VMM decides to remove a page from a working set, it must ask itself whether a copy of the page content exists in the paging file. If the page has never been written to the paging file or has been modified since the last time it was written, its content must be saved to the file, before it can be reused. A page that needs to be saved has a PTE with bit `_MMPTE.u.Hard.Dirty` and `_MMPTE.u.Hard.Dirty1` set. Furthermore, such a page has `_MMPFN.u3.e1.Modified` set.

We saw in sec. 26.6.2 on p. 164 how a page begins its life as dirty. We will see later when a page becomes clean and when it becomes dirty again.

A dirty page being removed is added to the Modified list. This is represented by the thick arrow on the state diagram below:

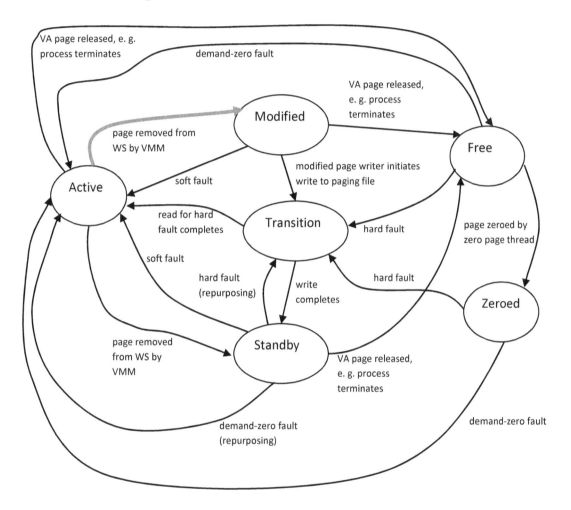

Figure 27 - Dirty Page Removal

A page on the Modified list is waiting to be written to the paging file to become reusable. While on the list, it can be faulted back into the working set at any time as soon as an instruction touches it. The PTE and _MMPFN are set up to aid the VMM in performing these tasks.

29.1.2   Modified Lists Details

With a little digging around we can see that the VMM uses three static instances of
`_MMPFNLIST` to keep track of the Modified list.

MmModifiedPageListHead does not actually point to list elements, because its `Flink` and
`Blink` members are always set to 0xFFFFFFFF`FFFFFFFF (or -1), which represents an empty
list. However, `MmModifiedPageListHead.Total` stores the total number of Modified
pages in the system, that is its value appears to always be equal to the total showed by
Sysinternals' Process Explorer.

MmModifiedPageListByColor is actually the head of a linked list of `_MMPFN` instances. The
`Flink` member holds the index (not the address) of the first `_MMPFN` instance in the PFN
database. In turn, the `_MMPFN.u1.Flink` member of each instance stores the index of the
next one in the list. The `_MMPFN`s which are part of the list have
`_MMPFN.u3.e1.PageLocation` = 3, which corresponds to
`_MMLISTS.ModifiedPageList`.

In spite of its name, the list does not appear to group pages with the same color, but rather,
it generally includes pages of any color. Furthermore, MmModifiedPageListByColor is not the
address of an array (possibly indexed by color) but of a single instance of `_MMPFNLIST`.

MmModifiedProcessListByColor is the head of yet another list, with the same structure as the
previous one.

It appears that the pages in the MmModifiedPageListByColor were mapping addresses in the
system address range before entering the Modified state, while the ones pointed by
MmModifiedProcessListByColor were mapping user addresses. At least, this is what results
from a random exploration of the lists content.

As an example, we can examine the last node of the MmModifiedPageListByColor list. First,
we obtain the node index from the Blink member:

```
1: kd> dt nt!_MMPFNLIST Blink @@masm(nt!MmModifiedPageListByColor)
   +0x018 Blink : 0x2088f
```

Notice the use of the `@@masm()` construct to "force" Windbg to understand that what
follows is an expression resulting in the address. Without `@@masm()`, Windbg interprets
`nt!MmModifiedPageListByColor` as a member name and complains that it cannot find it
in `_MMPFNLIST`.

With the index, we then compute the _MMPFN address knowing that the PFN database begins at 0xFFFFFA80`00000000 and that each instance is 0x30 bytes in size. We feed the address to a `dt` command, to examine the PteAddress member:

```
1: kd> dt nt!_MMPFN PteAddress @@masm(fffffa8000000000 + 2088f * 30)
   +0x010 PteAddress : 0xfffff6fb`80008400 _MMPTE
```

This is the address of the PTE which was using the physical page to map a virtual address. Remember that a page on the Modified list still holds the memory content (unsaved, actually) and that the PTE which was pointing to it still "points" to the physical page, even though the P bit is clear. The `!pte` extension gives us the VA mapped by the PTE with this address:

```
1: kd> !pte 0xfffff6fb`80008400
                              VA fffff70001080000

PXE @ FFFFF6FB7DBEDF70    PPE at FFFFF6FB7DBEE000    PDE at FFFFF6FB7DC00040    PTE at FFFFF6FB80008400
contains 000000002B241863  contains 000000002B282863  contains 000000002B283863  contains 0000000021600863
pfn 2b241     ---DA--KWEV  pfn 2b282     ---DA--KWEV  pfn 2b283     ---DA--KWEV  pfn 21600     ---DA-
KWEV
```

The address that follows "VA" is the virtual address which was mapped to our page and we can see it's a system range address. This seems to always be the case and suggests that this list is for system addresses.

In the output from `!pte`, the shaded value (0000000021600863) is the PTE value, i.e. the 8 bytes stored at the PTE address grouped as a quadword. This value reminds us of a fact which can be easily forgotten, because it does not seem to have any relationship with the _MMPFN we started from. First of all, it's an odd value, so the PTE has bit 0, i.e. the P bit, set, thus it is a valid PTE, actively mapping a virtual address. Also, the PFN of the page, which is in bits 47:12 is set to 0x21600, not 0x2088F, which is the index of our _MMPFN.

This happens because the paging structures range maps the paging structures of the *current* address space, which happens not to be the one our dirty page belongs to. In other words, the `!pte` command is looking at *another* PTE, the one found at address 0xFFFFF6FB`80008400 in the current address space.

However, the fact that this PTE maps address 0xFFFFF700`01080000 is always true in *any* address space, because is an implication of how the paging structures are mapped (see sec. 15.2 on p. 63), so we can use `!pte` to get the mapped address from the PTE address.

Finally, it is useful to observe that the mapped VA 0xFFFFF700`01080000 is part of the Hyperspace region, which is private of each address space. This explains why the PTE content changes across address spaces. For other system range regions, the virtual to physical mapping is identical across address spaces and we would not observe the apparent inconsistency between the PTE content and the _MMPFN.

If we perform the same exploration on nodes of the list pointed by MmModifiedProcessListByColor, we usually find _MMPFN instances for user range addresses.

29.1.3   How to Observe Dirty Pages Being Moved

It is possible to observe the Working Set Manager at work moving dirty pages to the two lists with the following procedure:

- Write a program which reserves and commits a great amount of memory (around 70% of the total physical memory) with VirtualAllocEx; the program must also write to all the pages (it is enough to write one byte for each page), to ensure that physical pages are faulted in and treated as dirty ones (remember, in sec. 26.6.2.1 on p. 165 we saw that reading the pages is not enough).

- Run an instance of the program and obtain the address of its _EPROCESS instance with

    ```
    !process 0 0 executable_name
    ```

- Set breakpoints on writes to the _MMPFNLIST.Total member of the list heads. Since this is actually the first member of the structure, it is enough to set the breakpoints at the symbol addresses. Use the /p option to make the breakpoint valid for the test program only:

    ```
    ba w 8 /p eprocess_address nt!MmModifiedPageListByColor
    ba w 8 /p eprocess_address nt!MmModifiedProcessListByColor
    ```

- Run another instance of the program

The second program instance kicks out dirty pages from the first and this triggers the breakpoint. When this happens, usually we find that the current thread is the Working Set Manager, attached to the first instance of the process, working to insert a page into one of the Modified lists. Below is a typical example:

```
Breakpoint 1 hit
nt!MiInsertPageInList+0x152:
fffff800`0288a8b2 488b4f18        mov     rcx,qword ptr [rdi+18h]

0: kd> !thread @$thread
THREAD ffffa8000cf7680  Cid 0004.0064  Teb: 0000000000000000 Win32Thread:
0000000000000000 RUNNING on processor 0
Not impersonating
```

```
DeviceMap                       fffff8a002236700
Owning Process                  fffffa8000cd36f0        Image:          System
Attached Process                fffffa800327a7b0        Image:          MemTests.EXE
Wait Start TickCount            6815405         Ticks: 0
Context Switch Count            199852
UserTime                        00:00:00.000
KernelTime                      00:05:31.296
Win32 Start Address nt!KeBalanceSetManager (0xfffff800028877ac)
Stack Init fffff88003139db0 Current fffff88003139710
Base fffff8800313a000 Limit fffff88003134000 Call 0
Priority 16 BasePriority 8 UnusualBoost 0 ForegroundBoost 0 IoPriority 2 PagePriority 5
Child-SP          RetAddr          : Args to Child
: Call Site
fffff880`03139740 fffff800`0288b4fc : 00000000`00000011 fffffa80`00786b70
00000000`00000000 2aaaaaaa`aaaaaaab : nt!MiInsertPageInList+0x152

fffff880`031397d0 fffff800`028bad45 : fffffa80`002734b0 00000000`00000001
ffffffff`ffffffff fffff800`02878e52 : nt!MiPfnShareCountIsZero+0x19c

fffff880`03139840 fffff800`0294372f : fffffa80`0327ab48 fffff880`03139a50
fffffa80`00000000 fffffa80`00000002 : nt!MiFreeWsleList+0x285

fffff880`03139a30 fffff800`028f39c3 : 00000000`00000377 fffffa80`0002bec2
00000000`00000005 00000000`00000000 : nt!MiTrimWorkingSet+0x14f

fffff880`03139ae0 fffff800`028876e2 : 00000000`0000a2f8 00000000`00000000
00000000`00000000 00000000`00000000 : nt! ?? ::FNODOBFM::`string'+0x498d1

fffff880`03139b80 fffff800`0288796f : 00000000`00000008 fffff880`03139c10
00000000`00000001 fffffa80`00000000 : nt!MmWorkingSetManager+0x6e

fffff880`03139bd0 fffff800`02b16166 : fffffa80`00cf7680 00000000`00000080
fffffa80`00cd36f0 00000000`00000001 : nt!KeBalanceSetManager+0x1c3

fffff880`03139d40 fffff800`02851486 : fffff800`029ebe80 fffffa80`00cf7680
fffff800`029f9c40 00000000`00000000 : nt!PspSystemThreadStartup+0x5a

fffff880`03139d80 00000000`00000000 : fffff880`0313a000 00000000`00000000
00000000`00000000 00000000`00000000 : nt!KxStartSystemThread+0x16
```

When execution is stopped at *MiInsertPageInList*+0x152 as in this example, `rdi` holds the address of the list where the page is being added and `rbp` the PFN of the page. In the current example we had:

```
0: kd> ln @rdi
(fffff800`029e7ba8)   nt!MmModifiedProcessListByColor   |   (fffff800`029e7bd0)
nt!MiInitialPoolFreed
Exact matches:
    nt!MmModifiedProcessListByColor = <no type information>

0: kd> r @rbp
rbp=000000000002823d
```

29.1.4   PTE and _MMPFN of a Modified Page

The PTE for a page on the Modified list is represented by an instance of
`_MMPTE_TRANSITION`. Here is a typical example:

```
1: kd> dt nt!_mmpte u.trans. 0xfffff683`ff7ede80
   +0x000 u          :
      +0x000 Trans    :
         +0x000 Valid     : 0y0
         +0x000 Write     : 0y1
         +0x000 Owner     : 0y1
         +0x000 WriteThrough : 0y0
         +0x000 CacheDisable : 0y0
         +0x000 Protection : 0y00100 (0x4)
         +0x000 Prototype : 0y0
         +0x000 Transition : 0y1
         +0x000 PageFrameNumber : 0y000000000000000000000111111001011010 (0x7e5a)
         +0x000 Unused    : 0y1000110010100000 (0x8ca0)
```

The `Valid` bit is 0, which makes the PTE invalid.

`Write`, `Owner`, `WriteThrough` and `CacheDisable` are bits R/W, U/S, PWT, PCD of the
hardware (i.e. processor-defined) PTE and seem to have retained the value they had when
the PTE was valid.

`Protection` spans bits 5-9 and is the VMM-defined encoding for the page protection, e. g.
the one originally coming from the VAD and resulting from the protection attribute passed to
the memory allocation function. When the PTE is made valid as we saw in Chapter 26, the
previous PTE value, with the VMM protection in bits 5-9, is copied into
`_MMPFN.OriginalPte`, so the VMM has this value available when the page is moved to the
Modified list. We will see in Chapter 31 (p. 236) on soft faults that when a page fault occurs
on an address mapped by a PTE like this one, the protection bits are used to establish the
actual hardware protection of the page, much like with a demand zero fault. So, placing the
protection back in the PTE keeps it ready for an eventual fault.

`Transition` is set to 1 to mark this PTE as being a transition one, i.e. pointing to a page
which is either on the Modified or the Standby list (which are collectively called *transition
lists*). Note that, for a valid PTE the same bit (bit 11), is available to software and used by the
VMM to mark a writable page. However, valid PTEs have bit 0 set to 1; when bit 0 is clear, bit
11 denotes a transition PTE.

`PageFrameNumber` spans bits 12-47 and holds the PFN of the page which is still storing the
virtual page content. This field has the same value it had when the PTE was valid.

We will see in Chapter 31 (p. 236) how, when a reference to a VA mapped by this PTE is attempted, a soft fault occur, i.e. the VMM takes the page from the Modified list and maps it back into the address space. The VMM obviously needs the PFN to be able to set up the PTE and to reach the `_MMPFN` instance. The solution here is to simply leave the PFN untouched in the PTE itself.

An `_MMPFN` on the Modified list has the following characteristics:

- `u1.Flink` and `u2.Blink` are used to link the instance in the list. When the page was in use, `u1` stored the working set index and `u2` the share count; both data are no longer of use after the page has been removed from the working set.

- `PteAddress` still holds the virtual address of the PTE mapping the page.

- `u3.e1.PageLocation` is set to 3, i.e. `_MMLISTS.ModifiedPageList`.

- `OriginalPte` has the same value it had when the page was in the working set, i.e. bits 5-9 are set to the software protection value. The same value is now in bits 5-9 of the actual PTE, as we just saw. The other bits of OriginalPte are usually 0, for an `_MMPFN` on the Modified list.

29.1.5   TLB Invalidation

When a page is moved to the Modified list, the P bit is cleared in the corresponding PTE. To ensure that this change is perceived by all the processors, the VMM must invalidate the corresponding TLB entry. The VMM invalidates the entry on the executing processor and sends inter-processor interrupts to the other ones, to direct them to do the same.

29.1.6   Synchronization During Page Removal

Removing a page consists of multiple operations because both the PTE and the `_MMPFN` must be updated, so the VMM must be prepared to handle a page fault on a page which is in the process of being removed. This is accomplished by means of the working set pushlock (`_EPROCESS.Vm.WorkingSetMutex`). The WSM acquires the pushlock calling *MiAttachAndLockWorkingSet* before updating the page state and releases it when all the state information has been updated. As we saw in sec. 26.1 on p. 139, the page fault handler attempts to acquire this pushlock at the very beginning of the fault handling so, if it is already owned by the WSM, a faulting thread is suspended, until page removal is complete.

The working set pushlock has been introduced in Chapter 25 (p. 136).

29.2 Writing the Page Content to the Paging File

29.2.1   Standby Lists Details

When a page is outpaged, it goes to the Standby list. We already saw in sec. 26.4.3.4.3.2 on p. 161 that there are actually 8 lists organized by page priority. By analyzing a function named *MiRemoveLowestPriorityStandbyPage*, we can see that the static MmStandbyPageListByPriority is an array of 8 _MMPFNLIST structures with an item for each priority. Item 0 is the head of the list of pages at priority 0 and so forth. In the following, we will refer generically to "the Standby list" when it is not important to refer to a particular sublist.

29.2.2   The Modified Page Writer Thread

The Modified Page Writer (MPW) is a system thread running at priority 17 and executing the *MiModifiedPageWriter* function, which writes modified pages to the paging file and moves them to the Standby list.

This thread waits on three synchronization objects ([1], p. 813):

1. MmModifiedPageWriterGate (a gate object) which is signaled under various conditions, including the following:

    •   The Working Set Manager finds out that the combined size of the Zeroed and Free lists is below 20,000 pages.

    •   The Working Set Manager finds out that the number of available pages stored at MmAvailablePages is less than 262,144 (i.e. 1 GB)

    •   An explicit request to flush all the pages is issued.

2. The MiRescanPageFilesEvent event.

3. An event inside the "paging file header" (MmPagingFileHeader). Presumably, this is a data structure used to manage the paging file.

All these synchronization objects are used by the VMM to awaken the MPW when the time has come to consolidate the content of modified pages into the paging file.

We can see the MPW at work by placing breakpoints as follows. First, we find the address of the MPW's _ETHREAD by dumping the system process with the !process command and looking for the thread with *MiModifiedPageWriter* as its Win32 start address:

```
        THREAD fffffa8000cf5530  Cid 0004.005c  Teb: 0000000000000000 Win32Thread:
0000000000000000 RUNNING on processor 1
        Not impersonating
        DeviceMap                 fffff8a002236700
        Owning Process            fffffa8000cd36f0        Image:      System
        Attached Process          fffffa8000e96370        Image:      MemTests.EXE
        Wait Start TickCount      9710145        Ticks: 65 (0:00:00:01.015)
        Context Switch Count      41961
        UserTime                  00:00:00.000
        KernelTime                00:00:41.531
        Win32 Start Address nt!MiModifiedPageWriter  (0xfffff8000280b9c0)
```

Then, we place two breakpoints on writes to MmModifiedProcessListByColor and
MmModifiedPageListByColor from this thread. These are the addresses of the page counts
for the modified lists and the MPW updates them as it process modified pages. The
breakpoints are placed with the following commands:

```
ba w 8 /t fffffa8000cf5530 nt!MmModifiedPageListByColor
ba w 8 /t fffffa8000cf5530 nt!MmModifiedProcessListByColor
```

Afterwards, it is just a matter of generating some paging activity with some processes, until
one of the breakpoints is hit. We see a call stack like the following one:

```
Child-SP          RetAddr           Call Site
fffff880`0312b260 fffff800`0280bd5d nt!MiUnlinkPageFromLockedList+0x6dd
fffff880`0312b2f0 fffff800`02946443 nt!MiReferencePageForCluster+0x7d
fffff880`0312b320 fffff800`0280b471 nt!MiBuildPageFileCluster+0x633
fffff880`0312bc00 fffff800`0280bb7b nt!MiGatherPagefilePages+0x271
fffff880`0312bce0 fffff800`02b16166 nt!MiModifiedPageWriter+0x1bb
fffff880`0312bd40 fffff800`02851486 nt!PspSystemThreadStartup+0x5a
fffff880`0312bd80 00000000`00000000 nt!KxStartSystemThread+0x16
rax=00000000000d10b8 rbx=fffffa8000656d90 rcx=fffffa8000000000
rdx=0000000000001c32 rsi=0000000000000001 rdi=fffff800029e7ba8
rip=fffff800028944dd rsp=fffff8800312b260 rbp=fffff80002aab1e0
 r8=0000058000000000  r9=fffffa8000000008 r10=0000000000000000
r11=2aaaaaaaaaaaaaab r12=0000000000000000 r13=0000000000000000
r14=0000000000000001 r15=0000000000000000
iopl=0         nv up ei pl nz na pe nc
cs=0010  ss=0018  ds=002b  es=002b  fs=0053  gs=002b              efl=00000202
nt!MiUnlinkPageFromLockedList+0x6dd:
fffff800`028944dd 393511e11700    cmp     dword ptr [nt!MiMirroringActive
(fffff800`02a125f4)],esi ds:002b:fffff800`02a125f4=00000000
```

29.2.3   Page State During the Write I/O

Writing a page to the paging file means executing an actual disk I/O operation, which takes
time to complete, so the MPW issues an asynchronous write and goes on executing while the
I/O is in progress. When the write is done, an APC interrupts the MPW, which brings the page
into its final state. This behavior will be showed in detail in sec. 29.2.6.3 on p. 211.

The VMM tracks the fact that a write is in progress for the page by setting `_MMPFN.u3.e1.WriteInProgress` = 1, which means the page is in the Transition state, as defined in sec. 21.4 on p. 130.

It is important not to confuse the Transition state with the transition *lists*, i.e. the Standby and Modified list: a page in this state is not on any list and has an I/O in progress; a page on the Standby or Modified list has no I/O in progress.

When the write operation ends, the page is moved to the Standby list.

These state transitions are represented by the two thick arrows in the state diagram below.

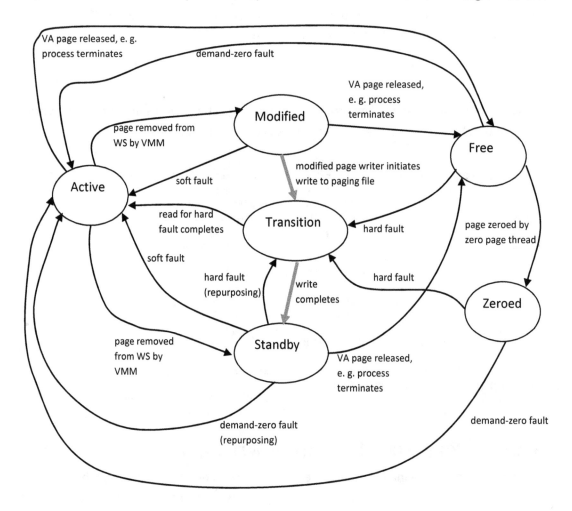

Figure 28 - Writing the Page to the Paging File

29.2.4   Final Status of the _MMPFN and PTE for a Standby Page

The most relevant `_MMPFN` members are:

`u1.Flink`, `u2.Blink`: link the instance to the rest of the list

`PteAddress`: still points to the PTE that mapped the page when it was active

`u3.e1.PageLocation` = `_MMLISTS.StandByPageList` (i.e. 2).

`u3.e1.Modified` = 0

`OriginalPte.u.Soft.Protection`: still set to the VMM defined protection mask

`OriginalPte.u.Soft.PageFileLow`: set to an index which selects the paging file (Windows supports multiple paging files). We will add more details on this index in sec. 34.3 on p. 256.

`OriginalPte.u.Soft.PageFileHigh`: offset into the paging file (in pages, i.e. shifted right by three hex digits, b/c they are always 0).

In section 29.2.6.3 on p. 211 we will see these members during a debug session tracking a page being moved to the Standby list. The same section will show that the PTE is not updated by the page writing logic, i.e. it retains the value it had when the page was a Modified one.

29.2.5   Support for Clustered Reads

The VMM tries to optimize paging file access by reading multiple pages. We will see when analyzing in-paging in Chapter 34 (p. 249), that, instead of reading a single page to resolve a fault, it reads a block, made of the required page and a few ones before and after it, operating on the principle that, when a process accesses an address, it is likely that it will soon access other addresses in its proximity. Such a block of pages is called a *cluster*. Since program instructions operate on *virtual addresses*, a cluster is made of contiguous *virtual page numbers*. Consider for instance an instruction which incurs an hard fault on virtual address 0x5234: the VMM needs to read the content to be mapped at VA 0x5000, but it actually reads a cluster consisting of VPNs 0x4000, 0x5000, 0x6000 (this is only an example, the actual cluster size will be detailed later). The *physical* pages used for the mapping need not be contiguous and they may very well be at sparse addresses, because the criteria used for their allocation are based on where to allocate them from: Free, Zeroed, Standby list, page color, NUMA node, etc.

In order for clustering to be effective, pages in a cluster should have their content at contiguous offsets in the paging file, to minimize disk seek time. To achieve this, the VMM attempts to write *blocks* of contiguous virtual pages to contiguous paging file offsets. This means that the MPW does not randomly grab pages from the Modified list and write them into the first available slot of the paging file, but, rather, builds a list of contiguous pages, looks for a free paging file region big enough to hold them all and writes them in a single operation, thus optimizing the write I/O and placing the swapped out content so that clustered reads will perform better.

The MPW must therefore be able to build lists of pages that were mapped at contiguous virtual addresses, before they were moved to the Modified list. Furthermore, for user range pages, they must belong to the *same* address space, because a clustered read will look for swapped out content for a specific address space later. Again, this has nothing to do with the pages *physical* addresses at the moment of the write.

This poses two problems:

1. The MPW needs to know the address space owning a page on the Modified list

2. It must be able to examine that address space, looking for other modified pages surrounding the original page.

In other words, pages on the modified list can come from any address space and virtual address range, but the MPW must have a way to organize them by address space and address range, to optimize paging file allocation.

In [1], p. 813 is stated that the MPW looks at `_MMPFN.OriginalPte` for this information, but this cannot be correct: at this stage, `OriginalPte` only stores an instance of `_MMPTE` with `_MMPTE.u.Soft.Protection` set to the page protection and the other fields zeroed. There is no information on the virtual address the page was mapped at, much less on which address space it was part of.

The solution appears to lay in the `_MMPFN.u4.PteFrame` member: we already know that it stores the PFN of the parent paging structure in the mapping, which means that:

*   For a page mapping a virtual page, it stores the PFN of the page table.

*   For a page table, it stores the PFN of the page directory.

*   For a page directory, it stores the PFN of the page directory pointers table.

*   For a page directory pointers table, it stores the PFN of the page map level 4.

Note: a page on the modified list is not actually mapping a VA, because the PTE which was referencing it has already been made invalid, i.e. it's P bit is clear. However, the PTE still stores the page PFN and can be made valid again if a soft fault occurs. The _MMPFN for such a page still holds the PFN of the page table in u4.PteFrame.

By design, a PFN is also the index of the _MMPFN instance for the page, which is located at

  0xFFFFFA80`00000000 + PFN * 0x30

so the VMM can access the _MMPFN of all the paging structures mapping a particular page.

We know that _MMPFN.u1 has different meanings depending on the state of a page, e. g.:

- for an page in a working set, it stores the WS index (u1.WsIndex)

- for a page on a list, it stores the pointer to the next element (u1.Flink), etc.

It turns out that this member is used in a peculiar way in the _MMPFN of the PML4: *it stores the address of the _EPROCESS owning the address space*. This makes sense, because the information usually stored in u1 is not needed for the PML4: it has a fixed WS index, it's never put into a list, etc.

Also, the _MMPFN of a PML4 is easily recognizable from at least two of its members:

- PteAddress is set to 0xFFFFF6FB`7DBEDF68, i.e. the address of the auto-entry (see sec. 15.2.3 on p. 69).

- u4.PteFrame is set to the PFN of the entry itself. Of course, this member is available, because there is no upper level paging structure to point to.

In summary, given an _MMPFN on the modified list, the MPW can easily extract the pointer to the _EPROCESS which owned the page.

Incidentally, this gives a way to know the address space for pages in the Active state in the PFN database.

The MPW then calls *MiForceAttachProcess* with the _EPROCESS pointer in rcx, *attaching* itself to the process address space. Now it has access to all of the process PTEs; it also has the address of the PTE for the page we started with, from its _MMPFN.PteAddress, so it can examine the surrounding PTEs to build a list of pages to be written.

In short, the MPW uses the same trick employed by the Working Set Manager: it attaches to address spaces; to accomplish this, it follows the _MMPFN hierarchy to get to the _PROCESS pointer.

The next sections will describe how this behavior can be verified.

29.2.6   Watching the MPW at Work

This section shows how the concepts stated so far can be observed with WinDbg. It gives evidence supporting the statements of the previous sections and provides additional details on the MPW.

29.2.6.1   Obtaining the _EPROCESS for a Modified Page

In this section we are going to discover the _EPROCESS owning the first page in the MmModifiedProcessByColor list.

First, we get the PFN from the list head:

```
1: kd> dt nt!_mmpfnlist Flink @@masm(nt!MmModifiedProcessListByColor)
   +0x010 Flink : 0x1d60e
```

We use the PFN found in Flink as the index into the PFN database and examine a few fields in the page's _MMPFN:

```
1: kd> dt nt!_mmpfn PteAddress u3.e1. OriginalPte.u. u4.PteFrame
@@masm(fffffa8000000000 + 1d60e*30)
   +0x010 PteAddress      : 0xfffff680`003bd740 _MMPTE
   +0x018 u3              :
      +0x002 e1           :
         +0x000 PageLocation   : 0y011
         +0x000 WriteInProgress : 0y0
         +0x000 Modified       : 0y1
         +0x000 ReadInProgress : 0y0
         +0x000 CacheAttribute : 0y01
         +0x001 Priority       : 0y101
         +0x001 Rom            : 0y0
         +0x001 InPageError    : 0y0
         +0x001 KernelStack    : 0y0
         +0x001 RemovalRequested : 0y0
         +0x001 ParityError    : 0y0
   +0x020 OriginalPte     :
      +0x000 u             :
         +0x000 Long       : 0x80
         +0x000 VolatileLong : 0x80
         +0x000 Hard       : _MMPTE_HARDWARE
         +0x000 Flush      : _HARDWARE_PTE
         +0x000 Proto      : _MMPTE_PROTOTYPE
         +0x000 Soft       : _MMPTE_SOFTWARE
         +0x000 TimeStamp  : _MMPTE_TIMESTAMP
```

```
      +0x000 Trans            : _MMPTE_TRANSITION
      +0x000 Subsect          : _MMPTE_SUBSECTION
      +0x000 List             : _MMPTE_LIST
   +0x028 u4         :
      +0x000 PteFrame         : 0y0000000000000000000000000000000000000001101100100100101
(0xd925)
```

Now we use the same command with the PFN taken from `u4.PteFrame`; we do it all the way up until we reach the `_MMPFN` of the PML4.

`_MMPFN` of the PT:

```
1: kd> dt nt!_mmpfn u4.PteFrame @@masm(fffffa8000000000 + d925*30)
   +0x028 u4         :
      +0x000 PteFrame         : 0y0000000000000000000000000000000000000010101010000010010101
(0x2a095)
```

`_MMPFN` of the PD:

```
1: kd> dt nt!_mmpfn PteAddress u4.PteFrame @@masm(fffffa8000000000 + 2a095*30)
   +0x010 PteAddress : 0xfffff6fb`7da00008 _MMPTE
   +0x028 u4         :
      +0x000 PteFrame         : 0y0000000000000000000000000000000000000001000010010101010100
(0x10954)
```

`_MMPFN` of the PDPT:

```
1: kd> dt nt!_mmpfn PteAddress u4.PteFrame @@masm(fffffa8000000000 + 10954*30)
   +0x010 PteAddress : 0xfffff6fb`7dbed000 _MMPTE
   +0x028 u4         :
      +0x000 PteFrame         : 0y0000000000000000000000000000000000000001111111011101010
(0xfeea)
```

`_MMPFN` of the PML4:

```
1: kd> dt nt!_mmpfn PteAddress u4.PteFrame @@masm(fffffa8000000000 + feea*30)
   +0x010 PteAddress : 0xfffff6fb`7dbedf68 _MMPTE
   +0x028 u4         :
      +0x000 PteFrame         : 0y0000000000000000000000000000000000000001111111011101010
(0xfeea)
```

Notice how the last `_MMPFN` has `u4.PteFrame` set to its own index. This instance has `u1.Flink` set to the `_EPROCESS` address, which we can feed to the !process command:

```
1: kd> dt nt!_mmpfn u1.Flink PteAddress u4.PteFrame @@masm(fffffa8000000000 + feea*30)
   +0x000 u1         :
      +0x000 Flink            : 0xfffffa80`00ad5060
   +0x010 PteAddress : 0xfffff6fb`7dbedf68 _MMPTE
   +0x028 u4         :
      +0x000 PteFrame         : 0y0000000000000000000000000000000000000001111111011101010
(0xfeea)
1: kd> !process 0xfffffa80`00ad5060
PROCESS fffffa8000ad5060
    SessionId: 1  Cid: 0b8c    Peb: 7fffffd3000  ParentCid: 04e8
```

```
DirBase: 0feea000  ObjectTable: fffff8a001daa290  HandleCount:  23.
Image: cmd.exe
VadRoot ffffffa8000e6e8b0 Vads 38 Clone 0 Private 270. Modified 1767. Locked 0.
DeviceMap fffff8a0020fe120
Token                        fffff8a00139ca90
ElapsedTime                  23 Days 19:23:50.468
UserTime                     00:00:00.000
KernelTime                   00:00:00.046
QuotaPoolUsage[PagedPool]    0
QuotaPoolUsage[NonPagedPool] 0
Working Set Sizes (now,min,max)  (51, 50, 345) (204KB, 200KB, 1380KB)
PeakWorkingSetSize           787
VirtualSize                  38 Mb
PeakVirtualSize              42 Mb
PageFaultCount               6804
MemoryPriority               BACKGROUND
BasePriority                 8
CommitCharge                 788
```

Now we know we found a page of cmd.exe.

We can further verify that our conclusion is correct; first, we switch to this process' context:

```
1: kd> .cache forcedecodeptes

Max cache size is        : 1048576 bytes (0x400 KB)
Total memory in cache    : 0 bytes (0 KB)
Number of regions cached: 0
0 full reads broken into 0 partial reads
    counts: 0 cached/0 uncached, 0.00% cached
    bytes : 0 cached/0 uncached, 0.00% cached
** Transition PTEs are implicitly decoded
** Virtual addresses are translated to physical addresses before access
** Prototype PTEs are implicitly decoded

1: kd> .process 0xffffffa80`00ad5060
Implicit process is now ffffffa80`00ad5060
```

Then we feed the address of the PTE pointing to the Modified page to the !pte command. This address is in the PteAddress member of the page's _MMPFN:

```
1: kd> dt nt!_mmpfn PteAddress u3.e1. OriginalPte.u. u4.PteFrame
@@masm(fffffa8000000000 + 1d60e*30)
   +0x010 PteAddress      : 0xfffff680`003bd740 _MMPTE
   +0x018 u3              :
     +0x002 e1            :
        +0x000 PageLocation   : 0y011
        +0x000 WriteInProgress : 0y0
        +0x000 Modified       : 0y1
        +0x000 ReadInProgress : 0y0
        +0x000 CacheAttribute : 0y01
        +0x001 Priority       : 0y101
        +0x001 Rom            : 0y0
        +0x001 InPageError    : 0y0
```

```
        +0x001 KernelStack      : 0y0
        +0x001 RemovalRequested : 0y0
        +0x001 ParityError      : 0y0
   +0x020 OriginalPte     :
      +0x000 u              :
         +0x000 Long         : 0x80
         +0x000 VolatileLong : 0x80
         +0x000 Hard         : _MMPTE_HARDWARE
         +0x000 Flush        : _HARDWARE_PTE
         +0x000 Proto        : _MMPTE_PROTOTYPE
         +0x000 Soft         : _MMPTE_SOFTWARE
         +0x000 TimeStamp    : _MMPTE_TIMESTAMP
         +0x000 Trans        : _MMPTE_TRANSITION
         +0x000 Subsect      : _MMPTE_SUBSECTION
         +0x000 List         : _MMPTE_LIST
   +0x028 u4              :
      +0x000 PteFrame       : 0y000000000000000000000000000000000000001101100100100101
(0xd925)


1: kd> !pte 0xfffff680`003bd740
                               VA 0000000077ae8000

PXE @ FFFFF6FB7DBED000    PPE at FFFFF6FB7DA00008    PDE at FFFFF6FB40001DE8    PTE at FFFFF680003BD740
contains 1590000010954867  contains 12E000002A095867  contains 1A4000000D925867  contains B08000001D60E886
pfn 10954    ---DA--UWEV  pfn 2a095     ---DA--UWEV  pfn d925     ---DA--UWEV  not valid
                                                                  Transition: 1d60e
                                                                  Protect: 4 - ReadWrite
```

We can see that the PTE is not valid, in transition and the PFN is 1d60e, which is the PFN we
took from the modified list head at the beginning. This confirms that we found the correct
address space for the page.

29.2.6.2   Watching the MPW Attaching To Processes

We can catch the MPW reading the _EPROCESS from the _MMPFN, by placing a breakpoint
on read accesses from the MPW thread to _MMPFN.u1.Flink. Here is what we get when we
place it on the _MMPFN for the PML4 of MemTests.exe:

```
0: kd> bl
 0 e fffffa80`000efe50 r 8 0001 (0001)
    Match thread data fffffa80`0095fb60

0: kd> g
Breakpoint 0 hit
nt!MiBuildPageFileCluster+0x14d:
fffff800`029a3f5d 488d542430     lea     rdx,[rsp+30h]
```

Access breakpoint stops at the instruction after the access, so we use ub to see the actual
access:

```
0: kd> ub
nt!MiBuildPageFileCluster+0x133:
fffff800`029a3f43 488bc1         mov     rax,rcx
```

```
fffff800`029a3f46 49c1e504         shl     r13,4
fffff800`029a3f4a 4c2bea           sub     r13,rdx
fffff800`029a3f4d 498b4d28         mov     rcx,qword ptr [r13+28h]
fffff800`029a3f51 4923c9           and     rcx,r9
fffff800`029a3f54 483bc8           cmp     rcx,rax
fffff800`029a3f57 75e6             jne     nt!MiBuildPageFileCluster+0x12f
(fffff800`029a3f3f)
fffff800`029a3f59 498b7d00         mov     rdi,qword ptr [r13]
```

This tells us that the address of _MMPFN.u1.Flink is in r13. Now, using !thread, we see that
the thread is not attached to any process:

```
0: kd> !thread @$thread
THREAD fffffa800095fb60  Cid 0004.005c  Teb: 0000000000000000 Win32Thread:
0000000000000000 RUNNING on processor 0
Not impersonating
DeviceMap                 fffff8a000006090
Owning Process            fffffa80008da990      Image:        System
Attached Process          N/A             Image:        N/A
Wait Start TickCount      12888628        Ticks: 48959 (0:00:12:44.984)
Context Switch Count      95522
UserTime                  00:00:00.000
KernelTime                00:01:09.265
Win32 Start Address nt!MiModifiedPageWriter (0xfffff800028699c0)
Stack Init fffff8800312bdb0 Current fffff8800312ba80
Base fffff8800312c000 Limit fffff88003126000 Call 0
Priority 17 BasePriority 8 UnusualBoost 0 ForegroundBoost 0 IoPriority 2 PagePriority 5
Child-SP          RetAddr           : Args to Child
: Call Site
fffff880`0312b320 fffff800`02869471 : fffffa80`018c1078 fffffa80`00000000
00000000`00004edf fffffa80`00000021 : nt!MiBuildPageFileCluster+0x14d

fffff880`0312bc00 fffff800`02869b7b : fffffa80`00004edf fffff880`00000000
00000000`00004edf 00000000`00000000 : nt!MiGatherPagefilePages+0x271

fffff880`0312bce0 fffff800`02b74166 : fffffa80`0095fb60 00000000`00000000
00000000`00000080 00000000`00000001 : nt!MiModifiedPageWriter+0x1bb

fffff880`0312bd40 fffff800`028af486 : fffff800`02a49e80 fffffa80`0095fb60
fffff800`02a57c40 00000000`00000000 : nt!PspSystemThreadStartup+0x5a

fffff880`0312bd80 00000000`00000000 : fffff880`0312c000 fffff880`03126000
fffff880`0312ba80 00000000`00000000 : nt!KxStartSystemThread+0x16
```

Stepping into the code for a while, we eventually arrive at a call to *MiForceAttachProcess*,
with rcx set to the _EPROCESS address loaded at the breaking instruction (i.e. the
_EPROCESS address is passed to the function as its first parameter). After the call, the MPW
is attached to the process:

```
0: kd>
nt!MiBuildPageFileCluster+0x1dd:
fffff800`029a3fed e85a1cf4ff      call    nt!MiForceAttachProcess (fffff800`028e5c4c)
```

```
0: kd> p
nt!MiBuildPageFileCluster+0x1e2:
fffff800`029a3ff2 413bc7          cmp     eax,r15d


0: kd> !thread @$thread
THREAD fffffa800095fb60  Cid 0004.005c  Teb: 0000000000000000 Win32Thread:
0000000000000000 RUNNING on processor 0
Not impersonating
DeviceMap                fffff8a0020fe120
Owning Process           fffffa80008da990      Image:        System
Attached Process         fffffa8000cef970      Image:        MemTests.EXE
Wait Start TickCount     12937618      Ticks: 1 (0:00:00:00.015)
Context Switch Count     95523
UserTime                 00:00:00.000
KernelTime               00:01:09.765
Win32 Start Address nt!MiModifiedPageWriter (0xfffff800028699c0)
Stack Init fffff8800312dbd0 Current fffff8800312afd0
Base fffff8800312c000 Limit fffff88003126000 Call 0
Priority 17 BasePriority 8 UnusualBoost 0 ForegroundBoost 0 IoPriority 2 PagePriority 5
Child-SP          RetAddr          : Args to Child
: Call Site
fffff880`0312b320 fffff800`02869471 : fffffa80`018c1078 fffffa80`00000000
00000000`00004edf fffffa80`00000021 : nt!MiBuildPageFileCluster+0x1e2

fffff880`0312bc00 fffff800`02869b7b : fffffa80`00004edf fffff880`00000000
00000000`00004edf 00000000`00000000 : nt!MiGatherPagefilePages+0x271

fffff880`0312bce0 fffff800`02b74166 : fffffa80`0095fb60 00000000`00000000
00000000`00000080 00000000`00000001 : nt!MiModifiedPageWriter+0x1bb

fffff880`0312bd40 fffff800`028af486 : fffff800`02a49e80 fffffa80`0095fb60
fffff800`02a57c40 00000000`00000000 : nt!PspSystemThreadStartup+0x5a

fffff880`0312bd80 00000000`00000000 : fffff880`0312c000 fffff880`03126000
fffff880`0312ba80 00000000`00000000 : nt!KxStartSystemThread+0x16
```

29.2.6.3   Watching the MPW Writing a Modified Page

We can intercept the MPW while it is writing a Modified page setting a breakpoint at *MiBuildPageFileCluster*+0x62e, one of the addresses on the call stack shown on p. 201. Actually, the call stack shows *MiBuildPageFileCluster*+0x633, because it shows the call return address; at +0x62e is the call to *MiReferencePageForCluster*, with rbp and rcx both storing the _MMPFN address of the page about to be written. Using the /t option, we set a breakpoint which can be triggered by the MPW only:

```
1: kd> bp /t fffffa80`0095fb60 nt!MiBuildPageFileCluster+0x62e
```

When the breakpoint stops rbp stores the _MMPFN address:

```
0: kd> r
rax=0000000000000080 rbx=84a000000ca23886 rcx=fffffa800025e690
```

```
rdx=0000000000000000 rsi=0000000000000000 rdi=0000000000000000
rip=fffff800029a443e rsp=fffff8800312b320 rbp=fffffa800025e690
 r8=000000000000ca23  r9=fffff6800000c130 r10=0000000000000000
r11=0000000001836000 r12=0000000000000001 r13=0000000000000001
r14=fffff6800000c1b0 r15=000000000000ca23
iopl=0         nv up ei pl zr na po nc
cs=0010  ss=0018  ds=002b  es=002b  fs=0053  gs=002b          efl=00000246
nt!MiBuildPageFileCluster+0x62e:
fffff800`029a443e e89d58ecff      call    nt!MiReferencePageForCluster
(fffff800`02869ce0)
```

We see the MPW is attached to an instance of svchost.exe:

```
0: kd> !thread @$thread
THREAD fffffa800095fb60  Cid 0004.005c  Teb: 0000000000000000 Win32Thread:
0000000000000000 RUNNING on processor 0
Not impersonating
DeviceMap                 fffff8a0008fd9f0
Owning Process            fffffa80008da990        Image:         System
Attached Process          fffffa80024d5b30        Image:         svchost.exe
Wait Start TickCount      15146512       Ticks: 0
Context Switch Count      112890
UserTime                  00:00:00.000
KernelTime                00:01:36.718
Win32 Start Address nt!MiModifiedPageWriter (0xfffff800028699c0)
Stack Init fffff8800312bdb0 Current fffff8800312b010
Base fffff8800312c000 Limit fffff88003126000 Call 0
Priority 17 BasePriority 8 UnusualBoost 0 ForegroundBoost 0 IoPriority 2 PagePriority 5
Child-SP       RetAddr        : Args to Child
: Call Site
fffff880`0312b320 fffff800`02869471 : fffffa80`018bc078 fffffa80`00000000
00000000`0001ebf1 fffffa80`00000100 : nt!MiBuildPageFileCluster+0x62e

fffff880`0312bc00 fffff800`02869b7b : fffffa80`0001ebf1 fffff880`00000000
00000000`0001ebf1 00000000`00000000 : nt!MiGatherPagefilePages+0x271

fffff880`0312bce0 fffff800`02b74166 : fffffa80`0095fb60 00000000`00000000
00000000`00000080 00000000`00000001 : nt!MiModifiedPageWriter+0x1bb

fffff880`0312bd40 fffff800`028af486 : fffff800`02a49e80 fffffa80`0095fb60
fffff800`02a57c40 00000000`00000000 : nt!PspSystemThreadStartup+0x5a

fffff880`0312bd80 00000000`00000000 : fffff880`0312c000 fffff880`03126000
fffff880`0312b010 00000000`00000000 : nt!KxStartSystemThread+0x16
```

Looking at the _MMPFN, we see that PageLocation = 3 (_MMLISTS.ModifiedPageList)
and we have the PTE address in PteAddress:

```
0: kd> dt nt!_mmpfn u1.Flink u2.Blink u3.e1. PteAddress OriginalPte.u.Soft. @rbp
   +0x000 u1                 :
     +0x000 Flink            : 0xc8b
   +0x008 u2                 :
```

```
     +0x000 Blink                   : 0xa522
   +0x010 PteAddress                : 0xffffff680`0000c1b1 _MMPTE
   +0x018 u3                        :
     +0x002 e1                      :
       +0x000 PageLocation          : 0y011
       +0x000 WriteInProgress       : 0y0
       +0x000 Modified              : 0y1
       +0x000 ReadInProgress        : 0y0
       +0x000 CacheAttribute        : 0y01
       +0x001 Priority              : 0y010
       +0x001 Rom                   : 0y0
       +0x001 InPageError           : 0y0
       +0x001 KernelStack           : 0y0
       +0x001 RemovalRequested      : 0y0
       +0x001 ParityError           : 0y0
   +0x020 OriginalPte               :
     +0x000 u                       :
       +0x000 Soft                  :
         +0x000 Valid               : 0y0
         +0x000 PageFileLow         : 0y0000
         +0x000 Protection          : 0y00100 (0x4)
         +0x000 Prototype           : 0y0
         +0x000 Transition          : 0y0
         +0x000 UsedPageTableEntries : 0y0000000000 (0)
         +0x000 InStore             : 0y0
         +0x000 Reserved            : 0y000000000 (0)
         +0x000 PageFileHigh        : 0y00000000000000000000000000000000 (0)
```

Note how `_MMPTE.u3.e1.Modified` = 1, in accordance with the page being dirty.

We can also verify that the `_MMPFN` is linked to a list by observing that the `_MMPFN` with indexes equal `Flink` and `Blink` point to the instance above. First, we compute the index of the `_MMPFN` above, whose address is into `rbp`:

```
0: kd> ? (@rbp - ffffffa8000000000) / 30
Evaluate expression: 51747 = 00000000`0000ca23
```

Then, we look at the instance pointed by the current `Blink` and verify that it has `Flink` set to the index computed above:

```
0: kd> dt nt!_mmpfn u1.Flink @@masm(ffffffa8000000000 + 30*a522)
   +0x000 u1          :
     +0x000 Flink     : 0xca23
```

Same check for the instance pointed by the current `Flink`:

```
0: kd> dt nt!_mmpfn u2.Blink @@masm(ffffffa8000000000 + 30*c8b)
   +0x008 u2          :
     +0x000 Blink     : 0xca23
```

Note also how the PteAddress has bit 0 set; it is used as a lock bit to exclusively access the _MMPFN. The MPW has the _MMPFN locked and other threads needing to update it would busy-wait in a loop until the bit is clear, as explained in sec. 25.2 on p. 137.

_MMPTE.OriginalPte.PageFileHigh is 0, which tells us that the offset of the page into the paging file has not yet been determined.

Since the MPW is attached to the process, the address space of the latter is active, so we can examine the PTE content:

```
0: kd> !pte 0xfffff680`0000c1b0
                        VA 0000000001836000

PXE @ FFFFF6FB7DBED000    PPE at FFFFF6FB7DA00000    PDE at FFFFF6FB40000060    PTE at FFFFF6800000C1B0
contains 550000001938C867  contains 488000001940F867  contains 021000000E4C3867  contains 84A000000CA23886
pfn 1938c    ---DA--UWEV  pfn 1940f    ---DA--UWEV  pfn e4c3    ---DA--UWEV  not valid
                                                            Transition: ca23
                                                            Protect: 4 - ReadWrite
```

The value above corresponds to a not valid PTE with:

```
_MMPTE.u.Trans.Protection = 4
_MMPTE.u.Trans.Transition = 1
_MMPTE.u.Trans.PageFrameNumber = 0xca23
```

Note how PageFrameNumber is set to the index of the _MMPFN instance.

We can further follow this page while it is written to the paging file. The first step is to set a breakpoint on write accesses to _MMPFN.OriginalPte, where the MPW is going to write the paging file offset. We stop at *MiUpdatePfnBackingStore*+0x85, with the _MMPFN address in rbx:

```
0: kd> r
rax=0001ebf200000000 rbx=fffffa800025e690 rcx=0001ebf200000080
rdx=0000000000000000 rsi=000000000001ebf2 rdi=0000000000000000
rip=fffff80002869ca5 rsp=fffff8800312b2f0 rbp=0000000000000000
 r8=000000000001ebf2  r9=0000000000000001 r10=000000000183d001
r11=000000000184f000 r12=0000000000000000 r13=0000000000000001
r14=fffff6800000c278 r15=fffffa80018bc0b0
iopl=0         nv up ei pl nz na pe nc
cs=0010  ss=0018  ds=002b  es=002b  fs=0053  gs=002b              efl=00000202
nt!MiUpdatePfnBackingStore+0x85:
fffff800`02869ca5 f0836310fe      lock and dword ptr [rbx+10h],0FFFFFFFEh
ds:002b:fffffa80`0025e6a0=0000c1b1
```

The _MMPFN is set as follows:

```
0: kd> dt nt!_mmpfn u1.Flink u2.Blink u3.e1. PteAddress OriginalPte.u.Soft. @rbx
   +0x000 u1                     :
      +0x000 Flink              : 0
```

```
+0x008 u2                        :
    +0x000 Blink                 : 0
+0x010 PteAddress                : 0xfffff680`0000c1b1 _MMPTE
+0x018 u3                        :
    +0x002 e1                    :
        +0x000 PageLocation      : 0y011
        +0x000 WriteInProgress   : 0y1
        +0x000 Modified          : 0y0
        +0x000 ReadInProgress    : 0y0
        +0x000 CacheAttribute    : 0y01
        +0x001 Priority          : 0y010
        +0x001 Rom               : 0y0
        +0x001 InPageError       : 0y0
        +0x001 KernelStack       : 0y0
        +0x001 RemovalRequested  : 0y0
        +0x001 ParityError       : 0y0
+0x020 OriginalPte               :
    +0x000 u                     :
        +0x000 Soft              :
            +0x000 Valid               : 0y0
            +0x000 PageFileLow         : 0y0000
            +0x000 Protection          : 0y00100 (0x4)
            +0x000 Prototype           : 0y0
            +0x000 Transition          : 0y0
            +0x000 UsedPageTableEntries : 0y0000000000 (0)
            +0x000 InStore             : 0y0
            +0x000 Reserved            : 0y000000000 (0)
            +0x000 PageFileHigh        : 0y00000000000000011110101111110010 (0x1ebf2)
```

We can see that now `Modified` = 0 and `WriteInProgress` = 1. The latter will remain set
after the MPW will have released the lock on the `_MMPFN`, tracking that a write is in progress.
`OriginalPte` now includes the paging file offset. The `_MMPFN` is still locked, because
`PteAddress` is an odd value. `Flink` and `Blink` are set to 0, so the `_MMPFN` is not linked to
the list anymore. The PTE is not shown, but it is unchanged. Below is the MPW status:

```
0: kd> !thread @$thread
THREAD fffffa800095fb60  Cid 0004.005c  Teb: 0000000000000000 Win32Thread:
0000000000000000 RUNNING on processor 0
Not impersonating
DeviceMap               fffff8a0008fd9f0
Owning Process          fffffa80008da990       Image:        System
Attached Process        fffffa80024d5b30       Image:        svchost.exe
Wait Start TickCount    15146513        Ticks: 0
Context Switch Count    112890
UserTime                00:00:00.000
KernelTime              00:01:36.734
Win32 Start Address nt!MiModifiedPageWriter (0xfffff800028699c0)
Stack Init fffff8800312bdb0 Current fffff8800312b010
Base fffff8800312c000 Limit fffff88003126000 Call 0
Priority 17 BasePriority 8 UnusualBoost 0 ForegroundBoost 0 IoPriority 2 PagePriority 5
```

```
Child-SP         RetAddr           : Args to Child
: Call Site
fffff880`0312b2f0 fffff800`029a468c : 00000000`00000001 00000580`00000000
00000000`00000000 00000000`0001ebf2 : nt!MiUpdatePfnBackingStore+0x85

fffff880`0312b320 fffff800`02869471 : fffffa80`018bc078 fffffa80`00000000
00000000`0001ebf1 fffffa80`00000100 : nt!MiBuildPageFileCluster+0x87c

fffff880`0312bc00 fffff800`02869b7b : fffffa80`0001ebf1 fffff880`00000000
00000000`0001ebf1 00000000`00000000 : nt!MiGatherPagefilePages+0x271

fffff880`0312bce0 fffff800`02b74166 : fffffa80`0095fb60 00000000`00000000
00000000`00000080 00000000`00000001 : nt!MiModifiedPageWriter+0x1bb

fffff880`0312bd40 fffff800`028af486 : fffff800`02a49e80 fffffa80`0095fb60
fffff800`02a57c40 00000000`00000000 : nt!PspSystemThreadStartup+0x5a

fffff880`0312bd80 00000000`00000000 : fffff880`0312c000 fffff880`03126000
fffff880`0312b010 00000000`00000000 : nt!KxStartSystemThread+0x16
```

Setting a breakpoint at *MiBuildPageFileCluster*+0x87c, which is the first return address on the stack, we catch the MPW on its way back to the caller:

```
Breakpoint 2 hit
nt!MiBuildPageFileCluster+0x87c:
fffff800`029a468c 4103dd          add     ebx,r13d
```

We can see that now the _MMPFN is unlocked (PteAddress has bit 0 clear) and still has WriteInProgress set. Other VMM components may access the _MMPFN, but they will know that the page has an I/O in progress.

```
0: kd> dt nt!_mmpfn u1.Flink u2.Blink u3.e1. PteAddress OriginalPte.u.Soft.
fffffa800025e690
   +0x000 u1                :
      +0x000 Flink          : 0
   +0x008 u2                :
      +0x000 Blink          : 0
   +0x010 PteAddress        : 0xfffff680`0000c1b0 _MMPTE
   +0x018 u3                :
      +0x002 e1             :
         +0x000 PageLocation      : 0y011
         +0x000 WriteInProgress   : 0y1
         +0x000 Modified          : 0y0
         +0x000 ReadInProgress    : 0y0
         +0x000 CacheAttribute    : 0y01
         +0x001 Priority          : 0y010
         +0x001 Rom               : 0y0
         +0x001 InPageError       : 0y0
         +0x001 KernelStack       : 0y0
         +0x001 RemovalRequested  : 0y0
         +0x001 ParityError       : 0y0
   +0x020 OriginalPte       :
      +0x000 u                :
```

```
+0x000 Soft                      :
   +0x000 Valid                 : 0y0
   +0x000 PageFileLow           : 0y0000
   +0x000 Protection            : 0y00100 (0x4)
   +0x000 Prototype             : 0y0
   +0x000 Transition            : 0y0
   +0x000 UsedPageTableEntries : 0y0000000000 (0)
   +0x000 InStore               : 0y0
   +0x000 Reserved              : 0y000000000 (0)
   +0x000 PageFileHigh          : 0y00000000000000011110101111110010 (0x1ebf2)
```

By setting breakpoints on the return addresses on the stack, we eventually stop at *MiModifiedPageWriter*+0x1bb:

```
0: kd> !thread @$thread
THREAD ffffa800095fb60  Cid 0004.005c  Teb: 0000000000000000 Win32Thread:
0000000000000000 RUNNING on processor 0
IRP List:
   ffffa8001090860: (0006,03a0) Flags: 00060003  Mdl: ffffa80018bc078
Not impersonating
DeviceMap              fffff8a000006090
Owning Process         ffffa80008da990      Image:        System
Attached Process       N/A          Image:        N/A
Wait Start TickCount   15146517     Ticks: 0
Context Switch Count   112890
UserTime               00:00:00.000
KernelTime             00:01:36.796
Win32 Start Address nt!MiModifiedPageWriter (0xfffff800028699c0)
Stack Init fffff8800312bdb0 Current fffff8800312b010
Base fffff8800312c000 Limit fffff88003126000 Call 0
Priority 17 BasePriority 8 UnusualBoost 0 ForegroundBoost 0 IoPriority 2 PagePriority 5
Child-SP          RetAddr         : Args to Child
: Call Site
fffff880`0312bce0 fffff800`02b74166 : ffffa80`0095fb60 00000000`00000000
00000000`00000080 00000000`00000001 : nt!MiModifiedPageWriter+0x1bb

fffff880`0312bd40 fffff800`028af486 : fffff800`02a49e80 ffffa80`0095fb60
fffff800`02a57c40 00000000`00000000 : nt!PspSystemThreadStartup+0x5a

fffff880`0312bd80 00000000`00000000 : fffff880`0312c000 fffff880`03126000
fffff880`0312b010 00000000`00000000 : nt!KxStartSystemThread+0x16
```

When we are here, the _MMPFN still has WriteInProgress = 1 and is unlocked:

```
0: kd> dt nt!_mmpfn u1.Flink u2.Blink u3.e1. PteAddress OriginalPte.u.Soft.
ffffa800025e690
   +0x000 u1                    :
      +0x000 Flink              : 0
   +0x008 u2                    :
      +0x000 Blink              : 0
   +0x010 PteAddress            : 0xfffff680`0000c1b0 _MMPTE
   +0x018 u3                    :
      +0x002 e1                 :
         +0x000 PageLocation    : 0y011
         +0x000 WriteInProgress : 0y1
```

```
      +0x000 Modified          : 0y0
      +0x000 ReadInProgress     : 0y0
      +0x000 CacheAttribute     : 0y01
      +0x001 Priority           : 0y010
      +0x001 Rom                : 0y0
      +0x001 InPageError        : 0y0
      +0x001 KernelStack        : 0y0
      +0x001 RemovalRequested   : 0y0
      +0x001 ParityError        : 0y0
  +0x020 OriginalPte       :
    +0x000 u              :
      +0x000 Soft            :
        +0x000 Valid           : 0y0
        +0x000 PageFileLow     : 0y0000
        +0x000 Protection      : 0y00100 (0x4)
        +0x000 Prototype       : 0y0
        +0x000 Transition      : 0y0
        +0x000 UsedPageTableEntries : 0y0000000000 (0)
        +0x000 InStore         : 0y0
        +0x000 Reserved        : 0y000000000 (0)
        +0x000 PageFileHigh    : 0y00000000000000011110101111110010 (0x1ebf2)
```

The fact that the MPW has moved on and returned to its top level function while
WriteInProgress is still 1 tells us that the MPW issues an asynchronous I/O write and moves
on while the operation is in progress, as stated in sec. 29.2.3 on p. 201.

We can observe the write final steps by setting a breakpoint for write accesses to u3.e1 on
our _MMPFN instance, catching the MPW when it updates WriteInProgress. When the
breakpoint is hit, rbx is set to the _MMPFN address:

```
0: kd> r
rax=0000000000000001 rbx=fffffa800025e690 rcx=fffffa800025e690
rdx=0000000000000000 rsi=fffffa80018bc8a8 rdi=0000000000000000
rip=fffff80002907fb7 rsp=fffff8800312ae20 rbp=0000000000000001
 r8=0000000000000000  r9=0000000000000000 r10=0000000000000000
r11=fffff80002a85d40 r12=0000000000000000 r13=0000000000000002
r14=0000000000000000 r15=0000000000000000
iopl=0         nv up ei pl nz na pe nc
cs=0010  ss=0018  ds=002b  es=002b  fs=0053  gs=002b          efl=00000202
nt!MiWriteCompletePfn+0x43:
fffff800`02907fb7 0fb74318        movzx   eax,word ptr [rbx+18h]
ds:002b:fffffa80`0025e6a8=0001
```

The thread status is as follows:

```
0: kd> !thread @$thread
THREAD fffffa800095fb60  Cid 0004.005c  Teb: 0000000000000000 Win32Thread:
0000000000000000 RUNNING on processor 0
Not impersonating
DeviceMap              fffff8a000006090
Owning Process         fffffa80008da990      Image:         System
Attached Process       N/A        Image:         N/A
Wait Start TickCount   15146517      Ticks: 1 (0:00:00:00.015)
```

```
Context Switch Count      112890
UserTime                  00:00:00.000
KernelTime                00:01:36.812
Win32 Start Address nt!MiModifiedPageWriter (0xfffff800028699c0)
Stack Init fffff8800312bdb0 Current fffff8800312b010
Base fffff8800312c000 Limit fffff88003126000 Call 0
Priority 17 BasePriority 8 UnusualBoost 0 ForegroundBoost 0 IoPriority 2 PagePriority 5
Child-SP          RetAddr          : Args to Child
: Call Site
fffff880`0312ae20 fffff800`02908514 : 00026ffd`00000001 00000000`00000000
00000000`00000000 fffffa80`01515290 : nt!MiWriteCompletePfn+0x43

fffff880`0312ae90 fffff800`028bae67 : ffffffa80`018bc010 00000000`00000000
00000000`00000000 ffffffa80`018bc0b0 : nt!MiWriteComplete+0x1b4

fffff880`0312af50 fffff800`028ad92f : ffffffa80`0095fb60 ffffffa80`0095fbb0
ffffffa80`00e3af80 00000000`00000001 : nt!IopCompletePageWrite+0x57

fffff880`0312af80 fffff800`028adce7 : fffff880`0312b301 00000000`00000000
00000000`00000000 00000000`00000000 : nt!KiDeliverApc+0x1d7

fffff880`0312b000 fffff800`02975dbb : fffff880`0312bb20 00000000`00000000
00000000`00000001 00000000`00000000 : nt!KiApcInterrupt+0xd7 (TrapFrame @
fffff880`0312b000)

fffff880`0312b190 fffff800`02d545da : 00030010`00000000 75000029`00000001
850021c8`00000001 fffff880`0312b301 : nt!KeThawExecution+0x26b

fffff880`0312b210 fffff800`02935b01 : fffff880`0312b300 fffff880`0312baa8
fffff800`02a49e80 00000000`00000000 : nt!KdExitDebugger+0x7a

fffff880`0312b240 fffff800`02d5303f : fffff880`0312b300 fffff880`0312b800
fffff880`0312bb50 fffff800`02909ca1 : nt! ?? ::FNODOBFM::`string'+0x19491

fffff880`0312b280 fffff800`0290b1a6 : fffff880`0312baa8 fffff880`0312bb50
fffff880`0312bb50 ffffffa80`018bc010 : nt!KdpTrap+0x2f

fffff880`0312b2d0 fffff800`028d0542 : fffff880`0312baa8 ffffffa80`0095fb60
fffff880`0312bb50 ffffffa80`008da990 : nt!KiDispatchException+0x126

fffff880`0312b970 fffff800`028ce374 : ffffffa80`015ff900 ffffffa80`01906070
ffffffa80`015ff900 ffffffa80`01090860 : nt!KiExceptionDispatch+0xc2

fffff880`0312bb50 fffff800`02869b7c : ffffffa80`0001ecf1 fffff880`00000000
00000000`0001ebf1 00000000`00000000 : nt!KiBreakpointTrap+0xf4 (TrapFrame @
fffff880`0312bb50)

fffff880`0312bce0 fffff800`02b74166 : ffffffa80`0095fb60 00000000`00000000
00000000`00000080 00000000`00000001 : nt!MiModifiedPageWriter+0x1bc

fffff880`0312bd40 fffff800`028af486 : fffff800`02a49e80 ffffffa80`0095fb60
fffff800`02a57c40 00000000`00000000 : nt!PspSystemThreadStartup+0x5a

fffff880`0312bd80 00000000`00000000 : fffff880`0312c000 fffff880`03126000
fffff880`0312b010 00000000`00000000 : nt!KxStartSystemThread+0x16
```

The current thread is still 0xFFFFFA80`0095FB60, i.e. the MPW; it is not attached to the process anymore and is updating `WriteInProgress` from a function called by *KiDeliverApc*. This means the I/O completion is signaled by an APC, as stated in sec. 29.2.3 on p. 201. Unfortunately, the call stack is a bit dirty, with a trap frame created by *KiBreakpointTrap*, which seems due to the debugger. This is probably caused by the write operation raising the APC interrupt before the debugger returns control from the previous breakpoint, so we see the APC interrupting while the thread context was being restored.

The `_MMPFN` now is locked again, because the MPW is in the process of updating it, and WriteInProgress is 0:

```
0: kd> dt nt!_mmpfn u1.Flink u2.Blink u3.e1. PteAddress OriginalPte.u.Soft.
fffffa800025e690
   +0x000 u1                 :
      +0x000 Flink            : 0
   +0x008 u2                 :
      +0x000 Blink            : 0
   +0x010 PteAddress         : 0xfffff680`0000c1b1 _MMPTE
   +0x018 u3                 :
      +0x002 e1               :
         +0x000 PageLocation      : 0y011
         +0x000 WriteInProgress   : 0y0
         +0x000 Modified          : 0y0
         +0x000 ReadInProgress    : 0y0
         +0x000 CacheAttribute    : 0y01
         +0x001 Priority          : 0y010
         +0x001 Rom               : 0y0
         +0x001 InPageError       : 0y0
         +0x001 KernelStack       : 0y0
         +0x001 RemovalRequested  : 0y0
         +0x001 ParityError       : 0y0
   +0x020 OriginalPte        :
      +0x000 u                 :
         +0x000 Soft             :
            +0x000 Valid                 : 0y0
            +0x000 PageFileLow           : 0y0000
            +0x000 Protection            : 0y00100 (0x4)
            +0x000 Prototype             : 0y0
            +0x000 Transition            : 0y0
            +0x000 UsedPageTableEntries  : 0y0000000000 (0)
            +0x000 InStore               : 0y0
            +0x000 Reserved              : 0y000000000 (0)
            +0x000 PageFileHigh          : 0y0000000000000000011110101111110010 (0x1ebf2)
```

Setting a breakpoint on the first return address, we find the `_MMPFN` still locked, `u3.e1.PageLocation` set to 2 (`_MMLISTS.StandByPageList`) and Flink and Blink chaining the instance into a list. The MPW is moving along, bringing the `_MMPFN` into the Standby state, but has not yet released it.

```
Breakpoint 5 hit
```

```
nt!MiWriteComplete+0x1b4:
fffff800`02908514 4533ff          xor      r15d,r15d

0: kd> dt nt!_mmpfn u1.Flink u2.Blink u3.e1. PteAddress OriginalPte.u.Soft.
fffffa800025e690
   +0x000 u1                    :
      +0x000 Flink              : Oxffffffff`ffffffff
   +0x008 u2                    :
      +0x000 Blink              : 0x2ac58
   +0x010 PteAddress            : 0xfffff680`0000c1b1 _MMPTE
   +0x018 u3                    :
      +0x002 e1                 :
         +0x000 PageLocation    : 0y010
         +0x000 WriteInProgress : 0y0
         +0x000 Modified        : 0y0
         +0x000 ReadInProgress  : 0y0
         +0x000 CacheAttribute  : 0y01
         +0x001 Priority        : 0y010
         +0x001 Rom             : 0y0
         +0x001 InPageError     : 0y0
         +0x001 KernelStack     : 0y0
         +0x001 RemovalRequested: 0y0
         +0x001 ParityError     : 0y0
   +0x020 OriginalPte           :
      +0x000 u                  :
         +0x000 Soft            :
            +0x000 Valid              : 0y0
            +0x000 PageFileLow        : 0y0000
            +0x000 Protection         : 0y00100 (0x4)
            +0x000 Prototype          : 0y0
            +0x000 Transition         : 0y0
            +0x000 UsedPageTableEntries : 0y0000000000 (0)
            +0x000 InStore            : 0y0
            +0x000 Reserved           : 0y000000000 (0)
            +0x000 PageFileHigh       : 0y0000000000000000111101011111110010 (0x1ebf2)
```

The next return address on the stack is *IopCompletePageWrite*+0x57; here the _MMPFN is unlocked:

```
Breakpoint 6 hit
nt!IopCompletePageWrite+0x57:
fffff800`028bae67 488b5c2430      mov      rbx,qword ptr [rsp+30h]

0: kd> dt nt!_mmpfn u1.Flink u2.Blink u3.e1. PteAddress OriginalPte.u.Soft.
fffffa800025e690
   +0x000 u1                    :
      +0x000 Flink              : 0xa522
   +0x008 u2                    :
      +0x000 Blink              : 0x2ac58
   +0x010 PteAddress            : 0xfffff680`0000c1b0 _MMPTE
   +0x018 u3                    :
      +0x002 e1                 :
         +0x000 PageLocation    : 0y010
         +0x000 WriteInProgress : 0y0
```

```
    +0x000 Modified            : 0y0
    +0x000 ReadInProgress       : 0y0
    +0x000 CacheAttribute       : 0y01
    +0x001 Priority             : 0y010
    +0x001 Rom                  : 0y0
    +0x001 InPageError          : 0y0
    +0x001 KernelStack          : 0y0
    +0x001 RemovalRequested     : 0y0
    +0x001 ParityError          : 0y0
 +0x020 OriginalPte       :
    +0x000 u              :
       +0x000 Soft           :
          +0x000 Valid             : 0y0
          +0x000 PageFileLow       : 0y0000
          +0x000 Protection        : 0y00100 (0x4)
          +0x000 Prototype         : 0y0
          +0x000 Transition        : 0y0
          +0x000 UsedPageTableEntries : 0y0000000000 (0)
          +0x000 InStore           : 0y0
          +0x000 Reserved          : 0y000000000 (0)
          +0x000 PageFileHigh      : 0y0000000000000000011110101111110010 (0x1ebf2)
```

We can look at the final status of the PTE, but we have to switch into the context of the process the MPW was originally attached to (it has by now detached). In this particular debug session, .cache forcedecodeptes was not functioning properly, so .process /i was used:

```
0: kd> .process /i fffffa80024d5b30
You need to continue execution (press 'g' <enter>) for the context
to be switched. When the debugger breaks in again, you will be in
the new process context.
0: kd> g
Break instruction exception - code 80000003 (first chance)
nt!DbgBreakPointWithStatus:
fffff800`028c8f60 cc              int     3
```

Since we let the system run, it is better to verify that the _MMPFN did not change:

```
0: kd> dt nt!_mmpfn u1.Flink u2.Blink u3.e1. PteAddress OriginalPte.u.Soft.
fffffa800025e690
   +0x000 u1           :
      +0x000 Flink          : 0xa522
   +0x008 u2           :
      +0x000 Blink          : 0x2ac58
   +0x010 PteAddress       : 0xfffff680`0000c1b0 _MMPTE
   +0x018 u3           :
      +0x002 e1           :
         +0x000 PageLocation      : 0y010
         +0x000 WriteInProgress   : 0y0
         +0x000 Modified          : 0y0
         +0x000 ReadInProgress    : 0y0
         +0x000 CacheAttribute    : 0y01
         +0x001 Priority          : 0y010
         +0x001 Rom               : 0y0
```

```
    +0x001 InPageError        : 0y0
    +0x001 KernelStack        : 0y0
    +0x001 RemovalRequested   : 0y0
    +0x001 ParityError        : 0y0
 +0x020 OriginalPte    :
    +0x000 u                  :
    +0x000 Soft               :
       +0x000 Valid               : 0y0
       +0x000 PageFileLow         : 0y0000
       +0x000 Protection          : 0y00100 (0x4)
       +0x000 Prototype           : 0y0
       +0x000 Transition          : 0y0
       +0x000 UsedPageTableEntries : 0y0000000000 (0)
       +0x000 InStore             : 0y0
       +0x000 Reserved            : 0y000000000 (0)
       +0x000 PageFileHigh        : 0y00000000000000011110101111110010 (0x1ebf2)
```

The _MMPFN has the same `PteAddress` and `PageFileHigh`, so we can safely assume that
the page state did not change. A look at the PTE shows that it has not been changed at all
during the whole process:

```
0: kd> !pte 0xfffff680`0000c1b0
                          VA 0000000001836000

PXE @ FFFFF6FB7DBED000    PPE at FFFFF6FB7DA00000    PDE at FFFFF6FB40000060    PTE at FFFFF6800000C1B0
contains 550000001938C867   contains 488000001940F867   contains 021000000E4C3867   contains 84A000000CA23886
pfn 1938c     ---DA--UWEV  pfn 1940f     ---DA--UWEV  pfn e4c3      ---DA--UWEV  not valid
                                                                   Transition: ca23
                                                                   Protect: 4 - ReadWrite
```

Thus, as far as the PTE is concerned, it does not matter whether the page state is Modified or
Standby.

In summary, we observed a page on the modified list being processed by the MPW, going
into Transition with WriteInProgress = 1 and ending up as a Standby page, with its paging file
offset saved into OriginalPte.

29.2.6.4   Watching the MPW Processing a Block of Contiguous Pages

The MPW can also be observed while it builds a block of pages by placing a break point at
MiBuildPageFileCluster+0x62e (the same offset used in sec. 29.2.6.3 on p. 211). When the
breakpoint is hit, the !thread command shows the MPW attached to one of the existing
processes. `rcx` holds the address of the _MMPFN of the modified page being added to the list,
so we can obtain the PTE address from it.

We see the breakpoint being hit multiple times, with _MMPFNs for contiguous PTEs being
processed. Below is an example of a PTE range observed while the MPW was attached to
explorer.exe:

```
hit #1:     +0x010 PteAddress : 0xfffff680`00047a01 _MMPTE
hit #2:     +0x010 PteAddress : 0xfffff680`00047a09 _MMPTE
hit #3:     +0x010 PteAddress : 0xfffff680`00047a11 _MMPTE
hit #4:     +0x010 PteAddress : 0xfffff680`00047a19 _MMPTE
hit #5:     +0x010 PteAddress : 0xfffff680`00047a21 _MMPTE
```

Note that actual PTE addresses are multiple of 8 and have bit 0 clear. Bit 0 of
`_MMPFN.PteAddress` is set, because the `_MMPFN is locked`.

Given the relationship between PTE addresses and mapped addresses, contiguous PTEs
correspond to contiguous virtual pages.

`_MMPFN.OriginalPte. u.Soft.PageFileHigh` stores the paging file offset for a page
which has been written to the paging file and, at this stage, this member is still set to 0. We
can catch the MPW updating it by placing a breakpoint for writes to it. We discover that the
write is at *MiUpdatePfnBackingStore*+0x85 (actually is at *MiUpdatePfnBackingStore*+0x81,
because access breakpoints hit on the instruction *after* the access). By placing a breakpoint
here, we see multiple hits, each setting ...`PageFileHigh` to consecutive offsets (here the
`_MMPFN` address is stored into `rbx`:

```
hit #1:
0: kd> dt nt!_mmpfn OriginalPte.u.Soft. @rbx
   +0x020 OriginalPte        :
      +0x000 u               :
         +0x000 Soft              :
            +0x000 Valid               : 0y0
            +0x000 PageFileLow         : 0y0000
            +0x000 Protection          : 0y00100 (0x4)
            +0x000 Prototype           : 0y0
            +0x000 Transition          : 0y0
            +0x000 UsedPageTableEntries : 0y0000000000 (0)
            +0x000 InStore             : 0y0
            +0x000 Reserved            : 0y000000000 (0)
            +0x000 PageFileHigh        : 0y00000000000000111001000101101010 (0x3916a)
0: kd> k
Child-SP          RetAddr           Call Site
fffff880`0312b2f0 fffff800`029a468c nt!MiUpdatePfnBackingStore+0x85
fffff880`0312b320 fffff800`02869471 nt!MiBuildPageFileCluster+0x87c
fffff880`0312bc00 fffff800`02869b7b nt!MiGatherPagefilePages+0x271
fffff880`0312bce0 fffff800`02b74166 nt!MiModifiedPageWriter+0x1bb
fffff880`0312bd40 fffff800`028af486 nt!PspSystemThreadStartup+0x5a
fffff880`0312bd80 00000000`00000000 nt!KxStartSystemThread+0x16

hit #2: +0x000 PageFileHigh        : 0y00000000000000111001000101101011 (0x3916b)
hit #3: +0x000 PageFileHigh        : 0y00000000000000111001000101101100 (0x3916c)
...
```

29.2.7   Writing Active Pages to the Paging File

29.2.7.1   Basic Concept

When performing the analysis of the previous section, it is possible to observe the MPW processing *valid* PTEs, i.e. PTEs actively mapping VAs. This is could be done to handle a situation where the MPW finds a block of contiguous Modified pages, with some Active pages interspersed among them. If the MPW were to limit itself to strictly writing Modified pages, it would have to issue multiple writes, possibly to scattered areas of the paging file. By writing Active pages as well, the MPW can perform a single write operation and allocate a contiguous paging file block for the whole range of pages.

The VMM regards an Active page which has been written to the paging file as clean: it can be moved on the Standby list and, eventually, repurposed. This is tracked in a few control bits related to the page. The PTE has:

```
_MMPFN.u.Hard.Valid = 1
_MMPFN.u.Hard.Dirty1 = 0
_MMPFN.u.Hard.Dirty = 0
_MMPFN.u.Hard.Write = 1
```

Note that `Dirty1` is bit 1, i.e. the hardware R/W bit of the processor; clearing it means setting the page as read only, so that a write into the page will cause a page fault. We will return on this later, however we can understand that this is a way for the VMM to take control when the page is modified and the copy in the paging file becomes out of date.

`Dirty` is the actual processor dirty bit and is cleared to be consistent with the page being clean.

`Write` is ignored by the processor and used by the VMM to recognize the page as writable. The first write into the page will cause a page fault because `Dirty1` is clear, but the VMM will know that the page is actually writable from `Writable` being set.

The `_MMPFN` has:

```
_MMPFN.u3.e1.Modified = 0
```

These three bits are all set to 1 when a page is first mapped to satisfy a demand-zero fault (see sec. 26.5 on p. 162, sec. 26.6.2 on p. 164), because the page begins its life as "dirty"; now we have seen one of the events that change its state to clean.

Another, perhaps more common, event which results in the same state is when a page on the Standby list is faulted back into the working set. We will return on this subject in sec. 31.1.1 on p. 238.

29.2.7.2   Evidence from a Debug Session

This section is meant to provide evidence of the concepts explained in the previous one, so readers willing to take them at face value may choose to skip it.

To catch the MPW while it is writing an active page, we set again a breakpoint at *MiBuildPageFileCluster*+0x62e (see sec. 29.2.6.3 on p. 211), where `rbp` and `rcx` both store the `_MMPFN` address of the page about to be written. This time, we set a conditional breakpoint which looks at the value of `rbp->u3.e1.PageLocation` and resumes execution when it's not `_MMLISTS.ActiveAndValid` (i.e. 6). Such a breakpoint can be set with the following command:

```
1: kd> bp /t fffffa80`0095fb60 nt!MiBuildPageFileCluster+0x62e "j ((poi(@rbp + 1a) & 7)
== 6) ''; 'gc'"
```

When the breakpoint stops `rbp` stores the `_MMPFN` address:

```
nt!MiBuildPageFileCluster+0x62e:
fffff800`029a443e e89d58ecff     call    nt!MiReferencePageForCluster
(fffff800`02869ce0)

0: kd> r
rax=0000000000000000 rbx=f3600000077bc805 rcx=fffffa8000167340
rdx=0000000000000000 rsi=0000000000000000 rdi=0000000000000000
rip=fffff800029a443e rsp=fffff8800312b320 rbp=fffffa8000167340
 r8=0000000000000000  r9=fffff6800001ddc8 r10=0000000000000000
r11=0000000003bc8000 r12=0000000000000000 r13=0000000000000001
r14=fffff6800001de40 r15=00000000000077bc
iopl=0         nv up ei pl nz na pe nc
cs=0010  ss=0000  ds=002b  es=002b  fs=0053  gs=002b        efl=00000202
nt!MiBuildPageFileCluster+0x62e:
fffff800`029a443e e89d58ecff     call    nt!MiReferencePageForCluster
(fffff800`02869ce0)
```

We see the MPW is attached to an instance of svchost.exe:

```
0: kd> !thread @$thread
THREAD fffffa800095fb60  Cid 0004.005c  Teb: 0000000000000000 Win32Thread:
0000000000000000 RUNNING on processor 0
IRP List:
    fffffa8000e2ba00: (0006,03a0) Flags: 00060003  Mdl: fffffa80018bc078
Not impersonating
DeviceMap               fffff8a000006090
Owning Process          fffffa80008da990       Image:       System
Attached Process        fffffa800248e1d0       Image:       svchost.exe
```

```
Wait Start TickCount      13496591        Ticks: 3428 (0:00:00:53.562)
Context Switch Count      97646
UserTime                  00:00:00.000
KernelTime                00:01:32.843
Win32 Start Address nt!MiModifiedPageWriter (0xfffff800028699c0)
Stack Init fffff8800312bdb0 Current fffff8800312ba80
Base fffff8800312c000 Limit fffff88003126000 Call 0
Priority 17 BasePriority 8 UnusualBoost 0 ForegroundBoost 0 IoPriority 2 PagePriority 5
Child-SP          RetAddr             : Args to Child
: Call Site
fffff880`0312b320 fffff800`02869471 : fffffa80`018c1078 fffffa80`00000000
00000000`00031006 fffffa80`000000ca : nt!MiBuildPageFileCluster+0x62e

fffff880`0312bc00 fffff800`02869b7b : fffffa80`00031006 fffff880`00000000
00000000`00031006 00000000`00000000 : nt!MiGatherPagefilePages+0x271

fffff880`0312bce0 fffff800`02b74166 : fffffa80`0095fb60 00000000`00000000
00000000`00000080 00000000`00000001 : nt!MiModifiedPageWriter+0x1bb

fffff880`0312bd40 fffff800`028af486 : fffff800`02a49e80 fffffa80`0095fb60
fffff800`02a57c40 00000000`00000000 : nt!PspSystemThreadStartup+0x5a

fffff880`0312bd80 00000000`00000000 : fffff880`0312c000 fffff880`03126000
fffff880`0312ba80 00000000`00000000 : nt!KxStartSystemThread+0x16
```

Looking at the _MMPFN, we see that `PageLocation` is 6 and we have the PTE address in
`PteAddress`:

```
0: kd> dt nt!_mmpfn u3.e1. PteAddress OriginalPte.u. @rbp
   +0x010 PteAddress       : 0xfffff680`0001de41 _MMPTE
   +0x018 u3               :
      +0x002 e1            :
         +0x000 PageLocation   : 0y110
         +0x000 WriteInProgress : 0y0
         +0x000 Modified       : 0y1
         +0x000 ReadInProgress : 0y0
         +0x000 CacheAttribute : 0y01
         +0x001 Priority       : 0y101
         +0x001 Rom            : 0y0
         +0x001 InPageError    : 0y0
         +0x001 KernelStack    : 0y0
         +0x001 RemovalRequested : 0y0
         +0x001 ParityError    : 0y0
   +0x020 OriginalPte      :
      +0x000 u               :
         +0x000 Long           : 0x80
         +0x000 VolatileLong   : 0x80
         +0x000 Hard           : _MMPTE_HARDWARE
         +0x000 Flush          : _HARDWARE_PTE
         +0x000 Proto          : _MMPTE_PROTOTYPE
         +0x000 Soft           : _MMPTE_SOFTWARE
         +0x000 TimeStamp      : _MMPTE_TIMESTAMP
         +0x000 Trans          : _MMPTE_TRANSITION
         +0x000 Subsect        : _MMPTE_SUBSECTION
         +0x000 List           : _MMPTE_LIST
```

Note how the PTE address has bit 0 set; we know by now that it is used as a lock bit to exclusively access the _MMPFN (see sec. 25.2 on p. 137). Since the MPW is attached to the process, the address space of the latter is active, so we can examine the PTE content:

```
0: kd> !pte 0xfffff680`0001de40
                         VA 0000000003bc8000

PXE @ FFFFF6FB7DBED000    PPE at FFFFF6FB7DA00000    PDE at FFFFF6FB400000E8    PTE at FFFFF6800001DE40
contains 02E000001B2CF867  contains 044000001B252867  contains 01D000000F277867  contains F3600000077BC805
pfn 1b2cf    ---DA--UWEV  pfn 1b252    ---DA--UWEV  pfn f277    ---DA--UWEV  pfn 77bc    -------
UR-V
```

The value reported corresponds to a valid PTE with:

```
_MMPTE.u.Hard.Valid = 1
_MMPTE.u.Hard.Dirty1 = 0
_MMPTE.u.Hard.Dirty = 0
_MMPTE.u.Hard.Write = 1
```

This confirms that the MPW is writing an active page to the paging file and also shows that it has already marked the PTE as clean, which implies setting it to read only (for the processor).

We can further follow this page while it is written to the paging file. The first step is to set a breakpoint on write accesses to _MMPFN.OriginalPte, where the MPW is going to write the paging file offset. We stop at *MiUpdatePfnBackingStore*+0x85, with the _MMPFN address in rbx:

```
0: kd> r
rax=0003100600000000 rbx=fffffa8000167340 rcx=0003100600000080
rdx=0000000000000000 rsi=0000000000031006 rdi=0000000000000000
rip=fffff80002869ca5 rsp=fffff8800312b2f0 rbp=0000000000000000
 r8=0000000000031006  r9=0000000000000000 r10=0000000003bfc005
r11=0000000003c12000 r12=0000000000000000 r13=0000000000000001
r14=fffff6800001e090 r15=fffffa80018c10a8
iopl=0         nv up ei pl nz na pe nc
cs=0010  ss=0018  ds=002b  es=002b  fs=0053  gs=002b             efl=00000202
nt!MiUpdatePfnBackingStore+0x85:
fffff800`02869ca5 f0836310fe      lock and dword ptr [rbx+10h],0FFFFFFFEh
ds:002b:fffffa80`00167350=0001de41
```

The _MMPFN is set as follows:

```
0: kd> dt nt!_mmpfn u3.e1. PteAddress OriginalPte.u. @rbx
   +0x010 PteAddress      : 0xfffff680`0001de41 _MMPTE
   +0x018 u3              :
     +0x002 e1            :
        +0x000 PageLocation   : 0y110
        +0x000 WriteInProgress : 0y1
        +0x000 Modified       : 0y0
        +0x000 ReadInProgress : 0y0
        +0x000 CacheAttribute : 0y01
        +0x001 Priority       : 0y101
```

```
      +0x001 Rom               : 0y0
      +0x001 InPageError       : 0y0
      +0x001 KernelStack       : 0y0
      +0x001 RemovalRequested  : 0y0
      +0x001 ParityError       : 0y0
   +0x020 OriginalPte    :
      +0x000 u                 :
      +0x000 Long              : 0x31006`00000080
      +0x000 VolatileLong      : 0x31006`00000080
      +0x000 Hard              : _MMPTE_HARDWARE
      +0x000 Flush             : _HARDWARE_PTE
      +0x000 Proto             : _MMPTE_PROTOTYPE
      +0x000 Soft              : _MMPTE_SOFTWARE
      +0x000 TimeStamp         : _MMPTE_TIMESTAMP
      +0x000 Trans             : _MMPTE_TRANSITION
      +0x000 Subsect           : _MMPTE_SUBSECTION
      +0x000 List              : _MMPTE_LIST
```

We can see that now `Modified` is 0 and `WriteInProgress` is 1. The latter will remain set after the MPW will have released the lock on the `_MMPFN`, tracking that a write is in progress. `OriginalPte` now includes the paging file offset. The `_MMPFN` is still locked, because `OriginalPte` is an odd value. The PTE is not shown, but it is unchanged. Below is the MPW status:

```
0: kd> !thread @$thread
THREAD fffffa800095fb60  Cid 0004.005c  Teb: 0000000000000000 Win32Thread:
0000000000000000 RUNNING on processor 0
Not impersonating
DeviceMap               fffff8a000006090
Owning Process          fffffa80008da990        Image:        System
Attached Process        fffffa800248e1d0        Image:        svchost.exe
Wait Start TickCount    13500021        Ticks: 1 (0:00:00:00.015)
Context Switch Count    97646
UserTime                00:00:00.000
KernelTime              00:01:32.890
Win32 Start Address nt!MiModifiedPageWriter (0xfffff800028699c0)
Stack Init fffff8800312bdb0 Current fffff8800312ba80
Base fffff8800312c000 Limit fffff88003126000 Call 0
Priority 17 BasePriority 8 UnusualBoost 0 ForegroundBoost 0 IoPriority 2 PagePriority 5
Child-SP          RetAddr           : Args to Child
: Call Site
fffff880`0312b2f0 fffff800`029a468c : 00000000`00000000 00000580`00000000
00000000`00000000 00000000`00031006 : nt!MiUpdatePfnBackingStore+0x85

fffff880`0312b320 fffff800`02869471 : fffffa80`018c1078 fffffa80`00000000
00000000`00031006 fffffa80`000000ca : nt!MiBuildPageFileCluster+0x87c

fffff880`0312bc00 fffff800`02869b7b : fffffa80`00031006 fffff880`00000000
00000000`00031006 00000000`00000000 : nt!MiGatherPagefilePages+0x271

fffff880`0312bce0 fffff800`02b74166 : fffffa80`0095fb60 00000000`00000000
00000000`00000080 00000000`00000001 : nt!MiModifiedPageWriter+0x1bb
```

```
fffff880`0312bd40 fffff800`028af486 : fffff800`02a49e80 fffffa80`0095fb60
fffff800`02a57c40 00000000`00000000 : nt!PspSystemThreadStartup+0x5a

fffff880`0312bd80 00000000`00000000 : fffff880`0312c000 fffff880`03126000
fffff880`0312ba80 00000000`00000000 : nt!KxStartSystemThread+0x16
```

Setting a breakpoint at *MiBuildPageFileCluster*+0x87c, which is the first return address on the stack, we catch the MPW on its way back to the caller:

```
Breakpoint 2 hit
nt!MiBuildPageFileCluster+0x87c:
fffff800`029a468c 4103dd              add       ebx,r13d
```

We can see that now the _MMPFN is unlocked (PteAddress has bit 0 clear) and still has WriteInProgress set. Other VMM components may access it, but they will know that the page has an I/O in progress.

```
0: kd> dt nt!_mmpfn u3.e1. PteAddress OriginalPte.u. fffffa8000167340
   +0x010 PteAddress      : 0xfffff680`0001de40 _MMPTE
   +0x018 u3              :
      +0x002 e1           :
         +0x000 PageLocation    : 0y110
         +0x000 WriteInProgress : 0y1
         +0x000 Modified        : 0y0
         +0x000 ReadInProgress  : 0y0
         +0x000 CacheAttribute  : 0y01
         +0x001 Priority        : 0y101
         +0x001 Rom             : 0y0
         +0x001 InPageError     : 0y0
         +0x001 KernelStack     : 0y0
         +0x001 RemovalRequested : 0y0
         +0x001 ParityError     : 0y0
   +0x020 OriginalPte     :
      +0x000 u             :
         +0x000 Long            : 0x31006`00000080
         +0x000 VolatileLong    : 0x31006`00000080
         +0x000 Hard            : _MMPTE_HARDWARE
         +0x000 Flush           : _HARDWARE_PTE
         +0x000 Proto           : _MMPTE_PROTOTYPE
         +0x000 Soft            : _MMPTE_SOFTWARE
         +0x000 TimeStamp       : _MMPTE_TIMESTAMP
         +0x000 Trans           : _MMPTE_TRANSITION
         +0x000 Subsect         : _MMPTE_SUBSECTION
         +0x000 List            : _MMPTE_LIST
```

By setting breakpoints on the return addresses on the stack, we eventually stop at *MiModifiedPageWriter*+0x1bb:

```
0: kd> !thread @$thread
THREAD fffffa800095fb60  Cid 0004.005c  Teb: 0000000000000000 Win32Thread:
0000000000000000 RUNNING on processor 0
IRP List:
```

```
    fffffa8002788010: (0006,03a0) Flags: 00060003  Mdl: fffffa80018c1078
Not impersonating
DeviceMap                 fffff8a000006090
Owning Process            fffffa80008da990        Image:        System
Attached Process          N/A              Image:        N/A
Wait Start TickCount      13500031         Ticks: 0
Context Switch Count      97646
UserTime                  00:00:00.000
KernelTime                00:01:33.031
Win32 Start Address nt!MiModifiedPageWriter (0xfffff800028699c0)
Stack Init fffff8800312bdb0 Current fffff8800312ba80
Base fffff8800312c000 Limit fffff88003126000 Call 0
Priority 17 BasePriority 8 UnusualBoost 0 ForegroundBoost 0 IoPriority 2 PagePriority 5
Child-SP          RetAddr          : Args to Child
: Call Site
fffff880`0312bce0 fffff800`02b74166 : fffffa80`0095fb60 00000000`00000000
00000000`00000080 00000000`00000001 : nt!MiModifiedPageWriter+0x1bb

fffff880`0312bd40 fffff800`028af486 : fffff800`02a49e80 fffffa80`0095fb60
fffff800`02a57c40 00000000`00000000 : nt!PspSystemThreadStartup+0x5a

fffff880`0312bd80 00000000`00000000 : fffff880`0312c000 fffff880`03126000
fffff880`0312ba80 00000000`00000000 : nt!KxStartSystemThread+0x16
```

When we are here, the _MMPFN still has WriteInProgress = 1 and is unlocked:

```
0: kd> dt nt!_mmpfn u3.e1. PteAddress OriginalPte.u. fffffa8000167340
   +0x010 PteAddress      : 0xfffff680`0001de40 _MMPTE
   +0x018 u3              :
      +0x002 e1           :
         +0x000 PageLocation    : 0y110
         +0x000 WriteInProgress : 0y1
         +0x000 Modified        : 0y0
         +0x000 ReadInProgress  : 0y0
         +0x000 CacheAttribute  : 0y01
         +0x001 Priority        : 0y101
         +0x001 Rom             : 0y0
         +0x001 InPageError     : 0y0
         +0x001 KernelStack     : 0y0
         +0x001 RemovalRequested : 0y0
         +0x001 ParityError     : 0y0
   +0x020 OriginalPte     :
      +0x000 u             :
         +0x000 Long        : 0x31006`00000080
         +0x000 VolatileLong : 0x31006`00000080
         +0x000 Hard        : _MMPTE_HARDWARE
         +0x000 Flush       : _HARDWARE_PTE
         +0x000 Proto       : _MMPTE_PROTOTYPE
         +0x000 Soft        : _MMPTE_SOFTWARE
         +0x000 TimeStamp   : _MMPTE_TIMESTAMP
         +0x000 Trans       : _MMPTE_TRANSITION
         +0x000 Subsect     : _MMPTE_SUBSECTION
         +0x000 List        : _MMPTE_LIST
```

The fact that the MPW has moved on and returned to its top level function while
WriteInProgress is still 1 tells us that the MPW issues an asynchronous I/O write and moves
on while the operation is in progress.

We can observe the write final steps by setting a breakpoint for write accesses to u3.e1 on
our _MMPFN instance, catching the MPW when it clears WriteInProgress. When the
breakpoint is hit, rbx is set to the _MMPFN address:

```
0: kd> r
rax=0000000000000001 rbx=ffffffa8000167340 rcx=fffffa8000167340
rdx=0000000000000000 rsi=fffffa80018c16f8 rdi=0000000000000000
rip=fffff80002907fb7 rsp=fffff8800312ae20 rbp=0000000000000001
 r8=0000000000000000  r9=0000000000000000 r10=0000000000000000
r11=fffff80002a85790 r12=0000000000000000 r13=0000000000000002
r14=0000000000000000 r15=0000000000000000
iopl=0         nv up ei pl nz na pe nc
cs=0010  ss=0018  ds=002b  es=002b  fs=0053  gs=002b        efl=00000202
nt!MiWriteCompletePfn+0x43:
fffff800`02907fb7 0fb74318        movzx   eax,word ptr [rbx+18h]
ds:002b:fffffa80`00167358=0002
```

The thread status is as follows:

```
0: kd> !thread @$thread
THREAD fffffa800095fb60  Cid 0004.005c  Teb: 0000000000000000 Win32Thread:
0000000000000000 RUNNING on processor 0
Not impersonating
DeviceMap               fffff8a000006090
Owning Process          fffffa80008da990      Image:        System
Attached Process        N/A            Image:        N/A
Wait Start TickCount    13500031       Ticks: 1 (0:00:00:00.015)
Context Switch Count    97646
UserTime                00:00:00.000
KernelTime              00:01:33.046
Win32 Start Address nt!MiModifiedPageWriter (0xfffff800028699c0)
Stack Init fffff8800312bdb0 Current fffff8800312ba80
Base fffff8800312c000 Limit fffff88003126000 Call 0
Priority 17 BasePriority 8 UnusualBoost 0 ForegroundBoost 0 IoPriority 2 PagePriority 5
Child-SP          RetAddr          : Args to Child
: Call Site
fffff880`0312ae20 fffff800`02908514 : 000228cc`00000001 00000000`00000000
00000000`00000000 00000000`00000000 : nt!MiWriteCompletePfn+0x43

fffff880`0312ae90 fffff800`028bae67 : fffffa80`018c1010 00000000`00000000
00000000`00000000 fffffa80`018c10a8 : nt!MiWriteComplete+0x1b4

fffff880`0312af50 fffff800`028ad92f : fffffa80`0095fb60 fffffa80`0095fbb0
fffff880`0312b301 fffff800`02817939 : nt!IopCompletePageWrite+0x57

fffff880`0312af80 fffff800`028adce7 : fffff880`0312b301 00000000`00000000
00000000`00000000 00000000`00000000 : nt!KiDeliverApc+0x1d7
```

```
fffff880`0312b000 fffff800`02975dbb : fffff880`0312bb20 00000000`00000000
00000000`00000001 00000000`00000000 : nt!KiApcInterrupt+0xd7 (TrapFrame @
fffff880`0312b000)

fffff880`0312b190 fffff800`02d545da : 00030010`00000000 75000029`00000001
850021c8`00000001 fffff880`0312b301 : nt!KeThawExecution+0x26b

fffff880`0312b210 fffff800`02935b01 : fffff880`0312b300 fffff880`0312baa8
fffff800`02a49e80 0053002b`002b0010 : nt!KdExitDebugger+0x7a

fffff880`0312b240 fffff800`02d5303f : fffff880`0312b300 fffff880`0312b800
fffff880`0312bb50 fffff800`02909ca1 : nt! ?? ::FNODOBFM::`string'+0x19491

fffff880`0312b280 fffff800`0290b1a6 : fffff880`0312baa8 fffff880`0312bb50
fffff880`0312bb50 fffffa80`018c1010 : nt!KdpTrap+0x2f

fffff880`0312b2d0 fffff800`028d0542 : fffff880`0312baa8 fffffa80`0095fb60
fffff880`0312bb50 fffffa80`008da990 : nt!KiDispatchException+0x126

fffff880`0312b970 fffff800`028ce374 : fffffa80`015ff900 fffffa80`01906070
fffffa80`015ff900 fffffa80`02788010 : nt!KiExceptionDispatch+0xc2

fffff880`0312bb50 fffff800`02869b7c : fffffa80`000310d0 fffff880`00000000
00000000`00031006 00000000`00000000 : nt!KiBreakpointTrap+0xf4 (TrapFrame @
fffff880`0312bb50)

fffff880`0312bce0 fffff800`02b74166 : fffffa80`0095fb60 00000000`00000000
00000000`00000080 00000000`00000001 : nt!MiModifiedPageWriter+0x1bc

fffff880`0312bd40 fffff800`028af486 : fffff800`02a49e80 fffffa80`0095fb60
fffff800`02a57c40 00000000`00000000 : nt!PspSystemThreadStartup+0x5a

fffff880`0312bd80 00000000`00000000 : fffff880`0312c000 fffff880`03126000
fffff880`0312ba80 00000000`00000000 : nt!KxStartSystemThread+0x16
```

The current thread is still 0xFFFFFA80`0095FB60, i.e. the MPW; it is not attached to the process anymore and is updating `WriteInProgress` from a function called by *KiDeliverApc*. This means the I/O completion is signaled by an APC, which is normal behavior for the I/O manager. Unfortunately, the call stack is a bit dirty, with a trap frame created by *KiBreakpointTrap*, which seems due to the debugger. This is probably caused by the write operation raising the APC interrupt before the debugger returns control from the previous breakpoint, so we see the APC interrupting while the thread context was being restored.

The `_MMPFN` now is locked again, because the MPW is in the process of updating it, and WriteInProgress is 0:

```
0: kd> dt nt!_mmpfn u3.e1. PteAddress OriginalPte.u. fffffa8000167340
   +0x010 PteAddress     : 0xfffff680`0001de41 _MMPTE
   +0x018 u3             :
      +0x002 e1          :
         +0x000 PageLocation   : 0y110
         +0x000 WriteInProgress : 0y0
```

```
            +0x000 Modified       : 0y0
            +0x000 ReadInProgress : 0y0
            +0x000 CacheAttribute : 0y01
            +0x001 Priority       : 0y101
            +0x001 Rom            : 0y0
            +0x001 InPageError    : 0y0
            +0x001 KernelStack    : 0y0
            +0x001 RemovalRequested : 0y0
            +0x001 ParityError    : 0y0
      +0x020 OriginalPte    :
         +0x000 u              :
            +0x000 Long         : 0x31006`00000080
            +0x000 VolatileLong : 0x31006`00000080
            +0x000 Hard         : _MMPTE_HARDWARE
            +0x000 Flush        : _HARDWARE_PTE
            +0x000 Proto        : _MMPTE_PROTOTYPE
            +0x000 Soft         : _MMPTE_SOFTWARE
            +0x000 TimeStamp    : _MMPTE_TIMESTAMP
            +0x000 Trans        : _MMPTE_TRANSITION
            +0x000 Subsect      : _MMPTE_SUBSECTION
            +0x000 List         : _MMPTE_LIST
```

If we stop along the return addresses saved on the stack, we see that, when we arrive at *IopCompletePageWrite*+0x57, the _MMPFN is unlocked:

```
nt!IopCompletePageWrite+0x57:
fffff800`028bae67 488b5c2430        mov       rbx,qword ptr [rsp+30h]

0: kd> dt nt!_mmpfn u3.e1. PteAddress OriginalPte.u. fffffa8000167340
   +0x010 PteAddress     : 0xfffff680`0001de40 _MMPTE
   +0x018 u3             :
      +0x002 e1              :
         +0x000 PageLocation   : 0y110
         +0x000 WriteInProgress : 0y0
         +0x000 Modified       : 0y0
         +0x000 ReadInProgress : 0y0
         +0x000 CacheAttribute : 0y01
         +0x001 Priority       : 0y101
         +0x001 Rom            : 0y0
         +0x001 InPageError    : 0y0
         +0x001 KernelStack    : 0y0
         +0x001 RemovalRequested : 0y0
         +0x001 ParityError    : 0y0
   +0x020 OriginalPte    :
      +0x000 u              :
         +0x000 Long         : 0x31006`00000080
         +0x000 VolatileLong : 0x31006`00000080
         +0x000 Hard         : _MMPTE_HARDWARE
         +0x000 Flush        : _HARDWARE_PTE
         +0x000 Proto        : _MMPTE_PROTOTYPE
         +0x000 Soft         : _MMPTE_SOFTWARE
         +0x000 TimeStamp    : _MMPTE_TIMESTAMP
         +0x000 Trans        : _MMPTE_TRANSITION
         +0x000 Subsect      : _MMPTE_SUBSECTION
         +0x000 List         : _MMPTE_LIST
```

We can see the final status of the PTE, but we have to set the process context to the svchost instance the MPW was originally attached to, because, by now, it has detached:

```
0: kd> .cache forcedecodeptes

Max cache size is       : 1048576 bytes (0x400 KB)
Total memory in cache   : 0 bytes (0 KB)
Number of regions cached: 0
0 full reads broken into 0 partial reads
    counts: 0 cached/0 uncached, 0.00% cached
    bytes : 0 cached/0 uncached, 0.00% cached
** Transition PTEs are implicitly decoded
** Virtual addresses are translated to physical addresses before access
** Prototype PTEs are implicitly decoded
0: kd> .process fffffa800248e1d0
Implicit process is now fffffa80`0248e1d0
0: kd> !pte 0xfffff680`0001de40
                        VA 0000000003bc8000
PXE @ FFFFF6FB7DBED000    PPE at FFFFF6FB7DA00000    PDE at FFFFF6FB400000E8    PTE at FFFFF6800001DE40
contains 02E000001B2CF867  contains 044000001B252867  contains 01D000000F277867  contains F3600000077BC805
pfn 1b2cf    ---DA--UWEV pfn 1b252    ---DA--UWEV pfn f277    ---DA--UWEV pfn 77bc    -------
UR-V
```

The PTE is unchanged.

In summary, we observed an active modified page being processed by the MPW, going into transition with `WriteInProgress` = 1 and ending up as a clean page, with its paging file offset saved into `OriginalPte`.

29.2.8   A Note on Concurrent Page Accesses While the Write Is in Progress

While the write I/O is in progress, everything else is still going on in the system, so other threads can reference the page being written to the paging file. This situation will be described in Chapter 32 (p. 241).

30   Standby Pages Repurposing

We saw in section 26.4.3.4.3 on p. 158 that a page can be taken from the standby list and reused to resolve a page fault from a different address space, a process called *repurposing*. By following the transitions a page goes through to get to the Standby state we have therefore covered its life cycle up to the point it can be reused.

Standby is not, however, a state in which pages simply awaits to be repurposed. Pages in this state can be *returned* to the address space they were removed from - what we call a soft fault. The next chapter will deal with this scenario as well as soft faults for Modified pages.

31   Soft Faults

In the previous chapters, we saw how a physical page is added to an address space for the first time; what happens when it is removed from it and enters the Modified state; how it is moved from Modified to Standby.

The next logical step in our analysis of the life cycle of a page is to describe what happens when a page is returned to an address space from the Standby and Modified states, an event called soft fault, because it begins as a page fault but is resolved without reading the paging file.

It's worth remembering that a PTE whose page has been moved into Standby or Modified still has the page PFN in bits 12-48, so the VMM can easily access the `_MMPFN` for the page.

31.1 Soft Fault from the Standby State

This state transition is represented by the thick arrow in the following figure:

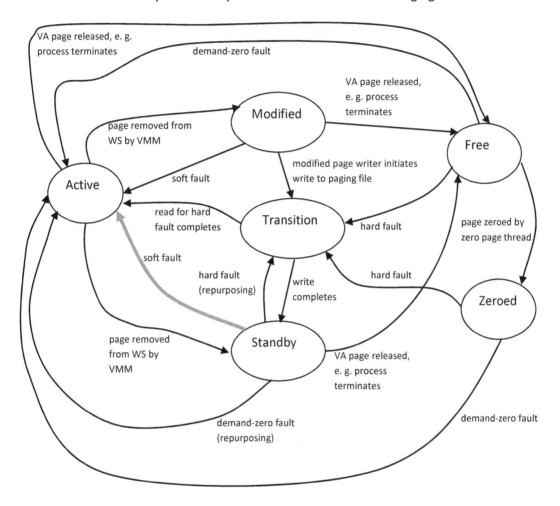

Figure 29 - Soft Fault from the Standby State

The fault can be caused by an attempt to read from or to write to the page, which results in different actions taken by the VMM.

31.1.1   Read Access

The VMM functions involved are *MmAccessFault*, *MiDispatchFault*, *MiResolveTransitionFault*, whose job is to:

- Unlink the _MMPFN from the Standby list

- Update the _MMPFN content to represent the page as being Active

- Update the PTE so that it maps the VA to the physical page

- Add an entry for the page to the working set list.

The final PTE value must be interpreted with the _MMPTE.u.Hard member, because it is a valid PTE, and it has:

> _MMPTE.u.Hard.Valid = **1**
> **_MMPTE.u.Hard.Dirty1 = 0**
> _MMPTE.u.Hard.Accessed = **1**
> **_MMPTE.u.Hard.Dirty = 0**
> **_MMPTE.u.Hard.Write = 1**

Dirty1, Dirty and Write have the same value we saw in sec. 29.2.7.1 on p. 225 for a *clean* page. This is something worth noting: when a page is faulted back from Standby *because of a read access*, it is clean, because a valid copy of it exists in the paging file. If the VMM decides to trim the working set, such a page can be removed from the address space (we will return on this in sec. 33.1 on p. 245) and placed directly into Standby, without going through Modified and without writing it again to the paging file. The clean page of sec. 29.2.7.1 had Accessed clear while here it is set, which is consistent with the fact that the page is being faulted back because an access to it has been attempted.

The final _MMPFN of the page has:

> _MMPFN.u1.WsIndex = **working set index entry**
> _MMPFN.u2.ShareCount = **1**
> _MMPFN.u3.ReferenceCount = **1**
> _MMPFN.u3.e1.PageLocation = **_MMLISTS.ActiveAndValid, i.e. 6**
> _MMPFN.u3.e1.Modified = **0, consistent with the page being clean.**
> _MMPFN.OriginalPte.u.Soft.Protection: **set to the VMM defined protection mask**

> `_MMPFN.OriginalPte.u.Soft.PageFileHigh` = offset in the paging file expressed in pages, i.e. 1 means 1 x 4096 bytes from byte 0.

It is interesting to observe how the offset in the paging file is retained in the `_MMPFN`, tracking where the page copy is and making it possible to move such a page directly to the Standby state. In contrast, a new page added to the working set by a demand-zero fault, is dirty and has `PageFileHigh` set to 0.

31.1.2 Write Access

When the faulting access is a memory write, it is handled in a similar fashion, but with a few important differences.

`_MMPFN.OriginalPte.u.Soft.PageFileHigh` is set to 0, which means the physical page is disassociated from its copy in the paging file, which is about to become out of date. Throwing away `PageFileHigh` means that the VMM does not even keep track of the copy position, i.e. the paging file slot for this page is freed. Further evidence of this behavior is a call from *MiResolveTransitionFault* to a function named *MiReleaseConfirmedPageFileSpace*, with `rcx` set to `OriginalPte` with the old value of `PageFileHigh`: possibly, this function updates the data structures keeping track of which parts of the paging file are in use.

The final PTE has:

> `_MMPTE.u.Hard.Valid` = 1
> **`_MMPTE.u.Hard.Dirty1`** = **1**
> `_MMPTE.u.Hard.Accessed` = 1
> **`_MMPTE.u.Hard.Dirty`** = **1**
> **`_MMPTE.u.Hard.Write`** = **1**

`Dirty1` = 1 means that the processor allows writes to the page, so there will be no page fault on a write and the VMM will not regain control. This is not a problem, because the VMM has already updated its data consistently with the page being dirty.

The final `_MMPFN` is similar to the read case with these differences:

> `_MMPFN.u3.e1.Modified` = 1
> `_MMPFN.OriginalPte.u.Soft.PageFileHigh` = 0

The PTE and the `_MMPFN` are set like in the demand-zero fault case: the page has lost its paging file copy, so it is as if it had just been allocated.

31.2 Soft Fault from the Modified State

This transition, which happens when a page on the Modified list is referenced before the Modified Page Writer writes its content into the paging file, is represented by the thick arrow in the diagram below:

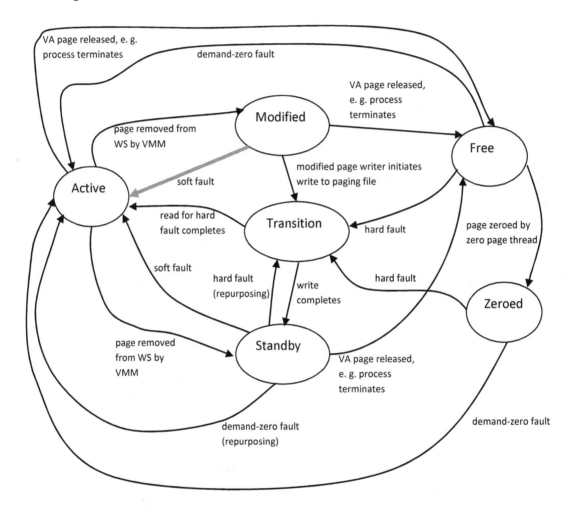

Figure 30 - Soft Fault from the Modified State

The actions taken are similar to the ones described in section 31.1.1 on p. 238; since the page was Modified, no paging file space had yet been assigned to it, so _MMPFN.OriginalPte.u.Soft.PageFileHigh was set to 0 when the fault occurred, and remains unchanged afterwards. The page becomes active, retaining its dirty state and the final PTE and _MMPFN are as follows:

_MMPTE.u.Hard.Valid = 1

_MMPTE.u.Hard.Dirty1 = 1

_MMPTE.u.Hard.Accessed = 1

_MMPTE.u.Hard.Dirty = 1

_MMPTE.u.Hard.Write = 1

_MMPFN.u1.WsIndex = working set index entry

_MMPFN.u2.ShareCount = 1

_MMPFN.u3.ReferenceCount = 1

_MMPFN.u3.e1.PageLocation = _MMLISTS.ActiveAndValid, i.e. 6

_MMPFN.u3.e1.Modified = 1, consistent with the page being dirty.

_MMPFN.OriginalPte.u.Soft.Protection: set to the VMM defined protection
     mask

_MMPFN.OriginalPte.u.Soft.PageFileHigh = 0

Also, *MiReleaseConfirmedPageFileSpace* is not called. The behavior is the same both for read and write accesses to the page. For a Standby page, a write required extra handling because the page changed from clean to dirty, but a Modified page is already dirty in the first place.

32   Access to a Page With a Write in Progress

Since writing a page to the paging file can take a while, it is possible for a thread to access a page for which a write is in progress, a fact which is also mentioned in [1] on p. 813, so we are now going to see how the VMM handles this case.

The main functions involved are *MiWriteComplete* and *MiWriteCompletePfn*, which are called by the APC triggered when the write completes. Regardless of whether the page has been reaccessed or not, *MiWriteCompletePfn* clears _MMPFN.u3.e1.WriteInProgress, which had been set by the Modified Page Writer at the beginning of the process.

32.1 Access to a Modified Page

32.1.1   Read Access

We can start by observing that a Modified page can be soft-faulted back to its address space regardless of the write in progress: since its content is still valid, there is no reason to keep the faulting thread waiting. The VMM will, however, do something different when the write will complete.

MiWriteCompletePfn looks at the page reference count (_MMPFN.u3.ReferenceCount) to check whether the page has been accessed. When the Modified Page Writer initiates the write, it increments the reference count. If the page has not been referenced by anyone else, the count is 1; if it has been mapped into an address space, the count becomes 2.

MiWriteCompletePfn decrements the reference count and chains the page to the Standby list only if it drops to 0, calling *MiPfnReferenceCountIsZero* to do the job. When this happens, `_MMPFN.u3.e1.PageLocation` is also set to `_MMLISTS.StandbyPageList`.

If, on the other hand, the final reference count is not 0, *MiWriteCompletePfn* skips the call to *MiPfnReferenceCountIsZero*, which means that the `_MMPFN` members used to link to a list (`u1`, `u2`) as well as `u3.e1.PageLocation` are left unchanged. It is interesting to note that these members must store values consistent with the page being mapped:

- `_MMPFN.u1.WsIndex` must be set to the WSL entry index

- `_MMPFN.u2.ShareCount` must be set to 1 (for private memory; we will discuss shared memory later)

- `_MPFN.u3.e1.PageLocation` must be set to `_MMLIST.ActiveAndValid`

These values are set by the VMM while it handles the soft fault which causes the page to be remapped and simply left unchanged when the write completes.

Furthermore, for a memory read access, the page copy into the paging file remains valid: the page is again mapped in an address space, but it is clean and the effort spent into writing it to the paging file is not wasted. *MiWriteCompletePfn* does not update `_MMPFN.OriginalPte.u.Soft.PagingFileHigh` were the paging file offset has been stored when the write was started.

32.1.2   Write Access

This situation must be handled differently, because the page copy in the paging file is no longer valid: there is no way to know if the write operation stored the page content before or after it was updated.

MiWriteComplete detects this situation because it finds `_MMPFN.u3.e1.Modified` set. We saw in the `_MMPFN` on p. 214 that this bit is found cleared inside *MiUpdatePfnBackingStore*, when the MPW is setting up the write operation; if it is later found set, it means that a fault for a write access to the page has been handled in the meantime. When this happens, *MiWriteComplete* calls *MiWriteCompletePfn* with the second parameter set to 2, which causes the latter function to call *MiReleaseConfirmedPageFileSpace* and set `_MMPFN.OriginalPte.u.Soft.PageFileHigh` to 0. This releases the paging file slot for the page and leaves the _MMPFN consistent with the page being dirty. In every other respect, *MiWriteCompletePfn* behaves as in the read access case.

The page fault handler sets _MMPFN.u3.e1.Modified when it detects a write access to the page, but cannot call *MiReleaseConfirmedPageFileSpace* because the write is still in progress, so this last step is left to the write completion code.

32.2 Access to an Active Page - One Reason Why Clean Pages Are Read-Only

We saw in sec. 29.2.7 on p. 225 that dirty pages can be written to the paging file while active, even if they have not been moved to the Modified list.

We can now understand better how the MPW manages to distinguish these writes from the ones for Modified pages: an Active page has the reference count set to 2 while the write is in progress and it drops to 1, instead of 0, when the write completes. *MiCompleteWritePfn* will not call *MiPfnReferenceCountIsZero* and the page will not be linked to the Standby list.

 These write operations face the same problem of the ones for Modified page, namely that the page can be accessed while the write is in progress.

A read access does not actually require any special handling: the written copy is valid and the page is left active and clean; this is the normal course of a write for an active page. The fact that the page may be read while this goes on is irrelevant.

A write access, however, must result in the paging file copy being discarded, just as it happens for a Modified page, so the VMM must be able to detect such an access. There is, however, a significant difference between this scenario and a Modified page: the PTE for the latter is not valid (P = 0), so *any* access to the page causes a page fault. This means the VMM takes control and can examine the fault error code, detect a write access and act accordingly.

On the other hand, an Active page has a *valid* PTE, so, in general, an access to the page does not cause a fault and the VMM has no way to take control of the situation. Here is where setting up the PTE for a clean page as read-only comes into play: a write to the page will cause a page fault, not because the PTE is not valid, but because, as far as the processor is concerned, the page cannot be written to.

We saw on p. 228 that the MPW clears _MMPTE.u.Hard.Dirty1, which is actually the processor R/W bit, early when setting up the page write, so while the write is in progress the page is already marked as read-only, a write access causes a fault and the VMM has the chance to set _MMPFN.u3.e1.Modified, which will inform *MiWriteComplete* that the MPW effort has been wasted and the write must be discarded. Note that we saw on p. 228 that `_MMPFN.u3.e1.Modified` is cleared while setting up the write, so *MiWriteComplete* will find it clear if the page is not written to.

33   Active Clean Page State Changes and PTE Dirty Bits

Having completed our analysis of how an active page becomes clean, we can now consider the transitions such a page can go through.

33.1 Clean Page Removal from a Working Set

A clean page can be removed from a WS just as a dirty one. This transition is represented by the thick arrow in the diagram below:

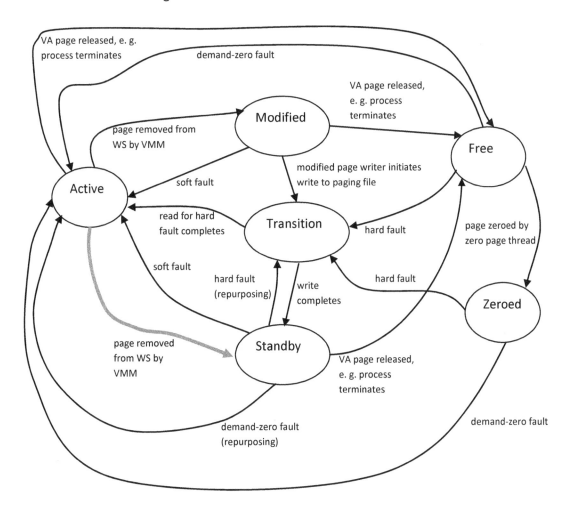

Figure 31 - Clean Page Removal from a Working Set

Compared to the removal a dirty page, the main difference is that the page goes straight into the Standby state.

We already saw in section 29.2.4 on p. 203 the PTE and the _MMPFN for a Standby page, which apply to this scenario also: the fact that the page did not go through the Modified state because it was clean while active does not make any difference.

33.2 Write to a Clean Active Page

A write access to a clean page makes the page dirty. We know by now that a clean page has a PTE with the processor R/W bit clear, marking it as read-only, therefore the write causes a page fault and the VMM intercepts it.

The main thing the VMM does is releasing the paging file copy of the page, since it is about to become invalid. This amounts to calling *MiReleaseConfirmedPageFileSpace* and setting `_MMPFN.OriginalPte.u.Soft.PageFileHigh` to 0. Afterwards, the VMM sets the PTE so that writes on the page are allowed and re-executes the faulting instruction.

We can observe the VMM at work performing these changes by allocating a block of memory, forcing the VMM to page it out by allocating other memory, then paging it back in by reading it. In this way, we end up with an active clean page and can see what happens when we write to it. Before performing the write, we set a breakpoint on writes to `_MMPFN.OriginalPte` and another one on *MiReleaseConfirmedPageFileSpace*, restricted to our test process (this function is executed by a lot of threads in the system). Then we attempt a write access to the page.

First, we see the test program hitting the breakpoint on writes to `_MMPFN.OriginalPte` and, by examining `_MMPFN`, we see that the `_MMPFN.OriginalPte.u.Soft.PageFileHigh` has just been set to 0. At this stage, the PTE is still read-only:

```
0: kd> !pte 5d0000
```

```
PXE at FFFFF6FB7DBED000    PPE at FFFFF6FB7DA00000    PDE at FFFFF6FB40000010    PTE at FFFFF68000002E80
contains 00C0000017471867   contains 0100000009C34867   contains 1150000006189867   contains DC800000105FD825
pfn 17471     ---DA--UWEV  pfn 9c34      ---DA--UWEV  pfn 6189      ---DA--UWEV  pfn 105fd      ----A--UR-V
```

Bits 0-11 of the PTE are set to 825, which corresponds to:

> 0y1000 0010 0101

the processor R/W bit is bit 1, which is still 0.

Afterwards, we hit the call to *MiReleaseConfirmedPageFileSpace*:

```
0: kd> !thread @$thread
THREAD fffffa80031f4060  Cid 0ba8.0a80  Teb: 000007fffffdd000 Win32Thread:
0000000000000000 RUNNING on processor 0
Not impersonating
DeviceMap                 fffff8a00113a310
Owning Process            fffffa800101e060       Image:         MemTests.EXE
Attached Process          N/A            Image:        N/A
```

```
Wait Start TickCount        6422019        Ticks: 6 (0:00:00.093)
Context Switch Count        17174
UserTime                    00:00:12.687
KernelTime                  00:00:06.765
Win32 Start Address MemTests!wmainCRTStartup (0x000000013f222f90)
Stack Init fffff88004b8adb0 Current fffff88004b8a7b0
Base fffff88004b8b000 Limit fffff88004b85000 Call 0
Priority 11 BasePriority 8 UnusualBoost 0 ForegroundBoost 2 IoPriority 2 PagePriority 5
Child-SP          RetAddr           : Args to Child
: Call Site
fffff880`04b8aab8 fffff800`02830140 : ffffffff`00000000 00000001`3f27e401
fffff880`04b8aca0 fffff800`0288afef : nt!MiReleaseConfirmedPageFileSpace

fffff880`04b8aac0 fffff800`02882fee : 00000000`00000001 00000000`00000000
00000000`001dbf01 fffffa80`00fdee60 : nt! ?? ::FNODOBFM::`string'+0x432d5

fffff880`04b8ac20 00000001`3f221402 : 00000001`3f27dad0 00000000`00000000
00000000`001dfc28 00000000`00000000 : nt!KiPageFault+0x16e (TrapFrame @
fffff880`04b8ac20)

00000000`001dfde0 00000001`3f27dad0 : 00000000`00000000 00000000`001dfc28
00000000`00000000 00000000`005d0000 : MemTests!PrvAllocTouchLoop+0x212
[d:\dati\bob\programm\memtests\memtests\main.cpp @ 284]

00000000`001dfde8 00000000`00000000 : 00000000`001dfc28 00000000`00000000
00000000`005d0000 0000000d`2bc00000 : MemTests!__xt_z+0x6f8
```

When control returns to the test program to retry the faulting write, the PTE has been updated so as to allow write access:

```
0: kd> !pte 5d0000
                                    VA 00000000005d0000
PXE at FFFFF6FB7DBED000   PPE at FFFFF6FB7DA00000   PDE at FFFFF6FB40000010   PTE at FFFFF68000002E80
contains 00C0000017471867  contains 0100000009C34867  contains 1150000006189867  contains DC800000105FD867
pfn 17471      ---DA--UWEV  pfn 9c34      ---DA--UWEV  pfn 6189      ---DA--UWEV  pfn 105fd      ---DA--UW-V
```

Bits 0-11:

   867 = 0y1000 0110 0111

This time, R/W = 1.

An interesting detail is that _MMPFN.u3.e1.Modified is left clear: since the page is dirty it would have seemed likely to find it set, but this is not the case. However, what matters is that the VMM must know that the page is dirty and must be written to disk before being reused; the VMM can infer this from:

- _MMPTE.OriginalPte.u.Soft.PageFileHigh being 0. This is a clear indication that no copy of the page exists

- The PTE having `_MMPTE.u.Hard.Dirty1` and `_MMPTE.u.Hard.Dirty` set.

33.3 Summary on PTE Dirty Bits Management

It is useful to summarize how the VMM sets the PTE of a page depending on its clean or dirty status.

First of all, a page is considered clean *only if a copy of its content exists in the paging file*.

The PTE for a *writable* clean page has:

- `_MMPTE.u.Hard.Dirty1` = 0. This is the processor R/W bit, so the page is actually read-only, as far as the processor is concerned.

- `_MMPTE.u.Hard.Dirty` = 0. This is the actual processor dirty bit.

- `_MMPTE.u.Hard.Write` = 1. This is bit 11 and is ignored by the processor. The VMM uses to track that the page is actually writable.

When the page is written to, a page fault occurs because R/W = 0. The VMM finds that `_MMPTE.u.Hard.Write` is set, meaning that a write is allowed, so it changes the page state to dirty and re-executes the faulting write.

The PTE for a dirty page has:

- `_MMPTE.u.Hard.Dirty1` = 1. This is what makes the page actually writable.

- `_MMPTE.u.Hard.Dirty` = 1. This is the actual processor dirty bit.

- `_MMPTE.u.Hard.Write` = 1 i.e. unchanged.

Once the PTE has R/W set, further writes to the page will not cause faults anymore. The VMM intercepts the first write in order to release the paging file allocation for the page, since its copy is no longer valid.

We also saw in sec. 32.2 on p. 243 how intercepting the first write access is used to handle active pages with an I/O write to the paging file in progress.

An actual *read-only* page has both `_MMPTE.u.Hard.Dirty1` and `_MMPTE.u.Hard.Write` clear. A write access results in a fault and the VMM, seeing the `Write` bit clear raises an exception to the faulting thread.

34   Hard Faults

In the previous chapters we followed the life cycle of a physical page, seeing how it is mapped into an address space, removed from it and written to the paging file, making it available for reuse.

We also saw how it can be mapped back by a soft fault before having been reused.

If, however, a page is reused or repurposed, the PTE that was mapping it stores an instance of `_MMPTE_SOFTWARE` with `PageFileHigh` set to the offset of the data in the paging file, expressed in pages, i.e. the byte offset is `PageFileHigh` x 0x1000.

When the VA is accessed, the VMM must read back the data from the paging file, or, as we will say, perform an in-paging I/O; this event is called an *hard fault* and is represented by the thick arrows in the following diagram; there are multiple possible paths as the physical page can come from different states:

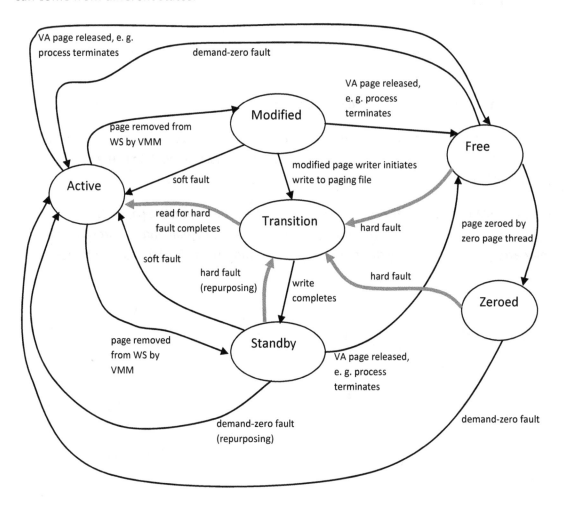

Figure 32 - Hard Fault

34.1 Clustering

34.1.1   Basic Concept

The VMM attempts to improve the efficiency of in-paging I/Os by reading paging file blocks bigger than a single page. When an hard fault occurs, the VMM attempts to read swapped out data for a few pages around the one where the fault occurred, counting on the fact that a process is likely to access more data at virtual addresses near the faulting one. Clustering is a form of prefetching, because it means reading data before it is actually needed, in an attempt to improve performances. We will therefore refer to the additional pages read as *prefetched* ones.

It is useful to define a *cluster* as a *group of contiguous PTEs*. Since there is a one-to-one correspondence between a PTE and the VA it maps, a cluster corresponds to a region of virtual addresses.

34.1.2   Determining the Cluster Boundaries

The clustering logic is implemented in a function named *MiResolvePageFileFault*. The VMM attempts to build a cluster made of the faulting PTE and of 15 more contiguous PTEs above it (that is at higher addresses). While doing this, it limits the cluster to PTEs stored in the same page table of the faulting one. Suppose, for instance that the PTE for the faulting address is the third to last of the page table, as in the following figure:

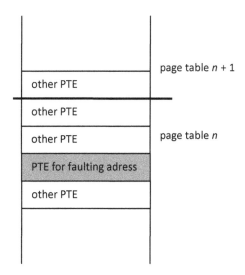

Figure 33 - Position of Faulting PTE vs. Page Table Boundary

In such a situation, the VMM includes in the cluster the 2 PTEs above the one of the fault and 13 PTEs *below* the latter, so that the cluster still spans 16 pages, but does not cross a page table boundary.

The reason for this behavior is probably that, at this stage, there is no guarantee that page table $n + 1$ is mapped in memory (paging structures are themselves pageable, as we will see in Chapter 36 - p. 288).

Another factor which determines the cluster boundaries are PTEs which cannot be updated by the clustered read. To understand why this happens, we must keep in mind that the purpose of the cluster is to read swapped out data from the paging file in a single operation and update the cluster PTEs making them point to the physical pages where the data has been loaded. The PTEs near the faulting one could be in such a state that reading content from the paging file is useless or even meaningless. In the following, we will refer to PTEs which cannot be updated as *excluded* from the cluster. The reasons for excluding a PTE from the cluster are given below.

- A valid PTE mapping a dirty page must be excluded, because, by design, the page has no copy in the paging file (see section 33.3 on p. 248), so there is nowhere to read it from.

- In general, *any* valid PTE is excluded, including the ones for clean pages, because it makes no sense to read data that is already in memory.

- A PTE must be excluded when it points to one of the transition lists, which again implies that there is already a copy of the page content in memory, so it is not read again. Note also that if the page is on the Modified list, it does not have a copy in the paging file.

- A PTE is excluded when it maps a virtual range which has not been reserved and committed, i.e. is completely invalid.

- While determining the cluster boundaries, *MiResolvePageFileFault* also excludes PTEs with _MMPTE_SOFTWARE.Protection different from the faulting one.

- Finally, the data position in the paging file may cause a PTE to be excluded. By design, the VMM reads a *contiguous* block of paging file during a clustered read, so PTEs pointing to other, scattered, positions in the file are excluded. This is depicted in the following figure:

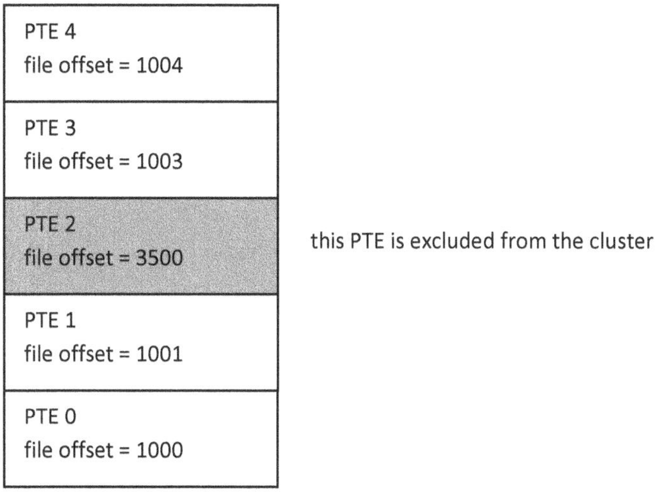

Figure 34 - Non-contiguous PTE Excluded from Cluster

PTE 2 (shaded) is excluded from the cluster, because of its paging file offset. Note however, that PTE 3 and PTE 4 will be part of the cluster, because, as we will see, the VMM uses a trick to "skip" excluded PTEs. Note also that, in order for PTE 3 to be included, its offset must be 1003, i.e. +3 from the offset of PTE 0. The VMM will point PTE 0 to the physical page loaded with the first 4 kB block of data read, PTE 1 to the second block read and so on. The data to which PTE 3 will point will be the one read at +3 x 4kB from the start (remember that offsets in PTEs are divide by 4k).

We can now understand that clustered reads have *two* goals: one is to prefetch pages around the one being faulted in, the other is to read contiguous *blocks* of data from the paging file, reducing latencies due to disk seek time. The VMM tries to accomplish this in spite of the fact that not all PTEs are updatable and that data may be scattered at non-contiguous positions. We saw in section 29.2.5 on p. 203 how the modified page writer strives to page out data into contiguous blocks of paging file, in order to support clustered in-paging.

When looking for the cluster boundaries, *MiResolvePageFileFault* scans 15 PTEs above the faulting one, or less, if the page table boundary is encountered. In the scanned range, excluded PTEs interspersed with includable ones become part of the cluster (they will be dealt with later); consider now the situation depicted in the following figure:

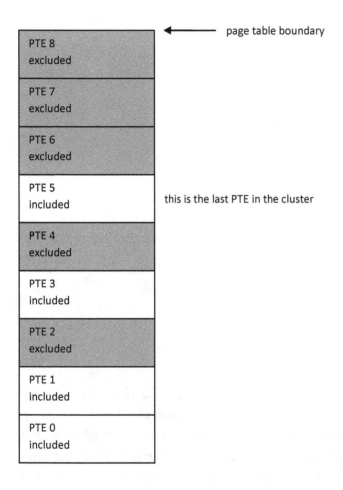

Figure 35 - Block of Excluded PTEs at Cluster End

In this example, the scan was limited to 9 PTEs by the PT boundary and the last three PTEs all have to be excluded (for any one of the reasons we saw). When *MiResolvePageFileFault* realizes this, it sets the cluster end at PTE 6. While there is a way to deal with excluded PTEs between included ones, it makes no sense to include in the cluster a tail of excluded PTEs.

If the upper boundary is such that the cluster spans less than 16 PTEs (counting the excluded ones mixed with included ones), *MiResolvePageFileFault* scans the PTEs *below* (meaning at lower addresses) the faulting one. If the cluster spans n PTEs above the faulting one, *MiResolvePageFileFault* scans 15 - n PTEs below (in the example above, it would scan 10 additional PTEs). Again, the scan stops earlier if the page table boundary is reached and a contiguous block of excluded PTEs at the cluster head is discarded. Given this logic, the final cluster might span less than 16 PTEs.

34.2 Allocating Physical Pages for the Read

34.2.1   List Search Order, Page Color and NUMA Support

Having set the cluster boundaries, *MiResolvePageFileFault* must allocate physical pages where the data read will ultimately be placed.

Allocation is attempted on the Free list first – a Zeroed page is not needed, because the page content will be overwritten by the read. The function looks into the singly linked list pointed by MiFreePageSlist first, then in the PFN linked one if the former is empty (the distinction between singly and PFN linked lists has been described in sec. 26.4.3 on p. 151). If the Free list is empty, it goes to the Zeroed list, then to the Standby list. See also sec. 26.4.3.4.3 on p. 158 for further details on allocating from the Standby list.

Since we are talking about *physical* pages, the VMM must account for page colors and NUMA nodes, as when a page is allocated for a demand-zero fault. The logic used is the same described in sec. 26.4 on p. 148; in particular, *MiResolvePageFileFault* goes through the same steps taken by *MiResolveDemandZeroFault* and described in sec. 26.4.2.1 on p. 151, to check whether a NUMA node was explicitly requested when the virtual memory range was allocated. In summary, the VMM uses the same logic to select the color and node, both when the physical page is being mapped for the first time and when it is being filled with content reloaded from the paging file.

34.2.2   Setting up the MDL

The Memory Descriptor List or MDL is a data structure passed to the I/O manager, to request the read of the paging file portion spanned by the offsets of the first and last cluster PTE. It includes an array storing the PFNs of the pages to be filled with the data read; the physical page selected by the first PFN is loaded with the first 4 kB of data and so on. When the read is started, the VMM updates the PTEs of the cluster with the PFNs from the array: the first PTE will have its PFN bits (i.e. bits 12-48) set to the first array element, etc.

MiResolvePageFileFault examines each PTE spanned by the cluster and, for included ones, allocates a physical page with the logic described in the previous section, storing the PFN in the corresponding array element.

Array elements corresponding to excluded PTEs are set to the PFN of a dummy page, whose content is ignored by the rest of the system. This is an actual physical page, which is used only to store useless data. When the read operation executes, data from the paging file portions corresponding to excluded PTEs will end up in this page, with each 4 kB block overwriting the previous content. This way, the I/O manager is still able to issue a single read operation for the file portion as a whole. Data blocks corresponding to excluded PTEs are lost in the single dummy page, but they were not going to be used anyway. When the VMM updates the PTEs with the PFNs from the array, it does not update PTEs whose corresponding array element stores the PFN of the dummy page; *this* is what preserves the excluded PTEs. For the more curious readers, the PFN of the dummy page is stored in MiDummyPage, which is referenced in *MiResolvePageFileFault* + 0xd9b.

34.3 Multiple Paging Files Support

34.3.1   Paging File Selection

So far, we have pretended that there was a single paging file, but this is not actually true, as multiple files (up to 16) can be configured on different logical discs. The modified page writer can therefore choose one of a set of paging files when writing a block of pages, but will have to store somewhere some information identifying which file has been selected.

We know by now that, when a page is written to a paging file, _MMPFN.OriginalPte is updated to record its position; more to the point, _MMPFN.OriginalPte.u.Soft.PageFileHigh is set to the file offset divided by 4 kB. Another member, _MMPFN.OriginalPte.u.Soft.PageFileLow records which file has been selected.

Paging files are identified by integer numbers, whose meaning is best explained after having introduced a few other data structures.

The static variable MmPagingFile is an array of pointers with one element for each paging file and with unused elements set to 0. Each element points to an instance of _MMPAGING_FILE. Below we can see these data structures for a system with 2 paging files:

```
0: kd> dq nt!MmPagingFile
fffff800`02a75440  fffffa80`02090d00 fffffa80`02043e10
fffff800`02a75450  00000000`00000000 00000000`00000000
fffff800`02a75460  00000000`00000000 00000000`00000000
fffff800`02a75470  00000000`00000000 00000000`00000000
fffff800`02a75480  00000000`00000000 00000000`00000000
fffff800`02a75490  00000000`00000000 00000000`00000000
fffff800`02a754a0  00000000`00000000 00000000`00000000
fffff800`02a754b0  00000000`00000000 00000000`00000000
```

Only the first two elements are different from 0. Below we interpret them as pointers to
_MMPAGING_FILE:

```
1: kd> dt nt!_MMPAGING_FILE @@masm(poi nt!MmPagingFile)
   +0x000 Size             : 0x1c400
   +0x008 MaximumSize      : 0x1f400
   +0x010 MinimumSize      : 0xc800
   +0x018 FreeSpace        : 0x172fe
   +0x020 PeakUsage        : 0x1f3ff
   +0x028 HighestPage      : 0
   +0x030 File             : 0xffffffa80`0209eaa0 _FILE_OBJECT
   +0x038 Entry            : [2] 0xffffffa80`020a2760 _MMMOD_WRITER_MDL_ENTRY
   +0x048 PageFileName     : _UNICODE_STRING "\??\C:\pagefile.sys"
   +0x058 Bitmap           : 0xffffffa80`020a3000 _RTL_BITMAP
   +0x060 EvictStoreBitmap : (null)
   +0x068 BitmapHint       : 0x9844
   +0x06c LastAllocationSize : 0x100
   +0x070 ToBeEvictedCount : 0
   +0x074 PageFileNumber   : 0y0000
   +0x074 BootPartition    : 0y1
   +0x074 Spare0           : 0y00000000000 (0)
   +0x076 AdriftMdls       : 0y0
   +0x076 Spare1           : 0y000000000000000 (0)
   +0x078 FileHandle       : 0xffffffff`80000240 Void
   +0x080 Lock             : 0
   +0x088 LockOwner        : 0xffffffa80`00cf71a1 _ETHREAD
1: kd> dt nt!_MMPAGING_FILE @@masm(poi(nt!MmPagingFile + 8))
   +0x000 Size             : 0x1f400
   +0x008 MaximumSize      : 0x1f400
   +0x010 MinimumSize      : 0xc800
   +0x018 FreeSpace        : 0x189a0
   +0x020 PeakUsage        : 0x1f3ff
   +0x028 HighestPage      : 0
   +0x030 File             : 0xffffffa80`020a2070 _FILE_OBJECT
   +0x038 Entry            : [2] 0xffffffa80`0218e010 _MMMOD_WRITER_MDL_ENTRY
   +0x048 PageFileName     : _UNICODE_STRING "\??\E:\pagefile.sys"
   +0x058 Bitmap           : 0xffffffa80`02194000 _RTL_BITMAP
   +0x060 EvictStoreBitmap : (null)
   +0x068 BitmapHint       : 0x15bf
   +0x06c LastAllocationSize : 0x100
   +0x070 ToBeEvictedCount : 0
   +0x074 PageFileNumber   : 0y0001
   +0x074 BootPartition    : 0y0
   +0x074 Spare0           : 0y00000000000 (0)
   +0x076 AdriftMdls       : 0y0
   +0x076 Spare1           : 0y000000000000000 (0)
   +0x078 FileHandle       : 0xffffffff`80000248 Void
   +0x080 Lock             : 0
   +0x088 LockOwner        : 0xffffffa80`032d2b61 _ETHREAD
```

We can see that the structure stores the file name in readable form, which, after a few hundreds of pages showing only hexadecimal data, is somehow refreshing.

We are now able to understand that `_MMPFN.OriginalPte.u.Soft.PageFileLow` stores the index for the paging file into the MmPagingFile array. This can be verified by intercepting an hard fault with the debugger. Here are a few excerpts from a debug session where MemTests.exe incurred an hard fault while trying to access address 0x570000. The first output has been obtained by setting a breakpoint on a read access to the PTE, which allows us to break into the VMM while the PTE is still pointing to the paging file:

```
1: kd> !pte 570000
                                     VA 0000000000570000

PXE at FFFFF6FB7DBED000   PPE at FFFFF6FB7DA00000   PDE at FFFFF6FB40000010   PTE at FFFFF68000002B80
contains 029000002E11C867  contains 02D000003B95F867  contains 0EB000000620C867  contains 00005E3E00000082
pfn 2e11c    ---DA--UWEV  pfn 3b95f    ---DA--UWEV  pfn 620c     ---DA--UWEV  not valid
                                                                              PageFile: 1
                                                                              Offset: 5e3e
                                                                              Protect: 4 - ReadWrite
```

Note how the !pte extension goes as far as displaying `PageFile: 1`. The PTE value 0x00005E3E00000082 corresponds to `_MMPTE.u.Soft.PageFileLow = 1`.

Here is where the VMM has been stopped:

```
1: kd> !Thread @$thread
THREAD fffffa8000e56830  Cid 06a4.0250  Teb: 000007fffffde000 Win32Thread:
0000000000000000 RUNNING on processor 1
Not impersonating
DeviceMap                 fffff8a00113a310
Owning Process            fffffa8000ec3060       Image:        MemTests.EXE
Attached Process          N/A         Image:     N/A
Wait Start TickCount      131828      Ticks: 0
Context Switch Count      11522
UserTime                  00:00:00.265
KernelTime                00:00:03.546
Win32 Start Address 0x000000013f182e90
Stack Init fffff880029afdb0 Current fffff880029af690
Base fffff880029b0000 Limit fffff880029aa000 Call 0
Priority 11 BasePriority 8 UnusualBoost 0 ForegroundBoost 2 IoPriority 2 PagePriority 5
Child-SP          RetAddr         : Args to Child
: Call Site
fffff880`029afac0 fffff800`02882fee : 00000000`00000000 00000000`00000000
00000000`001ebc01 fffffa80`02f32af0 : nt!MmAccessFault+0x1ef

fffff880`029afc20 00000001`3f18134b : 00000001`3f1dda40 00000000`00000000
00000000`001ef968 00000000`00000000 : nt!KiPageFault+0x16e (TrapFrame @
fffff880`029afc20)

00000000`001efb20 00000001`3f1dda40 : 00000000`00000000 00000000`001ef968
00000000`00000000 00000000`00570000 : 0x1`3f18134b

00000000`001efb28 00000000`00000000 : 00000000`001ef968 00000000`00000000
00000000`00570000 0000000d`0c800000 : 0x1`3f1dda40
```

Next, we are going to verify that the read operation will target the file pointed by MmPagingFile[1]. In order to do this, we set a breakpoint on *IoPageRead* for the current process only. This function is called to initiate the read with `rcx` set to the address of the `_FILE_OBJECT` of the file to read. The `_FILE_OBJECT` structure must not be confused with `_MMPAGING_FILE`: they are different types, however `_MMPAGING_FILE.File` stores the address of the `_FILE_OBJECT` for the file, i.e. the address passed to *IoPageRead*.

```
1: kd> bp /p @$proc nt!IoPageRead
1: kd> g
Breakpoint 2 hit
nt!IoPageRead:
fffff800`02876800 fff3              push    rbx
1: kd> r
rax=fffff98000000000 rbx=fffffa800312b2c0 rcx=fffffa8002087f21
rdx=fffffa800312b330 rsi=fffffa8000e56830 rdi=fffffa800312b270
rip=fffff80002876800 rsp=fffff880029af9e8 rbp=fffff880029afa60
 r8=fffffa800312b2d0  r9=fffffa800312b290 r10=0000000000c9d512
r11=00000000c0033333 r12=fffffa800312b290 r13=0000000000000000
r14=fffffa8000ec33f8 r15=fffffa8002087f21
iopl=0         nv up ei pl zr na po nc
cs=0010  ss=0018  ds=002b  es=002b  fs=0053  gs=002b         efl=00000246
nt!IoPageRead:
fffff800`02876800 fff3              push    rbx
```

Now, since `PageFileLow` was set to 1, we are going to compare `rcx` with the `_FILE_OBJECT` for the file with index 1:

```
1: kd> dt nt!_mmpaging_file @@masm(poi (nt!MmPagingFile + 8))
   ...
   +0x030 File              : 0xfffffa80`02087f20 _FILE_OBJECT
   +0x038 Entry             : [2] 0xfffffa80`02085010 _MMMOD_WRITER_MDL_ENTRY
   +0x048 PageFileName      : _UNICODE_STRING "\??\E:\pagefile.sys"
```

The two values are not exactly equal: the only difference is bit 0, which is set into `rcx` and clear in the `File` member. We can verify that this is always the case by performing the test again, so we can presume that `_FILE_OBJECT` is aligned so that bit 0 is always clear (actually, we can observe it aligned on 8 byte boundaries, so bits 0-3 are all clear) and the VMM uses it as an additional flag for some purpose. "Overloading" bits of aligned pointers in this way is a trick found often in VMM code.

Leaving bit 0 aside, this test confirms that the in-paging for `PageFileLow` = 1 targets MmPagingFile[1].

`PageFileLow` is 4 bits wide, so it allows for up to 16 paging files to be addressed.

Below we can see the thread call stack at the beginning of *IoPageRead*:

```
1: kd> !thread @$thread
```

```
THREAD fffffa8000e56830  Cid 06a4.0250  Teb: 000007fffffde000 Win32Thread:
0000000000000000 RUNNING on processor 1
Not impersonating
DeviceMap               fffff8a00113a310
Owning Process          fffffa8000ec3060      Image:        MemTests.EXE
Attached Process        N/A          Image:        N/A
Wait Start TickCount    131828       Ticks: 1 (0:00:00:00.015)
Context Switch Count    11522
UserTime                00:00:00.265
KernelTime              00:00:03.562
Win32 Start Address 0x000000013f182e90
Stack Init fffff880029afdb0 Current fffff880029af690
Base fffff880029b0000 Limit fffff880029aa000 Call 0
Priority 11 BasePriority 8 UnusualBoost 0 ForegroundBoost 2 IoPriority 2 PagePriority 5
Child-SP          RetAddr         : Args to Child
: Call Site
fffff880`029af9e8 fffff800`02876d55 : 00000000`00000000 00000000`00000000
fffffa80`0312b270 00000000`00000000 : nt!IoPageRead

fffff880`029af9f0 fffff800`028a009b : 00000000`00000000 00000000`00000000
ffffffff`ffffffff fffff880`00000000 : nt!MiIssueHardFault+0x255

fffff880`029afac0 fffff800`02882fee : 00000000`00000000 00000000`00000000
00000000`001ebc01 fffffa80`02f32af0 : nt!MmAccessFault+0x14bb

fffff880`029afc20 00000001`3f18134b : 00000001`3f1dda40 00000000`00000000
00000000`001ef968 00000000`00000000 : nt!KiPageFault+0x16e (TrapFrame @
fffff880`029afc20)

00000000`001efb20 00000001`3f1dda40 : 00000000`00000000 00000000`001ef968
00000000`00000000 00000000`00570000 : 0x1`3f18134b

00000000`001efb28 00000000`00000000 : 00000000`001ef968 00000000`00000000
00000000`00570000 0000000d`0c800000 : 0x1`3f1dda40
```

34.3.2   Paging Files Configuration

As explained in [1] on p. 780, the list of paging files configured on the system is stored in the registry value HKLM\SYSTEM\CurrentControlSet\Control\Session Manager\Memory Management\PagingFiles, which contains the name, minimum size, and maximum size of each paging file.

If the minimum and maximum sizes are set to 0 in the registry key, the default values of the following table are used:

Physical Memory Size	Paging File Minimum	Paging File Maximum
< 1 GB	1.5 x phys. mem. size	3 x phys. mem. size
>= 1 GB	1 x phys. mem. size	3 x phys. mem. size

It is also possible to configure Windows to delete the paging files on shutdown, which could be desirable for privacy reasons, since they store whatever had been outpaged by the MPW while the system was running. Setting the registry value HKLM\SYSTEM\CurrentControlSet\Control\Session Manager\Memory Management\ClearPageFileAtShutdown to 1 activates this feature.

34.4 State While the Read Is in Progress

34.4.1   Faulting Thread State

The faulting thread waits for the read to complete: since it needs the page content to resume its execution, there is not much it can do in the meanwhile. Note the difference with outpaging performed by the Modified Page Writer (sec. 29.2.3 on p. 201), which issues an asynchronous write and goes on about its business.

The VMM stores into _MMPFN.u1.Event the address of an event which is signaled when the read is complete.

We can catch the thread before it begins to wait by setting a breakpoint on *MiWaitForInPageComplete*+0xbd, which is where *KeWaitForSingleObject* is called. By doing this, we are able to observe the state of the PTEs and the _MMPFNs described in the next sections. Below is an example of call stack when the breakpoint is hit:

```
1: kd> kn
 # Child-SP          RetAddr           Call Site
00 fffff880`04bf5910 fffff800`028b1d8b nt!MiWaitForInPageComplete+0xbd
01 fffff880`04bf59f0 fffff800`028db09b nt!MiIssueHardFault+0x28b
02 fffff880`04bf5ac0 fffff800`028bdfee nt!MmAccessFault+0x14bb
03 fffff880`04bf5c20 00000001`3f7c140c nt!KiPageFault+0x16e
04 00000000`0012fbb0 00000001`3f81dae8 MemTests!PrvAllocTouchLoop+0x21c
[d:\dati\bob\programm\memtests\memtests\main.cpp @ 288]
05 00000000`0012fbb8 00000000`00000000 MemTests!__xt_z+0x710

1: kd> lsa MemTests!PrvAllocTouchLoop+0x21c
   284:                            *lpTouch = 1;
   285:                  } else {
   286:
   287:                          // read memory
 > 288:                          dummyByte = *lpTouch;
   289:                  }
   290:              }
   291:
```

34.4.2   PTEs State

Each PTE in the cluster is set as if it were pointing to a page on a transition list. By interpreting the content as an instance of `_MMPTE_TRANSITION`, we see that they are set as follows:

`Valid:`	0
`Protection:`	software protection value. This member has the same value it had before the fault, when the PTE pointed to the swapped out data.
`Transition:`	1. This, together with `Valid` = 0 identifies the PTE as a transition one.
`PageFrameNumber:`	PFN of the page allocated in the previous steps

Thus, as far as the PTE are concerned, it is as if the pages were on the Standby or Modified list. The `_MMPFN`s, however record the fact that there is a read in progress for each page.

34.4.3   _MMPFN State

The `_MMPFN` of each page is set as follows:

`u1.Event:`	address of the event which is signaled when the read is complete. All the `_MMPFN`s involved in a clustered read point to the same event and this pointer is passed into `rcx` in the call to *KeWaitForSingleObject* at *MiWaitForInPageComplete*+0xbd.
`u2.ShareCount:`	0. This accounts for the fact that the page is not yet mapped to a virtual address.
`u3.ReferenceCont:`	1. Accounts for the read in progress: the I/O manager and the file system driver are referencing the page.
`u3.e1.PageLocation:`	`_MMLISTS.StandbyPageList`. Note how the `_MMPFN` is "predisposed" to become part of the Standby list. The reason for this will be explained soon.
`u3.e1.ReadInProgress:`	1. *This* is what tracks the fact that a read is in progress.

OriginalPte: set to the `value` the PTE had when the fault occurred. This is the instance of `_MMPTE_SOFTWARE` storing the software protection and the paging file information (file number and offset). We will return on this member when describing the final `_MMPFN` state in the next section.

34.5 State When the Read Is Complete

34.5.1   State of the Faulting Virtual Page

We use the term faulting virtual page for the one including the address where the hard fault occurred. This page is obviously mapped to the corresponding physical page allocated when the cluster was built, so that the memory access can be resumed. The PTE becomes a valid one and the `_MMPFN` is set as appropriate for an active page.

If the fault occurred while trying to read from memory, the page is clean, so the PTE has `Dirty1` bit clear and `OriginalPte` in the `_MMPFN` still stores the location of the page content into the paging files (i.e. file number and offset). As usual, as long as a page is in this state, it can be moved to the Standby list, because its content is safely stored in the paging file.

If the fault happened while attempting a memory write, the page is set up as dirty as part of the fault handling. The paging file information is removed from `OriginalPte`, which implies that *MiReleaseConfirmedPageFileSpace* must be called.

It is worth noting how the final setup of the PTE and the `_MMPFN` is very similar to the one for a soft fault.

Naturally, `_MMPFN` also has u3.e1.ReadInProgress clear.

34.5.2   State of Prefetched Virtual Pages

These pages are the ones mapped by PTEs included in the cluster (excluding the faulting virtual page), which are left exactly as they were when the read operation started. These PTEs were set as if they were pointing to a page on one of the transition lists; after the read is completed, the `_MMPFN` for their physical pages are left in the Standby state, so the PTEs and `_MMPFN`s are consistent. This approach has some interesting implications.

First of all, an eventual access to a prefetched virtual page results in a soft fault, which is quickly resolved without further I/O. Thus, if the program accesses pages around the faulting one, we have the benefits of prefetching.

At the same time, leaving the physical pages in the Standby list makes them available for reuse. We know by now that the VMM uses Standby pages when there are no Zeroed or Free ones, because pages in this state have, by design, a copy of their content in the paging file. Of course, since these physical pages have just been read without even having been accessed, they fit the bill perfectly.

Finally, since the PTEs are left in transition, they have the P bit clear, which guarantees that *no* processor in the system has cached them in its TLB. This way, if these pages are repurposed, e. g. to satisfy a fault from some other address space, there is no need to flush any TLBs. This is not different from what happens when *any* Standby page is repurposed: pages which were trimmed from working sets are not cached in TLBs anymore, because the buffers are invalidated when the page changes state. This makes the Standby state especially well suited for clustered-read physical pages, which have been preloaded without actually having been accessed.

In summary, placing all the preloaded physical pages into Standby gives the benefits of prefetching and of reading the paging file in blocks larger than a single page, while, at the same time, leaving the physical memory available for reuse and without polluting the TLBs – quite a win-win combination.

This approach is based on the notion that free physical memory is actually *wasted* memory. Instead of having a heap of unused memory filled with garbage or zeroes, it is better to preload it in an attempt to anticipate hard faults before they happen.

The _MMPFN of the preloaded physical pages are only updated to place them into full-fledged Standby state:

- u1.Flink is used to chain the instance in the list. Previously, u1.Event (which overlaps with u1.Flink) held the pointer to the event for the read.

- u2.Blink, which was set to 0 while the read was in progress, chains the instance into the list as well.

- u3.e1.ReadInProgress is cleared.

Of course, among the members which are not modified is OriginalPte, which points to the paging file copy of the content, as for any other Standby page.

34.6 State of Excluded Virtual Pages

As already mentioned, excluded PTEs can be recognized by the presence of the dummy page PFN in the corresponding MDL element and are left unchanged when the read is initiated. Of course, they are not modified when the read is complete as well, so they are unaffected by the clustered read, while the file data is lost in dummy page.

35   In-paging Collisions

35.1 In-paging Collision Concept

At the time the VMM determines that a hard fault occurred, it is still exclusively holding the WS pushlock. Before entering the wait for the in-paging read to complete, the VMM releases the pushlock, so that other threads in the same address space can freely execute VMM code (e. g. a thread calling *VirtualAllocEx* or another thread encountering a page fault). This makes it possible for other threads to change the portion of virtual address space involved in the in-paging being performed, an event which we will name *in-paging collision*.

The following kinds of in-paging collisions are possible:

- Collided protection change: the protection of the page being read is changed (e.g. from read/write to read only).

- Collided memory release or decommit: the virtual region which includes the page being read is released; the virtual page being read is decommitted.

  Note: the *VirtualFreeEx* API only allows to release a range which has been previously reserved (and eventually committed) as a whole: the entire reserved range must be released. It is not possible to, say, release (i.e. decommit and "dereserve") a single page of the range. When a range is released it is neither reserved nor committed. On the other hand, it is possible to decommit subranges and even single pages of a previously reserved range; the subrange remains reserved, but is not committed anymore. This probably means that releasing virtual memory amounts to throwing away the VAD for the whole range, while decommitting subranges means setting their PTEs to decommitted (see sec. 20.1.2 on p. 103).

- Collided page fault: another thread tries to touch the virtual page being read, resulting in another page fault for the same virtual page.

  Furthermore, since the VMM implements clustering, for each of the collision types above, the page involved can be the one actually needed to resolve the fault or another page of the cluster for which in-paging is in progress. Multiple collisions on different pages of the cluster being read are also possible.

35.2 Collided Protection Change

35.2.1   Collision on the faulting PTE

We saw in section 34.4.2 on p. 262 that, while the read is in progress, the PTE is in transition. A call to *VirtualProtectEx* changing the page protection sets `_MMPTE.u.Trans.Protection` to the new value without changing other members, sot the PTE is still in transition and still pointing to the same physical page.

This kind of collision is detected inside *MiWaitForInPageComplete*, where the VMM waits for the read to complete. After the wait, this function acquires again the WS pushlock and calls *MiIsFaultPteIntact*, to check whether the PTE involved in the fault (and the rest of the paging structure hierarchy) have changed; this detects the protection change.

In this scenario, *MiWaitForInPageComplete* returns STATUS_PTE_CHANGED, which has two effects: the VMM leaves the PTE unchanged, i.e. in transition, and adds the `_MMPFN` to the Standby list. Afterwards, the VMM resumes the faulting instruction, which will cause yet another fault; the VMM checks that the attempted access is allowed under the protection stored in the PTE and, if this is the case, resolves the fault as a soft one, since now the page is in Standby. If the new protection forbids the attempted access, an access violation exception is raised.

The logic above means that the VMM resolves this kind of collision by re-evalutaing the fault with the new protection.

When the second fault is processed, the VMM does not initiate a read operation, so it keeps the WS pushlock acquired until it has finished updating the PTE making it valid.

35.2.2   Collision on a prefeteched PTE

This scenario occurs when the protection of a PTE being prefetched by a clustered read is changed. This simply results in `_MMPTE.u.Trans.Protection` being set to the new value. At the end of the read, the PTE will be left in transition and the page in Standby, as is the case when no collision occurs. If the prefetched page is later accessed, the soft fault will be handled according to the new protection in the PTE.

35.3 Collided Release and Decommit

35.3.1   Release or Decommit of the Faulting Page

In this scenario, the page being read is released or decommitted while the read is in progress. The behavior described here has been observed by calling *VirtualFreeEx* while the read was in progress.

When the API call returns, the PTE is set to 0, if the call parameters specified to release the memory range, or to 0x200 if the page was only being decommitted. This value corresponds to an _MMPTE_SOFTWARE with Protection = 0x10, which WinDbg translates as Decommitted, as in the following example:

```
1: kd> !pte 700000
                                     VA 0000000000700000

PXE at FFFFF6FB7DBED000   PPE at FFFFF6FB7DA00000   PDE at FFFFF6FB40000018   PTE at FFFFF68000003800
contains 03A00000014E2867  contains 02F0000001EA5867  contains 1C20000016E93867  contains 0000000000000200
pfn 14e2    ---DA--UWEV  pfn 1ea5    ---DA--UWEV  pfn 16e93   ---DA--UWEV  not valid
                                                                            PageFile:  0
                                                                            Offset:  0
                                                                            Protect: 10 - Decommitted
```

Before the call, the PTE was in transition and pointing to the physical page; after the call, the _MMPFN of the page has bit 1 of the PteAddress member set. This bit is always 0 in the actual address, because PTEs are 8-bytes aligned, so it doubles as a flag. When it is set, it indicates that this page is to be returned to the Free list after the read is complete. *MiWaitForInPageComplete* checks this bit when the event used to wait for the read data is signaled and acts accordingly, discarding the read data since the virtual page has been released or decommitted.

When the read is in-progress, the call stack is as follows:

```
fffff880`04d086a0 fffff800`028c8052 nt!KiSwapContext+0x7a
fffff880`04d087e0 fffff800`028ca1af nt!KiCommitThreadWait+0x1d2
fffff880`04d08870 fffff800`028b1cd2 nt!KeWaitForSingleObject+0x19f
fffff880`04d08910 fffff800`028b2d8b nt!MiWaitForInPageComplete+0xc2
fffff880`04d089f0 fffff800`028dc09b nt!MiIssueHardFault+0x28b
fffff880`04d08ac0 fffff800`028befee nt!MmAccessFault+0x14bb
fffff880`04d08c20 00000001`3f271758 nt!KiPageFault+0x16e
00000000`0042f8f0 00000001`3f2cd400 MemColls!AccessMemory+0xc8
[b:\programm\memtests\memcolls\main.cpp @ 194]
```

MemColls is the test program used in this analysis. For this kind of collision, *MiIssueHardFault* returns STATUS_PTE_CHANGED and, afterwards, *MmAccessFault* returns STATUS_SUCCESS, which tells *KiPageFault* to restore the context at the time of the fault and retry the faulting instruction. This will cause another page fault since the PTE is either 0 or 0x200 and this time the VMM will detect the access is for an invalid address and *MmAccessFault* will return `STATUS_ACCESS_VIOLATION`. *KiPageFault* will raise an exception in user mode which, unless catched by a __try/__except block will crash the process, deservingly so, because a program which releases memory without bothering to check whether one of its threads is still accessing it is asking for trouble.

35.3.2   Release or Decommit of Prefetched Pages

This event is similar to the one of the previous section (like before, the analysis has been conducted by calling *VirtualFreeEx*): a clustered read is in progress and one of the pages being prefetched is decommitted or the whole range they are part of is released.

When a page is decommitted, its PTE is set to 0x200 (`_MMPTE_SOFTWARE.Protection` = 0x10 = Decommitted); when a page is released its PTE is zeroed.

The `_MMPFN` for which the read is in progress has bit 1 of `PteAddress` set, which will cause the page to be returned to the Free list when the read completes.

35.4 Collided Page Faults

35.4.1   Initial Handling and the Support Block

This is perhaps the most complex kind of in-paging collision, because it involves concurrent accesses to the pages being read. A collided page fault is initially seen as a soft fault by the VMM code, because, while the read is in progress, the PTE is set up exactly as if the page were on the Standby or Modified list: it has `_MMPTE.u.Trans.Transition` set, `PageFrameNumber` stores the PFN of the physical page and the other members are set according to the page protection and caching policy.

The VMM detects the collision when it finds out that the relevant `_MMPFN` instance has `u3.e1.ReadInProgress` set.

To understand how collided page faults are handled, we need to add a few details on a data structure the VMM uses for in-paging. We already know that `_MMPFN.u1.Event` stores the address of an event which is signaled when the read completes. This event is part of a data structure storing other variables used during the in-paging. When the VMM is handling an hard fault, it allocates an instance of this data structure by calling *MiGetInPageSupportBlock*, so we will name this structure the *support block*. Unfortunately, there does not seem to be a declaration for this data structure among the public symbols of Windows, so we are going to provide a partial listing here:

```
@#@IN_PAGE_SUPPORT_BLOCK

...
+8h             Thread                  : Ptr32 _KTHREAD
+10h            ListEntry               : _LIST_ENTRY
+20h            Event1                  : _KEVENT
+38h            Event2                  : _KEVENT
...
+0x090          Unk-90                  : Uint1B
...
+0xb8           Unk-b8                  : Uint1B
...
+0x0c0          Mdl                     : _MDL
+0x0f0 PfnArray             : Uint8B [???]
+???            PmasterBlock            : Ptr64 @#@IN_PAGE_SUPPORT_BLOCK
```

The listing above mimics the output of WinDbg's dt command and the type name is prefixed with "@#@" to remark that this is not an actual declaration found among the actual symbols of Windows. We will explain the usage of the members above while describing the handling of collided page faults.

For starters, it is important to know that _MMPFN.u1.Event points to Event1 inside the @#@IN_PAGE_SUPPORT_BLOCK instance allocated to resolve the hard fault, so the VMM can get from the _MMPFN to the @#@IN_PAGE_SUPPORT_BLOCK.

The PfnArray member is an array storing the PFNs of the physical pages where the data read from the paging file will be loaded. They are the physical pages pointed by the PTEs of the cluster being in-paged.

The VMM can deal with a collided page fault in two different ways: it can make the second faulting thread wait for the read initiated by the first one to finish, or it can start a second read operation for the same virtual memory content in the second thread. We can refer to the first approach as *synchronous handling*, since the second thread synchronizes with the first, and, therefore, we will label the second strategy *asynchronous handling*.

 In the next sections we will describe this logic in greater detail and we will see why the VMM may choose to handle a collision asynchronously.

35.4.2   Synchronous Handling

35.4.2.1   Collisions on the Same Faulting PTE

The VMM code executed by the second faulting thread gets from the faulting PTE to the _MMPFN (the PTE is in transition, so it includes the PFN) and from the _MMPFN to the

@#@IN_PAGE_SUPPORT_BLOCK. It then increments a counter in the support block and waits for @#@IN_PAGE_SUPPORT_BLOCK.Event2 to become signaled.

Meanwhile, the first faulting thread is waiting on @#@IN_PAGE_SUPPORT_BLOCK.Event1 (pointed by _MMPFN.u1.Event), which is signaled by the I/O manager when the read operation completes. Event2 is not signaled directly by the I/O manager, so the first faulting thread is always the first one to resume execution.

There can be any number of collided threads waiting on Event2, each one of them trying to resolve a fault on the page being read (we will describe collisions on other PTEs in the cluster in the next section).

When Event1 is signaled, the VMM exclusively acquires the WS pushlock and sets up the _MMPFN for the Active state. Then it checks the counter in the support block incremented by colliding threads and, when it finds it to be greater than zero, signals Event2. This will awake all the collided threads, however the VMM code executed by them tries to acquire the WS pushlock, so they block again.

While holding on to the pushlock, the first thread updates the page PTE changing it into a valid one mapping the VA to the physical page just read. It then releases the pushlock and resumes the faulting instruction so that user mode code can go on about its business.

The collided threads acquire the WS pushlock (one at a time) and detect that the PTE has changed, so they don't try to update it and simply resume their faulting instruction which will succeed since the PTE is now valid.

Each collided thread decrements the counter in the support block; the thread which detects to be the last one using the support block releases it.

35.4.2.2   Collisions on Other PTEs in the Cluster

This scenario is not too different from the one of the previous section: while the read is in progress all the PTEs of the cluster are in transition and the _MMPFNs they point to are marked as having a read in progress. At this stage, the PTE and _MMPFN for the faulting address don't differ from the other ones in the cluster.

The colliding threads still wait for Event2 to become signaled, then for the WS pushlock. When the first thread releases the pushlock, the other PTEs in the cluster are in transition and the corresponding _MMPFNs are in Standby. Thus, what the colliding threads have to do is resolve an actual soft fault, which they do. When all the collided faults have been resolved their PTEs are valid, while the other cluster PTEs are left in transition.

This scenario greatly benefits from prefetching: instead of performing a disk access, the colliding threads just wait for the first one to finish their job for them and prefetching is effective even when it has not completed yet.

35.4.3   Asynchronous Handling

35.4.3.1   When Does Asynchronous Handling Take Place

In this section, we are going to describe two conditions which result in asynchronous handling. While we cannot be sure that this are the *only* situations where the VMM chooses this course of action, it is a fact that it does so in the following scenarios.

35.4.3.1.1   ActiveFaultCount Greater than Zero

One condition which results in asynchronous handling is the thread incurring a page fault when _ETHREAD.ActiveFaultCount is greater than 0. This counter is incremented before initiating the read and decremented after returning from *MiWaitForInPageComplete*. When the VMM detects a collided page fault, it examines this counter and, if finds it to be greater than 0, handles the collision asynchronously.

Below is the current instruction of a thread caught inside *MiResolveTransitionFault*, where it finds that ActiveFaultCount is greater than 0:

```
0: kd> r
rax=0000000000000000 rbx=0000000000000001 rcx=fffffa80023e3db0
rdx=fffffa8000ab1660 rsi=fffffa8003a1c70 rdi=00000000ffffffff
rip=fffff800028ee2bc rsp=fffff880034dc380 rbp=fffff6fc50007380
 r8=0000000000000000  r9=00000000135ed880 r10=0000000000000000
r11=0000000000000000 r12=0000000000000000 r13=fffff80002a04b40
r14=fffff8a000e70eb0 r15=fffff880034dc680
iopl=0          nv up ei pl zr na po nc
cs=0010  ss=0000  ds=002b  es=002b  fs=0053  gs=002b           efl=00000246
nt! ?? ::FNODOBFM::`string'+0x35d41:
fffff800`028ee2bc 389a56040000    cmp     byte ptr [rdx+456h],bl
ds:002b:fffffa80`00ab1ab6=01
```

Here, rdx points to the _ETHREAD instance for the current thread and at +0x456 is ActiveFaultCount, which is currently 1. To catch this event, the following conditional breakpoint was used:

```
fffff800`028ee2bc     0001 (0001) nt! ?? ::FNODOBFM::`string'+0x35d41 "j
((poi(@rdx+456) & ff) != 0) '';'gc'"
```

This is a conditional breakpoint inside *MiResolveTransitionFault* which automatically resumes execution if the byte value at rdx + 0x456 is 0 and breaks otherwise. The numerical breakpoint address is 0xFFFFF800`028EE2BC and is, quite unfortunately translated into "nt!

?? ::FNODOBFM::`string'+0x35d41", because of how the function code is laid out. It is quite common in x64 Windows to find functions with a block of code located in a region outside the one spanned by the main function body. This block (sometimes more than one) is often located at an address *lower* than the one corresponding to the function symbol and addresses inside the block are displayed this way, which makes looking at disassembly code much more fun. It is also annoying that this symbolic notation cannot be translated back to the numerical value, e. g. you cannot enter

        u nt! ?? ::FNODOBFM::`string'+0x35d41

to disassemble that particular instruction, and, since nt is not loaded at a fixed address, there's no guarantee that the instruction will always have the numerical address shown here. One way to get around this problem is to compute the instruction offset from nt's base address and use it to obtain the absolute address later. This particular instruction is at nt + 0xE62BC. In the example below, the `lm` command was used to obtain nt's base address and the offset to locate the same instruction:

```
1: kd> lm m nt
start              end              module name
fffff800`0284e000 fffff800`02e2b000  nt         (pdb symbols)

1: kd> u fffff800`0284e000 + 0xe62bc
nt! ?? ::FNODOBFM::`string'+0x35d41:
fffff800`029342bc 389a56040000     cmp      byte ptr [rdx+456h],bl
```

Below we can see the status of the thread caught by our breakpoint:

```
0: kd> !thread @$thread
THREAD fffffa8000ab1660  Cid 07dc.04f4  Teb: 000007fffffa6000 Win32Thread:
0000000000000000 RUNNING on processor 0
Not impersonating
DeviceMap              fffff8a000006090
Owning Process         fffffa8000a5bb30       Image:        SearchIndexer.exe
Attached Process       N/A          Image:        N/A
Wait Start TickCount   262311       Ticks: 0
Context Switch Count   453
UserTime               00:00:00.000
KernelTime             00:00:00.015
Win32 Start Address MSSRCH!CBackoffTimerThread::Thread (0x000007fef7bb5740)
Stack Init fffff880034dcdb0 Current fffff880034dc050
Base fffff880034dd000 Limit fffff880034d7000 Call 0
Priority 8 BasePriority 8 UnusualBoost 0 ForegroundBoost 0 IoPriority 2 PagePriority 5
Child-SP          RetAddr          : Args to Child
: Call Site
fffff880`034dc380 fffff800`02896506 : 00000000`00000000 fffff8a0`00e70eb0
00000000`02ba9121 fffff800`02a04b40 : nt! ?? ::FNODOBFM::`string'+0x35d41

fffff880`034dc410 fffff800`028944d1 : 00000008`00000101 00000000`00000000
00000000`00181800 00000000`00060001 : nt!MiDispatchFault+0x946
```

```
fffff880`034dc520 fffff800`02877fee : 00000000`00000000 fffff8a0`00e70eb0
fffff6fb`7dbf0000 00000000`00000000 : nt!MmAccessFault+0x8f1

fffff880`034dc680 fffff800`02b5ed9c : 00000000`00000000 00000000`00000000
00000000`00000000 00000000`00000000 : nt!KiPageFault+0x16e (TrapFrame @
fffff880`034dc680)

fffff880`034dc810 fffff800`02b5ec15 : fffff880`00b45000 ffffffff`7c1e0000
00000000`00183000 00000000`00000000 : nt!MiApplyCompressedFixups+0x40

fffff880`034dc860 fffff800`02b4c17c : fffffa80`00000000 fffffa80`00ab1660
00000000`00000000 fffffa80`00000000 : nt!MiPerformFixups+0x65

fffff880`034dc8b0 fffff800`0286b4ac : fffffa80`002b5030 fffffa80`00ebc5f0
00000000`00000000 fffffa80`02287c00 : nt!MiRelocateImagePfn+0x114

fffff880`034dc910 fffff800`0286bd8b : fffffa80`00ebc530 fffff880`034dca80
fffffa80`00a5bec8 00000000`00000000 : nt!MiWaitForInPageComplete+0x89c

fffff880`034dc9f0 fffff800`0289509b : 00000000`00000000 00000000`00000000
ffffffff`ffffffff 00000000`00000000 : nt!MiIssueHardFault+0x28b

fffff880`034dcac0 fffff800`02877fee : 00000000`00000000 00000000`00000003
fffff880`00000001 fffffa80`00a755e0 : nt!MmAccessFault+0x14bb

fffff880`034dcc20 00000000`76f94014 : 00000000`00000000 000007fe`fcfb93f4
00000000`00000003 00000000`00000003 : nt!KiPageFault+0x16e (TrapFrame @
fffff880`034dcc20)

00000000`02a2e980 000007fe`fcfb93f4 : 00000000`00000003 00000000`00000003
00000000`00000000 000007fe`f7bb0000 : ntdll!RtlInitUnicodeString+0x24

00000000`02a2e990 000007fe`fcfb9632 : 00000000`00000003 00000000`009ee060
00000000`009e87f0 00000000`00000011 : KERNELBASE!BasepGetModuleHandleExW+0x94

00000000`02a2ee60 000007fe`f7bb5511 : 00000000`01011bf0 00000000`009eb190
00000000`009e8a60 00000000`009e8ff0 : KERNELBASE!GetModuleHandleW+0x1e

00000000`02a2ee90 000007fe`f7bb55a9 : 00000000`00000000 00000000`00000000
00000000`00000001 00000000`00000003 :
MSSRCH!CGatheringService::SetPropStoreCacheMode+0x15

00000000`02a2eec0 000007fe`f7bb5aff : 00000000`009e90a0 00000000`009e8ff0
00000000`009e8ff0 00000000`009eb1c8 : MSSRCH!CBackOffController::PossiblyFlush+0x65

00000000`02a2eef0 000007fe`f7bb586d : 00000000`00000000 00000000`009e9078
00000000`009e9078 00000000`009e90a0 : MSSRCH!CBackOffController::DoBackOffLogic+0x53a

00000000`02a2eff0 00000000`76e3f56d : 00000000`00000000 00000000`00000000
00000000`00000000 00000000`00000000 : MSSRCH!CBackoffTimerThread::Thread+0x1c0

00000000`02a2fa00 00000000`76f73281 : 00000000`00000000 00000000`00000000
00000000`00000000 00000000`00000000 : kernel32!BaseThreadInitThunk+0xd
```

```
00000000`02a2fa30 00000000`00000000 : 00000000`00000000 00000000`00000000
00000000`00000000 00000000`00000000 : ntdll!RtlUserThreadStart+0x1d
```

The call stack tells us an interesting story: the thread encountered a page fault inside *RtlInitUnicodeString*. Each fault results in a trap frame with the context at the time of the fault saved on the stack and visible in the call stack above. Afterwards, the thread entered *MiWaitForInPageComplete*, where ActiveFaultCount has already been incremented and, *before* returning from this function, it called *MiRelocateImagePfn*, which caused a second fault inside *MiApplyCompressedFixups*, as shown by the trap frame visible in the upper portion of the call stack. This second fault was a collided one, so the VMM code inside *MiResolveTransitionFault* reached the breakpoint where `ActiveFaultCount` is checked. Since the thread is still inside *MiWaitForInPageComplete*, the count is found to be 1 and this will cause the second fault to be handled asynchronously.

The logic behind this design is probably that waiting for the collided fault to complete could lead to a deadlock. `ActiveFaultCount` greater than 0 means our thread (let's call it thread A) is in the process of resolving an earlier fault (as the call stack clearly shows). Blocking thread A on a wait for another thread (thread B) to resolve the latest (collided) fault could lead to a situation where thread B blocks waiting for thread A to resolve the earlier fault and the two threads end up waiting for each other.

Instead, performing a second, independent I/O guarantees that sooner or later the current thread will move forward (we will see later how the VMM handles concurrent reads for the same virtual page).

35.4.3.1.2 First Faulting Thread Has I/O Priority Lower than Two

It may be useful to briefly introduce the concept of I/O priority, in order to better understand this section.

A thread has an I/O priority, which is stored in `_ETHREAD.ThreadIoPriority` and is also displayed by WinDbg as in the following example:

```
1: kd> !thread @$thread
THREAD ffffffa8000b1b660  Cid 0124.05ac  Teb: 000007fffffdc000 Win32Thread:
0000000000000000 RUNNING on processor 1
Not impersonating
DeviceMap               fffff8a001070ee0
Owning Process          ffffffa80024a08c0          Image:          MemColls.EXE
Attached Process        N/A            Image:          N/A
Wait Start TickCount    8104           Ticks: 0
Context Switch Count    29
UserTime                00:00:00.000
KernelTime              00:00:00.000
Win32 Start Address 0x000000013fee1690
```

```
Stack Init fffff880031a7db0 Current fffff880031a6ff0
Base fffff880031a8000 Limit fffff880031a2000 Call 0
Priority 9 BasePriority 8 UnusualBoost 0 ForegroundBoost 0 IoPriority 2 PagePriority 5
```

On most threads, the I/O priority is found to be 2 as in the example above. It is stored in a field 3 bits wide, so it can range from 0 to 7.

This attribute is honored by the file system driver stack which queues I/O operations of threads with higher priority ahead of other ones. One application of I/O priority is to improve the responsiveness of applications which play video, music, etc, so that their output does not have glitches.

A thread's I/O priority can be modified by calling the *SetThreadPriority* API with `nPriority` set to THREAD_MODE_BACKGROUND_BEGIN, which sets it to 0.

When the VMM must read data from the paging file, it checks the I/O priority of the current thread (thread A) and, if it is less than 2, it sets bit 2 of `@#@IN_PAGE_SUPPORT_BLOCK.Unk-90` and goes on about its business of performing the I/O. If, later, thread B collides with thread A, the VMM code executed by thread B checks the I/O priority. When the priority is 2 or greater, it checks bit 2 of `Unk-90` and, if set, resolves the fault asynchronously.

The logic behind this design is that thread A is in-paging at low I/O priority and thread B needs the same virtual page and has a normal (or higher) I/O priority, so it would be detrimental to make B wait for A. Better to have B start another read at its own I/O priority.

This optimization appears to be used in Superfetch, a Windows component which prefetches swapped out content when there is enough unused memory, placing the prefetched pages in the Standby list. This is the same approach described for clustered in-paging, but on a larger scale: Superfetch keeps track of memory usage by processes trying to predict which virtual pages are more likely to be needed. When physical memory becomes available, instead of letting it sit around on the Free list, it starts prefeteching swapped out content. However, Superfetch appears to do so at a low I/O priority, as shown by the following thread status, where the function names are related to Superfetch and the I/O priority is 0:

```
1: kd> !thread @$thread
THREAD fffffa8000a2a660  Cid 0358.01b0   Teb: 000007fffffa6000 Win32Thread:
0000000000000000 RUNNING on processor 1
Impersonation token:  fffff8a00187c670 (Level Impersonation)
Owning Process            ffffa80024b9b30       Image:        svchost.exe
Attached Process          ffffa80027f0640       Image:        sppsvc.exe
Wait Start TickCount      254594        Ticks: 0
Context Switch Count      359
UserTime                  00:00:00.000
```

```
KernelTime                      00:00:10.906
Win32 Start Address sysmain!PfRbPrefetchWorker (0x000007fefa747ac0)
Stack Init fffff880038ebdb0 Current fffff880038eb270
Base fffff880038ec000 Limit fffff880038e6000 Call 0
Priority 8 BasePriority 7 UnusualBoost 0 ForegroundBoost 0 IoPriority 0 PagePriority 1
Child-SP          RetAddr           : Args to Child
: Call Site
fffff880`038eb3b8 fffff800`02949ebc : fffffa80`00a2a720 00000000`00000000
00000000`00000000 00000000`00000000 : nt!MiResolvePageFileFault

fffff880`038eb3c0 fffff800`028eef23 : ffffffff`ffffffff 00000000`00000000
ffffffa80`026a07a0 fffff800`028c709c : nt! ?? ::FNODOBFM::`string'+0x36a16

fffff880`038eb4d0 fffff800`029ef8fb : 00000000`00000000 fffffa80`00a2a660
00000000`00000000 00000000`00000000 : nt!MmAccessFault+0x343

fffff880`038eb630 fffff800`029effbf : 00000000`00000001 00000000`00000000
fffffa80`027f0640 00000000`00000000 : nt!MiPrefetchVirtualMemory+0x2ab

fffff880`038eb6b0 fffff800`02d13e1a : ffffffa80`027f0640 00000000`00000010
ffffffa80`018c7390 fffff8a0`02247000 : nt!MmPrefetchVirtualMemory+0x14f

fffff880`038eb760 fffff800`02d39b9b : fffff8a0`00000000 fffff8a0`00000006
fffff8a0`00000004 00000000`000000a8 : nt!PfpPrefetchPrivatePages+0x1da

fffff880`038eb810 fffff800`02d3a7b7 : 00000000`00000000 fffff880`038ebca0
fffff880`038eba08 fffff8a0`059f4060 : nt!PfpPrefetchRequestPerform+0x28b

fffff880`038eb960 fffff800`02d46d8e : fffff880`038eba08 00000000`00000001
ffffffa80`02432300 00000000`00000000 : nt!PfpPrefetchRequest+0x176

fffff880`038eb9d0 fffff800`02d4b4be : 00000000`00000000 00000000`01ecfa00
00000000`0000004f 00000000`00000001 : nt!PfSetSuperfetchInformation+0x1ad

fffff880`038ebab0 fffff800`028d4153 : ffffffa80`00a2a660 00000000`00000000
00000000`00000001 00000000`00000001 : nt!NtSetSystemInformation+0xb91

fffff880`038ebc20 00000000`77b715aa : 00000000`00000000 00000000`00000000
00000000`00000000 00000000`00000000 : nt!KiSystemServiceCopyEnd+0x13 (TrapFrame @
fffff880`038ebc20)

00000000`01ecf9d8 00000000`00000000 : 00000000`00000000 00000000`00000000
00000000`00000000 00000000`00000000 : ntdll!NtSetSystemInformation+0xa
```

This makes a lot of sense: although trying to make the most of free memory is a good thing, it would not be wise to keep the disk subsystem busy with prefetching activity; other processes may need to access the disk to respond to the user. So Superfetch behaves and runs with its I/O priority set to 0. However, if another thread collides on a page being "superprefetched" it would not do to keep it waiting for the low priority read to complete. Now that page is needed as soon as possible, not just because of Superfetch's guessing game, so another read is started, with normal I/O priority to shove Superfetch out of the way.

35.4.3.2   How Is the Asynchronous Read Set up

Once the VMM has determined that it must start a second read operation, it allocates a new physical page to be loaded with content from the paging file and a new support block, which is chained to the one for the read already in progress through its `ListEntry` member. This support block stores the PFN of the new page in its `PfnArray`. We will refer to the support block for the first I/O as the *master* one. As for the synchronous case, the VMM gets from the PFN in the transition PTE to the `_MMPFN` and from the event pointer `_MMPFN.u1.Event` to the master support block, because the pointed event is `@#@IN_PAGE_SUPPORT_BLOCK.Event1` (i.e. `_MMPFN.u1.Event` points at +0x20 into the support block).

The new support block, which we are going to call *secondary* one, is for reading the single page on which the collision occurred, i.e. the read about to be started is not for a cluster, just for one page.

Notice how the new read uses a *different* physical page than the original one: the two reads are independent operations, each loading the same 4kB chunk of paging file into a different physical page.

This scenario can involve multiple threads: there can be one master support block with multiple secondary ones, each due to a different thread which collided on the page involved. In the following, we will use the terms master or secondary also in connection with the thread which allocated the master or one of the secondary support blocks, respectively.

When a secondary operation is set up, the PTE is not updated: it still stores the PFN of the physical page allocated for that particular virtual one when the master thread set up the clustered read. The reads performed by secondary threads are going to target physical pages that, at this stage are only "known" in the secondary support blocks.

The VMM code executing in a secondary thread holds the WS pushlock while it detects that a collision occurred and that an asynchronous I/O is in order. This code will wait on `Event1` in its own secondary `@#@IN_PAGE_SUPPORT_BLOCK` instance for the read to complete but, before doing so, it will release the WS pushlock.

Each thread, including the master one, tries to acquire the WS pushlock when its read operation completes, so we have different scenarios, depending on whether the master thread or one of the secondary ones "wins", i.e. acquires the pushlock first.

35.4.3.3   Scenario A: the Master Thread Wins

35.4.3.3.1   Actions Taken by the Master Thread

After acquiring the pushlock, the master thread detects that there are secondary support blocks chained to its own. These secondary blocks can be for collisions on the faulting PTE or on other PTEs in the cluster. When the master thread owns the pushlock, it has finished reading *all* the pages in the cluster so it discards all the read operations of secondary threads.

It does so by setting a flag which signals to each secondary thread that its read operation has to be discarded. This flag is bit 1 of `PteAddress` in the `_MMPFN` instance for the physical page targeted by the secondary read. Notice how this bit, which we are going to call the *discard flag*, is the same one used when a page is decommitted or released while being read (see section 35.3.1 on p. 267). In all these scenarios, it is used to signal to a thread which just completed a read that it was all for naught, because while it was waiting things have changed.

To set the discard flag, the master thread scans the list of support blocks linked to its own and gets the PFN of the page from each block. From there it's just a matter of arithmetic to compute the `_MMPFN` address and set the flag. Besides setting the flag, the master thread also unchains each block from the list.

Afterwards, the master thread completes the in-paging as usual: maps the faulting page as Active and puts the ones for prefetched PTEs in Standby; releases the WS pushlock; resumes the faulting instruction.

The master thread also checks its own support block share count and eventually signals `@#@IN_PAGE_SUPPORT_BLOCK.Event2`, as explained in sec. 35.4.2.1 on p. 269, to awake other threads which collided and opted for synchronous handling. For instance, a thread with `ActiveFaultCount` equal to zero can collide with the master one and wait on `@#@IN_PAGE_SUPPORT_BLOCK.Event2`, while another one with `ActiveFaultCount` greater than zero starts an asynchronous read.

35.4.3.3.2   Actions Taken by the Secondary Threads

After acquiring the pushlock, each secondary thread finds its own support block not part of any chain and detects the discard flag set in the `_MMPFN` of the page where it has just loaded the data. Each thread returns the page to the free list without updating the PTE, releases the pushlock and resumes the faulting instruction, which will succeed because the PTE has already been made valid by the master thread.

35.4.3.4   Scenario B: One of the Secondary Threads Wins

35.4.3.4.1   Actions Performed by the Winning Secondary Thread

The first thread acquiring the pushlock will find its support block is still part of a chain, so it will access the master support block through
`@#@IN_PAGE_SUPPORT_BLOCK.PmasterBlock`.

This member requires some additional explanation (see `@#@IN_PAGE_SUPPORT_BLOCK` on p. 269): it is located after the array of PFNs which has variable length, however `@#@IN_PAGE_SUPPORT_BLOCK.Mdl.Size` gives the number of bytes spanned by `@#@IN_PAGE_SUPPORT_BLOCK.Mdl` plus the PFN array, so the address of `PmasterBlock` can be computed. This member, in turn, points to the master block.

The thread scans the list of PFNs in the master block, looking for the one in collision. The master block PFN array stores multiple elements, because the master read is clustered, so the secondary thread must find the one involved in the collision. In order to do this, the secondary thread looks at `PteAddress` inside its own `_MMPFN` instance (the one for the physical page it used in the read); this member points to the PTE for the VA where the collision occurred. For each PFN in the master block array, it accesses `_MMPFN.PteAddress`, looking for the one pointing to the same PTE. It then sets bit 1 of `PteAddress`, thereby signaling the master thread that this page must be discarded (at this stage, the master thread is still waiting for its read to complete or to acquire the pushlock).

In this scenario, the secondary thread "knows" it has won, because its support block was still chained in the list, so it updates the PTE replacing the PFN pointing to the physical page allocated by the master thread with the PFN of its own physical page. This is what throws away the master read and makes the secondary one actually resolve the fault.

The winning thread still has to deal with other secondary threads which collided on the same VPN and lost the race, so it scans all the other support blocks chained to the master one and checks if the PFN (a secondary block has a single PFN) is for the collided `PteAddress`. If this is the case, it unchains the block and sets bit 1 of the related `_MMPFN.PteAddress` to 1, to signal to the other secondary thread that it must discard its page.

Note how the winning thread does not unchain all the secondary blocks, because there may be block in the chain for collisions on other PTEs in the cluster. When the winning thread has finished cleaning things up, the master block may still be chained to other ones, related to different collisions.

At any rate, the winning thread goes on by making the PTE valid, releasing the pushlock and resuming the faulting instruction.

35.4.3.4.2   Actions Performed by the Master Thread

The master thread returns to the free list the pages for which bit 1 of `_MMPFN.PtreAddress` is set and does not update the PTEs for which they were meant to be used.

Pages for other prefetched PTEs are still put into Standby and the PTEs are left in transition, as when no collision occurs.

Afterwards, the master thread releases the pushlock and resumes the faulting instruction.

35.4.3.4.3   Actions Performed by the Losing Secondary Threads

These threads find themselves in a situation similar to when the master thread wins: their support block is not part of a chain and their physical page has bit 1 of `_MMPFN.PteAddress` set. Each of them returns its physical page to the free list, releases the pushlock and resumes the faulting instruction.

35.4.3.5   Collisions on Prefetched PTEs

When the master thread wins, all secondary reads are discarded, regardless of whether they are for the faulting PTE or one of the prefetched ones, as explained in sec. 35.4.3.3.1 on p. 278. The master thread leaves all the prefetched PTEs in transition and their physical pages in Standby.

When one of the secondary threads wins, it invalidates the read results for its particular PTE from all other colliding threads, as explained previously. It then makes the PTE valid, because the secondary thread is not just prefetching it: it incurred a fault on it. The other threads, finding their own read invalidated will not touch the PTE.

In summary, a secondary thread winning the race on an access to a PTE which was being prefetched can go on independently, mapping the VA and resuming the faulting instruction. Looking back at the description of Superfetch in sec. 35.4.3.1.2 on p. 274, we can see that this is a good thing, because it is likely that Superfetch in-pages clusters of PTEs at low priority, so a thread needing any one of these PTEs should be allowed to in-page it at its own priority.

35.5 Experiments on In-Paging Collisions

35.5.1   Overview

This section explain how to perform some experiments with in-paging collision and may be of interest for readers willing to verify or further investigate the concepts explained in this chapter.

A word of caution: these experiments involve using a test driver and tweaking the execution of kernel code by updating processor registers, so there is a *high* risk of crashing the system. It would be best to use a virtual machine for these tests.

The main problem to solve is how to cause the desired events to occur at the same time, e.g. how to decommit a page, or cause a collided fault while an in-paging is in progress.

To solve this problem, we can start by observing that at *MiWaitForInPageComplete*+0xbd is the call to *KeWaitForSingleObject* where the VMM waits for `_MMPFN.u1.Event` to become signaled. At the moment of the call, `rcx` is set to the address of the event. A test kernel mode driver has been developed, named WrkEvent, which creates an array of 5 events available for these tests. We can therefore place a breakpoint at *MiWaitForInPageComplete*+0xbd and set `rcx` to the address of one of the events controlled by WrkEvent. As long as this event is not signaled, the thread which started the in-paging is kept suspended, as if the read operation was still in progress. This makes it possible to cause all sorts of collisions and analyze what the VMM does.

A client program for WrkEvent (WrkEvClient) allows to interactively set or clear its events and an application program named MemColls performs memory access operations in separate threads, to cause the desired collisions. All these programs are included in the download package for this book.

Important note: the tests described in the following sections have been performed on a system with UAC turned off.

35.5.2   The Test Driver and Its Client

Caution: the test driver described here *only* works for Windows 7 x64 RTM (i.e. pre-SP1, *no updates installed*). *It will crash the system on any other version of Windows*, because it calls unexported functions of ntkrnlmp.exe using fixed offsets valid only on a particular build.

The driver (WrkEvent.sys) and the client (WrkEvClient.exe) must be copied in the same directory. The client does not require any command line parameter and, when launched, it loads the driver then displays a menu of options.

The code for loading the driver is based on the code of w2k_lib.dll, written by Sven Schreiber and included in the companion CD to [12]. The CD content is available for download at

> http://undocumented.rawol.com

The test driver is not digitally signed, which would normally make it unusable on an x64 system. However, Windows allows loading an unsigned driver if a kernel debugger is attached to the system. When the driver is loaded (usually after a few seconds), Windows still shows the following dialog box stating that the driver did not load:

Figure 36 - Non-signed Driver Warning

but the message is misleading since the driver was actually loaded. This can be confirmed by looking at the debugger console, where the following messages, should be visible:

```
WrkEvent - Device created

WrkEvent - Object addresses:
   WrkEvent[0] address  : 0XFFFFFA8000C679B8
```

```
     WrkEvent[1] address   : 0XFFFFFA8000C679D0
     WrkEvent[2] address   : 0XFFFFFA8000C679E8
     WrkEvent[3] address   : 0XFFFFFA8000C67A00
     WrkEvent[4] address   : 0XFFFFFA8000C67A18
     Ev ptr array address : 0XFFFFFA8000C67A30
     Gate address          : 0XFFFFFA8000C67A58
WrkEvent - Work event driver successfully loaded.
```

Since the tests we want to perform require a debugger anyway, we can use an unsigned driver.

The WrkEvClient program displays a simple menu with options for printing the event addresses into the debugger console, signaling an event and clearing an event. The menu options are self explanatory and after performing the requested action, the program returns to the menu itself. When the option for setting or clearing an event is selected, the program asks for the zero-based index of the event to act upon.

When the *Print objects addresses option* is selected, the driver prints the addresses into the debugger console, as shown above. The output includes:

- The addresses of 5 KEVENTs available for tests.

- The address of an array of 5 pointers to the events. This is used in tests which will be explained in a later chapter.

- The address of a gate (an instance of KGATE). This too will be used in a later chapter.

For the tests described in the next sections, only the event addresses will be used.

35.5.3   MemColls

MemColls is a simple test program which can perform a set of memory operations like touching a range of memory, changing protection, decommitting, etc. It displays a simple menu with self-explanatory options for each operation. The requested operation is carried out in a newly created thread. This makes it possible, for instance to start a memory touch operation which causes in-paging, suspend the in-paging by means of a driver-controlled event and start other colliding operations in the same instance of MemColls. The main menu is managed by a dedicated thread, so the program continues to respond to commands while the in-paging thread is suspended.

When launched, MemColls reserves and commits a virtual memory range. Its command line requires two parameters, the range size in bytes and its protection, where the latter must be a valid numerical value for the `flProtect` parameter of *VirtualAllocEx*, e.g.:

```
PAGE_READWRITE 4
PAGE_READONLY  2
```

Both parameters can be specified on the command line either as hexadecimal or decimal quantities. A pure number is interpreted as a decimal value, while the form 0x... is interpreted as an hexadecimal one.

The operations available through the menu act on the allocated region.

Two operations (c and t) control whether MemColls causes a break into the debugger before performing its operations. When breaking is active, MemColls calls the *DebugBreak* API before performing the requested operation and it does so in the context of the thread about to perform it. This breaks into the debugger with the calling thread being the current one (and MemColls being the current process) and makes it easier to examine the PTEs of MemColls (e.g. there is no need to switch to it with !process /P or /i) and set breakpoints valid for this thread only with

```
bp /t @$thread ...
```

@$thread is WinDbg's pseudo-register for the current thread. The flip side of the coin is that if breaking is active and a debugger is not attached to the system, MemColls crashes when it calls *DebugBreak*.

The current breaking status is displayed together with the menu and the memory region addresses.

35.5.4   Example: Suspending an In-Paging Operation

In this section we will assume that:

- A kernel debugger is attached to the system.

- WrkEvent.sys, WrkEvClient.exe, MemColls.exe are in the current directory.

By following the steps below, we can suspend an in-paging operation:

- Launch WrkEvClient; it is better to do it in a separate process by entering

```
start WrkEvClient
```

so that the driver control program is ready to be used when needed. The driver will list the event addresses in the debugger console:

```
WrkEvent - Device created
   WrkEvent[0] address: 0XFFFFFA8000C6B1C8
```

```
WrkEvent[1] address: 0XFFFFFA8000C6B1E0
WrkEvent[2] address: 0XFFFFFA8000C6B1F8
WrkEvent[3] address: 0XFFFFFA8000C6B210
WrkEvent[4] address: 0XFFFFFA8000C6B228
```

- Launch MemColls specifying a memory region with a size of about 90% of the physical memory.

- Select the *Write entire region* option to write the entire memory region. This will force the VMM to map physical pages for all the region. While MemColls touches the whole range, the virtual pages at its beginning are likely to be swapped out, to free physical memory.

- Select the *Activate breaking mode* option to do what it says.

- Select the *Access subrange* option to access a memory subrange and enter the region starting address, a size of 1 page (0x1000) or less, a memory access type (read or write, anything will do).

Since breaking is now active, the debugger will take control, with the thread about to perform the memory access being the current one. We can now examine the PTE of the range first page and it is likely that it will be swapped out. The output of the !pte extension should look like this:

```
1: kd> !pte 560000
                        VA 0000000000560000

PXE @ FFFFF6FB7DBED000    PPE at FFFFF6FB7DA00000    PDE at FFFFF6FB40000010    PTE at FFFFF68000002B00
contains 00C0000006570867  contains 0100000001D73867  contains 04B0000005D89867  contains 0000E47400000080
pfn 6570      ---DA--UWEV pfn 1d73      ---DA--UWEV  pfn 5d89      ---DA--UWEV  not valid
                                                      PageFile: 0
                                                      Offset: e474
                                                      Protect: 4 - ReadWrite
```

Hint: if the page is in transition, try repeating the previous steps with a larger region. The point is to have a region big enough to force the VMM to repurpose part of it.

At this stage, it is useful to take note of the current process and current thread addresses by entering

```
        ? @$proc
```

and

```
        ? @$thread
```

These are the addresses of the _EPROCESS and _ETHREAD instances and can later be used to examine the process status.

- Examine a few PTEs for higher addresses, e.g. 561000, 562000 for the example above (remember that each PTE maps 0x1000 byte). They are likely to be swapped out at contiguous offsets.

- Place a breakpoint for the current thread on the call where the VMM waits on _MMPFN.u.Event1 with the following command:

```
bp /t @$thread nt!MiWaitForInPageComplete+0xbd
```

- Resume execution. When the breakpoint is hit, the VMM has set up the clustered read and is about to wait for the read operation to complete. The faulting PTE is now in transition and it is likely that the ones after it are in transition too, because they have been included in the cluster.

Here `rcx` is set to the event address taken from _MMPFN.u1.Event. Remember that this is also +0x20 inside the support block, so, from `rcx`, it is possible to examine the rest of the support block.

At this stage, the thread call stack should be similar to the following one:

```
1: kd> k
Child-SP          RetAddr           Call Site
fffff880`024d5910 fffff800`028acd8b nt!MiWaitForInPageComplete+0xbd
fffff880`024d59f0 fffff800`028d609b nt!MiIssueHardFault+0x28b
fffff880`024d5ac0 fffff800`028b8fee nt!MmAccessFault+0x14bb
fffff880`024d5c20 00000001`3f421758 nt!KiPageFault+0x16e
00000000`3628f7e0 00000001`3f47d400 MemColls!AccessMemory+0xc8 00000000`3628f7e8
00000000`00000298 MemColls!__xt_z+0x30
```

Hint: if the debugger is not using the symbols of MemColls, enter `.reload /user`.

Note also that MemColls reprints the menu in a separate thread from the one performing the memory access, which is also the one hitting the breakpoint. When this happens, the menu handling thread could be in the process of listing the menu options and, since the whole system freezes when the debugger takes control, we might end up with a partially printed menu. This does not mean that something is going wrong: when we will resume execution, MemColls will finish displaying the menu.

- Set `rcx` to the address of one of the event controlled by the test driver.

- Remove the breakpoint (e.g. `bc*` removes all breakpoints). This is important because, even though it is filtered for the current thread, it slows down the system quite badly. This suggests that the breakpoint actually causes the debugger to take control when the instruction is reached in every thread. It is therefore the debugger which examines the filter condition and resumes execution automatically when the latter is not satisfied.

- Resume execution. The thread which was accessing the page will now be frozen until we signal the event with the driver client. Meanwhile, we can launch colliding operations (page fault, decommit, etc.) with MemColls.

We can also break again with the debugger by hitting Ctrl-C and examine the thread we "freezed".

- First, we instruct the debugger to switch to the memory context of MemColls entering

  `0: kd> .process /P` address of _EPROCESS

- Then we set our thread as the current one by entering

  `.thread` *address of _ETHREAD*

- Finally, we print the call stack:

```
0: kd> k
  *** Stack trace for last set context - .thread/.cxr resets it
Child-SP          RetAddr           Call Site
fffff880`024d56a0 fffff800`028c2052 nt!KiSwapContext+0x7a
fffff880`024d57e0 fffff800`028c41af nt!KiCommitThreadWait+0x1d2
fffff880`024d5870 fffff800`028abcd2 nt!KeWaitForSingleObject+0x19f
fffff880`024d5910 fffff800`028acd8b nt!MiWaitForInPageComplete+0xc2
fffff880`024d59f0 fffff800`028d609b nt!MiIssueHardFault+0x28b
fffff880`024d5ac0 fffff800`028b8fee nt!MmAccessFault+0x14bb
fffff880`024d5c20 00000001`3f421758 nt!KiPageFault+0x16e
00000000`3628f7e0 00000001`3f47d400 MemColls!AccessMemory+0xc8
```

Note how we are inside KeWaitForSingleObject and the thread is suspended.

To "unfreeze" the thread, we go to the driver client and set the event whose address we put into `rcx` before.

It is interesting to note that, if we choose the *Quit* option which terminates MemColls, the program does not exit until we signal the event. Windows does not terminate the thread, and hence the process, until it finishes its read operation.

36   Paging of Paging Structures

36.1 Basic Concept

The paging structures (i.e. PDPTs, PDs and PTs) are themselves pageable, which means that, for a given VA, one of more of them can be missing. For instance, the PT can be missing, which means that the PDE selected by the VA will have the P bit clear; both the PT and the PD can be missing; finally, the PDPT can be missing as well, so that only an invalid PML4 entry exists for the address.

When this happens, a paging structure (PS) can be missing for several reasons; the most obvious is when we are accessing for the first time a VA mapped by it, so that the PS itself has never been initialized. However, this is not the only scenario: the physical page storing a PS can be reused just like any other one.

In the following, we are going to use the term *leaf page* to refer to a physical page storing the content of a virtual page, because such a page is a leaf in the tree of the paging structures hierarchy, whose root is the PML4. A leaf page stores the content (e.g. program data, program code, etc.) visible at a given VA. Conversely, a *paging structure page* stores a paging structure used to map VAs to their leaf pages.

We already know that leaf pages go through a life cycle, e.g they become Active, then Standby/Modified, etc. PS pages follow the same cycle: they can be moved to a transition list, repurposed and restored at a later time. Thus, a paging structure that has been initialized and used can become missing, because its physical page is in transition or its content has been swapped out.

It is useful to keep in mind what happens when an instruction references a VA for which all the PSs are present, but the leaf page is not, i.e. the PTE has the P bit clear: the processor raises a page fault exception, with CR2 set to the faulting VA.

Now suppose that a VA is being referenced for which the PDPT and PD are present, but the PDE has the P bit clear, i.e. the PT and hence the PTE is missing. The processor generates a page fault exception with CR2 still set to the VA referenced by the instruction, *not* the VA of the missing PTE. This becomes obvious when we think that what makes the PTE visible at a certain VA is the auto-entry in the PML4, which is not something defined by the processor architecture. We could, conceivably, change the auto-entry and completely unmap all the PSs from virtual space but they would still be used to map VAs referenced by instructions. In short, the processor knows nothing about the VAs at which PSs are visible and simply sets

CR2 to the VA the instruction was trying to access, for which a virtual to physical translation is not possible.

This means that it is the job of the page fault handler to determine the cause of the fault: whether it is just a missing leaf page or other levels in the PS hierarchy. *MmAccessFault* does so early in the process of handling a fault: it examines every level of the hierarchy starting with the PML4E and checking whether the P bit is set. If this is not the case, it takes the appropriate actions to make the entry valid (e.g. pointing it to a brand new page or retrieving a previously removed one) then moves on to the next level, until the PML4E, the PDPTE, and the PDE are all valid and pointing to a physical page. Afterward, the leaf page is handled as explained previously.

36.2 First Initialization of a Paging Structure

When this scenario occurs, the entry of the parent structure is set to 0. For instance, a PML4E set to 0 means that the PDPT must be initialized. This also implies that all the levels of the hierarchy below the zeroed entry must be initialized as well, since all the virtual range mapped by the zeroed entry has never been accessed before. In the previous example, the PDPT must be initialized, so all its children PDs and their children PTs have never been initialized as well. Of course, this does not mean that the VMM will initialize 512 PDs and 512 PTs for each PD, because it would mean to consume 262.144 physical pages or 1GB of physical memory for the paging structures alone. It will only initialize the PD and the PT needed to map the faulting address.

A PS entry set to 0 may also result from an instruction trying to access an invalid address (a region which has not been properly reserved and committed), so the VMM calls *MiCheckVirtualAddress* to check the VADs and, if this is the case, raises an access violation exception. The remainder of this section describes what happens when the address is valid.

For each PS entry in the hierarchy found to be 0, *MmAccessFault* calls *MiDispatchFault*, which in turns calls *MiResolveDemandZeroFault*. The latter allocates a new physical page much in the same way it is done for a leaf page, accounting for cache color, for the priority in which page lists are searched, etc. A new paging structure page must be filled with zeroes, as is the case for a leaf page, because this represents the fact that its entries are uninitialized, i.e. a child paging structure has never been created for them. This way, when *MmAccessFault* moves to the next level in the hierarchy, it finds yet another zeroed entry and performs the same steps. This goes on until the PT is allocated and the PDE pointed to it. Afterwards, the fault handling will take place as described in section 26.2.1 on p. 140.

Using the same logic to map both virtual addresses and paging structures is made possible by the way paging structures are mapped in the virtual address space (see section 15.2, p. 63). The relationship between a VA and the VA of its PTE is the same relationship found between the VA of a PTE and the VA of the PDE mapping the PT; the same applies to PDPTE/PD and to PML4E/PDPT.

It is interesting to note that *MiCheckVirtualAddress* can actually be called multiple times: once for every missing level of the hierarchy (in the worst scenario the PDPT, PD and PT can be all missing) and one more time when finding the PTE set to 0, as explained in section 26.2.1. This is a little inefficient, but it only happens when a page is accessed for the first time. It does not happen, for instance, when the paging structures have been swapped out: no call to *MiCheckVirtualAddress* is needed since it already occurred for the first fault.

For a PS, `_MMPFN.u3.e1.PageLocation` is set to `_MMLISTS.ActiveAndValid` as it happens for a leaf page.

A new PS is added to the process working set in the same way that leaf pages are: an entry is added to the working set list for the VPN of the paging structure.

We can see such entries are part of the WSL of every process. As an example, consider the following status of an instance of notepad.exe:

```
PROCESS fffffa80014a2060
    SessionId: 1  Cid: 0b08    Peb: 7fffffd3000  ParentCid: 074c
    DirBase: 23e3f000  ObjectTable: fffff8a0079b8500  HandleCount:   77.
    Image: notepad.exe
    VadRoot fffffa800157fe20 Vads 61 Clone 0 Private 340. Modified 4. Locked 0.
    DeviceMap fffff8a000e8fe70
    Token                             fffff8a0068b9060
    ElapsedTime                       00:00:10.140
    UserTime                          00:00:00.000
    KernelTime                        00:00:00.000
    QuotaPoolUsage[PagedPool]         0
    QuotaPoolUsage[NonPagedPool]      0
    Working Set Sizes (now,min,max)   (1460, 50, 345) (5840KB, 200KB, 1380KB)
    PeakWorkingSetSize                1460
    VirtualSize                       71 Mb
    PeakVirtualSize                   75 Mb
    PageFaultCount                    1522
    MemoryPriority                    BACKGROUND
    BasePriority                      8
    CommitCharge                      432
```

We can examine the virtual address space with !vad; here is an excerpt of the output:

```
0: kd> !vad fffffa800157fe20
VAD              level      start      end     commit
fffffa8001584c60 ( 5)        10        1f         0 Mapped     READWRITE
fffffa8000edfc50 ( 4)        20        26         0 Mapped     READONLY
fffffa80017b3ed0 ( 5)        30        33         0 Mapped     READONLY
fffffa800156ded0 ( 3)        40        41         0 Mapped     READONLY
fffffa8000dc23a0 ( 5)        50        50         1 Private    READWRITE
...
```

The last entry above tells us that the virtual range 0x50000 – 0x50fff is valid. Below is the status of the paging structures for this range:

```
0: kd> !pte 50000
                                 VA 0000000000050000

PXE at FFFFF6FB7DBED000   PPE at FFFFF6FB7DA00000   PDE at FFFFF6FB40000000   PTE at FFFFF68000000280
contains 531000001AE2D867 contains 011000002F970867 contains 012000002E7B1867 contains B5D0000038237867
pfn 1ae2d    ---DA--UWEV  pfn 2f970    ---DA--UWEV  pfn 2e7b1    ---DA--UWEV  pfn 38237    ---DA--UW-V
```

This tells us that the VA is mapped and all the PSs needed to translate it are in place. If we dump the WS list, we see that there are indeed entries for the PSs:

```
0: kd> !wsle 1

Working Set @ fffff70001080000
    FirstFree      5b4  FirstDynamic       5
    LastEntry      660  NextSlot           5  LastInitialized      76e
    NonDirect        0  HashTable          0  HashTableSize        0

Reading the WSLE data .................

Virtual Address        Age  Locked  ReferenceCount
...
fffff6fb40000009         0       0   1                 <-- entry for the PD
...
fffff68000000009         0       0   1                 <-- entry for the PT
...
fffff6fb7da00009         0       0   1                 <-- entry for the PDPT
```

Furthermore, we already know that an entry for the PML4 itself is always present in the list (see sec. 20.3.3.1.1 on p. 118).

When a PS is initialized, its share count (u2.ShareCount of the _MMPFN for the PS page) is set to 1. Whenever an entry of a PS is made valid, the share count is incremented, so that it is usually equal to the number of valid entries plus one.

Furthermore, UsedPageTableEntries of the _MMPFN for the PS is incremented each time an entry is made valid and linked to a child page. There is an important difference between this member and the share count: a valid entry can later become invalid while the child page is first moved to a transition list and then repurposed. When the repurposing happens, the share count is decremented (we will return on this in the next section), but

`UsedPageTableEntries` is not, because the entry is still in use. The latter is decremented when memory is released and entries become truly unused. It also appears that `UsedPageTableEntries` is not used for leaf pages and is usually set to 0 for them.

`UsedPageTableEntries` is found to be 0 in `_MMPFN` instances for PSs mapping system addresses. We will return on this in sec. 44.3.3 on p. 419.

36.3 Transition of a Paging Structure from Active to Modified or Standby

If we start by considering an Active PT, we know it has a share count which started at 1 and then has been incremented each time one of its entries has been made valid.

Eventually, the leaf page pointed by one entry is moved to Modified or Standby as part of the VMM trimming activity. When this happens, the share count is *not* decremented. To understand why, we must consider that the share count is used to decide when the PT itself can be moved into Modified or Standby: a share count set to 1 means the PT can change state. After a PS has entered one of the transition state, the VMM can repurpose it as part of its normal operation, without further updating the `_MMPFN`s of its leaf pages. This poses two problems.

First, for a Standby or Modified leaf page `_MMPFN.u4.PteFrame` is set to the PFN of the PT (see sec. 26.4.3.4.3.1 on p. 158). If the VMM were to repurpose the PT, the physical page that was storing it would be reused for something else, while the `_MMPFN`s of leaf pages are still pointing to it.

Second, suppose the leaf page eventually enters the Standby state and is later repurposed; the PTE pointing to it must be updated recording the paging file offset into it. If, at this stage, the VMM had already repurposed the PT, it would have to reload it from the paging file to update the PTE.

These problems are avoided by repurposing a PT only when all the used PTEs point to leaf pages which have been themselves repurposed, i.e. they point into the paging file. When this is true, there are no `_MMPFN`s on transition lists left around pointing back to the PT, because they have all been repurposed. The bottom line is that the VMM decrements the share count of a PT when a leaf page is *repurposed*, not when it is moved to a transition list.

Thus, leaf pages follow their life cycle from Active to Standby/Modified and are eventually repurposed while the PT share count decreases. When it has dropped to 1, the VMM knows the PT is eligible for being itself moved to the Modified state. Since the PT has an entry in the WS list, it will eventually be moved as part of WS trimming or page replacement.

While this process goes on, `_MMPFN.UsedPageTableEntries` is not decremented and keeps track of how many entries are in use, regardless of the fact that they point to swapped out leaf pages. It is also possible that the VMM uses this information to prioritize page removal from the working set: a leaf page with `UsedPageTableEntries` equal to 0 is removed before a PT; removing a page means unmapping 4kB of virtual range, while a PT covers a 2MB range, so it is much more likely that the latter will be soon needed back. This hypothesis has not been verified by the author.

The process outlined so far also applies to the upper levels of the PS hierarchy: when a PT is repurposed, the PDE which was pointing to it is updated to store the paging file offset and the PD share count is decremented; when it drops to 1, the PD can be repurposed, thereby decrementing the PDPT share count and so on.

A PS page on the Modified list will be moved to the Standby one like any other page: the modified page writer will write its content into the paging file and mark the page as clean. From there, the page can be repurposed if the need for physical memory arises.

36.4 Bringing Back a Paging Structure from Transition or the Paging File

Sooner or later, a page fault will occur for which one of the PSs is either on a transition list or swapped out. From the logic described in the previous section, we can understand that all the PSs below the first missing one have been swapped out, e.g. if the PDPT is present and the PD is missing, the PT is swapped out (but the PD can still be in transition). Likewise, if the PDPT is missing, the PD and the PT are swapped out.

The VMM checks the entire hierarchy beginning with the PML4E and, if the entry has the P bit clear, calls *MiDispatchFault*. This is the same function which handles Standby, Modified and swapped out leaf pages in the way we described in previous chapters. When it is invoked for a leaf page, the latter is pointed by a PTE; when it is invoked for a PS page, the needed page is pointed by a PDE, a PDPTE or a PML4E. These entries have the same layout of a PTE and *MiDispatchFault* performs essentially the same steps it does for a leaf page to make the referring PxE valid. If the entry is in transition, it invokes *MiResolveTransitionFault*; if the content is swapped out it invokes *MiResolvePageFileFault* and returns an NTSTATUS which directs its caller to invoke *MiIssueHardFault*. The latter function, in turn, reads the page from the paging file. This is the same process performed for a leaf page and results in the PxE being pointed to a physical page storing the PS; this is done for every level of the hierarchy up to the PDE. Once the PT is back into place, the fault is handled as described in previous chapters.

36.5 State Diagram for Paging Structures Pages

Figure 37 shows the state diagram for PS pages. It is similar to the one for leaf pages, but there are no state transitions triggered by faults, since paging structures are never "faulted back" but, rather restored by the VMM as needed.

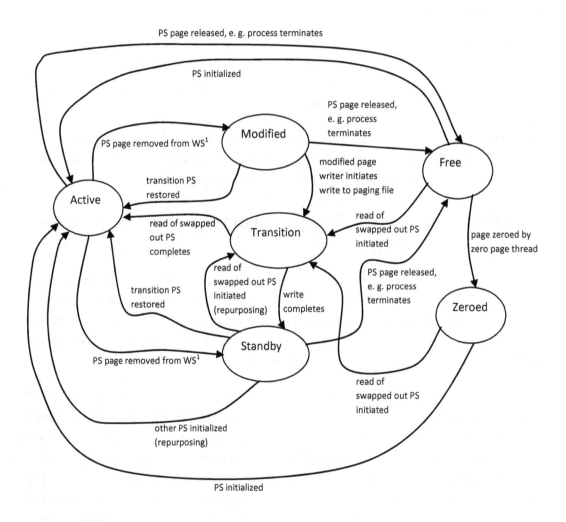

Figure 37 – Paging Structures State Diagram

Notes

1. PS are removed only when all the entries are either unused or referring to swapped out content in the paging file.

37   User Range Shared Memory

37.1 Basic Concept

The VMM provides functionalities to allow different processes to share a region of memory. This is achieved by setting the PTEs of the sharing processes to point to the same physical pages. The VMM uses a number of data structures to keep track of shared pages, which we are going to analyze in detail shortly.

These data structures also form the basis for another VMM functionality: file mapping, i.e. the ability to map a portion of the virtual address space to the content of a file. In broad terms, this is done by treating the file as if it were the paging file, so that memory content is read from and written to the file through in-paging and out-paging operations. We will describe file mapping in Chapter 38 (p. 338).

37.2 APIs for Shared Memory, Section Objects and Prototype PTEs

This section is a short overview of the APIs and data structure used to implement shared memory and is meant to give a broad outline of the general picture. We will examine these concepts in greater detail later in this chapter.

To allocate a shared memory region, we must first call *CreateFileMapping*, which creates a *file mapping object*, also called *section object* (we will use the latter term in the following). This call creates the internal data structures needed to track the status of shared pages and returns an handle to the section object. Simply creating the section object does not make the shared memory accessible: this is done by calling *MapViewOfFileEx*, which maps the section object into the virtual address space, and returns the region address.

So far, the allocated memory is not yet shared with anyone else, however, another process can map the *same* section object into its address space, by passing an handle to it in a call to *MapViewOfFileEx*. When this is done, the two processes see the same physical memory. A process can obtain an handle to a section object created by another one in several ways, e.g.

the creating process can specify a name for the section in the call to *CreateFileMapping* and the second process does the same, thus, not actually creating a section object, but rather opening the existing one.

The names of these APIs refer to the file mapping capabilities of the VMM, because a section object can be used to map a file, but it is easier to understand how it works by examining "plain" shared memory first. Given the similarities between memory sharing and file mapping, it does not come as a surprise that file mappings can be shared too, so that multiple processes "see" the content of the same file and we will see how this is the foundation for loading and sharing DLLs.

The first parameter to *CreateFileMapping* is the handle of the file to map and, if we only want to allocate shared memory, we just have to set it to INVALID_HANDLE_VALUE. This gives us a section object not tied to the content of a particular file.

A section object which actually maps a file, is said to be *backed by the file*, because the content of its memory pages is read from the file and written to it when physical memory is repurposed. In keeping with this terminology, a section object created solely for the purpose of sharing memory is said to be *backed by the paging file*, since its content is stored and reloaded from the latter.

Among the data structures created with the section object is a set of special PTEs called *prototype PTEs*. They are special, because they are not actually used by the processor to translate virtual addresses, since they reside in memory pages not pointed by the paging structure hierarchy. We still call them PTEs because they are instances of _MMPTE, but they are working copies that the VMM uses to later fill the "real" PTEs used by the processors. To understand how prototype PTEs are used, we can depict the status of two processes sharing a newly allocated page of memory, when neither process has touched the page yet:

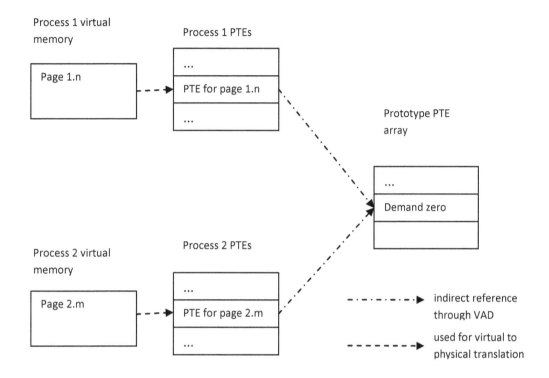

Figure 38 - Untouched Shared Page

The PTE which translates virtual page n of process 1 indirectly refers to a prototype PTE, which means it is an invalid PTE (P = 0) with a layout defined by the VMM to refer to a prototype PTE. We will call this PTE format a *proto-pointer* PTE, and it is defined as _MMPTE_PROTOTYPE among the kernel types. The prototype PTE, in turn, is set to a value which means that a zeroed page will have to be mapped for the first process touching the page. This value is an instance of _MMPTE_SOFTWARE with all the members set to 0, except for Protection, which is set to 4 for a read/write page.

If we suppose that process 1 touches the page first, the situation changes as follows:

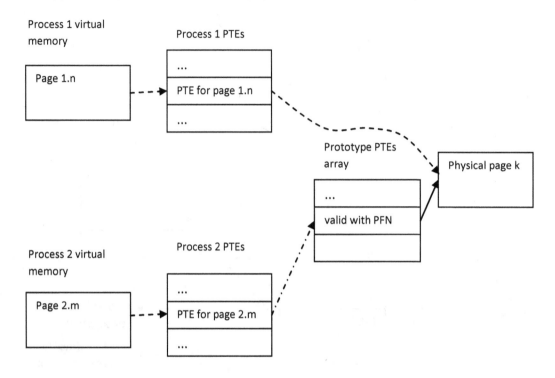

Figure 39 - Shared Page Touched by Process 1

The VMM sets both the PTE of process 1 and the prototype PTE as valid, with the PFN of physical page k. Process 1 now "sees" page k, because the processor translates virtual addresses in page 1.n to physical ones in page k. The PTE of process 2 has not been changed.

If, later, process 2 accesses the page, we have the following scenario:

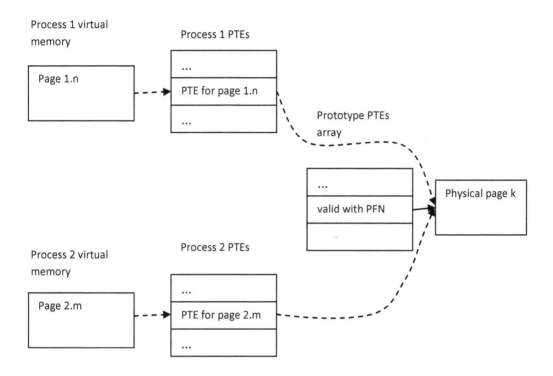

Figure 40 - Shared Page Touched by Both Processes

The VMM has set the PTE for process 2 with the PFN taken from the prototype PTE.

In general, a prototype PTE is used to fill the actual PTE of each process sharing the same memory range: if, later, process 3 maps the same section object and accesses the same page, the VMM looks into the prototype PTE to find the PFN of the physical page.

We will see in the next sections how the prototype PTE is used to implement out-paging as well: the shared page is removed from the working set of a process by setting its PTE back to a proto-pointer PTE. When the shared page has been removed from all the working sets, the physical page is moved to the Modified or Standby list and the prototype PTE is set accordingly.

The prototype PTE remains the single place where information allowing to fault back the page is stored: as long as the page is in transition, the prototype PTE stores the page PFN; if the page is repurposed, the prototype PTE stores the paging file offset; in turn, the sharing processes refer to the prototype PTE through their proto-pointers.

37.3 Setting up a Shared Memory Region

This section describes in deeper detail the data structures created when a shared region is set up.

37.3.1   Effect of CreateFileMapping

The handle returned by *CreateFileMapping* refers to an instance of _SECTION_OBJECT, whose Segment member stores the address of an instance of _SEGMENT. It's worth noting that the Segment member is defined as a pointer to _SEGMENT_OBJECT in the Windows symbols, however the content of the area pointed by it is consistent with the layout of _SEGMENT.

_SEGMENT.PrototypePte stores the address of the prototype PTE array. For shared memory, the array usually begins at the address of the member named _SEGMENT.ThePtes, i.e. at + 0x48 bytes from _SEGMENT. Below is an example of a _SEGMENT for a 1GB section:

```
0: kd> dt nt!_SEGMENT 0xfffff8a0`01a00000
   +0x000 ControlArea      : 0xfffffa80`02b83010 _CONTROL_AREA
   +0x008 TotalNumberOfPtes : 0x40000
   +0x00c SegmentFlags     : _SEGMENT_FLAGS
   +0x010 NumberOfCommittedPages : 0x40000
   +0x018 SizeOfSegment    : 0x40000000
   +0x020 ExtendInfo       : (null)
   +0x020 BasedAddress     : (null)
   +0x028 SegmentLock      : _EX_PUSH_LOCK
   +0x030 u1               : <unnamed-tag>
   +0x038 u2               : <unnamed-tag>
   +0x040 PrototypePte     : 0xfffff8a0`01a00048 _MMPTE
   +0x048 ThePtes          : [1] _MMPTE
```

_SEGMENT is located at 0xFFFFF8A0`01A00000 and PrototypePte is set to +0x48 from there. At this address begins the array of prototype PTEs, which are instances of _MMPTE. In this example, the page protection requested was read/write, so the PTEs are instances of _MMPTE_SOFTWARE, with Protection set to 4.

```
1: kd> dq 0xfffff8a0`01a00048
fffff8a0`01a00048  00000000`00000080 00000000`00000080
fffff8a0`01a00058  00000000`00000080 00000000`00000080
fffff8a0`01a00068  00000000`00000080 00000000`00000080
fffff8a0`01a00078  00000000`00000080 00000000`00000080
fffff8a0`01a00088  00000000`00000080 00000000`00000080
fffff8a0`01a00098  00000000`00000080 00000000`00000080
```

```
fffff8a0`01a000a8   00000000`00000080 00000000`00000080
fffff8a0`01a000b8   00000000`00000080 00000000`00000080
```

We can interpret the first occurrence with the `!pte` extension:

```
0: kd> !pte 0xfffff8a0`01a00048 1
                          VA fffff8a001a00048

PXE @ FFFFF8A001A00048    PPE at FFFFF8A001A00048    PDE at FFFFF8A001A00048    PTE at FFFFF8A001A00048
contains 0000000000000080        unavailable
not valid
DemandZero
Protect: 4 - ReadWrite
```

As the debugger shows, this value represents a demand-zero PTE, because it is not valid (bit 0 is clear), it is not in transition (bit 11 is clear) and the upper 32 bit (i.e. `_MMPTE_SOFTWARE.PageFileHigh`) where the paging file offset is stored are set to 0. When an actual PTE (meaning one used by the processor) is set to such a value, an attempt to access the mapped address results in a zero-filled page being mapped, hence the name. In summary, for a newly allocated section, the prototype PTEs are initialized as demand-zero ones. This is similar to what happens for actual PTEs with private memory, when a region is partially committed (as we saw in sec. 20.1.1 on p. 98).

`_SEGMENT.ControlArea` points to an instance of `_CONTROL_AREA`, whose `Segment` member points back to the segment. A `_CONTROL_AREA` can be interpreted with the `!ca` debugger extension:

```
0: kd> !ca 0xfffffa80`02b83010

ControlArea  @ fffffa8002b83010
  Segment       fffff8a001a00000  Flink      0000000000000000  Blink        0000000000000000
  Section Ref            1  Pfn Ref              0  Mapped Views          0
  User Ref               1  WaitForDel           0  Flush Count           0
  File Object  0000000000000000  ModWriteCount        0  System Views          0
  WritableRefs           0
  Flags (2000) Commit


Segment @ fffff8a001a00000
  ControlArea      fffffa8002b83010  ExtendInfo     0000000000000000
  Total Ptes            40000
  Segment Size       40000000  Committed            40000
  CreatingProcess fffffa8002e84b30  FirstMappedVa         0
  ProtoPtes       fffff8a001a00048
  Flags (80000) ProtectionMask


Subsection 1 @ fffffa8002b83090
  ControlArea  fffffa8002b83010  Starting Sector      0  Number Of Sectors  0
  Base Pte     fffff8a001a00048  Ptes In Subsect  40000  Unused Ptes        0
  Flags                 8  Sector Offset        0  Protection         4
```

The control area points to a subsection, described by an instance of _SUBSECTION. For shared memory (as opposite to mapped files), there is usually a single instance of subsection, so it does not add much to the information already provided by the segment, however its importance will become clearer with mapped files. Note how the base PTE address points to the prototype PTE array. It is worth noting that the protection which ends up in the prototype PTEs is stored in the subsection. The protection is encoded using the same values detailed in Table 3 on p. 104

The control area does not have an explicit pointer to the subsection, which appears to be located after the former, i.e. at +0x80 (the size of _CONTROL_AREA) from the control area address.

We can see how creating the section object does not, by itself, reserve, much less commit virtual address space. Rather, it results in the creation of a set of data structures which can be employed later to map a shared region into the address space of one or more processes. The VA at which the region is mapped in the address spaces is not stored in these data structures and will be established only when MapViewOfFileEx is called. These structures describe a range of virtual addresses of a given size, without tying it to a particular starting address.

The diagram below summarizes the relationships among these data structures.

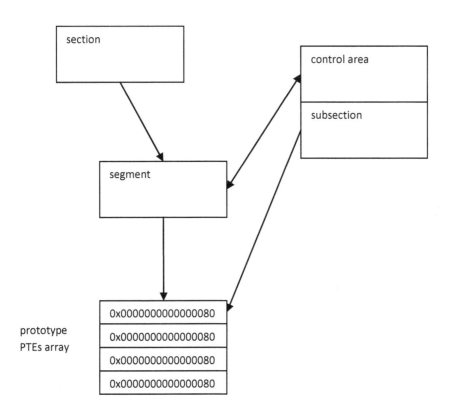

Figure 41 - Data Structures Created by *CreateFileMapping*

37.3.2   Effect of MapViewOfFileEx

37.3.2.1   Virtual Address of the Mapping in Different Processes

MapViewOfFileEx maps the shared region into the virtual address space of the calling process and returns the map starting address. The caller can specify the virtual address at which the region should be mapped, or can let the system choose a suitable address. This brings us to a concept we managed to avoid, so far, i.e. that shared memory is not necessarily mapped at the same virtual address in different processes.

The `dwNumberOfBytesToMap` parameter to *MapViewOfFileEx* specifies the size of the view, i.e. the length of the virtual region which is mapped to the section (it is possible to map a subrange of a section). The mapping succeeds only if a free range of the required size is available at the chosen starting address. Since different processes can have a different distribution of free ranges in their virtual address spaces, the VMM may choose a different starting address for the mapping. Even if the caller specifies a starting address, the mapping will fail if it would overlap a region of virtual addresses already in use. The bottom line is that a section can, and often will, be mapped at different virtual addresses among different processes.

Therefore, when we say that two processes access the same page of a section, we are not actually saying that they access the same virtual address. Rather, each process accesses some virtual address that, in its own address space, maps to the same physical page of the section. After a process has mapped a section, each mapped virtual page corresponds to a certain offset from the section start, e.g. the first mapped page corresponds to the first 0x1000 bytes of the section, the second one to the range 0x1000 - 0x1FFF and so on. The offset from the section start determines which prototype PTE is used to map the virtual range (e.g. the first PTE maps the range with offset between 0 and 0xFFF and so on) and, ultimately, which physical page is seen at the virtual address. Putting it all together, two processes see the same physical page at a virtual address which is at the same offset from the section start.

For the sake of completeness, it is worth to point out that *MapViewOfFileEx* also allows to specify an offset from the section starting address for the mapping. Thus, the address at offset 0 from the mapping starting address may be at offset *x* from the section starting address. However, when it comes to identifying which physical page is seen at a given VA, what matters is the offset from the beginning of the section, which must be computed accounting for an eventual offset passed to *MapViewOfFileEx*.

37.3.2.2   Data Structures Created by the Mapping

Since *MapViewOfFileEx* maps the section pages into a region of virtual addresses, it creates an entry in the VAD tree for the region. Below we can see an excerpt of the output from `!vad` for our test process with a 1GB mapped view:

```
VAD               level      start      end      commit
fffffa8002cacd70 ( 4)         10       1f          0 Mapped      READWRITE
...
fffffa8000a0a010 ( 3)        4d0     404cf          0 Mapped      READWRITE
...
Total VADs:    21  average level:    3  maximum depth: 4
```

Here we have part of the content of the `_MMVAD` instance for the region:

```
1: kd> dt -b nt!_mmvad fffffa8000a0a010
...
   +0x018 StartingVpn      : 0x4d0
   +0x020 EndingVpn        : 0x404cf
   +0x028 u                : <unnamed-tag>
         +0x000 Protection     : 0y00100 (0x4)
...
   +0x048 Subsection       : 0xfffffa80`02b83090
   +0x048 MappedSubsection : 0xfffffa80`02b83090
   +0x050 FirstPrototypePte : 0xfffff8a0`01a00048
   +0x058 LastContiguousPte : 0xfffff8a0`01c00040
   +0x060 ViewLinks        : _LIST_ENTRY [ 0xfffffa80`02b83080 - 0xfffffa80`02b83080 ]
      +0x000 Flink            : 0xfffffa80`02b83080
      +0x008 Blink            : 0xfffffa80`02b83080
...
```

There are a few things worth mentioning here:

- StartingVpn and EndingVpn are set to the region boundaries.

- u.Protection is set to the protection of the section. Actually, *MapViewOfFileEx* allows to specify a desired access to the section through its dwDesiredAccess parameter. Here we specified read/write access and since the section had been created with read/write protection, the internal encoding for read write (i.e. 4) ended up in the VAD. If we repeat the test requesting read only access, we end up with a protection of 1 in the VAD, which corresponds to read only page protection (see Table 3 on p. 104).

- Subsection points to the subsection created with the section.

- FirstPrototypePte points to the beginning of the PTE array.

This VAD resulted from calling MapViewOfFileEx with the offset from the beginning of the section set to 0. A nonzero offset would have resulted in FirstPrototypePte pointing to the prototype PTE corresponding to the offset. Note that the offset must be a multiple of 64k and hence is also a multiple of the page size. The first byte of the view will always be the first byte of a page, and FirstPrototypePte points to the prototype PTE used to map that page.

It is also interesting to examine the PTEs for the virtual address of the mapping:

```
1: kd> !pte 4d0000
                        VA 00000000004d0000
PXE @ FFFFF6FB7DBED000   PPE at FFFFF6FB7DA00000   PDE at FFFFF6FB40000010   PTE at FFFFF68000002680
contains 03A000001A5A2867  contains 02F0000019DA5867  contains 0000000000000000
pfn 1a5a2     ---DA--UWEV    pfn 19da5     ---DA--UWEV
```

In this particular case, the PDE is not valid, i.e. the PT for this VA has yet to be allocated. The VMM will look at the VAD to resolve the fault caused by the first access to this page.

37.3.2.3   NUMA Support

MapViewOfFileExNuma extends the functionality of *MapViewOfFileEx* allowing to specify a preferred NUMA node for the physical pages to be used. It works in a way similar to *VirtualAllocExNuma* (see sec. 20.1.4 on p. 105): `_MMVAD.u5.VadFlags3.PreferredNode` is set to `nndPreferred` (the node number passed to the API) + 1. The page fault handler uses this value as described in sec. 26.4.2 on p. 150 to allocate physical pages from the specified node when possible.

37.4 First Access to a Shared Page

Beginning with this section, we are going to describe the life cycle of a shared page with an approach similar to the one used for private memory. After the call to *MapViewOfFileEx*, virtual addresses in a shared page are not yet mapped to a physical one, as far as the processor is concerned, because their PTEs are still not valid or even missing. We are therefore going to begin our analysis with the first access to a page, which will cause a page fault.

In the following, we will use the term *hardware PTE* to refer to a PTE actually used to translate virtual to physical addresses, to distinguish it from a prototype PTE, which is simply a working copy used by the VMM. With this terminology, an hardware PTE is an 8 bytes *slot* which is accessed by the processor to perform a virtual to physical translation. We will not use the term hardware PTE to refer to a particular format of a PTE *content*, e.g. a valid PTE value, with the P bit set and a valid PFN in it. An hardware PTE can therefore store values with different formats, including ones with the P bit clear and other bits set to values defined by the VMM.

Since we are interested in virtual addresses mapped to a section, there will always be two PTEs involved: the hardware one and the prototype one.

When the first access occurs, the VMM allocates a zero-filled page and updates both the prototype and the hardware PTE so that they have the P bit set and the PFN field pointing to the physical page.

For a read/write mapping and view, the final prototype PTE has:

    `_MMPTE_HARDWARE.Dirty1` = 1, which makes the page writable (processor defined R/W bit)

_MMPTE_HARDWARE.Dirty = 1, which, together with Dirty1, marks the page as dirty.

_MMPTE_HARDWARE.Write = 1, which marks the page as writable to the VMM (software defined bit)

_MMPTE_HARDWARE.Owner = 0, which makes the page accessible only from kernel mode

_MMPTE_HARDWARE.Global = 1, which tells the processor not to invalidate a TLB entry for the page when CR3 is loaded. This is normally used for system range addresses, where the virtual to physical mapping is the same in all the address spaces.

Notes

1. For further details on the Dirty1 and Write bits see sections 26.6.2 on p. 164 and 33.3 on p. 248.

2. We are interpreting these bits as if this were an hardware PTE, however the prototype PTE itself is just a working copy. If an hardware PTE were to be filled with this content, these bits would have the effect detailed here.

The hardware PTE has:

_MMPTE_HARDWARE.Dirty1 = 1 if the access is a write, otherwise it is set to 0

_MMPTE_HARDWARE.Dirty = 1 if the access is a write, otherwise it is set to 0

_MMPTE_HARDWARE.Write = 1

_MMPTE_HARDWARE.Owner = 1, which makes the page accessible from kernel mode *and* user mode

_MMPTE_HARDWARE.Global = 0, which tells the processor to invalidate a TLB entry for the page when CR3 is loaded.

Notes

1. we know from sec. 26.6.2 on p. 164 that a page which has been mapped to resolve a demand-zero fault and has not yet written to the paging file should be considered dirty, regardless of the type of access, because a copy of the page content (even if it's just filled with zeroes) does not exist in the paging file yet. Remember that "clean" does not mean "never written to" but, rather, "equal to its paging file copy".

It might therefore seem wrong to set the hardware PTE as clean for a read access. However, by experimenting with test programs, we can see that the VMM moves such a page to the Modified list, when trimming occurs. At this stage, the VMM has at least two pieces of information which mark the page as dirty: the prototype PTE and the _MMPFN, which has u3.e1.Modified set.

2. Note how, when it comes to the hardware PTE, Owner and Global are set consistently with addresses in the user mode range.

It is also important to examine the content of the _MMPFN for the page assigned to the virtual address.

_MMPFN.u2.ShareCount = 1. This count will increase each time another process maps the section and accesses the page.

_MMPFN.u3.e1.Modified = 1.

_MMPFN.u3.ReferenceCount = 1. This count is *not* incremented when other processes access the same page. Whether the page is included in one or more working sets, this contributes with a single unit to the reference count. The reference count is incremented when other components lock the page in memory (see also sec. 28.5 on p. 192).

_MMPFN.OriginalPte: the initial value of the *prototype* PTE is copied here (i.e. 0x80 for a read/write section).

_MMPFN.PteAddress: set to the address of the *prototype* PTE.

_MMPFN.u4.PteFrame: set to the PFN of the physical page storing the *prototype* PTE.

_MMPFN.u4.ProtoTypePte = 1.

There are a few important things to point out about the _MMPFN.

OriginalPte, PteAddress and PteFrame are used to manage the page along its life cycle as it goes from Active to Modified/Standby and is eventually repurposed. All these fields refer to the prototype PTE, rather than the hardware one, because it is the former which refers to the page or the swapping file offset. The hardware PTEs only refer directly to the physical page when they are valid, otherwise they relate (indirectly, as we will see shortly) to the prototype PTEs in all other stages of the life cycle.

The `ProtoTypePte` flag is what tells the VMM components that manage pages that this page is part of a section. We will see shortly how this information is used by the working set manager. The `!pfn` extension (see: Appendix A on p.565 for more details on this extension) prints the "Shared" label for a page with this bit set, e.g.:

```
1: kd> !pfn 6148
    PFN 00006148 at address FFFFFA8000123D80
    flink        00000187  blink / share count 00000001  pteaddress FFFFF8A001A00048
    reference count 0001    used entry count  0000      Cached      color 0   Priority 5
    restore pte 00000080  containing page         02A714  Active      MP
    Modified Shared

1: kd> dt -b nt!_mmpfn FFFFFA8000123D80
    ...
    +0x028 u4                  : <unnamed-tag>
        +0x000 PteFrame          : 0y000000000000000000000000000000000001010100111000010100
(0x2a714)
        +0x000 Unused            : 0y000
        +0x000 PfnImageVerified : 0y0
        +0x000 AweAllocation     : 0y0
        +0x000 PrototypePte      : 0y1
        +0x000 PageColor         : 0y000000 (0)
```

If other processes access the same page, the corresponding hardware PTE is set up in the same way and the page share count is incremented. Note that, for this to happen, the other processes have to actually access the page. Simply mapping the same section only results in creating the VAD, but, as long as the page is not "touched" the hardware PTE is not set up with the page PFN and the share count is not incremented.

37.5 Removing a Shared Page from a Working Set

37.5.1   Actions Performed for All the Processes Where the Page Is Active

When a page which is part of a section is removed from the working set of a process, the VMM must perform different actions than the ones suitable for a private page.

For one thing, the hardware PTE must be set so that it refers to the prototype one, whereas for a private page it has to be set in transition. We can observe that the *FreeWsleList* function, executed by the working set manager, checks `_MMPFN.u4.PrototypePte` and acts accordingly.

This function sets the hardware PTE to an instance of `_MMPTE_PROTOTYPE`, which we are going to call a *proto-pointer*, to avoid confusing it with prototype PTEs.

The proto-pointer has:

```
_MMPTE_PROTOTYPE.Valid = 0
_MMPTE_PROTOTYPE.Prototype = 1
```

and this bit combination identifies the PTE content as a proto-pointer.

The WSM also sets `_MMPTE_PROTOTYPE.Protection` from the working set list entry for the page. When the WSM is in the process of removing the page, the latter still has a WSLE, with `_MMWSLENTRY.Protection` set to the page protection. As is the case for VADs and various PTE types, the protection is represented by numerical values unrelated to the processor-defined protection bits (see Table 3 on p. 104). The WSM copies `_MMWSLENTRY.Protection` into `_MMPTE_PROTOTYPE.Protection`.

This is interesting, because it is what makes possible to change the protection of a section page. After having mapped a section, we can use *VirtualProtectEx* to change the protection of some of its pages, in the context of a particular process. In broad terms, this does not work for every combination of original and new protection values, but, rather, when the protection change seeks to restrict access to the pages. At any rate, there are combinations for which the change is allowed, e.g. from read/write to read only.

This poses the problem of where to store the new protection while the page is in the working set and the PTE is valid.

For a private page, the VMM defined protection is stored in the hardware PTE when it is not valid; in the following, we are going to refer to the PTE *content* at this stage as the *software PTE* (it is an instance of `_MMPTE_SOFTWARE`). When eventually the hardware PTE becomes valid, the software PTE is copied into `_MMPFN.OriginalPte`, where it will eventually be updated with the paging file offset, still preserving the protection value. The key point is that, as long as the physical page is referenced by the hardware PTE, the `_MMPFN` is available to store the software PTE. This is true even when the page is in transition, because the hardware PTE still refers to it. The software PTE value must be evicted from the `_MMPFN` when the page is repurposed, because the `_MMPFN` instance will be updated to reflect whatever purpose the page has been reassigned to. At this stage, however, the hardware PTE is completely available, because it needs not to store the PFN anymore, so `OriginalPte`, which includes the protection, is copied back into the hardware PTE itself.

If we use *VirtualProtectEx* with a private page, the software PTE is updated and the new protection will remain in effect while the software PTE moves back and forth between the hardware PTE and `_MMPFN.OriginalPte`.

This cannot be done for a section page, because the `_MMPFN` is shared among all the processes. We need a per-process structure where to "park" the software PTE while the hardware PTE is valid. We cannot use the VAD, because, although it is a per-process structure, it is used to store the protection for the whole virtual region mapped to the section, while *VirtualProtectEx* allows to change the protection of single pages within the region. So, in the end, the VMM uses the working set list, to solve this problem.

It can be observed that the VMM appears to always copy the page protection into `_MMWSLENTRY.Protection`, and from there to `_MMPTE_PROTOTYPE.Protection`, not just for pages for which *VirtualProtectEx* has been used.

Another important member of `_MMPTE_PROTOTYPE` is `ProtoAddress`. As its name implies, it should be used to store the address of the prototype PTE, but this is not always the case. Before delving further into how it is used, we should point out that this member is 48 bits wide, so it cannot store a full 64 bit pointer. This is not a problem, however, because addresses must be in canonical form, so the upper 16 bits are simply equal to bit 47 and can be discarded. When `ProtoAddress` is actually used to store the address of a prototype PTE, the complete address can be computed by or-ing 0xFFFF000000000000 to its value, since prototype PTEs are in the system region, where bits 63-47 are set.

For sections mapped in the user region, `ProtoAddress` does not usually point to the prototype PTE, but, rather, it is set to 0xFFFFFFFFFFFF, which tells the VMM that it has to look into the VAD to eventually resolve a fault involving this PTE. At the end of the day, the VMM will still read the prototype PTE to resolve a fault, but it will find it by looking at the VAD, which in turn stores the addresses of the subsection and of the prototype PTE array. The offset of the faulting address from the start of the region described by the VAD will be used to compute the offset of the prototype PTE from the start of the array. It is interesting to observe that the debugger interprets such a proto-pointer as referring to a VAD:

```
0: kd> !pte 4e0000
                              VA 00000000004e0000
PXE at FFFFF6FB7DBED000   PPE at FFFFF6FB7DA00000   PDE at FFFFF6FB40000010   PTE at FFFFF68000002700
contains 00C0000023103867  contains 010000000CD46867  contains 05B0000029B60867  contains FFFFFFFF00000480
pfn 23103    ---DA--UWEV   pfn cd46    ---DA--UWEV   pfn 29b60    ---DA--UWEV   not valid
                                                                                Proto: VAD
```

Proto-pointers with `ProtoAddress` set to an actual address can be found with sections mapped by the cache manager, but we are not going to analyze them here, and with sections of executable files, which will be described shortly.

When a section page is removed from a WS, the VMM also performs the following actions:

- Decrements the share count of the PT to which the PTE belongs, as is the case for private pages

- Decrements the share count of the physical page being removed from the WS.

The prototype PTE is not updated as long as there are other processes where the page is Active, i.e. where a valid hardware PTE refers to the page.

37.5.2   Additional Actions for the Last Process Where the Page Is Active

The VMM detects that it is removing a section page from the last process actively using it when the share count drops to 0.

This scenario occurs when there are one or more processes mapping a view of the section and a particular physical page of the section is about to be removed (e.g. by WS trimming) from the last address space using it, i.e. the last valid hardware PTE pointing to that page is about to be set to a proto-pointer value. We can represent this situation with the following diagram:

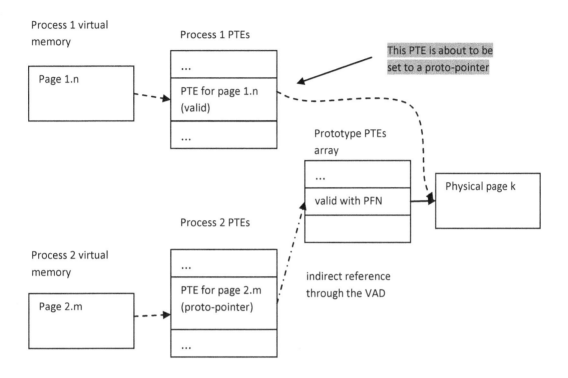

Figure 42 - Removal from the Last Working Set

When this happens, the reference count is decremented. If it is still greater than zero, some component has locked the page in memory, as explained in section 28.5 on p. 192.

If, on the other hand, the reference count becomes zero as well, the page is moved to the Modified or Standby list and the prototype PTE is set in transition, much in the same way this is done for the hardware PTE of a private page, i.e. it becomes an instance of `_MMPTE_TRANSITION` with:

> `_MMPTE_TRANSITION.Valid = 0`
> `_MMPTE_TRANSITION.Protection` = set to the protection from `_MMPFN.OriginalPte` (bits 5-9)
> `_MMPTE_TRANSITION.Transition` = 1 this bit, together with Valid = 0 marks the PTE as in transition
> `_MMPTE_TRANSITION.PageFrameNumber` still set to the PFN of the physical page

The `_MMPFN` is set accordingly to the page being on a transition list, with

`_MMPTE.u1.Flink`, `_MMPTE.u2.Blink` linking the instance to the Modified or
  Standby list

`_MMPTE.u3.ReferenceCount` = 0

`_MMPFN.u3.e1.PageLocation` set according to the list
  (`_MMLISTS.ModifiedPageList` or `_MMLISTS.StandbyPageList`)

`_MMPFN.PteAddress`, `_MMPFN.OriginalPte` and `_MMPFN.u4.PteFrame`:
  unchanged and still referring to the prototype PTE and its original software PTE
  value.

37.6 Writing a Section Page to the Paging File

When a page used for a section is written to the paging file, goes from the Modified to the
Standby list. As for a private page, `_MMPFN.OriginalPte.u.Soft.PageFileHigh` is set
to the paging file offset. By setting access breakpoints on members of `_MMPFN`, we can
observe that the page is written asynchronously by the Modified Page Writer (while the write
is in progress, `_MMPFN.u3.e1.WriteInProgress` is set), as it happens for private pages.

37.7 Soft Faults

A soft fault for a page which is part of a section can happen for several reasons.

A process can touch a virtual address whose page has been removed from its working set,
but whose prototype PTE is still valid and pointing to the physical page. In this scenario, at
the time of the fault the hardware PTE is set to a proto-pointer, but the prototype PTE is still
valid.

A similar scenario can take place, but with the prototype PTE and the physical page in
transition: the prototype PTE is not actually valid, but the physical page is still available on
the Modified or Standby list.

A process mapping a section touches a page for the first time and the prototype PTE is either
valid or in transition.

In all these situations the prototype PTE refers to a physical page with the desired content,
which is what makes the event a soft fault. The VMM brings the page into the Active state, if
it was in transition, and updates the hardware PTE involved so that it is valid as well and
pointing to the same physical page. It also increments the share count of the physical page
and updates the bits tracking whether the page is dirty or clean. Here are some of the
possible combinations:

- if the page was on the Standby list and the access is a read, the paging file offset in _MMPFN.OriginalPte is preserved and _MMPTE.u3.e1.Modified is clear, so the page remains clean. The hardware PTE has:

  _MMPTE.u.Hard.Dirty1 = 0, this makes the page read-only for the processor, so the first write attempt will cause a fault which will change the page status to dirty (see also sec. 33.3 on p. 248).

  _MMPTE.u.Hard.Dirty = 0

  _MMPTE.u.Hard.Write = 1, which tells the VMM this is actually a read/write page

- if the page was on the Standby list but the access is a write, it becomes dirty:

  _MMPFN.OriginalPte.u.Soft.PageFileHigh = 0

  _MMPTE.u3.e1.Modified = 1.

  The hardware PTE is read/write (_MMPTE.u.Hard.Dirty1 = 1), because there is no need to intercept the first write access.

- if the page was on the Modified list, it was and remains dirty. The hardware PTE is still set up as read-only if the access is a read.

Even without enumerating all the possible combinations of page states and types of access, the general rule is that the VMM tracks in the _MMPFN whether the page is clean or dirty and sets up the hardware PTE to detect when a clean page becomes dirty.

37.8 Section Page Repurposing

This part of the life cycle is similar for private and shared pages. The PTE pointing to the page is replaced with the content _MMPFN.OriginalPte, which stores the paging file offset and the VMM defined page protection. This unties the PTE from the physical page, which can be reused for something else.

For section pages, the _MMPFN refers to the prototype PTE, i.e.:

- _MMPFN.PteAddress is set to the address of the prototype PTE

- _MMPFN.u4.PteFrame stores the PFN of the page containing the prototype PTE

Thus, repurposing results in updating the prototype PTE, which is the right thing to do, since the hardware PTEs mapping the section by now are set to the proto-pointer to the VAD and must not be changed.

The overall situation after repurposing is depicted in the following diagram:

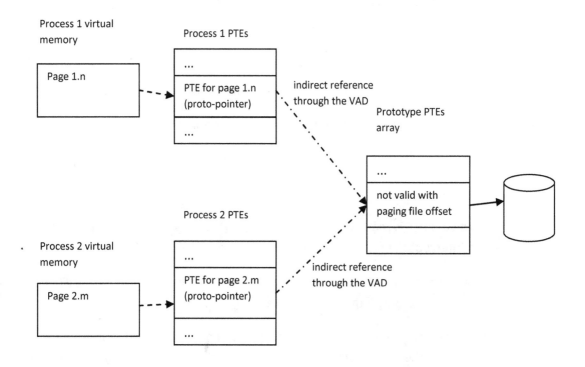

Figure 43 - Section Page After Repurposing

37.9 Writing to a Clean Section Page

This occurrence is handled in a way similar to a write to a private page (see sec. 33.2 on p. 246):

- The hardware PTE bits `Dirty1`, `Dirty` and `Accessed` are set

- The paging file allocation is released and `_MMPFN.OriginalPte.u.Soft.PagingFileHigh` is set to zero.

- `_MMPFN.u3.e1.Modified` is *not* set, as for a private page, however, it can be observed that this bit is set when the page is removed from the working set; we can therefore conclude that the VMM checks the PTE bits and updates the `_MMPFN` accordingly.

37.10   Hard Faults

As for private pages, a physical page is allocated and filled with content retrieved from the paging file. Afterwards, both the prototype PTE and the hardware PTE are set as valid and pointing, through the PFN field, to the new physical page, which is also added to the working set.

The page and PTE are configured as clean if the access is a read and as dirty otherwise.

37.11   Paging of Prototype PTEs

So far, we have turned a blind eye over one problem related to section objects implementation. The VMM must allocate a prototype PTE for each page of the section. For instance, a 1GB section spans 262,144 pages, so the same number of 8-bytes PTEs must be allocated in kernel memory, occupying 2MB of memory. If all the PTE arrays of all the sections were to be kept resident in physical memory, there would be a significant overhead. We have not covered memory mapped files yet, however they are based on section objects and every DLL and executable is accessed through memory mapping. The cache manager creates section objects for data files as well so the bottom line is there are a lot of section objects in a running system.

The VMM is therefore smart enough to page out prototype PTEs, to save physical memory. Before exploring this subject, we must say a few words about the *paged pool*.

37.11.1   Paged Pool Overview

The paged pool is a region of system virtual addresses mapped to pageable memory. The VMM offers APIs (actually, in kernel mode parlance the acronym DDI for Device Driver Interface is used, so we will adopt it from now on) to allocate and deallocate a region from the pool. A kernel component or driver who allocates a region is free to access that virtual range, but must be aware that its content can be unmapped at any time. For kernel mode code this is not irrelevant, because, under certain conditions, page faults cannot be generated. When the code *can* incur page faults it can freely access paged pool regions while the VMM takes care of handling any fault.

Kernel-mode code allocating from the paged pool can specify a four byte *tag* which identifies its allocations and is displayed by various tools to track pool usage. One such tool is the `!pool` debugger extension, which we are going to use in the next section.

37.11.2   Dumping Section Data Structures in Paged Pool

We can use the !pool extension to confirm that some of the data structures used to implement memory sections are in paged pool. Below is the output from !vad for a process with a 1GB view of a section:

```
1: kd> !vad ffffffa8000aeabc0
VAD             level     start     end      commit
...
fffffa8000a81320 ( 3)      490     4048f         0 Mapped       READWRITE
...
Total VADs:    21  average level:   3  maximum depth: 4
```

By examining the VAD, we find the addresses of the subsection and the prototype PTE array:

```
1: kd> dt nt!_mmvad fffffa8000a81320
...
   +0x048 Subsection       : 0xfffffa80`026dab90 _SUBSECTION
   +0x048 MappedSubsection : 0xfffffa80`026dab90 _MSUBSECTION
   +0x050 FirstPrototypePte : 0xfffff8a0`02800048 _MMPTE
   +0x058 LastContiguousPte : 0xfffff8a0`02a00040 _MMPTE
...
```

We can now feed the address of the prototype PTE array to the !pool extension:

```
1: kd> !pool 0xfffff8a0`02800048
Pool page fffff8a002800048 region is Paged pool
*fffff8a002800000 : large page allocation, Tag is MmSt, size is 0x201000 bytes
               Pooltag MmSt : Mm section object prototype ptes, Binary : nt!mm
```

This tells us that the address is indeed part of a paged pool region, allocated with the tag MmSt. We can also see that the pool region size is 0x201000, i.e. 2 MB plus one page, which is consistent with the fact that the segment is in the same region. To better understand this, we can retrieve the segment address from the subsection:

```
1: kd> dt nt!_subsection 0xfffffa80`026dab90
   +0x000 ControlArea      : 0xfffffa80`026dab10 _CONTROL_AREA
...
1: kd> !ca 0xfffffa80`026dab10

ControlArea  @ fffffa80026dab10
  Segment      fffff8a002800000   Flink      0000000000000000  Blink
0000000000000000
```

The segment is located immediately before the prototype PTEs array, at the beginning of the paged pool region. As we said before, a 1 GB region requires 262144 PTEs occupying 2MB. Since the PTEs begin at +0x48 inside the first page of the region, because of the segment instance, the region must span an extra page to accommodate them all (assuming that the

VMM rounds the region size up to the first multiple of the page size when allocating from the pool).

The paged pool has an associated working set, not unlike the ones used for process address spaces, keeping track of which virtual addresses are currently mapped to physical pages. We can therefore say that a physical page is added to the paged pool working set when it is used to map a virtual region of the pool.

Other section-related data structures are not kept in paged pool. For instance, if we use `!pool` with the control area address we get:

```
Pool page fffffa80026dab10 region is Nonpaged pool
 fffffa80026da000 size:   80 previous size:    0  (Allocated)  Even (Protected)
 fffffa80026da080 size:   30 previous size:   80  (Free)       IoUs
 fffffa80026da0b0 size:   60 previous size:   30  (Allocated)  Io
 fffffa80026da110 size:  150 previous size:   60  (Allocated)  File (Protected)
 fffffa80026da260 size:   90 previous size:  150  (Allocated)  Vad
 fffffa80026da2f0 size:  100 previous size:   90  (Allocated)  MmCa
 fffffa80026da3f0 size:   30 previous size:  100  (Allocated)  MmSi
 fffffa80026da420 size:  1e0 previous size:   30  (Allocated)  MmCi
 fffffa80026da600 size:  500 previous size:  1e0  (Allocated)  Thre (Protected)
*fffffa80026dab00 size:   d0 previous size:  500  (Allocated) *MmCa
          Pooltag MmCa : Mm control areas for mapped files, Binary : nt!mm
 fffffa80026dabd0 size:   c0 previous size:   d0  (Allocated)  FMfc
 fffffa80026dac90 size:  150 previous size:   c0  (Allocated)  File (Protected)
 fffffa80026dade0 size:   c0 previous size:  150  (Allocated)  FMfc
 fffffa80026daea0 size:  160 previous size:   c0  (Allocated)  Ntfx
```

Which tells us the control area is in *nonpaged* pool memory, which, as the name suggests, is not pageable. Paged pool memory is usually found at addresses in the range 0xFFFFF8A0`00000000 – 0xFFFFF8BF`FFFFFFFF.

37.11.3   Prototype PTEs Paging Logic

In general, paged pool (PP) physical pages can be removed from the PP working set at any time by the VMM, much like user range pages, to reuse physical memory for other purposes. It is the job of the VMM to fault back physical memory as needed, when PP memory is accessed.

Prototype PTEs, however, pose a special problem. Consider, for instance an Active section page: the prototype PTE refers to it with its PFN field and the _MMPFN of the page refers to the page containing the PTE with its `u4.PteFrame` member, as in the following diagram:

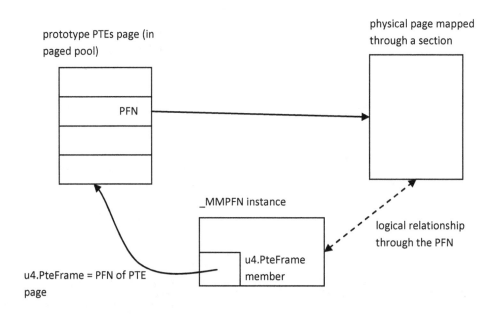

Figure 44 - Relationship between Prototype Page, _MMPFN and Mapped Page

Now suppose that the prototype page (i.e. the page storing the prototype PTEs) is reused, saving its content in the paging file, for some other purpose, e.g. to resolve a demand-zero fault. `_MMPFN.u4.PteFrame` would still point to the physical page, even though the latter is not storing the prototype PTEs anymore, which would obviously lead to a disaster. The fact alone that the VMM can restore swapped out PP content when needed is not enough for prototype PTEs: the VMM itself needs to make sure that the *same* physical page is present, when it needs to access the prototype PTEs. Thus, pages storing prototype PTEs are handled in a special way.

When a prototype PTE is set to valid and pointed to a physical page, the share count *of the page storing the prototype PTE* is incremented. This is not unlike what happens for private pages. For instance, when a demand-zero fault is resolved, both for private and for section pages, *MiInitializePfn* is called and it is this function which increments the share count of the PTE page. For a private page, the PTE page is the actual PT, while for a section page the PTE page is the one containing the prototype PTE. This is consistent with the general concept that the _MMPFN of a section page relates to the prototype PTE with all the members that would normally refer to an hardware PTE for a private page (`PteAddress`, `OriginalPte`, `u4.PteFrame`).

The prototype page share count is decremented when one of its PTEs is disassociated from the physical page it was pointing to (e.g., the PTE is set to point into the paging file, or is released altogether). In general, a PTE is associated with a physical page when it is valid or in transition. Again, this is the same logic used for private pages, only applied to the prototype page instead of the page table.

It's worth pointing out that other kernel-mode components outside the VMM, e.g. kernel-mode drivers, cannot manipulate the share count of paged pool pages: this is an internal logic of the VMM itself.

For a PP page, the share count is used much in the same way it is for a user range page: it is incremented when the page is used to map the PP virtual address (i.e. added to the PP working set) and decremented when the VA is unmapped. When the share count drops to zero, the reference count is decremented; when the reference count drops to zero, the page is moved to a transition list.

Now suppose that the VMM decides to remove a set of physical pages from the PP working set, to attempt to reuse memory, and that a prototype page is among them. The share count of this page will be decremented but, as long as there are one or more PTEs referencing physical pages, it will not drop to zero, so the reference count is not decremented and the page remains active. This is a peculiar situation, because we have a page with a nonzero share count, which is not actually part of any working set; normally, the share count of a physical page is equal to the number of working sets including it.

So far so good, the VMM has a way to ensure the page is not grabbed (notably, by *its own* working set manager) as long as it is needed. It must however deal with the fact that the PP virtual region corresponding to the page might be unmapped. When the WSM removes the page from the PP working set, it sets the PTE mapping it in transition, so attempting to access the prototype PTE at their regular virtual address could cause a page fault.

The VMM code accounts for this possibility by mapping the page at a work VA address at which to access it. This happens, for instance, inside *MiPfnShareCountIsZero*, when the VMM needs to set a prototype PTE in transition: the PFN of the prototype page is taken from `_MMPFN.u4.PteFrame` of the page mapped by the PTE and used to make the prototype page visible at a work virtual range, where the prototype PTE is updated. This extra work is done only for prototype PTEs, while hardware ones are updated directly at their virtual address in the paging structures region (and outside *MiPfnShareCountIsZero*).

Another stage of the paging logic where the VMM needs to update the PTE is when a page is repurposed and the PTE must be changed from a transition one to a software one pointing into the paging file. The code performing this operation always maps the page storing the PTE at a work address by calling *MiMapPageInHyperSpaceWorker* as explained in sec. 26.4.3.4.3.1 on p. 158. This works both for hardware and prototype PTEs: the `_MMPFN.u4.PteFrame` member of the page being repurposed gives access to the relevant page table (either a "real" page table or a prototype page) and the PTE is updated.

In summary, all the stages where the VMM needs to touch a prototype PTE work thanks to the fact that the physical page is still available (because of the nonzero share count) and it does not matter whether the PP virtual address is currently mapped to it or not.

When all the prototype PTEs in a page have no relationship with other physical pages and when the page is removed from the PP working set, the share count drops to zero and the page can be safely moved to a transition list.

This logic complements the regular paging activity performed on PP pages, to manage those special ones which can be referenced by `_MMPFN`s. This is done in an elegant fashion, by the coupling of two criteria:

- The share count of a page storing prototype PTEs accounts for the number of entries referring to physical pages, in the same way the share count of an hardware page table does.

- The paged pool physical pages are subject to the share count/reference count rules as any other physical page in the system.

37.11.4   Resolving a Fault When the Prototype PTEs Are Swapped out

In the previous section, we saw how the VMM *avoids* bringing prototype pages out of the active state when it cannot be done. At some point, however, prototype pages can be repurposed, so, sooner or later, a fault will happen for which the prototype page is swapped out.

This is not terribly different from what happens when the paging structures for private pages are swapped out (see sec. 36.4 on p. 293) and is handled by calling *MiDispatchFault* with `rdx` set to the address of the prototype PTE which must be paged in. Below is an excerpt from a debug session where the prototype PTE was swapped out.

The process was attempting to access address 0x4A0000, which was part of a section and whose PTE was not valid:

```
1: kd> !pte 4a0000
                                VA 00000000004a0000

PXE at FFFFF6FB7DBED000   PPE at FFFFF6FB7DA00000   PDE at FFFFF6FB40000010   PTE at FFFFF68000002500
contains 00C0000034005867  contains 0100000014D08867  contains 1B80000013AA7847  contains FFFFFFFF00000480
pfn 34005   ---DA--UWEV   pfn 14d08   ---DA--UWEV   pfn 13aa7   ---D---UWEV   not valid
                                                                               Proto: VAD
                                                                               Protect: 4 - ReadWrite
```

Below is the address of the VAD for the section range:

```
1: kd> !vad ffffffa8002d9b6c0
VAD               level     start     end     commit
...
ffffffa80010ca2b0 ( 4)        4a0    2049f         0 Mapped       READWRITE
Pagefile-backed section
...
Total VADs:    21  average level:    3  maximum depth: 4
```

The VAD gives us the address of the prototype PTE:

```
1: kd> dt nt!_mmvad ffffffa80010ca2b0
...
   +0x048 Subsection        : 0xffffffa80`00fc9090 _SUBSECTION
   +0x048 MappedSubsection  : 0xffffffa80`00fc9090 _MSUBSECTION
   +0x050 FirstPrototypePte : 0xfffff8a0`0283c048 _MMPTE
   +0x058 LastContiguousPte : 0xfffff8a0`0293c040 _MMPTE
```

The PTE address is not valid:

```
1: kd> dq 0xfffff8a0`0283c048
fffff8a0`0283c048  ????????`???????? ????????`????????
fffff8a0`0283c058  ????????`???????? ????????`????????
fffff8a0`0283c068  ????????`???????? ????????`????????
fffff8a0`0283c078  ????????`???????? ????????`????????
fffff8a0`0283c088  ????????`???????? ????????`????????
fffff8a0`0283c098  ????????`???????? ????????`????????
fffff8a0`0283c0a8  ????????`???????? ????????`????????
fffff8a0`0283c0b8  ????????`???????? ????????`????????
```

By using !pte with the address of the prototype PTE, we see that the page storing it is in the paging file:

```
1: kd> !pte 0xfffff8a0`0283c048
                                    VA fffff8a00283c048

PXE at FFFFF6FB7DBEDF88   PPE at FFFFF6FB7DBF1400   PDE at FFFFF6FB7E2800A0   PTE at FFFFF6FC500141E0
contains 000000003D144863  contains 0000000000BB5863  contains 000000002D417863  contains 000278B000000080
pfn 3d144   ---DA--KWEV   pfn bb5   ---DA--KWEV   pfn 2d417   ---DA--KWEV   not valid
                                                                               PageFile:  0
                                                                               Offset:  278b0
```

By tracing the fault processing we arrive at a call to *MiDispatchFault* with rdx set to the prototype PTE address:

```
1: kd> r
rax=fffff88004e4fbc0 rbx=0000000000000000 rcx=0000000000000000
rdx=fffff8a00283c048 rsi=0000000000000000 rdi=ffffffffffffffff
rip=fffff800028e5bc0 rsp=fffff88004e4fab8 rbp=fffff88004e4fb40
 r8=0000000000000000  r9=0000000000000000 r10=0000000000000000
r11=fffffa8000fc9090 r12=fffffa8003204b60 r13=fffff8a00283c048
r14=fffff88004e4fc20 r15=fffff80002a54b40
iopl=0         nv up ei pl zr na po nc
cs=0010  ss=0018  ds=002b  es=002b  fs=0053  gs=002b             efl=00000246
nt!MiDispatchFault:
fffff800`028e5bc0 fff3            push    rbx
```

Here is the call stack of the thread at the beginning of *MiDispatchFault*

```
1: kd> !thread @$thread
THREAD fffffa8003204b60  Cid 0718.02a4  Teb: 000007fffffde000 Win32Thread:
0000000000000000 RUNNING on processor 1
Not impersonating
DeviceMap               fffff8a000e8fe70
Owning Process          fffffa8001cbc9e0       Image:        MemTests.EXE
Attached Process        N/A         Image:        N/A
Wait Start TickCount    7055785       Ticks: 2 (0:00:00:00.031)
Context Switch Count    7842
UserTime                00:00:05.296
KernelTime              00:00:07.531
Win32 Start Address 0x000000013f9944c0
Stack Init fffff88004e4fdb0 Current fffff88004e4f690
Base fffff88004e50000 Limit fffff88004e4a000 Call 0
Priority 11 BasePriority 8 UnusualBoost 0 ForegroundBoost 2 IoPriority 2 PagePriority 5
Child-SP          RetAddr           : Args to Child
: Call Site
fffff880`04e4fab8 fffff800`028e5828 : ffffffff`ffffffff 00000000`004a0000
00000000`00000000 00000000`00000000 : nt!MiDispatchFault

fffff880`04e4fac0 fffff800`028c7fee : 00000000`00000000 00000000`00000000
00000000`00000001 fffffa80`0194c6c0 : nt!MmAccessFault+0x1c48

fffff880`04e4fc20 00000001`3f991951 : 00000001`3f9eeac0 00000001`3f9eeaa0
00000000`004a0000 00000000`004a1000 : nt!KiPageFault+0x16e (TrapFrame @
fffff880`04e4fc20)

00000000`0019fc90 00000001`3f9eeac0 : 00000001`3f9eeaa0 00000000`004a0000
00000000`004a1000 00000000`20000000 : 0x1`3f991951

00000000`0019fc98 00000001`3f9eeaa0 : 00000000`004a0000 00000000`004a1000
00000000`20000000 00000000`00000000 : 0x1`3f9eeac0

00000000`0019fca0 00000000`004a0000 : 00000000`004a1000 00000000`20000000
00000000`00000000 00000000`00000020 : 0x1`3f9eeaa0
```

MiDispatchFault is the workhorse function called to resolve most kinds of faults and is capable of going all the way to the paging file and back to retrieve the prototype PTEs.

37.12   Releasing Shared Memory

Releasing shared memory is a two-step process. First, *UnmapViewOfFile* is called to disassociate the virtual range from the section object. Among other things, this decrements the share count of all the pages that were part of the working set of the process calling the function.

It's interesting to remember that when a section is mapped by *n* processes the page share count is not necessarily equal to *n* for all the pages. A sharing process contributes to the share count only when it actually accesses the page: it is at this stage that the VAD is consulted and the hardware PTE filled from the prototype one. So, in general, active physical pages of the section can have any share count between 1 and *n*. When *UnmapViewOfFile* is called, the share count of the pages which are part of the working set of the calling process is decremented. For some pages, this may result in the share count dropping to 0, which causes them to be moved to the Standby or Modified list.

When there are no processes left mapping a view of a section, all the section pages are on a transition list.

The second step in releasing shared memory is closing the handle of the section object. As long as there are processes with an open handle to the section object, the section data structures (control area, subsections, segment) are retained and the section pages are left on the transition lists. Modified pages continue to be outpaged by the modified page writer and Standby pages can be repurposed, but this does not necessarily happen, if there is other memory available.

It is worth to point out how this differs from when private memory is released. With this kind of memory, the physical pages are immediately added to the free list, since their content is not needed anymore: once we release memory, there is no way we can get back its content. Paging file blocks used by clean, outpaged physical pages and by swapped out content will be released as well, for the same reason. On the other hand, for shared memory, as long as the section exists, its content can't be discarded, so it is either in pages on a transition list or swapped out.

The section is destroyed when the last handle to it is closed. Again, when this happen, the memory content cannot be retrieved anymore. At this stage, the physical pages consumed by the section are moved to the free list and paging file space is released.

This behavior can be observed with the MemTests program (included in the download package and described later in section 38.7 on p. 371) and with an utility like Process Explorer by Sysinternals, which displays the amount of Free, Standby and Modified pages.

First, we start an instance of MemTests and allocate a section object big enough to stick out in the memory counters, e.g. 512 MB on a 1GB system. We can do this with the *Memory section test* option.

Then we use the *Access region* option to write to the entire region, so that the section consumes physical pages. Process explorer will show an increase in used physical memory. The following figure shows the physical memory usage for a 512MB section on a virtual machine with 1GB:

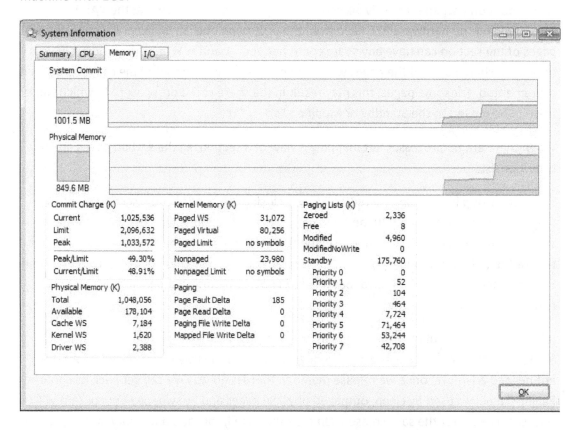

Figure 45 - Physical Memory Usage After Accessing a Memory Section

We then start a second instance of MemTests, use the *Open existing file mapping* option to open the same section and read the entire region, so that the second process is actually referencing the physical pages.

Afterwards, we use the *Release file mapping* option to unmap the view and close the section handle in one MemTests instance. We can see that the Standby and Modified counters don't change (other than their normal fluctuation), because the section physical pages are still mapped in the second MemTests process. The following figure is a snapshot taken at this stage:

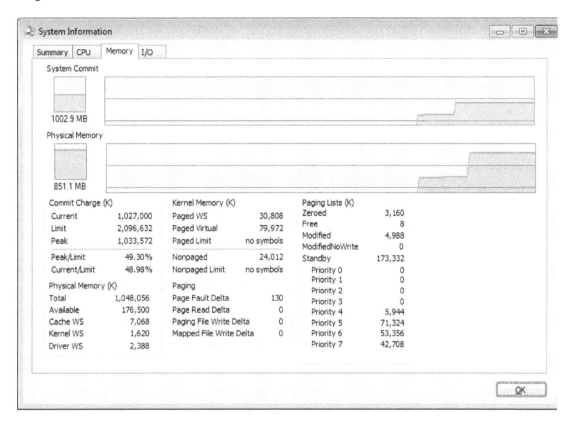

Figure 46 - Physical Memory Usage with One Remaining Mapping

When we unmap the view from the second instance as well and before closing the handle, we see a sharp increase in the Modified list:

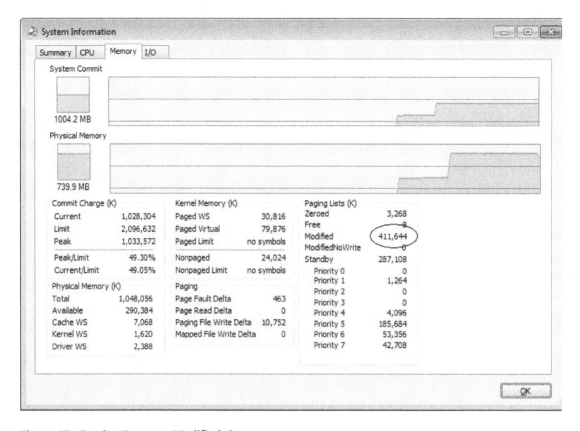

Figure 47 - Section Pages on Modified List

These are the section pages which are not part of a working set anymore and have been moved on the Modified list. They are dirty, hence they don't go to the Standby list, because we wrote to the memory region earlier. The physical memory graph shows the beginning of a downward ramp, due to the modified page writer which is outpaging and moving pages to the Standby list.

When we close the second and last handle to the section, all the section content is discarded. Both the pages still on the Modified list and those moved to the Standby list are added to the Free list and then Zeored. In the end, the Zeroed counter has increased significantly while the Modified and Stanby ones have dropped:

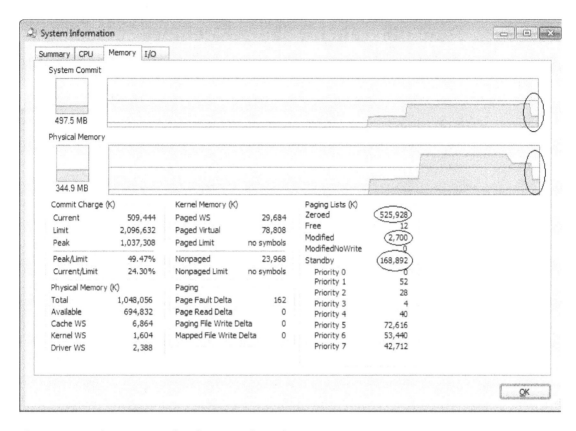

Figure 48 - Section Destroyed and Pages Released

We can also see that the commit charge has dropped, since the section just released needed to be backed either by memory or paging file.

37.13   State Diagram for Shared Memory

Figure 49 shows the page state diagram with the transitions for shared memory highlighted in bold.

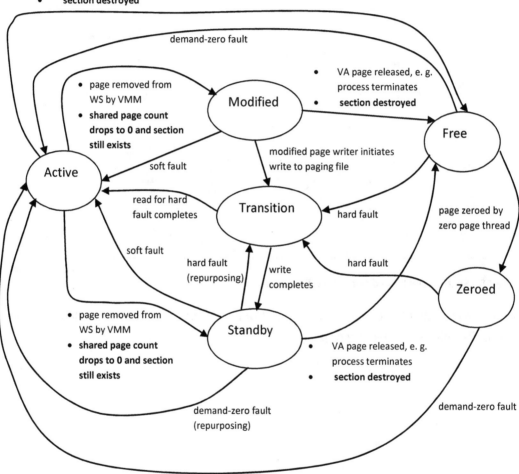

Figure 49 - State Diagram with Section Objects Transitions

37.14   Shared Memory and Working Set List Entries

37.14.1   How the VMM Can Get from a VA to Its WSLE

In section 20.3.6 on p. 123 we saw how the VMM stores inside the _MMPFN the WSLE index of a page active in a working set (in the u1.WsIndex member). This is done to be able to get from a valid VA to its WSLE. WSLEs are in random order inside the WSL and there is no easy way to find the entry for a particular VA simply by looking at the list. Instead, the VMM can easily get from the VA to the PTE, from the PTE to the page _MMPFN and find the WSLE index there.

37.14.2   The Problem (and the Non-problem) for Shared Memory

The approach outlined in the previous section works well for private pages which are mapped at most in a single WS, but shared memory poses a new problem. The same physical page can be added first to a working set and later to another one (or several other ones). The VMM cannot be sure that the same WSLE is available in all the WSs, since WSLEs are allocated depending on the order in which each process accesses memory, and freed for a number of events, including the VMM trimming activity. So a shared page can be associated with different WSL indexes in different WSs.

The VMM can detect this situation when it follows its usual path to find the WSLE: it can read the index from the _MMPFN and access the WSLE selected by it. The WSLE contains the VA it refers to, so the VMM can compare the VA from the WSLE with the one it started from. If the two are not the same, it knows the WSLE is not the correct one. When this happens, the VMM needs a way to get to the correct entry.

Before looking at how the VMM solves this problem, it's worth spending a few words on something that is *not* part of the problem. So far, we concentrated on WSLE indexes, which may be different across WSs. The same applies for the VA at which the page is mapped: a shared page can be mapped at different VAs in different address spaces. However, this is not a problem when it comes to get from VA to WSLE.

Consider two address spaces *A* and *B* where the same shared page is mapped at different VAs *VAa* and *VAb*, but suppose the VMM has been able to use the same WSLE with index *i* in both WSs. When the address space *A* is current the VMM can get to the _MMPFN from the PTE and get index *i*, which is valid. When address space *B* is current, the PTE for *VAb* points to the same _MMPFN, allowing again to extract index *i*. In summary, different VAs are not a problem because, in the end, they map to the same page; different WSLEs, instead *are* a problem.

The scenario with different VAs and same index can actually be observed by experimenting a little with memory sections.

37.14.3   The Solution: the Hash Table (in General)

The VMM solves this problem by using an hash table. Actually, there are two hash tables and we will analyze them in more details shortly, but, for now, it is enough to think of a single, logical, hash table which associates a VA with a WSL index. Whenever the VMM discovers that the WSLE selected by _MMPFN.u1.WsIndex is for another VA, it uses the hash table to get from the VA to the correct index. Each WS has its own hash table (in the Hyperspace region, which is process-private), so each table has the correct indexes for the WS it belongs to. We are now going to describe when the VMM decides to create hash table entries.

The logic described from now on is implemented in the following VMM functions: *MiUpdateWsle, MiUpdateWsleHash, MiSwapWslEntries.*

The first thing to note is that a plain WSLE for a private page has the Direct bit set, like the one below:

```
1: kd> ?? ((nt!_mmwsl *) 0xfffff70001080000)->Wsle[0x1f6].u1.e1
struct _MMWSLENTRY
   +0x000 Valid            : 0y1
   +0x000 Spare            : 0y0
   +0x000 Hashed           : 0y0
   +0x000 Direct           : 0y1
   +0x000 Protection       : 0y00000 (0)
   +0x000 Age              : 0y000
   +0x000 VirtualPageNumber : 0y0000000000000000000000000000000000000000000000011000000
(0xc0)
```

When a shared page is added to a working set and is not already part of another WS, the WSLE is set up like the one before, with the Direct bit set. The VMM detects this condition from _MMPFN.u1.WsIndex, which is 0 for such a page. After the page has been added to the WS, _MMPFN.u1.WsIndex will be set to the WSLE index.

When a shared page is being added to a WS and it already has a value in _MMPFN.u1.WsIndex, the VMM attempts to use the same index in the new WS.

If the WSLE is free in the WS it is used, however the Direct bit is not set. It therefore appears that Direct is only set in the WS which first assigned the page its WS index.

If the WSLE is in use, the VMM *moves* its content to another free entry and reuses the entry for the page being added to the WS. Thus, even in this scenario, the WSLE for the page is the one whose index is found in the _MMPFN. However, when this happens, the VMM also creates an hash table entry for the VA. This entry will tie the VA at which the page is mapped with the WSLE index, even though this index is the same one found in the `_MMPFN`. Furthermore, the entry will have the `Direct` bit clear and the `Hashed` bit set, like the following one:

```
1: kd> ?? ((nt!_mmwsl *) 0xfffff700`01080000)->Wsle[0x207].u1.e1
struct _MMWSLENTRY
   +0x000 Valid             : 0y1
   +0x000 Spare             : 0y0
   +0x000 Hashed            : 0y1
   +0x000 Direct            : 0y0
   +0x000 Protection        : 0y00100 (0x4)
   +0x000 Age               : 0y000
   +0x000 VirtualPageNumber : 0y0000000000000000000000000000000000000000000001011111
(0x5f)
```

In general, the `Hashed` bit seems to indicate the presence of an hash table entry. Creating the hash table entry in this scenario is a wasted effort. The entry will eventually be used if the WSLE is eventually relocated in the future, ending up at an index which is not the one in the `_MMPFN` anymore.

When the VMM moves an WSLE as we just saw there are two possible scenarios: the WSLE being moved can be associated with a private or shared physical page.

When the former applies, `_MMPFN.u1.WsIndex` is updated with the index of the new WSLE assigned to the page. The WSLE still has `Direct` set and it has no hash table entry. It is as if it had been loaded into the final WSLE from the beginning.

If the WSLE being moved is for a shared page, `_MMPFN.u1.WsIndex` cannot be changed. There could be other WSs including the same page at that index and they need the `_MMPFN` to stay the same to be accessible. So the WSLE being moved becomes the one really in need of an hash table entry: it is about to end up in an WSLE with an index *different* from `_MMPFN.u1.WsIndex`. The VMM creates an hash table entry for the VA (if one did not exist already) and records into it the new index of the WSLE.

With this logic, the last VA "targeting" a WSLE wins and the VA previously tracked by the entry is relocated. Possibly, the reasoning behind this is that older WSLEs have an higher chance of being evicted from the WSL by the Working Set Manager before they need to be accessed by means of the hash table. The WSM scans WSs not VAs, so it needs not to go through the hash table.

37.14.4   Hash Tables Details

The concepts in this section can be observed by analyzing the *MiUpdateWsleHash* function.

There are actually two hash tables, pointed by the _MMWSL structure usually located at address 0xFFFFF700`01080000.

37.14.4.1   Non Direct Hash Table

The first one is pointed by _MMWSL.NonDirectHash and is 1 page in size. It is usually at address 0xFFFFF704`40000000, i.e. at +17GB inside the hyperspace region. Its entries are of type _MMWSLE_NONDIRECT_HASH

```
1: kd> dt -v  nt!_MMWSLE_NONDIRECT_HASH

struct _MMWSLE_NONDIRECT_HASH, 2 elements, 0x10 bytes
   +0x000 Key              : Ptr64 to Void
   +0x008 Index            : Uint4B
```

and is 0x10 bytes long, so the table can store up to 0x100 entries. The VMM looks into this table to find the WSL index for a given VA. It uses bits 0-7 of the Virtual Page Number (i.e. bits 12 - 19 of the VA) as an index into the table. Of course, collisions are possible, i.e. two VAs with the same value for bits 12-19 select the same entry. The Key member of the entry stores the complete VA the entry is actually referring to, so the VMM checks it to see if it has selected the correct hash table entry. If this is not the case, it scans the table sequentially looking for the VA in the Key member. (Key is actually set to the VA OR-ed with 1, so it has bit 0 set; this is accounted for when searching for the correct entry; remember that WSLEs are associated with page aligned addresses).

Since this hash table is limited to 0x100 entries it can become full. When this happens, *MiConvertWsleHash* is called (e. g. by *MiUpdateWsleHash*), probably to convert the hash table in a direct one, discussed in the next section.

37.14.4.2   Direct Hash Table

The direct hash table address is stored in _MMWSL.HashTableStart, which is usually set to 0xFFFFF704`40001000, i.e. right after the non direct one. The table itself is an array of _MMWSLE_HASH indexed as follows:

- To locate the entry for a given VA, _MMWSL.LowestPagableAddress is subtracted from the address itself.

- The result is shifted right by 12 bits.

- The final result is the index into the array. An _MMWSLE_HASH is 4 bytes in size, so the entry offset is the index multiplied by 4.

`_MMWSL.LowestPagableAddress` is usually 0, however the name suggests that, if a WS has a non-pageable region in its lower range, this member points to the beginning of the pageable range. This saves array space, because associates element 0 of the array with the first movable page of memory. Pages that are not pageable don't need to be accounted for in the WSL.

The result of the subtraction is right-shifted 12 times because each WSLE is associated with a virtual page number, so entry 0 is for page 0, entry 1 is for page 0x1000, etc. (assuming the lowest pageable address is 0).

From the logic above we can see that this array is not actually an hash table, but rather a direct access array. Collisions are not possible since there is a one to one relationship between VPNs and array indexes. For this reason the array element type `_MMWSLE_HASH` does not include a key member like in the non direct case and it simply stores the WSLE index.

The direct hash has an entry for every possible VPN in the 8TB user mode range, so its size is given by:

    (800`00000000 >> 0xc) * 4 = 0x2`00000000 = 8GB

This fact alone tells us that the VMM cannot map physical memory for the entire table in advance - and there is an hash table for every process! What happens is that the VMM maps a page in the hash table range when it needs to create an hash table entry, so the virtual region in the hash table has "holes".

As an example, below is the address of the PTE mapping the first hash table page for an instance of explorer.exe:

```
1: kd> !pte @@( ((nt!_mmwsl *) 0xfffff70001080000)->HashTableStart )
                                VA fffff70440001000

PXE at FFFFF6FB7DBEDF70   PPE at FFFFF6FB7DBEE088   PDE at FFFFF6FB7DC11000   PTE at FFFFF6FB82200008
contains 000000000B642863  contains 000000000C476863  contains 000000000C675863  contains 800000000B8C6863
pfn b642     ---DA--KWEV  pfn c476     ---DA--KWEV  pfn c675     ---DA--KWEV  pfn b8c6     ---DA--KW-V
```

If we dump this PTE and the one immediately following it we see that PTEs set to 0, corresponding to invalid virtual pages, alternate with valid ones:

```
1: kd> dq FFFFF6FB82200008
fffff6fb`82200008  80000000`0b8c6863 80000000`0bcde863
fffff6fb`82200018  00000000`00000000 00000000`00000000
fffff6fb`82200028  00000000`00000000 00000000`00000000
fffff6fb`82200038  80000000`0beea863 80000000`38304863
fffff6fb`82200048  80000000`38186863 80000000`0a23d863
fffff6fb`82200058  00000000`00000000 80000000`09b50863
```

```
fffff6fb`82200068  80000000`07625863 80000000`09f4b863
fffff6fb`82200078  80000000`09ac3863 80000000`08d56863
```

We see a block of 4 zeroed PTEs starting at 0xFFFFF6FB`82200018, followed by nonzero ones. We can confirm that the first nonzero one following the zeroed ones maps direct hash entries by examining the memory content. First, we get the mapped address from the !pte extension:

```
1: kd> !pte fffff6fb`82200038
                              VA fffff70440007000

PXE at FFFFF6FB7DBEDF70    PPE at FFFFF6FB7DBEE088    PDE at FFFFF6FB7DC11000    PTE at FFFFF6FB82200038
contains 000000000B642863  contains 000000000C476863  contains 000000000C675863  contains 800000000BEEA863
pfn b642      ---DA--KWEV pfn c476      ---DA--KWEV pfn c675      ---DA--KWEV pfn beea      ---DA--KW-V
```

By examining the memory content starting from 0xFFFFF704`40007000, we find the following nonzero hash table entries:

```
1: kd> dd fffff704`40007c80
fffff704`40007c80  0000030e 0000030d 000001b6 000001b7
fffff704`40007c90  000001b8 000001b9 000001ba 000001bb
fffff704`40007ca0  00000000 00000000 000001c0 000001c1
fffff704`40007cb0  000001c2 000001c3 000001c4 000001c5
fffff704`40007cc0  000015d3 000001be 00000000 00000000
fffff704`40007cd0  00000000 00000000 00000000 00000000
fffff704`40007ce0  00000000 00000000 00000000 00000000
fffff704`40007cf0  00000000 00000000 0000187f 0000045b
```

Now let's compute the VA to which the entry at 0xFFFFF704`40007C80 refers to:

```
1: kd> ? ((fffff704`40007c80  - fffff70440001000) / 4 ) << c
Evaluate expression: 28442624 = 00000000`01b20000
```

The expression above computes the entry index and shift it left by 12 bits, reversing the formula used to compute the index (_MMWSL.LowestPagableAddress is 0). This tells us that the entry is for VA 0x1B20000. Let's see if this is consistent with the WSL:

```
1: kd> ?? ((nt!_mmwsl *) 0xfffff70001080000)->Wsle[0x30e].u1.e1
struct _MMWSLENTRY
   +0x000 Valid            : 0y1
   +0x000 Spare            : 0y0
   +0x000 Hashed           : 0y1
   +0x000 Direct           : 0y0
   +0x000 Protection       : 0y00001 (0x1)
   +0x000 Age              : 0y110
   +0x000 VirtualPageNumber : 0y00000000000000000000000000000000000000000001101100100000
(0x1b20)
```

We have used 0x30E, i.e. the value found in the hash table entry as an index into the WSL and we found a WSLE for VPN 0x1B20. This confirms that the memory content after the "hole" of 4 non valid PTEs is consistent with the direct hash table.

The physical pages used to store the hash table are accounted for as *process metapages*. This concept is described in greater detail in sec. 48.1 on p. 533.

37.14.4.3   Which Hash Table Is Used

MiUpdateWsleHash calls *MiConvertWsleHash* when the non direct hash is full. This suggests that a process starts its life using the non direct hash table and switches to the direct one later, if the need arises. As an example, MemTests is usually found to use the non direct hash table while explorer.exe, cmd.exe and notepad.exe use the direct one.

For a process using the non direct table the following is usually observed:

- `_MMWSL.NonDirectHash` is nonzero and usually set to 0xFFFFF704`40000000.

- The page pointed by the member above is valid.

- `_MMWSL.HashTableStart` is set to the usual direct table address 0xFFFFF704`40001000.

- The direct hash table starting page is not valid.

While for a process using the direct table:

- `_MMWSL.NonDirectHash` is zero.

- The page at 0xFFFFF704`40000000 is not valid.

- `_MMWSL.HashTableStart` is set to the direct table address, usually 0xFFFFF704`40001000.

- There are valid pages in the direct hash table range.

Strangely, the `!wsle` extension always reports 0 for the hash table size and address, regardless of which one is in use. Below is the output for MemTests using the non direct table:

```
Working Set @ fffff70001080000
    FirstFree      1c7  FirstDynamic       5
    LastEntry    10288  NextSlot           5  LastInitialized    1036e
    NonDirect      b7  HashTable          0  HashTableSize        0
```

while this is the result fr explorer.exe, using the direct one:

```
Working Set @ fffff70001080000
    FirstFree      852  FirstDynamic       5
```

```
LastEntry      2102  NextSlot          5  LastInitialized    216e
NonDirect         0  HashTable         0  HashTableSize         0
```

One interesting difference is the "NonDirect" value which corresponds to `_MMWSL.NonDirectCount` and is nonzero for MemTests.exe.

38   Memory Mapped Files

38.1 Basic Concept

Mapping a file in memory means making its content visible from a given starting virtual address. Once a file is mapped, it can be read and written to simply by accessing virtual memory. The VMM takes care of making the file content visible in the virtual range and of updating the file by paging out the memory content. The mapped file is handled in a way similar to the paging file: when a portion of it is accessed for the first time, a page fault occurs and the VMM maps a physical page filled with content from the file into the address space. When the process working set is trimmed or the file mapping is closed, pages that were modified go to the Modified list and will later be written to the mapped file.

The VMM uses section objects to map files, but initializes them in such a way that they associate virtual addresses with offsets into the mapped file. Section objects of this kind are said to be backed by the mapped file, while section objects not mapping a file are said to be backed by the paging file. This terminology reflects where the data in memory is read from and written to when paging occurs.

Mapped files come in two kinds: data and executable, also called image files, because they represent a snapshot of how executable code is loaded in memory. They are mapped in different ways: data files are mapped exactly as the file content is visible from disk, i.e. if the mapping starts at memory address *x*, the byte at offset *o* from the beginning of the file ends up at address *x* + *o* in memory. Image files are mapped differently, so that the relationship between file offset and mapping offset is a bit more complex.

The main APIs for section objects are *CreateFileMapping* and *MapViewOfFileEx*, which were described in the previous chapter.

Many of the concepts related to paging file backed section objects are valid for mapped file backed ones, so we will only describe the differences between the two kinds of objects.

38.2 Mapped Data Files

38.2.1   The Section Object for a Mapped Data File

38.2.1.1   Section Object Data Structures

To map a file, a program must call *CreateFileMapping* with the hFile parameter set to the handle of the file.

The protection specified by the flProtect parameter must be consistent with the access requested when opening the file, e.g., if the file is opened with GENERIC_READ access and later flProtect is set to PAGE_READWRITE, *CreateFileMapping* fails and *GetLastError* returns ERROR_ACCESS_DENIED.

dwMaximumSizeHigh and dwMaximumSizeLow specify the size of the mapping: setting them to less than the file length only maps a portion of the file, while specifying a size greater than the length extends the file. Finally, setting them both to 0 automatically creates a mapping with size equal to the file length.

The call to *CreateFileMapping* creates a set of data structures similar to the ones used for shared memory. The handle returnd by CreateFileMapping refers to an instance of a _SECTION_OBJECT, as in the following example:

```
1: kd> !handle @@(*lphMap)

PROCESS fffffa80011a0700
    SessionId: 1  Cid: 09f4    Peb: 7ffffffd7000  ParentCid: 053c
    DirBase: 14b05000  ObjectTable: fffff8a002991540  HandleCount:    9.
    Image: MemTests.EXE

Handle table at fffff8a00176a000 with 9 entries in use

0024: Object: fffff8a001b92eb0  GrantedAccess: 000f0007 Entry: fffff8a00176a090
Object: fffff8a001b92eb0  Type: (fffffa8000ccc790) Section
    ObjectHeader: fffff8a001b92e80 (new version)
        HandleCount: 1  PointerCount: 2
        Directory Object: fffff8a005b0f160  Name: map

1: kd> dt nt!_SECTION_OBJECT fffff8a001b92eb0
    +0x000 StartingVa         : 0xfffffa80`011a0700 Void
    +0x008 EndingVa           : 0xfffff8a0`05b0f160 Void
    +0x010 Parent             : 0xfffff880`0576fa01 Void
    +0x018 LeftChild          : (null)
    +0x020 RightChild         : 0xfffff8a0`05b0f0f0 Void
    +0x028 Segment            : 0xfffff8a0`018e74e0 _SEGMENT_OBJECT
```

Segment appears to be the address of an instance of _MAPPED_FILE_SEGMENT, while for paging file backed sections it pointed to an instance of _SEGMENT. The former is actually a subset of the latter:

```
struct _MAPPED_FILE_SEGMENT, 8 elements, 0x30 bytes
   +0x000 ControlArea       : Ptr64 to struct _CONTROL_AREA, 16 elements, 0x80 bytes
   +0x008 TotalNumberOfPtes : Uint4B
   +0x00c SegmentFlags      : struct _SEGMENT_FLAGS, 12 elements, 0x4 bytes
   +0x010 NumberOfCommittedPages : Uint8B
   +0x018 SizeOfSegment     : Uint8B
   +0x020 ExtendInfo        : Ptr64 to struct _MMEXTEND_INFO, 2 elements, 0x10 bytes
   +0x020 BasedAddress      : Ptr64 to Void
   +0x028 SegmentLock       : struct _EX_PUSH_LOCK, 7 elements, 0x8 bytes

struct _SEGMENT, 12 elements, 0x50 bytes
   +0x000 ControlArea       : Ptr64 to struct _CONTROL_AREA, 16 elements, 0x80 bytes
   +0x008 TotalNumberOfPtes : Uint4B
   +0x00c SegmentFlags      : struct _SEGMENT_FLAGS, 12 elements, 0x4 bytes
   +0x010 NumberOfCommittedPages : Uint0B
   +0x018 SizeOfSegment     : Uint8B
   +0x020 ExtendInfo        : Ptr64 to struct _MMEXTEND_INFO, 2 elements, 0x10 bytes
   +0x020 BasedAddress      : Ptr64 to Void
   +0x028 SegmentLock       : struct _EX_PUSH_LOCK, 7 elements, 0x8 bytes
   +0x030 u1  : union <unnamed-tag>, 2 elements, 0x8 bytes
      +0x000 ImageCommitment : Uint8B
      +0x000 CreatingProcess : Ptr64 to struct _EPROCESS, 135 elements, 0x4d0 bytes
   +0x038 u2  : union <unnamed-tag>, 2 elements, 0x8 bytes
      +0x000 ImageInformation : Ptr64 to struct _MI_SECTION_IMAGE_INFORMATION, 2
elements, 0x48 bytes
      +0x000 FirstMappedVa : Ptr64 to Void
   +0x040 PrototypePte      : Ptr64 to struct _MMPTE, 1 elements, 0x8 bytes
   +0x048 ThePtes           : [1] struct _MMPTE, 1 elements, 0x8 bytes
```

One important difference is that the prototype PTEs are not part of the segment like for paging file backed sections. They are still inside a region allocated from paged pool, but a separate one. Also, _SEGMENT.PrototypePte which, for shared memory stored the address of the first prototype PTE, is not included in _MAPPED_FILE_SEGMENT (if we try to dump the memory content as a _SEGMENT, we get meaningless values for PrototypePte), so we need some other way to find the PTEs and we will see later how this is where the subsection comes handy. _MAPPED_FILE_SEGMENT.ControlArea stores the address of an instance of _CONTROL_AREA:

```
0: kd> dt nt!_MAPPED_FILE_SEGMENT 0xffffff8a0`018e74e0
   +0x000 ControlArea       : 0xffffffa80`00ecae10 _CONTROL_AREA
   +0x008 TotalNumberOfPtes : 0x100
   +0x00c SegmentFlags      : _SEGMENT_FLAGS
   +0x010 NumberOfCommittedPages : 0
   +0x018 SizeOfSegment     : 0x100000
   +0x020 ExtendInfo        : (null)
   +0x020 BasedAddress      : (null)
   +0x028 SegmentLock       : _EX_PUSH_LOCK
```

```
0: kd> dt nt!_CONTROL_AREA 0xfffffa80`00ecae10
   +0x000 Segment          : 0xfffff8a0`018e74e0 _SEGMENT
   +0x008 DereferenceList  : _LIST_ENTRY [ 0x00000000`00000000 - 0x0 ]
   +0x018 NumberOfSectionReferences : 1
   +0x020 NumberOfPfnReferences : 0
   +0x028 NumberOfMappedViews : 1
   +0x030 NumberOfUserReferences : 2
   +0x038 u                : <unnamed-tag>
   +0x03c FlushInProgressCount : 0
   +0x040 FilePointer      : _EX_FAST_REF
   +0x048 ControlAreaLock  : 0n0
   +0x04c ModifiedWriteCount : 0
   +0x04c StartingFrame    : 0
   +0x050 WaitingForDeletion : (null)
   +0x058 u2               : <unnamed-tag>
   +0x068 LockedPages      : 0n1
   +0x070 ViewList         : _LIST_ENTRY [ 0xfffffa80`010d0620 - 0xfffffa80`010d0620 ]
```

The control area address can also be fed to the !ca extension:

```
0: kd> !ca 0xfffffa80`00ecae10


ControlArea  @ fffffa8000ecae10
  Segment       fffff8a0018e74e0  Flink     0000000000000000  Blink        0000000000000000
  Section Ref                  1  Pfn Ref                  0  Mapped Views                1
  User Ref                     2  WaitForDel               0  Flush Count                 0
  File Object   fffffa8001466340  ModWriteCount            0  System Views                0
  WritableRefs                 2
  Flags (80) File


      File: \Apps\TestApp\testmap.tmp

Segment @ fffff8a0018e74e0
  ControlArea      fffffa8000ecae10  ExtendInfo      0000000000000000
  Total Ptes                    100
  Segment Size               100000  Committed                       0
  Flags (c0000) ProtectionMask


Subsection 1 @ fffffa8000ecae90
  ControlArea  fffffa8000ecae10  Starting Sector          0  Number Of Sectors  100
  Base Pte     fffff8a0017eb010  Ptes In Subsect        100  Unused Ptes          0
  Flags                      d  Sector Offset            0  Protection           6
  Accessed
  Flink        0000000000000000  Blink     0000000000000000  MappedViews          1
```

!ca shows that _CONTROL_AREA refers to a file named testmap.tmp and this information is kept in _CONTROL_AREA.FilePointer, which stores the address of a _FILE_OBJECT:

```
0: kd> dt nt!_CONTROL_AREA FilePointer. 0xfffffa80`00ecae10
   +0x040 FilePointer  :
      +0x000 Object     : 0xfffffa80`01466341 Void
```

```
   +0x000 RefCnt       : 0y0001
   +0x000 Value        : 0xfffffa80`01466341
```

Object is set to the address of a _FILE_OBJECT and the RefCnt member suggests that bits 0-3 are used as a reference count, so we must mask them to get the actual address:

```
0: kd> dt nt!_FILE_OBJECT 0xfffffa80`01466340
   +0x000 Type         : 0n5
...
   +0x058 FileName     : _UNICODE_STRING "\Apps\TestApp\testmap.tmp"
...
```

In turn, the _FILE_OBJECT points back to the _CONTROL_AREA with its SectionObjectPointer member:

```
0: kd> ?? ((nt!_FILE_OBJECT *) 0xfffffa80`01466340)->SectionObjectPointer
struct _SECTION_OBJECT_POINTERS * 0xfffffa80`00facf68
   +0x000 DataSectionObject : 0xfffffa80`00ecae10 Void
   +0x008 SharedCacheMap    : (null)
   +0x010 ImageSectionObject : (null)
```

SectionObjectPointer stores the address of a _SECTION_OBJECT_POINTERS instance whose DataSectionObject member points to the _CONTROL_AREA.

Also, !ca shows the _SUBSECTION, which is stored after the _CONTROL_AREA: the latter is at address 0xFFFFFA80`00ECAE10 and the former is at 0xFFFFFA80`00ECAE90, i.e. at + 0x80 bytes which is the size of _CONTROL_AREA. The subsection is the key to gain access to the prototype PTEs, whose address is kept into _SUBSECTION.SubsectionBase and listed as "Base Pte" in the !ca output above; they are shown to be at 0xFFFFF8A0`017EB010. Note how the prototype PTEs are not part of the segment which is at 0xFFFFF8A0`018E74E0.

It can be observed, by repeating file mapping tests several times, that prototype PTEs are sometimes allocated when the section object is created, as it happened in this example, while at other times they are allocated only when a view of the section is mapped by *MapViewOfFileEx*. When this happens, _SUBSECTION.SubsectionBase is set to 0 until the actual allocation happens.

38.2.1.2   Section Objects with More than One Subsection

A section object can actually include more than one subsection. We will see a scenario where this happens in section 38.7.3 on p. 373 and below is an example of such a section:

```
ControlArea  @ fffffa8000bdf980
   Segment      fffff8a0008945b0  Flink        0000000000000000  Blink         0000000000000000
   Section Ref              2     Pfn Ref                  501   Mapped Views              2
   User Ref                 2     WaitForDel                 0   Flush Count               0
   File Object  fffffa8002362ea0  ModWriteCount              0   System Views              1
```

```
WritableRefs                 2
Flags (c080) File WasPurged Accessed


     File: \Apps\TestApp\testmap.tmp

Segment @ fffff8a0008945b0
  ControlArea     fffffa8000bdf980  ExtendInfo    0000000000000000
  Total Ptes               600
  Segment Size          600000  Committed                    0
  Flags (c0000) ProtectionMask


Subsection 1 @ fffffa8000bdfa00
  ControlArea  fffffa8000bdf980  Starting Sector        0  Number Of Sectors  100
  Base Pte     fffff8a0058c7010  Ptes In Subsect      100  Unused Ptes          0
  Flags                       d  Sector Offset          0  Protection           6
  Accessed
  Flink        0000000000000000  Blink   fffffa80023feb70  MappedViews          1

Subsection 2 @ fffffa8000b9de40
  ControlArea  fffffa8000bdf980  Starting Sector      100  Number Of Sectors  200
  Base Pte     fffff8a00bc00000  Ptes In Subsect      200  Unused Ptes          0
  Flags                       d  Sector Offset          0  Protection           6
  Accessed
  Flink        0000000000000000  Blink   fffffa80023feb70  MappedViews          1

Subsection 3 @ fffffa8001601a80
  ControlArea  fffffa8000bdf980  Starting Sector      300  Number Of Sectors  200
  Base Pte     fffff8a001a69000  Ptes In Subsect      200  Unused Ptes          0
  Flags                       d  Sector Offset          0  Protection           6
  Accessed
  Flink        0000000000000000  Blink   fffffa80023feb70  MappedViews          1

Subsection 4 @ fffffa800106f9e0
  ControlArea  fffffa8000bdf980  Starting Sector      500  Number Of Sectors  100
  Base Pte     fffff8a006206000  Ptes In Subsect      100  Unused Ptes        100
  Flags                       d  Sector Offset          0  Protection           6
  Accessed
  Flink        0000000000000000  Blink   0000000000000000  MappedViews          1
```

Each subsection maps a block of file whose length is given by the number of PTEs in the subsection (_SUBSECTION.PtesInSubsection, listed as Ptes In Subsect by !ca) multiplied by the page size. In the example above, subsection #1 has 0x100 PTEs, so maps the block 0 – 0xFFFFF. Since this is a data file, it is mapped in memory with the same layout it has on disk, so subsection #2 begins at the next byte, i.e. at offset 0x100000 in the file. In general, the offset of a subsection from the beginning of the file is given by the page size multiplied by the total count of PTEs found in previous subsections. This count is stored in _SUBSECTION.StartingSector (Starting Sector), so it's worth noting that, in spite of its name, this member does not store a disk sector number. We will see in sec. 38.4.3 on p. 364 that, for image files, this member is an actual sector offset.

We already know that the first subsection is located after the control area, but now we need a way to find the other subsections. It appears that _SUBSECTION.NextSubsection stores the address of the next subsection and is set to 0 in the last one. Below is the content of this member for the first, second and last subsection listed in the !ca output above:

```
0: kd> dt nt!_subsection 0xfffffa80`00bdfa00
...
   +0x010 NextSubsection   : 0xfffffa80`00b9de40 _SUBSECTION

0: kd> dt nt!_subsection 0xfffffa80`00b9de40
...
   +0x010 NextSubsection   : 0xfffffa80`01601a80 _SUBSECTION

0: kd> dt nt!_subsection 0xfffffa80`0106f9e0
...
   +0x010 NextSubsection   : (null)
```

We saw in sec. 37.3.2.2 on p. 304 that the VAD created by *MapViewOfSectionEx* points to the subsection, but now we have more than one, so it is worth pointing out that the VAD still has just one subsection pointer, which refers to the first subsection in the chain.

38.2.1.3   Section Object Diagram

The next figure shows the diagram of Figure 41 on p. 303 revised for a mapped file backed section:

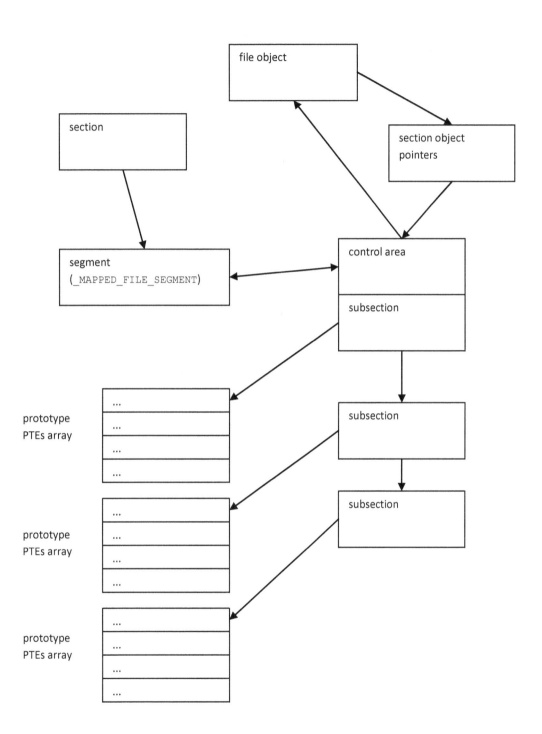

Figure 50 - Mapped File Backed Section

38.2.1.4   Prototype PTEs of a Mapped File Section

We saw that in a paging file backed section, the prototype PTEs are set up as demand-zero PTEs initially and later they are used to eventually track the memory content into the paging file. For such a section, the file to be used is, implicitly, the paging file, so the only information needed are *which* paging file and the *offset* into the file, which are stored into `_MMPTE.u.Soft.PageFileLow` and `_MMPTE.u.Soft.PageFileHigh`, respectively (the former is simply an index, see sec. 34.3 on p. 256).

For a mapped file section, things are different. First of all, it does not make sense to initialize the prototype PTEs as demand-zero ones, because when a section page is first accessed, it must be filled with data read from the file. Furthermore, the prototype PTEs must somehow identify the file on the entire file system, since it is not the paging file anymore.

To solve these problems, the protype PTEs are initialized as instances of `_MMPTE_SUBSECTION` with `SubsectionAddress` pointing to the `_SUBSECTION` describing the virtual range mapped by the prototype PTE. From the `_SUBSECTION`, the VMM can get to the `_CONTROL_AREA` and to the `_FILE_OBJECT`. The prototype PTEs don't explicitly store an offset into the file, because this information can be derived from:

- The offset of the PTE from the first PTE in the subsection, whose address is given by `_SUBSECTION.SubsectionBase`. A PTE at *base* + *n**8 maps the portion of the file at *subsection_start* + 0x1000 * *n*. Note how the offset into the subsection is implicit in the PTE position in the array.

- The offset of the block described by the subsection from the beginning of the file, i.e. *subsection_start*, which is given by `_SUBSECTION.StartingSector` multiplied by the page size.

Thus, protype PTEs belonging to a subsection are all initialized to the same value, pointing to the subsection itself. Here is an example:

```
ControlArea  @ ffffffa8002899d10
   Segment       fffff8a0013497e0  Flink    0000000000000000  Blink        0000000000000000
   Section Ref               1  Pfn Ref                 0  Mapped Views                1
   User Ref                  2  WaitForDel              0  Flush Count                 0
   File Object  ffffffa80025fae50  ModWriteCount           0  System Views                0
   WritableRefs              2
   Flags (80) File


     File: \Apps\TestApp\test500GB.tmp

Segment @ fffff8a0013497e0
   ControlArea       ffffffa8002899d10  ExtendInfo      0000000000000000
```

```
Total Ptes                    20001
Segment Size           20000001  Committed                    0
Flags (c0000) ProtectionMask


Subsection 1 @ fffffa8002899d90
  ControlArea   fffffa8002899d10  Starting Sector       0  Number Of Sectors 20000
  Base Pte      fffff8a00265d000  Ptes In Subsect   20001  Unused Ptes          0
  Flags             10000d  Sector Offset           1  Protection           6
  Accessed
  Flink         0000000000000000  Blink   0000000000000000  MappedViews          1
```

Below are the prototype PTE values found in the array

```
1: kd> dq fffff8a00265d000
fffff8a0`0265d000   fa800289`9d9004c0 fa800289`9d9004c0
fffff8a0`0265d010   fa800289`9d9004c0 fa800289`9d9004c0
fffff8a0`0265d020   fa800289`9d9004c0 fa800289`9d9004c0
fffff8a0`0265d030   fa800289`9d9004c0 fa800289`9d9004c0
fffff8a0`0265d040   fa800289`9d9004c0 fa800289`9d9004c0
fffff8a0`0265d050   fa800289`9d9004c0 fa800289`9d9004c0
fffff8a0`0265d060   fa800289`9d9004c0 fa800289`9d9004c0
fffff8a0`0265d070   fa800289`9d9004c0 fa800289`9d9004c0
```

We can see how the PTE are all set to the same value. WinDbg is capable of interpreting an instance of _MMPTE_SUBSECTION:

```
1: kd> !pte fffff8a00265d000 1
                          VA fffff8a00265d000

PXE @ FFFFF8A00265D000    PPE at FFFFF8A00265D000    PDE at FFFFF8A00265D000    PTE at FFFFF8A00265D000
contains FA8002899D9004C0         unavailable
not valid
 Subsection: FFFFFA8002899D90
 Protect: 6 - ReadWriteExecute
```

The subsection address shown is consistent with the one displayed by !ca.

It is interesting to observe how prototype PTEs of a paging file backed section need to store the paging file offset, since the page can be written anywhere into the paging file, while for a mapped file backed section the file offset is derived by the PTE position in the array and thus is not part of the PTE content.

We can notice from the output of !pte above that the PTE protection is set to 6 - ReadWriteExecute. This section object was for a data file with read/write protection, so the "Execute" part is surprising. We will see in sec. 38.2.2.3 on p. 352 that the actual protection of the hardware PTE does not allow execute access.

38.2.1.5   _MMPTE_SUBSECTION vs _MMPTE_PROTOTYPE

We saw in the previous section that _MMPTE_SUBSECTION defines the layout of a prototype
PTE entry pointing to a subsection and in sec. 37.5.1 on p. 309 that _MMPTE_PROTOTYPE is
the format of a proto-pointer, pointing to a prototype PTE. If we look at these two data
types, we see that there is no bit uniquely identifying a PTE value as of being of one type or
the other. Both are identified by having bit 0 clear and bit 10 set. It is interesting to note that
WinDbg interprets such a PTE value depending on the address region it belongs to: if it is in
the paging structures region, it is interpreted as a proto-pointer, otherwise as a subsection
pointer. We can confirm this by using the !pte extension on the same value at two different
addresses. The value:

0xCBA98765`43210400

has bit 0 clear, bit 10 set and the address part of the proto/subsection set to
0xCBA9`87654321. It is useful to remember that both _MMPTE_PROTOTYPE and
_MMPTE_SUBSECTION only store 48 bits of the address, because the upper 16 bits must be
equal to bit 47 (canonical form). Here is how !pte interprets this value inside the paging
structures region:

```
1: kd> dq FFFFF68000002B80 l1
fffff680`00002b80   cba98765`43210400

1: kd> !pte FFFFF68000002B80

                              VA 0000000000570000
PXE at FFFFF6FB7DBED000    PPE at FFFFF6FB7DA00000    PDE at FFFFF6FB40000010    PTE at FFFFF68000002B80
contains 00C0000005E9C867  contains 010000003041F867  contains 0EA000000AF4C867  contains CBA9876543210400
pfn 5e9c     ---DA--UWEV    pfn 3041f    ---DA--UWEV    pfn af4c    ---DA--UWEV    not valid
                                                                                  Proto: FFFFCBA987654321
```

We see it is interpreted as a protopointer. Note also how WinDbg assumes that the 16 upper
bits of the address are set to 1.

Below we see what happens when the same value is at a user mode address (any address
outside the paging structures region gives the same result):

```
1: kd> dq 570000 l1
00000000`00570000   cba98765`43210400

1: kd> !pte 570000 1
                              VA 0000000000570000
PXE at 0000000000570000    PPE at 0000000000570000    PDE at 0000000000570000    PTE at
0000000000570000
contains CBA9876543210400
not valid
Subsection: FFFFCBA987654321
```

```
Protect: 0
```

This time, the PTE is interpreted as a subsection pointer.

This confirms the *same* value has different meaning depending on its address and suggests that proto-pointers are only found in the paging structures region.

38.2.1.6   Section Object and Virtual Address Spaces

It is worth to recall a concept already introduced with shared memory: the section object, by itself, does not establish the virtual address at which the file content will be visible in a particular process. This is done when *MapViewOfFileEx* is called and the information is stored into the VAD. The section object ties together the prototype PTEs and the file, so that paging I/O can be performed on the file itself, without reference to the address range at which the file is visible in one of the potentially many processes mapping it.

38.2.2   First Access to a Mapped File Page

Beginning with this section, we are going to describe the relevant differences between the life cycle of paging file backed pages and mapped file backed ones.

In general, paging is similar to what happens for paging file backed objects, but the memory content is read from and written to the mapped file.

When the first access occurs, an _MMPFN for an active page is set up, so that it is similar to the one for a paging file backed object, but there are a few differences.

38.2.2.1   Clean/Dirty Status

We saw in section 37.4 on p. 306 that a paging file backed page is initialized as dirty since there is no copy of its content in the paging file, much as it happens for private memory.

A page backed by a mapped file is a different story, since it is initialized with content read from the file when the first access occurs. If the access is a read, the page is initialized as clean, because is identical to its file copy. More specifically, when such an access occurs the prototype PTE is set as follows:

_MMPTE_HARDWARE.Dirty1 = 0, which makes the page read-only (processor defined R/W bit)

_MMPTE_HARDWARE.Dirty = 0, which, together with Dirty1, marks the page as clean.

_MMPTE_HARDWARE.Write = 1, which marks the page as writable to the VMM (software
  defined bit)

This is different from what we have for paging file backed pages which have Dirty and
Dirty1 set. The hardware PTE stores the same values for these bits and the _MMPFN for the
page has u3.e1.Modified = 0, while for a paging file backed page it is set to 1. Thus, all
the bits related to dirtiness are clear and it can be observed that when such a page is brought
out of the Active state, it is moved directly to the Standby list, i.e. it is considered clean.

This stems from the difference between the life cycle of mapped file backed pages and
paging file backed ones: the former are initialized with content from the file, so a copy of
their content on disk already exists when they are added to a working set; the latter are filled
with zeroes and no copy of their content exists until they are written to the paging file.

Since a mapped file backed page must be filled with the file content, the first access to such a
page is actually an hard fault rather than a demand-zero one, which also mean that the Free
list is searched first to allocate the physical page. Thus, this kind of fault is represented by the

thick arrows in the state diagram below:

- VA page released, e. g. process terminates
- **section destroyed**

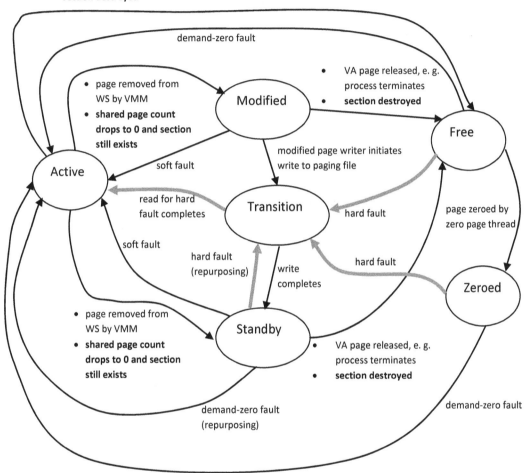

Figure 51 - First Access to Mapped Pages Is an Hard Fault

Finally, it can be observed that, when the first access is a write, the prototype PTE still has `Dirty` and `Dirty1` clear, `_MMPFN.u3.e1.Modified` is also clear, but the hardware PTE has `Dirty` and `Dirty1` set and this is enough to cause the page to be moved to the Modified list when it exits the Active state. More to the point, since such a page can be shared among different processes, each address space were the page has been written to has `Dirty` and `Dirty1` set in its hardware PTE. When the page is removed from such an address space, the VMM sets `_MMPFN.u3.e1.Modified`; if there are other address spaces mapping the page, the latter remains active, but the modified state has now been propagated into the _MMPFN so that, when it will be removed from the last address space, the page will be added to the Modified list.

38.2.2.2   Content of `OriginalPte`

For a paging file backed page, this member stores an _MMPTE_SOFTWARE with the page protection and, eventually, the paging file offset. For a mapped file backed page, it stores an _MMPTE_SUBSECTION pointing to the subsection which covers the file page mapped by the PTE.

38.2.2.3   Executable Protection

We already saw on p. 347 that prototype PTEs for a read/write section are initialized with their software protection set to 6, interpreted by WinDbg as ReadWriteExecute, which contrasts with the section protection. When the prototype PTEs are set to point to a physical page their content is defined by the processor and bit 63 specifies whether the page is executable (bit clear) or not. The prototype value indeed has bit 63 clear, so that the page is executable, a fact reported by WinDbg through the "E" flag; below is an example:

```
1: kd> !pte 0xfffff8a0`01ca1800 1
                             VA fffff8a001ca1800

PXE at FFFFF8A001CA1800   PPE at FFFFF8A001CA1800   PDE at FFFFF8A001CA1800   PTE at FFFFF8A001CA1800
contains 0000000007770963  contains 0000000007770963  contains 0000000007770963  contains 0000000007770963
pfn 7770      -G-DA--KWEV  pfn 7770      -G-DA--KWEV  pfn 7770      -G-DA--KWEV  pfn 7770      -G-DA--KWEV
```

However, the final hardware PTE is actually not executable, i.e. with bit 63 set:

```
1: kd> !pte 530000
                             VA 0000000000530000

PXE at FFFFF6FB7DBED000   PPE at FFFFF6FB7DA00000   PDE at FFFFF6FB40000010   PTE at FFFFF68000002980
contains 0100000023554867  contains 01200000234D7867  contains 00B0000023F6B867  contains 86A0000007770867
pfn 23554     ---DA--UWEV  pfn 234d7     ---DA--UWEV  pfn 23f6b     ---DA--UWEV  pfn 7770      ---DA--UW-V
```

This shows that the inconsistency between the protection specified by the parameters passed to *CreateFileMapping* and *MapViewOfFileEx* and the prototype PTE protection is only apparent; it is important to always remember that a prototype PTE is only a working copy from which the actual hardware PTE is derived.

It can be verified with a few experiments that, for a page to be executable, *MapViewOfFileEx* must be called requesting FILE_MAP_EXECUTE access and this fails if the mapping object was created with PAGE_READWRITE protection. In general, to have an actually executable page, this kind of access must be specified at all the levels, i.e.:

- when the file is opened

- when the section object is created

- when the view is mapped

38.2.3   Removing a Mapped File Page from a Working Set

Page removal is handled in a similar way for paging file backed (see sec. 37.5 on p. 309) and mapped file backed pages. The hardware PTE stores a proto-pointer referring to the VAD; when the page share count drops to 0, the prototype PTE is set in transition and referring to the physical page; the page is brought on the Modified or Standby list.

38.2.4   Writing a Mapped File Page to its File

An important difference between paging file backed and mapped file backed pages is that the VMM uses a dedicated thread to write to mapped files, called the *mapped page writer*. Its job is to write the content of pages on the modified list which are being used to map files, i.e. essentially the same task performed by the modified page writer for pages backed by the paging file.

Another small difference can be observed when the page goes from the Modified to the Standby list. For a paging file backed page, this is when the paging file offset is allocated and recorded into `_MMPFN.OriginalPte`, which, up until this moment, stored a demand-zero PTE. `_MMPFN.OriginalPte` will be the only place where the paging file offset is stored, until the page is eventually repurposed and its value is copied to the prototype PTE. For a mapped file backed page, `_MMPFN.OriginalPte` is not updated: it always stores an `_MMPTE_SUBSECTION` pointing to the subsection covering the page. This is enough information to know where the page content is stored in the file (see also sec. 38.2.1.4 on p. 346) and this value will be put back into the prototype PTE when the page is repurposed.

38.2.5   Mapped File Page Repurposing

When this happens, the prototype PTE is set back to the subsection pointer. For a paging file backed page, the prototype PTE stores the offset into the paging file.

38.2.6   Writing to a Clean Mapped File Page

For a paging file backed page, when this event occurs, the paging file block storing the copy of the page is released, since it has become outdated, and `_MMPFN.OriginalPte.u.Soft.PageFileLow` and `PageFileHigh` are set to 0. When the time will come to write again the page to disk, a new paging file block will be allocated.

For a mapped file backed page, `OriginalPte` is not modified since it stores the subsection pointer. The on-disk copy of the page is obviously always at the same offset from the beginning of the file. When the page will be written to disk, the corresponding file block will be updated.

38.2.7   Releasing Mapped File Memory

We saw in sec. 37.12 on p. 325 how memory for a paging file backed section is released. The process is similar for a mapped file backed section, but with an important difference.

A paging file backed section is used to manage a region of virtual memory mapped by one or more processes. When all these processes have unmapped their views and closed their handles to the section, the memory content can be destroyed. After all, no one expects the VMM to save the content of deallocated memory anywhere, and there is no point in writing it to the paging file. Thus, the section is destroyed as soon as the last process closes its handle.

A mapped file backed section is a different story: any dirty page in the section *must* be written to the file, because file mapping is designed to ensure that any modification made in memory is reflected into the underlying file. This can occur even after the processes mapping the section terminate: dirty pages are written by the mapped page writer when the VMM decides to do it and this is not synchronized with the life of processes.

Thus, for mapped files, the section object is retained, as long as there are dirty pages. If no process is mapping views of the section, the pages will be kept on the modified list. Even when no process has an open handle to the section, the latter is retained, at least as long as it has pages on the Modified list.

It can be observed experimentally that sections for large files (e.g. 1GB) are retained for some time even when their pages are clean, which means they are kept on the Standby list. This is probably a form of caching: after a large file has been brought into memory, it is kept on the Standby list (if there is enough free memory), where it can be quickly retrieved, should it be needed again. If, later, a process calls *MapViewOfFileEx* for the same file, the existing section is reused, with all the content in Standby pages readily available with no need for I/O.

The state diagram shown in Figure 49 on p. 330 is still valid, with the additional consideration that mapped file backed sections are destroyed only after the dirty pages have been flushed to the file and even after that, the section can be retained for some time.

In sec. 21.2 on p. 129, we stated that a page enters the Modified state when it is removed from a working set by trimming. We are now ready to understand that, for mapped files, the Modified state is also entered upon memory deallocation.

38.2.8   Mapped Files and Regular File System I/O

38.2.8.1   I/O by Means of Section Objects

Mapped files are more than a handy way for programmers to access a file content: they are at the very heart of file system I/O in Windows. When a file is accessed by means of *ReadFile* or *WriteFile*, behind the scenes a section object is created. The cache manager maps views of this section in a virtual address range in the system region, retrieving and updating the file data from there.

We are now going to see this happening by digging into the file data structures as the I/O APIs are called to read the first byte of a 1GB file (see sec. 38.7.4 on p. 377 for an experiment on this). The crucial piece of information is the `SectionObjectPointer` member of `_FILE_OBJECT`: it stores the address of an instance of `_SECTION_OBJECT_POINTERS`, whose `DataSectionObject` member holds the address of the `_CONTROL_AREA` for the section.

After the call to *CreateFile* and before the call to *ReadFile*, all the `_SECTION_OBJECT_POINTERS` members, including `DataSectionObject`, are set to null. Here is the `!handle` output for the file:

```
Handle table at fffff8a0022ab000 with 7 Entries in use
001c: Object: ffffffa80017bdd10  GrantedAccess: 0012019f Entry: fffff8a0022ab070
Object: ffffffa80017bdd10  Type: (ffffffa8000959a30) File
    ObjectHeader: ffffffa80017bdce0 (new version)
        HandleCount: 1  PointerCount: 1
        Directory Object: 00000000  Name: \Apps\TestApp\testmap4.tmp {HarddiskVolume2}
```

and below is the content of `_SECTION_OBJECT_POINTERS`:

```
0: kd> ?? ((nt!_FILE_OBJECT *) 0xffffffa80017bdd10)->SectionObjectPointer
struct _SECTION_OBJECT_POINTERS * 0xffffffa80`00b12868
   +0x000 DataSectionObject : (null)
   +0x008 SharedCacheMap    : (null)
   +0x010 ImageSectionObject : (null)
```

After a call to *ReadFile* to read the first byte, `DataSectionObject` stores an address:

```
1: kd> ?? ((nt!_FILE_OBJECT *) 0xffffffa80017bdd10)->SectionObjectPointer
struct _SECTION_OBJECT_POINTERS * 0xffffffa80`00b12868
   +0x000 DataSectionObject : 0xffffffa80`023f9d00
   +0x008 SharedCacheMap    : 0xffffffa80`01042010
```

```
    +0x010 ImageSectionObject : (null)
```

If we feed this address to the `!ca` extension, we see the control area content:

```
1: kd> !ca 0xfffffa80`023f9d00


ControlArea  @ fffffa80023f9d00
   Segment       fffff8a0013d88e0  Flink      0000000000000000  Blink       0000000000000000
   Section Ref                  1  Pfn Ref                   1  Mapped Views               1
   User Ref                     0  WaitForDel                0  Flush Count                0
   File Object fffffa80017bdd10  ModWriteCount             0  System Views               1
   WritableRefs                 0
   Flags (8080) File WasPurged


        File: \Apps\TestApp\testmap4.tmp

Segment @ fffff8a0013d88e0
   ControlArea      fffffa80023f9d00  ExtendInfo     0000000000000000
   Total Ptes                 40000
   Segment Size            40000000  Committed                     0
   Flags (c0000) ProtectionMask


Subsection 1 @ fffffa80023f9d80
   ControlArea   fffffa80023f9d00  Starting Sector        0  Number Of Sectors 40000
   Base Pte      fffff8a00e320000  Ptes In Subsect    40000  Unused Ptes               0
   Flags                        d  Sector Offset          0  Protection                6
   Accessed
   Flink         0000000000000000  Blink   0000000000000000  MappedViews               1
```

It is interesting to observe that the subsection includes 0x40000 PTEs, i.e. enough of them to map the whole file: even though a single byte has been read, the 1GB file has been completely mapped. However, the kernel has only built the data structures to keep track of the mapping, it has not actually allocated 0x40000 physical pages. We can confirm this by looking at the prototype PTEs at the address listed as `Base Pte` among the subsection data:

```
1: kd> dq fffff8a00e320000
fffff8a0`0e320000   00000000`0d954921 fa80023f`9d8004c0
fffff8a0`0e320010   fa80023f`9d8004c0 fa80023f`9d8004c0
fffff8a0`0e320020   fa80023f`9d8004c0 fa80023f`9d8004c0
fffff8a0`0e320030   fa80023f`9d8004c0 fa80023f`9d8004c0
fffff8a0`0e320040   fa80023f`9d8004c0 fa80023f`9d8004c0
fffff8a0`0e320050   fa80023f`9d8004c0 fa80023f`9d8004c0
fffff8a0`0e320060   fa80023f`9d8004c0 fa80023f`9d8004c0
fffff8a0`0e320070   fa80023f`9d8004c0 fa80023f`9d8004c0
```

Only the first PTE points to a physical page, while the other ones are instances of `_MMPTE_SUBSECTION` pointing to the subsection. We clearly see this when we dump the 1st and the 2nd prototype PTE:

```
1: kd> !pte fffff8a00e320000 1
```

```
                          VA fffff8a00e320000

PXE @ FFFFF8A00E320000     PPE at FFFFF8A00E320000     PDE at FFFFF8A00E320000     PTE at FFFFF8A00E320000
contains 000000000D954921  contains 000000000D954921  contains 000000000D954921  contains 000000000D954921
pfn d954      -G--A--KREV pfn d954      -G--A--KREV pfn d954      -G--A--KREV pfn d954          -G--A--
KREV


1: kd> !pte fffff8a00e320008 1
                          VA fffff8a00e320008

PXE @ FFFFF8A00E320008     PPE at FFFFF8A00E320008     PDE at FFFFF8A00E320008     PTE at FFFFF8A00E320008
contains FA80023F9D8004C0        unavailable
not valid
 Subsection: FFFFFA80023F9D80
 Protect: 6 - ReadWriteExecute
```

Thus, only the single physical page storing the accessed byte has actually been mapped. The prototype PTEs do consume physical memory, though, but they are in paged pool, so the VMM can eventually reclaim the pages as long as the PTEs don't point to a physical page (see sec. 37.11 on p. 317).

Given what we have just seen, we can understand that *any file read in the system is actually handled as a page fault*: the data is requested to the cache manager, which maps a view of the section and accesses it. If the data is in memory (i.e. it has been cached) it is simply returned to the caller, otherwise a page fault occurs and the data is brought into memory.

We can perform a similar experiment for a file write getting similar results: a mapping for the file is created and the page storing the modified byte is allocated. This tells us that the file content is first brought into memory and then modified. Afterwards, the mapped page writer will update the actual content on the file system.

When we call *CreateFileMapping* for a file for which a control areas does not exist, i.e. `_SECTION_OBJECT_POINTERS.DataSectionObject` is set to null, the same member is set to the address of the control area after the call. In other words, it does not matter if the control area is created implicitly by a file read/write or explicitly by *CreateFileMapping*, its address is stored in `DataSectionObject`.

38.2.8.2 More on Section Objects and File Caching

The page fault incurred by the cache manager can also be a soft one. This can happen because a previously active page has been placed on a transition list, but also thanks to prefetching. A section page can be prefetched while resolving an hard fault as a result of clustered in-paging (see sec. 34.1 on p. 250), but this is not the only reason, since the cache manager performs prefetching too.

We can now understand that the Standby list is *at the core of file caching*: cached file content is kept in transition pages, which eventually become Standby ones. They can either be formerly active pages or they can have been placed directly into the Standby list by prefetching logic. Whatever their "past history", they are available to make file content visible into the cache manager virtual address space without accessing the file system. As long as the VMM does not need to repurpose pages, the data can be kept in memory on the Standby list.

It is interesting to observe how file caching *is made possible* by prototype PTEs. For a Standby page which is not part of a section there must be an hardware PTE in the paging structures of some process pointing to it (an instance of _MMPTE_TRANSITION with bit 0 clear). In turn, the _MMPFN of the page refers to this hardware PTE through PteAddress and u4.PteFrame. Thus, such a Standby page *cannot exist* without having a slot of virtual address space assigned to it: the 4k range mapped by the PTE. This also applies to non-section pages prefetched by clustered in-paging: they too are pointed by PTEs in transition.

If Standby pages prefetched by the cache manager were to be managed this way, the size of the cache would be limited by the availability of virtual space in the system region, because each Standby page would consume one PTE.

With section objects instead, the *prototype* PTEs point to Standby pages and are pointed back by the _MMPFN, so a Standby page (or a Modified one) which is part of a section *is not tied to any particular virtual address and does not consume an hardware PTE*.

For each cached file there is a section with its arrays of prototype PTEs, and the kernel is free to build as many sections and arrays as it sees fit, because *it is not necessary to map all these PTEs at the same time*. If this were the case, the total number of PTEs pointing to cached file data in the system would have to be less than or equal to the virtual address range available to the cache manager divided by the page size.

Instead, the cache manager maps *views* of these sections when it needs to access their content. It has its own logic to keep track of how it is using its own virtual address range, but there is no need to cram all the prototype PTEs into it at once. This allows to have unlimited standby pages, i.e. to cache file data as long as physical memory is available.

This not only means that the cache manager can retain accessed data: it means it is *free to prefetch data as well*. If there is free physical memory, the cache manager can attempt to anticipate file accesses and prefetch pages before they are actually needed. Superfetch is a component which takes advantage of this scheme.

38.2.8.3   Memory Sections Sharing

An important implication of what we have seen in the previous sections, is that when a file is accessed by more than one process, the memory section is shared among them and this is what implements concurrent file access. This automatically makes the cache shared as it should be: all processes go through the same memory section and if a page is cached in Standby is available to all off them.

Also, if we call *CreateFileMapping* for a file which already has a section (pointed by its `SectionObjectPointer`), the same control area is reused. Here is an example from the previous test; after reading the file, the program called *CreateFileMapping* and got the following handle:

```
Handle table at fffff8a0022ab000 with 9 Entries in use
0024: Object: fffff8a001cf6c50  GrantedAccess: 000f0007 Entry: fffff8a0022ab090
Object: fffff8a001cf6c50  Type: (fffffa800095a6a0) Section
    ObjectHeader: fffff8a001cf6c20 (new version)
        HandleCount: 1  PointerCount: 2
        Directory Object: fffff8a0058812f0  Name: map
```

We can get from the `_SECTION_OBJECT` to the `_CONTROL_AREA` address:

```
0: kd> ?? (nt!_SECTION_OBJECT *) 0xfffff8a001cf6c50
struct _SECTION_OBJECT * 0xfffff8a0`01cf6c50
   +0x000 StartingVa      : 0xfffffa80`01c6f060
   +0x008 EndingVa        : 0xfffff8a0`058812f0
   +0x010 Parent          : 0xfffff880`02e80a01
   +0x018 LeftChild       : (null)
   +0x020 RightChild      : 0xfffff8a0`05881280
   +0x028 Segment         : 0xfffff8a0`013d88e0 _SEGMENT_OBJECT

0: kd> ?? (nt!_MAPPED_FILE_SEGMENT *) 0xfffff8a0`013d88e0
struct _MAPPED_FILE_SEGMENT * 0xfffff8a0`013d88e0
   +0x000 ControlArea     : 0xfffffa80`023f9d00 _CONTROL_AREA
   +0x008 TotalNumberOfPtes : 0x40000
   +0x00c SegmentFlags    : _SEGMENT_FLAGS
   +0x010 NumberOfCommittedPages : 0
   +0x018 SizeOfSegment   : 0x40000000
   +0x020 ExtendInfo      : (null)
   +0x020 BasedAddress    : (null)
   +0x028 SegmentLock     : _EX_PUSH_LOCK
```

The control area address is the same previously found in `_FILE_OBJECT.SectionObjectPointer->DataSectionObject`.

One way of looking at this is that *CreateFileMapping* and *MapViewOfFileEx* allow application code to directly perform what the I/O manager and the cache manager do under the hood. They use services provided by the VMM manager and these APIs expose the same services to programs.

38.3 Section Offset

It is worth to summarize some concepts we just saw, to define the concept of section offset.

A section object includes an ordered list of prototype PTEs, composed by the ones of the first subsection, followed by the ones of the next subsection and so on.

Each of these prototype PTEs is logically associated with a block of file data in the sense that, when they are set to point to a new physical page, the page is initialized with content read from the file at a certain offset . Also, if the page content is modified, it will at some point replace the same block into the file.

For mapped data files, the relationship between file data and prototype PTEs is straightforward: the first PTE maps the first 4k of file data, the second maps data between file offsets 0x1000 – 0x1fff and so on. This is not the only possibility, though: we are about to see that for image files the relationship is different. However, in both cases each prototype PTE logically refers to 4k of data somewhere in the file.

A section, through its list of prototype PTEs, defines the content of the virtual memory ranges where a view of the section is mapped. Mapping the view, merely establishes the starting address at which the range is visible, but the range content is defined by the section alone and its relationship with the file content.

If we picture the section content as it would be mapped in an address space and assign addresses to its byte starting from 0, we obtain a logical address associated with each byte of section content. We will call this logical address the *section offset*. When a view of the section is mapped at a starting address, the VA of each byte is the sum of the starting address and its section offset. The section offset is the offset from the section first byte *after* the memory layout of the file content has been established by associating (i.e. mapping) each file block to its prototype PTE.

MapViewOfFileEx allows to specify an offset into the section object at which the view starts through its `dwFileOffsetHigh` and `dwFileOffsetLow` parameters. Their meaning is what we just defined as the section offset: the byte mapped at the view starting address is the byte with section offset equal to the value specified.

It is worth noting that the function documentation states that these values specify an offset into the file, as their name implies, but this is accurate only for mapped data files, were section offsets and file offsets are equal. For image files which we are about to examine, the two values have different meaning, due to how the file is mapped in memory and `dwFileOffsetHigh`, `dwFileOffsetLow` specify a *section offset*, i, e. an offset into the content *after* it has been mapped to the prototype PTEs.

38.4 Mapped Image Files

38.4.1   Use of Image File Mapping

Image file mapping is Windows' way of loading executable in memory: both a process executable and the DLLs it loads are made visible in the virtual address space as mapped image files. When a process calls *LoadLibrary* to dinamically load a DLL, image file mapping takes place behind the scenes. The ability of the VMM to page mapped files makes it possible to page executables much like the rest of the virtual address space.

Since executables are mapped files, they have a section object, which can be found, for instance, through the VAD covering the virtual region. Below is an excerpt of the output from `!vad` for an instance of calc.exe:

```
0: kd> !vad fffffa8003567370
VAD             level     start     end     commit
[...]
fffffa8000eff590 ( 6)      ff0a0    ff182         6 Mapped  Exe   EXECUTE_WRITECOPY
\Windows\System32\calc.exe
```

The VAD instance gives the address of the 1st subsection:

```
0: kd> ?? ((nt!_MMVAD *) 0xfffffa8000eff590)->Subsection
struct _SUBSECTION * 0xfffffa80`01f68d30
   +0x000 ControlArea      : 0xfffffa80`01f68cb0 _CONTROL_AREA
   +0x008 SubsectionBase   : 0xfffff8a0`00443898 _MMPTE
   +0x010 NextSubsection   : 0xfffffa80`01f68d68 _SUBSECTION
   +0x018 PtesInSubsection : 1
   +0x020 UnusedPtes       : 0
   +0x020 GlobalPerSessionHead : (null)
   +0x028 u                : <unnamed-tag>
   +0x02c StartingSector   : 0
   +0x030 NumberOfFullSectors : 3
```

From the subsection, we can get the control area:

```
0: kd> ?? ((nt!_SUBSECTION *) ((nt!_MMVAD *) 0xfffffa8000eff590)->Subsection)-
>ControlArea
struct _CONTROL_AREA * 0xfffffa80`01f68cb0
   +0x000 Segment          : 0xfffff8a0`00443850 _SEGMENT
[...]
```

The address of the `ControlArea` can be fed directly to the `!ca` extension; we have to use the `@@()` operator to specify the use of the C++ evaluator (before it was not needed since `??` defaults to C++):

```
0: kd> !ca @@( ((nt!_SUBSECTION *) ((nt!_MMVAD *) 0xfffffa8000eff590)->Subsection)-
>ControlArea )


ControlArea  @ fffffa8001f68cb0
   Segment      fffff8a000443850  Flink      0000000000000000  Blink      fffffa8003538738
   Section Ref              1     Pfn Ref              8c  Mapped Views              1
   User Ref                 2     WaitForDel            0  Flush Count               0
   File Object  fffffa800312d840  ModWriteCount         0  System Views           ffff
   WritableRefs       c000000f
   Flags (40a0) Image File Accessed


       File: \Windows\System32\calc.exe

Segment @ fffff8a000443850
   ControlArea      fffffa8001f68cb0  BasedAddress  00000000ff0a0000
   Total Ptes              e3
   Segment Size          e3000  Committed                 0
   Image Commit             5  Image Info    fffff8a000443fb0
   ProtoPtes      fffff8a000443898
   Flags (820000) ProtectionMask


Subsection 1 @ fffffa8001f68d30
   ControlArea  fffffa8001f68cb0  Starting Sector       0  Number Of Sectors    3
   Base Pte     fffff8a000443898  Ptes In Subsect       1  Unused Ptes          0
   Flags                     2   Sector Offset         0  Protection           1

Subsection 2 @ fffffa8001f68d68
   ControlArea  fffffa8001f68cb0  Starting Sector       3  Number Of Sectors  307
   Base Pte     fffff8a0004438a0  Ptes In Subsect      61  Unused Ptes          0
   Flags                     6   Sector Offset         0  Protection           3
[...]
```

We can see that the section is made of multiple subsections and we will analyze shortly the relationship between the image file structure and the section object one.

An important effect of loading executables by mapping them is that they are *shared*: if we start a second instance of calc we see it uses the *same* section object, so only a copy of the executable code is present in physical memory. This sharing occurs both for executables and DLLs and, while it is very useful to save precious physical memory, it also raises a question: how can each process have a private copy of the static variables included in the executable or DLL? The answer will become clear when we will discuss copy-on-write protection in sec. 38.6 on p. 369.

We saw in sec. 38.2.8.1 on p. 355 that a file accessed by means of read/write APIs or mapped as a data file stores the address of the control area in _SECTION_OBJECT_POINTERS.DataSectionObject. When a file is mapped as an image file (we are going to explain shortly how this is achieved), the control area address is stored in `_SECTION_OBJECT_POINTERS.ImageSectionObject`. Thus, there are different members for the two different kinds of memory sections.

38.4.2   Overview of Image Files Format

This section contains a short introduction to the format of executable files, which described in much greater detail in [13].

x64 Image files are in the portable executable 32+ format (PE32+) and are composed of a set of headers and of blocks called *sections*, which is quite unfortunate, given they should not be confused with the file's *section object*. To avoid confusion, we will use the term *file section* when referring to file content.

There are separate file sections for code, data and other information stored into executables (e.g. resources).

File sections are aligned within the file, i.e. their offset from the file beginning is an integer multiple of a value called *file alignment*. The file alignment can have different values, however the most common is 0x200, which is also the size of a disk sector on most hard disks.

A PE32+ file also has a *section alignment* which specifies the in-memory alignment of data from a file section once it is mapped in an address space. The VA of the first byte of a file section must be a multiple of the section alignment. The section alignment must itself be a multiple of the page size and is often equal to it.

The most common alignment values are therefore 0x200 for the file alignment and 0x1000 for the section alignment.

A PE32+ file specifies the section offset (as defined in the previous – er – section) at which each file section must be mapped. In PE32+ parlance the section offset is called Relative Virtual Address. As an example, below is an excerpt from a dump of calc.exe:

```
Microsoft (R) COFF/PE Dumper Version 9.00.21022.08
Copyright (C) Microsoft Corporation.  All rights reserved.


Dump of file \\krnltest\c\apps\testapp\calc.exe

PE signature found

File Type: EXECUTABLE IMAGE
[...]
SECTION HEADER #1
   .text name
```

```
    60CC9 virtual size
     1000 virtual address (0000000100001000 to 0000000100061CC8)
    60E00 size of raw data
      600 file pointer to raw data (00000600 to 000613FF)
        0 file pointer to relocation table
        0 file pointer to line numbers
        0 number of relocations
        0 number of line numbers
 60000020 flags
          Code
          Execute Read
[...]

SECTION HEADER #2
   .rdata name
    10EC4 virtual size
    62000 virtual address (0000000100062000 to 0000000100072EC3)
[...]

SECTION HEADER #3
    .data name
     4E80 virtual size
    73000 virtual address (0000000100073000 to 0000000100077E7F)
[...]
```

The highlighted values are the RVAs or section offsets of each section. The first file section must be at +0x1000 from the beginning of the memory section, the second at +0x62000 and so on. This dump is created by dumpbin.exe, a tool which is included in the Windows SDK. To extract this information, simply launch:

```
dumpbin /headers calc_path\calc.exe
```

38.4.3   The Section Object for a Mapped Image File

We must tell *CreateFileMapping* that we want to map an image file by OR-ing SEC_IMAGE to the desired protection passed into the `flProtect` parameter. This is what tells the function to examine the file content and map it accordingly. If we don't specify this flag, an image file is treated as a data file and mapped as a single contiguous block. If we are feeling mischievous and pass SEC_IMAGE for a file which is not an executable, *CreateFileMapping* fails and *GetLastError* returns ERROR_BAD_EXE_FORMAT.

It is interesting to note that the error is returned by *CreateFileMapping*, not by *MapViewOfFileEx*: it is the former which creates the section object and associates the prototype PTEs with the file content and it does so by "understanding" the PE32+ format, so it is the same function which complains if the file is bad.

With a valid executable, a section object is created, which appears to have a distinct _SUBSECTION instances for each file section. Let's look again at the dump for calc.exe:

```
Microsoft (R) COFF/PE Dumper Version 9.00.21022.08
Copyright (C) Microsoft Corporation.  All rights reserved.


Dump of file \\krnltest\c\apps\testapp\calc.exe

PE signature found

File Type: EXECUTABLE IMAGE

FILE HEADER VALUES
            8664 machine (x64)
               6 number of sections
        4A5BC9D4 time date stamp Tue Jul 14 01:57:08 2009
               0 file pointer to symbol table
               0 number of symbols
              F0 size of optional header
              22 characteristics
                   Executable
                   Application can handle large (>2GB) addresses

OPTIONAL HEADER VALUES
...

SECTION HEADER #1
   .text name
   60CC9 virtual size
    1000 virtual address (0000000100001000 to 0000000100061CC8)
   60E00 size of raw data
     600 file pointer to raw data (00000600 to 000613FF)
       0 file pointer to relocation table
```

Above we see data for the first file section; we are now going to examine it together with the output from !ca for the section object (excerpt below).

```
ControlArea  @ fffffa8000aee680
   Segment       fffff8a0010e3040  Flink       0000000000000000  Blink       fffffa8002920208
   Section Ref               1  Pfn Ref              2b  Mapped Views             0
   User Ref                  1  WaitForDel            0  Flush Count              0
   File Object   fffffa8002874c10  ModWriteCount         0  System Views          ffff
   WritableRefs        c000000f
   Flags (40a0) Image File Accessed


      File: \Apps\TestApp\calc.exe

Segment @ fffff8a0010e3040
   ControlArea     fffffa8000aee680  BasedAddress   00000000ff130000
   Total Ptes                e3
   Segment Size            e3000  Committed                 0
   Image Commit               5  Image Info     fffff8a0010e37a0
   ProtoPtes       fffff8a0010e3088
   Flags (820000) ProtectionMask


Subsection 1 @ fffffa8000aee700
```

```
     ControlArea   fffffa8000aee680   Starting Sector     0   Number Of Sectors     3
     Base Pte      fffff8a0010e3088   Ptes In Subsect     1   Unused Ptes           0
     Flags                        2   Sector Offset       0   Protection            1

Subsection 2 @ fffffa8000aee738
     ControlArea   fffffa8000aee680   Starting Sector     3   Number Of Sectors   307
     Base Pte      fffff8a0010e3090   Ptes In Subsect    61   Unused Ptes           0
     Flags                        6   Sector Offset       0   Protection            3
[...]
```

Let's begin by noting that the file dump shows, for file section #1, a value of 0x600 for `file pointer to raw data`. This is the offset of the file section from the beginning of the file and tells us that there are 0x600 bytes of other data (the file headers) before it. This initial block of data is mapped by subsection 1.

We can confirm this by mapping a view of the file and examining the first page content, which is equal to the file content. This is an excerpt from the file content:

```
000000   4d 5a 90 00 03 00 00 00 04 00 00 00 ff ff 00 00   MZ..........ÿÿ..
000010   b8 00 00 00 00 00 00 00 40 00 00 00 00 00 00 00   ¸.......@.......
000020   00 00 00 00 00 00 00 00 00 00 00 00 00 00 00 00   ................
000030   00 00 00 00 00 00 00 00 00 00 00 00 f0 00 00 00   ............ð...
000040   0e 1f ba 0e 00 b4 09 cd 21 b8 01 4c cd 21 54 68   ..º..´.Í!¸.LÍ!Th
000050   69 73 20 70 72 6f 67 72 61 6d 20 63 61 6e 6e 6f   is program canno
000060   74 20 62 65 20 72 75 6e 20 69 6e 20 44 4f 53 20   t be run in DOS
000070   6d 6f 64 65 2e 0d 0d 0a 24 00 00 00 00 00 00 00   mode....$.......
```

and below is the memory content:

```
00000000`ff2f0000   4d 5a 90 00 03 00 00 00-04 00 00 00 ff ff 00 00   MZ..............
00000000`ff2f0010   b8 00 00 00 00 00 00 00-40 00 00 00 00 00 00 00   ........@.......
00000000`ff2f0020   00 00 00 00 00 00 00 00-00 00 00 00 00 00 00 00   ................
00000000`ff2f0030   00 00 00 00 00 00 00 00-00 00 00 00 f0 00 00 00   ................
00000000`ff2f0040   0e 1f ba 0e 00 b4 09 cd-21 b8 01 4c cd 21 54 68   .........!..L.!Th
00000000`ff2f0050   69 73 20 70 72 6f 67 72-61 6d 20 63 61 6e 6e 6f   is program canno
00000000`ff2f0060   74 20 62 65 20 72 75 6e-20 69 6e 20 44 4f 53 20   t be run in DOS
00000000`ff2f0070   6d 6f 64 65 2e 0d 0d 0a-24 00 00 00 00 00 00 00   mode....$.......
```

We can also see that subsection 1 has `Starting Sector` set to 0, which means that the page content must be read at file offset 0.

Things become more interesting with subsection 2. First of all, let's concentrate on the section offset of its 1st byte: subsection 1 is made of a single prototype PTE (`Ptes In Subsect` is equal to 1), so the section offset of subsection 2 is 0x1000. The same value is reported as the RVA of file section #1 from the file content, dumped as `virtual address`. This fact alone tells us that subsection 2 stores the content of file section #1. Furthermore, file section #1 has a listed virtual size equal to 0x60cc9 and subsection 2 has 0x61 prototype PTEs, so it stores file section #1 completely.

Also, subsection 2 has `Starting Sector` set to 3. If we multiply it by the file alignment for this file, which is 0x200, we get 0x600 (the file alignment is listed among the file `OPTIONAL HEADER VALUES` by dumpbin, which here are omitted). The file dump shows that file section #1 has `file pointer to raw data` equal to the same value, so `Starting Sector` is used to record where, in the file, the subsection data is found: it is equal to the file offset of the data divided by the file alignment.

What we have seen so far tells us that *CreateFileMapping* creates a subsection to map the file headers and a subsection for file section 1 which follows it.

If we examine other file sections and subsections, we can confirm that the number of prototype PTEs preceding each subsection is such that the section offset is equal to the RVA of a file section. For instance, Subsection 2 has `Ptes In Subsect` equal to 0x61, so collectively subsections 1 and 2 span 0x62 PTEs or 0x62000 bytes of virtual address space and the RVA for the next file section (#2, dumped below) is 0x62000.

Here are the dumpbin output and `!ca` output for the pair:

```
SECTION HEADER #2
  .rdata name
  10EC4 virtual size
  62000 virtual address (0000000100062000 to 0000000100072EC3)
  11000 size of raw data
  61400 file pointer to raw data (00061400 to 000723FF)
```

!ca output:

```
Subsection 3 @ fffffa8000aee770
  ControlArea  fffffa8000aee680  Starting Sector      30a  Number Of Sectors  88
  Base Pte     fffff8a0010e3398  Ptes In Subsect       11  Unused Ptes         0
  Flags                       2  Sector Offset          0  Protection          1
```

And the file offset is:

`Starting Sector` x *file alignment* = 0x30a x 0x200 = 0x61400 = `file pointer to raw data`

We can examine the remaining file sections (there are 6 of them) and confirm that each is mapped by its own subsection.

It's also worth noting that this analysis shows that `Starting Sector` must be multiplied by the file alignment to get the file offset, while we saw in section 38.2.1.2 on p. 342 that, for data files, it has to be multiplied by the page size.

File section #3 looks particularly interesting:

```
SECTION HEADER #3
   .data name
   4E80 virtual size
  73000 virtual address (0000000100073000 to 0000000100077E7F)
   4E00 size of raw data
  72400 file pointer to raw data (00072400 to 000771FF)
      0 file pointer to relocation table
      0 file pointer to line numbers
      0 number of relocations
      0 number of line numbers
C0000040 flags
        Initialized Data
        Read Write
```

The dump shows that the virtual size is 0x80 bytes greater than the raw data. For other file sections is the opposite, with the raw data equal to the virtual size rounded up to a multiple of the file alignment, but here we have that in memory the content is longer than on disk. This implies the *CreateFileMapping* does more than simply reading the file section content into memory, but, rather, it translates the data stored in the file somehow.

This brings us to a question: if the page content is modified, how can it be written back to the file, considering it has been transformed when loaded? The answer is it is not. If we look at the protection of the subsection, we see it is equal to 5, which means copy-on-write. We will describe this protection in more detail in sec. 38.6 on p. 369, however it's effect is that the original file is not updated.

In summary, an image file is mapped by a section object with distinct subsections for each mapped file section; these subsections are arranged so that each begins at a section offset equal to the one specified in the file; the content of some subsections is *derived* from the file section content, not simply a copy of it.

Mapping each file section to a distinct subsection allows file sections to have different memory protections, because the latter is specified at the subsection level. This makes it possible to have image files with read-only portions, executable portions, etc.

It appears from this that *CreateFileMapping* actually implements part of the executable loader. We must not forget, however, that actual loading requires more than mapping file sections (for instance, dependencies must be resolved).

38.4.4   Hardware PTEs for Mapped Image Files

Hardware PTEs are treated in a slightly different way than those of mapped data files: when the page is removed from a working set, the corresponding hardware PTE is set to a proto-pointer with an actual prototype PTE address. For data files the address part is usually set to 0xF...F which means "refer to the VAD".

38.5 Implications of Associating Sections with Files

A paging file backed section may refer to parts of the paging file only, without involving other files in the system.

Conversely, a mapped file backed section refer to regular files on the system, which are not under the exclusive control of the VMM like the paging file is. Consider the following scenario: a process maps a large file, updates it in memory and then quits. The VMM retains the section object and the pages on the modified list until the mapped page writer has finished writing them to the file. While the writing is in progress (or before it begins), another process erases the file. This is entirely possible, since no one has an handle open to the file after the first process terminates. In this situation, the VMM is made aware that the file no longer exists and it releases the dirty pages at once. This behavior is quite interesting to observe, so it will be the subject of an experiment in section 39.3.2 on p. 389.

In general, the components responsible for file I/O must interact with the I/O manager to account for these implications.

This brings us to a further question: let's consider again a mapped file which has been updated and closed and suppose its content is still on the Modified list, so that the on-disk file has not been actually updated, at least not completely. Since the file is closed and no one has an handle to it, another process can open it and read it with *ReadFile*. Will this process see the stale content of the on-disk copy? Perhaps corrupted content, only partially updated? No, thanks to the fact that a single section object is used for all accesses to the file, including those made with *ReadFile* and *WriteFile* (see sec. 38.2.8 on p. 355).

We can now understand how *fundamental* it is that all file accesses go through the section object: since outpaging is done asynchronously by the mapped page writer, the only updated copy of the file content is in the section object. The on-disk copy will be up to date at a later, undetermined time. As long as the section object exists, it *must* be used to access the file.

38.6 Copy on Write

Earlier in sec. 38.4.1 on p. 361 we saw that image file sections are shared among processes and we asked ourselves how can a process have a private copy of a module's static variables. The answer is in the protection of the section pages, which is set to copy-on-write.

When such a page is active, the hardware PTE has `_MMPTE.Hard.Dirty1` clear, which makes it a read-only page as far as the processor is concerned, and `_MMPTE.Hard.CopyOnWrite` set, which is ignored by the processor and tells the VMM this is a copy-on-write page.

An attempt to write to the page causes a page fault and the handler allocates a new physical page, copies the shared page content into it and points the hardware PTE to it. The new page is private to the process where the fault occurs, i.e. it has no relationship with the memory section: `_MMPFN.PteAddress` and `_MMPFN.u4.PteFrame` refer to the hardware PTE, not the prototype one; `_MMPFN.u4.PrototypePte` is clear; `_MMPFN.OriginalPte` is not set to a subsection pointer anymore, but rather to an `_MMPTE_SOFTWARE` with only the protection member set according to the page protection (minus the copy-on-write status – it is usually set to read/write). If such a page is later written to the backing store, it goes into the paging file instead of going into the file mapped by the section. In short, the process has now a private copy of the page.

This clearly has the effect of leaving the shared page untouched and providing the process which needed to update it with a private copy where the memory write takes place. This is what happens when a static variable in an image is updated.

The memory section is updated accordingly when this scenario occurs, i.e. the shared page share count is decremented, as if the process updating the page had called UnmapViewOfFile, which is consistent with the fact the shared page is not mapped in the process VA space anymore.

An image file specifies the protection of each file section as part of its content, so file sections are mapped by memory subsections with the requested protection. Read/write file sections such .data (where static variables are found) are implicitly mapped as copy-on-write. We don't need to explicitly specify copy-on-write protection when we call *CreateFileMapping* to map a file as an image.

However, copy-on-write protection is not reserved to image file only. If we call *CreateFileMapping* passing `PAGE_WRITECOPY` into `flProtect`, we can create a mapping for a data file with copy-on-write protection. We cannot pass `PAGE_WRITECOPY` to *VirtualAllocEx* when allocating non-section memory, because it does not make sense since copy on write is meant to automatically create private copies of section pages.

A copy on write page has software protection equal to 5. This value is stored in `_MMVAD.u.VadFlags.Protection` for a file mapped as data and in `_SUBSECTION.u.SubsectionFlags.Protection` for a copy-on-write subsection of a file mapped as image. This software protection tells the VMM how to set up the hardware PTE when a physical page is mapped.

38.7 Experiments on Mapped Files

38.7.1   The MemTests program

The MemTests program included in the download package for this book is a small program to test various VMM APIs. It has a main menu of options to map a private memory region, open a file, map the open file, access a memory region, etc.

Most tests start by asking the user all the required parameters, then prompts the user before each significant API call. At each prompt, the user can choose to abort the test, to go on, or to break. The last choice calls the *DebugBreak* function, which breaks into a debugger. This call is meant to be used when a kernel debugger is attached to the system where the program is running. *DebugBreak* breaks into the debugger with MemTests being the current process, so we have immediately access to the `_EPROCESS` and the address space, without having to look for the process and switch context. When the debugger takes control, it is very handy to use the `$proc` pseudo-register, which is set to the address of the `_EPROCESS` for the current process, and `$thread`, which points to the current `_ETHREAD`.

Since MemTests is mostly used in debugging sessions, the download package includes the source and symbol files, which should be placed in the debugger source and symbol paths.

When the program breaks into the debugger, execution is stopped inside `KERNELBASE!DebugBreak` and we can use the command

```
g @$ra
```

to return inside MemTests. If the debugger does not show the current line in the source code of MemTests, the problem can usually be fixed by reloading the symbols for user mode with

```
.reload /user
```

which should make it possible to step inside MemTests code at source level. After the `g @$ra` we are inside the MemTests function which prompts the user for a choice, so we must step until it returns to arrive at the operation about to be performed.

MemTests includes a set of tests operating on files, e.g. for reading or mapping creation, which use a file handle kept in a static variable. A menu option allows to open a file and stores the handle in the static variable, while other options operate on the open file, including one for closing it. The static variable is used to keep the handle available for the various tests until it is closed. Since MemTests is a test program, there are few checks on what the user does, e.g. it is possible to open a new file without closing the one already open, which "leaks" the handle.

Another static handle is used for the section object which can be created with the *Memory section test* option. Here the overall logic is similar: once a mapping has been created it can be reused by other menu options.

MemTests can allocate two distinct memory regions: a non-section one, allocated with *VirtualAllocEx* and a view of a section allocated with *MapViewOfFileEx*. The addresses of these regions are also kept in static variables, so that other menu options can access the region pages.

38.7.2   A Note about Breaking into the VMM with Data Breakpoints

A good technique to watch the VMM at work is to place data breakpoints with the `ba` command on PTEs and `_MMPFN`s while MemTests is working. For instance, MemTests allows to break immediately before accessing a memory region. When the debugger is in control, we can place a breakpoint on a PTE about to be accessed to regain control when the VMM updates it. There a few things to keep in mind on this subject.

A breakpoint on a PTE access must be enabled only for a specific address space, because the paging structures region is a per-process one. To do this, we must use the `/p` option of `ba`. If the breakpoint is for the current address space we can write

```
ba access size /p @$proc address
```

(the @ character is recommended to help the debugger understand that $proc is a pseudo-register and not a debug symbol). Conversely, a breakpoint on an `_MMPFN` member does not need the `/p` option since the PFN database is in a global system region.

If we want a break point valid for the current thread only, we must use the `/t` option:

```
ba access size /t @$thread address
```

It is not possible to break on many *prototype* PTE updates with a data breakpoint, because these PTEs are often mapped to a work virtual address in the system region and updated using this temporary virtual address instead of their regular one.

A good way to follow a page along its life cycle, e.g. from Active to Modified, to Standby, etc., is to set a conditional breakpoint on memory writes which clear bit 0 of `_MMPFN.PteAddress`. This bit is used to lock a particular `_MMPFN` instance for update, i.e. the bit is exclusively set before changing the instance content. When the update is complete and the `_MMPFN` is in a consistent state, the bit is cleared. By breaking when it is cleared we can observe the _MMPFN immediately after each state change. To set such a breakpoint, enter:

```
ba w 1 mmpfn_address + 10 "j ((poi(mmpfn_address + 10) & 1) == 0) '';'gc'"
```

+0x10 from the _MMPFN address is the offset of _MMPFN.PteAddress; the j command evaluates the expression in parentheses, which uses poi() to dereference an address; if the overall expression is nonzero (which happens when the term to the left of the == operator *is* zero), no further command is executed and the debugger takes control; if the expression is zero, the gc command is executed which causes execution to resume. Such a breakpoint is triggered every time the rightmost 8 bits of PteAddress are updated and automatically resumes execution when bit 0 is set, stopping only when is clear.

38.7.3 Creating a Memory Section with Multiple Subsections

In 38.2.1.2 on p. 342 we saw that a section for a file mapped as data can have multiple subsections. Normally, however, when we map a file, even a big one, the VMM creates a single subsection to map it. One scenario where we find multiple subsections, is when we incrementally grow the file. For instance, if we open a new file for writing and then write to it, we see that the VMM allocates an initial subsection, usually consisting of 0x100 PTEs, covering 1MB of file content. If the file grows beyond this limit, additional subsections are added.

This behavior can be observed with the *Create test file* option of MemTests. *Caution: this test creates a file, overwriting an eventual existing file with the same name*. After selecting the main menu option for the test, we provide a file name, select incremental expansion and provide a file size (e.g. 0x1000000 for 16 MB).

We then choose to break before the file is created, so we can step until after the call to *CreateFileWr* (a wrapper for *CreateFile*) and look at the section object pointers when the file has just been created:

```
1: kd> !handle @@(hRet)

PROCESS fffffa80038ac060
    SessionId: 1  Cid: 07ec    Peb: 7fffffd7000  ParentCid: 0890
    DirBase: 0f0a6000  ObjectTable: fffff8a001ed97b0  HandleCount:    7.
    Image: MemTests.EXE

Handle table at fffff8a001c60000 with 7 entries in use

001c: Object: fffffa8003847300  GrantedAccess: 0012019f Entry: fffff8a001c60070
Object: fffffa8003847300  Type: (fffffa8000ce6de0) File
```

```
    ObjectHeader: fffffa80038472d0 (new version)
        HandleCount: 1  PointerCount: 1
        Directory Object: 00000000  Name: \Apps\TestApp\multisubs.tmp {HarddiskVolume3}


1: kd> ?? ((nt!_FILE_OBJECT *) 0xfffffa8003847300)->SectionObjectPointer
struct _SECTION_OBJECT_POINTERS * 0xfffffa80`0322df68
   +0x000 DataSectionObject : (null)
   +0x008 SharedCacheMap    : (null)
   +0x010 ImageSectionObject : (null)
```

We then resume execution and, at the prompt of MemTests, choose again to break before the file is expanded, i.e. before *WriteFile* is called for the 1st time. We step until the first call to *WriteFileWr* returns and dump the section object pointers again:

```
1: kd> ?? ((nt!_FILE_OBJECT *) 0xfffffa8003847300)->SectionObjectPointer
struct _SECTION_OBJECT_POINTERS * 0xfffffa80`0322df68
   +0x000 DataSectionObject : 0xfffffa80`00ec4b70 Void
   +0x008 SharedCacheMap    : 0xfffffa80`02ecbc40 Void
   +0x010 ImageSectionObject : (null)
```

This time, `DataSectionObject` points to a control area, so we can dump it:

```
1: kd> !ca 0xfffffa80`00ec4b70


ControlArea @ fffffa8000ec4b70
   Segment      fffff8a001f07bd0  Flink      0000000000000000  Blink      0000000000000000
   Section Ref             1  Pfn Ref              1  Mapped Views            1
   User Ref               0  WaitForDel          0  Flush Count            0
   File Object  fffffa8003847300  ModWriteCount       0  System Views            1
   WritableRefs           0
   Flags (8080) File WasPurged


        File: \Apps\TestApp\multisubs.tmp


Segment @ fffff8a001f07bd0
   ControlArea      fffffa8000ec4b70  ExtendInfo      0000000000000000
   Total Ptes            100
   Segment Size       100000  Committed               0
   Flags (c0000) ProtectionMask


Subsection 1 @ fffffa8000ec4bf0
   ControlArea  fffffa8000ec4b70  Starting Sector        0  Number Of Sectors  100
   Base Pte     fffff8a001912800  Ptes In Subsect      100  Unused Ptes          0
   Flags                     d  Sector Offset          0  Protection           6
   Accessed
   Flink        0000000000000000  Blink      0000000000000000  MappedViews          1
```

This control area has a single subsection with 0x100 PTEs.

Afterwards, we let execution go on until the menu is displayed again, then we take control with the debugger by selecting Debug->Break and dump the control area again:

```
1: kd> !ca 0xfffffa80`00ec4b70


ControlArea  @ fffffa8000ec4b70
  Segment     fffff8a001f07bd0  Flink      0000000000000000  Blink      0000000000000000
  Section Ref                1  Pfn Ref                1001  Mapped Views              1
  User Ref                   0  WaitForDel                0  Flush Count               0
  File Object fffffa8003847300  ModWriteCount             0  System Views              1
  WritableRefs               0
  Flags (c080) File WasPurged Accessed


        File: \Apps\TestApp\multisubs.tmp

Segment @ fffff8a001f07bd0
  ControlArea     fffffa8000ec4b70  ExtendInfo     0000000000000000
  Total Ptes                 1100
  Segment Size            1100000  Committed                 0
  Flags (c0000) ProtectionMask


Subsection 1 @ fffffa8000ec4bf0
  ControlArea fffffa8000ec4b70  Starting Sector        0  Number Of Sectors  100
  Base Pte    fffff8a001912800  Ptes In Subsect      100  Unused Ptes          0
  Flags                     d  Sector Offset          0  Protection           6
  Accessed
  Flink       fffffa8003506740  Blink     fffffa80034e9e00  MappedViews          0

Subsection 2 @ fffffa80035066f0
  ControlArea fffffa8000ec4b70  Starting Sector      100  Number Of Sectors  200
  Base Pte    fffff8a001d64000  Ptes In Subsect      200  Unused Ptes          0
  Flags                     d  Sector Offset          0  Protection           6
  Accessed
  Flink       fffffa8003829980  Blink     fffffa8000ec4c40  MappedViews          0

Subsection 3 @ fffffa8003829930
  ControlArea fffffa8000ec4b70  Starting Sector      300  Number Of Sectors  200
  Base Pte    fffff8a001f27000  Ptes In Subsect      200  Unused Ptes          0
  Flags                     d  Sector Offset          0  Protection           6
  Accessed
  Flink       fffffa8003828bc0  Blink     fffffa8003506740  MappedViews          0

Subsection 4 @ fffffa8003828b70
  ControlArea fffffa8000ec4b70  Starting Sector      500  Number Of Sectors  200
  Base Pte    fffff8a001f28000  Ptes In Subsect      200  Unused Ptes          0
  Flags                     d  Sector Offset          0  Protection           6
  Accessed
  Flink       fffffa8001f91e30  Blink     fffffa8003829980  MappedViews          0

Subsection 5 @ fffffa8002ec08f0
  ControlArea fffffa8000ec4b70  Starting Sector      700  Number Of Sectors  200
  Base Pte    fffff8a001f29000  Ptes In Subsect      200  Unused Ptes          0
  Flags                     d  Sector Offset          0  Protection           6
```

```
   Accessed
   Flink            fffffa8002e1f230   Blink    fffffa8001f91e30   MappedViews           0

Subsection 6 @ fffffa8002e1f1e0
   ControlArea      fffffa8000ec4b70   Starting Sector      900   Number Of Sectors   200
   Base Pte         fffff8a001f2b000   Ptes In Subsect      200   Unused Ptes           0
   Flags                          d    Sector Offset          0   Protection            6
   Accessed
   Flink            fffffa8002f146c0   Blink    fffffa8002ec0940   MappedViews           0

Subsection 7 @ fffffa80034e4110
   ControlArea      fffffa8000ec4b70   Starting Sector      b00   Number Of Sectors   200
   Base Pte         fffff8a001f2c000   Ptes In Subsect      200   Unused Ptes           0
   Flags                          d    Sector Offset          0   Protection            6
   Accessed
   Flink            fffff80002a4f600   Blink    fffffa8003860ba0   MappedViews           0

Subsection 8 @ fffffa8001f91de0
   ControlArea      fffffa8000ec4b70   Starting Sector      d00   Number Of Sectors   200
   Base Pte         fffff8a001f2d000   Ptes In Subsect      200   Unused Ptes           0
   Flags                          d    Sector Offset          0   Protection            6
   Accessed
   Flink            fffffa8002ec0940   Blink    fffffa8003828bc0   MappedViews           0

Subsection 9 @ fffffa8000dea860
   ControlArea      fffffa8000ec4b70   Starting Sector      f00   Number Of Sectors   200
   Base Pte         fffff8a001f2e000   Ptes In Subsect      200   Unused Ptes           0
   Flags                          d    Sector Offset          0   Protection            6
   Accessed
   Flink            0000000000000000   Blink    0000000000000000   MappedViews           1
```

This time, the section has 9 subsections which have been created while the file was growing. The initial subsection is made of 0x100 prototype PTEs and the other 8 ones are 0x200 PTEs long, so in total the control area covers 0x1100 PTEs, which can span 0x1100000 or 17MB, covering the whole file.

We can also confirm that this subsection is the same one we get when we call *CreateFileMapping* with the following steps.

After resuming execution, select *Memory section test* on the main menu and select *mapped file* for the map type (the other type, *shared memory*, is for a paging file backed section). Enter a valid protection, e.g. 4, enter 0 for the size, which means we are going to map the whole file and enter a name for the mapping. The remaining prompts are for the call to *MapViewOfFileEx* which this test also performs; enter a valid required access, e.g. 6, and 0 for both the size and the offset (i.e. the view covers the whole section); choose to not specify the NUMA node to avoid extra questions. The program displays a summary of the input data and prompts for a key, then it prompts again just before calling *CreateFileMapping*. We choose to break here, and step until after the call to *CreateFileMapping*, dumping the returned handle:

```
1: kd> !handle @@(*lphMap)

PROCESS ffffffa80038ac060
    SessionId: 1  Cid: 07ec    Peb: 7fffffd7000  ParentCid: 0890
    DirBase: 0f0a6000  ObjectTable: fffff8a001ed97b0  HandleCount:    9.
    Image: MemTests.EXE

Handle table at fffff8a001c60000 with 9 entries in use

0024: Object: fffff8a001c62bb0  GrantedAccess: 000f0007 Entry: fffff8a001c60090
Object: fffff8a001c62bb0  Type: (ffffffa8000ce5790) Section
    ObjectHeader: fffff8a001c62b80 (new version)
        HandleCount: 1  PointerCount: 2
        Directory Object: fffff8a005b56860  Name: map
```

We then use a C++ expression to navigate the data types up to the control area address. The expression is a bit involved, because we need to cast `_SECTION_OBJECT.Segment`, which is declared as a pointer to a `_SEGMENT_OBJECT`, into a pointer to a `_MAPPED_FILE_SEGMENT`:

```
1: kd> ? @@( ((nt!_MAPPED_FILE_SEGMENT *) ((nt!_SECTION_OBJECT *) 0xfffff8a001c62bb0)-
>Segment)->ControlArea)
```

```
Evaluate expression: -6047298466960 = ffffffa80`00ec4b70
```

We are rewarded with a control area address which is exactly the same stored into the `_SECTION_OBJECT_POINTERS` for the file.

38.7.4   Section Object Created for File Read

This experiment shows how, under the hood, the kernel creates a section object for a file to process a call to *ReadFile*.

First, we are going to create a 1GB file exploiting the fact that the creation of a section object longer than the file it maps extends the file. We choose *Create test file* at the main menu of MemTests and provide a name (*caution: if the file already exists it is overwritten*), then we select no incremental expansion and enter a key to go on at the prompt. This results in calling *CreateFile* for the file, without writing anything to it, so we have an handle to an empty file.

Now we create a 1GB mapping for this file. We select *Memory section test* at the main menu, select *mapped file*, protection 4 (read/write), size 0x40000000 (1 GB), a valid name, view access 6 (read/write), offset 0, size 0 (the view is for the whole mapping), we don't specify a NUMA node. From the view access on, the data we specify are parameters for the call to *MapViewOfFileEx*. They are not actually needed, because we will abort the test after the call to *CreateFileMapping*, but MemTests asks for all the parameters before making the two calls. MemTests shows a summary of the input data and prompts for a key to continue. We go on and MemTests prompts again before calling *CreateFileMapping*. Again, we move forward and the next prompt is before the call to *CreateViewOfFileEx* (this is when MemTests prints the message "about to map the view"). When we are here, *CreateFileMapping* has already created a 1GB mapping and this extends the file to the same size, so we can choose *cancel* at the prompt and, then close MemTests at the main menu. We see a 1GB file created in the current directory.

To perform a clean experiment, we need to be sure to evict the section object we just created from memory, because it can remain resident even after the program has terminated. The simplest way to ensure this is to reboot the system.

Now we are going to read 1 byte from our file and see the section object.

At the main menu, we choose *File read test*, enter the name of the file created in the prevlous step, 0xc0000000 for the access (read/write) and we break before the file is opened. We step until the call to *MyOpenFile* returns and examine the file object:

```
1: kd> !handle @@(hFileGlob)

PROCESS fffffa8000d39b30
    SessionId: 1  Cid: 0358    Peb: 7fffffde000  ParentCid: 0890
    DirBase: 0d0c8000  ObjectTable: fffff8a005ba8f00  HandleCount:   7.
    Image: MemTests.EXE

Handle table at fffff8a0017b0000 with 7 entries in use

001c: Object: fffffa80020a69d0  GrantedAccess: 0012019f Entry: fffff8a0017b0070
Object: fffffa80020a69d0  Type: (fffffa8000ce6de0) File
    ObjectHeader: fffffa80020a69a0 (new version)
        HandleCount: 1  PointerCount: 1
        Directory Object: 00000000  Name: \Apps\TestApp\big.tmp {HarddiskVolume3}


1: kd> ?? ((nt!_FILE_OBJECT *) 0xfffffa80020a69d0)->SectionObjectPointer
struct _SECTION_OBJECT_POINTERS * 0xfffffa80`00e98ea8
   +0x000 DataSectionObject : (null)
   +0x008 SharedCacheMap    : (null)
   +0x010 ImageSectionObject : (null)
```

So far, no section exists for the file.

We resume execution, enter 0 for the offset and 1 for the length, to read 1 byte. MemTests prompts before calling *SetFilePointerEx*, which is used to move to the offset specified. We are not interested in observing this call, so we enter a key to continue.

The next prompt is before the call to *ReadFile*, so we break here. We stop immediately before the call to ReadFile and confirm that the section ojbect pointers are still set to null:

```
1: kd> ?? ((nt!_FILE_OBJECT *) 0xfffffa80020a69d0)->SectionObjectPointer
struct _SECTION_OBJECT_POINTERS * 0xfffffa80`00e98ea8
   +0x000 DataSectionObject : (null)
   +0x008 SharedCacheMap    : (null)
   +0x010 ImageSectionObject : (null)
```

We then execute the call to *ReadFile* and examine them again:

```
1: kd> ?? ((nt!_FILE_OBJECT *) 0xfffffa80020a69d0)->SectionObjectPointer
struct _SECTION_OBJECT_POINTERS * 0xfffffa80`00e98ea8
   +0x000 DataSectionObject : 0xfffffa80`030535c0 Void
   +0x008 SharedCacheMap    : 0xfffffa80`00ecca80 Void
   +0x010 ImageSectionObject : (null)
```

Now `DataSectionObject` points to a control area, which we dump:

```
1: kd> !ca 0xfffffa80`030535c0


ControlArea   @ fffffa80030535c0
  Segment       fffff8a0012075f0  Flink     0000000000000000  Blink      0000000000000000
  Section Ref                  1  Pfn Ref                 20  Mapped Views              1
  User Ref                     0  WaitForDel               0  Flush Count               0
  File Object   fffffa80020a69d0  ModWriteCount            0  System Views              1
  WritableRefs                 0
  Flags (8080) File WasPurged


       File: \Apps\TestApp\big.tmp

Segment @ fffff8a0012075f0
  ControlArea      fffffa80030535c0  ExtendInfo     0000000000000000
  Total Ptes               40000
  Segment Size          40000000  Committed                0
  Flags (c0000) ProtectionMask


Subsection 1 @ fffffa8003053640
  ControlArea   fffffa80030535c0  Starting Sector        0  Number Of Sectors 40000
  Base Pte      fffff8a002000000  Ptes In Subsect    40000  Unused Ptes              0
  Flags                        d  Sector Offset          0  Protection               6
  Accessed
  Flink         0000000000000000  Blink     0000000000000000  MappedViews            2
```

The data section has a single subsection spanning 0x40000 PTEs i.e. 0x40000000 bytes or 1GB, so the read of a single byte results in the creation of a section for the whole file.

39   Tweaking the MPW and the MAPW

39.1 Introduction

With these experiments we will block the modified page writer and the mapped page writer, so that the VMM is not able to repurpose physical pages anymore. Without these two threads, dirty pages stay on the Modified list indefinitely.

This experiment allows to observe the state of Modified pages before they are moved to the Standby list and it is also interesting in confirming empirically the fundamental role of these two threads.

We will use the test driver described in sec. 35.5 on p. 281, with the same warning: this driver can be used only with Windows 7 RTM (pre-SP1) and *will crash* any other version of Windows.

Furthermore, the system *deadlocks* when all physical memory is exhausted and the two writers are kept blocked. This is actually interesting to observe with a debugger attached, because after a timeout a message is printed in the console, warning that the system would have crashed if no debugger was attached.

We can pinpoint the modified page writer (MPW) and the mapped page writer (MAPW) with data breakpoints on writes to `_MMPFN.u3.e1` of dirty pages.

39.2 MPW Blocking

39.2.1   Overview

Using data breakpoints, we can see that the MPW is a thread belonging to the System process and executing the *MiModifiedPageWriter* function. Its status, when idle, is as follows:

```
        THREAD fffffa800097a680  Cid 0004.005c  Teb: 0000000000000000 Win32Thread:
0000000000000000 WAIT: (WrFreePage) KernelMode Non-Alertable
        fffff80002a384e0  Gate
    Not impersonating
    DeviceMap              fffff8a000006090
    Owning Process         fffffa8000956ae0      Image:         System
    Attached Process       N/A             Image:         N/A
    Wait Start TickCount   556173          Ticks: 16318 (0:00:04:14.968)
    Context Switch Count   328
    UserTime               00:00:00.000
    KernelTime             00:00:00.031
    Win32 Start Address nt!MiModifiedPageWriter (0xfffff8000281b9c0)
    Stack Init fffff8800312bdb0 Current fffff8800312ba80
    Base fffff8800312c000 Limit fffff88003126000 Call 0
```

```
        Priority 17 BasePriority 8 UnusualBoost 0 ForegroundBoost 0 IoPriority 2
PagePriority 5
        Child-SP          RetAddr           : Args to Child
: Call Site
        fffff880`0312bac0 fffff800`0288a052 : fffffa80`0097a680 fffffa80`0097a680
00000000`00000000 00000000`00000000 : nt!KiSwapContext+0x7a

        fffff880`0312bc00 fffff800`028ca4c5 : 00000000`0000000c fffff800`00b96080
00000000`00000000 fffff800`0281b9c0 : nt!KiCommitThreadWait+0x1d2

        fffff880`0312bc90 fffff800`0281ba1a : fffffa80`0097a680 fffff880`00000008
00000000`00000001 fffffa80`00956ae0 : nt!KeWaitForGate+0x101

        fffff880`0312bce0 fffff800`02b26166 : fffffa80`0097a680 00000000`00000000
00000000`00000080 00000000`00000001 : nt!MiModifiedPageWriter+0x5a

        fffff880`0312bd40 fffff800`02861486 : fffff800`029fbe80 fffffa80`0097a680
fffff800`02a09c40 00000000`00000000 : nt!PspSystemThreadStartup+0x5a

        fffff880`0312bd80 00000000`00000000 : fffff880`0312c000 fffff880`03126000
fffff880`0312ba80 00000000`00000000 : nt!KxStartSystemThread+0x16
```

This thread waits for work to do at *MiModifiedPageWriter* + 0x55 by calling *KeWaitForGate*, which is unexported and undocumented. The code before the call loads the address of a static named `MmModifiedPageWriterGate` into `rcx`, suggesting that the first function parameter is the gate address.

The test driver creates a KGATE which can be used to block the MPW. We can set a breakpoint at *MiModifiedPageWriter* + 0x55 and generate some dirty pages. The MPW is awakened and reaches the breakpoint while trying to entering the wait state again. When the breakpoint is hit, we alter `rcx` so that it points to the KGATE managed by the driver (these steps are described in greater detail later).

With this technique, we are actually capturing the MPW when it is about to enter a waiting state, not when it is awakening. However, it can be observed that, when the available physical memory is a fraction of the total and there are many dirty pages, the MPW repeatedly executes the call at *MiModifiedPageWriter* + 0x55, transitioning from waiting to running state, while writing blocks of pages to disk. Thus, we will see that we can intercept it when there are still many dirty pages waiting to be written to the paging file.

The functions for working with KGATES are undocumented and are not exported by the kernel. By analyzing VMM code, we can see that the MPW gate is signaled by calling *KeSignalGateBoostPriority*. An example of such a call can be found at *MiObtainFreePages* + 0x4b, where `rcx` is set to the address of `MmModifiedPageWriterGate`, which suggests that the function first parameter is the address of the gate being signaled.

The test driver calls *KeSignalGateBoostPriority* with the address of its own KGATE and this correctly awakens the MPW when it is waiting on it. The gate appears to be automatically set to non-signaled after the thread is resumed, i.e. if we cause the MPW to wait on the same gate again, it blocks until we signal it once more.

With a bit of guesswork on function names, we see that the kernel has a function named *KeInitializeGate*. To be on the safe side, WrkEvent.sys calls this function inside its initialization routine.

Since the gate functions are not exported by ntkrnlmp.exe, the driver computes their addresses using their offset from *KeSetEvent*, which is exported. These offsets have been extracted with WinDbg for the RTM build of Windows 7 x64 and are likely to be incorrect for any other Windows version. This is the reason why the test driver would crash on a different windows version: it would attempt function calls to invalid addresses.

39.2.2   Experiment

For this experiment we will need the following programs:

- WrkEvent.sys – the test driver

- WrkEvClient.exe – the driver client

- MemTests.exe – the memory allocation program.

In the following, we will assume that a kernel debugger is attached to the system.

The first thing to do is start WrkEvClient and MemTests in separate processes, so that they are ready when needed. WrkEvClient loads the driver, which, in turn, prints the addresses of its waitable objects in the debugger console. We should note the address of the KGATE, since we are going to need it later.

We then allocate a private memory region with a size equal to about 90% of the available physical memory, which we will use to generate dirty pages. We can do this with the *VirtualAllocEx() test* option, specifying 0x3000 (i.e. MEM_COMMIT | MEM_RESERVE) for flAllocationType and 4 (read/write) for flProtect.

Next, we break with the debugger and set the following breakpoint to catch the MPW before it calls *KeWaitForGate*:

```
bp nt!MiModifiedPageWriter + 0x55
```

We then write to the region with the *Access region* option and, while the memory write is in progress, the breakpoint should be hit.

When this happens, we set `rcx` to the address of the driver `KGATE` noted before and resume:

```
Breakpoint 1 hit
nt!MiModifiedPageWriter+0x55:
fffff800`0281ba15 e8aae90a00      call    nt!KeWaitForGate (fffff800`028ca3c4)
0: kd> r rcx=0XFFFFFA8000DEC768
0: kd> g
```

The MPW will stay blocked until we signal the gate with the driver client. If we monitor the physical memory usage, we should see something akin to the following graph (obtained with Sysinternal's Process Explorer):

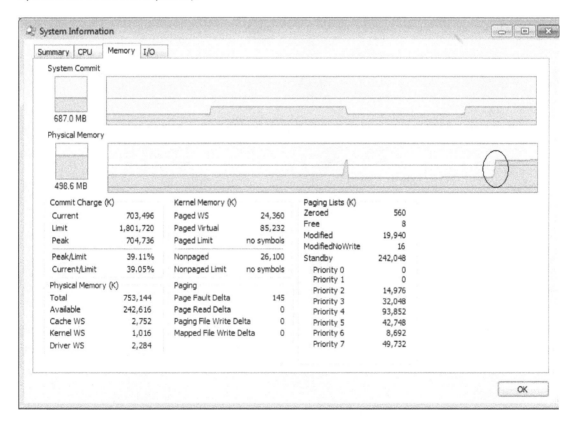

Figure 52 - Memory Usage with Blocked MPW

We see the abrupt increase in memory usage, followed by an almost flat line, indicating that dirty pages are not being written to disk. This test was performed on a virtual machine with 736MB of physical memory and an allocation size of 265MB.

We can launch another instance of MemTests and allocate other physical memory, almost exhausting all of it, and still the VMM is unable to free physical pages, because of the blocked MPW:

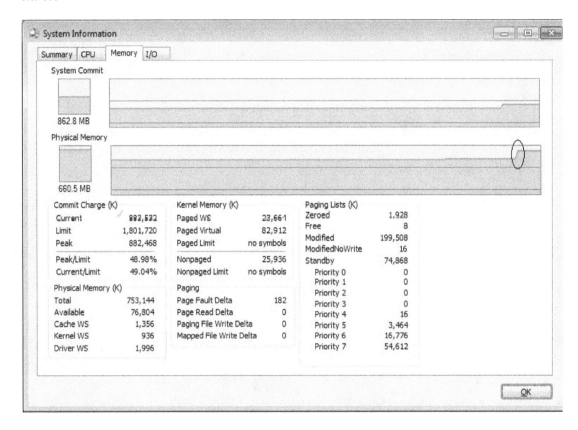

Figure 53 - Memory Usage with Blocked MPW

The second allocation was 150.000.000 bytes in size.

If we examine the working sets of the 2 MemTests instances, we see they have been partially trimmed (their working sets are less than the allocation size), while the VMM was attempting to free physical memory:

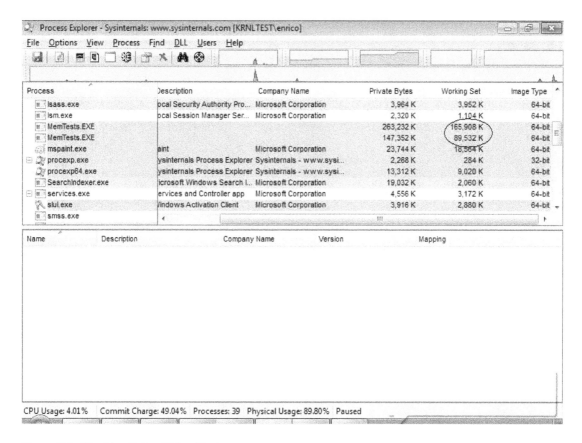

Figure 54 - Working Sets of MemTests

We can further reduce the working set size by selecting the *Shrink WS* option in both instances:

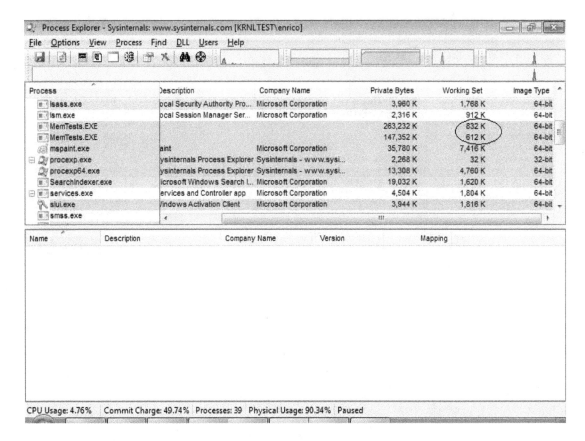

Figure 55 - Working Sets of MemTests after Self-Shrink

but the physical memory is still almost completely used:

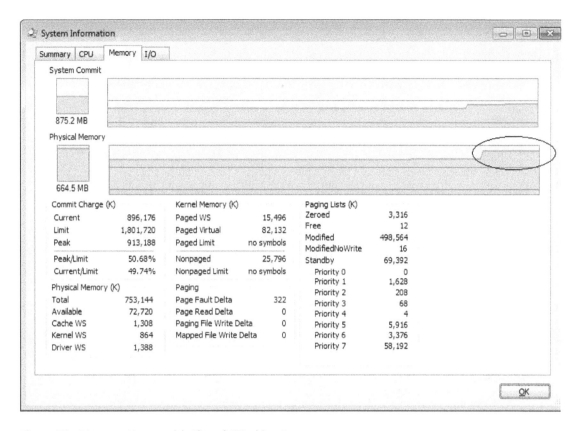

Figure 56 - Memory Usage with Shrunk Working Sets

It is not enough to remove pages from the working sets to free memory. This only puts them on the Modified list, but they will not be free (i.e. ready to be repurposed) until written to disk, and the writer is not doing its job. We can also notice the high value for the Modified list: 498,564 kB. These are our pages waiting to be written.

As soon as we signal the driver gate with the *Signal gate* option, memory is freed and, after a while, the breakpoint is hit again. This means that the MPW is trying to enter the wait state again. We can disable the breakpoint and leave the MPW alone. The System Information graph clearly shows the moment when the gate was signaled:

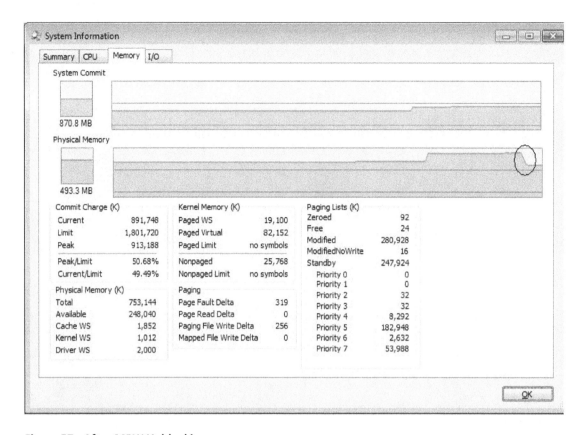

Figure 57 - After MPW Unblocking

39.3 MAPW Blocking

39.3.1   Introduction

The MAPW is another system thread, which executes *MiMappedPageWriter*:

```
      THREAD fffffa8000975040  Cid 0004.0060  Teb: 0000000000000000 Win32Thread:
0000000000000000 WAIT: (WrFreePage) KernelMode Non-Alertable
          fffff80002a4ef80  SynchronizationEvent
          fffff80002a4ef98  SynchronizationEvent
          fffff80002a4efb0  SynchronizationEvent
          fffff80002a4efc8  SynchronizationEvent
          fffff80002a4efe0  SynchronizationEvent
          fffff80002a4eff8  SynchronizationEvent
          fffff80002a4f010  SynchronizationEvent
          fffff80002a4f028  SynchronizationEvent
          fffff80002a4f040  SynchronizationEvent
          fffff80002a4f058  SynchronizationEvent
          fffff80002a4f070  SynchronizationEvent
          fffff80002a4f088  SynchronizationEvent
          fffff80002a4f0a0  SynchronizationEvent
          fffff80002a4f0b8  SynchronizationEvent
```

```
        fffff80002a4f0d0  SynchronizationEvent
        fffff80002a4f0e8  SynchronizationEvent
        fffff80002a4f100  SynchronizationEvent
    Not impersonating
    DeviceMap               fffff8a000006090
    Owning Process          fffffa8000956ae0      Image:        System
    Attached Process        N/A          Image:        N/A
    Wait Start TickCount     425997       Ticks: 146494 (0:00:38:08.968)
    Context Switch Count     20
    UserTime                00:00:00.000
    KernelTime              00:00:00.000
    Win32 Start Address nt!MiMappedPageWriter (0xfffff800028ba0c0)
    Stack Init fffff88003132db0 Current fffff88003132790
    Base fffff88003133000 Limit fffff8800312d000 Call 0
    Priority 17 BasePriority 8 UnusualBoost 0 ForegroundBoost 0 IoPriority 2
PagePriority 5
        Child-SP          RetAddr           : Args to Child
: Call Site
    fffff880`031327d0 fffff800`0288a052 : fffffa80`00975040 fffffa80`00975040
00000000`00000000 00000000`00000000 : nt!KiSwapContext+0x7a

    fffff880`03132910 fffff800`0288654b : 00000000`01000000 00000000`00000000
00000000`00000000 00000000`00000003 : nt!KiCommitThreadWait+0x1d2

    fffff880`031329a0 fffff800`028ba16b : 00000000`00000011 fffff880`03132c90
fffffa80`00000001 fffff8a0`00000008 : nt!KeWaitForMultipleObjects+0x271

    fffff880`03132c50 fffff800`02b26166 : fffffa80`00975040 00000000`00000080
fffffa80`00956ae0 00000000`00000000 : nt!MiMappedPageWriter+0xab

    fffff880`03132d40 fffff800`02861486 : fffff800`029fbe80 fffffa80`00975040
fffffa80`0097a680 00000000`00000000 : nt!PspSystemThreadStartup+0x5a

    fffff880`03132d80 00000000`00000000 : fffff880`03133000 fffff880`0312d000
fffff880`03132790 00000000`00000000 : nt!KxStartSystemThread+0x16
```

It waits for work calling *KeWaitForMultipleObjects* at *MiMappedPageWriter* + 0xa6. This
function is documented and requires an array of pointers to waitable objects, like events, on
which the thread will wait. We will use the array provided by WrkEvent.sys to block this
thread.

39.3.2   Experiment

For this experiment we will use the same programs of sec. 39.2.2 (p. 382) and the system
must be attached to a kernel debugger.

The first step is to start the driver client and MemTests in separate processes. We must note
the address of the event array (not of the individual events), which will be used later.

Now we need to map a file to generate dirty mapped pages, so that the MAPW is awakened
and hits the breakpoint when it tries to wait again. To do so, we use the *Memory section test*

option of MemTests, choosing *mapped file*. Note that it does not make sense to allocate a paging file backed section with the *shared memory* option, because its pages would be written by the MPW, not by the MAPW. If a file is not currently open, MemTests allows to create one (it is better not to select *incremental expansion*, to avoid waiting for the file to be expanded). We set the map protection to read/write and use a size of about 90% of the available physical memory; for the view, we set the access to read/write (i.e. 6 which is FILE_MAP_READ | FILE_MAP_WRITE) as well and 0 for the offset and size (the view spans the whole mapping).

Afterwards, we use the debugger to set a breakpoint at *MiMappedPageWriter* + 0xa6.

We then write to the mapped region with the *Access region* option. We must remember to write to the region, because we want to create dirty pages. Note that, as was the case with the MPW, the breakpoint catches the MAPW when it is about to enter a waiting state. The MAPW behavior looks different from the MPW one: it usually hits the breakpoint when it has written most of the pages to disk. We can see this from the fact that, while MemTests is writing to the region, the used physical memory comes close to 90%, then this value drops sharply while the MAPW is at work and the breakpoint is hit afterwards.

When the breakpoint is hit, the MAPW is about to call *KeWaitForMultipleObjects*, whose first two parameters are the count of objects to be waited on and the address of the array of waitable objects. We replace these two parameters, passed into rcx and rdx respectively, with a count of 1 and the address of the array of events created by WrkEvent.sys:

```
0: kd> r rcx=1
0: kd> r rdx=0XFFFFFA80014EA240
0: kd> g
```

We can then write to the entire region again, so that all the pages are dirty and observe that the used physical memory counter does not decrease anymore, because the MAPW is not working. The counter may vary slightly, due to the fact that the MPW is still working, but the huge memory usage caused by MemTests cannot be reduced.

Now we can observe an interesting implication of file mapping. This feature is designed to guarantee that the updated memory content is flushed to the file by the MAPW, so that the file is updated as one would expect. This can occur after the process updating the file has terminated, since the MAPW works asynchronously, but it *must* happen. Dirty pages mapped to a file are not moved to the Free list when the program mapping the file terminates: they stay on the Modified list until they have been written to the file. This is quite different from what happens with paging file backed memory: when the last process mapping such a section terminates (or simply closes the handle), this memory is immediately released to the

Free list, because there is no need to write to the paging file the content of an address space which has been destroyed.

Thus, if we close MemTests, we see that the used physical memory remains more or less the same, because the dirty pages are still there.

Another interesting implication is that now no process has an handle to the file, therefore we can delete it from a command prompt (so that it is really erased, not just moved to the recycle bin). We see the used memory drop sharply as the dirty pages are released: since the file is gone, there is no need (and no way) to update it anymore, so the VMM releases the pages.

It is also interesting to note the if we delete the file in Windows Explorer, which moves it to the recycle bin, physical memory is not released: the file is still around, so it still has to be updated.

To clean everything up, we should signal event 0 of WrkEvent.sys unblocking the MAPW. Normally, it hits the breakpoint again shortly. We can then clear the breakpoint and resume execution.

Note that if we close the driver client before unblocking the MAPW, the thread is still waiting on the KEVENT stored inside the device extension of the driver. This memory is released when the driver unloads, so the MAPW is left waiting on an invalid memory address, which will results in a system crash.

39.4 Bringing it All Down

A final experiment shows what happens if we completely exhaust physical memory, by keeping the MAPW and the MPW blocked. We can repeat the steps of the previous section, using a map size greater than the available physical memory. We also block both the MPW and the MAPW with the techniques described before. If we then write to the entire region, all of the physical memory is used. This causes the system to freeze completely and, after a while, the debugger takes control and prints the following messages:

```
Without a debugger attached, the following bugcheck would have occurred.
  eb 39e0c 143 1 c0000054
Without a debugger attached, the following bugcheck would have occurred.
  eb 39e0c 143 1 c0000054
Break instruction exception - code 80000003 (first chance)
nt!MiNoPagesLastChance+0x17f:
fffff800`0295a54f cc                int     3
```

Bugcheck 0xeb is DIRTY_MAPPED_PAGES_CONGESTION and we can also see the telltale name of the function: *MiNoPagesLastChance.*

40   Large Pages

40.1 Why Large Pages and Limitations

x64 processors have the ability to map so-called large pages. The idea behind large pages is to use a smaller portion of the VA for the indexes into the paging structures and use more bits for the page offset. The number of offset bits determines the page size, so increasing them means having larger pages. Why go through all this trouble? Because each translation for a physical page starting address is cached in a TLB entry. Increasing the page size means that a single TLB entry applies to a larger range of physical memory, thereby saving TLB space. Since the TLB is quite small, this can give better performances. There is, of course, a flip side of the coin, which we will see shortly.

To reduce the number of bits used as indexes, a level of translation is removed: instead of indexing into the PML4, the PDPT, the PD and the PT, only the first three level of tables are used, getting rid of the PT. Thus, the 9 bits which would be used to index into the PT are now part of the offset, which increases from 12 to 21 bits, corresponding to a page size of 2 MB. The physical address stored in the PDE, becomes the address of the physical page itself and the offset is added to it.

A virtual to physical translation of this kind, maps a 2MB virtual region to a 2MB physical region, so a *physically contiguous* free range of this size is needed to be able to map a large page. Furthermore, the processor architecture imposes that the physical page starting address be aligned at a multiple of its size, i.e. 2MB. We thus need a free physical range which satisfies both constraints: 2MB in size and aligned on a 2MB boundary. Since small 4kB pages are far more common, the physical memory can become so fragmented that finding a suitable range can be impossible. When this happens, the memory allocation APIs return an error, indicating that not enough resources are available (e.g. GetLastError() returns ERROR_NO_SYSTEM_RESOURCES or 1450). This is the price we pay for the improved TLB usage. As an example, on a 1GB system, letting the system run for about 30' can result in this error when allocating as little as 4MB of memory (i.e. 2 large pages).

Large pages are implicitly non-pageable, for a couple of reasons. First, outpaging a single large page means performing a 2MB write, so the usual VMM paging activity could result in too much I/O being performed. The other reason is that, when a large page needs to be paged in, a suitable free physical range may not available. This would be a difficult situation to handle: it is one thing to fail a memory allocation returning an error, but once memory has been allocated, the VMM cannot say "sorry, I swapped it out and now I don't know how to bring it back".

Given this, the process token must have the SeLockMemoryPrivilege to allocate large pages, otherwise it gets an ERROR_PRIVILEGE_NOT_HELD error. This privilege is normally disabled, even for those accounts who hold it, so it must be enabled with a call to *AdjustTokenPrivileges* before attempting the allocation. The privilege must be forst granted to the account under which the program is run, if the account itself does not hold it. Afterwards, it must also be enabled before the allocation can finally be performed. The source code of MemTests found in the download package shows examples of how to add and enable the privilege. The code for adding the privilege is based on the sample code found in [15].

40.2 Private Large Pages

40.2.1   Allocation

This kind of pages can be allocated by calling *VirtualAllocEx* OR-ing `MEM_LARGE_PAGES` to the `flAllocationType` parameter.

If we try setting `flAllocationType` to MEM_RESERVE | MEM_LARGE_PAGES, without also OR-ing MEM_COMMIT, *VirtualAllocEx* fails with ERROR_INVALID_PARAMETER (87). This happens because large pages must be resident in memory once allocated, so they must also be committed.

An interesting behavior occurs when we call *VirtualAllocEx* with `flAllocationType` set to `MEM_RESERVE` and later we call it a second time for the same range with `flAllocationType = MEM_COMMIT | MEM_LARGE_PAGES`. This is allowed, because we can call the function to only reserve pages and commit them later. What happens is that both calls succeed, but we end up using regular pages. The next sections will show how the paging structures and _MMPFNs are set up for large pages, but, in this scenario, it can be observed that they are set up for regular 4 kB pages.

The bottom line is that to actually allocate large pages we must set flAllocationType to:

```
MEM_RESERVE | MEM_COMMIT | MEM_LARGE_PAGES
```

40.2.2   PxEs and _MMPFN

After a successful allocation, the paging structures for an address mapped by a large page are set as follows:

```
1: kd> !pte a00000
                        VA 0000000000a00000

PXE @ FFFFF6FB7DBED000    PPE at FFFFF6FB7DA00000    PDE at FFFFF6FB40000028    PTE at FFFFF68000005000
contains 03A000002B18F867  contains 02F000002B312867  contains 80000000258008E7  contains 0000000000000000
pfn 2b18f     ---DA--UWEV  pfn 2b312     ---DA--UWEV  pfn 25800     --LDA--UW-V  LARGE PAGE pfn 25800
```

The PDE control bits are set to 0x8e7, with bit 7 (the PS bit) set to 1, which tells the processor this PDE directly maps a 2MB page. the `!pte` extension decodes the PDE content accordingly. This is the content of the paging structures immediately following the call to *VirtualAllocEx*, so physical memory is allocated by this function and not when the virtual range is accessed, as is the case for regular, pageable 4kB pages.

The PFN database has an entry for each 4 kB range of physical memory. These entries still exist when a 2MB range is covered by a PDE, so they are set to meaningful values, even though they don't actually relate to physical pages. A PDE spans 512 PFN entries. Below we can see the first two entries for the PDE above:

```
1: kd> !pfn 25800
    PFN 00025800 at address FFFFFA8000708000
    flink        FFFFFA8000F71B30  blink / share count 00000001  pteaddress FFFFF6FB4000002A
    reference count 0001    used entry count  0000      Cached     color 0    Priority 1
    restore pte 00000001  containing page       02B312  Active      R
        ReadInProgress
1: kd> !pfn 25801
    PFN 00025801 at address FFFFFA8000708030
    flink        FFFFFA8000F71B30  blink / share count 00000001  pteaddress FFFFF6FB4000002A
    reference count 0001    used entry count  0000      Cached     color 0    Priority 5
    restore pte 00000001  containing page       02B312  Active      M
    Modified
```

We can notice the following:

- `flink (_MMPFN.u1.Flink)` is set to the address of the _EPROCESS of the allocating process.

- `pteaddress (_MMPFN.PteAddress)` is the address of the PDE with bit 1 set. This bit acts as a flag of sorts since PxE addresses are multiple of 8 and have bits 0-2 clear.

- `restore pte (_MMPFN.u4.OriginalPte)` is set to 1. This member normally stores the software PTE to be copied into the hardware one when the page is repurposed. This page is locked and never repurposed, so this member is used for some other purpose.

- containing page (`_MMPFN.u4.PteFrame`) is set the PFN of the PDE.

- The first entry has `ReadInProgress` (`_MMPFN.u3.e1.ReadInProgress`) set. Obviously, this has some special meaning, since the page is locked and no I/O will ever occur for it.

All the page life cycle we analyzed in previous sections does not apply to large pages, since they are not pageable. Once mapped, they are simply left Active until released. So how does the VMM know not to page them. According to [14]: " The memory is part of the process private bytes but not part of the working set", so it's likely that WS entries are not created for these pages and the WSM simply knows nothing about them, because it looks at the WS list for pages to trim. This is confirmed by `_MMPFN.u1` being set to the address of `_EPROCESS`: for pages which are accounted in the working set, this member stores the index of the WSL entry for the address.

40.3 Memory Section Large Pages

40.3.1   Allocation and Section Object

Besides allocating private large pages, we can also allocate a shareable section object made of large pages. This is only allowed for paging file backed sections, not mapped file backed ones. This limitation stems from the fact that these pages are not pageable, like private large ones, hence so-called "paging file backed" pages don't actually go to the paging file and there is no way to transfer the content of large pages from and to another (mapped) file.

To create such a memory section, we must call *CreateFileMapping* OR-ing SEC_COMMIT and SEC_LARGE_PAGES to `flProtect`. When we do that, we see that a section object like the following one is created:

```
ControlArea  @ fffffa8000e5ae00
  Segment       fffff8a001f68000  Flink      0000000000000000  Blink      0000000000000000
  Section Ref             1  Pfn Ref                  0  Mapped Views             0
  User Ref                1  WaitForDel               0  Flush Count              0
  File Object  0000000000000000  ModWriteCount            0  System Views             0
  WritableRefs            0
  Flags (2000) Commit


Segment @ fffff8a001f68000
  ControlArea     fffffa8000e5ae00  ExtendInfo      0000000000000000
  Total Ptes              200
  Segment Size         200000  Committed                   200
  CreatingProcess fffffa8000e90b30  FirstMappedVa               0
  ProtoPtes       fffff8a001f68048
  Flags (80800) LargePages ProtectionMask
```

```
Subsection 1 @ fffffa8000e5ae80
  ControlArea   fffffa8000e5ae00  Starting Sector        0  Number Of Sectors    0
  Base Pte      fffff8a001f68048  Ptes In Subsect      200  Unused Ptes          0
  Flags                        8  Sector Offset          0  Protection           4
```

These data structure were dumped *before* any view of the section was mapped. It's interesting to observe the prototype PTEs of this section, while remembering that we saw in sec. 37.3.1 on p.300 that for small pages, these PTEs are initialized as demand-zero. Here the situation is different:

```
1: kd> dq fffff8a001f68048
fffff8a0`01f68048  80000000`25e00867 80000000`25e01867
fffff8a0`01f68058  80000000`25e02867 80000000`25e03867
fffff8a0`01f68068  80000000`25e04867 80000000`25e05867
fffff8a0`01f68078  80000000`25e06867 80000000`25e07867
fffff8a0`01f68088  80000000`25e08867 80000000`25e09867
fffff8a0`01f68098  80000000`25e0a867 80000000`25e0b867
fffff8a0`01f680a8  80000000`25e0c867 80000000`25e0d867
fffff8a0`01f680b8  80000000`25e0e867 80000000`25e0f867
```

Each PTE stores the physical address of a 4 kB range: the first one points to 0x25e00000, the second one to 0x25e01000, etc. These addresses, other than the first one, don't have an actual meaning for the processor: as we are going to see, when the virtual to physical mapping is established, the PDE is set to point to 0x25e00000 and the processor architecture *implies* that a 2 MB range of physical memory will be used by the translation, starting from there. The processor "knows" nothing of address 0x25e01000, etc.

But why are these prototype PTEs created at all, then? Since the page size is now 2 MB, why create a bunch of logical PTEs to describe each 4 kB chunk of the page? We will answer this question shortly.

We can see from the dump above that all the prototype PTEs are set as valid ones, with the P bit set. If we examine the _MMPFN instances for their physical addresses, we see that they are all in Active state, which tells us that physical memory is allocated at the time the section object is created. This contrasts with what happens for small pages, were physical memory is allocated only when a virtual address is referenced.

As is the case for private large pages, _MMPFN entries for physical addresses other than the first one, don't actually refer to a "page" in the processor sense. As far as the processor is concerned, there will be a single 2 MB page beginning at the physical address associated with the first entry. However, the VMM uses _MMPFN entries to keep track of the status of physical memory in 4 kB chunks, so it updates all the entries spanned by the page to record the fact that these physical memory blocks are in use, and this is done when the section object is created, not when a mapped view is referenced. In the following we will use the term *block* to refer to a 4 kB region of physical memory whose state is tracked by an `_MMPFN` instance, to avoid using the term page.

We saw in sec. 37.11 on p. 317 how the memory pages storing the prototype PTEs can be themselves swapped out, since they are part of the paged pool. We also saw that this can happen only when all the prototype PTEs don't refer to physical pages, because, otherwise, the `_MMPFN`s point back to the prototype PTE page through `u4.PteFrame`. This is managed by incrementing the share count of the prototype PTEs page for each valid or transition PTE. According to this logic, the pages storing the prototype PTEs above could not be paged out, since all the prototype PTEs stored are valid ones. However, if we examine the share count of the prototype PTE page, we see that it is actually set to 1, i.e. the valid PTEs are not accounted for. This makes sense when we consider that the value of `_MMPFN.u4.PteFrame` for each block pointed by the prototype PTEs is normally used when moving the page to a transition list or when repurposing it and this does not happen for large pages since they are non-pageable. We will see in a short while that `_MMPFN.u4.PteFrame` does not actually refer to the prototype PTE page.

So, even though we still have to understand *why* these prototype PTEs are created in the first place, we can at least conclude that they are pageable and the physical memory they consume can be reclaimed. If this happens, they will have to be brought back when a new view of the section is mapped, because they are used to build the hardware PDE.

Let's analyze the `_MMPFN` for the first block of the section:

```
1: kd> !pfn 25e00
   PFN 00025E00 at address FFFFFA800071A000
   flink       FFFFFA8000E90B30  blink / share count 00000001  pteaddress FFFFF8A001F68048
   reference count 0001    used entry count  0000       Cached     color 0    Priority 5
   restore pte 00000080  containing page       FFFFFFFFFFFFF  Active      MPR
   Modified Shared ReadInProgress
```

- `flink` (`_MMPFN.u1.Flink`) stores the address of the `_EPROCESS` of the section creator.

- `share count` (`_MMPFN.u2.ShareCount`) is set to 1, even though no view of this section is mapped. Furthermore, when one or more views of this section are mapped, this count remains set to 1. This beavior is consistent with the pages being non-pageable.

- `pteaddress` (`_MMPFN.PteAddress`) points to the prototype PTE.

- `containing page (_MMPFN.u4.PteFrame)` is set to -1 and does not point to the prototype PTE page, as we anticipated.

- `ReadInProgress (_MMPFN.u3.e1.ReadInProgress)` is set, as was the case for private large pages. It must have some special meaning, since these pages are non-pageable.

If we examine the next `_MMPFN` instance

```
1: kd> !pfn 25e01
    PFN 00025E01 at address FFFFFA800071A030
    flink       FFFFFA8000E90B30  blink / share count 00000001  pteaddress FFFFF8A001F68050
    reference count 0001    used entry count  0000      Cached     color 0   Priority 0
    restore pte 00000080  containing page         FFFFFFFFFFFF  Active      P
      Shared
```

we notice that `pteaddress` points to the next prototype PTE, confirming this member is set in a different way from the private large page case. Also, this `_MMPFN` and the following ones don't have `ReadInProgress1` set.

40.3.2   View Mapping with No Offset

When we map a view of the section with no offset, we find a PDE for a large page set as follows:

```
1: kd> !pte @@(*lplpRegion)
                            VA 0000000000800000

PXE @ FFFFF6FB7DBED000    PPE at FFFFF6FB7DA00000    PDE at FFFFF6FB40000020    PTE at FFFFF68000004000
contains 0290000031DD7867  contains 02D00000316DA867  contains 8000000025E008E7  contains 0000000000000000
pfn 31dd7     ---DA--UWEV  pfn 316da     ---DA--UWEV  pfn 25e00    --LDA--UW-V  LARGE PAGE pfn 25e00
```

which is not particularly remarkable, being a PDE for a large page like the ones we saw for private memory. Again, the PDE is initialized as valid, without waiting for the memory to be actually accessed. The prototype PTE and the `_MMPFN` are unchanged.

If other processes map additional views, the effect is the same: a PDE is initialized in their paging structures, but the prototype PTEs and `_MMPFN`s are unaffected.

40.3.3   View Mapping with Offset

40.3.3.1   Mapping the View

Now we are finally going to understand why the prototype PTEs are created: they are needed to map a view with an offset within the 2MB range.

This is something the APIs for secton objects allow: creating a section and then mapping a view of it, which starts at a given offset from the section first byte. This offset must be a multiple of 64k on x64 Windows, but this is the only requirement. We can therefore map a view of a section made of large pages, which begins at +64 k from the first byte.

This can't be obtained with a large page PDE in the mapping address space: the processor requires that the physical address stored in the PDE must be a multiple of 2 MB. To solve this problem, the VMM *does not use large pages* in the mapping process. Instead, it builds a set of small pages PDEs and PTEs, with the starting virtual address pointing at the section address plus the offset.

We must therefore be aware that by using an offset for the view, we *loose the improvement given by large pages*. Another interesting point is that, depending on which address space is curently active, the same physical address can be mapped in different ways: it can fall inside a single 2MB page or it can fall inside a 4kB page itself contained in the 2 MB range.

It's interesing to compare the `!vad` output for a view without offset and for one with offset:

```
1: kd> !vad @@(*lplpMappedRegion)
VAD             level     start     end     commit
fffffa8002ba1010 (-1)       800     9ff          0 Mapped  LargePagSec READWRITE

1: kd> !vad @@(*lplpMappedRegion)
VAD             level     start     end     commit
fffffa80010101c0 (-1)       720     81f          0 Mapped          READWRITE
```

The first listing is for a view without offset, while the second is for a view with an 1 MB offset and shows how the label `LargePageSec` is missing, which tells us the VAD is initialized differently.

Now let's take a look at the paging structures in the process using the offset:

```
1: kd> !pte @@(*lplpMappedRegion)
                         VA 0000000000720000

PXE @ FFFFF6FB7DBED000     PPE at FFFFF6FB7DA00000     PDE at FFFFF6FB40000018     PTE at FFFFF68000003900
contains 029000002C1B4867  contains 02D000002C177867  contains 18A0000037DC4867  contains 0000000000000000
pfn 2c1b4    ---DA--UWEV   pfn 2c177    ---DA--UWEV   pfn 37dc4    ---DA--UWEV
```

The PDE has the PS bit clear, so a PTE is needed to complete the mapping. the PTE is currently set to 0. This is similar to what happens for small pages, where PTEs are initialized only when memory is referenced. Since the VMM has to create PTEs here, it is resorting to its usual lazy techniques of doing the job only when it is actually needed.

The PTE above is invalid, so we can't see the physical address that will be mapped at VA 0x720000. However, we can do what the VMM does, and look at the VAD:

```
1: kd> dt nt!_mmvad fffffa80010101c0
   +0x000 u1                 : <unnamed-tag>
   +0x008 LeftChild          : (null)
   +0x010 RightChild         : (null)
   +0x018 StartingVpn        : 0x720
   +0x020 EndingVpn          : 0x81f
   +0x028 u                  : <unnamed-tag>
   +0x030 PushLock           : _EX_PUSH_LOCK
   +0x038 u5                 : <unnamed-tag>
   +0x040 u2                 : <unnamed-tag>
   +0x048 Subsection         : 0xfffffa80`00e5ae80 _SUBSECTION
   +0x048 MappedSubsection   : 0xfffffa80`00e5ae80 _MSUBSECTION
   +0x050 FirstPrototypePte  : 0xfffff8a0`01f68848 _MMPTE
   +0x058 LastContiguousPte  : 0xfffff8a0`01f69040 _MMPTE
   +0x060 ViewLinks          : _LIST_ENTRY [ 0xfffffa80`02bbd280 - 0xfffffa80`00e5ae70 ]
   +0x070 VadsProcess        : 0xfffffa80`02fd64c1 _EPROCESS
```

The prototype PTE is at +0x800 from the first subsection PTE dumped on p. 396. Since PTEs are 8 bytes in size, the first PTE of the view is at +0x100 PTEs from the first one, with the corresponding virtual address being at +0x100000 or 1 MB from byte 0 of the section, which is consistent with our offset.

When the first byte of the view is accessed, the VMM performs these steps to retrieve the prototype PTE and uses its content to fill the hardware one. *This*, is the reason for having prototype PTEs for 4 kB blocks: they are needed if we map a view with an offset and have to resort to small pages.

It is useful to review the concept of large pages section in light of these facts. When we create a section, we don't create any actual virtual to physical mapping: no hardware PxEs are updated. We just initialize a set of data structures which will later be used to create the translation; this can occur when a view is mapped, or possibly when memory is actually referenced. Hence, a section does not include actual, used-by-the-processor mappings, regardless of page size. A large page section is *predisposed* to be mapped with large pages, because it begins at a physical address which is a multiple of 2 MB and because its made of 2 MB chunks. Note, by the way, how the physical range spanned by the section needs not to be contiguous as a whole: 2MB blocks are enough to map a view with large pages; such a section will consist of 0x200 contiguous 4 kB blocks, followed by another such region, but these two regions can be at unrelated addresses. Hence, when the VMM succeeds in allocating enough physical memory blocks satisfying these requirements, i.e. when *CreateFileMapping* does not fail with ERROR_NO_SYSTEM_RESOURCES, we have a section that *can* later be mapped by means of large pages, but that *can also* be mapped with small pages, depending on *how* it is mapped, i.e. if we use an offset or not.

However, we must be careful not to assume that such a section differs from a small pages one only in the layout of its physical memory. It remains true that a large pages section is initialized as unpageable: the prototype PTEs are always valid and `_MMPFN.u4.PteFrame` does not refer to the prototype PTE page. Thus, large pages sections *are* different, but it is useful to be aware that the actual *pages* in the processor sense are not defined by the section alone.

In light of this, we can say that the prototype PTEs, which always exist, describe the section physical memory as a set of 4 kB *blocks*. Whether these blocks will become *pages* in the processor sense remains to be seen.

40.3.3.2   Referencing the View

After we reference the first byte of the view, the PxEs are as follows:

```
1: kd> !pte @@(lpTouch)
                              VA 0000000000720000

PXE @ FFFFF6FB7DBED000    PPE at FFFFF6FB7DA00000    PDE at FFFFF6FB40000018    PTE at FFFFF68000003900
contains 029000002C1B4867  contains 02D000002C177867  contains 18A0000037DC4867  contains 9F70000025F00867
pfn 2c1b4    ---DA--UWEV pfn 2c177    ---DA--UWEV pfn 37dc4    ---DA--UWEV pfn 25f00    ---DA--
UW-V
```

Note how the PTE is valid and points at +0x100000 from the 1st section block (whose physical address is 0x25e00000 as can be seen in the first prototype PTE on p. 396). This stems from the fact that the first 2 MB of the section are contiguous, so the virtual offset of the view becomes the physical offset.

It is also interesting to observe that the share count of the block *is* incremented, something that does not happen when large pages are used. Possibly, this happens because the logic mapping the view is the same used for small pages section.

```
1: kd> !pfn 25f00
    PFN 00025F00 at address FFFFFA800071D000
    flink        FFFFFA8000E90B30  blink / share count 00000002  pteaddress FFFFF8A001F68848
    reference count 0001    used entry count  0000      Cached    color 0    Priority 5
    restore pte 00000080  containing page        FFFFFFFFFFFFF Active      P
      Shared
```

If we examine the PTEs after the one of the touched page, we observe that 7 more have been made valid and filled with the corresponding prototype ones. It appears that the VMM does a "pre-mapping" of pages, possibly for the same reasons it performs prefetching from the paging file: to anticipate the process memory requirements. This operation is inexpensive because it just requires updating hardware PTEs.

40.4 Experimenting with Large Pages

Readers can use the MemTests program to allocate large pages, both with the *VirtualAllocEx() test* and with the *Memory section test*. As we already mentioned, the account running the program must hold the SeLockMemoryPrivilege and the privilege must be enabled in the token for the process. If these conditions are not satisfied, allocation attempts fail with *GetLastError* returning 1314 (ERROR_PRIVILEGE_NOT_HELD).

The MemTests main menu includes the *Enable SeLockMemoryPrivilege* option, which does just what it says. This only applies to the token of the running MemTests instance: if we quit MemTests and run it again, we must enable the privilege again.

Enabling the privilege fails with the message "Privilege SeLockMemoryPrivilege not assigned. Must add privilege to account." if the account does not hold the privilege. When this happens, the privilege can be added with the *Add SeLockMemoryPrivilege privilege* menu option. We must logoff and logon again for the change to be in effect, but, afterwards, it is permanent.

If large pages allocations fail with error 1450 (ERROR_NO_SYSTEM_RESOURCES), the VMM was unable to find enough free memory blocks with the correct size and alignment. When this happens, rebooting the system may help.

41   User Mode Stacks

The stack used when a thread is running in user mode is allocated when the process is created. It is allocated as a 1 MB region of reserved memory, with only a small portion of it actually committed and a guard page below it.

As we saw in sec. 26.9 on p. 173, this guard page is handled by the VMM in a special way, so that, when it is touched, a STATUS_GUARD_PAGE_VIOLATION is not raised to the process (as with normal guard pages). Instead, the VMM commits more pages to the stack region and resumes the faulting instruction. Kernel mode stacks will be analyzed later, in Chapter 47 (p. 521).

42   User Mode Heaps

42.1 Basic Heap Manager Features

Windows exposes features to allocate memory blocks which are smaller than a page and don't need to be aligned on a 64 kB boundary, like allocations made with *VirtualAllocEx* do.

These features are implemented in the heap manager which consists of both user-mode code, in subsystem DLLs and ntdll.dll, and of kernel code.

Internally, the heap manager allocates virtual memory pages and uses its own logic and data structures to hand out pointers to memory blocks inside these pages.

A process can have multiple heaps: each one is a separate virtual region from which small blocks of memory can be allocated. A program specifies which heap to allocate from passing a heap handle to the memory allocation functions.

Each process has a single default heap whose handle is returned by *GetProcessHeap* and can create and release additional heaps calling *HeapCreate* and *HeapDestroy*.

When creating a heap, a process can specify the `HEAP_NO_SERIALIZE` option, to disable the internal serialization the heap manager uses when more than one thread call heap functions. The heap functions are faster this way, but this is safe only if the process threads synchronize among themselves before calling them (the simplest scenario where this option can be used is a single-threaded process).

A heap can be created with an absolute maximum size, specified by the `dwMaximumSize` parameter of *HeapCreate*. Such a heap, called a fixed size heap, cannot grow beyond the maximum. Setting `dwMaximumSize` to 0 creates a heap that can grow as long as there is virtual address space available.

To allocate and release memory from a heap, a process calls *HeapAlloc* and *HeapFree*.

Heaps created with *HeapCreate* consist of private memory allocated through VirtualAlloc, whose content is only visible in the creating process. The system can create special heaps backed by memory section objects, whose content can be shared between different processes or between user-mode and kernel-mode components.

42.2 Low Fragmentation Heap

As a program allocates and frees memory from a heap, the latter can become fragmented. Memory allocations can fail even if there is enough free memory in the heap, because the free blocks are small and scattered among used ones. If the program is a multithreaded one, the heap can also suffer from contention on its internal variables, when accesses made to them must be synchronized among different threads. The heap manager includes logic to reduce the impact of these two problems in the low fragmentation heap (LFH), which is layered over the core heap management features. In Windows 7, the LFH is used by default.

In some special cases, the LFH is turned off and only the core heap manager is used. This happens when the heap has been created with the `HEAP_NO_SERIALIZE` option, when it has been created as a fixed size heap and when certain heap debugging tools are used.

The technique used by the LFH to reduce fragmentation consists of dividing the heap memory in chunks called *buckets*. Each bucket is used for a specific range of memory allocation sizes: bucket 1 is used for allocations requesting 1 to 8 bytes; bucket 2 is used for allocations between 9 and 16 bytes, etc.

The number of size values covered by a bucket is its *granularity*. The granularity of bucket 1 is 8, because it covers 8 size values from 1 to 8; the granularity of bucket 2 is 8 as well. All the buckets up to #32 have a granularity of 8, with bucket 32 covering sizes from 249 to 256.

The granularity of buckets from 33 to 48 is 16 and higher numbered buckets have higher granularities, according to the following table ([1], p. 733):

Buckets	Granularity	Allocation size range
1-32	8	1-256
33-48	16	257-512
49-64	32	513-1,024
65-80	64	1,025-2,048
81-96	128	2,049-4,096
97-112	256	4,097-8,194
113-128	512	8,195-16,384

Allocations above 16 kB are not satisfied from any bucket: the LFH is bypassed and memory is allocated by the core heap manager logic.

42.3 Security Features and !heap

The heap virtual memory region is used by the heap manager to store its own internal data, called metadata, which it uses to manage allocations. The metadata live in the heap region, side by side with memory blocks handed out by the manager to the calling process.

There are malicious programs which exploit application bugs to corrupt the metadata. By tricking the application into writing past the end or before the start of an allocated heap block, they can alter the metadata surrounding the block. This, in turn, can result in executing unwanted, malicious code.

To prevent this kind of threat, the heap manager protects the metadata by randomizing them, so that they don't have a simple well-known layout. For this reason, it is hard to examine the heap content by simply dumping it with the debugger. It is better to use the `!heap` command extension which is able to interpret the metadata.

42.4 Debugging Features

The heap manager offers a set of debugging features to help detect bugs in heap memory usage.

Tail checking: a signature is stored at the end of each allocated block of memory. If the allocating program writes past the end of the block, the signature is overwritten and the heap manager reports the error.

Free checking: free blocks are filled with a known pattern which the heap manager checks as part of its logic when invoked. If the pattern is found modified, it means that the program is using a stray pointer (perhaps to a block which was allocated and then freed).

Parameter checking: extra checks are performed on parameters passed to heap functions.

Heap validation: the entire heap is validated each time an heap function is called.

Heap tagging and stack traces support: heap allocations are marked with a tag and call stacks of allocations are traced.

These options can be enabled with the gflags utility, part of the Debugging Tools for Windows package. Enabling any of these options causes the LFH to be disabled (heap allocations will be performed using only the core heap management functions).

42.5 Pageheap

The first three debugging options listed in the previous section may end up detecting a corruption of the heap long after it has occurred, making it hard to pinpoint the bug inside the code. Pageheap is another debugging feature which can catch an invalid access to an address inside the heap right when it happens.

This feature works by allocating a separate virtual page for each heap allocation and placing the allocated block at the end of the page. If the allocating code accesses an address past the end of the block, this triggers an access violation exception, caused by an invalid address at the beginning of the next page.

Also, Pageheap can protect a page storing a block that has been allocated and then freed, so that any access inside the page will cause an access violation. Thus, a buggy program that frees an heap block and later tries to access it is caught red handed.

The price to pay for these useful features is a huge waste of both virtual address space and physical memory: every single heap allocation requires its own page. For this reason, Pageheap is a debugging feature and must be enabled with the Gflags tool. It is also possible to filter which allocations are handled by Pageheap, e.g. based on size, address range and which DLL the allocation call came from.

Part V - System Range Memory Management

43   Overview of System Range Memory Management

43.1 Types of System Regions

Beginning with this chapter, we are going to describe how the VMM manages the upper part of the address range, i.e. the region beginning at 0xFFFF8000`00000000. We already saw in sec. 15.3.1 on p. 74 that the system range starts at 0xFFFFF680`00000000, with all the addresses below this one being unused (their PML4Es are zeroed).

As its name implies, this range is used by system code, so its pages are protected and can only be accessed by code running at CPL = 0, also called ring 0 code.

It is divided into a set of fixed regions which we will detail in the next sections, e.g. a region for paged pool, another one for loaded drivers, etc.

We can classify these regions in two categories, based on how they are used. This will allow us, at least for one of the two kinds, to describe some VMM concepts which apply to multiple regions. While this classification is useful to outline general behaviors common to different regions, each one has its own peculiarities, which will be detailed later.

For regions of the first kind, which we are going to call *dynamically allocated* ones, the VMM implements logic to allocate and release portions of the virtual address space as their content changes while the system runs. For instance, there is a region where kernel mode drivers are loaded; when a new driver must be loaded in memory, the VMM looks for a free range inside this region where the driver image can be loaded. Later, the driver can be unloaded, thus freeing the range.

We will call regions of the second kind *special purpose* ones. They are not managed by the allocation logic used for dynamically allocated regions, and are dedicated to store specific data structures used by the kernel. An example is the hyperspace region where the process working set and other data structures are stored.

43.2 Virtual Address Space Management of Dynamically Allocated Regions

The VMM must keep track of virtual addresses in these regions, i.e. it needs to know which ones are in use and which are available. For user range memory this information is stored in VADs and the UMAB; for the system range it is kept in bitmaps.

A bitmap consists of an instance of `_RTL_BITMAP`, whose `Buffer` member points to a buffer, where each bit represents a resource. For these regions, each bit represents a PDE: if the bit is set, the PDE is in use, i.e. the virtual range mapped by it has already been allocated for some purpose. This means that dynamically allocated regions are allocated in blocks of 2MB, which is the virtual size mapped by a single PDE.

However, when a page fault occurs, these bitmaps are not used to check whether the faulting address is valid. In the user mode range, the VMM checks the VADs whenever it is invoked for a fault on a PTE which is set to 0 or missing altogether (i.e. the PT is not mapped). In the system range, the VMM looks at the paging structures only, ignoring these bitmaps, to decide whether the attempted access is allowed or not.

In the following sections, we will detail the known bitmaps used to manage dynamically allocated regions.

The *MiObtainSystemVa* function is usually called to allocate a block from these regions, with a parameter specifying which region to allocate from. The possible values of this parameter are defined by the `_MI_SYSTEM_VA_TYPE` enumeration:

```
0: kd> dt nt!_MI_SYSTEM_VA_TYPE
   MiVaUnused = 0n0
   MiVaSessionSpace = 0n1
   MiVaProcessSpace = 0n2
   MiVaBootLoaded = 0n3
   MiVaPfnDatabase = 0n4
   MiVaNonPagedPool = 0n5
   MiVaPagedPool = 0n6
   MiVaSpecialPoolPaged = 0n7
   MiVaSystemCache = 0n8
   MiVaSystemPtes = 0n9
   MiVaHal = 0n10
   MiVaSessionGlobalSpace = 0n11
   MiVaDriverImages = 0n12
   MiVaSpecialPoolNonPaged = 0n13
   MiVaMaximumType = 0n14
```

We will see how some of these values are used while discussing the different regions in more detail.

43.3 Page Fault Handling

This section contains a general description of page fault handling in the system range. There are exceptions to the logic detailed here, which will be covered in region-specific sections.

As soon as *MmAccessFault* detects that the faulting address is in the system range, it checks whether the value of the code segment register at the moment of the fault (saved in the

_KTRAP_FRAME on the stack) has bit 0 clear. The ring 0 CS is 0x10, while the ring 3 one is 0x33, so this is a way of checking whether the code trying to access a system address is running at ring 0. It is interesting to observe that a CS with bit 0 clear could also be a CPL 2 segment, i.e. with bit 1 set, since *MmAccessFault* checks bit 0 only. However, Windows only uses CPL 0 and 3.

If bit 0 0f the saved CS is set, MmAccessFault immediately returns STATUS_ACCESS_VIOLATION, since ring 3 code is not allowed to access system memory.

Afterwards, *MmAccessFault* examines all the paging structures up to the PDE. If any of them has the P bit clear, the address is invalid and the system bugchecks.

Otherwise, all the paging structures up to the page table are present, so the VMM checks the PTE. If the latter is 0, the address is invalid and, again, this brings everything down. If it is a valid PTE, the fault is resolved and the access is reattempted.

For instance, the PTE could be set to 0x80, which means it is an _MMPTE_SOFTWARE, with read/write protection and no copy of it exists in the paging file (_MMPTE_SOFTWARE.PageFileLow and PageFileHigh are 0). In this scenario, the fault must be resolved by mapping a zero filled page and *MmAccessFault* calls *MiDispatchFault* to do the job. The latter is the same function used to resolve most faults in the user mode range.

In general, if the fault is for a valid access and must be resolved, *MmAccessFault* always calls *MiDispatchFault* to do the job.

If the PTE is for a repurposed page (_MMPTE_SOFTWARE.PageFileLow and PageFileHigh are not 0), *MiDispatchFault* returns an appropriate status code and *MmAccessFault* calls *MiIssueHardFault* to perform in-paging, as is the case for the user mode range.

Given how the VMM checks the paging structures for these regions, we can understand that the structures themselves are not pageable in the system range: if either the PML4E, the PDPTE or the PDE have the P bit clear, the VMM crashes the system; no attempt is made to in-page anything from the paging file.

As is the case for user mode addresses, large pages are not pageable: a PDE may have the PS bit set, but this will implicitly lock the mapped memory.

When a page fault is resolved, an instance of _MMSUPPORT provides the pointer to a working set (_MMWSL) for the memory region. While in the user range each process has its own working set, in the system range there are working sets, i.e. instances of _MMSUPPORT and

_MMWSL, for the various regions, which will be detailed later. *MmAccessFault* determines the region where the faulting address falls and selects the appropriate _MMSUPPORT instance.

43.4 Synchronization

When *MmAccessFault* has determined which instance of _MMSUPPORT must be used, it attempts to exclusively lock the pushlock stored in the _MMSUPPORT.WorkingSetMutex member. If the pushlock is already locked, the thread is blocked (these steps occur at IRQL < DISPATCH, so the thread can block). This ensures that only one thread in the system can handle a fault on the region covered by the selected working set.

After successfully locking the _MMSUPPORT instance, MmAccessFault sets a bit flag in the _ETHREAD for the current thread, to record the fact that the thread owns the working set. These flag bits are checked during the initial steps of *MmAccessFault* and, if any one is set, the function returns the undocumented NTSTATUS value 0xD0000006. Thus, this value is returned if a thread causes a page fault in the system region while already owning a working set (including the process working set, used when resolving faults in the user mode range).

MmAccessFault releases the pushlock and clears the flag before returning.

It can also be observed that the VMM sets and clears bit 0 of the PteAddress member of _MMPFNs at various stages, e.g. while moving a paged pool page from the relevant working set to the Modified list. This suggests that this bit is used to lock an instance for exclusive access, as it happens when the VMM resolves faults on user range addresses (see sec. 25.2 on p. 137).

43.5 Invalid System Addresses vs. Invalid User Ones

The VMM provides a function named *MmProbeAndLockPages* which allows a driver to probe a virtual address in the user range and, if the address is valid, ensures it is mapped to physical memory (it actually locks the memory pages as its name implies). If the address is invalid, it raises an access violation exception, which can be caught with a __try/__except block. It is worth explaining why the same is not true for an invalid system range address, i.e. why, even with a __try/__except block, touching an invalid address crashes the system (even a call to this very function results in a system crash if it is used with an MDL pointing to an invalid system address).

When *MmAccessFault* detects a reference to an invalid user address, it returns an error NTSTATUS (usually 0xC0000005) to its caller, i.e. to *KiPageFault*. The latter has built a _KTRAP_FRAME with the status of the interrupted thread and would have reissued the faulting instruction, had *MmAccessFault* returned a success code. Upon receiving an error code, *KiPageFault* modifies the saved context so that execution resumes in system code which creates the data structures for a Windows-define exception and looks for an exception handler. Thus, if the code performing the invalid access has installed an handler with __try/__except, it resumes control.

On the other hand, MmAccessFault behaves in a different way when the invalid address is in the system range: it calls *KeBugCheckEx*, which crashes the system. This is the reason why an exception handler does not stand a chance: no attempt is made to resume the faulting context, because execution never returns from *MmAccessFault*.

44 System Regions

The following layout for the system range is derived from [2], which is a great source of information on this topic:

Start	End	Size	Description
FFFF8000`00000000	FFFFF67F`FFFFFFFF	118,5TB	Unused System Space
FFFFF680`00000000	FFFFF6FF`FFFFFFFF	512GB	Paging Structures Space
FFFFF700`00000000	FFFFF700`00FFFFFF	16MB	UMAB (see 20.2.1, p. 106)
FFFFF700`01000000	FFFFF700`0107FFFF	512kB	UMPB (see 20.2.2, p. 108)
FFFFF700`01080000	FFFFF700`01080487	1,160B	_MMWSL
FFFFF700`01080488	?	?	Process WS list
FFFFF704`40000000	FFFFF704`40000FFF	4K	Non direct hash table (see 37.14.4.1, p. 334)
FFFFF704`40001000	?	?	Direct hash table (see 37.14.4.2, p. 334)
FFFFF780`00000000	FFFFF780`00000FFF	4K	Shared System Page
FFFFF780`00001000	FFFFF7FF`FFFFFFFF	512GB - 4K	System WS lists
FFFFF800`00000000	FFFFF87F`FFFFFFFF	512GB	Initial Loader Mappings
FFFFF880`00000000	FFFFF89F`FFFFFFFF	128GB	Sys PTEs[1]
FFFFF8A0`00000000	*MmPagedPoolEnd		Paged Pool Area[1]
MmPagedPoolEnd + 1	FFFFF8FF`FFFFFFFF		Unused[1]
FFFFF900`00000000	FFFFF97F`FFFFFFFF	512GB	Session Space
FFFFF980`00000000	FFFFFA7F`FFFFFFFF	1TB	Dynamic Kernel VA Space
FFFFFa80`00000000	dynamically computed		PFN Database
dynamically computed	dynamically computed		Free and Zeroed Lists by Color
*MmNonPagedPoolStart	dynamically computed	512GB Max	Non-Paged Pool
FFFFFFFF`FFC00000	FFFFFFFF`FFFFFFFF	4MB	HAL and Loader Mappings

Notes

1. MmPagedPoolEnd is usually set to 0xFFFFF8BF`FFFFFFFF and the range from
    0xFFFFF8C0`00000000 to 0xFFFFF900`00000000 is normally not used (this will be
    explained in sec 44.9.1 on p. 476). The 512GB region at 0xFFFFF880`00000000 is
    therefore organized as follows:

    - 128GB for system PTEs (detailed in sec. 44.8 on p. 440).
    - 128GB for paged pool (detailed in sec. 44.9 on p. 476)
    - 256GB not used

When analyzing this layout is useful to remember that a PML4 entry maps a 512GB region, so
several of the regions above correspond to a single PML4E. The next sections analyze each
region in greater detail.

The shaded regions all fall in the range 0xFFFFF700`00000000 - 0xFFFFF77F`FFFFFFFF which is
commonly called hyperspace. It is important to remember that this range is process-private:
each PML4 has a different entry for this range.

44.1 The 8TB Limitation

Before further analyzing the various regions, we are going to explain why system addresses
lower than 8TB from the top of the VA space are subject to limitations. Interestingly, due to
these limitations, there are various sources stating that the system range is 8TB in size, while
it is actually 9.5TB, as shown in the table above. If the system range were 8TB in size it would
begin at 0xFFFFF800`00000000, leaving out paging structures, hyperspace and the system
working sets lists, which are documented by various sources (e.g. [1] and [2]) and show up in
several experiments throughout this book.

It is true, however that all the dynamically allocated regions are above the 8TB limit. Since
the DDIs which allocate virtual ranges for other kernel mode components return addresses
from these regions, it can be said that the system range "available" to other component is
8TB in size. This is not entirely correct either, because the upper 8TB range includes regions
which the VMM reserves for itself, like the PFN database. The bottom line is that the whole
system range is 9.5TB in size and only part of it is available for memory allocations from
kernel mode components.

What makes the higher 8TB so special are linked lists. Windows uses the _SLIST_HEADER
data structure to store the head of a singly linked list. The system builds all kinds of lists of
data structures, pointed by instances of _SLIST_HEADER. For performance reasons, it is

important to be able to compare and modify an `_SLIST_HEADER` with a single processor instruction. This allows to update the head of a list exclusively, i.e. ensuring that no other processor in the system updates it, without having to protect the structure with a lock, a fact which would degrade the scalability of the system.

The Intel architecture defines the CMPXCHG instruction, which can be used for this purpose. This instruction compares the value of processor register EAX with a value in memory. If the two values are equal, it replaces the value in memory with the content of a second register, otherwise it leaves the memory unaffected. So, if we want to exclusively modify a value in memory we first load it into EAX, load the updated value in the second register (e.g. EBX) and execute a CMPXCHG. If some other processor has modified the memory content, the comparison with EAX fails and the memory is left untouched. The code can detect this by checking the processor flags and retry the update. If, on the other hand, the memory content did not change between the loading into EAX and the CMPXCHG, it is updated with our new value.

In this short overview we used the names of 32 bits registers, which means the instruction operates on 4 bytes of memory, but there are variations of it for smaller and bigger sizes.

On earlier 64 bit processors, CMPXCHG could operate on at most 8 bytes, so any data structure meant to be updated with this instruction, like `_SLIST_HEADER`, had to fit into this size. An `_SLIST_HEADER` must store a pointer to the first list node along with other list information but, on 64 bit Windows, the pointer alone is 8 bytes long, leaving no room for the additional data. To solve this problem (see [1], p. 749) the pointer is truncated. `_SLIST_HEADER` is a union with the following declaration (dumped with WinDbg):

```
union _SLIST_HEADER, 5 elements, 0x10 bytes

   +0x000 Alignment        : Uint8B
   +0x008 Region           : Uint8B
   +0x000 Header8          : <unnamed-tag>
      +0x000 Depth : Pos 0, 16 Bits
      +0x000 Sequence : Pos 16, 9 Bits
      +0x000 NextEntry : Pos 25, 39 Bits
      +0x008 HeaderType : Pos 0, 1 Bit
      +0x008 Init  : Pos 1, 1 Bit
      +0x008 Reserved : Pos 2, 59 Bits
      +0x008 Region : Pos 61, 3 Bits
   +0x000 Header16         : <unnamed-tag>
      +0x000 Depth : Pos 0, 16 Bits
      +0x000 Sequence : Pos 16, 48 Bits
      +0x008 HeaderType : Pos 0, 1 Bit
      +0x008 Init  : Pos 1, 1 Bit
      +0x008 Reserved : Pos 2, 2 Bits
      +0x008 NextEntry : Pos 4, 60 Bits
   +0x000 HeaderX64        : <unnamed-tag>
```

```
+0x000 Depth : Pos 0, 16 Bits
+0x000 Sequence : Pos 16, 48 Bits
+0x008 HeaderType : Pos 0, 1 Bit
+0x008 Reserved : Pos 1, 3 Bits
+0x008 NextEntry : Pos 4, 60 Bits
```

The `Header8` member squeezes the 3 members `Depth`, `Sequence` and `NextEntry` into 8 bytes, by truncating the pointer to 39 bits. This member also includes 8 additional bytes (the bitfields starting at +008), but their content does not need to be updated when the list content changes, e.g. when a node is added or removed. This makes it possible to exclusively update the list using a CMPXCHG on the first 8 bytes only.

The price for this is truncating the pointer to 39 bits. This does not mean, however, that node addresses are really limited to only 39 bits. List nodes are stored at addresses multiple of 16, so the lower 4 bits are known to be 0, which gives a pointer size of 43 bits, i.e. addresses ranging from 0 to 8TB -1.

For lists in the user mode range, this is not a problem, since the range size is actually 8TB, and [1] implies at p. 750 that this is actually where the user range size comes from.

In the system range, 43 bits for the address mean we have to assume that bits 43-47 are all set to 1 (remember that in this range bits 48-63 are always 1 for a canonical address), so list nodes can only reside in the range 0xFFFFF800`00000000 – 0xFFFFFFFF`FFFFFFFF, i.e. the upper 8TB of the range.

This means that the initial portion of the system range is not entirely available for all purposes. The region 0xFFFFF680`00000000 – 0xFFFFF7FF`FFFFFFFF, which is 1.5TB in size cannot be used for data structures which are part of linked lists. This is not a big issue, because the lower 1.5TB range is fixedly allocated to store kernel data structures which don't need linked lists.

Another implication of this pointer truncation is that a list header must reside in the same range of the list nodes: for an header in the user region, the 43 bits are assumed to represent a user mode address, i.e. with bits 43-63 set to 0, while for an header in the system region bits 43-63 are assumed to be 1. This also implies that a list cannot include a mix of nodes from both the system and the user mode range, since each node can become the first of the list and be pointed by the `_SLIST_HEADER`. None of these constraints is a real problem, because Windows does not need to mix structure instances from the two ranges: user mode code cannot even access the system range anD system code stays away from the user mode range, since its content is unprotected and at risk of any kind of wrongdoing from application code.

The other two members of `_SLIST_HEADER`, `Header16` and `HeaderX64` are actually alternate layouts since this data structure is a union and this is clearly shown by their offset being 0. These two declarations are essentially equivalent and can only be used with more recent processors implementing the CMPXCHG16B instruction, which allows to exclusively modify 16 bytes, because the `NextEntry` member is now at offset +8. When this layout can be used, it removes the need to truncate the pointer, which becomes 60 bits in length (we can still do without the lower 4 bits using addresses multiple of 16).

So, there are two layout defined for this data structure, but which one is used? It appears that this decision is taken at runtime.

Bit 0 of byte +8, which is called `HeaderType` and is declared in all the layouts, identifies the type of header: if the bit is clear, the header content must be interpreted according to the `Header8` declaration while, when it is set, the alternate layout is in effect.

For instance, the code of *RtlpInterlockedPopEntrySList*, which pops an entry from a list, tests `HeaderType` and treats the `_SLIST_HEADER` instance accordingly. The instructions executed when `HeaderType` is set include a CMPXCHG16B which can be executed only on a processor supporting it, but, as long as `HeaderType` is clear, the function takes a different code path which performs a CMPXCHG on the first 8 bytes of `_SLIST_HEADER`. The CMPXCHG1B instruction, unknown to an older processor, is never executed and its presence in the code causes no harm: it is just an handful of bytes the processor will never stumble upon. Thus, the way an instance of `_SLIST_HEADER` is initialized determines *at runtime* whether support for CMPXCHG16B is needed or not.

This books analyzes a few linked lists used by the VMM, which turn out to have `HeaderType` set and a 60 bits pointer. Actually, the nodes of these lists happen to be in the higher regions of the system range (above 0xFFFFFA80`00000000) so that they could have been handled with a 43 bits pointer, but they have `HeaderType` set anyway. This analysis has been performed on a system with an Intel Core i7 mobile processor, which supports CMPXCHG16B, and these findings suggest that, on such a system, the kernel code uses the `Header16`/`HeaderX64` layout, because it detects that this is possible (the code can discover whether the processor supports CMPXCHG16B using the CPUID instruction). Possibly, on a different machine with an older processor, the `_SLIST_HEADER`s would be set up according to the `Header8` layout.

This means that the code which makes use of lists already can handle list nodes at any address in the system range (and even below the current system range start), if the processor supports CMPXCHG16B. However, the fact that the code for the Header8 layout is also present, suggests that, as of Windows 7, list nodes are kept above the 8TB line. The code dealing with lists is ready for when support for older processor will be dropped, the system range extended and list nodes moved to lower addresses.

In the next sections, we are going to describe the various regions of the system range.

44.2 Unused System Space

As the name implies, this region is unused. It spans 237 PML4Es which are set to 0. Touching an address inside this region from code running at CPL 0 will cause a system crash (user mode code gets a STATUS_ACCESS_VIOLATION exception when it touches an address anywhere in the system region).

It's worth to note how only a small fraction of the system range is used: the entire range is 128 TB in size, with an unused region of 118.5 TB and only 9.5 TB in use.

44.3 PTE Space

44.3.1   Description

This region is where the auto-entry maps the paging structures and it's a special purpose one.

44.3.2   Virtual Address Space Management

The VA space in this region has its own peculiar life cycle. Portions of it become mapped when the VMM updates the paging structures.

Consider a PML4 for an address space where the auto-entry is the only valid one. The only valid page in the entire virtual address space is the one where the PML4 itself is visible at address 0xFFFFF6FB`7DBED000, which is inside this region.

At some point, the VMM will create the PML4 entry for, say, the first 512 GB of the virtual address space (in the user mode range); this PML4E will point to a PDPT. As soon as the PML4E is pointed to a physical page and made valid, the content of the PDPT materializes in the PTE Space region, at the beginning of the PDPTE range, i.e. in the range 0xFFFFF6FB`7DA00000-0xFFFFF6FB`7DA00FFF. When the VMM points the first PDPTE to a physical page for the PD, the PD content becomes visible at 0xFFFFF6FB`40000000-0xFFFFF6FB`40000FFF, and so on.

In summary, while the VMM fills PxEs to map portions of the VA, the paging structures content pops up into this virtual region.

44.3.3   Page Fault Handing

The VMM does not normally cause page faults in this range. Consider for instance a user mode address ADDR whose page table has been repurposed, i.e. whose PDE points into the paging file. The PT is not retrieved from the paging file by accessing the PTE address, thereby causing and resolving a page fault. Instead, the VMM notices that the PDE is invalid while resolving the fault on ADDR and reads back the PT. It does not, in other words, incur a nested page fault by touching the address of the PTE. See also Chapter 36 on p. 288.

As for system range addresses, paging structures are not even pageable: if the VMM finds that any of them is missing while resolving a fault, it considers the address invalid and crashes the system.

A look at the logic of *MmAccessFault* for this region seems to confirm that page faults are not a normal occurrence. The function behaves differently, depending on the address mapped by the paging structure.

When *MmAccessFault* detects that the fault address is inside the paging structures region, it computes the VA which would be mapped by the paging entry if it were present. This is always possible, even if the PxE is not present, given the relationship between mapped VA and PxE VA (see sec. 15.2 on p. 63). The code performing the translation is located at +0x5e0 inside the function.

If the VA mapped by the not present PxE is in the system range, *MmAccessFault* crashes the system with bug check code 0x50.

If the mapped VA is in the user range, the fault is resolved and the paging structure containing the PxE is mapped to a physical page. However, when the process where this happens terminates, the system bugchecks with code 0x50, which means the VMM state is corrupted. This can be verified with MemTests, as we will see in sec. 45.4 on p. 504. Possibly, this code path of MmAccessFault is executed under particular conditions, however the fact remains that an actual page fault in this region ends up in a crash.

For the sake of completeness, we should point out that this behavior only occurs if the PxEs above the not present one in the hierarchy are themselves present. Examples of this scenario are: a PTE in a not mapped PT, for which the PD and PDPT are present; a PDE in a not mapped PD for which the PDPTE is present. If other PSs above the one where the fault occurs are also missing, the system bugchecks immediately, with code 0x50.

It's important to remember that only a buggy kernel mode component can cause these crashes, since an access from user mode to any address in the system range, including the

PTE Space, simply results in an access violation exception being raised to the thread in user mode.

The content of an `_MMPFN` for a PS page for user mode range has already been discussed in sec. 36.2 on p. 289. The main difference concerning a PS for the system range appears to be that `_MMPFN.UsedPageTableEntries` is always 0. This is probably because PS for the system range are not pageable. This member is used in the user mode range to keep track of in-use entries so that the share count can be decremented and PSs can be unmapped when it drops to 1. If no paging is going to occur, the share count alone is enough to track the number of in use entries.

44.3.4   Working Set for the Region

Paging structures mapping addresses in user range have an entry in the process working set. As an example, on a running system an instance of explorer.exe had the following allocated VA ranges:

```
VAD                 level      start     end    commit
fffffa8002940ec0 ( 7)            10      1f          0 Mapped        READWRITE
fffffa8000c0aac0 ( 6)            20      21          0 Mapped        READONLY
fffffa8000c52f80 ( 7)            30      33          0 Mapped        READONLY
fffffa8000c51160 ( 5)            40      41          0 Mapped        READONLY
```

The paging structures for the first page of the first range are:

```
0: kd> !pte 10000
                        VA 0000000000010000
PXE @ FFFFF6FB7DBED000    PPE at FFFFF6FB7DA00000    PDE at FFFFF6FB40000000    PTE at FFFFF68000000080
contains 02E0000028DB7867  contains 01300000284BA867  contains 014000002843B867  contains A6A0000021E5A867
pfn 28db7    ---DA--UWEV  pfn 284ba    ---DA--UWEV  pfn 2843b    ---DA--UWEV  pfn 21e5a    ---DA--
UW-V
```

The PFN of the page table is 0x2843B and has the following content:

```
0: kd> !pfn 2843b
    PFN 0002843B at address FFFFFA800078CB10
    flink        00000014  blink / share count 0000005B  pteaddress FFFFF6FB40000000
    reference count 0001    used entry count  0064       Cached    color 0    Priority 5
    restore pte 00000080    containing page         0284BA  Active    M
    Modified
```

The flink member of a page which is tracked in a working set list stores the index of the working set entry for that page, so we take a look at entry 0x14 of the process working set list:

```
0: kd> ?? ((nt!_MMWSL *) 0xfffff70001080000)->Wsle[0x14].u1
union <unnamed-tag>
   +0x000 VirtualAddress    : 0xfffff680`00000009
```

```
+0x000 Long              : 0xfffff680`00000009
+0x000 e1                : _MMWSLENTRY
+0x000 e2                : _MMWSLE_FREE_ENTRY
```

The entry is for VA 0xFFFFF680`00000000 (WS list entries always track virtual page numbers, i.e. page aligned virtual addresses, with the rightmost three digits equal to 0; the value 9 of the rightmost digit results from flag bits encoded into it). If we look again at the output of !pte, we can confirm that the PTE is at address 0xFFFFF680`00000080 and thus the virtual page containing it is at 0xFFFFF680`00000000, i.e. the address stored in the WS list entry. In other words, this entry in the process WS list is for the page table. We can find similar results for the PD, and the PDPT.

On the other hand, paging structures mapping system range addresses don't seem to be tracked into any working set and their flink member is often 0. This should not surprise us, since these PSs are not pageable. One exception to this rule are the paging structures mapping the VA of the working set list itself (0XFFFFF700`01080000):

- The PT, whose VA is usually entry 3 of the list

- The PD, which is entry 2

- The PDPT is entry 1

- The PML4 itself is entry 0

44.4 Hyperspace

This special purpose region is process-private and spans an entire PML4 entry, so each process has a different entry in its own PML4. It is used to manage per process information, like the working set list.

The next sections describe each hyperspace subregion.

44.4.1   UMAB Subregion

This 16MB range is reserved for the UMAB, detailed in sec. 20.2.1 on p. 106.

A page fault in this region is handled in a way similar to one in the user range and, if a physical page is eventually mapped, an entry is added to the process working set. Normally, a process has a valid PTE for the first page of this region and all the PTEs beyond it are set to 0. If a page fault occurs for an address mapped by one of the zeored PTEs, *MmAccessFault* calls *MiCheckVirtualAddress*, which determines that the address is invalid, so that the fault raises a

STATUS_ACCESS_VIOLATION exception. This behavior can be verified with MemTests (see Chapter 45 - p. 500).

On the other hand, if the faulting PTE is not 0, the fault can be handled and a page mapped. As an example, if the PTE is set to 0x80, the value for a committed read/write page, a fault results in a physical page being mapped and added to the process working set. This behavior can be verified by setting a PTE (e.g. for the page 0xFFFFF700`00001000) to 0x80 with WinDbg and touching the page with MemTests.

44.4.2   UMPB Subregion

This is 512kB range stores the UMPB analyzed in sec. 20.2.2 on p. 108.

Page faults in this range are handled much like those in the UMAB region. The invalid PTEs for this region are all set to 0x80 (those of the UMAB are set to 0), so page faults don't cause exceptions or crashes and are resolved mapping a physical page and adding an entry to the process WS. This behavior too can be verified with MemTests.

44.4.3   WSL Region

44.4.3.1   Region Content

This region stores the array of WSLEs making up the process working set list. Only the beginning of this region is usually mapped, with PTEs for higher addresses set to 0. The mapped region appears to be extended as the working set increases and the list grows.

We already saw in sec. 20.3.4 on p. 120 that _MMWSL.LastInitializedWsle is the index of the last entry of the valid VA range (i.e. the last 8 bytes of the last mapped page). We can observe how the mapped range changes when MemTests allocates and touches a 512MB range, thereby increasing its working set list.

Before the memory allocation, _MMWSL.LastInitializedWsle is set to 0x36e. Since WSLEs are 8 bytes in size this yields an address of

0xFFFFF700`01080488 + 0x36E * 8 = 0xFFFFF700`01081FF8

The address of the PTE mapping this VA is:

```
1: kd> !pte  0xFFFFF700`01081FF8
                                 VA fffff70001081ff8
PXE at FFFFF6FB7DBEDF70   PPE at FFFFF6FB7DBEE000   PDE at FFFFF6FB7DC00040   PTE at FFFFF6FB80008408
contains 000000000E798863   contains 0000000000319863   contains 0000000010C9A863   contains 8000000010953863
pfn e798     ---DA--KWEV  pfn 319      ---DA--KWEV  pfn 10c9a    ---DA--KWEV  pfn 10953    ---DA--KW-V
```

Also, the address of the 1st PTE mapping the WSLE is:

```
1: kd> !pte  0xFFFFF700`01080488
                                    VA fffff70001080488

PXE at FFFFF6FB7DBEDF70    PPE at FFFFF6FB7DBEE000    PDE at FFFFF6FB7DC00040    PTE at FFFFF6FB80008400
contains 000000000E798863  contains 0000000000319863  contains 0000000010C9A863  contains 000000000589B863
pfn e798    ---DA--KWEV  pfn 319    ---DA--KWEV  pfn 10c9a   ---DA--KWEV  pfn 589b    ---DA--KWEV
```

that is, the 2 PTEs are right one after the other. We can examine the content of the PTE range extending a little (0x10 PTEs) beyond the one for the last entry:

```
1: kd> dq FFFFF6FB80008400 FFFFF6FB80008408 + 0x10 * 8
fffff6fb`80008400   00000000`0589b863 80000000`10953863
fffff6fb`80008410   00000000`00000000 00000000`00000000
fffff6fb`80008420   00000000`00000000 00000000`00000000
fffff6fb`80008430   00000000`00000000 00000000`00000000
fffff6fb`80008440   00000000`00000000 00000000`00000000
fffff6fb`80008450   00000000`00000000 00000000`00000000
fffff6fb`80008460   00000000`00000000 00000000`00000000
fffff6fb`80008470   00000000`00000000 00000000`00000000
fffff6fb`80008480   00000000`00000000 00000000`00000000
```

As we can see, the PTEs beyond the one for the last entry are all set to 0, so the WSLE, right now, is consuming only 2 physical pages.

It's interesting to perform the same analysis after MemTests touches a 512MB region. The test was performed on a virtual machine with 1GB of RAM, so the VMM lets the working set of MemTests grow. These are the values for _MMWSL.LastInitializedWsle, the WSLE address and the PTE address:

```
1: kd> ?? ((nt!_mmwsl *) 0xfffff70001080000)->LastInitializedWsle
unsigned long 0x2036e

1: kd> ? 0xFFFFF700`01080488 + 0x2036e * 8
Evaluate expression: -9895586291720 = fffff700`01181ff8

1: kd> !pte fffff700`01181ff8
                                    VA fffff70001181ff8

PXE at FFFFF6FB7DBEDF70    PPE at FFFFF6FB7DBEE000    PDE at FFFFF6FB7DC00040    PTE at FFFFF6FB80008C08
contains 000000000E798863  contains 0000000000319863  contains 0000000010C9A863  contains 80000000173CE863
pfn e798    ---DA--KWEV  pfn 319    ---DA--KWEV  pfn 10c9a   ---DA--KWEV  pfn 173ce    ---DA--KW-V
```

The number of valid PTEs is now:

```
1: kd> ? (FFFFF6FB80008C08 + 8 - FFFFF6FB80008400) / 8
Evaluate expression: 258 = 00000000`00000102
```

0x102 or 258 PTEs, hence 258 physical pages (about 1MB) consumed by the WSL. If we dump the PTE content, we can confirm that they are as expected (only an excerpt is shown):

```
1: kd> dq FFFFF6FB80008400 FFFFF6FB80008C08 + 0x10 * 8
fffff6fb`80008400  00000000`0589b863 80000000`10953863
fffff6fb`80008410  80000000`0dfb7863 80000000`0c1b8863
[...]
fffff6fb`80008bf0  80000000`0e8b4863 80000000`2413a863
fffff6fb`80008c00  80000000`02d44863 80000000`173ce863
fffff6fb`80008c10  00000000`00000000 00000000`00000000
fffff6fb`80008c20  00000000`00000000 00000000`00000000
fffff6fb`80008c30  00000000`00000000 00000000`00000000
fffff6fb`80008c40  00000000`00000000 00000000`00000000
fffff6fb`80008c50  00000000`00000000 00000000`00000000
fffff6fb`80008c60  00000000`00000000 00000000`00000000
fffff6fb`80008c70  00000000`00000000 00000000`00000000
fffff6fb`80008c80  00000000`00000000 00000000`00000000
```

The physical pages for the WSL does not appear to be part of the WSL itself. If we examine their _MMPFNs, we find that _MMPFN.u1.WsIndex is usually 0. As an example, the next to last PTE above maps PFN 0x2D44, which has:

```
1: kd> !pfn 0x2d44
    PFN 00002D44 at address FFFFFA8000087CC0
    flink       00000000  blink / share count 00000001  pteaddress FFFFF6FB80008C00
    reference count 0001   used entry count  0000     Cached    color 0   Priority 5
    restore pte 00000080  containing page       010C9A  Active    M
    Modified
```

The exception is the page mapping the WSL itself (0xFFFFF700`08010000), which is always entry #4 of the WSLE.

The VMM releases physical pages when the working set shrinks and the WSLE can be shortened. Below is the situation after MemTests called *SetProcessWorkingSetSize* to shrink its own WS:

```
1: kd> ?? ((nt!_mmwsl *) 0xfffff70001080000)->LastInitializedWsle
unsigned long 0x36e

1: kd> ? 0xFFFFF700`01080488 + 0x36e * 8
Evaluate expression: -9895587340296 = fffff700`01081ff8

1: kd> !pte 0xFFFFF700`01080488 + 0x36e * 8
                                   VA fffff70001081ff8

PXE at FFFFF6FB7DBEDF70   PPE at FFFFF6FB7DBEE000   PDE at FFFFF6FB7DC00040   PTE at FFFFF6FB80008408
contains 0000000004D81863  contains 0000000004D82863  contains 0000000004D83863  contains 800000002430D863
pfn 4d81      ---DA--KWEV  pfn 4d82     ---DA--KWEV  pfn 4d83     ---DA--KWEV  pfn 2430d     ---DA--KW-V


1: kd> dq FFFFF6FB80008400 FFFFF6FB80008408 + 0x10 * 8
fffff6fb`80008400  00000000`04d84863 80000000`2430d863
fffff6fb`80008410  00000000`00000000 00000000`00000000
fffff6fb`80008420  00000000`00000000 00000000`00000000
fffff6fb`80008430  00000000`00000000 00000000`00000000
fffff6fb`80008440  00000000`00000000 00000000`00000000
```

```
fffff6fb`80008450   00000000`00000000  00000000`00000000
fffff6fb`80008460   00000000`00000000  00000000`00000000
fffff6fb`80008470   00000000`00000000  00000000`00000000
fffff6fb`80008480   00000000`00000000  00000000`00000000
```

We are back to a two-pages list.

44.4.3.2   Page Fault Handling

An analysis of *MmAccessFault* shows that page faults in this region are handled by the same code path used for the System PTE region (detailed later in sec. 44.8.3 on p. 472). This suggests that the VMM prevents page faults from happening in this region, because, if the PTE is such that a physical page is mapped, an entry for the address is added to the System PTE working set. This makes little sense, because there is a single instance of this WS and the content of this region is process-private. The fault for a given WSLE address can occur more than once in different processes, so that multiple WSL entries for the same address would be added to the System PTE WS. Possibly, the VMM avoids page faults in this region altogether, mapping physical pages when it needs to grow the WSLE before any fault can happen.

This is also confirmed by the fact that `_MMPFN`s for physical pages in this region (other than the one for page 0xFFFFF700`01080000) have `_MMPFN.u1.WsIndex` = 0. If a page were to be mapped as part of the handling of a fault, it would have an index corresponding to the System PTE WS entry. This can be verified by setting a zeroed PTE for this region to 0x80 and touching the range with MemTests. This experiment corrupts the system state since such a WS entry is not meant to be, so the system should be rebooted afterwards.

44.4.4   Hash Tables Regions

The next two subregions store the 2 working set hashtables: the single page non direct one described in sec. 37.14.4.1 on p. 334 and the direct one (sec. 37.14.4.2, p. 334). We have already analyzed how the virtual ranges for the two tables are mapped as the need for hash table entries arises.

A page fault in this reason would be treated in the same way as one in the WSL region (see the previous section), so the same considerations apply.

44.5 Shared System Page

This special purpose one page region is used to share content between code executing in user mode and code executing in kernel mode. It's layout is given by the _KUSER_SHARED_DATA structure ([2]).

The PTE mapping address 0xFFFFF780`00000000 forbids access from user mode code since it has the U/S bit clear, however, every process maps the same physical page pointed by this PTE at address 0x7FFE0000 and this mapping is accessible from user mode, albeit in read-only (bit R/W of the PTE is clear).

This special page actually has an entry in the VAD tree, which is somewhat peculiar:

```
VAD             level    start    end     commit
fffffa80033df990 ( 6)       10      1f          0 Mapped        READWRITE
[...]
fffffa8002f5b650 ( 1)     7ffe0    7ffef       -1 Private       READONLY
```

the number of committed pages is -1.

Also, the _MMPFN for the physical page has _MMPFN.u1 set to the address of KiInitialProcess, a static instance of _EPROCESS inside the kernel for the logical process Idle, to which the idle threads (one for each processor) belong.

44.6 System Working Sets

System WSs are similar to process ones, but for the system range, where several regions are pageable like the user mode range. To keep track of WS size and currently mapped VAs, the VMM uses a set of _MMSUPPORT instances, each pointing to an instance of _MMWSL. The _MMSUPPORT instances are static variables inside the kernel image and their VmWorkingSetList members point to _MMWSL instances inside this region, which is a special purpose one, dedicated to these data structures.

If we analyze the function named *MiSwapWslEntries*, we discover that it compares a pointer to an _MMSUPPORT instance with the address of two static variables, MmPagedPoolWs and MmSystemPtesWs, taking different actions for them than for a "regular" instance of _MMSUPPORT, describing the user range of a process. This suggests that MmPagedPoolWs and MmSystemPtesWs are instances of _MMSUPPORT, a fact confirmed both by their content and by the code of *MmAccessFault*. With a little guesswork, we can look for all the symbols ending in Ws inside the kernel, coming up with the following list:

```
1: kd> x nt!*ws
...
fffff800`02afa518 nt!MiSessionSpaceWs = <no type information>
...
fffff800`02a4f440 nt!MmSystemPtesWs = <no type information>
...
fffff800`02a4ee00 nt!MmSystemCacheWs = <no type information>
fffff800`02a4eb40 nt!MmPagedPoolWs = <no type information>
```

For now, we will ignore MiSessionSpaceWs until we will discuss session-private memory; we will return on it in sec. 44.10.2.1.2 on p. 489. The other three variables appear to actually be instances of _MMSUPPORT and each points to a different _MMWSL:

```
0: kd> dt nt!_mmsupport VmWorkingSetList @@masm(nt!MmSystemPtesWs)
   +0x068 VmWorkingSetList : 0xfffff780`00001000 _MMWSL
0: kd> dt nt!_mmsupport VmWorkingSetList @@masm(nt!MmSystemCacheWs)
   +0x068 VmWorkingSetList : 0xfffff780`c0000000 _MMWSL
0: kd> dt nt!_mmsupport VmWorkingSetList @@masm(nt!MmPagedPoolWs)
   +0x068 VmWorkingSetList : 0xfffff781`c0000000 _MMWSL
```

We can see that these _MMWSL instances fall in the system working sets region.

These working sets appear to be identified by the value of _MMSUPPORT.Flags.WorkingSetType:

```
1: kd> dt nt!_mmsupport Flags.WorkingSetType @@masm(nt!MmSystemCacheWs)
   +0x084 Flags           :
      +0x000 WorkingSetType     : 0y010   i.e. 2

1: kd> dt nt!_mmsupport Flags.WorkingSetType @@masm(nt!MmPagedPoolWs)
   +0x084 Flags           :
      +0x000 WorkingSetType     : 0y011   i.e. 3

1: kd> dt nt!_mmsupport Flags.WorkingSetType @@masm(nt!MmSystemPtesWs)
   +0x084 Flags           :
      +0x000 WorkingSetType     : 0y100   i.e. 4
```

This is corroborated by the analysis of the *MiMapProcessMetaPage* function: it includes a block of logic which uses a pointer to an instance of _MMSUPPORT and releases its WorkingSetMutex member, which is a pushlock protecting the instance. After releasing it, the function clears one of a set of flags inside the _ETHREAD of the current thread, depending on the value of Flags.WorkingSetType. The relationship between the cleared flag and WorkingSetType is given by the following table:

WorkingSetType	_ETHREAD flag cleared	Implied WS type
0	OwnsProcessWorkingSetExclusive	Process
1	OwnsSessionWorkingSetExclusive	Session
2	OwnsSystemCacheWorkingSetExclusive	System cache
3	OwnsPagedPoolWorkingSetExclusive	Paged pool
4	OwnsSystemPtesWorkingSetExclusive	System PTE

The flag names suggest that 1 is the type for the session working set and so on. The types implied by the flag names match with the values extracted from the `_MMSUPPORT` instances. Furthemore, the same logic for setting and clearing these flags is found in *MmAccessFault*.

All these instances of `_MMSUPPORT` and their associated `_MMWSL` track ranges of system VAs in the same way a process WSL does: by storing counters for the WS and the list of mapped VAs, with their ages.

44.6.1   System Cache Working Set

The system cache working set (MmSystemCacheWs) keeps track of physical pages used by the Windows file cache, thus MmSystemCacheWs.WorkingSetSize gives the number of physical pages used by it.

These pages are mapped at addresses in the Dynamic Kernel VA Space region, whose content will be analyzed later. For now, it is enough to say that this region includes pageable addresses, which are tracked by this working set.

It is worth noting that [1] states, on p. 833, that MmSystemCacheWs.WorkingSetSize does not give the size of the file cache WS alone, but, rather, the combined sizes of three working sets: system cache, paged pool and system PTEs ([1] does not mention the system PTEs WS explicitly, but, rather, pageable code and mapped views, which are in the System PTE range). However, [1] refers to the Vista VMM and it appears that in Windows 7 things are different. [1] states that the value of the file cache working set *alone* is given by a variable named MmSystemCachePage and by the performance counter named Memory: System Cache Resident Bytes. In Windows 7, MmSystemCachePage no longer exists and the performance counter shows exactly the same value extracted from MmSystemCacheWs (albeit in bytes rather than in pages). [1] also lists other performance counters to obtain the sizes of the paged pool working set and of the System PTE working set. In Windows 7, these counters perfectly match the values extracted from MmPagedPoolWs and MmSystemPtesWs. In summary, the three kinds of system working sets are managed by three distinct instances of `_MMSUPPORT` in Windows 7, while [1] implies that in Vista it was not so (and the same was stated in the older *Inside Windows 2000* book). [1] also states on p. 856 that the Cache Bytes counter reports the size of the global system working set, which includes file cache, nonpaged pool and system PTEs, while the System Cache Resident Bytes counter gives the size of the file cache working set alone. In Windows 7 this two counters have the same value and they are both equal to MmSystemCacheWs.WorkingSetSize.

Below is a dump of the _MMWSL instance for this working set:

```
1: kd> ?? ((nt!_MMSUPPORT*) @@(nt!MmSystemCacheWS))->VmWorkingSetList
struct _MMWSL * 0xfffff780`c0000000
   +0x000 FirstFree         : 0x3068
   +0x004 FirstDynamic      : 1
   +0x008 LastEntry         : 0x35ed
   +0x00c NextSlot          : 1
   +0x010 Wsle              : 0xfffff780`c0000488 _MMWSLE
   +0x018 LowestPagableAddress : 0xfffff980`00000000 Void
   +0x020 LastInitializedWsle : 0x376e
   +0x024 NextAgingSlot     : 0x306c
   +0x028 NumberOfCommittedPageTables : 0
   +0x02c VadBitMapHint     : 0
   +0x030 NonDirectCount    : 0x13
   +0x034 LastVadBit        : 0
   +0x038 MaximumLastVadBit : 0
   +0x03c LastAllocationSizeHint : 0
   +0x040 LastAllocationSize : 0
   +0x048 NonDirectHash     : 0xfffff781`7ffff000 _MMWSLE_NONDIRECT_HASH
   +0x050 HashTableStart    : 0xfffff781`80000000 _MMWSLE_HASH
   +0x058 HighestPermittedHashAddress : 0xfffff781`c0000000 _MMWSLE_HASH
   +0x060 MaximumUserPageTablePages : 0
   +0x064 MaximumUserPageDirectoryPages : 0
   +0x068 CommittedPageTables : (null)
   +0x070 NumberOfCommittedPageDirectories : 0
   +0x078 CommittedPageDirectories : [128] 0
   +0x478 NumberOfCommittedPageDirectoryParents : 0
   +0x480 CommittedPageDirectoryParents : [1] 0
```

The dump shows that the _MMWSL instance is in the system working set region and that the WSLE array immediately follows it.

LowestPagableAddress is set to the starting address of the dynamic kernel VA space region, confirming this WS tracks VAs in that range.

It is a bit surprising to see NonDirectCount with a nonzero value. It is useful to recall its meaning, which is fully explained in sec. 37.14 on p. 331).

For a page which is part of a process working set, _MMPFN.u1.WsIndex stores the index of the working set entry for the VA mapped to the page. When more processes share a physical page of memory, the VMM cannot always use the same WSLE in all the working sets, because in some WSs that entry may be in use. For the WSs where the index stored in the _MMPFN is not the correct one, the VMM creates an hash table entry associating the VA with the correct index.

All of the above stems from a basic fact: pages mapping user range addresses can be shared among different working sets.

However, the system cache working set keeps track of system range addresses (specifically, in the dynamic kernel VA region) and we would expect that physical pages mapping these addresses were not part of any other working set. Other system working sets like the System PTE one, the nonpaged pool one and the session one, are for other system regions and have nothing to do with the VAs in the system cache working set. If the VAs in the cache WS are mapped by pages which can only be part of that WS, there is no need for hash table entries: `_MMPFN.u1.WsIndex` can simply store the correct index for the cache working set.

The explanation lies in how the kernel uses section objects to access files (see Chapter 38 on p. 338). A file is *always* accessed by creating a section object and by mapping views of it. If a program uses file access APIs like *ReadFile*, the kernel creates the section object behind the scenes and, together with the file system driver, copies data from the section into the program buffer. But where is the view of this section mapped? In the VA region used by the cache manager, which is inside the dynamic kernel VA space region. So, basically, when *ReadFile* returns data, kernel mode code is reading it from some VA assigned to the cache manager where a view of the section for the file is mapped. The system cache WS tracks these VAs, i.e. its entries are for them.

So far so good, we know what the VAs in the cache WS are for, but we still don't know why they need hash table entries.

In sec. 38.2.8.1 on p. 355 we saw that, no matter how we access a file, a single section object is created: if we use regular I/O functions, it is created by the I/O manager; if we use file mapping functions we create it explicitly; if we do both things, the same section object is used for both purposes. There is *one* section object in the whole system for a given file, no matter what kind of access was created for. The only exception is when we create a file mapping for an image file: it can be mapped both as a data file and as an image one and two distinct sections are created. However, it still holds true that there is a single section for a given access mode.

Having a single section means caching: if parts of the section are in physical memory pages, these are available to all the processes mapping views of the section. Now, suppose we have a file which has been accessed with *ReadFile* in one process and with file mapping APIs in another. The cache manager has loaded parts of the file in physical pages and mapped them in its own virtual range. The process mapping the file, maps the *same* physical pages into its own address range. These pages are now part of *two* working sets: the system cache WS and the process WS. This is why hash table entries may be needed.

We are now going to observe the above scenario in a debug session. Below is a partial dump of the non direct hash table of the cache WS:

```
1: kd> dq 0xfffff781`7ffff000
fffff781`7ffff000  00000000`00000000 00000000`000004fd
fffff781`7ffff010  fffff980`04401001 00000000`000006d2
```

The entry on the second line shows that VA 0xFFFFF980`04401000 (the rightmost 1 is due to a flag bit) has index 0x6D2 in the WS list (remember that these entries are of type _MMWSLE_NONDIRECT_HASH). We can confirm this by examining the WSL entry in the system cache WS:

```
1: kd> ?? ((nt!_mmwsl*) 0xfffff780`c0000000)->Wsle[0x6d2].u1.e1
struct _MMWSLENTRY
   +0x000 Valid            : 0y1
   +0x000 Spare            : 0y0
   +0x000 Hashed           : 0y1
   +0x000 Direct           : 0y0
   +0x000 Protection       : 0y00000 (0)
   +0x000 Age              : 0y110
   +0x000 VirtualPageNumber : 0y1111111111111111111111001100000000000001000100000000001
(0xfffff98004401)
```

The VirtualPageNumber member stores the VPN for our address. With !pte and !pfn we can look at _MMPFN.u1.WsIndex:

```
1: kd> !pte fffff980`04401000
                                      VA fffff98004401000

PXE at FFFFF6FB7DBEDF98    PPE at FFFFF6FB7DBF3000    PDE at FFFFF6FB7E600110    PTE at FFFFF6FCC0022008
contains 00000000272B2863  contains 00000000272B1863  contains 0000000017DCE863  contains 6D2000001837D901
pfn 272b2    ---DA--KWEV   pfn 272b1    ---DA--KWEV   pfn 17dce    ---DA--KWEV   pfn 1837d    -G-----KREV
```

```
1: kd> !pfn 1837d
   PFN 0001837D at address FFFFFA800048A770
   flink        00000C5F   blink / share count 00000007   pteaddress FFFFF8A001330008
   reference count 0001    used entry count  0000       Cached       color 0   Priority 6
   restore pte FA8002EF559004C0  containing page         017DD0    Active      P
     Shared
```

Clearly, the _MMPFN has the wrong WSL index.

Now, since this page is in the cache WS, it is part of a section. We know that restore pte shown above is _MMPFN.OriginalPte, which, for such a page, is an instance of _MMPTE_SUBSECTION pointing to the subsection. We can use it to get to the control area for the file:

```
1: kd> ?? ((nt!_mmpfn*) 0xFFFFFA800048A770)->OriginalPte.u.Subsect
struct _MMPTE_SUBSECTION
   +0x000 Valid            : 0y0
   +0x000 Unused0          : 0y0000
   +0x000 Protection       : 0y00110 (0x6)
   +0x000 Prototype        : 0y1
   +0x000 Unused1          : 0y00000 (0)
```

```
   +0x000 SubsectionAddress : 0y1111101010000000000001011101111010101010110010000
(0xfa8002ef5590)
```

The subsection address above is only 48 bits in size because bits 48-63 are known to be set. To rebuild the complete address we must OR it with these set bits:

```
1: kd> ?? (nt!_subsection *)(((unsigned int64) ((nt!_mmpfn*) 0xFFFFFA800048A770)-
>OriginalPte.u.Subsect.SubsectionAddress) | (0xffff << 48) )
struct _SUBSECTION * 0xfffffa80`02ef5590
   +0x000 ControlArea        : 0xfffffa80`02ef5510 _CONTROL_AREA
   +0x008 SubsectionBase     : 0xfffff8a0`01330000 _MMPTE
   +0x010 NextSubsection     : (null)
   +0x018 PtesInSubsection   : 0x940
   +0x020 UnusedPtes         : 0
   +0x020 GlobalPerSessionHead : (null)
   +0x028 u                  : <unnamed-tag>
   +0x02c StartingSector     : 0
   +0x030 NumberOfFullSectors : 0x940
```

This gives us the subsection content and, in particular, the control area address, which can be given to the !ca extension to get to the file name:

```
1: kd> !ca @@( ((nt!_subsection *)(((unsigned int64) ((nt!_mmpfn*) 0xFFFFFA800048A770)-
>OriginalPte.u.Subsect.SubsectionAddress) | (0xffff << 48) ))->ControlArea)


ControlArea  @ fffffa8002ef5510
   Segment      fffff8a00132c2e0  Flink      0000000000000000  Blink      0000000000000000
   Section Ref             7  Pfn Ref                 e0  Mapped Views            7
   User Ref                c  WaitForDel               0  Flush Count             0
   File Object  fffffa8002eef4f0  ModWriteCount            0  System Views            1
   WritableRefs            0
   Flags (c080) File WasPurged Accessed


      File: \Windows\Fonts\StaticCache.dat

Segment @ fffff8a00132c2e0
   ControlArea    fffffa8002ef5510  ExtendInfo      0000000000000000
   Total Ptes             940
   Segment Size        940000  Committed                0
   Flags (c0000) ProtectionMask



Subsection 1 @ fffffa8002ef5590
   ControlArea  fffffa8002ef5510  Starting Sector         0  Number Of Sectors  940
   Base Pte     fffff8a001330000  Ptes In Subsect       940  Unused Ptes          0
   Flags                     d  Sector Offset           0  Protection           6
   Accessed
   Flink        0000000000000000  Blink      0000000000000000  MappedViews          7
```

We see above that Mapped Views is 7, which tells us that there are multiple views of this section besides the one in the system range we started from. To find one of these other views, we look at the control area content:

```
1: kd> ?? ((nt!_subsection *)(((unsigned int64) ((nt!_mmpfn*) 0xFFFFFA800048A770)-
>OriginalPte.u.Subsect.SubsectionAddress) | (0xffff << 48) ))->ControlArea
struct _CONTROL_AREA * 0xffffffa80`02ef5510
   +0x000 Segment          : 0xfffff8a0`0132c2e0 _SEGMENT
   +0x008 DereferenceList  : _LIST_ENTRY [ 0x00000000`00000000 - 0x0 ]
   +0x018 NumberOfSectionReferences : 7
   +0x020 NumberOfPfnReferences : 0xe0
   +0x028 NumberOfMappedViews : 7
   +0x030 NumberOfUserReferences : 0xc
   +0x038 u                : <unnamed-tag>
   +0x03c FlushInProgressCount : 0
   +0x040 FilePointer      : _EX_FAST_REF
   +0x048 ControlAreaLock  : 0n0
   +0x04c ModifiedWriteCount : 0
   +0x04c StartingFrame    : 0
   +0x050 WaitingForDeletion : (null)
   +0x058 u2               : <unnamed-tag>
   +0x068 LockedPages      : 0n1
   +0x070 ViewList         : _LIST_ENTRY [ 0xffffffa80`031d7c90 - 0xffffffa80`02eefec0 ]
```

The `ViewList` member links the control area with a list of VADs mapping its views. Inside the `_MMVAD` structure the link member is at +0x60, so the highlighted address above is the address of a VAD +0x60. With this knowledge we can dump the VAD content:

```
1: kd> ?? (nt!_mmvad*) (0xffffffa80`031d7c90 - 0x60)
struct _MMVAD * 0xffffffa80`031d7c30
   +0x000 u1               : <unnamed-tag>
   +0x008 LeftChild        : 0xffffffa80`0316f260 _MMVAD
   +0x010 RightChild       : 0xffffffa80`011a5150 _MMVAD
   +0x018 StartingVpn      : 0x3790
   +0x020 EndingVpn        : 0x40bf
   +0x028 u                : <unnamed-tag>
   +0x030 PushLock         : _EX_PUSH_LOCK
   +0x038 u5               : <unnamed-tag>
   +0x040 u2               : <unnamed-tag>
   +0x048 Subsection       : 0xffffffa80`02ef5590 _SUBSECTION
   +0x048 MappedSubsection : 0xffffffa80`02ef5590 _MSUBSECTION
   +0x050 FirstPrototypePte : 0xfffff8a0`01330000 _MMPTE
   +0x058 LastContiguousPte : 0xfffff8a0`01334978 _MMPTE
   +0x060 ViewLinks        : _LIST_ENTRY [ 0xffffffa80`0117e110 - 0xffffffa80`02ef5580 ]
   +0x070 VadsProcess      : 0xffffffa80`0148cb31 _EPROCESS
```

We must remember that a VAD describes a portion of the *user* range of a process. We are seeing where it is that some process is mapping in its user range a view of the section for our file.

We see that the prototype PTE at 0xFFFFF8A0`01330000 is mapped to VPN 0x3790. Looking back at the `!pfn` output for our physical page, we see that `pteaddress` is 0xFFFFF8A0`01330008. Thus, the page is mapping a prototype PTE at +8 from the first one mapped by the VAD. Since PTEs are 8 bytes in size, this means our page is mapping the next prototype PTE, i.e. the next virtual page in this address space or address 0x3791000.

The `VadsProcess` member gives us the address of the `_EPROCESS` for this address space. Since `_EPROCESS` structures are aligned on even addresses, we can mask off the rightmost 1 and see that the process is mmc.exe:

```
1: kd> !process 0xfffffa80`0148cb30
PROCESS fffffa800148cb30
    SessionId: 1  Cid: 0938    Peb: 7fffffd5000  ParentCid: 006c
    DirBase: 2f0a7000  ObjectTable: fffff8a0019684e0  HandleCount: 388.
    Image: mmc.exe
```

Knowing the `_EPROCESS` address, we can make this address space current and examine the PTE for virtual address 0x3791000:

```
1: kd> .process /P 0xfffffa80`0148cb30
Implicit process is now fffffa80`0148cb30
.cache forcedecodeptes done

1: kd> !pte 3791000
                           VA 0000000003791000

PXE at FFFFF6FB7DBED000   PPE at FFFFF6FB7DA00000   PDE at FFFFF6FB400000D8   PTE at FFFFF6800001BC88
contains 01F0000027D48867   contains 012000002BB4C867   contains 3BF0000028160847   contains C5F000001837D005
pfn 27d48   ---DA--UWEV  pfn 2bb4c   ---DA--UWEV  pfn 28160   ---D---UWEV  pfn 1837d   -------UR-V
```

We see that this VA is mapped to PFN 0x1837d, i.e. the same physical page for our original system address, which confirms what we have found so far. Now we can see that the WSL index stored in the `_MMPFN` (i.e. 0xC5F), which was not correct for the cache WS, is valid in this process WS:

```
1: kd> ?? ((nt!_mmwsl*) 0xfffff70001080000)->Wsle[0xc5f].u1.e1
struct _MMWSLENTRY
   +0x000 Valid            : 0y1
   +0x000 Spare            : 0y0
   +0x000 Hashed           : 0y1
   +0x000 Direct           : 0y0
   +0x000 Protection       : 0y00001 (0x1)
   +0x000 Age              : 0y001
   +0x000 VirtualPageNumber : 0y0000000000000000000000000000000000000011011110010001
(0x3791)
```

In summary, `_MMPFN.u1.WsIndex` stores an index valid for this (and perhaps other) process WS, but not valid for the cache WS, hence the need for the hash table entry in the latter.

44.6.2   Paged Pool Working Set

The WS managed by MmPagedPoolWs tracks the VAs assigned to the paged pool, which we will discuss later. In broad terms, it is a range of pageable memory, available to kernel modules through a set of allocation/deallocation functions, which performs a role similar to what the heap does for a process. At any rate, the VMM needs to manage the virtual addresses of this range to implement the paged pool functionality, so it uses an _MMSUPPORT to do the job.

From the _MMSUPPORT we can see that both the _MMWSL and the _MMWSLE array fall in the system working sets region:

```
0: kd> ?? ((nt!_mmsupport*) @@(nt!MmPagedPoolWs))->VmWorkingSetList
struct _MMWSL * 0xfffff781`c0000000
   +0x000 FirstFree         : 0x2ca3
   +0x004 FirstDynamic      : 1
   +0x008 LastEntry         : 0x443f
   +0x00c NextSlot          : 1
   +0x010 Wsle              : 0xfffff781`c0000488 _MMWSLE
   +0x018 LowestPagableAddress : 0xfffff8a0`00000000 Void
   +0x020 LastInitializedWsle : 0x456e
   +0x024 NextAgingSlot     : 0x3e19
   +0x028 NumberOfCommittedPageTables : 0
   +0x02c VadBitMapHint     : 0
   +0x030 NonDirectCount    : 0
   +0x034 LastVadBit        : 0
   +0x038 MaximumLastVadBit : 0
   +0x03c LastAllocationSizeHint : 0
   +0x040 LastAllocationSize : 0
   +0x048 NonDirectHash     : (null)
   +0x050 HashTableStart    : 0xfffff782`80000000 _MMWSLE_HASH
   +0x058 HighestPermittedHashAddress : 0xfffff782`80000000 _MMWSLE_HASH
   +0x060 MaximumUserPageTablePages : 0
   +0x064 MaximumUserPageDirectoryPages : 0
   +0x068 CommittedPageTables : (null)
   +0x070 NumberOfCommittedPageDirectories : 0
   +0x078 CommittedPageDirectories : [128] 0
   +0x478 NumberOfCommittedPageDirectoryParents : 0
   +0x480 CommittedPageDirectoryParents : [1] 0
```

We can see how LowestPagableAddress is set to the starting address of the paged pool.

Physical pages mapping paged pool VAs are part of this working set only, so there is no need for hash table entries: NonDirectCount is 0 and the direct hash table is not even mapped:

```
0: kd> dd @@( ((nt!_mmsupport*) @@(nt!MmPagedPoolWs))->VmWorkingSetList->HashTableStart )
fffff782`80000000  ???????? ???????? ???????? ????????
fffff782`80000010  ???????? ???????? ???????? ????????
fffff782`80000020  ???????? ???????? ???????? ????????
fffff782`80000030  ???????? ???????? ???????? ????????
fffff782`80000040  ???????? ???????? ???????? ????????
fffff782`80000050  ???????? ???????? ???????? ????????
fffff782`80000060  ???????? ???????? ???????? ????????
fffff782`80000070  ???????? ???????? ???????? ????????
```

44.6.3   System PTE Working Set

MmSystemPtesWs manages another region in the system range which will also be explained later. For now, we can regard it as just another chunk of pageable virtual address space whose current state is tracked by this `_MMSUPPORT` instance.

It is worth noting that `MmSystemPtesWs.WorkingSetSize` is exactly equal to the sum of two statics cited in [1], p. 833: MmSystemDriverPage and MmSystemCodePage. We will return on this in sec. 44.8.4 on p. 473.

Again, we can see that the `_MMWSL` and the WSLEs are in our region and that the hash tables are not mapped:

```
0: kd> ?? ((nt!_mmsupport*) @@(nt!MmSystemPtesWs))->VmWorkingSetList
struct _MMWSL * 0xfffff780`00001000
   +0x000 FirstFree        : 0x3bb
   +0x004 FirstDynamic     : 1
   +0x008 LastEntry        : 0xebb
   +0x00c NextSlot         : 1
   +0x010 Wsle             : 0xfffff780`00001488 _MMWSLE
   +0x018 LowestPagableAddress : 0xfffff800`00000000 Void
   +0x020 LastInitializedWsle : 0xf6e
   +0x024 NextAgingSlot    : 0x411
   +0x028 NumberOfCommittedPageTables : 0
   +0x02c VadBitMapHint    : 0
   +0x030 NonDirectCount   : 0
   +0x034 LastVadBit       : 0
   +0x038 MaximumLastVadBit : 0
   +0x03c LastAllocationSizeHint : 0
   +0x040 LastAllocationSize : 0
   +0x048 NonDirectHash    : 0xfffff780`7ffff001 _MMWSLE_NONDIRECT_HASH
   +0x050 HashTableStart   : 0xfffff780`80000000 _MMWSLE_HASH
   +0x058 HighestPermittedHashAddress : 0xfffff780`a8000000 _MMWSLE_HASH
   +0x060 MaximumUserPageTablePages : 0
   +0x064 MaximumUserPageDirectoryPages : 0
   +0x068 CommittedPageTables : (null)
   +0x070 NumberOfCommittedPageDirectories : 0
   +0x078 CommittedPageDirectories : [128] 0
   +0x478 NumberOfCommittedPageDirectoryParents : 0
   +0x480 CommittedPageDirectoryParents : [1] 0

0: kd> dd @@( ((nt!_mmsupport*) @@(nt!MmSystemPtesWs))->VmWorkingSetList->NonDirectHash
)
fffff780`7ffff001  ???????? ???????? ???????? ????????
fffff780`7ffff011  ???????? ???????? ???????? ????????

0: kd> dd @@( ((nt!_mmsupport*) @@(nt!MmSystemPtesWs))->VmWorkingSetList-
>HashTableStart )
fffff780`80000000  ???????? ???????? ???????? ????????
fffff780`80000010  ???????? ???????? ???????? ????????
```

It's interesting to observe that `LowestPagableAddress` points below the System PTE region, i.e. at the beginning of the Initial Loader Mappings region, which stores kernel mode images loaded in the early stages of system boot, e.g. the kernel and the HAL. Since these images have pageable sections, they too must be tracked by a working set, which appears to be this one. This is consistent with the fact that MmSystemCodePage contributes to the value of `MmSystemPtesWs.WorkingSetSize`: the former is the count of physical pages used to map the kernel image ([1], p. 833), which are mapped in the Initial Loader Mappings region.

44.6.4   Page Fault Handling

The code of *MmAccessFault* shows that page faults in this region are handled by the same logic used for the System PTE region (detailed later in sec. 44.8.3 on p. 472). This suggests that the VMM prevents page faults from happening in this region (i.e. it maps VAs to physical pages before accessing them), a fact also confirmed by the `_MMPFN`s for physical pages in this region which have `_MMPFN.u1.WsIndex` = 0.

44.7 Initial Loader Mapping

44.7.1   Region Content

This region is used, as its name implies, to store code and data structures initialized when Windows starts up. It is more similar to a dynamically allocated region than to a special purpose one, because it contains executable code and parts of it are pageable. However, there are no known kernel functions to allocate portions of this region, whose content appears to be determined at system boot time and to remain the same for the lifetime of the system.

The kernel and the hal are loaded here, as well as the kernel debugger dll. We will analyze later in Chapter 46 (p. 507) how kernel mode executables are loaded in memory.

This region also includes the `_KPCR` instance for processor 0. This data structure, named Processor Control Region, stores status information for a processor. It's address is given by gs:[0], i.e. it's offset 0 in the segment pointed by GS. The segment descriptor pointed by GS is one of the few ones which has a nonzero base. Instead, its base is set to point to the beginning of the `_KPCR` for the processor. Since each processor has its own GDT, each has a distinct descriptor for GS (even though the value of GS is 0x2B an all processors), so, on every processor, GS:[0] points to the beginning of the `_KPCR`.

`_KPCR.Self` stores the VA of the `_KPCR` instance, which can be used to access the `_KPCR` content through the DS register (the one we are always implicitly using when we "forget" about segmentation), whose base address is implicitly 0. Every time we use VAs in debugger commands they are implicitly interpreted as offset into the DS segment. So, in order to examine the _KPCR, we can do the following: knowing that _KPCR.Self is at +0x18 inside the structure, we can examine it with dq:

```
1: kd> dq gs:[18] l1
002b:00000000`00000018  fffff880`009e7000
```

This gives us the VA of the _KPCR, which can be used with dt or C++ expressions. For instance, the expression below examines _KPCR.Self again and confirms that our address is correct:

```
1: kd> ?? (void*) ((nt!_kpcr*) 0xfffff880`009e7000)->Self
void * 0xfffff880`009e7000
```

Knowing this, we can see that the _KPCR for processor 0 is in this region (the ~0 command switches the debugger to processor 0):

```
1: kd> ~0
0: kd> dq gs:[18] l1
002b:00000000`00000018  fffff800`02a08d00
```

Possibly, this fundamental data structure for processor 0 is initialized during system boot (it's likely that id 0 is assigned to the boot processor), so it's stored in this region, which is used in the early steps of boot. Other processors are initialized later and their _KPCRs end up in the System PTE region, e.g.:

```
0: kd> ~1
1: kd> dq gs:[18] l1
002b:00000000`00000018  fffff880`009e7000
```

This region also includes the stack for one of the idle threads. When the system is fully running, there is an idle thread for each processor and it appears that the one of processor 0 has its stack here, while the other ones have theirs in the System PTE region. The address of the _EPROCESS for the Idle process is stored in KiInitialProcess, so we can examine the threads stacks with the following command:

```
1: kd> !process nt!KiInitialProcess 6
PROCESS fffff80002a17140
    SessionId: none  Cid: 0000    Peb: 00000000  ParentCid: 0000
    DirBase: 00187000  ObjectTable: fffff8a0000018c0  HandleCount: 640.
    Image: Idle

        THREAD fffff80002a16c40  Cid 0000.0000  Teb: 0000000000000000 Win32Thread:
0000000000000000 RUNNING on processor 0
[...]
        Win32 Start Address nt!KiIdleLoop (0xfffff800028986a0)
[...]
```

```
        Child-SP          RetAddr               : Args to Child
: Call Site
        fffff800`00b9c9c8 fffff800`02857b93 : fffffa80`02f175b8 00000000`00032636
fffff780`00000320 00000000`0002625a : nt!DbgBreakPointWithStatus

        fffff800`00b9c9d0 fffff800`02e0f090 : 00000000`00000000 fffff800`00b9cb80
fffff800`02e2a3c0 00000000`00000000 : nt! ?? ::FNODOBFM::`string'+0x6cb0
[...]




        THREAD fffff880009f1f40  Cid 0000.0000  Teb: 0000000000000000 Win32Thread:
0000000000000000 RUNNING on processor 1
[...]
        Win32 Start Address nt!KiIdleLoop (0xfffff800028986a0)
[...]
        Child-SP          RetAddr               : Args to Child
: Call Site
        fffff880`02f1bc98 fffff800`0289da3a : 00000000`00369e99 fffffa80`023b1c08
fffff880`009f1f40 00000000`00000001 : intelppm!C1Halt+0x2

        fffff880`02f1bca0 fffff800`028986cc : fffff880`009e7180 fffff880`00000000
00000000`00000000 fffff800`029471d0 : nt!PoIdle+0x53a
[...]
```

From the command output above, we see that the stack of the thread running on processor 1 is in the System PTE region. The whole situation is similar to the what happens with the _KPCRs: the initial loader mapping region is used for the boot processor and the System PTE region for the other ones.

Kernel Stacks will be analyzed in Chapter 47 (p. 521).

It is also interesting to note that the addresses of the _ETHREADs (shown to the right of the label THREAD above) follow the same pattern: only the one running on processor 0 is in the initial loader mapping region.

44.7.2   Page Fault Handling

Page faults in this region are handled as the ones occurring in the System PTE region (described in sec. 44.8.3 on p. 472).

One scenario where page faults can take place in this region is when a not present address of the kernel is referenced. This can happen since sections of the kernel are pageable (Chapter 46, p. 507, describes in greater detail how the kernel is loaded and paged). When this happens, the fault is resolved and the newly mapped VA is accounted into the System PTE working set, which therefore has entries for this region as well.

As an example, below we see the address range where the kernel is loaded:

```
1: kd> lm m nt
start            end              module name
fffff800`02857000 fffff800`02e34000   nt           (pdb symbols)
```

Address 0xFFFFF800`02CF2000 is inside this range and below we can see the details of the _MMPFN for its page:

```
1: kd> !pte fffff80002cf2000
                                          VA fffff80002cf2000

PXE at FFFFF6FB7DBEDF80    PPE at FFFFF6FB7DBF0000    PDE at FFFFF6FB7E0000B0    PTE at FFFFF6FC00016790
contains 0000000000199063  contains 0000000000198063  contains 00000000001DC063  contains 0100000002CF2101
pfn 199      ---DA--KWEV pfn 198      ---DA--KWEV pfn 1dc      ---DA--KWEV pfn 2cf2      -G-----KREV
```

```
1: kd> !pfn 2cf2
    PFN 00002CF2 at address FFFFFA8000086D60
    flink          00000010  blink / share count 00000001  pteaddress FFFFF6FC00016790
    reference count 0001    used entry count  0000       Cached    color 0    Priority 5
    restore pte 00000060  containing page        0001DC  Active    M
    Modified
```

We know that the value printed to the right of flink is _MMPFN.u1.WsIndex, so we use it as an index into the System PTE working set to confirm that the WSL entry is actually for this VA:

```
1: kd> ?? ((nt!_mmsupport*) @@(nt!MmSystemPtesWs))->VmWorkingSetList->Wsle[0x10].u1.e1
struct _MMWSLENTRY
    +0x000 Valid         : 0y1
    +0x000 Spare         : 0y0
    +0x000 Hashed        : 0y0
    +0x000 Direct        : 0y1
    +0x000 Protection    : 0y00000 (0)
    +0x000 Age           : 0y011
    +0x000 VirtualPageNumber : 0y1111111111111111111111100000000000000000010110011110010
(0xfffff80002cf2)
```

This confirms that the System PTE working set also has entries for the initial loader mappings region.

44.8 System PTE

44.8.1   Region Content

44.8.1.1   Region Purpose and Name

This is a dynamically allocated region.

The name of this region is an unfortunate one, because it is misleading. In spite of it, this region does not store any PTEs. We already know that the actual PTEs used by the processor are mapped in the PTE space region. Even prototype PTEs, which are software defined working copies of PTEs are stored somewhere else, namely in the paged pool region. As we are about to see, this range is reserved for dynamically mapping and unmapping a number of kernel mode related "stuff" in the virtual address space. The PTEs mapping this (system) range are thus available for these mappings and the virtual range takes its name from them.

Another reason for this peculiar name could be the fact that the virtual address range of this region can be allocated in page units. Other dynamically allocated regions manage the virtual address space in PDE units, so each allocation is a multiple of 2MB in size and aligned on a 2MB boundary. For this region, additional logic and data structures exist, allowing to allocate single *PTEs*, rather than PDEs, hence, possibly, the region name. We will examine how virtual address space management is implemented for this region later, in sec. 44.8.2 on p. 442.

The next sections describe the different kinds of content found in this region.

44.8.1.2   MDL Mappings

An MDL is a data structure commonly used by kernel mode components to interact with the memory manager. One common use of MDLs is to allow a kernel mode component to access a data buffer allocated by user mode code. This could be done, for instance, in a kernel mode driver, which passes the buffer content to a device or fills the buffer with data coming from a device. A user mode buffer is mapped only in the context of the process which allocated it; on the other hand, it is often necessary, for a driver, to be able to access the buffer in an arbitrary process context (e.g. in a function invoked by an interrupt). This is accomplished by mapping the physical pages of the buffer in the System PTE region. The physical pages are still mapped to the original user mode addresses, so there will be two different virtual ranges mapped to the same pages: the original one and a range in the System PTE region, with the latter valid in any process context.

An MDL can be used to perform this additional mapping. This structure can store both an array of PFNs and the address of the VA range mapped to the physical pages. Initially, the VA address is set to the user mode address of the buffer. At this stage, the PFN array content is not valid, because a user mode range is pageable, so its PTEs are not necessarily pointing to physical pages: they could be in transition, swapped out or demand zero ones. Thus, the next step is to call *MmProbeAndLockPages* while in the context of the process which allocated the buffer. This DDI maps the virtual range to actual memory and locks the physical pages, so that the PTEs remain valid and pointing to the same PFN. It also copies the PFNs of the range into the array in the MDL. The content of this array remains valid as long as the pages are locked. Finally, a call to *MmGetSystemAddressForMdlSafe* maps the PFNs in the array into a virtual range in the System PTE region. More information on this subject can be found in [18] and in the WDK documentation.

There are other possible ways of using MDLs, but we are not going to dig further on this subject.

It is important not to confuse the VA where the MDLs structures are allocated, with the VA mapped to the PFNs in the array. MDLs are allocated in nonpaged pool, so their addresses are found in that region, while the PFNs in the array, when mapped, become visible in the System PTE region.

44.8.1.3   Other Kinds of Content

This region is also used for the following kinds of content

- Kernel mode drivers are loaded in this region. We will see in Chapter 46 on p. 507 more details on how they are brought into memory.

- Kernel stacks, i.e. the stacks threads use when they execute in kernel mode (more on this in Chapter 47 on p. 521).

- Device memory mappings: some devices are mapped by hardware at physical memory addresses, so that the processor can interact with them simply by reading and writing at these addresses. As usual, processor instructions work with virtual addresses, so these special physical ones must be mapped somewhere in the virtual space and this region is used for this purpose.

- We will also see in sec. 44.10.2.1.1 on p. 487 that an instance of _MM_SESSION_SPACE for each session in the system is mapped inside this region.

44.8.2   Virtual Address Space Management

44.8.2.1   The Allocation Granularity Problem

This section describes the region VA management in detail. Since many concepts found here are undocumented, sec. 44.8.2.6 on p. 448 will present supporting evidence.

The address space of this region is controlled by a bitmap named MiSystemPteBitmap, where each bit represents a PDE, spanning 2MB of virtual address space.

Many allocations performed in this region, however, are for VA sizes much smaller than 2MB. For instance, this region is used to map MDL described buffers, which can be as small as 1 page. Also, thread kernel stacks are allocated here and their size amounts to some kilobytes. Forcing every such allocation to begin on a 2MB boundary would waste a lot of virtual address space, so the VMM implements logic to manage this region in page sized blocks.

An example of this behavior is the *MmMapLockedPagesSpecifyCache* DDI, which maps a buffer described by an MDL in this region and returns page aligned, rather than PDE aligned addresses. Another example are thread kernel mode stacks (detailed later in Chapter 47 - p. 521), which are delimited by page aligned addresses.

44.8.2.2   The Solution: Yet More Bitmaps

The VMM maintains two static instances of _MI_SYSTEM_PTE_TYPE to manage allocations from this region, named MiSystemPteInfo and MiKernelStackPteInfo. Below is the type declaration from the WinDbg dt command:

```
struct _MI_SYSTEM_PTE_TYPE, 12 elements, 0x48 bytes
   +0x000 Bitmap             : struct _RTL_BITMAP, 2 elements, 0x10 bytes
   +0x010 Flags              : Uint4B
   +0x014 Hint               : Uint4B
   +0x018 BasePte            : Ptr64 to struct _MMPTE, 1 elements, 0x8 bytes
   +0x020 FailureCount       : Ptr64 to Uint4B
   +0x028 Vm                 : Ptr64 to struct _MMSUPPORT, 21 elements, 0x88 bytes
   +0x030 TotalSystemPtes    : Int4B
   +0x034 TotalFreeSystemPtes : Int4B
   +0x038 CachedPteCount     : Int4B
   +0x03c PteFailures        : Uint4B
   +0x040 SpinLock           : Uint8B
   +0x040 GlobalMutex        : Ptr64 to struct _KGUARDED_MUTEX, 7 elements, 0x38 bytes
```

The Bitmap member is what its name suggests and each bit represent a page in the System PTE region. Allocations from this region are performed by calling *MiReservePtes* ([2]), which takes the address of the instance of _MI_SYSTEM_PTE_TYPE to use for the allocation as its first parameter.

Before examining in detail how these structures are used, let's concentrate on why there are two of them. According to [2], the reason is to avoid VA fragmentation: an instance is used for allocations which are retained longer, like kernel mode stacks, the other for shorter lived ones, like MDLs. Thus, having two instances covering different subranges avoids having, say, two stacks with a small unused hole between them caused by an MDL that has been allocated and released.

Another possible benefit of having two instances is that it reduces contention for exclusive access to the bitmap itself. E.g. MDL allocations don't block stack allocations, etc.

44.8.2.3   Bitmap Buffers Maximum Size and Address

Both bitmaps have a buffer big enough to cover the entire System PTE region (we will soon see why).

The region spans 128GB and, knowing the bitmap buffer must have a bit for each page in this range, we can compute the buffer maximum size as:

0x20`00000000 / 0x1000 / 8 = 0x400000 bytes = 4MB

The first division computes the number of pages, i.e. of bits and the second one accounts for having 8 bits in each bitmap byte.

Below are the buffer addresses dumped from our two instances:

```
0: kd> ?? ((nt!_mi_system_pte_type*) @@(nt!MiSystemPteInfo))->Bitmap
struct _RTL_BITMAP
   +0x000 SizeOfBitMap    : 0xfe00
   +0x008 Buffer          : 0xfffff880`00000000  -> 0xffffffff

0: kd> ?? ((nt!_mi_system_pte_type*) @@(nt!MiKernelStackPteInfo))->Bitmap
struct _RTL_BITMAP
   +0x000 SizeOfBitMap    : 0x4e00
   +0x008 Buffer          : 0xfffff880`00400000  -> 0xffffffff
```

First of all, we can see that these buffers are stored in the System PTE region itself. Then we see that the buffer for MiKernelStackPteInfo lays next to the one for MiSystemPteInfo. Both are 4MB in size, so the first 8MB of the System PTE region are set aside for this purpose. We should never see MDLs, kernel stacks or loaded image files in the range 0xFFFFF880`00000000 - 0xFFFFF880`00800000.

Each bit in the bitmap represents a page of the System PTE range: bit 0 of the first byte corresponds to the range 0xFFFFF880`00000000 - 0xFFFFF880`00000FFF, etc. Interestingly, since the first 8MB of the range are used for the buffers themselves, the first

0x800000 / 0x1000 / 8 = 0x100

bytes of the bitmaps will always be set to 0xFF.

44.8.2.4   Buffer Actual Size and Expansion

Even though each bitmap has 4MB of virtual addresses set aside for it, only part of this range is mapped to physical pages. `_RTL_BITMAP.SizeOfBitmap` gives the number of valid bits in the bitmap and is usually much lower than 4MB * 8. The two bitmaps are expanded only when an allocation in the region cannot be satisfied with the current bitmap content.

This is easier to understand if we look at how the bitmaps are initialized during system startup. The function responsible for initializing the two instances of `_MI_SYSTEM_PTE_TYPE` is *MiInitializeSystemPtes* ([2]), which sets `SizeOfBitmap` to 8 and maps all the virtual pages of the buffer to a single physical page filled with 0xFF. This is interesting: the virtual content of both 4MB buffers represents a fully utilized bitmap, but only a single physical page is consumed.

So, since all the bitmap bits are set to 1, it is `SizeOfBitmap` that tells us how many of those 1s are actually in use pages. It's initial value of 8 means that the bitmap is completely empty, i.e. no part of its buffer is valid. We will return on this in sec. 44.8.2.6 on p. 448.

The master bitmap MiSystemPteBitmap is initialized with its first byte set to 0xF and the rest of its buffer set to 0. This represents the fact that the first 4 PDEs, i.e. the first 8MBs of the region are in use (because they are reserved for the secondary bitmaps).

The first allocation made from a secondary bitmap during initialization is usually for 0x40 pages to be allocated from MiKernelStackPteInfo. A PDE, which covers 0x200 pages is set aside from the master bitmap, whose first byte becomes 0x1F and the secondary bitmap is updated.

The first virtual page of its buffer is mapped to an actual page, so that its content can be set to other than 0xFF in every byte.

`SizeOfBitmap` is set to 0xA00. To understand this value, we must remember that the first 8MB of the region are used for the buffers. This correspond to 0x800 pages, i.e. bitmap bits, which will always be set to 1. Then a PDE, which spans 0x200 bits has just been added to the bitmap, so its final size is 0xA00. This means that, of the bits visible in the bitmap buffer, 0xA00 have actual meaning, i.e. 0 means free page and 1 means allocated page, while all the others must be ignored.

Normally, the bits beyond index 0xA00 in the first buffer page are set to 1 as if they represented in-use pages. All the other pages of the buffer are still mapped to the physical page filled with 0xFF, so their bits are 1 as well. In other words, all the bits beyonf 0xA00 (i.e. `SizeOfBitmap` are set to 1).

The first 0xA00 bits, i.e. 0x140 bytes of the bitmap are set to values representing the actual state of PTEs: the first 0x800 bits are set to 1 and, since the allocation is for 0x40 pages, the next 0x40 bits are set to 1 as well. The remaining bits, up to bit 0x9FF are clear and represent the fact that these virtual pages, now managed by the secondary bitmap are free for allocation.

Note how, to include in the secondary bitmap the pages allocated from the primary one, we had to adjust its content so that the 0x800 in-use pages preceding them are represented correctly. As long as SizeOfBitmap was 8, the bitmap content did not really matter. Now that it has become 0xA00, all the 0xA00 bits must be set to their correct value.

This process is repeated every time one of the two secondary bitmap must be expanded: the master one is consulted, to find free PDEs, then the buffer size and content are adjusted to include the new free pages assigned to the bitmap and all the set bits corresponding to already allocated pages which had to be included.

This expansion is performed by *MiExpandPtes*, which calls *MiObtainSystemVa* specifying MiVaSystemPtes for the page type ([2]). A detailed analysis of it is included in sec. 44.8.2.6 on p. 448.

As we see, each secondary bitmap is expanded when needed, extending the virtual size covered by its buffer so that it acquires new free pages.

There are also kernel functions which allocate directly from the master bitmap MiSystemPteBitmap. This means that, at the next secondary bitmap expansion, a certain number of bits set in the master one will have to be included, to reach clear bits. This is the same thing that happened with the first 0x800 bits corresponding to the buffer range. In other words, when expanding a secondary bitmap, a number of PDEs following the pre-expansion bitmap size will be found in use. It does not matter if they were allocated by the other secondary bitmap or directly from the master one. They simply have to be incorporated in the bitmap being expanded as set bits for the corresponding pages.

All these allocations occur in random order, so we end up with the scenario depicted in Figure 58.

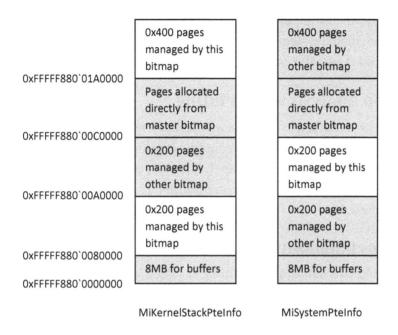

Figure 58 - Distribution of System PTE VA across Bitmaps

The left diagram in Figure 58, depicts the virtual address space from the perspective of the MiKernelStackPteInfo bitmap. Shaded boxes represent ranges not allocated to the bitmap and incorporated as set bits during expansions. The bits for these ranges will always be set in this bitmap. White boxes represent ranges allocated to the bitmap, so that their bits can be set or clear, depending on the page state. The right diagram has the same meaning, but for the MiSystemPteInfo bitmap. The first 8MB as well as regions allocated directly from the master bitmap are shaded in both diagrams, since those ranges are not controlled by any of the two bitmaps.

The diagram shows that the subregions managed by the two bitmaps alternate with each other, depending on the order of allocations, so the System PTE range is not simply split into two subregions for the two bitmaps.

Finally, the VMM can decide to reduce a secondary bitmap, returning a portion of its range under control of the master one.

44.8.2.5   Additional System PTEs

This is not the whole story. An analysis of the Free System PTEs performance counter suggests that there are additional system PTEs available in some other part of the system range. This will be analyzed in sec. 50.8 on p. 552.

44.8.2.6   Bitmap Analysis with WinDbg

This section shows the logic described in the previous one at work while the system is initializing. Its purpose is to offer evidence of the concepts explained before, so readers willing to take the author's word for them may skip it. However, sec. 44.8.2.6.4 on p. 468 may still be of interest because it gives a little glimpse on the internals of the *MmAllocateMappingAddress* DDI.

44.8.2.6.1   Bitmaps Initialization

To be able to debug the bitmaps initialization, WinDbg has been launched with the -d command line option, which causes the debugger to take control of the system very early during boot. This allows us to set a breakpoint on *MiInitializeSystemPtes* and examine the bitmaps before and after their initialization. When the breakpoint is hit, we see the following situation:

```
Breakpoint 0 hit
nt!MiInitializeSystemPtes:
fffff800`02cc8180 488bc4          mov     rax,rsp

kd> ?? ((nt!_rtl_bitmap*) @@(nt!MiSystemPteBitmap))
struct _RTL_BITMAP * 0xfffff800`02b017a0
   +0x000 SizeOfBitMap     : 0x10000
   +0x008 Buffer           : 0xfffff800`02a80b00  -> 0

kd> ln @@( ((nt!_rtl_bitmap*) @@(nt!MiSystemPteBitmap))->Buffer )
(fffff800`02a80b00)   nt!MiSystemPteBits   |   (fffff800`02a82b00)
nt!MiSystemVaTypeCount
Exact matches:
    nt!MiSystemPteBits = <no type information>
```

The master bitmap is already initialized with size equal to 0x10000. Since each bit represents a PDE, this size covers the 128GB of the System PTE range:

$$0x10000 * 0x200000 = 0x20`00000000 = 128GB$$

We can also notice that the master bitmap buffer is itself a static area inside `nt` and its address has the symbol MiSystemPteBits. The output above shows that the first byte is set to 0 (as is the rest of the buffer).

Let's take a look now at the secondary bitmaps:

```
kd> ?? ((nt!_mi_system_pte_type*) @@(nt!MiKernelStackPteInfo))
struct _MI_SYSTEM_PTE_TYPE * 0xfffff800`02a7dec0
   +0x000 Bitmap            : _RTL_BITMAP
   +0x010 Flags             : 0
   +0x014 Hint              : 0
   +0x018 BasePte           : (null)
   +0x020 FailureCount      : (null)
   +0x028 Vm                : (null)
   +0x030 TotalSystemPtes   : 0n0
   +0x034 TotalFreeSystemPtes : 0n0
   +0x038 CachedPteCount    : 0n0
   +0x03c PteFailures       : 0
   +0x040 SpinLock          : 0
   +0x040 GlobalMutex       : (null)

kd> ?? ((nt!_mi_system_pte_type*) @@(nt!MiKernelStackPteInfo))->Bitmap
struct _RTL_BITMAP
   +0x000 SizeOfBitMap      : 0
   +0x008 Buffer            : (null)

kd> ?? ((nt!_mi_system_pte_type*) @@(nt!MiSystemPteInfo))
struct _MI_SYSTEM_PTE_TYPE * 0xfffff800`02a7e720
   +0x000 Bitmap            : _RTL_BITMAP
   +0x010 Flags             : 0
   +0x014 Hint              : 0
   +0x018 BasePte           : (null)
   +0x020 FailureCount      : (null)
   +0x028 Vm                : (null)
   +0x030 TotalSystemPtes   : 0n0
   +0x034 TotalFreeSystemPtes : 0n0
   +0x038 CachedPteCount    : 0n0
   +0x03c PteFailures       : 0
   +0x040 SpinLock          : 0
   +0x040 GlobalMutex       : (null)

kd> ?? ((nt!_mi_system_pte_type*) @@(nt!MiSystemPteInfo))->Bitmap
struct _RTL_BITMAP
   +0x000 SizeOfBitMap      : 0
   +0x008 Buffer            : (null)
```

We find that the control structures are filled with zeroes. We are now going to see how things change after *MiInitializeSystemPtes* has done its job:

```
kd> g @$ra
nt!MmInitNucleus+0x1fc:
fffff800`02df0e5c 85c0              test    eax,eax
```

Below is the content of the master bitmap:

```
kd> ?? ((nt!_rtl_bitmap*) @@(nt!MiSystemPteBitmap))
struct _RTL_BITMAP * 0xfffff800`02b017a0
   +0x000 SizeOfBitMap      : 0x10000
```

```
+0x008 Buffer              : 0xfffff800`02a80b00  -> 0xf
```

The buffer first byte is now set to 0xF, i.e. the first 4 bits are set. The rest of the buffer is filled with zeroes:

```
kd> dq 0xfffff800`02a80b00
fffff800`02a80b00  00000000`0000000f 00000000`00000000
fffff800`02a80b10  00000000`00000000 00000000`00000000
fffff800`02a80b20  00000000`00000000 00000000`00000000
fffff800`02a80b30  00000000`00000000 00000000`00000000
fffff800`02a80b40  00000000`00000000 00000000`00000000
fffff800`02a80b50  00000000`00000000 00000000`00000000
fffff800`02a80b60  00000000`00000000 00000000`00000000
fffff800`02a80b70  00000000`00000000 00000000`00000000
```

This means the first 8MB of range are allocated and we know that they are set aside for the secondary bitmaps. We are now going to look at these bitmaps' control structures:

```
kd> ?? ((nt!_mi_system_pte_type*) @@(nt!MiKernelStackPteInfo))
struct _MI_SYSTEM_PTE_TYPE * 0xfffff800`02a7dec0
   +0x000 Bitmap            : _RTL_BITMAP
   +0x010 Flags             : 3
   +0x014 Hint              : 0x800
   +0x018 BasePte           : 0xfffff6fc`40000000 _MMPTE
   +0x020 FailureCount      : 0xfffff800`02a7defc  -> 0
   +0x028 Vm                : 0xfffff800`02a56440 _MMSUPPORT
   +0x030 TotalSystemPtes   : 0n0
   +0x034 TotalFreeSystemPtes : 0n0
   +0x038 CachedPteCount    : 0n0
   +0x03c PteFailures       : 0
   +0x040 SpinLock          : 0
   +0x040 GlobalMutex       : (null)

kd> ?? ((nt!_mi_system_pte_type*) @@(nt!MiKernelStackPteInfo))->Bitmap
struct _RTL_BITMAP
   +0x000 SizeOfBitMap      : 8
   +0x008 Buffer            : 0xfffff880`00400000  -> 0xffffffff

kd> ?? ((nt!_mi_system_pte_type*) @@(nt!MiSystemPteInfo))
struct _MI_SYSTEM_PTE_TYPE * 0xfffff800`02a7e720
   +0x000 Bitmap            : _RTL_BITMAP
   +0x010 Flags             : 3
   +0x014 Hint              : 0x800
   +0x018 BasePte           : 0xfffff6fc`40000000 _MMPTE
   +0x020 FailureCount      : 0xfffff800`02a7e75c  -> 0
   +0x028 Vm                : 0xfffff800`02a56440 _MMSUPPORT
   +0x030 TotalSystemPtes   : 0n0
   +0x034 TotalFreeSystemPtes : 0n0
   +0x038 CachedPteCount    : 0n0
   +0x03c PteFailures       : 0
   +0x040 SpinLock          : 0
   +0x040 GlobalMutex       : (null)

kd> ?? ((nt!_mi_system_pte_type*) @@(nt!MiSystemPteInfo))->Bitmap
```

```
struct _RTL_BITMAP
   +0x000 SizeOfBitMap      : 8
   +0x008 Buffer            : 0xfffff880`00000000  -> 0xffffffff
```

The control structures are now initialized, including the bitmap buffer addresses. Here is how the first buffer is mapped:

```
kd> !pte @@( ((nt!_mi_system_pte_type*) @@(nt!MiSystemPteInfo))->Bitmap.Buffer )
                                    VA fffff88000000000

PXE at FFFFF6FB7DBEDF88    PPE at FFFFF6FB7DBF1000    PDE at FFFFF6FB7E200000    PTE at FFFFF6FC40000000
contains 000000003C084863  contains 000000003C083863  contains 000000003C082863  contains 000000003C080121
pfn 3c084    ---DA--KWEV  pfn 3c083     ---DA--KWEV  pfn 3c082    ---DA--KWEV  pfn 3c080     -G--A--KREV
```

The first page is mapped to PFN 0x3C080. We can quickly examine the PTEs fo the following pages by dumping the memory content at the PTE address:

```
kd> dq FFFFF6FC40000000
fffff6fc`40000000   00000000`3c080121 00000000`3c080121
fffff6fc`40000010   00000000`3c080121 00000000`3c080121
fffff6fc`40000020   00000000`3c080121 00000000`3c080121
fffff6fc`40000030   00000000`3c080121 00000000`3c080121
fffff6fc`40000040   00000000`3c080121 00000000`3c080121
fffff6fc`40000050   00000000`3c080121 00000000`3c080121
fffff6fc`40000060   00000000`3c080121 00000000`3c080121
fffff6fc`40000070   00000000`3c080121 00000000`3c080121
```

The PTEs all have the same value, i.e. the VAs are all mapped to the same physical page. Note also how the !pte output above shows that these mappings have read-only protection. We can further confirm that all the buffer is mapped this way by dumping the last two PTEs. First, we use !pte again to compute their address:

```
kd> !pte fffff880`00400000 - 2000
                                    VA fffff880003fe000

PXE at FFFFF6FB7DBEDF88    PPE at FFFFF6FB7DBF1000    PDE at FFFFF6FB7E200008    PTE at FFFFF6FC40001FF0
contains 000000003C084863  contains 000000003C083863  contains 000000003C001863  contains 000000003C080121
pfn 3c084    ---DA--KWEV  pfn 3c083     ---DA--KWEV  pfn 3c001    ---DA--KWEV  pfn 3c080     -G--A--KREV


kd> dq FFFFF6FC40001FF0 12
fffff6fc`40001ff0   00000000`3c080121 00000000`3c080121
```

The content visible with this mapping is a page filled with 0xFF:

```
kd> db ffffff880`00000000
fffff880`00000000   ff ff ff ff ff ff ff ff-ff ff ff ff ff ff ff ff   ................
fffff880`00000010   ff ff ff ff ff ff ff ff-ff ff ff ff ff ff ff ff   ................
fffff880`00000020   ff ff ff ff ff ff ff ff-ff ff ff ff ff ff ff ff   ................
fffff880`00000030   ff ff ff ff ff ff ff ff-ff ff ff ff ff ff ff ff   ................
fffff880`00000040   ff ff ff ff ff ff ff ff-ff ff ff ff ff ff ff ff   ................
fffff880`00000050   ff ff ff ff ff ff ff ff-ff ff ff ff ff ff ff ff   ................
fffff880`00000060   ff ff ff ff ff ff ff ff-ff ff ff ff ff ff ff ff   ................
```

```
fffff880`00000070  ff ff ff ff ff ff ff ff-ff ff ff ff ff ff ff ff   ................
```

The second buffer is mapped in the same way:

```
kd> !pte @@( ((nt!_mi_system_pte_type*) @@(nt!MiKernelStackPteInfo))->Bitmap.Buffer )
                                    VA fffff88000400000

PXE at FFFFF6FB7DBEDF88    PPE at FFFFF6FB7DBF1000    PDE at FFFFF6FB7E200010    PTE at FFFFF6FC40002000
contains 000000003C084863  contains 000000003C083863  contains 000000003C106863  contains 000000003C080121
pfn 3c084    ---DA--KWEV  pfn 3c083    ---DA--KWEV  pfn 3c106    ---DA--KWEV  pfn 3c080    -G--A--KREV
```

```
kd> dq FFFFF6FC40002000
fffff6fc`40002000  00000000`3c080121 00000000`3c080121
fffff6fc`40002010  00000000`3c080121 00000000`3c080121
fffff6fc`40002020  00000000`3c080121 00000000`3c080121
fffff6fc`40002030  00000000`3c080121 00000000`3c080121
fffff6fc`40002040  00000000`3c080121 00000000`3c080121
fffff6fc`40002050  00000000`3c080121 00000000`3c080121
fffff6fc`40002060  00000000`3c080121 00000000`3c080121
fffff6fc`40002070  00000000`3c080121 00000000`3c080121
```

This allows us to confirm that the second buffer size is 4MB, by observing that the mapping is set up this way exactly up to the end address resulting from this size. The following `!pte` output gives us the address of the PTE for the last page of the 4MB range:

```
kd> !pte @@( ((nt!_mi_system_pte_type*) @@(nt!MiKernelStackPteInfo))->Bitmap.Buffer ) +
400000 - 1000

                                    VA fffff880007ff000

PXE at FFFFF6FB7DBEDF88    PPE at FFFFF6FB7DBF1000    PDE at FFFFF6FB7E200018    PTE at FFFFF6FC40003FF8
contains 000000003C084863  contains 000000003C083863  contains 000000003C105863  contains 000000003C080121
pfn 3c084    ---DA--KWEV  pfn 3c083    ---DA--KWEV  pfn 3c105    ---DA--KWEV  pfn 3c080    -G--A--KREV
```

And below is the PTEs content:

```
kd> dq FFFFF6FC40003FF8
fffff6fc`40003ff8  00000000`3c080121 ????????`????????
fffff6fc`40004008  ????????`???????? ????????`????????
fffff6fc`40004018  ????????`???????? ????????`????????
fffff6fc`40004028  ????????`???????? ????????`????????
fffff6fc`40004038  ????????`???????? ????????`????????
fffff6fc`40004048  ????????`???????? ????????`????????
fffff6fc`40004058  ????????`???????? ????????`????????
fffff6fc`40004068  ????????`???????? ????????`????????
```

confirming that a 4MB range is mapped to PFN 0x3C080.

44.8.2.6.2   Bitmaps Expansion

To go on with our analysis, we will now set a few breakpoints. The first one will be on *MiExpandPtes*, which is called to expand the range covered by the secondary bitmaps (which so far is empty). Another one will be for writes to the first qword of the master bitmap buffer, to intercept code allocating VAs from there. Two more breakpoints will catch writes to `_MI_SYSTEM_PTE_TYPE.Bitmap.SizeOfBitMap`, so that we can break when the secondary bitmaps are being expanded. Note that `SizeOfBitmap` is at offset 0 inside the `_MI_SYSTEM_PTE_TYPE` structure, so the breakpoint will be at the structure instance addresses. This is our breakpoint list:

```
kd> bl
 0 e fffff800`0290eef0     0001 (0001) nt!MiExpandPtes
 1 e fffff800`02a80b00 w 8 0001 (0001) nt!MiSystemPteBits
 2 e fffff800`02a7dec0 w 4 0001 (0001) nt!MiKernelStackPteInfo
 3 e fffff800`02a7e720 w 4 0001 (0001) nt!MiSystemPteInfo
```

The first breakpoint hit is the one on *MiExpandPtes*:

```
kd> g
Breakpoint 0 hit
nt!MiExpandPtes:
fffff800`0290eef0 48895c2408      mov     qword ptr [rsp+8],rbx
kd> k
Child-SP          RetAddr           Call Site
fffff800`00b9c4a8 fffff800`028ad9ec nt!MiExpandPtes
fffff800`00b9c4b0 fffff800`02b0ba7c nt!MiReservePtes+0x5e4
fffff800`00b9c540 fffff800`02df0e96 nt!MmInitializeProcessor+0x1c
fffff800`00b9c570 fffff800`02df51e5 nt!MmInitNucleus+0x236
fffff800`00b9c600 fffff800`02dfa205 nt!MmInitSystem+0x15
fffff800`00b9c630 fffff800`02b18cce nt!InitBootProcessor+0x385
fffff800`00b9c860 fffff800`02b05d7c nt!KiInitializeKernel+0x84e
fffff800`00b9cbf0 00000000`00000000 nt!KiSystemStartup+0x19c
```

`rcx` is set to the address of the control structure for the bitmap to expand, which for this call is MiKernelStackPteInfo:

```
kd> ln @rcx
(fffff800`02a7dec0)   nt!MiKernelStackPteInfo   |   (fffff800`02a7e710)
nt!MiPteTrackingBitmap
Exact matches:
    nt!MiKernelStackPteInfo = <no type information>
```

We will also see shortly that `rdx` is set to the number of pages to allocate to the bitmap, so this call is allocating 0x40 pages:

```
kd> r
rax=0000000000000000 rbx=fffff80002a43e80 rcx=fffff80002a7dec0
rdx=0000000000000040 rsi=fffff80002a7dec0 rdi=0000000000000040
rip=fffff8000290eef0 rsp=fffff80000b9c4a8 rbp=fffff88000400000
 r8=0000000000000000  r9=0000000000000007 r10=ffffffffffffffff
r11=0000000000000040 r12=00000000ffffffff r13=0000000000000001
r14=0000000000000000 r15=0000000000000001
iopl=0         nv up ei ng nz na po cy
cs=0010  ss=0018  ds=002b  es=002b  fs=0053  gs=002b             efl=00000287
nt!MiExpandPtes:
```

```
fffff800`0290eef0 48895c2408      mov     qword ptr [rsp+8],rbx
ss:0018:fffff800`00b9c4b0={nt!MiKernelStackPteInfo (fffff800`02a7dec0)}
```

The master bitmap allocates virtual addresses in 2MB blocks, which amount to 0x200 pages, so this amount will actually be allocated to the secondary bitmap, with only 0x40 of them used and the rest available for further allocations.

Before resuming execution, we add one more breakpoint for the current thread to the return address from *MiExpandPtes*, so that we will know when the call to this function is complete:

```
kd> bp /t @$thread fffff800`028ad9ec
kd> bl
 0 e fffff800`0290eef0      0001 (0001)  nt!MiExpandPtes
 1 e fffff800`02a80b00  w 8 0001 (0001)  nt!MiSystemPteBits
 2 e fffff800`02a7dec0  w 4 0001 (0001)  nt!MiKernelStackPteInfo
 3 e fffff800`02a7e720  w 4 0001 (0001)  nt!MiSystemPteInfo
 4 e fffff800`028ad9ec      0001 (0001)  nt!MiReservePtes+0x5e4
     Match thread data fffff800`02a51c40
```

When we resume execution we see the breakpoint on the master bitmap buffer being hit:

```
kd> g
Breakpoint 1 hit
nt!RtlSetBits+0x3d:
fffff800`028e218d 488b742440      mov     rsi,qword ptr [rsp+40h]

kd> k
Child-SP          RetAddr           Call Site
fffff800`00b9c2f0 fffff800`0290e0e5 nt!RtlSetBits+0x3d
fffff800`00b9c320 fffff800`0290ef57 nt!MiObtainSystemVa+0x2c5
fffff800`00b9c410 fffff800`028ad9ec nt!MiExpandPtes+0x67
fffff800`00b9c4b0 fffff800`02b0ba7c nt!MiReservePtes+0x5e4
fffff800`00b9c540 fffff800`02df0e96 nt!MmInitializeProcessor+0x1c
fffff800`00b9c570 fffff800`02df51e5 nt!MmInitNucleus+0x236
fffff800`00b9c600 fffff800`02dfa205 nt!MmInitSystem+0x15
fffff800`00b9c630 fffff800`02b18cce nt!InitBootProcessor+0x385
fffff800`00b9c860 fffff800`02b05d7c nt!KiInitializeKernel+0x84e
fffff800`00b9cbf0 00000000`00000000 nt!KiSystemStartup+0x19c
```

It's interesting to observe how MiExpandPtes has called MiObtainSystemVa, which is the general VA allocation routine used also for other system regions.

Below we find how the master bitmap buffer has changed:

```
kd> dq @@( ((nt!_rtl_bitmap*) @@(nt!MiSystemPteBitmap))->Buffer) l 1
fffff800`02a80b00  00000000`0000001f
```

The first byte changed from 0xF to 0x1F, i.e. 1 PDE has been allocated, corresponding to the range 0xFFFFF880`00800000 - 0XFFFFF880`00BFFFFF.

Resuming execution, we break on the updating of the secondary bitmap size:

```
kd> g
Breakpoint 2 hit
nt!MiExpandPtes+0x33a:
fffff800`0290f22a e92ffeffff      jmp      nt!MiExpandPtes+0x16e (fffff800`0290f05e)

kd> bl
 0 e fffff800`0290eef0     0001 (0001) nt!MiExpandPtes
 1 e fffff800`02a80b00 w 8 0001 (0001) nt!MiSystemPteBits
 2 e fffff800`02a7dec0 w 4 0001 (0001) nt!MiKernelStackPteInfo
 3 e fffff800`02a7e720 w 4 0001 (0001) nt!MiSystemPteInfo
 4 e fffff800`028ad9ec     0001 (0001) nt!MiReservePtes+0x5e4
     Match thread data fffff800`02a51c40
```

The secondary bitmap has now changed. For one thing, the first buffer page is now mapped to a different page, with read/write protection:

```
kd> !pte @@( ((nt!_mi_system_pte_type*) @@(nt!MiKernelStackPteInfo))->Bitmap.Buffer )
                         VA fffff88000400000

PXE at FFFFF6FB7DBEDF88   PPE at FFFFF6FB7DBF1000   PDE at FFFFF6FB7E200010   PTE at FFFFF6FC40002000
contains 000000003C084863 contains 000000003C083863 contains 000000003C106863 contains 000000003C088963
pfn 3c084    ---DA--KWEV  pfn 3c083    ---DA--KWEV  pfn 3c106    ---DA--KWEV  pfn 3c088    -G-DA--KWEV
```

The buffer size changed from 8 to 0xA00:

```
kd> ?? ((nt!_mi_system_pte_type*) @@(nt!MiKernelStackPteInfo))->Bitmap
struct _RTL_BITMAP
   +0x000 SizeOfBitMap     : 0xa00
   +0x008 Buffer           : 0xfffff880`00400000  -> 0xffffffff
```

Let's see how this value is computed: in the master bitmap 4 bits were already set for the buffers range, corresponding to 8MB or 0x800 pages. Now a bit has been allocated, i.e. a PDE, for a size of 2MB or 0x200 pages. The secondary bitmap is now including this whole range: the first 0x800 pages have been included as in-use, i.e. as set bits and the last 0x200 as pages actually available for allocations from this bitmap. In the buffer, this corresponds to a byte range of

   0xA00 / 8 = 0x140 bytes

which is completely contained in the first virtual page, now mapped to a real, updatable page. At this stage, the buffer range is full of 0xFF as if all the pages were in-use, but we will see that upon returning from *MiExpandPtes* free pages will have their bits zeroed:

```
kd> dq @@( ((nt!_mi_system_pte_type*) @@(nt!MiKernelStackPteInfo))->Bitmap.Buffer ) l
140 /8
fffff880`00400000  ffffffff`ffffffff ffffffff`ffffffff
fffff880`00400010  ffffffff`ffffffff ffffffff`ffffffff
fffff880`00400020  ffffffff`ffffffff ffffffff`ffffffff
fffff880`00400030  ffffffff`ffffffff ffffffff`ffffffff
fffff880`00400040  ffffffff`ffffffff ffffffff`ffffffff
fffff880`00400050  ffffffff`ffffffff ffffffff`ffffffff
```

```
fffff880`00400060   ffffffff`ffffffff ffffffff`ffffffff
fffff880`00400070   ffffffff`ffffffff ffffffff`ffffffff
fffff880`00400080   ffffffff`ffffffff ffffffff`ffffffff
fffff880`00400090   ffffffff`ffffffff ffffffff`ffffffff
fffff880`004000a0   ffffffff`ffffffff ffffffff`ffffffff
fffff880`004000b0   ffffffff`ffffffff ffffffff`ffffffff
fffff880`004000c0   ffffffff`ffffffff ffffffff`ffffffff
fffff880`004000d0   ffffffff`ffffffff ffffffff`ffffffff
fffff880`004000e0   ffffffff`ffffffff ffffffff`ffffffff
fffff880`004000f0   ffffffff`ffffffff ffffffff`ffffffff
fffff880`00400100   ffffffff`ffffffff ffffffff`ffffffff
fffff880`00400110   ffffffff`ffffffff ffffffff`ffffffff
fffff880`00400120   ffffffff`ffffffff ffffffff`ffffffff
fffff880`00400130   ffffffff`ffffffff ffffffff`ffffffff
```

Resuming execution again, we hit the breakpoint on the return address from *MiExpandPtes*:

```
kd> g
Breakpoint 4 hit
nt!MiReservePtes+0x5e4:
fffff800`028ad9ec 4885c0          test    rax,rax
kd> bl
 0 e fffff800`0290eef0     0001 (0001) nt!MiExpandPtes
 1 e fffff800`02a80b00 w 8 0001 (0001) nt!MiSystemPteBits
 2 e fffff800`02a7dec0 w 4 0001 (0001) nt!MiKernelStackPteInfo
 3 e fffff800`02a7e720 w 4 0001 (0001) nt!MiSystemPteInfo
 4 e fffff800`028ad9ec     0001 (0001) nt!MiReservePtes+0x5e4
     Match thread data fffff800`02a51c40
```

Now the buffer shows some zeroes:

```
kd> dq @@( ((nt!_mi_system_pte_type*) @@(nt!MiKernelStackPteInfo))->Bitmap.Buffer ) 1
140 / 8
fffff880`00400000   ffffffff`ffffffff ffffffff`ffffffff
fffff880`00400010   ffffffff`ffffffff ffffffff`ffffffff
fffff880`00400020   ffffffff`ffffffff ffffffff`ffffffff
fffff880`00400030   ffffffff`ffffffff ffffffff`ffffffff
fffff880`00400040   ffffffff`ffffffff ffffffff`ffffffff
fffff880`00400050   ffffffff`ffffffff ffffffff`ffffffff
fffff880`00400060   ffffffff`ffffffff ffffffff`ffffffff
fffff880`00400070   ffffffff`ffffffff ffffffff`ffffffff
fffff880`00400080   ffffffff`ffffffff ffffffff`ffffffff
fffff880`00400090   ffffffff`ffffffff ffffffff`ffffffff
fffff880`004000a0   ffffffff`ffffffff ffffffff`ffffffff
fffff880`004000b0   ffffffff`ffffffff ffffffff`ffffffff
fffff880`004000c0   ffffffff`ffffffff ffffffff`ffffffff
fffff880`004000d0   ffffffff`ffffffff ffffffff`ffffffff
fffff880`004000e0   ffffffff`ffffffff ffffffff`ffffffff
fffff880`004000f0   ffffffff`ffffffff ffffffff`ffffffff
fffff880`00400100   ffffffff`ffffffff 00000000`00000000
fffff880`00400110   00000000`00000000 00000000`00000000
fffff880`00400120   00000000`00000000 00000000`00000000
fffff880`00400130   00000000`00000000 00000000`00000000
```

Let's examine its content in more detail: bytes 0 - 0xFF correspond to bit indexes 0 - 0x7ff, which cover the first 8MB of address space. These bits have been incorporated as set in the bitmap, since they were already set in the master one. From 0x100 begin the 0x200 bits of the PDE just assigned to this bitmap. Of these, the first 64 or 0x40 are set, which is consistent with the value of rdx when *MiExpandPtes* was called.

This shows how the bitmap has been extended to encompass all the already allocated pages and the new ones assigned to it.

We can also see that the return value from *MiExpandPtes* is the address of the PTE mapping the beginning of the range assigned to the bitmap:

```
kd> r
rax=fffff6fc40004000  rbx=fffff80002a43e80  rcx=0000000000000042
rdx=fffffa800000001e  rsi=fffff80002a7dec0  rdi=0000000000000040
rip=fffff800028ad9ec  rsp=fffff80000b9c4b0  rbp=fffff88000400000
 r8=0000000000000000   r9=0000000000000001  r10=0000000000000000
r11=0000000000000001  r12=00000000ffffffff  r13=0000000000000001
r14=0000000000000000  r15=0000000000000001
iopl=0         nv up ei ng nz na pe nc
cs=0010  ss=0018  ds=002b  es=002b  fs=0053  gs=002b             efl=00000282
nt!MiReservePtes+0x5e4:
fffff800`028ad9ec 4885c0          test    rax,rax

kd> !pte @rax
                                        VA fffff88000800000
PXE at FFFFF6FB7DBEDF88   PPE at FFFFF6FB7DBF1000   PDE at FFFFF6FB7E200020   PTE at FFFFF6FC40004000
contains 000000003C084863  contains 000000003C083863  contains 000000003C089863  contains 0000000000000000
pfn 3c084     ---DA--KWEV  pfn 3c083     ---DA--KWEV  pfn 3c089     ---DA--KWEV  not valid
```

Now we will remove the breakpoint on the return address from *MiExpandPtes* and resume execution. We will see the same process repeated to expand the MiSystemPteInfo secondary bitmap and we will see how this bitmap will incorporate all the range covered by MiKernelStackPteInfo and will extend for an additional 0x200 pages.

```
kd> bc4
kd> g
Breakpoint 0 hit
nt!MiExpandPtes:
fffff800`0290eef0 48895c2408      mov     qword ptr [rsp+8],rbx
```

It's always interesting to look at the stack to see what's going on:

```
kd> k
Child-SP          RetAddr           Call Site
fffff800`00b9c428 fffff800`0285f3d8 nt!MiExpandPtes
fffff800`00b9c430 fffff800`02df39f3 nt! ?? ::FNODOBFM::`string'+0x1cfc6
fffff800`00b9c4a0 fffff800`02df46ec nt!MiInitializeBootProcess+0x3e3
fffff800`00b9c570 fffff800`02df51f3 nt!MiInitSystem+0xac
```

```
fffff800`00b9c600 fffff800`02dfa205 nt!MmInitSystem+0x23
fffff800`00b9c630 fffff800`02b18cce nt!InitBootProcessor+0x385
fffff800`00b9c860 fffff800`02b05d7c nt!KiInitializeKernel+0x84e
fffff800`00b9cbf0 00000000`00000000 nt!KiSystemStartup+0x19c
```

`rcx` and `rdx` give us the bitmap being expanded and the number of pages to allocate:

```
kd> ln @rcx
(fffff800`02a7e720)   nt!MiSystemPteInfo   |   (fffff800`02a7ef68)   nt!MiAdjustCounter
Exact matches:
    nt!MiSystemPteInfo = <no type information>
kd> r @rdx
rdx=0000000000000001
```

Even though just one page is requested, the bitmap must be expanded, because now it's empty.

Again, we set a breakpoint on the return address from *MiExpandPtes* and resume, hitting breakpoint #1 on the updating of the master bitmap:

```
kd> bp /t @$thread fffff800`0285f3d8
kd> g
Breakpoint 1 hit
nt!RtlSetBits+0x3d:
fffff800`028e218d 488b742440      mov     rsi,qword ptr [rsp+40h]
kd> bl
 0 e fffff800`0290eef0     0001 (0001) nt!MiExpandPtes
 1 e fffff800`02a80b00 w 8 0001 (0001) nt!MiSystemPteBits
 2 e fffff800`02a7dec0 w 4 0001 (0001) nt!MiKernelStackPteInfo
 3 e fffff800`02a7e720 w 4 0001 (0001) nt!MiSystemPteInfo
 4 e fffff800`0285f3d8     0001 (0001) nt! ?? ::FNODOBFM::`string'+0x1cfc6
    Match thread data fffff800`02a51c40
```

We can see how another PDE has been allocated, which results in the bitmap changing from 0x1F to 0x3F:

```
kd> dq @@( ((nt!_rtl_bitmap*) @@(nt!MiSystemPteBitmap))->Buffer) l 1
fffff800`02a80b00  00000000`0000003f
```

Resuming execution, we hit breakpoint #3 on the updating of the bitmap controlled by MiSystemPteInfo. We see that its buffer is now mapped to a normal physical page:

```
kd> g
Breakpoint 3 hit
nt!MiExpandPtes+0x33a:
fffff800`0290f22a e92ffeffff      jmp     nt!MiExpandPtes+0x16e (fffff800`0290f05e)
kd> bl
 0 e fffff800`0290eef0     0001 (0001) nt!MiExpandPtes
 1 e fffff800`02a80b00 w 8 0001 (0001) nt!MiSystemPteBits
 2 e fffff800`02a7dec0 w 4 0001 (0001) nt!MiKernelStackPteInfo
 3 e fffff800`02a7e720 w 4 0001 (0001) nt!MiSystemPteInfo
 4 e fffff800`0285f3d8     0001 (0001) nt! ?? ::FNODOBFM::`string'+0x1cfc6
```

```
       Match thread data fffff800`02a51c40

kd> !pte @@( ((nt!_mi_system_pte_type*) @@(nt!MiSystemPteInfo))->Bitmap.Buffer )
                                        VA fffff88000000000

PXE at FFFFF6FB7DBEDF88    PPE at FFFFF6FB7DBF1000    PDE at FFFFF6FB7E200000    PTE at FFFFF6FC40000000
contains 000000003C084863  contains 000000003C083863  contains 000000003C082863  contains 000000003C08A963
pfn 3c084    ---DA--KWEV  pfn 3c083    ---DA--KWEV  pfn 3c082    ---DA--KWEV  pfn 3c08a    -G-DA--KWEV
```

and that the buffer size has been increased:

```
kd> ?? ((nt!_mi_system_pte_type*) @@(nt!MiSystemPteInfo))->Bitmap
struct _RTL_BITMAP
   +0x000 SizeOfBitMap     : 0xc00
   +0x008 Buffer           : 0xfffff880`00000000  -> 0xffffffff
```

We saw earlier that the other secondary bitmap was expanded up to page 0xA00. This one
has now been expanded to include 0x200 pages beyond that, corresponding to 1 PDE. When
we resume execution, we hit breakpoint #4 on the return address from *MiExpandPtes*, where
we see the buffer of the secondary bitmap with the expected zeroes:

```
kd> g
Breakpoint 4 hit
nt! ?? ::FNODOBFM::`string'+0x1cfc6:
fffff800`0285f3d8 4885c0          test    rax,rax

kd> bl
 0 e fffff800`0290eef0     0001 (0001) nt!MiExpandPtes
 1 e fffff800`02a80b00 w 8 0001 (0001) nt!MiSystemPteBits
 2 e fffff800`02a7dec0 w 4 0001 (0001) nt!MiKernelStackPteInfo
 3 e fffff800`02a7e720 w 4 0001 (0001) nt!MiSystemPteInfo
 4 e fffff800`0285f3d8     0001 (0001) nt! ?? ::FNODOBFM::`string'+0x1cfc6
    Match thread data fffff800`02a51c40

kd> dq @@( ((nt!_mi_system_pte_type*) @@(nt!MiSystemPteInfo))->Bitmap.Buffer ) l @@(
((nt!_mi_system_pte_type*) @@(nt!MiSystemPteInfo))->Bitmap.SizeOfBitMap ) / 40
fffff880`00000000  ffffffff`ffffffff ffffffff`ffffffff
fffff880`00000010  ffffffff`ffffffff ffffffff`ffffffff
fffff880`00000020  ffffffff`ffffffff ffffffff`ffffffff
fffff880`00000030  ffffffff`ffffffff ffffffff`ffffffff
fffff880`00000040  ffffffff`ffffffff ffffffff`ffffffff
fffff880`00000050  ffffffff`ffffffff ffffffff`ffffffff
fffff880`00000060  ffffffff`ffffffff ffffffff`ffffffff
fffff880`00000070  ffffffff`ffffffff ffffffff`ffffffff
fffff880`00000080  ffffffff`ffffffff ffffffff`ffffffff
fffff880`00000090  ffffffff`ffffffff ffffffff`ffffffff
fffff880`000000a0  ffffffff`ffffffff ffffffff`ffffffff
fffff880`000000b0  ffffffff`ffffffff ffffffff`ffffffff
fffff880`000000c0  ffffffff`ffffffff ffffffff`ffffffff
fffff880`000000d0  ffffffff`ffffffff ffffffff`ffffffff
fffff880`000000e0  ffffffff`ffffffff ffffffff`ffffffff
fffff880`000000f0  ffffffff`ffffffff ffffffff`ffffffff
fffff880`00000100  ffffffff`ffffffff ffffffff`ffffffff
fffff880`00000110  ffffffff`ffffffff ffffffff`ffffffff
fffff880`00000120  ffffffff`ffffffff ffffffff`ffffffff
```

```
fffff880`00000130   ffffffff`ffffffff ffffffff`ffffffff
fffff880`00000140   00000000`00000001 00000000`00000000
fffff880`00000150   00000000`00000000 00000000`00000000
fffff880`00000160   00000000`00000000 00000000`00000000
fffff880`00000170   00000000`00000000 00000000`00000000
```

The buffer range up to +0x13F correspond to pages managed by other bitmaps and all its bits are set. At +0x140 are the bits for the last PDE allocated, of which only one is in use, since `rdx` was set to 1 when *MiExpandPtes* was called. As in the previous call, the returned `rax` gives the address of the allocated PTE:

```
kd> !pte @rax
                                        VA fffff88000a00000

PXE at FFFFF6FB7DBEDF88   PPE at FFFFF6FB7DBF1000   PDE at FFFFF6FB7E200028   PTE at FFFFF6FC40005000
contains 000000003C084863 contains 000000003C083863 contains 000000003C08B863 contains 0000000000000000
pfn 3c084    ---DA--KWEV   pfn 3c083    ---DA--KWEV   pfn 3c08b    ---DA--KWEV   not valid
```

We obtain the same value if we compute the address from the index of the set bit, which is bit 0 of the byte at +0x140, hence the offset in the System PTE region is:

offset = 0x140 * 8 * 0x1000 = 0xA00000

Or we can compare it with the index of the bit allocated from the master bitmap, which was bit 5, corresponding to an offset of:

5 * 0x200000 = 0xA00000

Removing breakpoint #4 and resuming execution, we see a few direct allocations from the master bitmap. These can be recognized from the fact that *MiExpandPtes* is not called and breakpoint #1, on the master bitmap update is hit. Bits are allocated without expanding any secondary bitmap. Below we see the first hit and the functions involved:

```
kd> bc4

kd> g
Breakpoint 1 hit
nt!RtlSetBits+0x3d:
fffff800`028e218d 488b742440      mov     rsi,qword ptr [rsp+40h]

kd> bl
 0 e fffff800`0290eef0     0001 (0001)  nt!MiExpandPtes
 1 e fffff800`02a80b00 w 8 0001 (0001)  nt!MiSystemPteBits
 2 e fffff800`02a7dec0 w 4 0001 (0001)  nt!MiKernelStackPteInfo
 3 e fffff800`02a7e720 w 4 0001 (0001)  nt!MiSystemPteInfo

kd> k
Child-SP          RetAddr           Call Site
fffff800`00b9c230 fffff800`0290e0e5 nt!RtlSetBits+0x3d
fffff800`00b9c260 fffff800`02c6de4d nt!MiObtainSystemVa+0x2c5
```

```
fffff800`00b9c350 fffff800`02dd5aee nt!MiReserveDriverPtes+0xad
fffff800`00b9c390 fffff800`02df4724 nt!MiReloadBootLoadedDrivers+0x25e
fffff800`00b9c570 fffff800`02df51f3 nt!MiInitSystem+0xe4
fffff800`00b9c600 fffff800`02dfa205 nt!MmInitSystem+0x23
fffff800`00b9c630 fffff800`02b18cce nt!InitBootProcessor+0x385
fffff800`00b9c860 fffff800`02b05d7c nt!KiInitializeKernel+0x84e
fffff800`00b9cbf0 00000000`00000000 nt!KiSystemStartup+0x19c
```

We can see that the master bitmap has one additional bit set:

```
kd> dq @@( ((nt!_rtl_bitmap*) @@(nt!MiSystemPteBitmap))->Buffer) l 1
fffff800`02a80b00  00000000`0000007f
```

This goes on for several direct allocations, until the master bitmap is set to 0x1FFF. Since there are now 13 bits set, this means that the highest allocated page offset is:

13 * 0x200 - 1 = 0x19FF

meanwhile, the secondary bitmaps are unchanged, so that MiKernelStackPteInfo only covers up to page offset 0x9FF and MiSystemPteInfo goes up to 0xBFF. Finally, an expansion occurs again, this time for MiKernelStackPteInfo, fow which 0x400 pages (2 full PDEs are requested):

```
kd> g
Breakpoint 0 hit
nt!MiExpandPtes:
fffff800`0290eef0 48895c2408      mov     qword ptr [rsp+8],rbx
kd> bl
 0 e fffff800`0290eef0     0001 (0001) nt!MiExpandPtes
 1 e fffff800`02a80b00 w 8 0001 (0001) nt!MiSystemPteBits
 2 e fffff800`02a7dec0 w 4 0001 (0001) nt!MiKernelStackPteInfo
 3 e fffff800`02a7e720 w 4 0001 (0001) nt!MiSystemPteInfo

kd> ln @rcx
(fffff800`02a7dec0)   nt!MiKernelStackPteInfo   |   (fffff800`02a7e710)
nt!MiPteTrackingBitmap
Exact matches:
    nt!MiKernelStackPteInfo = <no type information>
kd> r @rdx
rdx=0000000000000400
```

When we hit breakpoint #1, we see that two bits have been set in the master bitmap:

```
kd> g
Breakpoint 1 hit
nt!RtlSetBits+0x3d:
fffff800`028e218d 488b742440      mov     rsi,qword ptr [rsp+40h]
kd> bl
 0 e fffff800`0290eef0     0001 (0001) nt!MiExpandPtes
 1 e fffff800`02a80b00 w 8 0001 (0001) nt!MiSystemPteBits
 2 e fffff800`02a7dec0 w 4 0001 (0001) nt!MiKernelStackPteInfo
 3 e fffff800`02a7e720 w 4 0001 (0001) nt!MiSystemPteInfo
 4 e fffff800`02ddacc8     0001 (0001) nt!MiBuildPagedPool+0xf8
    Match thread data fffff800`02a51c40
```

```
kd> dq @@( ((nt!_rtl_bitmap*) @@(nt!MiSystemPteBitmap))->Buffer) l 1
fffff800`02a80b00  00000000`00007fff
```

When this expansion begins, the MiKernelStackPteInfo bitmap covers up to page offset
0x9FF, which corresponds to byte 0x13F in its buffer. On the other hand, the master bitmap
records that page offsets up to 0x19FF are in use, so the range 0xA00 - 0x19FF is
incorporated in the bitmap with the corresponding bits set. In terms of byte offsets in the
buffer this gives:

0xA00 / 8 = 0x140

0x19ff / 8 = 0x33F

Also, the starting address of the allocated region will have page offset 0x1A00 and, having
allocated two full PDEs they will require 0x400 bits or 0x80 bytes, bringing the final buffer
size to

0x1A00 + 0x400 = 0x1E00 (in bits) or

0x400 + 0x80 = 0x480 (in bytes).

This is consistent with what we see when we return from *MiExpandPtes*:

```
kd> ?? ((nt!_mi_system_pte_type*) @@(nt!MiKernelStackPteInfo))->Bitmap
struct _RTL_BITMAP
   +0x000 SizeOfBitMap     : 0x1e00
   +0x008 Buffer           : 0xfffff880`00400000  -> 0xffffffff
kd> dq @@( ((nt!_mi_system_pte_type*) @@(nt!MiKernelStackPteInfo))->Bitmap.Buffer ) l
@@( ((nt!_mi_system_pte_type*) @@(nt!MiKernelStackPteInfo))->Bitmap.SizeOfBitMap ) / 40
fffff880`00400000  ffffffff`ffffffff ffffffff`ffffffff
fffff880`00400010  ffffffff`ffffffff ffffffff`ffffffff
fffff880`00400020  ffffffff`ffffffff ffffffff`ffffffff
fffff880`00400030  ffffffff`ffffffff ffffffff`ffffffff
fffff880`00400040  ffffffff`ffffffff ffffffff`ffffffff
fffff880`00400050  ffffffff`ffffffff ffffffff`ffffffff
fffff880`00400060  ffffffff`ffffffff ffffffff`ffffffff
fffff880`00400070  ffffffff`ffffffff ffffffff`ffffffff
fffff880`00400080  ffffffff`ffffffff ffffffff`ffffffff
fffff880`00400090  ffffffff`ffffffff ffffffff`ffffffff
fffff880`004000a0  ffffffff`ffffffff ffffffff`ffffffff
fffff880`004000b0  ffffffff`ffffffff ffffffff`ffffffff
fffff880`004000c0  ffffffff`ffffffff ffffffff`ffffffff
fffff880`004000d0  ffffffff`ffffffff ffffffff`ffffffff
fffff880`004000e0  ffffffff`ffffffff ffffffff`ffffffff
fffff880`004000f0  ffffffff`ffffffff ffffffff`ffffffff
fffff880`00400100  ffffffff`ffffffff ffffffff`ffffffff
fffff880`00400110  ffffffff`ffffffff ffffffff`ffffffff
fffff880`00400120  ffffffff`ffffffff 00000001`ffffffff
fffff880`00400130  00000000`00000000 00000000`00000000
```

```
fffff880`00400140   ffffffff`ffffffff ffffffff`ffffffff
fffff880`00400150   ffffffff`ffffffff ffffffff`ffffffff
fffff880`00400160   ffffffff`ffffffff ffffffff`ffffffff
fffff880`00400170   ffffffff`ffffffff ffffffff`ffffffff
fffff880`00400180   ffffffff`ffffffff ffffffff`ffffffff
fffff880`00400190   ffffffff`ffffffff ffffffff`ffffffff
fffff880`004001a0   ffffffff`ffffffff ffffffff`ffffffff
fffff880`004001b0   ffffffff`ffffffff ffffffff`ffffffff
fffff880`004001c0   ffffffff`ffffffff ffffffff`ffffffff
fffff880`004001d0   ffffffff`ffffffff ffffffff`ffffffff
fffff880`004001e0   ffffffff`ffffffff ffffffff`ffffffff
fffff880`004001f0   ffffffff`ffffffff ffffffff`ffffffff
fffff880`00400200   ffffffff`ffffffff ffffffff`ffffffff
fffff880`00400210   ffffffff`ffffffff ffffffff`ffffffff
fffff880`00400220   ffffffff`ffffffff ffffffff`ffffffff
fffff880`00400230   ffffffff`ffffffff ffffffff`ffffffff
fffff880`00400240   ffffffff`ffffffff ffffffff`ffffffff
fffff880`00400250   ffffffff`ffffffff ffffffff`ffffffff
fffff880`00400260   ffffffff`ffffffff ffffffff`ffffffff
fffff880`00400270   ffffffff`ffffffff ffffffff`ffffffff
fffff880`00400280   ffffffff`ffffffff ffffffff`ffffffff
fffff880`00400290   ffffffff`ffffffff ffffffff`ffffffff
fffff880`004002a0   ffffffff`ffffffff ffffffff`ffffffff
fffff880`004002b0   ffffffff`ffffffff ffffffff`ffffffff
fffff880`004002c0   ffffffff`ffffffff ffffffff`ffffffff
fffff880`004002d0   ffffffff`ffffffff ffffffff`ffffffff
fffff880`004002e0   ffffffff`ffffffff ffffffff`ffffffff
fffff880`004002f0   ffffffff`ffffffff ffffffff`ffffffff
fffff880`00400300   ffffffff`ffffffff ffffffff`ffffffff
fffff880`00400310   ffffffff`ffffffff ffffffff`ffffffff
fffff880`00400320   ffffffff`ffffffff ffffffff`ffffffff
fffff880`00400330   ffffffff`ffffffff ffffffff`ffffffff
fffff880`00400340   ffffffff`ffffffff ffffffff`ffffffff
fffff880`00400350   ffffffff`ffffffff ffffffff`ffffffff
fffff880`00400360   ffffffff`ffffffff ffffffff`ffffffff
fffff880`00400370   ffffffff`ffffffff ffffffff`ffffffff
fffff880`00400380   ffffffff`ffffffff ffffffff`ffffffff
fffff880`00400390   ffffffff`ffffffff ffffffff`ffffffff
fffff880`004003a0   ffffffff`ffffffff ffffffff`ffffffff
fffff880`004003b0   ffffffff`ffffffff ffffffff`ffffffff
```

We see that at the end of the previous bitmap expansion, below +0x140, there were still a few available pages, but not enough to satisfy the current request for 0x400 ones. All the bits in the expansion range are set to 1, since the allocation covered exactly 2 full PDEs. Finally, the address corresponding to the PTE returned by *MiExpandPtes* is:

```
kd> !pte @rax
                                  VA fffff88001a00000
PXE at FFFFF6FB7DBEDF88   PPE at FFFFF6FB7DBF1000   PDE at FFFFF6FB7E200068   PTE at FFFFF6FC4000D000
contains 000000003C084863 contains 000000003C083863 contains 0000000000BD0863 contains 0000000000000000
pfn 3c084     ---DA--KWEV pfn 3c083    ---DA--KWEV pfn bd0      ---DA--KWEV not valid
```

as expected.

This confirms that the expansion of a secondary bitmap can take place after direct allocations from the master one. The bitmap is expanded to include all the in-use range and the newly allocated one, which is returned to the caller.

44.8.2.6.3   Relationship Between Bit Index and Virtual Address (MiSystemPteInfo)

This section gives further evidence of the fact that the bit index in MiSystemPteInfo represents a page offset in the System PTE region.

To capture the data presented here, a data breakpoint has been used on the bitmap buffer. The problem with this approach, was the need to know in advance *which* bits in the buffer were going to be set in response to an allocation from the bitmap, in order to place the data breakpoint on the right QWORD. This has been solved by looking at _MI_SYSTEM_PTE_TYPE.Hint, which appears to be the index at which the VMM starts looking for free pages in the bitmap.

For this test, we are going to use MemTests to call *MmMapLockedPagesSpecifyCache*, which allocates from MiSystemPteInfo.

First, we allocate a private buffer of 4 pages, then, from the system range tests menu, we initialize an MDL for it and probe and lock its pages. Finally, we call *MmMapLockePagesSpecifyCache* on the MDL, requesting a kernel mode mapping. When MemTests is about to call the driver, it displays a prompt where we can enter b to break into the debugger.

When the debugger takes control, the current thread is the MemTests one, so we can place a breakpoint on *MmMapLockedPagesSpecifyCache* for it and resume execution:

```
1: kd> bp /t @$thread nt!MmMapLockedPagesSpecifyCache
1: kd> g


KernelAllocs - MmMapLockedPagesSpecifyCacheTest
KernelAllocs - About to call MmMapLockedPagesSpecifyCache()
KernelAllocs     MemoryDescriptorList = 0xFFFFFA8003104010
KernelAllocs     AccessMode       = 0x0
KernelAllocs     CacheType        = 0x1
KernelAllocs     BaseAddress      = 0x0000000000000000
Breakpoint 0 hit
nt!MmMapLockedPagesSpecifyCache:
fffff800`0288f570 488bc4          mov     rax,rsp
```

We then extract the hint from MiSystemPteInfo:

```
1: kd> ?? ((nt!_mi_system_PTE_type *) @@(nt!MiSystemPteInfo))
struct _MI_SYSTEM_PTE_TYPE * 0xfffff800`02a34720
   +0x000 Bitmap           : _RTL_BITMAP
   +0x010 Flags            : 3
   +0x014 Hint             : 0xc446
   +0x018 BasePte          : 0xfffff6fc`40000000 _MMPTE
   +0x020 FailureCount     : 0xfffff800`02a3475c  -> 0
   +0x028 Vm               : 0xfffff800`02a0c440 _MMSUPPORT
   +0x030 TotalSystemPtes  : 0n4096
   +0x034 TotalFreeSystemPtes : 0n3223
   +0x038 CachedPteCount   : 0n0
   +0x03c PteFailures      : 0
   +0x040 SpinLock         : 0
   +0x040 GlobalMutex      : (null)
```

then, we can confirm that the bit pointed by the hint is clear:

```
1: kd> dq fffff880`00000000 + c446 / 8
fffff880`00001888  00000000`00000000 00000000`00000000
```

Afterwards, we place a breakpoint on the byte pointed by the hint and resume execution:

```
1: kd> ba w 8 /t @$thread fffff880`00000000 + c446 / 8
1: kd> g
Breakpoint 1 hit
nt!MmMapLockedPagesSpecifyCache+0x267:
fffff800`0288f7d7 0f858d060000    jne     nt!MmMapLockedPagesSpecifyCache+0x90a
(fffff800`0288fe6a)

1: kd> k
Child-SP          RetAddr           Call Site
fffff880`0522e890 fffff880`04579963 nt!MmMapLockedPagesSpecifyCache+0x267
fffff880`0522e950 fffff880`04578554 krnlallocs!MmMapLockedPagesSpecifyCacheTest+0x233
[b:\programm\wntsys\vmmtests\kernelallocs\driver\drvmain.cpp @ 1210]
fffff880`0522e9c0 fffff800`02b993a7 krnlallocs!DispatchDioc+0x164
[b:\programm\wntsys\vmmtests\kernelallocs\driver\drvmain.cpp @ 492]
fffff880`0522ea10 fffff800`02b99c06 nt!IopXxxControlFile+0x607
fffff880`0522eb40 fffff800`02880153 nt!NtDeviceIoControlFile+0x56
fffff880`0522ebb0 00000000`777fff2a nt!KiSystemServiceCopyEnd+0x13
00000000`0017fbb8 000007fe`fda7b399 ntdll!NtDeviceIoControlFile+0xa
00000000`0017fbc0 00000000`776a610f KernelBase!DeviceIoControl+0x75
00000000`0017fc30 00000001`3fba59db kernel32!DeviceIoControlImplementation+0x7f
00000000`0017fc80 00000000`00000000 0x1`3fba59db
```

After the hit, the bitmap has changed as follows:

```
1: kd> dq fffff880`00000000 + c446 / 8
fffff880`00001888  00000000`000003c0 00000000`00000000
```

Bits 6,7,8,9 are now set, as many as the pages we are locking. The byte offset of the bit pointed by the hint is given by:

```
1: kd> ? c446 % 8
Evaluate expression: 6 = 00000000`00000006
```

which is consistent with bit 6 being the first bit set.

If we assume that each bit in the bitmap represents a page in the System PTE region, the address corresponding to the first bit set is:

```
1: kd> ? c446 * 1000 + fffff880`00000000
Evaluate expression: -8246131400704 = fffff880`0c446000
```

Right now, the PTEs for this address and for the next 3 pages are not valid:

```
1: kd> !pte c446 * 1000 + fffff880`00000000
                                        VA fffff8800c446000

PXE at FFFFF6FB7DBEDF88    PPE at FFFFF6FB7DBF1000    PDE at FFFFF6FB7E200310    PTE at FFFFF6FC40062230
contains 000000003C084863  contains 000000003C083863  contains 000000003ADB0863  contains 0000000000000000
pfn 3c084    ---DA--KWEV   pfn 3c083    ---DA--KWEV    pfn 3adb0    ---DA--KWEV   not valid


1: kd> dq FFFFF6FC40062230 l 4
fffff6fc`40062230  00000000`00000000 00000000`00000000
fffff6fc`40062240  00000000`00000000 00000000`00000000
```

Now we let *MmMapLockedPagesSpecifyCache* complete and see how the situation changes:

```
1: kd> g @$ra
krnlallocs!MmMapLockedPagesSpecifyCacheTest+0x233:
fffff880`04579963 4889442440       mov     qword ptr [rsp+40h],rax
1: kd> r
rax=fffff8800c446000 rbx=ffffa80014ecf20 rcx=0000000000000001
rdx=0000000000000000 rsi=ffffa80014ecf20 rdi=ffffa8003102d40
rip=fffff88004579963 rsp=fffff8800522e950 rbp=fffff8800522eca0
 r8=0000000038e01000  r9=0000000000000000 r10=0000000000000000
r11=0000ffffffffff000 r12=0000000000000008 r13=0000000000000001
r14=0000000000000001 r15=ffffa80012bc060
iopl=0          nv up ei ng nz na pe nc
cs=0010  ss=0018  ds=002b  es=002b  fs=0053  gs=002b            efl=00000282
krnlallocs!MmMapLockedPagesSpecifyCacheTest+0x233:
fffff880`04579963 4889442440       mov     qword ptr [rsp+40h],rax
ss:0018:fffff880`0522e990=0000000000000001
```

The address returned in `rax` is the one computed from the hint. This confirms the relationship between the index of a bit and the System PTE region. Furthermore, the PTEs are now mapping valid addresses:

```
1: kd> dq FFFFF6FC40062230 l 4
fffff6fc`40062230  00000000`07756963 00000000`24b57963
fffff6fc`40062240  00000000`1dcd8963 00000000`252d9963
```

From the messages printed by the KrnlAllocs driver to the debugger console listed on p. 464, we see that the MDL address is 0xFFFFFA80`03104010. At +0x30 from the start is the array of PFNs mapped by the MDL, which turns out to be:

```
1: kd> dq FFFFFA8003104010 + 30 l 4
fffffa80`03104040  00000000`00007756 00000000`00024b57
fffffa80`03104050  00000000`0001dcd8 00000000`000252d9
```

i.e. the PFNs referenced by the PTEs.

Finally, we can see how the bitmap hint increased by 4 units:

```
1: kd> ?? ((nt!_mi_system_PTE_type *) @@(nt!MiSystemPteInfo))
struct _MI_SYSTEM_PTE_TYPE * 0xfffff800`02a34720
   +0x000 Bitmap            : _RTL_BITMAP
   +0x010 Flags             : 3
   +0x014 Hint              : 0xc44a
   +0x018 BasePte           : 0xfffff6fc`40000000 _MMPTE
   +0x020 FailureCount      : 0xfffff800`02a3475c  -> 0
   +0x028 Vm                : 0xfffff800`02a0c440 _MMSUPPORT
   +0x030 TotalSystemPtes   : 0n4096
   +0x034 TotalFreeSystemPtes : 0n3219
   +0x038 CachedPteCount    : 0n0
   +0x03c PteFailures       : 0
   +0x040 SpinLock          : 0
   +0x040 GlobalMutex       : (null)
```

A final interesting fact is how the bits are cleared: we can select the option of MemTests which calls *MmUnmapLockedPages* and break again into the debugger before the call to the driver. By placing again data breakpoints on the bits about to be cleared, we find out it is not the thread executing *MmUnmapLockedPages* which updates them. Rather, the breakpoint is hit asynchronously after the call to the DDI has completed and this is the thread updating them:

```
0: kd> k
Child-SP          RetAddr           Call Site
fffff880`031399e0 fffff800`02890dd4 nt!MiReplenishBitMap+0x11b
fffff880`03139af0 fffff800`02894609 nt!MiEmptyPteBins+0x10d
fffff880`03139b40 fffff800`028956b4 nt!MiAdjustPteBins+0x29
fffff880`03139b80 fffff800`0289596f nt!MmWorkingSetManager+0x40
fffff880`03139bd0 fffff800`02b24166 nt!KeBalanceSetManager+0x1c3
fffff880`03139d40 fffff800`0285f486 nt!PspSystemThreadStartup+0x5a
fffff880`03139d80 00000000`00000000 nt!KxStartSystemThread+0x16
```

The Working Set Manager is actually doing the job. Presumably, this happens because when system virtual addresses are freed, the corresponding TLB entries must be invalidated on all processors. Since this is an expensive operation, it makes sense to do it in batches and it appears that the WSM is used for this purpose.

44.8.2.6.4   Relationship Between Bit Index and Virtual Address (MiKernelStackPteInfo)

We can conduct a test similar to the previous one to confirm the relationship between bit index and virtual address for this bitmap as well.

For this purpose, we will use MemTests to call the *MmAllocateMappingAddress* DDI, which, it turns out, allocates from this bitmap. This DDI does not map physical pages from an MDL, but simply reserves an address range which can be later used with other functions. Interestingly, the DDI signature taken from [16] is:

```
PVOID
  MmAllocateMappingAddress (
    IN SIZE_T  NumberOfBytes,
    IN ULONG   PoolTag
    );
```

The second parameter is quite peculiar, since reserving a virtual address range has nothing to do with the system pools. We will see while performing this test that the tag is used by the VMM to mark the reserved range. This information is then used when the range is freed, to check that this is done properly.

The DDI to be called to free such a range is *MmFreeMappingAddress* and has the following signature:

```
VOID
  MmFreeMappingAddress (
    IN PVOID  BaseAddress,
    IN ULONG  PoolTag
    );
```

This function checks whether the input address is the beginning of a range marked with the same tag passed in the PoolTag parameter. If this is not the case, the DDI bugchecks with code 0xDA: SYSTEM_PTE_MISUSE.

For this test, we choose the *MmAllocateMappingAddress() test* in the System Range Tests menu of MemTests and break into the debugger before calling the driver. When the debugger takes control, the current thread is the one which will call the DDI. We expect MiReservePtes to be called to perform the allocation, so we place a breakpoint at the function address valid for this thread only and resume execution:

```
1: kd> bp /t @$thread nt!MiReservePtes
1: kd> g
KernelAllocs - MmAllocateMappingAddressTest
KernelAllocs - About to allocate mapping address
```

```
KernelAllocs    Size = 0x10000
Breakpoint 0 hit
nt!MiReservePtes:
fffff800`02863408 4489442418      mov      dword ptr [rsp+18h],r8d
```

As we see from the driver messages, in this test we are reserving 0x10 pages. The register values tell us a couple of interesting things:

```
1: kd> r
rax=0000000000000010 rbx=fffffa800106d070 rcx=fffff80002a33ec0
rdx=0000000000000012 rsi=0000000000000010 rdi=000000004b415453
rip=fffff80002863408 rsp=fffff8800522e8d8 rbp=fffff8800522eca0
 r8=0000000000000000  r9=0000000000000000 r10=0000000000000000
r11=fffff8800522e580 r12=0000000000000010 r13=0000000000000001
r14=0000000000000001 r15=fffffa80012bc060
iopl=0         nv up ei pl zr na po nc
cs=0010  ss=0018  ds=002b  es=002b  fs=0053  gs=002b          efl=00000246
nt!MiReservePtes:
fffff800`02863408 4489442418      mov      dword ptr [rsp+18h],r8d
ss:0018:fffff880`0522e8f0=00000001
```

First, rcx is the address of MiKernelStackPteInfo:

```
1: kd> ln @rcx
(fffff800`02a33ec0)   nt!MiKernelStackPteInfo   |   (fffff800`02a34710)
nt!MiPteTrackingBitmap
Exact matches:
    nt!MiKernelStackPteInfo = <no type information>
```

This suggests we are about to allocate from the corresponding bitmap, a fact which we are going to confirm with a data breakpoint on the bitmap itself.

Second, rdx is set to the number of paging we are reserving + 2. As we will see, the implementation of *MmAllocateMappingAddress* does indeed reserve two extra pages and uses their PTEs for its own purpose: the first one will contain the number of pages reserved and the second one a modified version of the input tag.

Going on with our test, here is the status of the bitmap:

```
1: kd> ?? (( nt!_mi_system_pte_type*) @@(nt!MiKernelStackPteInfo))
struct _MI_SYSTEM_PTE_TYPE * 0xfffff800`02a33ec0
   +0x000 Bitmap            : _RTL_BITMAP
   +0x010 Flags             : 3
   +0x014 Hint              : 0x4b38
   +0x018 BasePte           : 0xfffff6fc`40000000 _MMPTE
   +0x020 FailureCount      : 0xfffff800`02a33efc  -> 0
   +0x028 Vm                : 0xfffff800`02a0c440 _MMSUPPORT
   +0x030 TotalSystemPtes   : 0n8704
   +0x034 TotalFreeSystemPtes : 0n2150
   +0x038 CachedPteCount    : 0n7
   +0x03c PteFailures       : 0
   +0x040 SpinLock          : 0
   +0x040 GlobalMutex       : (null)
```

And below is the bitmap content at the index given by `Hint`:

```
1: kd> dq fffff880`00400000 + 4b38/8 l1
fffff880`00400967  fffffffe0`00001fc0
1: kd> ? 4b38 % 8
Evaluate expression: 0 = 00000000`00000000
```

This is an interesting case, because the hint points to bit 0 inside the byte at 0xFFFFF880`00400967, which is set to 0xC0. This means only 6 clear bits are found, then there is a group of set bit. Since we are requesting 0x10 (actually 0x12 for the reasons we saw) pages, the range corresponding to the hint cannot be used.

Since we want to place a data breakpoint on the bytes we are expecting to be updated, we are going to guess that the VMM will use the free range which begins within the next byte, which is set to 0x1F. This means bits 5,6,7 of this byte are free and we see from the output above that two more bytes and part of a third have clear bits as well. 0x12 pages can fit in this range, so we expect these bits to be modified and place our breakpoints accordingly. When we resume execution, this is what happens:

```
1: kd> g
Breakpoint 1 hit
Breakpoint 2 hit
nt!MiReservePtes+0x1c3:
fffff800`028635cb 0f8548040000    jne     nt!MiReservePtes+0x611 (fffff800`02863a19)
1: kd> dq fffff880`00400000 + 4b38/8 l1
fffff880`00400967  fffffffe0`7fffffc0
```

Note: we are seeing two breakpoints hit because two of them were actually set. Below is the call stack when the breakpoint is hit:

```
1: kd> k
Child-SP          RetAddr          Call Site
fffff880`0522e850 fffff800`02ba3c98 nt!MiReservePtes+0x1c3
fffff880`0522e8e0 fffff880`0457914d nt!MmAllocateMappingAddress+0x48
fffff880`0522e960 fffff880`04578494 krnlallocs!MmAllocateMappingAddressTest+0xfd
[b:\programm\wntsys\vmmtests\kernelallocs\driver\drvmain.cpp @ 926]
fffff880`0522e9c0 fffff800`02b993a7 krnlallocs!DispatchDioc+0xa4
[b:\programm\wntsys\vmmtests\kernelallocs\driver\drvmain.cpp @ 468]
fffff880`0522ea10 fffff800`02b99c06 nt!IopXxxControlFile+0x607
fffff880`0522eb40 fffff800`02880153 nt!NtDeviceIoControlFile+0x56
fffff880`0522ebb0 00000000`777fff2a nt!KiSystemServiceCopyEnd+0x13
00000000`0017fbd8 000007fe`fda7b399 ntdll!NtDeviceIoControlFile+0xa
00000000`0017fbe0 00000000`776a610f KERNELBASE!DeviceIoControl+0x75
00000000`0017fc50 00000001`3fba59db kernel32!DeviceIoControlImplementation+0x7f
00000000`0017fca0 00000000`00000000 MemTests!SendIoCtl+0x5b
[b:\programm\memtests\memtests\main.cpp @ 3790]
```

The following bits have been set:

- bits 5,6,7 of the byte at offset 0x4B38 / 8 + 1

- all the bits of the next byte

- bits 0-6 of the next byte

The number of bits which have been set is thus

3 + 8 + 7 = 18 = 0x12

which is consistent with our expectations. The index of the first bit set is:

0x4B38 + 1*8 + 5 = 0x4B45

Assuming this index corresponds to a page offset in the System PTE region, the expected address is:

(0x4B38 + 1*8 + 5) * 1000 + 0xFFFFF880`00000000 = 0xFFFFF880`04B45000

While we are still inside *MiReservePtes*, the corresponding PTEs are free:

```
1: kd> !pte (4b38 + 1*8 + 5) * 1000 + fffff880`00000000
                                        VA fffff88004b45000

PXE at FFFFF6FB7DBEDF88   PPE at FFFFF6FB7DBF1000   PDE at FFFFF6FB7E200128   PTE at FFFFF6FC40025A28
contains 000000003C084863  contains 000000003C083863  contains 000000000E44F863  contains 0000000000000000
pfn 3c084    ---DA--KWEV  pfn 3c083    ---DA--KWEV  pfn e44f    ---DA--KWEV  not valid


1: kd> dq FFFFF6FC40025A28 l 12
fffff6fc`40025a28  00000000`00000000 00000000`00000000
fffff6fc`40025a38  00000000`00000000 00000000`00000000
fffff6fc`40025a48  00000000`00000000 00000000`00000000
fffff6fc`40025a58  00000000`00000000 00000000`00000000
fffff6fc`40025a68  00000000`00000000 00000000`00000000
fffff6fc`40025a78  00000000`00000000 00000000`00000000
fffff6fc`40025a88  00000000`00000000 00000000`00000000
fffff6fc`40025a98  00000000`00000000 00000000`00000000
fffff6fc`40025aa8  00000000`00000000 00000000`00000000
```

Now we return to MmallocateMappingAddress and from there to our test driver, to see the address of the range we have got:

```
1: kd> g @$ra
nt!MmAllocateMappingAddress+0x48:
fffff800`02ba3c98 4885c0          test    rax,rax
1: kd> g @$ra
krnlallocs!MmAllocateMappingAddressTest+0xfd:
fffff880`0457914d 4c8bd8          mov     r11,rax
1: kd> r
rax=fffff88004b47000 rbx=fffffa800106d070 rcx=0000000000000000
```

```
rdx=0000000000000012 rsi=fffffa800106d070 rdi=fffffa8000fd82a0
rip=fffff8800457914d rsp=fffff8800522e960 rbp=fffff8800522eca0
 r8=000000004b415453  r9=0000000000000001 r10=0000000000000000
r11=fffff8800522e950 r12=0000000000000010 r13=0000000000000001
r14=0000000000000001 r15=fffffa80012bc060
iopl=0         nv up ei pl zr na po nc
cs=0010  ss=0018  ds=002b  es=002b  fs=0053  gs=002b          efl=00000246
krnlallocs!MmAllocateMappingAddressTest+0xfd:
fffff880`0457914d 4c8bd8          mov     r11,rax
```

The returned address is at +2 pages from the one computed earlier. Let's examine the PTEs from the latter:

```
1: kd> dq FFFFF6FC40025A28 1 12
fffff6fc`40025a28  00000012`00000000 00000000`4b415012
fffff6fc`40025a38  00000000`00000000 00000000`00000000
fffff6fc`40025a48  00000000`00000000 00000000`00000000
fffff6fc`40025a58  00000000`00000000 00000000`00000000
fffff6fc`40025a68  00000000`00000000 00000000`00000000
fffff6fc`40025a78  00000000`00000000 00000000`00000000
fffff6fc`40025a88  00000000`00000000 00000000`00000000
fffff6fc`40025a98  00000000`00000000 00000000`00000000
fffff6fc`40025aa8  00000000`00000000 00000000`00000000
```

The first PTE stores 0x12 in the upper DWORD, i.e. the overall range length and the second PTE is related to the tag. The test driver sets the tag as follows:

```
CHAR    MapRegionTag[] = {'S', 'T', 'A', 'K'};
```

which translates to the following values:

```
0: kd> db krnlallocs!MapRegionTag 14
fffff880`02bdd110  53 54 41 4b                                      STAK
```

As we see, 0x4b and 0x41 are present in the PTE. The other two bytes have been transformed in some way by the DDI. The range length in the first PTE is particularly interesting, since it explains why *MmFreeMappingAddress* does not have, among its parameters, the length of the range to be freed: the DDI reads it from the hidden PTE, found two PTEs before the one for the input address.

This analysis confirms that the bit index of the bitmap controlled by MiKernelStackPteInfo corresponds to a page offset from the start of the System PTE region. This section and the previous one show that the indexes of both bitmaps have the same meaning.

44.8.3   Page Fault Handling

Page faults in this regions are handled as explained in sec. 43.3 on p. 410. The _MMSUPPORT instance used is the static one at MmSystemPtesWs.

44.8.4   MmSystemPtesWs: a Working Set for Kernel Mode Images Only

We already mentioned in sec. 44.6.3 on p. 436 that MmSystemPtesWs.WorkingSetSize is equal to the sum of MmSystemDriverPage and MmSystemCodePage.

The meaning of these two statics is explained in [1] on p. 833: both the kernel and kernel mode drivers have pageable sections, which can therefore be not mapped. These counters store the number of physical pages currently used for mapped virtual pages of drivers and the kernel, respectively.

Thus, the working set size stored in MmSystemPtes accounts for pages mapping kernel mode images *only*.

But, what about the other possible kinds of contents of the System PTE region? They are not part of *any* working set, because they are not pageable by the working set manager. Let's analyze them one by one.

44.8.4.1   MDL Mappings

These VA are used to "see" physical pages tracked by MDLs, which had to be locked in memory before being mapped (see sec. 44.8.1.2 on p. 441), so they are not pageable.

The following example further expands on this subject by analyzing the mapping of an MDL for a user mode buffer.

The buffer is allocated by MemTests at 0x6b0000 and is 1MB in size, extending to 0x7affff.

```
1: kd> !vad 6b0000
VAD             level      start     end     commit
fffffa8003082300 (-1)       6b0      7af       256 Private       READWRITE
```

An MDL has been created for the buffer, the pages have been locked and mapped in the System PTE region, ending up in the range 0xFFFFF880`03B00000 - 0xFFFFF880`03BFFFFF. Below are the PTE and the _MMPFN for the first page:

```
1: kd> !pte 0xFFFFF88003B00000
                                       VA fffff88003b00000
PXE at FFFFF6FB7DBEDF88  PPE at FFFFF6FB7DBF1000  PDE at FFFFF6FB7E2000E8  PTE at FFFFF6FC4001D800
contains 000000003C084863  contains 000000003C083863  contains 000000001ADAE863  contains 00000000278C2963
pfn 3c084     ---DA--KWEV pfn 3c083     ---DA--KWEV pfn 1adae    ---DA--KWEV pfn 278c2     -G-DA--KWEV


1: kd> !pfn 278c2
    PFN 000278C2 at address FFFFFA800076A460
      flink        00000262  blink / share count 00000001  pteaddress FFFFF68000003580
```

```
reference count 0002    used entry count  0000     Cached   color 0   Priority 5
restore pte 00000080   containing page          027F41  Active     M
Modified
```

We see that `pteaddress` (`_MMPFN.PteAddress`) in the `_MMPFN` is quite different from the address of the PTE for the System PTE range. But of course: this physical page was originally allocated for the user mode buffer, so the `_MMPFN` content is consistent with the page usage in the process address space. Let's see the PTE for the user mode address:

```
1: kd> !process 0 0 memtests.exe
PROCESS ffffa80011a9060
    SessionId: 1 Cid: 09f8    Peb: 7fffffd9000  ParentCid: 09d8
    DirBase: 16137000  ObjectTable: fffff8a002281600  HandleCount:  31.
    Image: MemTests.EXE

1: kd> .process /P ffffa80011a9060
Implicit process is now ffffa80`011a9060
.cache forcedecodeptes done

1: kd> !pte 6b0000
                                  VA 00000000006b0000

PXE at FFFFF6FB7DBED000   PPE at FFFFF6FB7DA00000   PDE at FFFFF6FB40000018   PTE at FFFFF68000003580
contains 03C0000028930867  contains 0300000027DB3867  contains 2610000027F41867  contains A6200000278C2867
pfn 28930    ---DA--UWEV  pfn 27db3    ---DA--UWEV  pfn 27f41    ---DA--UWEV  pfn 278c2    ---DA--UW-V
```

The address of the PTE for the *user mode* address is the one found in the `_MMPFN`, and the PTE is also pointing to the correct physical page.

The second thing we notice is that the `_MMPFN` *does* have a working set index (`flink` is 0x262), but this should not surprise us: it's the index in the working set of the process. We can confirm this with the debugger:

```
1: kd> ?? ((nt!_MMWSL*) 0xfffff70001080000)->Wsle[0x262].u1.e1
struct _MMWSLENTRY
   +0x000 Valid             : 0y1
   +0x000 Spare             : 0y0
   +0x000 Hashed            : 0y0
   +0x000 Direct            : 0y1
   +0x000 Protection        : 0y00000 (0)
   +0x000 Age               : 0y000
   +0x000 VirtualPageNumber : 0y0000000000000000000000000000000000000000000011010110000
(0x6b0)
```

But could this physical page *also* be part of the System PTE working set? Let's see the same entry from the latter:

```
1: kd> ?? ((nt!_MMSUPPORT*) @@(nt!MmSystemPtesWs))->VmWorkingSetList->Wsle[0x262].u1.e1
struct _MMWSLENTRY
   +0x000 Valid             : 0y1
   +0x000 Spare             : 0y0
   +0x000 Hashed            : 0y0
```

```
    +0x000 Direct             : 0y1
    +0x000 Protection         : 0y00000 (0)
    +0x000 Age                : 0y000
    +0x000 VirtualPageNumber  : 0y11111111111111111111111110001000000000000001100100111010
(0xfffff8800193a)
```

This entry clearly does not refer neither to the user mode VA nor to the System PTE VA at which the physical page is mapped, so it's an entry for some other physical page.

We also know (see sections 37.14.3 on p. 332 and 37.14.4 on p. 333) that the WSL entry for a certain VA can be at a different index than the one found in the `_MMPFN`, if the page is shared. But this is managed by allocating an hash table for the working set and we already know (see sec. 44.6.3 on p. 436) that the System PTE WS does not have one.

The bottom line is that the System PTE WS does not account for MDL mappings, because the physical pages are already part of another WS and because it does not make sense to attempt to page them: they are mapped *only* after having been previously locked.

The test described here can be replicated with MemTests, which has menu options to allocate an MDL and to lock and map its pages. See Chapter 45 on p. 500.

44.8.4.2 Kernel Stacks

We will see in Chapter 47 on p. 521 why kernel stacks pages are paged in an entirely peculiar way, so that they are not part of any working set.

44.8.4.3 Device Memory Mappings

These are VA which are not even mapped to physical pages, so it does not make any sense to create working set entries for them.

44.8.4.4 _MM_SESSION_SPACE Instances

We will see in sec. 44.10.2.1.1 on p. 487 that instances of `_MM_SESSION_SPACE` are mapped in the System PTE region. The pages storing these instances don't seem to belong to any working set, because `_MMPFN.u1`, for them is set to the VA mapped to them.

44.8.4.5 Conclusion

Of the various kinds of content which are found in the System PTE region, only the driver code is accounted for in MmSystemPtesWs.

A final twist is that `MmSystemPtesWs.LowestPagableAddress` points below the System PTE region, at the beginning of the initial loader mappings region, which stores kernel mode images loaded in the early stages of system boot (e.g. the kernel and the HAL). Thus, this working set tracks the paging of these images as well, which, strictly speaking are *outside* the System PTE region. In summary, this working set job appears to be to track the pageable physical pages of all kernel mode images, both in the Initial Loader Mapping and the System PTE region.

44.9 Paged Pool

44.9.1   Region Content

This is a dynamically allocated region.

The paged pool (PP) is a sort of heap of pageable memory available to kernel mode components. The Executive exposes DDI to allocate and release memory from it like *ExAllocatePool* and *ExFreePool*.

The paged pool upper limit is stored in the static MmPagedPoolEnd ([2] and also tested at *MmAccessFault* + 0xe0b), which is usually set to 0xFFFFF8BF`FFFFFFFF, so that the pool virtual range has a size of 128GB. The range from 0xFFFFF8C0`00000000 to the next region (session space at 0xFFFFF900`00000000) appears to be unused because the PDPTEs mapping it are set to 0. This unused range spans 256GB.

The VMM defines more than one PP, to reduce contention among different threads on the data structures used to manage the pools. The different PPs are not visible to callers of *ExAllocatePool*, which just returns a memory chunk from "somewhere" in the PP region. The different pools are also allocated in virtual ranges mapped to different NUMA nodes, so that pool allocations are distributed evenly among nodes.

See also [1], pp. 721 - 728.

44.9.2   Virtual Address Space Management

The virtual address space of this region is controlled by the bitmap at MiPagedPoolVaBitmap. *MiObtainSystemVa* allocates from this region when the MiVaPagedPool memory type is requested.

44.9.3   Page Fault Handling

Page faults in this region are handled as detailed in sec. 43.3 on p. 410, using the static _MMSUPPORT instance named MmPagedPoolWs for the working set.

44.9.4   Outpaging and Repurposing

PP pages are outpaged and repurposed quite like user mode ones: the Working Set Manager removes pages form the PP WS, moving them to the Modified list when they are dirty. The Modified Page Writer outpages their content to the paging file and moves them to the Standby list, from where they are eventually repurposed.

This section shows excerpts from a debugging session where the transition of a PP page have been tracked by placing breakpoints on the _MMPFN instance and on the WSLE.

The page for which the analysis was conducted is the one mapping the first VPN of paged pool. This is the initial situation, with the page actively mapping the VPN:

```
0: kd> !pte fffff8a000000000
                                       VA fffff8a000000000

PXE at FFFFF6FB7DBEDF88   PPE at FFFFF6FB7DBF1400   PDE at FFFFF6FB7E280000   PTE at FFFFF6FC50000000
contains 000000003C004863 contains 0000000003113863 contains 0000000003112863 contains B420000003114943
pfn 3c004   ---DA--KWEV   pfn 3113   ---DA--KWEV   pfn 3112   ---DA--KWEV   pfn 3114      -G-D---KW-V


0: kd> !pfn 3114
   PFN 00003114 at address FFFFFA80000933C0
   flink       00003342  blink / share count 00000001  pteaddress FFFFF6FC50000000
   reference count 0001    used entry count  0000       Cached    color 0    Priority 5
   restore pte 00000080  containing page       003112  Active    M
   Modified
```

0x3342 is the index of the WSL entry for the page, so we can examine its content:

```
0: kd> ?? ((nt!_mmsupport*) @@(nt!MmPagedPoolWs))->VmWorkingSetList->Wsle[0x3342].u1.e1
struct _MMWSLENTRY
   +0x000 Valid             : 0y1
   +0x000 Spare             : 0y0
   +0x000 Hashed            : 0y0
   +0x000 Direct            : 0y1
   +0x000 Protection        : 0y00000 (0)
   +0x000 Age               : 0y110
   +0x000 VirtualPageNumber : 0y1111111111111111111110001010000000000000000000000000
(0xfffff8a000000)
```

So far, the page is part of the PP WS and is mapping the VA. To track the life of the page, two data breakpoints were used: one at +0x10 inside the _MMPFN, i.e. at _MMPFN.PteAddress. Bit 0 of this member is used to lock the instance for exclusive access, so most of the significant changes to the instance content are surrounded by accesses to this member, to set and clear the lock. The second data breakpoint was on the WSL entry.

Two instances of MemTests were running, one accessing a private region of 0x3c000000 bytes, the other a mapped file of 0x20000000; the system was a virtual machine with 1GB of memory, so the running programs were using all the available memory and forcing the system to swap out paged pool pages.

In the following, the addresses at which breakpoints are hit are the ones after the instruction performing the data access. This is normal behavior since the processor generates a trap when such a breakpoint is hit.

The first interesting breakpoint hit is on _MMPFN.PteAddress at *MiFreeWsleList*+0x4be to lock the instance. Below is the call stack at the breakpoint, showing that the running thread is the Working Set Manager:

```
0: kd> !thread @$thread
THREAD ffffffa8000ce0b60  Cid 0004.0064  Teb: 0000000000000000 Win32Thread:
0000000000000000 RUNNING on processor 0
Not impersonating
DeviceMap                 fffff8a000006090
Owning Process            ffffffa8000cbc6f0      Image:         System
Attached Process          N/A              Image:        N/A
Wait Start TickCount      561913           Ticks: 0
Context Switch Count      18583
UserTime                  00:00:00.000
KernelTime                00:00:00.546
Win32 Start Address nt!KeBalanceSetManager (0xfffff800028dd7ac)
Stack Init fffff88003139db0 Current fffff88003139620
Base fffff8800313a000 Limit fffff88003134000 Call 0
Priority 16 BasePriority 8 UnusualBoost 0 ForegroundBoost 0 IoPriority 2 PagePriority 5
Child-SP          RetAddr           : Args to Child
: Call Site
fffff880`03139840 fffff800`0299972f : fffff800`02a53b40 fffff880`03139a50
fffffa80`00000000 fffff800`00000012 : nt!MiFreeWsleList+0x4be

fffff880`03139a30 fffff800`029499c3 : 00000000`0000032d fffff800`00003437
00000000`00002d46 00000000`00000000 : nt!MiTrimWorkingSet+0x14f

fffff880`03139ae0 fffff800`028dd6e2 : 00000000`000022f0 00000000`00000000
00000000`00000000 00000000`00000000 : nt! ?? ::FNODOBFM::`string'+0x498d1

fffff880`03139b80 fffff800`028dd8e4 : 00000000`00000008 fffff880`03139c10
00000000`00000001 fffffa80`00000000 : nt!MmWorkingSetManager+0x6e

fffff880`03139bd0 fffff800`02b6c166 : fffffa80`00ce0b60 00000000`00000080
fffffa80`00cbc6f0 00000000`00000001 : nt!KeBalanceSetManager+0x138

fffff880`03139d40 fffff800`028a7486 : fffff800`02a41e80 fffffa80`00ce0b60
fffff800`02a4fc40 00000000`00000000 : nt!PspSystemThreadStartup+0x5a

fffff880`03139d80 00000000`00000000 : fffff880`0313a000 00000000`00000000
00000000`00000000 00000000`00000000 : nt!KxStartSystemThread+0x16
```

Shortly afterwards, the same breakpoint is hit again at *MiFreeWsleList*+0x4e1 and the
_MMPFN instance is unlocked. The _MMPFN has not been updated yet, but The PTE is now in
transition:

```
0: kd> !pte fffff8a000000000
                                        VA fffff8a000000000

PXE at FFFFF6FB7DBEDF88   PPE at FFFFF6FB7DBF1400   PDE at FFFFF6FB7E280000   PTE at FFFFF6FC50000000
contains 000000003C004863  contains 0000000003113863  contains 0000000003112863  contains B420000003114882
pfn 3c004    ---DA--KWEV  pfn 3113    ---DA--KWEV  pfn 3112    ---DA--KWEV  not valid
                                                                            Transition: 3114


Protect: 4 - ReadWrite

0: kd> !pfn 3114
    PFN 00003114 at address FFFFFA80000933C0
    flink       00003342  blink / share count 00000001  pteaddress FFFFF6FC50000000
    reference count 0001    used entry count  0000        Cached    color 0    Priority 5
    restore pte 00000080  containing page        003112  Active     M
    Modified
```

Note: the last `Modified` label in the output above represents the fact that the page is dirty
and does not mean that the page is on the Modified list. The label for the page state is the
shaded Active. See also Appendix A (p. 565) for more details on the output of `!pfn`.

Later, the breakpoint is hit again and, when the _MMPFN is unlocked at
MiFreeWsleList+0x2e0, it has been moved to the modified list:

```
0: kd> !pfn 3114
    PFN 00003114 at address FFFFFA80000933C0
    flink       FFFFFFFFFFFFFFFF  blink / share count 0002271E  pteaddress FFFFF6FC50000000
    reference count 0000    used entry count  0000        Cached    color 0    Priority 5
    restore pte 00000080  containing page        003112  Modified   M
    Modified
```

When a page is in the list, flink and blink are the PFNs of the next and previous list nodes.
Here `flink` set to 0xFFFFFFFF`FFFFFFFF means our page is at the tail of the list, so we can
easily confirm that it is on the list pointed by MmModifiedPageListByColor:

```
0: kd> ?? ((nt!_mmpfnlist*) @@(nt!MmModifiedPageListByColor))
struct _MMPFNLIST * 0xfffff800`02a3db80
   +0x000 Total          : 0x76d
   +0x008 ListName       : 3 ( ModifiedPageList )
   +0x010 Flink          : 0x6936
   +0x018 Blink          : 0x3114
   +0x020 Lock           : 0
```

The head `Blink` points to our PFN. We can also confirm that page 0x2271e, pointed by our
`blink` has `flink` set to our PFN:

```
0: kd> !pfn 2271e
    PFN 0002271E at address FFFFFA80006755A0
    flink        00003114  blink / share count 0000214A  pteaddress FFFFF6FC50007F68
    reference count 0000    used entry count  0000      Cached    color 0    Priority 5
    restore pte 00000080  containing page         0109B3  Modified    M
    Modified
```

So far, the WSL entry has not been updated yet, but, when execution is resumed, its breakpoint is hit at *MiRemoveWsle*+0x62 and we see that the `Valid` bit has been cleared. Other members will be updated afterwards.

```
0: kd> ?? ((nt!_mmsupport*) @@(nt!MmPagedPoolWs))->VmWorkingSetList->Wsle[0x3342].u1.e1
struct _MMWSLENTRY
    +0x000 Valid             : 0y0
    +0x000 Spare             : 0y0
    +0x000 Hashed            : 0y0
    +0x000 Direct            : 0y1
    +0x000 Protection        : 0y00000 (0)
    +0x000 Age               : 0y110
    +0x000 VirtualPageNumber : 0y1111111111111111111111110001010000000000000000000000000
(0xfffff8a000000)
```

After a few more hits on the `_MMPFN` we see at *MiGatherPagefilePages*+0x3a5 that the page is in the process of being written to disk:

```
0: kd> !pfn 3114
    PFN 00003114 at address FFFFFA80000933C0
    flink        00000000  blink / share count 00000000  pteaddress FFFFF6FC50000000
    reference count 0001    used entry count  0000      Cached    color 0    Priority 5
    restore pte 00000080  containing page         003112  Modified        W
         WriteInProgress
```

The current thread is the Modified Page Writer:

```
0: kd> !thread @$thread
THREAD fffffa8000cdd680  Cid 0004.005c  Teb: 0000000000000000 Win32Thread:
0000000000000000 RUNNING on processor 0
IRP List:
    fffffa80030f2160: (0006,03a0) Flags: 00060003  Mdl: fffffa8002c15078
    fffffa8000d9b3b0: (0006,03a0) Flags: 00060003  Mdl: fffffa8002c1f078
    fffffa800113a3f0: (0006,03a0) Flags: 00060003  Mdl: fffffa8002c147c8
Not impersonating
DeviceMap                 fffff8a000006090
Owning Process            fffffa8000cbc6f0       Image:         System
Attached Process          N/A            Image:         N/A
Wait Start TickCount      568965         Ticks: 2 (0:00:00.031)
Context Switch Count      7058
UserTime                  00:00:00.000
KernelTime                00:00:03.296
Win32 Start Address nt!MiModifiedPageWriter (0xfffff800028619c0)
Stack Init fffff8800312bdb0 Current fffff8800312b820
Base fffff8800312c000 Limit fffff88003126000 Call 0
Priority 17 BasePriority 8 UnusualBoost 0 ForegroundBoost 0 IoPriority 2 PagePriority 5
```

```
Child-SP          RetAddr          : Args to Child
: Call Site
fffff880`0312bc00 fffff800`02861b7b : fffffa80`00025deb fffff880`00000000
00000000`00025deb 00000000`00000000 : nt!MiGatherPagefilePages+0x3a5

fffff880`0312bce0 fffff800`02b6c166 : fffffa80`00cdd680 56173455`16325215
00000000`00000080 00000000`00000001 : nt!MiModifiedPageWriter+0x1bb

fffff880`0312bd40 fffff800`028a7486 : fffff800`02a41e80 fffffa80`00cdd680
fffffa80`00cddb60 2f34392f`343b2f36 : nt!PspSystemThreadStartup+0x5a

fffff880`0312bd80 00000000`00000000 : fffff880`0312c000 fffff880`03126000
fffff880`0312b820 00000000`00000000 : nt!KxStartSystemThread+0x16
```

Later, the _MMPFN is updated again and, when it is unlocked at
MiUpdatePfnBackingStore+0x8A (still in the context of the Modified Page Writer), we see
that `restore pte` now stores, in the upper DWORD, the paging file offset assigned to the
page:

```
0: kd> !pfn 3114
    PFN 00003114 at address FFFFFA80000933C0
    flink        00000000  blink / share count 00000000  pteaddress FFFFF6FC50000000
    reference count 0001   used entry count  0000      Cached    color 0   Priority 5
    restore pte 25DEE00000080  containing page       003112  Modified      W
            WriteInProgress
```

The write is still in progress, but, by now, the paging file offset has been assigned to the page
content.

Further on, the MPW hits the breakpoint again at *MiWriteComplete*+0x1c7 and we see the
page has been moved to the standby list:

```
0: kd> !pfn 3114
    PFN 00003114 at address FFFFFA80000933C0
    flink        FFFFFFFFFFFFFFFF  blink / share count 00000BD7  pteaddress FFFFF6FC50000000
    reference count 0000   used entry count  0000      Cached    color 0   Priority 5
    restore pte 25DEE00000080  containing page       003112  Standby
```

Again, `flink` tells us our page is the last of the list, which in our case will be the standby list
for priority 5, so it's worth to check the list head:

```
0: kd> ?? ((nt!_mmpfnlist*) @@(nt!MmStandbyPageListByPriority) + 5)
struct _MMPFNLIST * 0xfffff800`02a53d48
   +0x000 Total       : 0x62af
   +0x008 ListName     : 2 ( StandbyPageList )
   +0x010 Flink        : 0x2ea83
   +0x018 Blink        : 0x3114
   +0x020 Lock         : 0
```

To recapitulate, so far we have seen the Working Set Manager trim the PP working set and
move the page to the Modified list, then the Modified Page Writer copy the page content to

the paging file and move the page to the Standby list. The page is now clean and the paging file offset of its copy is stored into `_MMPFN.OriginalPte`.

As the two instances of MemTests go on asking for memory, the `_MMPFN` is eventually accessed again to be repurposed. The first hit is at *MiRemoveLowestPriorityStandbyPage+0x91* in the context of MemTest's thread:

```
0: kd> !thread @$thread
THREAD fffffa8001021060  Cid 00a8.03d0  Teb: 000007fffffdd000 Win32Thread:
0000000000000000 RUNNING on processor 0
Not impersonating
DeviceMap                fffff8a001447e10
Owning Process           fffffa8000ffa270      Image:          MemTests.EXE
Attached Process         N/A            Image:          N/A
Wait Start TickCount     569616         Ticks: 0
Context Switch Count     4928
UserTime                 00:00:00.296
KernelTime               00:00:04.843
Win32 Start Address 0x000000013f787500
Stack Init fffff88004d63db0 Current fffff88004d63050
Base fffff88004d64000 Limit fffff88004d5e000 Call 0
Priority 8 BasePriority 8 UnusualBoost 0 ForegroundBoost 0 IoPriority 2 PagePriority 5
Child-SP          RetAddr           : Args to Child
: Call Site
fffff880`04d63720 fffff800`02939380 : fffff8a0`060d0a40 fffff880`04d63800
00000000`00000000 fa800320`5f9004c0 : nt!MiRemoveLowestPriorityStandbyPage+0x91

fffff880`04d637a0 fffff800`028ef60d : fa800320`5f9004c0 ffffffff`00000480
fffff8a0`060d0a40 00000000`00000000 : nt! ?? ::FNODOBFM::`string'+0x2aa24

fffff880`04d63910 fffff800`028e4d9e : 00000000`00000001 00000000`1a7c8000
fffff680`000d3e40 fffffa80`00ffa608 : nt!MiResolveProtoPteFault+0x48d

fffff880`04d639b0 fffff800`028e2f23 : ffffffff`ffffff00 00000000`1a7c8000
ffffffff`ffffffff fffff800`00000000 : nt!MiDispatchFault+0x1de

fffff880`04d63ac0 fffff800`028c6fee : 00000000`00000001 00000000`00000000
00000000`00000001 00000000`00000000 : nt!MmAccessFault+0x343

fffff880`04d63c20 00000001`3f7817e7 : 00000001`3f7e1660 00000001`3f7e1648
00000000`00680000 00000000`20680000 : nt!KiPageFault+0x16e (TrapFrame @
fffff880`04d63c20)

00000000`0012f980 00000001`3f7e1660 : 00000001`3f7e1648 00000000`00680000
00000000`20680000 00000001`00000077 : 0x1`3f7817e7
```

The _MMPFN is still in Standby, but now it is locked, presumably because it is about to be repurposed:

```
0: kd> !pfn 3114
    PFN 00003114 at address FFFFFA80000933C0
    flink       00012DB8  blink / share count FFFFFFFFFFFFFFFF  pteaddress FFFFF6FC50000001
    reference count 0000     used entry count  0000        Cached      color 0    Priority 5
```

```
restore pte 25DEE00000080  containing page       003112  Standby
```

Up to this point, the PTE for PP address 0xFFFFF8A0`00000000 has remained the same, i.e. in transition but still pointing to our page:

```
0: kd> !pte fffff8a000000000
                                         VA fffff8a000000000

PXE at FFFFF6FB7DBEDF88   PPE at FFFFF6FB7DBF1400   PDE at FFFFF6FB7E280000   PTE at FFFFF6FC50000000
contains 000000003C004863 contains 0000000003113863 contains 0000000003112863 contains B420000003114882
pfn 3c004    ---DA--KWEV   pfn 3113    ---DA--KWEV   pfn 3112    ---DA--KWEV   not valid
                                                                             Transition: 3114
                                                                             Protect: 4 - ReadWrite
```

When the _MMPFN is unlocked at *MiRemoveLowestPriorityStandbyPage*+0x2d0, the PTE has changed and is now pointing into the paging file, at the offset at which the page was previously written:

```
0: kd> !pte fffff8a000000000
                                         VA fffff8a000000000

PXE at FFFFF6FB7DBEDF88   PPE at FFFFF6FB7DBF1400   PDE at FFFFF6FB7E280000   PTE at FFFFF6FC50000000
contains 000000003C004863 contains 0000000003113863 contains 0000000003112863 contains 00025DEE00000080
pfn 3c004    ---DA--KWEV   pfn 3113    ---DA--KWEV   pfn 3112    ---DA--KWEV   not valid
                                                                             PageFile:  0
                                                                             Offset: 25dee
                                                                             Protect: 4 - ReadWrite
```

As for the _MMPFN, it has been unchained from the list, `restore pte` does not store a paging file offset anymore and is, temporarily, in "bad" state:

```
0: kd> !pfn 3114
    PFN 00003114 at address FFFFFA80000933C0
    flink         00000000  blink / share count 00000000  pteaddress FFFFF6FC50000000
    reference count 0000     used entry count    0000      Cached    color 0   Priority 0
    restore pte 00000080  containing page       003112  Bad
```

Further breakpoint hits show the page with a read operation in progress and then finally becoming part of MemTests working set.

In summary, we see that the VMM pages system range addresses much like user mode ones: they are part of working sets examined by the Working Set Manager, so are eventually moved to the transition lists and repurposed.

By setting a breakpoint on the PTE address for the page we can also see the page being reloaded from the paging file. After the breakpoint is hit several times, we see the PTE being changed at *MiInitializeReadInProgressSinglePfn*+0x246:

```
0: kd> !pte fffff8a000000000
                                         VA fffff8a000000000
```

```
PXE at FFFFF6FB7DBEDF88   PPE at FFFFF6FB7DBF1400   PDE at FFFFF6FB7E280000   PTE at FFFFF6FC50000000
contains 000000003C004863  contains 0000000003113863  contains 0000000003112863  contains 00000000318AA880
pfn 3c004     ---DA--KWEV  pfn 3113     ---DA--KWEV  pfn 3112     ---DA--KWEV  not valid
                                                                               Transition: 318aa
                                                                               Protect: 4 - ReadWrite
```

The PTE is now in transition and pointing to a different physical page, for which a read I/O is in progress:

```
0: kd> !pfn 318aa
    PFN 000318AA at address FFFFFA8000949FE0
    flink        FFFFFA8003248250  blink / share count 00000000  pteaddress FFFFF6FC50000000
    reference count 0001    used entry count  0000       Cached      color 0    Priority 0
    restore pte 25DEE00000080  containing page         003112  Standby      R
        ReadInProgress
```

It's interesting to observe how the PTE pointing into the paging file has been saved into `_MMPFN.OriginalPte` (displayed as `restore pte`). This page starts its life as clean because a copy of it exists in the paging file.

Now that we have a PFN, we can set an additional breakpoint on writes to `_MMPFN.Lock` to further track the in-paging.

Eventually, the PTE is pointed to the page and a WSL entry is created for it:

```
0: kd> !pte fffff8a000000000
```

```
                                VA fffff8a000000000
PXE at FFFFF6FB7DBEDF88   PPE at FFFFF6FB7DBF1400   PDE at FFFFF6FB7E280000   PTE at FFFFF6FC50000000
contains 000000003C004863  contains 0000000003113863  contains 0000000003112863  contains A9100000318AA963
pfn 3c004     ---DA--KWEV  pfn 3113     ---DA--KWEV  pfn 3112     ---DA--KWEV  pfn 318aa    -G-DA--KW-V
```

```
0: kd> !pfn 318aa
    PFN 000318AA at address FFFFFA8000949FE0
    flink        00002A91  blink / share count 00000001  pteaddress FFFFF6FC50000000
    reference count 0001    used entry count  0000       Cached      color 0    Priority 5
    restore pte 00000080  containing page         003112  Active      M
    Modified
```

```
0: kd> ?? ((nt!_mmsupport*) @@(nt!MmPagedPoolWs))->VmWorkingSetList->Wsle[0x2a91].u1.e1
struct _MMWSLENTRY
    +0x000 Valid            : 0y1
    +0x000 Spare            : 0y0
    +0x000 Hashed           : 0y0
    +0x000 Direct           : 0y1
    +0x000 Protection       : 0y00000 (0)
    +0x000 Age              : 0y000
    +0x000 VirtualPageNumber : 0y1111111111111111111111000101000000000000000000000000000
(0xfffff8a000000)
```

We can notice that the page has "lost" its paging file copy, which is shown by `restore pte` being 0x80. This means the access which caused the fault was a write, the page content is about to be modified and the paging file copy has been released, because it will soon be stale.

Among the functions hitting the two breakpoints we find: *MiResolvePageFileFault*, *MiInitializeReadInProgressSinglePfn*, *MiFindActualFaultingPte* (called, indirectly, by *MiIssueHardFault*), *MiWaitForInPageComplete*. With additional breakpoints on `_MMPFN.u1.WsIndex` we can also catch *MiUpdateWsle* building the WSL entry. These functions are the same ones called for hard faults on user mode addresses.

44.9.5   Pages Not Belonging to Any Working Set

All the paging activity appears to be centered around the working set lists: the Working Set Manager scans these lists aging pages and removes the least recently accessed ones, when available memory is low. This implies that a page actively mapping a virtual address but not accounted for in any working set list is implicitly non-pageable, because is out of reach for the Working Set Manager. Such pages can be recognized by being Active and having a valid `_MMPFN.PteAddress`, while at the same time having `_MMPFN.u1.WsIndex` = 0.

As an example, we have already seen that paging structures for the system range are not pageable. Their `_MMPFN` normally have `u1.WsIndex` = 0, e.g.:

```
0: kd> !pte fffff880`00000000
                                        VA fffff88000000000

PXE at FFFFF6FB7DBEDF88   PPE at FFFFF6FB7DBF1000   PDE at FFFFF6FB7E200000   PTE at FFFFF6FC40000000
contains 000000003C004863  contains 000000003C003863  contains 000000003C002863  contains 000000003C08A963
pfn 3c004      ---DA--KWEV  pfn 3c003      ---DA--KWEV  pfn 3c002      ---DA--KWEV  pfn 3c08a      -G-DA--KWEV


0: kd> !pfn 3c002
    PFN 0003C002 at address FFFFFA8000B40060
    flink        00000000  blink / share count 00000003  pteaddress FFFFF6FB7E200000
    reference count 0001    used entry count  0000      Cached      color 0    Priority 0
    restore pte 00000080  containing page         03C003  Active      M
    Modified
```

0x3c002 is the PFN of the Page Table. We can see that many `_MMPFN` members are consistent with the page mapping this VA: `pteaddress` is correct (is the address of the PDE), `containing page` points to the PDPT page, even the share and reference counts are set up correctly. However, `flink`, i.e. `_MMPFN.u1.WsIndex` is 0 and there is no working set managing the paging structures for the system range (there is, alas, the System PTE working set, whose name is terribly misleading in this regard; it is *not* the working set of system PTEs, but, instead, the working set managing the System PTE *region*, which does not store PTEs at all).

This does not mean that these pages are never released. It is reasonable to think, for instance, that the VMM releases a PT for the system range when it's not mapping any pages, perhaps because the entire virtual range mapped by it has been released. In general, the VMM will free and recycle non-pageable pages which are not in use, but, as long as they are used, it does not *page* them, i.e., as long as they are used, their VAs are valid.

So, system paging structures and, in general, many pages of most special purpose regions are simply non-pageable, because they cannot be touched by the main paging actor, i.e. the Working Set Manager.

44.10   Session Space

44.10.1   Session Space Purpose

We can classify this region as a special purpose one, since *MiObtainSystemVa* does not seem to allow to allocate ranges from this region. However, kernel mode drivers are loaded in this region and part of it is used for a paged pool, so this region is also (internally) managed by the VMM as other dynamically allocated ones.

The main purpose of this region is to have a virtual range whose content is shared among all the processes belonging to a given session and, at the same time, is private among different sessions. In other words, processes belonging to different sessions have a different PML4E for it and map different physical pages into this range.

The system must maintain a separate set of data structures for each active session. For instance, each session must have its own state of the user interface. The Windows GUI is based on a hierarchy of system object: the session, the window station and the desktop (see for instance [17]). In the end, what we see on the screen is the state of a desktop belonging to the interactive windows station named Winsta0, whose session is currently connected with the screen and keyboard. While this goes on, other sessions exist in the system, each including windows stations and desktops. The system must therefore maintain all this state information for each session and this is accomplished by storing it into this region.

The region content can be classified as follows:

- Session control structures

- Session space image files

- Session paged pool

- Session mapped views

The following section describes each kind of content.

44.10.2   Region Content

44.10.2.1   Session Control Structures

These are data structures used to manage the session region itself. In these section we will provide a few examples although it is likely that many other undocumented data structures live in session space.

44.10.2.1.1 _MM_SESSION_SPACE

For each session the system creates an instance of _MM_SESSION_SPACE and each process has _EPROCESS.Session set to the address of the instance for the session it belongs to [2]. This address is outside session space (it's in the System PTE region) and is therefore always mapped to the same physical page, no matter what session the current address space belongs to.

By digging a little around the addresses of _MM_SESSION_SPACE instances we discover an interesting detail. Below, we see the address for an instance of explorer.exe:

```
1: kd> !process 0 0 explorer.exe
PROCESS ffffffa8002e8b060
    SessionId: 1  Cid: 03c4    Peb: 7fffffd5000  ParentCid: 036c
    DirBase: 2e532000  ObjectTable: fffff8a001a01c00  HandleCount: 855.
    Image: explorer.exe

1: kd> ?? ((nt!_eprocess*) 0xffffffa8002e8b060)->Session
void * 0xfffff880`03613000
```

As we said, the address is in the System PTE region, now let's have a look at its PTE and at the _MMPFN for its page:

```
1: kd> !pte @@( ((nt!_eprocess*) 0xffffffa8002e8b060)->Session )
                              VA fffff88003613000

PXE at FFFFF6FB7DBEDF88    PPE at FFFFF6FB7DBF1000    PDE at FFFFF6FB7E2000D8    PTE at FFFFF6FC4001B098
contains 000000003C004863  contains 000000003C003863  contains 0000000025147863  contains 0000000019DA4963
pfn 3c004     ---DA--KWEV pfn 3c003     ---DA--KWEV pfn 25147     ---DA--KWEV pfn 19da4     -G-DA--KWEV


1: kd> !pfn 19da4
    PFN 00019DA4 at address FFFFFA80004D8EC0
    flink        FFFFF88003613000  blink / share count 00000001  pteaddress FFFFF6FC80000000
    reference count 0001    used entry count  0000       Cached      color 0    Priority 0
    restore pte 000000C0  containing page       01A4A8  Active      M
    Modified
```

The _MMPFN content shows a few atypical values: `pteaddress` is not set to the PTE address reported by `!pte`; `containing page` (which is actually _MMPFN.u4.PteFrame) is not set to the PFN of the PT, also reported by `!pte` (it's the PFN in the PDE); `flink` is set 0xFFFFF880`03613000, i.e. the address of _MM_SESSION_SPACE itself, while, for an active page, this member is normally set to the WSL index or 0.

Let's turn now to `pteaddress` from the _MMPFN: it is actually the address of the PTE mapping the first page of session space, as we can see with `!pte`:

```
1: kd> !pte FFFFF6FC80000000
                                    VA fffff90000000000
PXE at FFFFF6FB7DBEDF90    PPE at FFFFF6FB7DBF2000    PDE at FFFFF6FB7E400000    PTE at
FFFFF6FC80000000
contains 0000000000000000
not valid
```

It is useful to remember that when `!pte` is used with a PTE address, it reports the PxEs for the address *mapped by* the given address. What we are seeing above is therefore that 0xFFFFF900`00000000 is mapped by the PTE at 0xFFFFF6FC`80000000, which is what we found in our _MMPFN.

So let's have a look at how session space is mapped when explorer.exe is the current process:

```
1: kd> .process /P 0xfffffa8002e8b060
Implicit process is now fffffa80`02e8b060
.cache forcedecodeptes done
1: kd> !pte fffff900`00000000
                                    VA fffff90000000000

PXE at FFFFF6FB7DBEDF90    PPE at FFFFF6FB7DBF2000    PDE at FFFFF6FB7E400000    PTE at FFFFF6FC80000000
contains 000000001A026863  contains 000000001A4A7863  contains 000000001A4A8863  contains 0000000019DA4863
pfn 1a026    ---DA--KWEV pfn 1a4a7    ---DA--KWEV pfn 1a4a8    ---DA--KWEV pfn 19da4    ---DA--KWEV
```

This is quite interesting: the first session space page is mapped by the same physical page storing the _MM_SESSION_SPACE instance.

So, to recapitulate: a process belongs to a session; an instance of _MM_SESSION_SPACE stores state information for this session; when the process address space is mapped, _MM_SESSION_SPACE is visible in the first session space page; _MM_SESSION_SPACE is also visible *in all memory contexts* at an address in the System PTE region, which can be found at _EPROCESS.Session.

Note how the System PTE region has been used to map something that needed to be accessible in an arbitrary session context. Conceptually, this is similar to mapping user mode buffers with MDLs to make them accessible in an arbitrary process context (see sec. 44.8.1.2 on p. 441).

Note also that `containing page` in the _MMPFN was 0x1A4A8, which is the PFN of the PT for 0xFFFFF900`00000000 visible in the `!pte` output above. In other words, the _MMPFN content is set up to reflect the mapping at the session space VA, rather than at the system PTE one.

A final note concerns the first `!pte` output for the session space address, which we obtained before issuing the `.process` command. As we can see, we were in a context where the PML4E for session space was set to 0 and therefore the entire session space was invalid. As it turns out, this is what we see when we have just broken into the debugger and the current context is the one of the System process: this context has no session space.

44.10.2.1.2 Session Working Set List

Subranges of the session space are pageable, so they are managed by means of a working set list like the other ones we have encountered in the past. _MM_SESSION_SPACE has a `Vm` member of type _MMSUPPORT:

```
1: kd> ?? &((nt!_mm_session_space*) ((nt!_eprocess*) 0xffffffa8001546b30)->Session)->Vm
struct _MMSUPPORT * 0xfffff880`03613c00
   +0x000 WorkingSetMutex   : _EX_PUSH_LOCK
   +0x008 ExitGate          : (null)
   +0x010 AccessLog         : 0xfffffa80`00e94000 Void
   +0x018 WorkingSetExpansionLinks : _LIST_ENTRY [ 0xfffffa80`02e7cee0 -
0xfffffa80`01073cd0 ]
   +0x028 AgeDistribution   : [7] 0x5f
   +0x044 MinimumWorkingSetSize : 0x400
   +0x048 WorkingSetSize    : 0x8df
   +0x04c WorkingSetPrivateSize : 0x659
   +0x050 MaximumWorkingSetSize : 0x408
   +0x054 ChargedWslePages  : 0
   +0x058 ActualWslePages   : 0
   +0x05c WorkingSetSizeOverhead : 6
   +0x060 PeakWorkingSetSize : 0xf94
   +0x064 HardFaultCount    : 0x3cb
   +0x068 VmWorkingSetList  : 0xfffff900`00812000 _MMWSL
   +0x070 NextPageColor     : 0x55d3
   +0x072 LastTrimStamp     : 0x3605
   +0x074 PageFaultCount    : 0x159e3
   +0x078 RepurposeCount    : 0xc300
   +0x07c Spare             : [2] 0
   +0x084 Flags             : _MMSUPPORT_FLAGS
```

The `VmWorkingSetList` member points inside session space. We can also see that the _WSLE array is in session space as well:

```
1: kd> ?? ((nt!_mm_session_space*) ((nt!_eprocess*) 0xfffffa8001546b30)->Session)-
>Vm.VmWorkingSetList
struct _MMWSL * 0xfffff900`00812000
```

```
[...]
   +0x010 Wsle              : 0xfffff900`00812488 _MMWSLE

[...]
```

This shows that the array is just after the `_MMWSL`.

There is also a static variable in the kernel image named MiSessionSpaceWs, which we first encountered in sec. 44.6 on p. 426. This variable stores the address of the session `_MMWSL`:

```
1: kd> dq nt!MiSessionSpaceWs l1
fffff800`02aff518  fffff900`00812000
```

which suggests that this address is the same for every session.

44.10.2.1.3 Session Space Bitmap

`_MM_SESSION_SPACE.DynamicVaBitMap` appears to store the address of a bitmap in session space:

```
1: kd> ?? ((nt!_mm_session_space*) ((nt!_eprocess*) 0xfffffa8001546b30)->Session)-
>DynamicVaBitMap
struct _RTL_BITMAP
   +0x000 SizeOfBitMap    : 0xfa00
   +0x008 Buffer          : 0xfffff900`00010000  -> 0x7ffff
```

which perhaps is used by the VMM to keep track of free/in use virtual addresses inside this region.

44.10.2.2   Session Space Image Files

Besides data structures, this region hosts kernel mode drivers implementing the windows GUI. We will return on this subject in greater detail in sec. 46.2 on p. 513, so for now we will just state that the VMM and image loader give each session a private copy of the read/write sections of these image files, and, therefore, of their static variables. Among the drivers loaded in this region are "Win32K.sys (Window Manager), CDD.DLL (Canonical Display Driver), TSDDD.dll (Frame Buffer Display Driver), DXG.sys (DirectX Graphics Driver)", [2]. By loading these drivers in session space, the VMM gives them a different copy of their static variables in each session, thus, the drivers themselves are not required to maintain per-session state.

44.10.2.3   Session Paged Pool

A portion of session space is used for a per-session paged pool. This allows other kernel mode components to make per-session allocations of pageable memory. The paged pool

limits are given by `_MM_SESSION_SPACE.PagedPoolStart` and
`_MM_SESSION_SPACE.PagedPoolEnd` ([2]):

```
1: kd> ?? ((nt!_mm_session_space*) ((nt!_eprocess*) 0xfffffa8001546b30)->Session)-
>PagedPoolStart
void * 0xfffff900`c0000000
1: kd> ?? ((nt!_mm_session_space*) ((nt!_eprocess*) 0xfffffa8001546b30)->Session)-
>PagedPoolEnd
void * 0xfffff920`bfffffff
```

44.10.2.4   Mapped Views

Several sources on this subject mention the existence of mapped views in session space. See
for instance [1], p. 741, or [17], which states that the desktop heap is among these views.
These should be views of memory sections allocated to share portions of memory between
an instance of session space and other virtual regions.

Also, [1] states on pp. 730,731 that Win32k.sys uses a heap "for sharing GDI and User objects
with user mode" stored in a memory section. It seems likely that this heap is the desktop
heap detailed in [17] and that views of this memory section are mapped in session space and
in user mode.

By digging through a few data structures it is possible to find some sections mapped both in
this region and in the user mode range of some processes (with read only protection), so that
user mode components can actually read portions of session space.

44.10.3   Page Fault Handling

MmAccessFault handles page faults in this region as described in sec. 43.3 on p. 410, with the
following peculiarities:

- If the current process is the System one, the function bugchecks, which makes sense
  when we think that the PML4 for System maps all the session space as invalid.

- The WSL used to track a new mapped virtual address is, of course, the session
  working set list.

44.11   Dynamic Kernel VA Space

44.11.1   Region Content

This is a dynamically allocated region used for: system cache views, paged special pool,
nonpaged special pool.

44.11.1.1   System Cache Views

These views are used to implement the file cache (in Chapter 49 - p. 543, we will see a few more details about the cache manager).

The cache manager does its job by creating a memory section object backed by the file to cache. We know that such a memory section does not make the file content visible in the virtual address space (see sec. 38.2.1.6 on p. 349 and also p. 302) and that, for this to happen, we must map a view of the section somewhere in virtual space. The cache manager allocates VA ranges from this region to map these views.

44.11.1.2   Paged and Nonpaged Special Pools

These are special variations of the paged and nonpaged pool used by Driver Verifier, a tool integrated in the system, which can be used to check drivers for bugs. Driver Verifier can be configured to intercept pool allocations from drivers and satisfy them from the special pool region, where the allocated memory is purposely surrounded by not mapped VAs. This way, if a buggy driver accesses memory outside its allocated pool block, a page fault occurs and the system crashes with the address of the driver's function reported as part of the blue screen data.

44.11.2   Virtual Address Space Management

The static MiSystemAvailableVa contains the number of 2MB ranges available in this region [2].

MiObtainSystemVa allocates from this region when MiVaSystemCache, MiVaSpecialPoolPaged or MiVaSpecialPoolNonPaged is specified for the memory type.

The bitmap used to manage this region is MiSystemVaBitmap.

44.11.3   Page Fault Handling

Page faults in this region are handled as described in sec. 43.3 on p. 410. Since this region is used for different types of content, the working set list to be used must be selected according to what is stored at the faulting address. For other dynamically allocated regions, the WSL to be used was implied by the region itself. The dynamic kernel VA region, however, is heterogeneous and its physical pages can belong to different WSLs.

MmAccessFault looks at the _MMPFN of the page table which contains the PTE mapping the address and checks the VaType member. Its value determines the WSL selected according to the following table:

_MMPFN.VaType	_MI_SYSTEM_VA_TYPE	Working Set List
7	MiVaSpecialPoolPaged	MmPagedPoolWs
8	MiVaSystemCache	MmSystemCacheWs
Any other value		MmSystemPtesWs

The table also shows that the symbolic values defined by _MI_SYSTEM_VA_TYPE are consistent with the WSL selected (see p. 410).

This gives us an hint as to the meaning of _MMPFN.VaType and tells us that, when allocating from this region, the VMM sets it to the memory type specified in the allocation. The VMM uses the _MMPFN of the page table, which is selected by the PDE mapping the address, so all the VAs mapped by a single PDE will have the same type. This is not a problem, since the minimum allocation unit of system VA ranges is a PDE i.e. 2MB.

44.12   PFN Database

44.12.1   Region Content

This special purpose region is where the _MMPFN array is stored, with an element for each physical memory page. We have been talking about _MMPFN instances throughout this book, so there is nothing much left to say about the content of this region.

This region is non-pageable, so that _MMPFN instances are always accessible at any IRQL.

44.12.2   The PFN Database and the Physical Address Space

44.12.2.1   Physical Address Space Map

The size of the PFN database is dictated by the amount of physical memory in the system and by the chipset configuration.

Several devices in the system are *memory mapped*, which means that they are accessed by the processor as if they were memory. There are ranges of physical addresses configured for them, so that when the processor reads and writes at these physical addresses it is actually interacting with these devices.

MemInfo, written by Alex Ionescu
(http://www.winsiderss.com/tools/meminfo/meminfo.htm), is a tool which has the ability to
dump a map of the physical address ranges which are actually mapped to physical memory
i.e. not mapped to devices. This is a sample MemInfo output from a real system:

```
C:\Windows>meminfo -r

MemInfo v1.11 - Show PFN database information
Copyright (C) 2007-2008 Alex Ionescu
www.alex-ionescu.com

Physical Memory Range: 0000000000001000 to 000000000009D000 (156 pages, 624 KB)
Physical Memory Range: 0000000000100000 to 000000009CE3F000 (642367 pages, 2569468 KB)
Physical Memory Range: 000000009CFFF000 to 000000009D000000 (1 pages, 4 KB)
Physical Memory Range: 0000000100000000 to 000000025FE00000 (1441280 pages, 5765120 KB)
MmHighestPhysicalPage: 2489856

C:\Windows>
```

This map shows that there are holes in the physical address space not mapped to memory,
e.g. the first one is between 0x9d000 and 0x100000.

44.12.2.2   Physical Address Space Size

MemInfo also shows the value of the MmHighestPhysicalPage static, although it actually
increments it by one. We can see this if we look at the same variable with WinDbg:

```
lkd> ? poi(nt!MmHighestPhysicalPage)
Evaluate expression: 2489855 = 00000000`0025fdff
```

This means the physical address space of this system is made of 0x25fe00 or 2,489,856 pages
with the last one having PFN 0x25fdff or 2,489,855.

Since each page is 4kB in size, 0x25fe00 pages give the following amount in bytes:

0x25fe00 x 0x1000 = 00000002`5fe00000 = 8GB + 0x5fe00000

This particular system has 8GB of RAM and the extra address space above this value is due to
memory mapped devices which shift actual physical memory toward higher addresses.

It is interesting to match these data with the value of the static MmNumberOfPhysicalPages,
which gives the amount of physical memory available to Windows:

```
lkd> dq nt!MmNumberOfPhysicalPages l1
fffff800`02f0c060  00000000`001fcbdc
```

This value is less than MmHighestPhysicalPage + 1, because it is the count of actual memory pages, while the other one is the total number of pages in the physical address space, including those mapped to devices.

To understand the relationship between these two values, we can start by computing the size of the "holes", i.e. ranges not mapped to memory (from the MemInfo output):

```
hole #1:
lkd> ? 100000 - 9D000
Evaluate expression: 405504 = 00000000`00063000

hole #2:
lkd> ? 9CFFF000 - 9CE3F000
Evaluate expression: 1835008 = 00000000`001c0000

hole #3:
lkd> ? 1`00000000 - 0`9D000000
Evaluate expression: 1660944384 = 00000000`63000000
```

The sum of these ranges gives 0x63223 pages, which must be subtracted from MmHighestPhysicalPage to find the number of actual memory pages. Furthermore, MemInfo shows that the first subrange mapped to physical memory begins at 0x1000, so an additional hole of 0x1000 byte, i.e. 1 page, is present at the very beginning of the physical address space. The pages of actual memory are therefore given by:

MmHighestPhysicalPage + 1 - 0x63223 - 1

which yields:

```
lkd> ? poi(nt!MmHighestPhysicalPage) + 1 - 0x63223 - 1
Evaluate expression: 2083804 = 00000000`001fcbdc
```

i.e. the same value found in MmNumberOfPhysicalPages.

Unfortunately, this leaves an unexplained detail: for some reason, the VMM is not using the whole 8GB of RAM. If it were, MmNumberOfPhysicalPages would be set to 0x200000. As it is, 13,348 pages, i.e. 54,673,408 are missing.

44.12.2.3   PFN Database Size

The PFN database is a simple array indexed by PFN. Since there are ranges of PFN values mapped to devices, the array elements corresponding to these ranges don't represent actual physical memory, but they exist in the database, because the VMM computes the address of the _MMPFN for any physical address as:

0xFFFFFA80`00000000 + sizeof(_MMPFN) * *PFN*

Given this, the database ending address can be easily computed from MmHighestPhysicalPage as:

$$\text{0xFFFFFA80`00000000} + \text{sizeof(\_MMPFN)} * (\text{MmHighestPhysicalPage} + 1)$$

On our test system this yields:

```
lkd> ?? 0xfffffa80`00000000 + sizeof(nt!_MMPFN) * (@@(poi MmHighestPhysicalPage) + 1)
unsigned int64 0xfffffa80`071fa000
```

We can see that the PFN database is immediately followed by the array of pages by color we saw in sec. 26.4.3.2 on p. 154:

```
lkd> dq nt!MmFreePagesByColor l1
fffff800`02e53f80  fffffa80`071fa000
```

The region for these lists will be described shortly in sec 44.13 on p. 497.

44.12.2.4 PFN Database Entries Corresponding to Mapped Devices

For PFNs not mapped to actual memory, the corresponding PFN entries appear to be filled with zeroes.

If a whole PFN db page corresponds to non-memory PFNs, the page is not mapped, i.e. the corresponding VA range in the PFN DB region is invalid.

44.12.2.5 Large Pages Usage

On certain systems a different behavior can be observed: the PFN DB is mapped with large pages, so even DB regions spanning whole 4k pages can be mapped, if they share the large page range with valid DB entries. When this happens, the invalid entries are filled with zeroes. This behavior can be observed on a system with 8GB of RAM:

```
lkd> !pte fffffa80`00000000
                                       VA fffffa8000000000
PXE at FFFFF6FB7DBEDFA8   PPE at FFFFF6FB7DBF5000   PDE at FFFFF6FB7EA00000   PTE at FFFFF6FD40000000
contains 0000000003254863 contains 0000000003255863 contains 00000001000009E3 contains 0000000000000000
pfn 3254     ---DA--KWEV pfn 3255     ---DA--KWEV pfn 100000   -GLDA--KWEV LARGE PAGE pfn 100000
```

Conversely, on a virtual machine with 1GB of RAM small pages are used.

```
1: kd> !pte fffffa80`00000000
                                       VA fffffa8000000000
PXE at FFFFF6FB7DBEDFA8   PPE at FFFFF6FB7DBF5000   PDE at FFFFF6FB7EA00000   PTE at FFFFF6FD40000000
contains 0000000004000863 contains 0000000004001863 contains 0000000004002863 contains 0000000004003963
pfn 4000     ---DA--KWEV pfn 4001     ---DA--KWEV pfn 4002     ---DA--KWEV pfn 4003     -G-DA--KWEV
```

Using large pages spares TLB entries and physical pages used for PTs, at the price of having physical memory mapped to unused DB entries. Possibly, the VMM chooses this approach when physical memory is plentiful. Also, more physical memory means a larger PFN DB range, which would consume more TLB entries and more PTs if small pages were used, so in the end it might be convenient to "waste" the physical memory mapped to invalid DB entries.

44.13   Free and Zeroed Lists by Color

Immediately after the PFN database are the page lists discussed in sections 26.4.3.1 (p. 151) and 26.4.3.2 (p. 154). This region is a special purpose one, dedicated to store the arrays of list heads.

The first array is the one storing the heads of the PFN linked lists of Zeroed pages. The starting address is:

```
lkd> dq nt!MmFreePagesByColor l1
fffff800`02e54f80  fffffa80`071fa000
```

which, as we saw earlier, is right after the PFN DB.

There is a separate list head for each color-NUMA index value. On the system analyzed in the previous sections, the color index is 7 bits wide and there is a single NUMA node, so the color-NUMA index is in the range 0 - 0x7F. Each list head is an instance of _MMPFNLIST, so the end address of the array is:

```
lkd> ? poi nt!MmFreePagesByColor + 80 * @@(sizeof(nt!_MMPFNLIST))
Evaluate expression: -6047194434560 = fffffa80`071fb400
```

We also know that the address of the array of list heads for the Free lists is:

```
lkd> dq nt!MmFreePagesByColor + 8 l1
fffff800`02e54f88  fffffa80`071fb400
```

In other words, the pointer to the Free lists is at MmFreePagesByColor + 8 and it points right after the array of Zeroed lists. There are 0x80 list heads for the Free lists as well, so they end at:

```
lkd> ? poi(nt!MmFreePagesByColor + 8) + 80 * @@(sizeof(nt!_MMPFNLIST))
Evaluate expression: -6047194429440 = fffffa80`071fc800
```

Following these two arrays are the corresponding ones for singly linked lists. The address of the array of Zeroed lists can be extracted as follows:

```
lkd> dq nt!MiZeroPageSlist l1
fffff800`02e96790  fffffa80`071fc800
```

and it immediately follows the Free PFN-linked lists. This array stores an _SLIST_HEADER for each color-NUMA value, so its ending address is:

```
lkd> ? poi nt!MiZeroPageSlist + 80 * @@(sizeof(nt!_SLIST_HEADER))
Evaluate expression: -6047194427392 = ffffa80`071fd000
```

and matches nicely with the pointer to the Free lists array:

```
lkd> dq nt!MiFreePageSlist l1
fffff800`02e967b0  ffffa80`071fd000
```

This last array ends at:

```
lkd> ? poi nt!MiFreePageSlist + 80 * @@(sizeof(nt!_SLIST_HEADER))
Evaluate expression: -6047194425344 = ffffa80`071fd800
```

and we see that the nonpaged pool starts on the next page:

```
lkd> dq nt!MmNonPagedPoolStart l1
fffff800`02f010a8  ffffa80`071fe000.
```

This region appears to be non-pageable, which makes sense, considering the VMM accesses these lists to resolve page faults. It is mapped with large pages (hence implicitly non-pageable) on the 8GB system examined:

```
lkd> !pte poi nt!MmFreePagesByColor
                                    VA ffffa80071fa000

PXE at FFFFF6FB7DBEDFA8   PPE at FFFFF6FB7DBF5000   PDE at FFFFF6FB7EA001C0   PTE at FFFFF6FD40038FD0
contains 0000000003254863 contains 0000000003255863 contains 0000000105E009E3 contains 0000000000000000
pfn 3254      ---DA--KWEV pfn 3255      ---DA--KWEV pfn 105e00    -GLDA--KWEV LARGE PAGE pfn 105ffa


lkd> !pte poi nt!MiFreePageSlist + 80 * @@(sizeof(nt!_SLIST_HEADER))
                                    VA ffffa80071fd800

PXE at FFFFF6FB7DBEDFA8   PPE at FFFFF6FB7DBF5000   PDE at FFFFF6FB7EA001C0   PTE at FFFFF6FD40038FE8
contains 0000000003254863 contains 0000000003255863 contains 0000000105E009E3 contains 0000000000000000
pfn 3254      ---DA--KWEV pfn 3255      ---DA--KWEV pfn 105e00    -GLDA--KWEV LARGE PAGE pfn 105ffd
```

On the 1GB system small pages are used, but they don't belong to a working set, so they are not pageable as well:

```
1: kd> !pte poi nt!MmFreePagesByColor
                                    VA ffffa8000c00000

PXE at FFFFF6FB7DBEDFA8   PPE at FFFFF6FB7DBF5000   PDE at FFFFF6FB7EA00030   PTE at FFFFF6FD40006000
contains 0000000004000863 contains 0000000004001863 contains 0000000004C07863 contains 0000000004C08963
pfn 4000      ---DA--KWEV pfn 4001      ---DA--KWEV pfn 4c07      ---DA--KWEV pfn 4c08      -G-DA--KWEV


1: kd> !pfn 4c08
   PFN 00004C08 at address FFFFFA80000E4180
      flink       00000000  blink / share count 00000001  pteaddress FFFFF6FD40006000
```

```
     reference count 0001    used entry count  0000      Cached    color 0    Priority 0
     restore pte 00000000  containing page        004C07  Active

1: kd> !pte poi nt!MiFreePageSlist + 80 * @@(sizeof(nt!_SLIST_HEADER))
                                    VA fffffa8000c03800


PXE at FFFFF6FB7DBEDFA8    PPE at FFFFF6FB7DBF5000    PDE at FFFFF6FB7EA00030    PTE at FFFFF6FD40006018
contains 0000000004000863  contains 0000000004001863  contains 0000000004C07863  contains 0000000004C0B963
pfn 4000      ---DA--KWEV  pfn 4001      ---DA--KWEV  pfn 4c07      ---DA--KWEV  pfn 4c0b      -G-DA--KWEV


1: kd> !pfn 4c0b
    PFN 00004C0B at address FFFFFA80000E4210
    flink      00000000  blink / share count 00000001  pteaddress FFFFF6FD40006018
    reference count 0001    used entry count  0000      Cached    color 0    Priority 0
    restore pte 00000000  containing page        004C07  Active
```

Note: in the computations for the 1GB system, we used a color range size equal to 0x80, because this system is a virtual machine running on the 8GB physical one. With VmWare player, the virtual processor has the same cache size as the physical one, so the VMM uses 7 bits for the color index in the virtual machine as well.

44.14   Nonpaged Pool

44.14.1   Region Content

This is a dynamically allocated region, dedicated to store the nonpaged pool. The static MmNonPagedPoolStart is set to its starting address.

The VMM uses large pages to map this region, to save TLB entries. For instance, on a test system with 1GB of RAM we find:

```
1: kd> dq nt!MmNonPagedPoolStart l1
fffff800`02af20a0  fffffa80`00c04000
```

A large page maps a range which is 2MB in size and aligned on 2MB boundaries (i.e. multiples of 0x200000). This starting address falls in the 0xFFFFFA80`00C00000 range, which also stores the page lists head. This range is mapped with small pages, probably because it is not entirely used for nonpaged pool:

```
1: kd> !pte fffffa80`00c04000
                                    VA fffffa8000c04000


PXE at FFFFF6FB7DBEDFA8    PPE at FFFFF6FB7DBF5000    PDE at FFFFF6FB7EA00030    PTE at FFFFF6FD40006020
contains 0000000004000863  contains 0000000004001863  contains 0000000004C07863  contains 000000003FF81963
pfn 4000      ---DA--KWEV  pfn 4001      ---DA--KWEV  pfn 4c07      ---DA--KWEV  pfn 3ff81      -G-DA--KWEV
```

However, as soon as we cross a 2MB boundary, we see that large pages are used. The first multiple of 0x200000 after our starting address is 0xFFFFFA80`00E00000; in the output below, note how the PDE address has increased by 8, confirming that we have moved to the next PDE and this one is set to map a large page:

```
1: kd> !pte fffffa80`00e00000
                                        VA fffffa8000e00000

PXE at FFFFF6FB7DBEDFA8   PPE at FFFFF6FB7DBF5000   PDE at FFFFF6FB7EA00038   PTE at FFFFF6FD40007000
contains 0000000004000863  contains 0000000004001863  contains 000000003FC009E3  contains 0000000000000000
pfn 4000      ---DA--KWEV pfn 4001      ---DA--KWEV pfn 3fc00      -GLDA--KWEV LARGE PAGE pfn 3fc00
```

Other kernel mode components can allocate pool blocks by calling DDIs like *ExAllocatePool* and specifying the desired number of bytes. These allocations can be of any size. Internally, the VMM manages the nonpaged pool in a way similar to a heap and, when it needs to grow its size, it calls *MiObtainSystemVa* and, eventually, maps physical memory to the new VA addresses.

See also [1], pp. 721 - 728.

44.14.2   Virtual Address Space Management

Virtual address space is allocated from this region by calling *MiObtainSystemVa* specifying MiVaNonPagedPool. The bitmap used to manage this region is MiNonPagedPoolVaBitmap ([2]).

44.15   HAL and Loader Mappings

This region is used during system startup ([2]).

45   System Range Experiments

45.1 A Word of Caution

The MemTests program comes with a kernel mode driver named KrnlAllocs.sys which allows to test a number of memory related DDIs. It also has a function for reading or writing at a system range address specified by the user. This function is executed at ring 0 and accesses the specified address.

All tests performed by the driver are potentially dangerous and there is a good chance that they will cause a blue screen.

The driver writes messages to the kernel debugger console, so it only makes sense to use it on a machine hooked up to a debugger.

KrnlAllocs.sys is not signed, so, normally, it would not be loaded by Windows. However, when a kernel debugger is attached to the system, such a driver can be loaded, even though the following (misleading) warning is displayed:

Figure 59 - Non-signed Driver Warning

To confirm that the driver was successfully loaded, look for the following messages in the debugger console:

```
KernelAllocs - driver, compiled Jun 10 2012 09:10:51

KernelAllocs - Device created
KernelAllocs - driver successfully loaded.
```

45.2 The System Range Tests Menu

The *System range tests* option of MemTests main menu opens the submenu for these tests.

The menu section titled *Driver control* contains one option to load driver and another one to unload it. When the driver is loaded, its service definition is created and it will be removed upon driver unloading.

The options in section *Tests* are mostly self-explanatory and allow to call a number of DDIs.

45.3 Touching a System Range

In the previous chapter, we analyzed how page faults are handled in the various system regions. We can use MemTests to cause such faults, in order to analyze *MmAccessFault* with WinDbg.

In the following example, we will access an invalid address in the System PTE region and break into *MmAccessFault*. When we will resume execution, the system will crash, because of the invalid access.

We begin by entering the *System Range Tests* submenu and selecting *Load kernel allocations driver*.

To find an invalid address, we can dump the PxEs of the region starting address we the `!pte` extension:

```
0: kd> !pte fffff880`00000000
                                  VA fffff88000000000

PXE at FFFFF6FB7DBEDF88    PPE at FFFFF6FB7DBF1000    PDE at FFFFF6FB7E200000    PTE at FFFFF6FC40000000
contains 000000003BF84863  contains 000000003BF83863  contains 000000003BF82863  contains 000000003C08A963
pfn 3bf84    ---DA--KWEV   pfn 3bf83    ---DA--KWEV   pfn 3bf82    ---DA--KWEV   pfn 3c08a    -G-DA--KWEV
```

Then, knowing that the region is allocated in units of 1 PDE, we can dump the PDEs following the first one, looking for entries set to 0, which are invalid PDEs:

```
0: kd> dq FFFFF6FB7E200000
fffff6fb`7e200000  00000000`3bf82863 00000000`3bf81863
fffff6fb`7e200010  00000000`3c006863 00000000`3c005863
fffff6fb`7e200020  00000000`3c089863 00000000`3c08b863
fffff6fb`7e200030  00000000`3c10c863 00000000`03103863
fffff6fb`7e200040  00000000`03104863 00000000`03105863
fffff6fb`7e200050  00000000`03106863 00000000`03107863
fffff6fb`7e200060  00000000`03108863 00000000`03110863
fffff6fb`7e200070  00000000`0310f863 00000000`d80009fb
0: kd> dq
fffff6fb`7e200080  00000000`1b928863 00000000`19fae863
fffff6fb`7e200090  00000000`19f73863 00000000`14eb0863
fffff6fb`7e2000a0  00000000`11a5f863 00000000`3d427863
fffff6fb`7e2000b0  00000000`240f6863 00000000`271d1863
fffff6fb`7e2000c0  00000000`27fbd863 00000000`2803e863
fffff6fb`7e2000d0  00000000`108ce863 00000000`251c7863
fffff6fb`7e2000e0  00000000`0f5e1863 00000000`23e68863
fffff6fb`7e2000f0  00000000`2258a863 00000000`2415a863
0: kd> dq
fffff6fb`7e200100  00000000`22a25863 00000000`1d2aa863
fffff6fb`7e200110  00000000`0f575863 00000000`0def1863
fffff6fb`7e200120  00000000`0b94e863 00000000`3b581863
fffff6fb`7e200130  00000000`36727863 00000000`32857863
fffff6fb`7e200140  00000000`00000000 00000000`00000000
fffff6fb`7e200150  00000000`00000000 00000000`00000000
```

```
fffff6fb`7e200160  00000000`00000000 00000000`00000000
fffff6fb`7e200170  00000000`00000000 00000000`00000000
```

The shaded entries are invalid. To know the address mapped by the first entry, we have to shift its address left by 18 bits. This kicks out the auto-entry index from the PML4 and PDPT index slots and aligns the indexes of the actual address into their slots. We must also set the 16 leftmost bits to 1, to make the address canonical:

```
0: kd> ?? (0xfffff6fb`7e200140 << 18) | ((int64) 0xffff << 48)
unsigned int64 0xfffff880`05000000
```

We then resume execution and, at the MemTests submenu, select the *Memory touch test* option. The program prompts us for the starting address and we use the one computed above (we must be careful to remove the inverted apostrophe from the value). We can accept the default values for the length of the accessed region and the access type (i.e. 0x1000 bytes and read access).

 When the program shows the prompt after the *About to call the driver* message, we must choose b, in order to break into the debugger. We need to do this to set up a breakpoint on *MmAccessFault*, otherwise the function would execute completely, crashing the system.

After selecting b, we must switch to the debugger, where the system is halted inside the thread about to call KrnlAllocs.sys. This is the thread which will incur the page fault, so we set a breakpoint on *MmAccessFault*, valid for this thread only, with the following command:

```
1: kd> bp /t @$thread nt!MmAccessFault
```

It is very important to specify a breakpoint for this thread only, because *MmAccessFault* is continuously called by lots of threads in the system.

We can now resume execution and we see a couple of messages from KrnlAllocs in the debugger console, followed by the breakpoint hit:

```
KernelAllocs - KmemTouchTest
KernelAllocs - About to touch region 0xFFFFF88005000000 - 0xFFFFF88005001000
Breakpoint 0 hit
nt!MmAccessFault:
fffff800`028d6be0 48895c2410      mov     qword ptr [rsp+10h],rbx
```

We can now follow *MmAccessFault* in its handling of the fault. For instance, we can place the following breakpoint:

```
1: kd> bp /t @$thread nt!MmAccessFault + 6ee
```

thereby specifying the offset of the instruction which reads the PDE from memory to check whether it is valid (note how we are always using /t to set a breakpoint for the current thread only). When we resume execution, we stop here:

```
1: kd> g
Breakpoint 1 hit
nt!MmAccessFault+0x6ee:
fffff800`028d72ce 498b1b          mov     rbx,qword ptr [r11]
```

The r command shows that r11 is set to the address of our PDE and that the latter is still set to 0:

```
1: kd> r
rax=fffff6fb7dbed000 rbx=fffff6fb7dbf1000 rcx=fffff70001080000
rdx=ffff080000000011 rsi=0000000000000000 rdi=fffff88005000000
rip=fffff800028d72ce rsp=fffff88004dfe650 rbp=fffff88004dfe6c0
 r8=0000000000000000  r9=fffff6fc40028000 r10=00000000000001f1
r11=fffff6fb7e200140 r12=fffff00004dfe7b0 r13=fffff00005000000
r14=0000000000000000 r15=0000000000000000
iopl=0         nv up ei pl nz na pe nc
cs=0010  ss=0018  ds=002b  es=002b  fs=0053  gs=002b             efl=00000202
nt!MmAccessFault+0x6ee:
fffff800`028d72ce 498b1b          mov     rbx,qword ptr [r11]
ds:002b:fffff6fb`7e200140=0000000000000000
```

Here *MmAccessFault* is about to discover that the address is invalid. If we step through the code for a few instructions, we arrive at a call to *KeBugCheckEx* which brings everything down.

45.4 Touching an Invalid Paging Structure for the User Range

This experiment shows the peculiar behavior described in sec.44.3.3 on p. 419: an access to a not present paging structure (we will use a page table) which would map an address in the user range is "resolved" mapping a physical page. However, when the process owning the paging structure terminates, the system bugchecks with code 0x50.

We will perform the same steps of section 45.3 on p. 502, but for a page table of the MemTests program itself.

After launching MemTests and loading the driver, we break into the debugger and look for the address of MemTests with the following command:

```
1: kd> !process 0 1 memtests.exe
```

Setting the option flags parameter to 1 has the effect of dumping various process data including the VAD tree address.

WinDbg thinks for a while, then presents us with the process data:

```
1: kd> !process 0 1 memtests.exe
PROCESS fffffa8000f5db30
    SessionId: 1  Cid: 0518    Peb: 7fffffdf000  ParentCid: 0964
    DirBase: 14a58000  ObjectTable: fffff8a002305580  HandleCount:   9.
    Image: MemTests.EXE
    VadRoot fffffa80034e28e0 Vads 26 Clone 0 Private 190. Modified 0. Locked 0.
    DeviceMap fffff8a00103e730
    Token                             fffff8a0023e9a90
    ElapsedTime                       00:00:11.546
    UserTime                          00:00:00.000
    KernelTime                        00:00:00.000
    QuotaPoolUsage[PagedPool]         0
    QuotaPoolUsage[NonPagedPool]      0
    Working Set Sizes (now,min,max)  (488, 50, 345) (1952KB, 200KB, 1380KB)
    PeakWorkingSetSize                488
    VirtualSize                       11 Mb
    PeakVirtualSize                   11 Mb
    PageFaultCount                    485
    MemoryPriority                    BACKGROUND
    BasePriority                      8
    CommitCharge                      210
```

We switch the debugger to the memory context of MemTests by feeding the address above to the .process metacommand:

```
1: kd> .process /P fffffa8000f5db30
Implicit process is now fffffa80`00f5db30
.cache forcedecodeptes done
```

We must be careful not to forget the /P option. Next, we examine the VAD tree to find an unallocated PDE:

```
1: kd> !vad fffffa80034e28e0
VAD              level    start      end    commit
fffffa8002f72170 ( 3)       10       1f         0 Mapped        READWRITE
fffffa80031b8730 ( 4)       20       2f         0 Mapped        READWRITE
fffffa800348d0d0 ( 2)       30       33         0 Mapped        READONLY
fffffa8000ec30d0 ( 4)       40       40         1 Private       READWRITE
fffffa8002f97380 ( 3)       50       b6         0 Mapped        READONLY
fffffa8002cbc940 ( 4)       c0      1bf        32 Private       READWRITE
fffffa8000eb5670 ( 1)      210      30f         7 Private       READWRITE
fffffa8000ec39e0 ( 5)      310      40f        32 Private       READWRITE
fffffa8002114850 ( 4)      410      50f        42 Private       READWRITE
fffffa8002d361f0 ( 5)      650      65f        10 Private       READWRITE
fffffa8000eb1300 ( 3)      680      68f         6 Private       READWRITE
fffffa800336a240 ( 4)    76d60    76e7e         4 Mapped   Exe  EXECUTE_WRITECOPY
fffffa8002f7b9d0 ( 2)    76f80    7712a        12 Mapped   Exe  EXECUTE_WRITECOPY
```

We can see a hole in the user region after the shaded range. Each PDE maps a 2MB range, i.e. a size of 0x200000 bytes in hexadecimal. We see from the VAD tree that the PDE for the range 0x600000 - 0x7FFFFF is allocated, because part of the range is allocated as well. The PDE for the range 0x800000 - 0x9FFFFF is not allocated. We can obtain the address of the first page table in this range with !pte:

```
1: kd> !pte 800000
                                  VA 0000000000800000

PXE at FFFFF6FB7DBED000    PPE at FFFFF6FB7DA00000    PDE at FFFFF6FB40000020    PTE at FFFFF68000004000
contains 03C0000029808867  contains 02F0000002BD0B867  contains 0000000000000000
pfn 29808    ---DA--UWEV    pfn 2bd0b    ---DA--UWEV    not valid
```

The output shows that the PDE is set to 0 and the PTE address is 0xFFFFF68000004000. Of course, this address is not mapped:

```
1: kd> db FFFFF68000004000
fffff680`00004000  ?? ?? ?? ?? ?? ?? ?? ??-?? ?? ?? ?? ?? ?? ?? ??  ????????????????
fffff680`00004010  ?? ?? ?? ?? ?? ?? ?? ??-?? ?? ?? ?? ?? ?? ?? ??  ????????????????
```

Now we can resume execution and use MemTests to touch this address. We do this in the same way we did in sec. 45.3 on p. 502, i.e. by breaking into the debugger before the memory access occurs and placing a breakpoint on nt!MmAccessFault, valid for the current thread only.

Note: when we break into the debugger by choosing b, it is better to check the PDE again, because it may have been mapped while MemTests was running. If this happened, we can use !vad again to find another invalid PDE, then resume execution with g, because the PTE address we specified in this run is now valid and no page fault will occur. From the MemTests menu, we can then repeat the test with the new PTE address.

When the breakpoint is hit, we can examine again the content of our PDE:

```
KernelAllocs - KmemTouchTest
KernelAllocs - About to touch region 0xFFFFF68000004000 - 0xFFFFF68000005000
Breakpoint 0 hit
nt!MmAccessFault:
fffff800`0289cbe0 48895c2410      mov      qword ptr [rsp+10h],rbx
0: kd> dq FFFFF6FB40000020 1 1
fffff6fb`40000020  00000000`00000000
```

The PDE is still set to 0.

Now we remove our breakpoint with bc* (which clears all the breakpoints), because MmAccessFault is continuously called and the breakpoint itself, even though it does not stop execution for other threads, slows down the system to the point of making it unusable. Then we let execution go on until MmAccessFault returns with the g @$ra command:

```
0: kd> bc*
0: kd> g @$ra
nt!KiPageFault+0x16e:
fffff800`02880fee 85c0                test    eax,eax
```

We stop inside *KiPageFault*, which is the caller of *MmAccessFault*. We can now look at our PDE, to see what MmAccessFault did:

```
0: kd> dq FFFFF6FB40000020 l 1
fffff6fb`40000020  1fb00000`13b4a867
```

The PDE is set to a valid mapping (bit 0 is set), which means that the PT is now mapped:

```
0: kd> db FFFFF68000004000
fffff680`00004000  00 00 00 00 00 00 00 00-00 00 00 00 00 00 00 00  ................
fffff680`00004010  00 00 00 00 00 00 00 00-00 00 00 00 00 00 00 00  ................
```

If we resume execution, the system seems to have survived the experiment. However, when MemTests closes, it usually crashes:

```
0: kd> g

KernelAllocs - Device closed
*** Fatal System Error: 0x00000050

(0xFFFFFA7FFFFFFFEA,0x0000000000000000,0xFFFFF800028B86FB,0x0000000000000007)
```

This tells us that such a page fault is not meant to happen and is a particular nasty one, because it corrupts the VMM data structures causing a crash *long after* the invalid access. It would be quite difficult to trace such a crash back to what caused it.

46   Kernel Mode Image Files Loading

46.1 Images Loaded Outside Session Space

This section analyzes the loading of images in the Initial Loader Mappings and System PTE regions.

46.1.1   Memory Sections Are Not Used

Kernel mode image files are executables loaded in the system range and executed at ring 0. The kernel image and hal belong to this category, together with all the kernel mode drivers loaded by the system, usually stored in files ending with a .sys extension.

These files are loaded in a different way from user mode ones, because memory sections are not used. This means that all the data structures that make up a memory section (section object, segment, subsections, prototype PTEs) are not created. This makes sense when we think that sections are used, for user mode images, to accomplish two things:

- Share the file sections which cannot be modified, e.g. code and read only data file sections, among all processes.

- Implement copy-on-write for sections which can be modified, i.e. share among processes the original copy from the image file and give each process a private copy as soon as it writes to it.

In the system range, none of this is necessary: the range content is already shared by all processes and this applies to read/write data sections of image files as well: if a kernel mode driver uses a static variable, it does not expect to see a different copy of it depending on which process is current.

The bottom line is that the VMM simply loads the image file content into memory mapped somewhere in the relevant region. For now, we are not going to discuss pageable sections of kernel mode drivers. For non-pageable sections, the mapping is fixed: the physical page is not part of any working set, so it is never repurposed.

We can verify this behavior by looking at the mapping for a kernel mode driver, e.g. ntfs.sys, the file system driver for NTFS. First, we find out the driver address:

```
0: kd> lm m ntfs
start               end                 module name
fffff880`0123c000 fffff880`013df000   Ntfs        (deferred)
```

Then we look at the PTE and _MMPFN for one of its pages, e.g. at +0x3000 or +3 pages from its starting address:

```
0: kd> !pte fffff880`0123c000 + 3000
                                        VA fffff8800123f000

PXE at FFFFF6FB7DBEDF88    PPE at FFFFF6FB7DBF1000    PDE at FFFFF6FB7E200048    PTE at FFFFF6FC400091F8
contains 000000003C004863  contains 000000003C003863  contains 0000000003105863  contains 0000000003481121
pfn 3c004     ---DA--KWEV  pfn 3c003    ---DA--KWEV  pfn 3105    ---DA--KWEV  pfn 3481     -G--A--KREV


0: kd> !pfn 3481
    PFN 00003481 at address FFFFFA800009D830
    flink         00000000  blink / share count 00000001  pteaddress FFFFF6FC400091F8
    reference count 0001    used entry count  0000        Cached    color 0    Priority 0
    restore pte 00000060  containing page        003105  Active    M
    Modified
```

We can see how the physical page is fixed since it has no working set index. Furthermore, we must remember that when a page is part of a memory section, `pteaddress` (`_MMPFN.PteAddress`) stores the address of the *prototype PTE* pointing to it and `containing page` (`_MMPFN.u4.PteFrame`) stores the PFN of the physical page for the prototype PTE. This allows the VMM to update the prototype PTE when it repurposes the page. However, the `!pfn` output above shows that `pteaddress` points to the hardware PTE and `containing page` matches the PFN of the hardware page table reported by the `!pte` extension above.

These are all clear signs that this physical page is not part of any shareable memory section, but, rather it is fixedly mapping a VA, where the image file content has been loaded.

Repeating this analysis for other addresses and for other kernel mode images, including the kernel image itself, yields the same results.

46.1.2   Pageable Sections of Kernel Mode Images

The loader and VMM allow a kernel mode driver to specify that some of its file sections are pageable. This is achieved by giving the file section a name which starts with "PAGE". With the Visual C compiler, this is done by means of the `#pragma alloc_text` directive, which takes a function name and a section name and places the code emitted for the function in a section with the specified name. Not all sections of a driver can be made pageable, since certain functions are called at `DISPATCH` IRQL or above.

We know that, with user mode image files, when a page is repurposed, its content is not saved to the paging file, because it is already available in the image file itself. This is made possible by the underlying file backed memory section, which associates the section content with offsets into the image file.

Since memory sections are not built for kernel mode image files, there is no way to associate a pageable virtual page with an offset into the file, so such a page is saved into the paging file when repurposed.

In general, a pageable virtual page of a loaded image is treated like any other pageable page in the system range (e.g. a paged pool page): it is part of a working set (the System PTE one) and can be brought into transition, outpaged and repurposed. When it is needed again, it is faulted back from the paging file.

We can verify this behavior with the krnlallocs.sys driver, which has a pageable function named *PageableFunction*. If we look at the PxEs mapping its address immediately after loading the driver, this is what we find:

```
0: kd> !pte krnlallocs!PageableFunction
                                    VA fffff8800357c010

PXE at FFFFF6FB7DBEDF88    PPE at FFFFF6FB7DBF1000    PDE at FFFFF6FB7E2000D0    PTE at FFFFF6FC4001ABE0
contains 000000003C004863  contains 000000003C003863  contains 00000000D6A6863  contains 000000003D4D6860
pfn 3c004     ---DA--KWEV  pfn 3c003    ---DA--KWEV  pfn d6a6     ---DA--KWEV  not valid
                                                                               Transition: 3d4d6
                                                                               Protect: 3 - ExecuteRead


0: kd> !pfn 3d4d6
    PFN 0003D4D6 at address FFFFFA8000B7E820
    flink      00002C25  blink / share count 00036321  pteaddress FFFFF6FC4001ABE0
    reference count 0000   used entry count  0000      Cached     color 0    Priority 2
    restore pte 00000060  containing page         00D6A6  Modified   M
    Modified
```

We see that the PTE is in transition and the page is on the Modified list. Thus, it appears that a pageable section is read into a page but not immediately made part of the working set.

We can select the *Call pageable function test* option in the submenu of MemTests to cause the function to be called. This function only writes the following message to the debugger console:

```
KernelAllocs - Device openedKernelAllocs - PageableFunction called
```

However, simply calling it causes the VMM to soft fault the page. This is the situation after the call:

```
0: kd> !pte krnlallocs!PageableFunction
                                    VA fffff8800357c010

PXE at FFFFF6FB7DBEDF88    PPE at FFFFF6FB7DBF1000    PDE at FFFFF6FB7E2000D0    PTE at FFFFF6FC4001ABE0
contains 000000003C004863  contains 000000003C003863  contains 00000000D6A6863  contains 0AB000003D4D6121
pfn 3c004     ---DA--KWEV  pfn 3c003    ---DA--KWEV  pfn d6a6     ---DA--KWEV  pfn 3d4d6    -G--A--KREV


0: kd> !pfn 3d4d6
    PFN 0003D4D6 at address FFFFFA8000B7E820
    flink      000000AB  blink / share count 00000001  pteaddress FFFFF6FC4001ABE0
    reference count 0001   used entry count  0000      Cached     color 0    Priority 5
    restore pte 00000060  containing page         00D6A6  Active     M
    Modified
```

The same page that was previously on the Modified list is now active and it is still dirty, because no copy of it exists in the paging file (restore pte is 0x60, so _MMPTE.u.Soft.PageFileHigh is 0). We can also confirm that the value 0xAB found in flink (_MMPTE.u1) is the working set list index for this VPN in the System PTE working set:

```
0: kd> ?? ((nt!_MMSUPPORT*) @@(nt!MmSystemPtesWs))->VmWorkingSetList->Wsle[0xab].u1.e1
struct _MMWSLENTRY
   +0x000 Valid           : 0y1
   +0x000 Spare           : 0y0
```

```
    +0x000 Hashed               : 0y0
    +0x000 Direct               : 0y1
    +0x000 Protection           : 0y00000 (0)
    +0x000 Age                  : 0y000
    +0x000 VirtualPageNumber : 0y111111111111111111111100010000000000000011010101111100
(0xfffff8800357c)
```

Finally, if we exhaust physical memory (e.g. by creating and mapping a file with a length equal to 90% of the physical memory and by writing to the mapped view), we can force the VMM to trim, outpage and repurpose the page. This is what we see afterwards:

```
0: kd> !pte krnlallocs!PageableFunction
                                      VA fffff8800357c010

PXE at FFFFF6FB7DBEDF88   PPE at FFFFF6FB7DBF1000   PDE at FFFFF6FB7E2000D0   PTE at FFFFF6FC4001ABE0
contains 000000003C004863 contains 000000003C003863 contains 000000000D6A6863 contains 0000E9A500000060
pfn 3c004   ---DA--KWEV pfn 3c003   ---DA--KWEV pfn d6a6   ---DA--KWEV not valid
                                                                        PageFile:  0
                                                                        Offset: e9a5
                                                                        Protect: 3 - ExecuteRead
```

These findings confirm that the driver code is outpaged to the paging file.

The final experiment we can perform with PageableFunction is to lock it in memory. To do this, we must select the *Lock pageable driver test* option in MemTests, which calls the *MmLockPagableCodeSection* DDI. This is the situation after the call:

```
1: kd> !pte krnlallocs!PageableFunction
                                      VA fffff8800357c010

PXE at FFFFF6FB7DBEDF88   PPE at FFFFF6FB7DBF1000   PDE at FFFFF6FB7E2000D0   PTE at FFFFF6FC4001ABE0
contains 000000003C004863 contains 000000003C003863 contains 000000000D6A6863 contains 006000001E3B2121
pfn 3c004   ---DA--KWEV pfn 3c003   ---DA--KWEV pfn d6a6   ---DA--KWEV pfn 1e3b2   -G--A--KREV


1: kd> !pfn 1e3b2
    PFN 0001E3B2 at address FFFFFA80005AB160
    flink        00000806  blink / share count 00000001  pteaddress FFFFF6FC4001ABE0
    reference count 0002     used entry count  0000       Cached    color 0   Priority 5
    restore pte E9A500000060  containing page      00D6A6  Active

1: kd> ?? ((nt!_mmsupport*) @@(nt!MmSystemPtesWs))->VmWorkingSetList->Wsle[0x806].u1.e1
struct _MMWSLENTRY
    +0x000 Valid                : 0y1
    +0x000 Spare                : 0y0
    +0x000 Hashed               : 0y0
    +0x000 Direct               : 0y1
    +0x000 Protection           : 0y00000 (0)
    +0x000 Age                  : 0y000
    +0x000 VirtualPageNumber : 0y111111111111111111111100010000000000000011010101111100
(0xfffff8800357c)
```

The VA is mapped to a physical page, which has a reference count of 2 and this will prevent it from being moved to a transition list. The page is currently part of the System PTE WS. If it is later removed from it, the share count drops to 0, the reference count to 1 and the page remains active.

An interesting implication of the way kernel mode images are loaded is that they can be deleted from the file system while they are loaded. The file is not locked in any way, which makes sense since the VMM does not need to read it again after loading its content. Even if the image has pageable sections, these are read at load time and placed into pages on the Modified list. Eventually, they may be written to the paging file and reloaded from there at a later time, but the image file will not be needed anymore. This can be verified by loading krnlallocs.sys and deleting the file. Not only the delete operation succeeds, but the driver remains loaded and working, as can be seen by calling it with MemTests.

46.1.3   Large Pages Usage

The kernel and the hal are mapped with large pages if there is enough physical memory on the system. For instance, on a virtual machine with 1GB of memory (which results in less than 1GB of memory as seen by Windows), small pages are used. On a physical machine with 8GB of RAM, large pages are found. This is what we see in the latter scenario:

```
lkd> lm m nt
start               end                 module name
fffff800`02c06000 fffff800`031f0000   nt         (pdb symbols)

lkd> !pte fffff800`02c06000
                                       VA fffff80002c06000

PXE at FFFFF6FB7DBEDF80    PPE at FFFFF6FB7DBF0000    PDE at FFFFF6FB7E0000B0    PTE at FFFFF6FC00016030
contains 0000000000199063  contains 0000000000198063  contains 000000002C009E3  contains 0000000000000000
pfn 199       ---DA--KWEV  pfn 198       ---DA--KWEV  pfn 2c00      -GLDA--KWEV  LARGE PAGE pfn 2c06


lkd> lm m hal
start               end                 module name
fffff800`031f0000 fffff800`03239000   hal        (deferred)

lkd> !pte fffff800`031f0000
                                       VA fffff800031f0000

PXE at FFFFF6FB7DBEDF80    PPE at FFFFF6FB7DBF0000    PDE at FFFFF6FB7E0000C0    PTE at FFFFF6FC00018F80
contains 0000000000199063  contains 0000000000198063  contains 0000000030009E3  contains 0000000000000000
pfn 199       ---DA--KWEV  pfn 198       ---DA--KWEV  pfn 3000      -GLDA--KWEV  LARGE PAGE pfn 31f0
```

As usual, the advantage of using large pages is that fewer TLB entries are needed to cache the VA range of these images. This comes with a price, however: a single PDE maps a 2MB range, defining its protection. The kernel image has several file sections that are loaded into ranges smaller than 2MB and have different protection requirements: the code sections should be read-only and executable; the data sections should be read/write. With large pages, the single PDE must be configured with the least restrictive protection, e.g. read/write/execute, since it maps all these subranges together. This means that a buggy kernel mode component can overwrite code from the kernel image through a stray pointer.

The system can be configured to use large pages for other kernel mode images, by adding a multistiring value named LargePageDrivers in the registry key HKLM\SYSTEM\CurrentControlSet\Control\Session Manager\Memory Management. This multistring must be set to the list of image file names ([1], p. 706).

46.2 Images Loaded in Session Space

46.2.1   Memory Sections Are Back in Play

We can start our analysis by considering two processes belonging to different sessions and by remembering that each has a different PML4E for the session space region. The kernel is thus faced with the following scenario:

- All the paging structures hierarchy for this region is made up of different structures: each process has its own PDPT, whose entries point to different PDs, which, in turn, point to different PTs, etc.

- Code loaded from images in this region must be shared among two such address spaces, in order to avoid wasting physical memory with unnecessary duplication.

- Each process should have a separate copy of read/write data sections of images. Better yet, copy on write should be implemented, so that two such address spaces share the same copy until one writes to it.

This is exactly the same problem the kernel has to solve for user mode images loaded in more than one process (e.g. DLLs), so it is solved in the same way: by building a memory section. We know that memory sections are not used outside session space, because the system VA ranges outside of it are simply shared as a result of having the same PML4Es in all address spaces and no copy on write behavior is required: both code and data are completely shared. In session space things are different, so sections come again into play.

46.2.2   I Think We Are Not in User Mode Anymore

There are, however, a few differences between sections used in session space the ones used in user mode.

It appears that the former are built as paging file backed sections. This is similar to what happens for other kernel mode images: the memory content is not tied to the image file once it has been loaded.

46.2.2.1   Finding the Memory Section for win32k.sys

Below we see the list of images in session space found on a test system:

```
fffff960`00020000 fffff960`0032f000   win32k    (deferred)
fffff960`00540000 fffff960`0054a000   TSDDD     (deferred)
fffff960`00670000 fffff960`00697000   cdd       (deferred)
```

We are now going to dig into the mapping of win32k.sys. Before doing this, it is useful to remember that when we break into the debugger, System is the current process and its PML4 has no valid entry for session space, so if we inspect the PxEs of win32k.sys we see this:

```
1: kd> !pte fffff960`00020000
                                          VA fffff96000020000

PXE at FFFFF6FB7DBEDF90   PPE at FFFFF6FB7DBF2C00   PDE at FFFFF6FB7E580000   PTE at FFFFF6FCB0000100
contains 0000000000000000
not valid
```

i.e. the PML4E is set to 0. In order to have a valid session space, the rest of this analysis has been performed on the address space of explorer.exe. Here the first page of win32k.sys looks different:

```
1: kd> !pte fffff960`00020000
                                          VA fffff96000020000

PXE at FFFFF6FB7DBEDF90   PPE at FFFFF6FB7DBF2C00   PDE at FFFFF6FB7E580000   PTE at FFFFF6FCB0000100
contains 000000001C64D863   contains 000000001C85E863   contains 000000001C8DD863   contains E420000008810201
pfn 1c64d    ---DA--KWEV pfn 1c85e   ---DA--KWEV pfn 1c8dd   ---DA--KWEV pfn 8810    C------KR-V
```

```
1: kd> !pfn 8810
    PFN 00008810 at address FFFFFA8000198300
    flink       00000642  blink / share count 00000001  pteaddress FFFFF8A000102048
    reference count 0001    used entry count  0000      Cached     color 0    Priority 5
    restore pte 298B000000A2  containing page        01D85F  Active      P
    Shared
```

The `!pfn` output shows that the page is shared and `pteaddress` is in the nonpaged pool region, not in the paging structures region, so it is pointing at a prototype PTE.

To get to the section data structures, we must perform a little bit of guesswork. It is often the case that, for paging file backed sections, the prototype PTEs array is located right at the end of the `_SEGMENT` structure, at +0x48 from the structure address. We can try to interpret the memory at `pteaddress` - 0x48 as a `_SEGMENT` instance and see what happens:

```
1: kd> ?? (nt!_SEGMENT*) ((char*) 0xFFFFF8A000102048 - 0x48)
struct _SEGMENT * 0xfffff8a0`00102000
   +0x000 ControlArea      : 0xfffffa80`02c525f0 _CONTROL_AREA
   +0x008 TotalNumberOfPtes : 0x30f
   +0x00c SegmentFlags     : _SEGMENT_FLAGS
   +0x010 NumberOfCommittedPages : 0x30f
   +0x018 SizeOfSegment    : 0x30f000
   +0x020 ExtendInfo       : 0xfffff97f`ff000000 _MMEXTEND_INFO
   +0x020 BasedAddress     : 0xfffff97f`ff000000 Void
   +0x028 SegmentLock      : _EX_PUSH_LOCK
   +0x030 u1               : <unnamed-tag>
   +0x038 u2               : <unnamed-tag>
   +0x040 PrototypePte     : 0xfffff8a0`00102048 _MMPTE
   +0x048 ThePtes          : [1] _MMPTE
```

If this is really a segment, `ControlArea` should point to an instance of `_CONTROL_AREA`, with a `Segment` member pointing back to the address we computed:

```
1: kd> ?? ((nt!_SEGMENT*) ((char*) 0xFFFFF8A000102048 - 0x48))->ControlArea->Segment
struct _SEGMENT * 0xfffff8a0`00102000
   +0x000 ControlArea      : 0xfffffa80`02c525f0 _CONTROL_AREA
   +0x008 TotalNumberOfPtes : 0x30f
[...]
```

The control area points back to the segment, so things are looking promising. Now it makes sense to try to feed the control area address to the `!ca` extension.

```
1: kd> !ca @@( ((nt!_SEGMENT*) ((char*) 0xFFFFF8A000102048 - 0x48))->ControlArea )

ControlArea @ fffffa8002c525f0

   Segment     fffff8a000102000  Flink     0000000000000000  Blink        0000000000000000
   Section Ref              1    Pfn Ref              0     Mapped Views             0
   User Ref                 1    WaitForDel           0     Flush Count              0
   File Object 0000000000000000  ModWriteCount        0     System Views             0
   WritableRefs             0
   Flags (2000) Commit


        Pagefile-backed section

Segment @ fffff8a000102000
   ControlArea     fffffa8002c525f0  ExtendInfo     fffff97fff000000
   Total Ptes               30f
   Segment Size          30f000  Committed                30f
   CreatingProcess           26  FirstMappedVa              0
   ProtoPtes       fffff8a000102048
   Flags (c0000) ProtectionMask


Subsection 1 @ fffffa8002c52670
   ControlArea  fffffa8002c525f0  Starting Sector      0    Number Of Sectors    0
   Base Pte     fffff8a000102048  Ptes In Subsect    30f    Unused Ptes          0
   Flags                      c   Sector Offset        0    Protection           6
```

There are two facts showing we are indeed looking at a control area:

- The segment address 0xFFFFF8A0`00102000 is the one we computed, i.e. -0x48 from `pteaddress`.

- The subsection shows a `Base Pte` value equal to the PTE address we began with.

In a short while, we are going to compare the prototype PTEs with the win32k.sys image and find further evidence of this being a section filled with the content of the file.

As we can see from the output above, this is a paging file backed section and, as is usual for these sections, it consists of a single subsection. This behavior is different from the one observed with user mode image files, where separate subsections are created for each file section. We are now going to analyze the subsection in greater detail.

46.2.2.2   Section prototype PTEs vs. win32k.sys Image

win32k.sys is made of different file sections which should be loaded with different protections. With user mode images, this is accomplished by creating a distinct subsection with the necessary page level protection for each file section. In session space, we see that the individual prototype PTEs of the single paging file backed section are set with the required protection.

Below is an excerpt of the output from dumpbin /headers (see sec. 38.4.2 on p. 363) for win32k.sys:

```
Microsoft (R) COFF/PE Dumper Version 9.00.30729.01
Copyright (C) Microsoft Corporation.  All rights reserved.


Dump of file win32k.sys
[...]
SECTION HEADER #1
   .text name
  29E88B virtual size
    1000 virtual address (FFFFF97FFF001000 to FFFFF97FFF29F88A)
  29EA00 size of raw data
     400 file pointer to raw data (00000400 to 0029EDFF)
       0 file pointer to relocation table
       0 file pointer to line numbers
       0 number of relocations
       0 number of line numbers
68000020 flags
         Code
         Not Paged
         Execute Read
```

We see that the first file section must be mapped at section offset (see sec. 38.3 on p. 360) 0x1000, i.e. it must be mapped by the second prototype PTE in the array, and that its protection is execute/read.

The corresponding PTEs in the array, match this protection. As an example, below is the content of the prototype PTEs for section offset 0x1000 and 0x2000:

```
1: kd> !pte fffff8a000102048 + 8 1
                                              VA fffff8a000102050

PXE at FFFFF8A000102050    PPE at FFFFF8A000102050    PDE at FFFFF8A000102050    PTE at FFFFF8A000102050
contains 0000298C00000062
not valid
  PageFile:  1
  Offset: 298c
  Protect: 3 - ExecuteRead
```

```
1: kd> !pte fffff8a000102048 + 8 + 8 1
                                              VA fffff8a000102058

PXE at FFFFF8A000102058    PPE at FFFFF8A000102058    PDE at FFFFF8A000102058    PTE at FFFFF8A000102058
contains 0000298D00000062
not valid
  PageFile:  1
  Offset: 298d
  Protect: 3 - ExecuteRead
```

It is also interesting to observe how, in this particular case, the section content has been outpaged. This further confirms that we are looking at a paging file backed section.

The state of the prototype PTE is consistent with the state of the hardware PTE for address +0x1000 into win32k.sys:

```
1: kd> !pte fffff960`00020000 + 0x1000
                                              VA fffff96000021000

PXE at FFFFF6FB7DBEDF90    PPE at FFFFF6FB7DBF2C00    PDE at FFFFF6FB7E580000    PTE at FFFFF6FCB0000108
contains 000000001C64D863  contains 000000001C85E863  contains 000000001C8DD863  contains F8A0001020500400
pfn 1c64d    ---DA--KWEV pfn 1c85e    ---DA--KWEV pfn 1c8dd    ---DA--KWEV not valid
                                                                            Proto: FFFFF8A000102050
```

```
1: kd> !pte fffff960`00020000 + 0x2000
                                              VA fffff96000022000

PXE at FFFFF6FB7DBEDF90    PPE at FFFFF6FB7DBF2C00    PDE at FFFFF6FB7E580000    PTE at FFFFF6FCB0000110
contains 000000001C64D863  contains 000000001C85E863  contains 000000001C8DD863  contains F8A0001020580400
pfn 1c64d    ---DA--KWEV pfn 1c85e    ---DA--KWEV pfn 1c8dd    ---DA--KWEV not valid
                                                                            Proto: FFFFF8A000102058
```

The hardware PTEs contain proto-pointers with the addresses of our prototype PTEs.

Alas, there is one thing which contrasts with the dumpbin output we saw earlier: the section is listed as "not paged" there, but we see it is swapped out. It appears that the VMM has different ideas in this regard. This reminds us that Windows, like the nature of the universe, can never be fully understood.

File section #1 has virtual size equal to 0x29E88B bytes, so it spans

  0x29E88B / 0x1000 + 1 = 671

pages, i.e. the same number of prototype PTE. The first prototype PTE mapping this file section has index 1, so the last one has index 671. We can examine this PTE and the one following it, which maps the first page of file section #2:

```
1: kd> !pte fffff8a000102048 + 0n671 * 8 1
                                            VA fffff8a000103540

PXE at FFFFF8A000103540   PPE at FFFFF8A000103540   PDE at FFFFF8A000103540   PTE at FFFFF8A000103540
contains 0000299000000062
not valid
 PageFile:  1
 Offset: 2990
 Protect: 3 - ExecuteRead
```

The last prototype PTE is consistent with file section 1.

```
1: kd> !pte fffff8a000102048 + 0n672 * 8 1
                                            VA fffff8a000103548

PXE at FFFFF8A000103548   PPE at FFFFF8A000103548   PDE at FFFFF8A000103548   PTE at FFFFF8A000103548
contains 8000000016C84021  contains 8000000016C84021  contains 8000000016C84021  contains 8000000016C84021
pfn 16c84     ----A--KR-V  pfn 16c84     ----A--KR-V  pfn 16c84     ----A--KR-V  pfn 16c84     ----A--KR-V
```

The next prototype PTE is for a read-only (not executable page). We can tell this by the leftmost digit being 8, which means bit 63 is set. This is the XD bit of the Intel 64 architecture, which forbids fetching instructions from the page. We can further confirm this by looking at the _MMPFN:

```
1: kd> !pfn 16c84
    PFN 00016C84 at address FFFFFA80004458C0
    flink       000002CF  blink / share count 00000002  pteaddress FFFFF8A000103548
    reference count 0001     used entry count  0000       Cached    color 0    Priority 5
    restore pte 00000020  containing page        01D45E  Active     MP
    Modified Shared
```

restore pte, i.e. _MMPFN.OriginalPte is 0x20. This is the original value of the prototype PTE, storing the page protection. Knowing its offset is +0x20, we can interpret it as a PTE:

```
1: kd> !pte FFFFFA80004458C0 + 20 1
                                            VA fffffa80004458e0

PXE at FFFFFA80004458E0   PPE at FFFFFA80004458E0   PDE at FFFFFA80004458E0   PTE at FFFFFA80004458E0
contains 0000000000000020
not valid
 DemandZero
 Protect: 1 - Readonly
```

And, again, we find read-only protection. Now, if we look at win32k.sys, we see that this protection is consistent with file section #2:

```
SECTION HEADER #2
  .rdata name
  23A70 virtual size
 2A0000 virtual address (FFFFF97FFF2A0000 to FFFFF97FFF2C3A6F)
  23C00 size of raw data
 29EE00 file pointer to raw data (0029EE00 to 002C29FF)
      0 file pointer to relocation table
      0 file pointer to line numbers
      0 number of relocations
      0 number of line numbers
48000040 flags
        Initialized Data
        Not Paged
        Read Only
```

Finally, we can have a look at the hardware PTE for the first page of file section #2, by adding its RVA to the base address of win32k.sys:

```
1: kd> !pte fffff960`00020000 + 2A0000
                                          VA fffff960002c0000

PXE at FFFFF6FB7DBEDF90   PPE at FFFFF6FB7DBF2C00   PDE at FFFFF6FB7E580008   PTE at FFFFF6FCB0001600
contains 000000001C64D863  contains 000000001C85E863  contains 000000001C95C863  contains A7E0000016C84021
pfn 1c64d     ---DA--KWEV  pfn 1c85e     ---DA--KWEV  pfn 1c95c     ---DA--KWEV  pfn 16c84     ----A--KR-V
```

and we find that it is mapped to the same physical page pointed by the prototype PTE, as it should be.

We can also verify that read/write file sections are mapped to copy on write pages. From dumpbin, we see that such a section is section #3:

```
SECTION HEADER #3
  .data name
  1CAA0 virtual size
 2C4000 virtual address (FFFFF97FFF2C4000 to FFFFF97FFF2E0A9F)
   CE00 size of raw data
 2C2A00 file pointer to raw data (002C2A00 to 002CF7FF)
      0 file pointer to relocation table
      0 file pointer to line numbers
      0 number of relocations
      0 number of line numbers
C8000040 flags
        Initialized Data
        Not Paged
        Read Write
```

From the file section RVA, we see that the first prototype PTE for it has index 0x2c4:

```
1: kd> !pte fffff8a000102048  + 2c4 * 8 1
                            VA fffff8a000103668
```

```
PXE at FFFFF8A000103668    PPE at FFFFF8A000103668    PDE at FFFFF8A000103668    PTE at FFFFF8A000103668
contains 0000025D000000A2
not valid
 PageFile:  1
 Offset: 25d
 Protect: 5 - ReadWriteCopy
```

Which, although currently swapped out, has the expected protection. Furthermore, the corresponding hardware PTE shows that, in the explorer.exe session, someone has indeed written to the page which is now mapped to a private copy:

```
1: kd> !pte fffff960`00020000 + 2c4000
                                        VA fffff960002e4000

PXE at FFFFF6FB7DBEDF90    PPE at FFFFF6FB7DBF2C00    PDE at FFFFF6FB7E580008    PTE at FFFFF6FCB0001720
contains 000000001C64D863  contains 000000001C85E863  contains 000000001C95C863  contains 959000001333A821
pfn 1c64d    ---DA--KWEV   pfn 1c85e    ---DA--KWEV   pfn 1c95c    ---DA--KWEV   pfn 1333a    ----A--KR-V
```

```
1: kd> !pfn 1333a
    PFN 0001333A at address FFFFFA8000399AE0
    flink        00000159  blink / share count 00000001  pteaddress FFFFF6FCB0001720
    reference count 0001    used entry count  0000     Cached    color 0    Priority 6
    restore pte 15E7700000080  containing page        01C95C  Active
```

We can tell this is a private copy from the fact that `pteaddress` and `containing page` in the `_MMPFN` point to the *hardware* PTE.

This copy is valid for the session of the current process, which is session 1:

```
1: kd> !process @$proc 0
PROCESS fffffa800327b370
    SessionId: 1  Cid: 02d8    Peb: 7fffffd8000  ParentCid: 03fc
    DirBase: 04ebe000  ObjectTable: fffff8a001f9d200  HandleCount: 793.
    Image: explorer.exe
```

We can look at the same page in session 0, by switching context to the csrss.exe instance running in that session:

```
PROCESS fffffa8002021750
    SessionId: 0  Cid: 0170    Peb: 7fffffdf000  ParentCid: 0154
    DirBase: 16d1b000  ObjectTable: fffff8a005ad7780  HandleCount: 399.
    Image: csrss.exe

PROCESS fffffa80021b6580
    SessionId: 1  Cid: 01ac    Peb: 7fffffdf000  ParentCid: 019c
    DirBase: 1caf1000  ObjectTable: fffff8a005b27590  HandleCount: 249.
    Image: csrss.exe

1: kd> .process /P fffffa8002021750
Implicit process is now fffffa80`02021750
.cache forcedecodeptes done


1: kd> !pte fffff960`00020000 + 2c4000
```

```
                                 VA fffff960002e4000

PXE at FFFFF6FB7DBEDF90   PPE at FFFFF6FB7DBF2C00   PDE at FFFFF6FB7E580008   PTE at FFFFF6FCB0001720
contains 000000001D4C0863 contains 000000001D765863 contains 000000001D4E3863 contains 9260000007C26801
pfn 1d4c0     ---DA--KWEV pfn 1d765     ---DA--KWEV pfn 1d4e3     ---DA--KWEV pfn 7c26     -------KR-V
```

The address is mapped to a different physical page.

Let's have a look at the first page of file section #2, which is a read-only section:

```
1: kd> !pte fffff960`00020000 + 2A0000
                                 VA fffff960002c0000

PXE at FFFFF6FB7DBEDF90   PPE at FFFFF6FB7DBF2C00   PDE at FFFFF6FB7E580008   PTE at FFFFF6FCB0001600
contains 000000001D4C0863 contains 000000001D765863 contains 000000001D4E3863 contains 87C0000016C84021
pfn 1d4c0     ---DA--KWEV pfn 1d765     ---DA--KWEV pfn 1d4e3     ---DA--KWEV pfn 16c84     ----A--KR-V
```

As expected, it is mapped to the same physical page pointed by the prototype PTE and used in session 1 (see p. 518). It is also interesting to compare the output above, with the one for the hardware PTE of session 1 (see p. 519): the leaf physical page is the same in both mappings (0x16c84), but the physical pages of the PDPT, PD and PT are different, because of the different PML4E for session space.

47   Kernel Mode Stacks

47.1 Why the Kernel Mode Stack Is Special

The kernel mode stack is a very important resource, because it is used by the processor itself to handle interrupts and exceptions. When one of these events occur, the processor saves on the stack the content of some registers (ss, rsp, rflags, cs, rip), followed, for some exceptions, by an error code, then transfers control to the handler address found in the IDT (see Chapter 4 - p. 8).

From the outline above, it is obvious that the processor needs a working stack to successfully transfer control to the handler. If the interruption occurred in user mode, the processor switches to kernel mode and loads the CPL0 rsp from the TSS before writing to the stack. If the event took place in kernel mode, the processor simply uses the current value of rsp. In both cases, a working ring 0 stack is needed.

But what if rsp points to an invalid address, e.g. to a not mapped VA? This is a quite difficult scenario for the processor, which generates a new exception: the *double fault exception* (vector #8). Note how, at this stage, the processor registers are still set as they were when the first exception took place.

Handling this problem by generating yet another exception does not seem a great idea, at first, since handling it requires a working stack as well. However, the trick is that the interrupt gate for the double fault specifies a nonzero index in the IST (interrupt stack table) field. This tells the processor to load rsp from the IST which is part of the TSS, before writing to the stack. The IST can store up to 7 pointers, to be loaded into rsp ([11], Vol 3A, p. 7-24). If an interruption occurs and its IDT descriptor has a nonzero IST index, rsp is loaded from the corresponding entry in the IST. This occurs both when the interrupted code was running at CPL 3 and when it was running at CPL 0. This way, if the "regular" ring 0 stack is unavailable, the interruption can still be handled successfully by the processor.

Windows sets up the interrupt gate for double fault with a nonzero IST index and the address of *KiDoubleFaultAbort*. This function crashes the system with bugcheck code 0x7F (UNEXPECTED_KERNEL_MODE_TRAP). Thus, even when the normal ring 0 stack is gone, the system can be shut down in a controlled manner.

For the sake of completeness, we should consider the case when rsp is still pointing to an invalid address when the processor tries to generate the double fault. This could happen if the double fault descriptor has the IST index set to 0 or if the address in the IST entry is invalid. In this (doomsday) scenario, the processor enters shutdown mode, which means it stops executing instructions. The processor can be brought out of shutdown mode only by a handful of signals, including the one for an hard reset. When entering shutdown, the processor signals what is going on its external pins and, usually, the chipset reacts by activating the reset signal and causing a complete restart. This is one scenario where a Windows system reboots without bugchecking first.

The !idt extension shows the rsp from the IST for vectors with nonzero IST index:

```
Dumping IDT:

[...]
02:     fffff800028bef00 nt!KiNmiInterrupt     Stack = 0xFFFFF880009F4F40
[...]
08:     fffff800028bf880 nt!KiDoubleFaultAbort          Stack = 0xFFFFF880009F0F40
[...]
12:     fffff800028c04c0 nt!KiMcheckAbort          Stack = 0xFFFFF880009F2F40
```

As we can see, only 3 vectors are set up to use the IST: non maskable interrupt, double fault and machine check. These are all serious interrupts/exceptions which don't normally occur.

47.2 Thread Kernel Stacks

47.2.1   Thread Stack vs. Context Switch

Each thread has its own kernel stack. Each processor in the system is always executing in the context of some thread and, when it goes from ring 3 to ring 0, rsp is loaded with the initial kernel stack for the current thread.

When the ring 3 - ring 0 transition is performed by Windows code (usually executing a `syscall` instruction), the kernel stack is set up by the kernel code to which control is transferred. When the transition occurs because of an interruption, the processor automatically loads the ring 0 stack from the TSS.

However, the processor does not know anything about threads: it simply loads the CPL0 rsp from the TSS (we are not considering vectors which use the IST here), so the per-thread implementation is up to Windows.

While a thread is running, the TSS entry for the CPL 0 rsp is set to the initial address of the kernel stack assigned to that thread. This value is also printed by the `!thread` extension as `Stack Init`:

```
1: kd> !thread @$thread
THREAD fffffa8000f88b60  Cid 0838.083c  Teb: 000007fffffde000 Win32Thread:
0000000000000000 RUNNING on processor 1
[...]
Stack Init fffff88004901db0 Current fffff88004901690
Base fffff88004902000 Limit fffff880048fc000 Call 0
[...]
```

This can be confirmed by dumping the TSS content and tells us that the scheduler code which changes the thread context updates the TSS as part of making a thread active. Thus, when an interruption occurs, the ring 0 stack for the current thread is already in place inside the TSS.

47.2.2   Allocation, Paging, _MMPFNs

Kernel stacks are allocated in the System PTE region when threads are created. Since the kernel stack is essential for the processor, as explained in sec. 47.1 on p. 521, its VA range cannot be invalidated by the working set manager. The system cannot survive a page fault at ring 0 caused by a not present stack page: the processor would attempt to use the same stack to push the registers to be saved, ending in a double fault exception. (Note, however, that these stacks *can*, under certain conditions, be swapped out, but this is handled by a dedicated VMM component, which we will describe later in sec 47.2.5 on p. 527).

Thus, we don't expect the physical pages mapping the stack to be part of any working set, which, normally translates in having `_MMPFN.u1.WsIndex` set to 0. As it turns out, this member has a different meaning for thread stack pages.

Let's start by looking at a thread with its initial stack pointer:

```
1: kd> !thread @$thread
THREAD ffffa8000f88b60  Cid 0838.083c  Teb: 000007fffffde000 Win32Thread:
0000000000000000 RUNNING on processor 1
Not impersonating
DeviceMap                 fffff8a0010ccf30
Owning Process            ffffa80010d0b30       Image:        MemTests.EXE
Attached Process          N/A       Image:       N/A
Wait Start TickCount      574666     Ticks: 0
Context Switch Count      549
UserTime                  00:00:00.015
KernelTime                00:00:00.046
Win32 Start Address 0x000000013fb87350
Stack Init fffff88004901db0 Current fffff88004901690
Base fffff88004902000 Limit fffff880048fc000 Call 0
```

Now let's have a look at the physical page for the 1st stack page:

```
1: kd> !pte fffff88004901db0
                          VA fffff88004901db0

PXE @ FFFFF6FB7DBEDF88   PPE at FFFFF6FB7DBF1000   PDE at FFFFF6FB7E200120   PTE at FFFFF6FC40024808
contains 00000000351C4863  contains 00000000351C3863  contains 000000000C358863  contains 8000000032038963
pfn 351c4     ---DA--KWEV pfn 351c3     ---DA--KWEV pfn c358     ---DA--KWEV pfn 32038     -G-DA--
KW-V
```

```
1: kd> !pfn 32038
    PFN 00032038 at address FFFFFA8000960A80
    flink         FFFFFA8000F88B61  blink / share count 00000001  pteaddress
FFFFF6FC40024808
      reference count 0001    used entry count  0000      Cached     color 0    Priority 5
      restore pte 000003E0  containing page       00C358   Active      M
      Modified
```

The content of `_MMPFN.u1`, which is labeled `flink` is the address of the `_ETHREAD` of the thread. Actually, it's equal to the address + 1, but this is likely due to the fact that `_ETHREAD` instances are aligned at multiples of some even number, so that bit 0 is known to be 0 in the actual address and used as a flag in the `_MMPFN`. `_MMPFN.u1` is a union and this usage is consistent with `_MMPFN.u1.KernelStackOwner`.

We can confirm that the next stack pages all show the same results (remember that, with stacks, "next" means lower addresses):

```
1: kd> !pte fffff88004900000
                          VA fffff88004900000
```

```
PXE @ FFFFF6FB7DBEDF88     PPE at FFFFF6FB7DBF1000     PDE at FFFFF6FB7E200120     PTE at FFFFF6FC40024800
contains 00000000351C4863  contains 00000000351C3863  contains 000000000C358863  contains 8000000022EE7963
pfn 351c4     ---DA--KWEV pfn 351c3     ---DA--KWEV pfn c358     ---DA--KWEV pfn 22ee7     -G-DA--
KW-V


1: kd> !pfn 22ee7
    PFN 00022EE7 at address FFFFFA800068CB50
    flink        FFFFFA8000F88B61  blink / share count 00000001  pteaddress
FFFFF6FC40024800
      reference count 0001    used entry count  0000      Cached      color 0    Priority 5
      restore pte 000003E0  containing page      00C358  Active     M
      Modified

1: kd> !pte fffff880048ff000
                              VA fffff880048ff000

PXE @ FFFFF6FB7DBEDF88     PPE at FFFFF6FB7DBF1000     PDE at FFFFF6FB7E200120     PTE at FFFFF6FC400247F8
contains 00000000351C4863  contains 00000000351C3863  contains 000000000C358863  contains 8000000023928963
pfn 351c4     ---DA--KWEV pfn 351c3     ---DA--KWEV pfn c358     ---DA--KWEV pfn 23928     -G-DA--
KW-V


1: kd> !pfn 23928
    PFN 00023928 at address FFFFFA80006AB780
    flink        FFFFFA8000F88B61  blink / share count 00000001  pteaddress
FFFFF6FC400247F8
      reference count 0001    used entry count  0000      Cached      color 0    Priority 5
      restore pte 000003E0  containing page      00C358  Active     M
      Modified
```

Below is the dump for the last (lowest address) stack page, labeled `Limit` in the `!thread` output, showing consistent results:

```
1: kd> !pte fffff880048fc000
                              VA fffff880048fc000

PXE @ FFFFF6FB7DBEDF88     PPE at FFFFF6FB7DBF1000     PDE at FFFFF6FB7E200120     PTE at FFFFF6FC400247E0
contains 00000000351C4863  contains 00000000351C3863  contains 000000000C358863  contains 80000000233EA963
pfn 351c4     ---DA--KWEV pfn 351c3     ---DA--KWEV pfn c358     ---DA--KWEV pfn 233ea     -G-DA--
KW-V


1: kd> !pfn 233ea
    PFN 000233EA at address FFFFFA800069BBE0
    flink        FFFFFA8000F88B61  blink / share count 00000001  pteaddress
FFFFF6FC400247E0
      reference count 0001    used entry count  0000      Cached      color 0    Priority 5
      restore pte 000003E0  containing page      00C358  Active     M
      Modified
```

47.2.3   Guard Pages

The VMM allocates a so-called guard page below the lowest page of a kernel mode thread stack. We have already encountered this term in user mode (see sec. 26.9 on p. 173) but here it is used with a different meaning. This guard page is actually an invalid PTE (which is found to be set to 0), so there is an invalid *virtual* page below the stack. If the thread uses all its stack space and rsp is moved below the last valid address, a page fault on the stack occurs, which, as we know by now, will end in a double fault and a system crash.

This is quite different from the usage of user mode guard pages: they too cause a page fault on the stack, but the ring 3 one. This is harmless enough, since the processor enters CPL 0 and loads the corresponding rsp from the TSS before attempting to write anything on the stack itself. Thus, the kernel page fault handler is invoked, as with any other page fault, detects that the cause was the guard page, commits another stack page and resumes execution.

For kernel mode thread stacks, guard pages are an extreme measure to avoid having a stack underflow overwriting other kernel mode data in the System PTE region. Rather than allowing that to happen and to cause hard to diagnose corruptions, the system crashes immediately, making it easier to find the culprit.

47.2.4   Stack Jumping

Some Windows components need more kernel stack space than the regular amount allotted to threads. An example are graphic system calls handled by win32k.sys. This module executes in kernel mode and may invoke user mode callbacks before returning to the caller. While executing the callback code, the processor can again enter kernel mode, e.g. because of an hardware interrupt, but, possibly, also for another system call invoked by the callback itself. In this situation there are two nested contexts on the kernel stack and more can be added if other mode transitions occur before returning. This kind of stack usage can lead to stack underflow.

To avoid this, the graphic subsystem uses a VMM facility which allocates an additional kernel mode stack to be used in place of the original one and "links" the two stacks, thus giving the nested contexts more stack space. As the nested contexts return, each additional stack is released and the previous one is restored as current. This facility is available to driver developers by calling the *KeExpandKernelStackAndCalloutEx* DDI.

The _MMPFN.u1 union has a member called NextStackPfn of type _SINGLE_LIST_ENTRY; both the name and the type suggest that it may be used to link different stacks together, perhaps as part of the implementation of *KeExpandKernelStackAndCalloutEx*.

47.2.5   The Swapper

47.2.5.1   Kernel Stack Outswapping

We saw in sec. 47.2.2 on p. 523 that translations for stack virtual pages cannot be unmapped by the working set manager. It would be a waste of precious physical memory, however to always keep every kernel stack resident. As long as a thread is not running, its stack is not needed: no code is ever going to touch that particular VA range. Thus, if a thread waits for a long time, e.g. for user input, it makes sense to swap out its stack and recycle physical pages.

The swapper is a system thread which executes *KeSwapProcessOrStack* and frees physical pages used by kernel mode stacks of threads which have been inactive for more than a certain maximum time. Below is the swapper status while it is in the process of recycling a page:

```
THREAD fffffa8000b76040  Cid 0004.0068  Teb: 0000000000000000 Win32Thread:
0000000000000000 RUNNING on processor 1
Not impersonating
DeviceMap                 fffff8a000006090
Owning Process            fffffa8000b51740      Image:         System
Attached Process          N/A            Image:       N/A
Wait Start TickCount      871309         Ticks: 0
Context Switch Count      187223
UserTime                  00:00:00.000
KernelTime                00:00:01.093
Win32 Start Address nt!KeSwapProcessOrStack (0xfffff800028b65e8)
Stack Init fffff88003140db0 Current fffff88003140a50
Base fffff88003141000 Limit fffff8800313b000 Call 0
Priority 23 BasePriority 8 UnusualBoost 0 ForegroundBoost 0 IoPriority 2 PagePriority 5
Child-SP          RetAddr         : Args to Child
: Call Site
fffff880`03140aa0 fffff800`028aaa6a : fffff880`04901000 00000000`00000000
fffff880`03140bd0 fffff6fc`400247d8 : nt!MiOutPageSingleKernelStack+0x207

fffff880`03140b20 fffff800`028aa878 : 00000000`00000000 00000000`00000004
fffff880`03140cd0 fffffa80`00f88b60 : nt!KeEnumerateKernelStackSegments+0x5a

fffff880`03140bb0 fffff800`028aa9c4 : 00000000`00000000 00000000`00000000
00000000`00000000 fffff800`0285cf03 : nt!MmOutPageKernelStack+0x34

fffff880`03140c90 fffff800`028b6630 : 00000000`00000000 00000000`00000080
fffffa80`00b51740 fffffa80`00b51700 : nt!KiOutSwapKernelStacks+0x11c

fffff880`03140d00 fffff800`02b65166 : 00000000`00000000 00000000`00000000
00000000`00000000 00000000`00000000 : nt!KeSwapProcessOrStack+0x48

fffff880`03140d40 fffff800`028a0486 : fffff800`02a3ae80 fffffa80`00b76040
fffffa80`00b75420 00000000`00000000 : nt!PspSystemThreadStartup+0x5a
```

```
fffff880`03140d80 00000000`00000000 : fffff880`03141000 00000000`00000000
00000000`00000000 00000000`00000000 : nt!KxStartSystemThread+0x16
```

The swapper can be intercepted by examining the _MMPFNs of a kernel mode stack and placing data access breakpoints on _MMPFN.OriginalPte.

As it turns out, the swapper is quite aggressive and unmaps kernel stacks of threads usually after less than 1' of inactivity. It's interesting to examine the stack of a thread which has been "taken care of" by the swapper:

```
0: kd> !thread fffffa8000f88b60
THREAD fffffa8000f88b60  Cid 0838.083c  Teb: 000007fffffde000 Win32Thread:
0000000000000000 WAIT: (WrLpcReply) UserMode Non-Alertable
    fffffa8000f88f20  Semaphore Limit 0x1
[...]
Stack Init fffff88004901db0 Current fffff88004901690
Base fffff88004902000 Limit fffff880048fc000 Call 0
[...]
        RetAddr              : Args to Child
: Call Site
fffff880`049016d0 fffff800`028c9052 : fffffa80`010c9420 fffffa80`00f88b60
fffff880`00000000 00000000`00000000 : nt!KiSwapContext+0x7a

fffff880`04901810 fffff800`028cb1af : 00000000`00000000 fffff800`02bbef4f
00000000`00000000 fffff800`028c69fa : nt!KiCommitThreadWait+0x1d2
```

The address labeled as Current (0xFFFFF880`04901690) is, possibly, the lowest address used on the stack. It's slightly below the value of rsp saved in the context of the thread:

```
0: kd> .thread fffffa8000f88b60
Implicit thread is now fffffa80`0f88b60
0: kd> r @rsp
Last set context:
rsp=fffff880049016d0
```

It is possible that *KiSwapContext*, the scheduler function which puts the thread into waiting state, sets Current to "tell" the memory manager how much of the stack is in use while the thread sleeps. In this example, given that Init is 0xFFFFF880`04901DB0, we understand that only the first stack page is storing useful context data. This is consistent with what we find when we examine the stack PTEs.

Let's start with the PTE for the address listed as current:

```
0: kd> !pte fffff88004901690
                        VA fffff88004901690
PXE @ FFFFF6FB7DBEDF88    PPE at FFFFF6FB7DBF1000    PDE at FFFFF6FB7E200120    PTE at FFFFF6FC40024808
contains 00000000351C4863  contains 00000000351C3863  contains 000000000C358863  contains 8000000032038BE2
pfn 351c4    ---DA--KWEV pfn 351c3    ---DA--KWEV pfn c358    ---DA--KWEV  not valid
                                                             Transition: 32038
                                                             Protect: 1f - ReadWriteCopyExecute  WC
```

The PTE is in transition, which makes sense: since the VA page is storing the saved thread context, this data can't be lost. If the page is not valid, it must be either in transition or in the paging file.

The strange protection `ReadWriteCopyExecute` appears to always be used for stack pages. We can see that the numeric value of the protection (`_MMPTE.u.Trans.Protection`) is 0x1F, i.e. al the 5 bits of `Protection` are set. Possibly, this value is a special one used for kernel stacks. This is further confirmed by the fact that the x64 WinDbg, v. 6.12.0002.633 actually lists a page with this protection value as `Outswapped kernel stack`. Here is a sample output:

```
0: kd> !pte fffff88004cd0fd0
                                  VA fffff88004cd0fd0

PXE at FFFFF6FB7DBEDF88   PPE at FFFFF6FB7DBF1000   PDE at FFFFF6FB7E200130   PTE at FFFFF6FC40026680
contains 000000003C084863 contains 000000003C083863 contains 000000001C5C5863 contains 80000000251B2BE2
pfn 3c084    ---DA--KWEV pfn 3c083    ---DA--KWEV pfn 1c5c5   ---DA--KWEV not valid
                                                                            Transition: 251b2
                                                                            Protect: 1f - Outswapped
kernel stack
```

The debugger output included in the remainder of this section has been obtained with the x86 WinDbg, v. 6.11.0001.404, connected to an x64 virtual machine, which lists the protection as `ReadWriteCopyExecute`.

Let's move now one page below, i.e. in a portion of stack which was not used, according to the value labeled as `Current`:

```
0: kd> !pte fffff88004901690 - 1000
                        VA fffff88004900690

PXE @ FFFFF6FB7DBEDF88   PPE at FFFFF6FB7DBF1000   PDE at FFFFF6FB7E200120   PTE at FFFFF6FC40024800
contains 00000000351C4863 contains 00000000351C3863 contains 000000000C358863 contains 00000000000003E0
pfn 351c4    ---DA--KWEV pfn 351c3    ---DA--KWEV pfn c358    ---DA--KWEV not valid
                                                                          DemandZero
                                                                          Protect: 1f - ReadWriteCopyExecute  WC
```

We find a demand zero page with the peculiar protection 0x1F. This PTE is neither in transition, nor does it refer to content saved in the paging file. The swapper noticed that the mapped page was not storing anything useful and simply repurposed it, without outpaging it first.

The same result is found for the next lower page:

```
0: kd> !pte fffff88004901690 - 2000
                        VA fffff880048ff690

PXE @ FFFFF6FB7DBEDF88   PPE at FFFFF6FB7DBF1000   PDE at FFFFF6FB7E200120   PTE at FFFFF6FC400247F8
contains 00000000351C4863 contains 00000000351C3863 contains 000000000C358863 contains 00000000000003E0
pfn 351c4    ---DA--KWEV pfn 351c3    ---DA--KWEV pfn c358    ---DA--KWEV not valid
```

```
                             DemandZero
                             Protect: 1f - ReadWriteCopyExecute  WC
```

Thus, the swapper efficiently reclaimed kernel stack pages of a thread which is not performing useful work.

It is also interesting to note that the first stack page being in transition is the "usual" way of caching things: the page can be saved to the paging file and moved to the standby list. It will then be available both for repurposing, if physical memory is needed, or for being restored to its thread (we are about to see how) should it come out of its slumber.

This behavior explains a curious phenomenon which is often found in WinDbg. Let's look again at our thread status:

```
1: kd> !thread fffffa8000f88b60
THREAD fffffa8000f88b60  Cid 0838.083c  Teb: 000007fffffde000 Win32Thread:
0000000000000000 WAIT: (WrLpcReply) UserMode Non-Alertable
    fffffa8000f88f20  Semaphore Limit 0x1
[...]
Kernel stack not resident.
Child-SP          RetAddr          : Args to Child
: Call Site
fffff880`049016d0 fffff800`028c9052 : fffffa80`010c9420 fffff8a0`0106f960
fffff880`04901af8 00000000`00000000 : nt!KiSwapContext+0x7a

fffff880`04901810 fffff800`028cb1af : fffffa80`010ca490 00000000`00000000
fffffa80`00000000 fffffa80`010ce601 : nt!KiCommitThreadWait+0x1d2
[...]
```

WinDbg reports `Kernel stack not resident`, then merrily goes on listing the call stack. Possibly, the explanation is that WinDbg is always able to extract the content of virtual pages mapped by PTEs in transition. This is something that can be observed with any such virtual page: when `!pte` lists the page as in transition, a `db` command dumps the page content instead of the rows of "?" we get for completely unmapped pages. For instance, here is our first stack page, in transition and yet visible:

```
0: kd> !pte fffff88004901690
                     VA fffff88004901690

PXE @ FFFFF6FB7DBEDF88    PPE at FFFFF6FB7DBF1000    PDE at FFFFF6FB7E200120    PTE at FFFFF6FC40024808
contains 00000000351C4863  contains 00000000351C3863  contains 000000000C358863  contains 8000000032038BE2
pfn 351c4     ---DA--KWEV pfn 351c3     ---DA--KWEV pfn c358       ---DA--KWEV not valid
                                                          Transition: 32038
                                                          Protect: 1f - ReadWriteCopyExecute  WC


0: kd> db fffff88004901690
fffff880`04901690  00 00 00 00 80 f8 ff ff-00 00 00 00 00 f8 ff ff  ................
fffff880`049016a0  00 e3 0c 01 80 fa ff ff-00 00 00 00 00 00 00 00  ................
[...]
```

WinDbg can do this because a PTE in transition still stores the PFN and the physical page is still valid.

So, the _ETHREAD is recording somewhere that the stack has been reclaimed by the swapper and this results in the `Kernel stack not resident` label but, at the same time, WinDbg is stubborn enough to try to access the stack anyway and, when this succeeds, to dump the call stack.

47.2.5.2   Kernel Stack Inswapping

As we saw in sec. 47.2.2 on p. 523, a page fault caused by an invalid kernel mode stack would bring the system down, so stack pages cannot be simply faulted back when the thread awakens. Rather, code in the thread scheduler triggers the swapper thread, which, in turn, remaps the stack. Pages that were brought into a transition list are put back into Active state, swapped out ones are read back from the paging file and PTEs set as demand zero are pointed to fresh zeroed pages. When the thread becomes active, all its stack pages, including demand zero ones are already in place.

The swapper can be observed while inswapping a stack by placing a write breakpoint on a stack PTE. Below is a sample call stack of the swapper in action. We can see how the thread performing the inswapping is the same one captured while outswapping the stack on p. 527.

```
0: kd> !thread @$thread
THREAD fffffa8000b76040  Cid 0004.0068  Teb: 0000000000000000 Win32Thread:
0000000000000000 RUNNING on processor 0
Not impersonating
DeviceMap               fffff8a000006090
Owning Process          fffffa8000b51740      Image:        System
Attached Process        N/A            Image:        N/A
Wait Start TickCount    1017942        Ticks: 31 (0:00:00:00.484)
Context Switch Count    249249
UserTime                00:00:00.000
KernelTime              00:00:01.468
Win32 Start Address nt!KeSwapProcessOrStack (0xfffff800028b65e8)
Stack Init fffff88003140db0 Current fffff88003140a50
Base fffff88003141000 Limit fffff8800313b000 Call 0
Priority 23 BasePriority 8 UnusualBoost 0 ForegroundBoost 0 IoPriority 2 PagePriority 5
Child-SP          RetAddr          : Args to Child
: Call Site
fffff880`03140860 fffff800`028de506 : 00000000`00000001 fffff880`04901000
00000000`00000002 fffff800`02a4d440 : nt!MiResolveTransitionFault+0x470

fffff880`031408f0 fffff800`028dc4d1 : 00000000`00000000 fffff800`028c7e52
00000000`00000246 fffff800`028d01ed : nt!MiDispatchFault+0x946

fffff880`03140a00 fffff800`028b6848 : 00000000`00000001 fffff6fc`400247e0
fffffa80`00adcb00 fffff880`03896cd0 : nt!MmAccessFault+0x8f1
```

```
fffff880`03140b60 fffff800`028b6a34 : fffffa80`00f88b60 00000000`00000000
fffff800`02a3ae80 fffff800`0285d0f2 : nt!MiInPageSingleKernelStack+0x134

fffff880`03140c70 fffff800`028b69cf : fffffa80`010d0b30 00000000`00000000
fffffa80`00b51740 00000000`00000000 : nt!MmInPageKernelStack+0x40

fffff880`03140cd0 fffff800`028b666c : 00000000`00000000 00000000`00000000
00000000`00000080 fffffa80`00b51740 : nt!KiInSwapKernelStacks+0x1f

fffff880`03140d00 fffff800`02b65166 : 00000000`00000000 00000000`00000000
00000000`00000000 00000000`00000000 : nt!KeSwapProcessOrStack+0x84

fffff880`03140d40 fffff800`028a0486 : fffff800`02a3ae80 fffffa80`00b76040
fffffa80`00b75420 00000000`00000000 : nt!PspSystemThreadStartup+0x5a

fffff880`03140d80 00000000`00000000 : fffff880`03141000 00000000`00000000
00000000`00000000 00000000`00000000 : nt!KxStartSystemThread+0x16
```

It is interesting to observe, in the call stack above, how the swapper *calls MmAccessFault* directly, without causing a page fault. This can be concluded from the fact that there is no trap frame in the call stack and there is no frame for *KiPageFault*. Below is an excerpt of a call stack where *MmAccessFault* is called after a page fault:

```
fffff880`027a5ac0 fffff800`028cefee : 00000000`00000001 00000000`00000000
fffffa80`014dc401 00000000`00000000 : nt!MmAccessFault+0x3c0

fffff880`027a5c20 00000001`3fa3131d : 00000001`3fa8d748 00000000`00000000
00000000`002dfb48 00000000`00000000 : nt!KiPageFault+0x16e (TrapFrame @
fffff880`027a5c20)
```

Most of the time, *MmAccessFault* is called bi *KiPageFault*, but the swapper is a different story and it calls the function directly.

Note that, conceivably, the swapper *could* have brought the pages in by touching them and causing a fault, because it would not have been a fault on *its own* stack. For the swapper, the stack being restored is just a piece of virtual memory in the system PTEs range.

47.3 DPC Stack

Windows switches to a different kernel stack when processing DPCs. A separate stack is kept for each processor in the system and used for this purpose to further insulate DPC triggered code from other code executed in regular thread context.

48   Obscure VMM Concepts

This section is about some VMM concepts that were encountered while researching the material for this book.

48.1 Process Metapages

Process metapages can be observed in the code managing the direct hash for a process working set (see sec. 37.14.4.2 on p. 334). *MiUpdateWsleHash* is called when an hash table entry must be added. When the working set is using the direct hash table, this function may have to map a virtual address in the direct hash range. In this range, only virtual pages actually needed to store table entries are mapped to physical pages, so, if the entry being added falls in a page which has not been mapped yet, the translation is set up by calling *MiMapProcessMetaPage*. The added page is accounted for in two counters: `_MMSUPPORT.WorkingSetSizeOverhead` and the static MiWsOverheadPages. The context in which these variables are used and their names suggest that their purpose is to track pages used in managing a working set list, but which are not part of the working set itself. Since a working set list manages pages, these are "pages on pages" or metapages. The counters observed can be useful when trying to account for overall physical memory usage.

48.2 Resident Available Memory

48.2.1   Basic Concept

To explain this concept, let's consider the creation of a thread. We know that a thread must have a kernel mode stack, which must be resident in physical memory when the thread runs. True, we also know that the stack can be swapped out when the thread is suspended, but the thread cannot run until its stack has been completely brought back into memory.

Given this, it makes sense to check whether there is enough available physical memory for the stack before creating a thread, since it would be pointless to create one and then not being able to run it.

This is what Resident Available Memory is about: it is a counter maintained by the VMM to check whether there is enough available physical memory to perform certain operations, which require at least a minimum amount of it.

Another example is the creation of a new process. Each process needs a minimum working set to run, so an attempt to create one may fail, if the system cannot guarantee that this amount of physical memory is available.

But what does it mean that physical memory is *available*? Normally, the amount of available pages is computed as the count of pages on the Zeroed, Free and Standby lists, because these are pages ready to be reused (Zeroed and Free ones are not used, Standby ones are ready to be repurposed). We could think that this is the value to check to see if there is enough memory for a new stack or process.

This approach would not be correct, however. Consider pages on the modified list: they are not counted as available, but they can be made available by flushing their content to disk. Also, a page currently part of a working set could be made available by trimming the latter, eventually flushing the page content to disk, if needed. This tells us that it would be too restrictive to fail the creation of a thread by checking the *current* amount of available pages.

Rather, the value we need to check is the amount of available physical memory we would have if everything was squeezed to its minimum: all the process working sets trimmed to their minimum, the paged pool swapped out, pageable kernel mode code swapped out, etc. If we determine that, even under these conditions, we would still lack enough memory for the attempted operation, then we must return failure.

The value we are interested in can be computed by subtracting from the total physical memory installed the amount of memory used by content that cannot be swapped out: the nonpaged pool, nonpaged driver and kernel code, etc. The result is the Resident Available Memory.

Given its meaning, we can understand that, for every operation that causes memory to be locked, the amount of memory that becomes non-pageable must be subtracted from the Resident Available count.

Going back to the thread creation example, if the operation succeeds, the size of the kernel stack must itself be subtracted from the Resident Available count, since that amount of memory becomes not pageable.

This adds a further twist: we know that, in fact, kernel stacks can be swapped out by the swapper thread, but this is not considered in the Resident Available computation. This is easier to understand if we think that, for this purpose, the system behaves as if kernel stacks were always resident. This ensures that all existing threads can have their stack resident, if the need arises, e.g. if none of them is suspended. The system does not allow to create a new thread if its stack cannot reside in physical memory together with all the other stacks (and all the other non-pageable content). That being said, if a thread remains suspended long enough, its stack is swapped out to free physical memory which, even though is not counted as Resident Available, can still be used for something useful, e.g. added to a working set, etc.

The same applies to processes: if all the threads of a process have been swapped out, the entire working set of the process is outswapped as well ([1], p.832), and its working set size drops to 0, i.e. below the working set minimum size. However, the barebone working set corresponding to the minimum size must be brought back into memory if a thread is to be run, so the minimum size is considered as if it were locked and subtracted from the Resident Available counter when a process is created ([1], p. 356).

Given how it is computed, the amount of Resident Available Memory is often found to be greater than the current available memory. The latter is what is currently available with all the working sets at their current size, while the former is what would be available if every working set was at its minimum (but with swapped out processes and stacks counted as resident).

This interpretation of Resident Available Memory has been inferred from [19], where an example of thread creation failure is reported; from [1], p. 356, which explains how the process working set minimum is subtracted from the count. The following sections report the results of a few tests which further confirm the interpretation proposed.

The current value of Resident Available Memory is included in the output of the !vm WinDbg extension:

```
1: kd> !vm

*** Virtual Memory Usage ***
        Physical Memory:      229246 (     916984 Kb)
        Page File: \??\C:\pagefile.sys
          Current:    1048576 Kb  Free Space:     107156 Kb
          Minimum:    1048576 Kb  Maximum:       2928820 Kb
unable to get nt!MmSystemLockPagesCount
        Available Pages:      100816 (     403264 Kb)
        ResAvail Pages:       202570 (     810280 Kb)
        Locked IO Pages:           0 (          0 Kb)
[...]
```

Normally, the value printed by !vm is found to be equal to the static variable MmResidentAvailablePages.

As described in [19], when the Resident Available count becomes too low, the system start malfunctioning, because various fundamental operations, like thread creation, fail.

48.2.2   Per Processor Counter Caching

One function which updates MmResidentAvailablePages is *MiChargeResidentAvailable* and its code shows an interesting behavior. Before updating the static, the function tries to subtract the value to be "charged" from a member of the _KPRCB of the executing processor named CachedResidentAvailable. If the value to be charged (i.e. subtracted) is less than _KPRCB.CachedResidentAvailable, it is subtracted from the latter and

MmResidentAvailablePages is not updated. If, on the other hand,
_KPRCB.CachedResidentAvailable is too small, the function subtracts the input count
from MmResidentAvailablePages.

Together, this logic and the member name suggest that a fraction of the total Resident
Available count is kept in the _KPRCB member. Since there is a _KPRCB for each processor,
this could be done to reduce traffic on the interprocessor bus caused by updates to the static
variable, which must be carried out atomically with a locked cmpxchg instruction, to ensure
a correct result. Instead of always accessing the single variable, each processor has a fraction
of the counter value in its own _KPRCB and deducts the charge from there.

The same function implements logic to "recharge" _KPRCB.CachedResidentAvailable:
if its value is found to be less than 64 and MmResidentAvailablePages is greater than 1024,
_KPRCB.CachedResidentAvailable is incremented to 128 and the amount of the
increment is subtracted from MmResidentAvailablePages. This "moves" a fraction of the
counter to the _KPRCB member, i.e. to the per processor cache.

Interestingly, this means that the value printed by !vm, which appears to be the same as
MmResidentAvailablePages, does not include the cached fractions in the PRCBs.

48.2.3   Test: Effect of Memory Locking

This test confirms that when a block of memory is locked, its size is subtracted from the
Resident Available count.

We allocate, with MemTests, a private block of 0x300000 bytes (3MB) and create an MDL
describing it. Then we call *MmProbeAndLockPages* to lock the buffer pages in memory.
MemTests allows us to break into the debugger before calling its driver. Within the debugger,
we place a breakpoint for the current thread at *MmProbeAndLockPages*. When the
breakpoint is hit, we are about to lock the pages and we find the following situation:

```
Breakpoint 0 hit
nt!MmProbeAndLockPages:
fffff800`028afd30 4489442418      mov     dword ptr [rsp+18h],r8d

1: kd> !vm

*** Virtual Memory Usage ***
        Physical Memory:     229246 (     916984 Kb)
        Page File: \??\C:\pagefile.sys
          Current:   1048576 Kb  Free Space:   1010896 Kb
          Minimum:   1048576 Kb  Maximum:      2914148 Kb
unable to get nt!MmSystemLockPagesCount
        Available Pages:     137433 (     549732 Kb)
        ResAvail Pages:      201124 (     804496 Kb)
```

```
            Locked IO Pages:           0 (            0 Kb)
            Free System PTEs:   33536630 ( 134146520 Kb)
            Modified Pages:         8930 (     35720 Kb)
            Modified PF Pages:      8909 (     35636 Kb)
            NonPagedPool Usage:     5861 (     23444 Kb)
            NonPagedPool Max:     163710 (    654840 Kb)
            PagedPool 0 Usage:     15680 (     62720 Kb)
            PagedPool 1 Usage:      2242 (      8968 Kb)
            PagedPool 2 Usage:       255 (      1020 Kb)
            PagedPool 3 Usage:       287 (      1148 Kb)
            PagedPool 4 Usage:       324 (      1296 Kb)
            PagedPool Usage:       18788 (     75152 Kb)
            PagedPool Maximum:  33554432 ( 134217728 Kb)
            Session Commit:         5164 (     20656 Kb)
            Shared Commit:          3549 (     14196 Kb)
            Special Pool:              0 (         0 Kb)
            Shared Process:         4286 (     17144 Kb)
            PagedPool Commit:      18796 (     75184 Kb)
            Driver Commit:          2694 (     10776 Kb)
            Committed pages:      110427 (    441708 Kb)
            Commit limit:         491390 (   1965560 Kb)

1: kd> dq nt!MmResidentAvailablePages l1
fffff800`02a1ac00  00000000`000311a4

1: kd> ? 311a4
Evaluate expression: 201124 = 00000000`000311a4
```

As we can see, MmResidentAvailablePages and !va give the same value. We must also
examine the counters fraction cached per processor:

```
1: kd> dq gs:[20] l1
002b:00000000`00000020  fffff880`009ea180

1: kd> ?? ((nt!_kprcb*) 0xfffff880`009ea180)->CachedResidentAvailable
unsigned long 0x6a

1: kd> ~0

0: kd> dq gs:[20] l1
002b:00000000`00000020  fffff800`02a08e80

0: kd> ?? ((nt!_kprcb*) 0xfffff800`02a08e80)->CachedResidentAvailable
unsigned long 0x7f
```

We exploited the fact that gs:[20] is _KPCR.CurrentPrcb and gives us the address of the
_KPRCB. As we can see, processor 1 has a cached count equal to 0x6A and the value for
processor 0 is 0x7F. The following expression gives the actual total of Resident Available:

```
0: kd> ? 0n201124 + 6a + 7f
Evaluate expression: 201357 = 00000000`0003128d
```

Now we resume execution with `g @$ra`, which will break again as soon as we return from *MmProbeAndLockPages*:

```
1: kd> g @$ra
krnlallocs!MmProbeAndLockPagesTest+0x1e5:
fffff880`0395ba25 eb2f          jmp     krnlallocs!MmProbeAndLockPagesTest+0x216
(fffff880`0395ba56)

1: kd> !vm

*** Virtual Memory Usage ***
        Physical Memory:     229246 (    916984 Kb)
        Page File: \??\C:\pagefile.sys
          Current:   1048576 Kb  Free Space:    1010896 Kb
          Minimum:   1048576 Kb  Maximum:       2914148 Kb
unable to get nt!MmSystemLockPagesCount
        Available Pages:     136665 (    546660 Kb)
        ResAvail Pages:      200461 (    801844 Kb)
        Locked IO Pages:          0 (         0 Kb)
        Free System PTEs:  33536630 ( 134146520 Kb)
        Modified Pages:        8930 (     35720 Kb)
        Modified PF Pages:     8909 (     35636 Kb)
        NonPagedPool Usage:    5861 (     23444 Kb)
        NonPagedPool Max:    163710 (    654840 Kb)
        PagedPool 0 Usage:    15680 (     62720 Kb)
        PagedPool 1 Usage:     2242 (      8968 Kb)
        PagedPool 2 Usage:      255 (      1020 Kb)
        PagedPool 3 Usage:      287 (      1148 Kb)
        PagedPool 4 Usage:      324 (      1296 Kb)
        PagedPool Usage:      18788 (     75152 Kb)
        PagedPool Maximum: 33554432 ( 134217728 Kb)
        Session Commit:        5164 (     20656 Kb)
        Shared Commit:         3549 (     14196 Kb)
        Special Pool:             0 (         0 Kb)
        Shared Process:        4286 (     17144 Kb)
        PagedPool Commit:     18796 (     75184 Kb)
        Driver Commit:         2694 (     10776 Kb)
        Committed pages:     110428 (    441712 Kb)
        Commit limit:        491390 (   1965560 Kb)
```

We stop inside the test driver (kernelallocs) where we once again compute the counter total:

```
1: kd> dq nt!MmResidentAvailablePages l1
fffff800`02a1ac00  00000000`00030f0d
1: kd> ? 30f0d
Evaluate expression: 200461 = 00000000`00030f0d

1: kd> ?? ((nt!_kprcb*) 0xfffff800`02a08e80)->CachedResidentAvailable
unsigned long 0x7f

1: kd> ?? ((nt!_kprcb*) 0xfffff880`009ea180)->CachedResidentAvailable
unsigned long 0

1: kd> ? 0n200461 + 7f
Evaluate expression: 200588 = 00000000`00030f8c
```

Finally, we compute the difference between the values before and after the call:

```
1: kd> ? 3128d - 30f8c
Evaluate expression: 769 = 00000000`00000301
```

The result above is the number of resident available pages consumed. 0x301 pages correspond to 0x301000 bytes which almost exactly match the size of our buffer. The extra page could be due to some other operation which took place while *MmProbeAndLockPages* was executing.

In general, repeating the same test we find that the Resident Available count decrement is close to the number of locked pages, which confirms that this operation is charged against the counter.

48.2.4   Test: Consuming More Resident Available Memory Than the Currently Available Memory

In this test we are going to lock a memory block with size greater than the available memory counter, but smaller than the Resident Available counter. We will see that this succeeds at the expense of swapping out other memory content.

First we allocate a private block of 0x30000000 (768MB or 0.75GB) bytes with MemTests. Then we create an MDL describing the buffer and finally, call *MmProbeAndLockPages* on it, thereby locking the pages in memory. When MemTests is about to call the driver, we choose to break into the debugger and place a breakpoint for the current thread on *MmProbeAndLockPages*. Figure 60 shows the memory status immediately before breaking into the debugger:

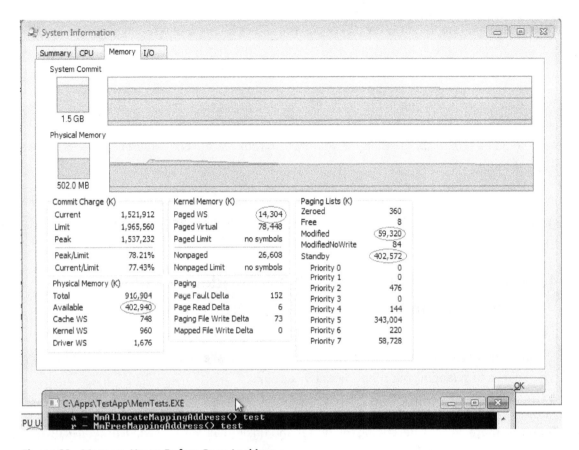

Figure 60 - Memory Usage Before Page Locking

We are about to see how the highlighted values are affected by this test. The first thing we notice is that the available memory (402,940kB) is less than the size of the buffer we are about to lock (768MB).

When the breakpoint at the beginning of *MmProbeAndLockPages* is hit, !vm reports the following:

```
KernelAllocs - MmProbeAndLockPagesTest
KernelAllocsAbout to probe and lock MDL pages
KernelAllocs     Mdl address = 0xFFFFFA800106A000
KernelAllocs     Access mode = 0
KernelAllocs     Operation   = 1
Breakpoint 0 hit
nt!MmProbeAndLockPages:
fffff800`028dbd30 4489442418      mov     dword ptr [rsp+18h],r8d


1: kd> !vm


*** Virtual Memory Usage ***
     Physical Memory:    229246 (    916984 Kb)
     Page File: \??\C:\pagefile.sys
```

```
        Current:   1048576 Kb  Free Space:       107156 Kb
        Minimum:   1048576 Kb  Maximum:         2928820 Kb
unable to get nt!MmSystemLockPagesCount
        Available Pages:        100816 (     403264 Kb)
        ResAvail Pages:         202570 (     810280 Kb)
        Locked IO Pages:             0 (          0 Kb)
        Free System PTEs:     33536665 ( 134146660 Kb)
        Modified Pages:          14756 (      59024 Kb)
        Modified PF Pages:       14736 (      58944 Kb)
        NonPagedPool Usage:       6653 (      26612 Kb)
        NonPagedPool Max:       163710 (     654840 Kb)
        PagedPool 0 Usage:       15801 (      63204 Kb)
        PagedPool 1 Usage:        2364 (       9456 Kb)
        PagedPool 2 Usage:         467 (       1868 Kb)
        PagedPool 3 Usage:         470 (       1880 Kb)
        PagedPool 4 Usage:         510 (       2040 Kb)
        PagedPool Usage:         19612 (      78448 Kb)
        PagedPool Maximum:    33554432 ( 134217728 Kb)
        Session Commit:           6753 (      27012 Kb)
        Shared Commit:            3352 (      13408 Kb)
        Special Pool:                0 (          0 Kb)
        Shared Process:           3638 (      14552 Kb)
        PagedPool Commit:        19620 (      78480 Kb)
        Driver Commit:            2694 (      10776 Kb)
        Committed pages:        380447 (    1521788 Kb)
        Commit limit:           491390 (    1965560 Kb)
```

We can see that the current Resident Available counter is greater than the buffer we are about to lock. We then resume execution with g@$ra and the first thing we notice is that we have to wait several minutes with the system accessing the disk, before the function returns. The VMM is frantically swapping out content to give us the physical pages we are requesting. When the function finally returns, the situation is as follows:

```
1: kd> g @$ra
krnlallocs!MmProbeAndLockPagesTest+0x1e5:
fffff880`03542a25 eb2f            jmp     krnlallocs!MmProbeAndLockPagesTest+0x216
(fffff880`03542a56)

0: kd> !vm

*** Virtual Memory Usage ***
        Physical Memory:        229246 (     916984 Kb)
        Page File: \??\C:\pagefile.sys
        Current:   1048576 Kb  Free Space:       440056 Kb
        Minimum:   1048576 Kb  Maximum:         2928820 Kb
unable to get nt!MmSystemLockPagesCount
        Available Pages:          5923 (      23692 Kb)
        ResAvail Pages:           6265 (      25060 Kb)
        Locked IO Pages:             0 (          0 Kb)
        Free System PTEs:     33536654 ( 134146616 Kb)
        Modified Pages:            249 (        996 Kb)
        Modified PF Pages:         217 (        868 Kb)
        NonPagedPool Usage:       6665 (      26660 Kb)
        NonPagedPool Max:       163710 (     654840 Kb)
```

```
PagedPool 0 Usage:      16387 (     65548 Kb)
PagedPool 1 Usage:       2350 (      9400 Kb)
PagedPool 2 Usage:        462 (      1848 Kb)
PagedPool 3 Usage:        445 (      1780 Kb)
PagedPool 4 Usage:        488 (      1952 Kb)
PagedPool Usage:        20132 (     80528 Kb)
PagedPool Maximum:   33554432 ( 134217728 Kb)
Session Commit:          6741 (     26964 Kb)
Shared Commit:           3346 (     13384 Kb)
Special Pool:               0 (         0 Kb)
Shared Process:          3758 (     15032 Kb)
PagedPool Commit:       20140 (     80560 Kb)
Driver Commit:           2694 (     10776 Kb)
Committed pages:       380713 (   1522852 Kb)
Commit limit:          491390 (   1965560 Kb)
```

We can see how Resident Available has dropped. Our buffer has been successfully locked, at the expense of other content which has been swapped out. We can confirm this by looking at the highlighted counters in this screenshot, taken before breaking on the return from *MmProbeAndLockPages*:

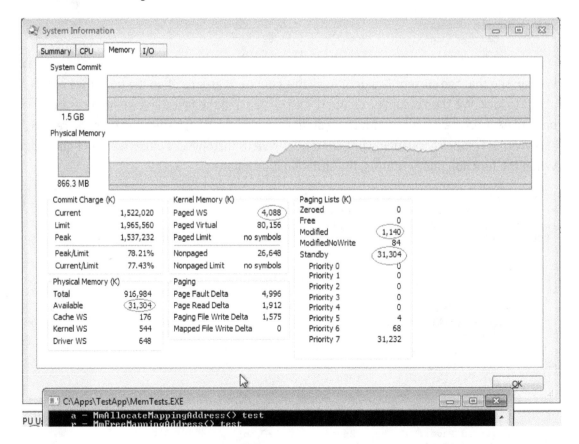

Figure 61 - Memory Usage After Page Locking

The Modified and Standby lists are now depleted and also the paged pool WS has been severely shrunk.

The Available memory from the screenshot (31,304k) is greater than the Resident Available value printed by `!vm` (25,060k), which is unusual. However this is caused by the fact that the System Explorer window is updated once per second, so the values we are seeing are the last sampled ones before `g @$ra` broke into the debugger and not the exact values at the time of break. This can be confirmed by looking again at the `!vm` output on p. 541, where the Available memory is listed at 23,692k, i.e. a little less than the Resident Available count.

49   Interactions with the Cache Manager

49.1 Cached Read Overview

This section provides an outline of how a read operation on a cached file works, which will allow us to explore the relationship between the cache manager (CM) and the VMM.

It is important to have a clear picture of the concepts exposed in Chapter 38 (p. 338), to better understand this section. Sec. 38.2.8 on p. 355 anticipates a few details about the CM.

For simplicity, we will consider a read of a file which has never been accessed since the system was started and we will temporarily forget about prefetching.

The call to *ReadFile* causes the file system driver which manages the file to be called. Since this is the first access to the file, the driver calls CM DDIs to initialize caching for it. These DDIs create the memory section backed by the file and other data structures used by the CM.

Afterwards, the file system driver calls a CM DDI, requesting the data block from the file.

The CM has a portion of the Dynamic Kernel VA region reserved for its own use, so this DDI maps into it a view of the memory section backed by the file.

The CM DDI accesses the view virtual range, where the data from the file should be, to read it and return it to the file system driver.

Since this is the first access to the file, the hardware PTE of the view is invalid (P bit clear) and points to the prototype PTE of the section; the latter, in turn, is invalid as well and points to the subsection. When the CM tries to read at the view address a page fault occurs and the VMM understands it must read the page from the file.

The VMM issues an I/O operation for the page, which ends up calling the file system driver again. This time, however, the I/O request is flagged as a non-cached read.

When the file system driver receives such a request, it knows the time has come to do its job: going down to the file system and retrieving the requested page. Note how, if the file system driver did not know, at this stage, that in-paging is being requested, it would call the CM again creating an infinite loop.

When the read completes, the page fault is resolved, the CM memory access is resumed and the data read is returned to the file system driver itself, which requested it in the first place. From the driver, the data read makes its way up the stack to the caller of *ReadFile*.

If the same file portion is accessed again later, here are some possible scenarios:

- The CM view is still mapped to the physical page with the data read, so the CM access to the view address does not cause a page fault. The data is read from memory, without performing I/O. This is how caching actually happens.

- The CM view is not mapped to the physical page anymore. Either the hardware PTE is invalid and points to the prototype PTE, or the view has been unmapped altogether (the hardware PTE is not in use or mapping something else). However, the memory section still exists and the prototype PTE is still valid and pointing to the physical page. Even though the mapping must be rebuilt, no I/O is performed and, again, this is caching at work.

- The next scenario is similar to the previous one, but the prototype PTE is in transition. The page is on the Standby list and still holds the data read. A soft fault will occur when the CM will try to access the data, but will not cause I/O, so, even in this situation, cached content was used.

- The memory section backed by the file is still existing (the CM keeps them alive according to its internal logic; also, the section is retained as long as there are open handles to the file), but the particular page needed has been repurposed. The prototype PTE is pointing again to the subsection. This time, I/O can't be avoided.

- Finally, the memory section may have been destroyed, and all the steps to access the file must be performed again.

49.2 Cache Physical Memory Usage

With this design, physical memory used by the CM is controlled by the VMM, in the same way the VMM itself manages all physical memory. Physical pages referenced by CM views are part of the CM working set, controlled by MmSystemCacheWs. The Working Set Manager can remove them from the working set if available memory is low and perform its usual steps: outpage, repurpose or soft-fault them back.

The CM continuously unmaps its views to reuse virtual address space. When this happens, the section physical pages are usually placed on the Standby or Modified list. There are exceptions: for instance, if another process has mapped a view of the same pages with *MapViewOfFileEx*, they remain Active, because their share count is greater than 0.

However, when the pages end up on the Standby list (eventually having passed through the Modified one), they can remain there for as long as there is physical memory available and the CM does not destroy the memory section. Thus, on a system with plenty of available RAM, large amounts of files can remain cached for a long time with no adverse effects, since Standby pages can be reused as soon as needed. This is another example of how the overall VMM design is aimed at *using* available memory.

As [1] points out on p. 858, it would therefore be wrong to think that the amount of data cached in memory is equal to the cache working set size. This is simply the amount of cached data currently mapped in the CM address space, but many more physical pages full of useful cached data may be on the Standby list, which acts as a unified memory cache for the system.

49.3 Prefetching

The CM design enables it to prefetch files as it sees fit. Once the memory section backed by a particular file is created, the CM can, and often does, prefetch parts of the file into physical pages which are put directly on the Standby list, with the corresponding prototype PTE set in transition. This way, file content is ready for use, while at the same time being stored in readily reusable physical pages.

For this reason, the outline given in section 49.1 on p. 543 is somewhat simplified. It may happen, for instance that the CM prefeteches the beginning of a file when it creates the memory section, so that the hard page fault does not actually occur. The overall logic remains valid, however: sooner or later, a piece of file which is not anywhere in memory (i.e. not even on the Standby list) will be needed and the hard fault will happen.

There are even higher level system components like the Prefetcher and Superfetch which proactively open and prefetch files without waiting for processes to access them. All these optimizations rely on the foundation provided by memory sections and the Standby list.

49.4 The Modified No-Write List

This list is made of _MMPFN instances linked together, and, like the Modified list includes instances referring to pages which must be written to their backing storage. However, the content of these pages is not written by the Modified Page Writer until an explicit call to the VMM is done.

This facility is used by file system drivers to control the order in which updates to the file system occur. This is important to try to maintain the file system in a recoverable state in case of a system crash. To achieve this, updates to the file system metadata should occur in a transactional fashion. If a crash occurs while the file system is being updated, it should be possible to either completely perform the changes or roll them back.

To this end, a file system driver writes into a log file the changes it is about to make to the metadata, before actually making them. When the block of changes written into the log is such that the file system would be in a consistent state after applying them, the actual metadata update can begin. If the system crashes while the metadata update is in progress, the log can be used to rollback or reapply the changes as a unit of work.

This scheme relies on the fact that the log file is updated *before* the metadata. However, metadata are themselves treated like files: they are cached and accessed by means of memory sections. Metadata updates are thus written to storage by the Modified Page Writer (although the CM also explicitly flushes cached content, to reduce the time during which the on-storage copy is out of date).

Without the Modified No-Write List, the Modified Page Writer could grab a few Modified pages of metadata and write them to disk before the log file has been updated. This does not happen because file system drivers place modified metadata pages on the Modified No-Write list and allow them to be flushed to storage only after having flushed updates to the log file.

50   Memory Object Performance Counters

In this chapter we are going to examine the meaning of some memory-related counters available through Performance Monitor. This is not a complete list: we are only going to analyze those counters whose meaning can be clarified with the concepts presented in this book.

For some counters, we will also refer to values reported by Process Explorer from Sysinternals, of which version 15.11 was used.

50.1 Available Bytes

Process Explorer name: Available, in the Physical Memory section (in kB)
Kernel variable: unknown

The combined size of the Free, Zeroed and Standby lists in bytes. This value is the sum of the following counters:

- Free & Zero Page List Bytes

- Standby Cache Core Bytes

- Standby Cache Normal Priority Bytes

- Standby Cache Reserve Bytes

Given the overall architecture of the VMM, this is the amount of physical memory available for use.

50.2 Cache Bytes

Process Explorer name: CacheWS, in the Physical Memory section (in kB)
Kernel variable: MmSystemCacheWs.WorkingSetSize (in pages)

The size of the file system cache working set in bytes. See sec. 44.6.1 on p. 428. See also Chapter 49 (p. 543) for an overview of the file system cache.

In Windows 7, this counter has the same value of the System Cache Resident Bytes counter.

50.3 Cache Faults/sec

Process Explorer name: N/A
Kernel variable: unknown

The number of page faults per second caused by accesses to content of the file system cache. This includes both soft and hard faults and is a count of faults, not of pages. See Chapter 49 (p. 543) for an overview of the file system cache.

50.4 Commit Limit

Process Explorer name: Limit, in the Commit Charge section (in kB)

Kernel variable: unknown

The maximum possible value of commit charge, computed as the sum of the physical memory size and the paging file(s) size. See the Committed Bytes counter for more details on commit charge.

Since pages counted in the commit charge must be stored either in RAM or in the paging file, the sum of their sizes gives the commit limit.

As an example, below is the output from the `!vm` extension:

```
0: kd> !vm 1

*** Virtual Memory Usage ***
        Physical Memory:     130942 (    523768 Kb)
        Page File: \??\C:\pagefile.sys
          Current:   1048576 Kb  Free Space:    894156 Kb
          Minimum:   1048576 Kb  Maximum:      3214180 Kb
[...]
        Commit limit:         393086 (   1572344 Kb)
```

The values on the left of the parentheses are expressed in pages. From the data above we have:

130942 + 1048576 / 4 = 393086

we have converted the paging file size in pages and obtained the commit limit.

Note that Windows is not always able to use all the physical RAM present on a system, due to how the chipset maps the physical address space, so the commit limit is not always exactly equal to the amount of *installed* memory plus the paging file size. However, if we use the memory actually available to Windows, as reported by `!vm`, the results usually match. There are, however, cases when the commit limit reported by `!vm` is a bit smaller than the one computed in this way.

The amount of available physical memory reported by `!vm` is the same listed by Process Explorer as Total in the Physical Memory section.

50.5 Committed Bytes

Process Explorer name: Current, in the Commit Charge section (in kB)

Kernel variable: unknown

50.5.1   Basic Concept

The systemwide commit charge. Its value represents the number of virtual pages which must be backed by RAM or the paging file.

Chapter 19 on p. 93 provides an introduction on the commit charge. Since this chapter was meant to be read much earlier in the book, we have to add a few concepts to its content.

In a demand paging system like Windows, a page of memory content can be stored either in memory or in the paging file. Thus, the systemwide maximum number of pages that can be allocated is the sum of the RAM size and the paging file length. The system increments the commit charge for every page for which storage must exist and fails an allocation if the resulting charge would be greater than the commit limit. In other words, the system considers the physical memory and the paging file (or files) as a global store, whose size is the commit limit and keeps track of how much of it has been consumed in the commit charge.

50.5.2   Effect of File Backed Memory Sections

An important implication of this logic is that pages of a memory section backed by a file (see Chapter 38 on p. 338) are not counted in the commit charge. File backed sections don't consume paging file space: when they are removed from memory, their content is moved to the file backing the section. When this happens, they *leave* the global store composed by RAM and paging file.

To further explain this concept, let's consider the following example: a system with 1 page of physical RAM, a paging file 1 page long and another file f, 100 pages long. The commit limit for this system is 2 pages: at any given time, we can have at most 1 page in memory and 1 in the paging file. However, if the commit charge is 1, i.e. a single page below the commit limit, we can map a view of a section which includes all the 100 pages of f. The VMM will use the single free RAM page as a window over the entire file content. It would be too restrictive to forbid the file mapping based on the commit limit, even though the file length is much greater.

We can verify with MemTests that the VMM applies this logic. When we map a view of a section, the commit charge is not incremented, no matter how big the view is.

This leads us to understand one of the pitfalls encountered when trying to estimate if a system has enough memory. It may seem a good idea to compare the commit charge with the physical memory size, under the notion that, when the former is much higher, more paging occurs. However, the commit charge does not account for file backed sections, so it may seem deceptively low.

As an example, the following screenshot has been taken from a system with 1GB of RAM, with a 768MB view of a file backed section mapped and accessed.

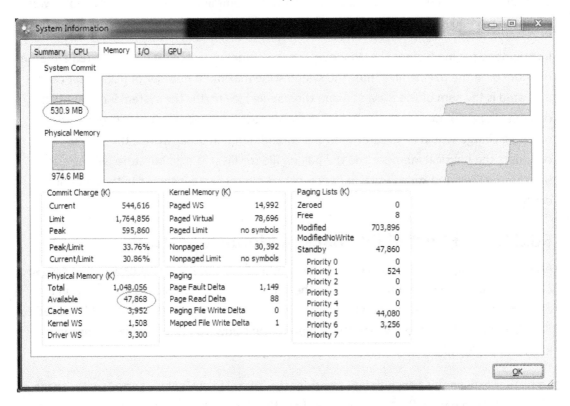

Figure 62 - Low Commit Charge with Low Free Memory

The commit charge is far less than the installed memory, so we may be tempted to think that there is an abundance of it. However, if we look at the available physical memory, we see that it is actually very low, and in fact the system was paging a lot and very slow during this test.

It was easier to make this mistake with the Windows XP Task Manager, which only showed a graph for the commit charge (called PF Usage):

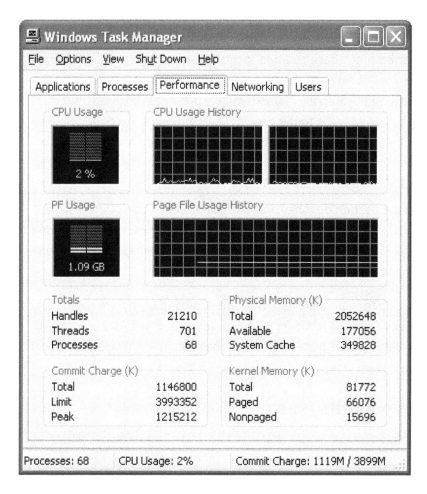

Figure 63 - Windows XP Task Manager

On the other hand, from the Process Explorer screenshot above, the lower graph for physical memory usage immediately tells us that we are running low on free memory, in spite of the low commit charge.

50.5.3   Demand Zero Faults

It is not completely accurate to state that a committed page has always content which is stored either in RAM or in the paging file. Consider a committed page which has not been accessed yet: the PTE is set as a demand zero one and does not reference a physical page. No copy of the page content exists in the paging file, since it has not even been accessed yet. Nevertheless, when this page has been committed, the commit charge has indeed been increment by one page. This is the way of the VMM to ensure at commit time that there will be room for the page either in RAM or in the paging file when physical storage will be needed.

50.5.4   Standby Pages

In previous sections, we stated that a page counted in the commit charge resides either in memory or in a paging file. For the sake of completeness, we must ponder on the fact that clean pages (both Active and on the Standby list) are actually present in both places. This does not mean they must be added twice to the commit charge though, since they can be removed from memory at any time, precisely because there is a valid copy in a paging file.

50.5.5   System Range Addresses

So far we have considered the user mode range, but the system range contributes to the commit charge as well. Each valid virtual page consumes 1 page of the overall store made of RAM and paging file, regardless of whether the page is for pageable addresses or fixed ones (non-pageable code, paging structures for the system range, etc).

Actually, when non-pageable pages are allocated, they are deducted both from the remaining commit charge *and* from the Resident Available count (see sec. 48.2 on p. 533). Such a page consumes 1 page of global store and leaves 1 page less of available physical memory for the rest of the system.

50.6 Demand Zero Faults/sec

Process Explorer name: N/A
Kernel variable: unknown

The rate of faults for demand zero pages. As an example, when a committed private page is referenced for the first time, one such fault is generated. A detailed analysis of demand zero faults processing can be found in Chapter 26 on p. 138.

50.7 Free and Zero Page List Bytes

Process Explorer name: displayed as separate values named Zeroed and Free in the Paging Lists section (in kB)
Kernel variable: unknown

The combined counts of pages on the Zeroed and Free list, converted in bytes. It represents the amount of memory available without repurposing transition pages. Repurposing is described in sec. 26.4.3.4.3 on p. 158.

50.8 Free System Page Table Entries

Process Explorer name: N/A

Kernel variable: see control structures detailed in sec. 44.8.2 on p. 442

System PTEs have been analyzed in sec. 44.8 on p. 440, and sec. 44.8.2 on p. 442 presents a detailed analysis of the bitmaps tracking their allocation.

This counter reports the number of available system PTEs and suggests the existence of an additional region for them. As an example, consider the screenshot below:

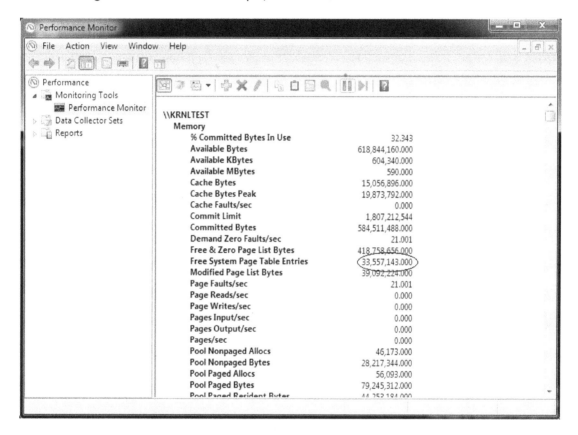

Figure 64 - Free System PTEs in Performance Monitor

The System PTE region at 0xFFFFF880`00000000 is 128GB in size, a fact which is consistent with the results of the analysis of sec. 44.8.2 on p. 442. The number of PTEs, i.e. of pages that can fit into the region is therefore:

0x20`00000000 / 0x1000 = 0x02000000 = 33,554,432

However, the number of free entries reported by Performance Monitor is higher than the total number of entries in this region. On p. 748 of [1], the region 0xFFFFF980`00000000 - FFFFFA7F`FFFFFFFF (which we called Dynamic Kernel VA Space) is described as follows:

" MM_SYSTEM_SPACE_START for a length of MI_DYNAMIC_KERNEL_VA_BYTES is managed by the MiSystemVaBitMap. This is typically 1TB and is used for the system cache, *system PTEs*, and special pool"

It is therefore possible that part of this region is used for additional system PTEs. This would also be consistent with the fact that the System PTE working set can be used for addresses in Dynamic Kernel VA Space, as we saw in sec. 44.11.3 on p. 492.

Also, the !vm extension reports an amount of free system PTEs which, although not exactly equal to the value printed by Performance Monitor, is close to it and corresponds to a virtual size greater than 128GB. Below are the results for the system were the screenshot above was taken, obtained breaking into WinDbg immediately after Performance Monitor refreshed its window:

```
0: kd> !vm 1

*** Virtual Memory Usage ***
        Physical Memory:        262014 (   1048056 Kb)
        Page File: \??\C:\pagefile.sys
          Current:     512000 Kb  Free Space:     488336 Kb
          Minimum:     512000 Kb  Maximum:       1024000 Kb
        Page File: \??\E:\pagefile.sys
          Current:     204800 Kb  Free Space:     182596 Kb
          Minimum:     204800 Kb  Maximum:        512000 Kb
Type information missing error for MiSystemVaTypeCount
        Available Pages:        151088 (    604352 Kb)
        ResAvail Pages:         216772 (    867088 Kb)
        Locked IO Pages:             0 (         0 Kb)
        Free System PTEs:     33557139 ( 134228556 Kb)
```

Note: even though WinDbg complains about missing type information the debugger was configured with the correct symbols.

The number of free system PTEs on the left of the parentheses is in pages and is close to the value reported by Performance Monitor.

Another tidbit of information comes from the !sysptes extension:

```
0: kd> !sysptes

System PTE Information
Unimplemented error for MiSystemVaTypeCount
  Total System Ptes 33558016
unable to get nt!MiPteBinMax
Unable to get syspte index array - skipping bins

    starting PTE: fffff6fc40000000
```

```
    free blocks: 19    total free: 2707     largest free block: 490


Kernel Stack PTE Information
Unable to get syspte index array - skipping bins

    starting PTE: fffff6fc40000000


  free blocks: 136   total free: 1513    largest free block: 114
```

If the amount labeled `Total System Ptes` is to be believed, it is interesting to convert it in hexadecimal:

```
0: kd> ? 0n33558016
Evaluate expression: 33558016 = 00000000`02000e00
```

This value is +0xE00 over 0x2000000, i.e. over the number of pages corresponding to 128GB. 0xE00 is a multiple of 0x200, which is the number of pages mapped by a PDE. Thus, this value implies that there is an additional block of

0xE00 / 0x200 = 7

PDEs somewhere, which are used for system PTEs.

These values were for a virtual machine with about 1GB of RAM. On a physical system with 8GB of RAM we find:

```
lkd> !sysptes

System PTE Information
Unimplemented error for MiSystemVaTypeCount
  Total System Ptes 33567232
unable to get nt!MiPteBinMax
Unable to get syspte index array - skipping bins

    starting PTE: fffff6fc40000000


  free blocks: 86   total free: 4010    largest free block: 348


Kernel Stack PTE Information
Unable to get syspte index array - skipping bins

    starting PTE: fffff6fc40000000


  free blocks: 355   total free: 3334    largest free block: 77
```

.

And here also the total number of system PTEs exceeds 0x2000000 by a whole number of PDEs:

```
lkd> ? 0n33567232
Evaluate expression: 33567232 = 00000000`02003200
lkd> ? 3200 % 200
Evaluate expression: 0 = 00000000`00000000
lkd> ? 3200 / 200
Evaluate expression: 25 = 00000000`00000019
```

It is also worth observing that the very small values labeled `total free` in the `!sysptes` output for the 1GB virtual machine are close to the values of free PTEs in the secondary bitmaps (see sec. 44.8.2 on p. 442):

```
0: kd> ?? ((nt!_mi_system_pte_type*) @@(nt!MiSystemPteInfo))
struct _MI_SYSTEM_PTE_TYPE * 0xfffff800`02a31720
   +0x000 Bitmap           : _RTL_BITMAP
   +0x010 Flags            : 3
   +0x014 Hint             : 0x4512
   +0x018 BasePte          : 0xfffff6fc`40000000 _MMPTE
   +0x020 FailureCount     : 0xfffff800`02a3175c  -> 0
   +0x028 Vm               : 0xfffff800`02a09440 _MMSUPPORT
   +0x030 TotalSystemPtes  : 0n3584
   +0x034 TotalFreeSystemPtes : 0n2707
   +0x038 CachedPteCount   : 0n4
   +0x03c PteFailures      : 0
   +0x040 SpinLock         : 0
   +0x040 GlobalMutex      : (null)

0: kd> ?? ((nt!_mi_system_pte_type*) @@(nt!MiKernelStackPteInfo))
struct _MI_SYSTEM_PTE_TYPE * 0xfffff800`02a30ec0
   +0x000 Bitmap           : _RTL_BITMAP
   +0x010 Flags            : 3
   +0x014 Hint             : 0x462a
   +0x018 BasePte          : 0xfffff6fc`40000000 _MMPTE
   +0x020 FailureCount     : 0xfffff800`02a30efc  -> 0
   +0x028 Vm               : 0xfffff800`02a09440 _MMSUPPORT
   +0x030 TotalSystemPtes  : 0n8704
   +0x034 TotalFreeSystemPtes : 0n1522
   +0x038 CachedPteCount   : 0n7
   +0x03c PteFailures      : 0
   +0x040 SpinLock         : 0
   +0x040 GlobalMutex      : (null)
```

There is one final twist left. The debugger data above was collected with WinDbg v. 6.12.0002.633, but, with v. 6.11.0001.404 we find different results. `!vm` reports a number of free entries which is both lower than the one reported by Performance Monitor and below the theoretical maximum of 33,554,432 (0x02000000). `!sysptes` reports a total number of entries below the same maximum. In summary, this version reports data consistent with the hypothesis that the only region used for system PTEs is the range 0xFFFFF880`00000000 – 0xFFFFF9FF`FFFFFFFF. Version 6.12 could be reporting wrong data (it appears to have an issue on nonpaged pool data, for instance), but its output is consistent with the performance counter value, itself above 33,554,432. It is therefore possible that version 6.12 has been updated to account for additional system PTEs of which version 6.11 had no knowledge.

50.9 Modified Page List Bytes

Process Explorer name: Modified, ModifiedNoWrite, in the Paging Lists section (in kB)
Kernel variable: see modified lists details in sec. 29.1.2 on p. 194

The combined sizes of the Modified and Modified No Write lists, converted in bytes. Process explorer gives separate values for the two lists, which, when added together, give the same value reported by this counter.

The size of the Modified list only, as reported by Process Explorer is also equal to:

    MmModifiedPageListHead.Total * 4

The kernel variable stores the count in pages, so multiplying it by 4 gives the amount in kB, as reported by Process Explorer.

50.10   Page Reads/sec

Process Explorer name: Page Read Delta in the Paging section
Kernel variable: unknown

Rate of read operations performed to resolve hard faults. Counts read operations, not pages, and a single read typically loads a cluster of multiple pages. Includes reads on the paging files, on mapped files and on cached files. We saw in Chapter 49 (p. 543) that, ultimately, an access to a cached file causes an access to a view of a section and, eventually, an hard fault.

Note how this means that this counter also includes reads caused by regular file I/O. This can be verified with MemTests by opening a big file, e.g. 1GB in size, and reading it (menu options: *Open existing test file* and *File read test*). While the read is in progress, we see this counter showing a sustained read rate.

50.11   Page Writes/sec

Process Explorer name: see description
Kernel variable: unknown

Rate of write operations performed to save the content of modified memory pages to the file system. The Performance Monitor counter description implies this is the overall rate and should therefore include writes to any file, not just the paging file. Process Explorer reports two distinct counters: Paging File Write Delta and Mapped File Write Delta, so their sum should be equal to this counter value.

Write operations to the paging file have been analyzed in sec. 29.2 on p. 200 and writes to mapped file in sec. 38.2.4 on p. 353.

Since the file system cache accesses files by mapping them, this counter includes writes resulting from regular file I/O.

50.12   Pool Nonpaged Bytes

Process Explorer name: see description
Kernel variable: unknown

There appears to be some confusion on the definition of this counter in the sources examined.

According to [1], p. 722, which applies to Windows Vista and Windows Server 2008, it represents the "Size of the initial nonpaged pool. This can be reduced automatically by the system if memory demands dictate."

in [20], which applies to Windows Server 2003, we find the following description:

"Shows the size, in bytes, of the nonpaged pool. Pool Nonpaged Bytes is calculated differently than Process\Pool Nonpaged Bytes, so it might not equal Process(_Total)\Pool Nonpaged Bytes."

However, it is likely that this counter actually reports the current nonpaged pool usage.

We can better understand this issue if we turn our attention on the data needed to describe the nonpaged pool (NPP) status. The VMM computes the maximum size for the NPP as 75% of available RAM or 128GB, whichever is smaller ([21]). The actual size of the pool is, in general, smaller than this value. If the pool is becoming fully allocated and its size is below the maximum, the VMM expands it. Thus, we have two pool sizes defined: the maximum size and the current size. Finally, at any given time, only a certain amount of NPP is in use, which gives us a third quantity describing the NPP state: its current usage.

It seems more likely that the Pool Nonpaged Bytes counter represents the current NPP usage, rather than the current size, for several reasons.

In [21] we find the following statement:

"There are three performance counters that indicate pool *usage*:

•Pool nonpaged bytes

•Pool paged bytes (virtual size of paged pool – some may be paged out)

•Pool paged resident bytes (physical size of paged pool)"

Also, while [1] states on p. 722 that this counter is the "Size of the initial nonpaged pool [...]" it also states that it is equal to the value of MmSizeOfNonPagedPoolInBytes. However, we can see that this variable is not equal to the counter value. As an example, below we find a screenshot of Performance Monitor followed by WinDbg data:

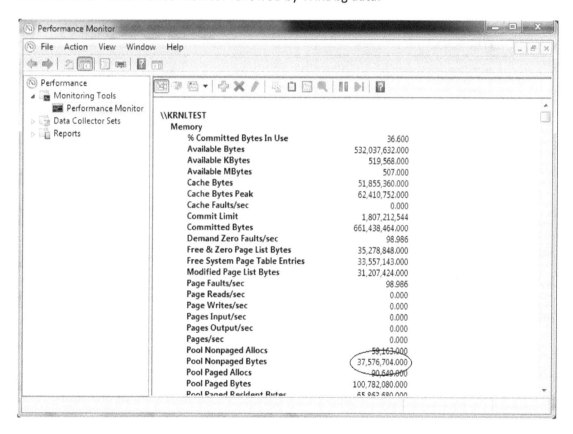

Figure 65 - Pool Nonpaged Bytes

```
0: kd> ? poi(nt!MmSizeOfNonPagedPoolInBytes)
Evaluate expression: 44023808 = 00000000`029fc000
```

It seems more likely that the static is storing the current NPP size, as its name suggests, while the counter represents current usage, which, naturally, is below the size.

Another piece of evidence comes from Process Explorer, which reports the value named Nonpaged, which matches the counter, albeit expressed in kB:

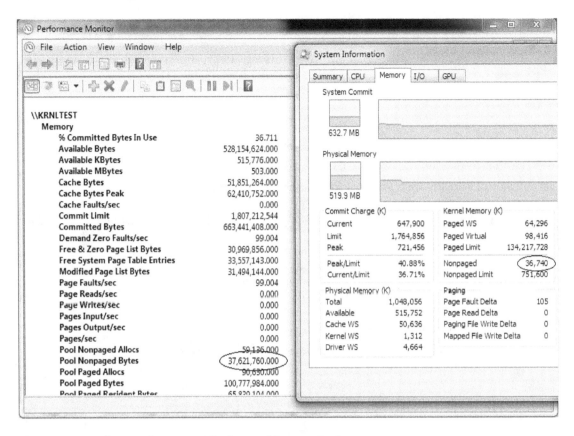

Figure 66 - NPP from Performance Monitor and Process Explorer

By converting Nonpaged in bytes we have:

36,740 * 1,024 = 37,621,760

Finally, it can be noticed that, while the system runs, Pool Nonpaged Bytes is continuously changing and it seems unlikely that the VMM adjusts the pool size so often, while it is perfectly reasonable to have a continuous fluctuation in pool usage.

50.13   Pool Paged Resident Bytes

Process Explorer name: Paged WS (in kB)
Kernel variable: `MmPagedPoolWs.WorkingSetSize` (in pages)

The size in bytes of the paged pool working set.

50.14   Standby Cache Counters

Process Explorer name: see description

Kernel variable: see sec. 29.2.1 on p. 200 for details on the Standby list

The three counters named Standby Cache Core Bytes, Standby Cache Normal Priority Bytes and Standby Cache Reserve Bytes are computed by summing the page counts of Standby lists at different priorities.

By comparing their values with the ones reported by Process Explorer for each priority we can see that:

- Standby Cache Core Bytes is the sum of page counts for priorities 6-7

- Standby Cache Normal Priority Bytes is the page count for priority 5

- Standby Cache Reserve Bytes is the sum of page counts for priorities 0-4

50.15   System Cache Resident Bytes

Process Explorer name: Cache WS, in the Physical Memory section (in kB)
Kernel variable: `MmSystemCacheWs.WorkingSetSize` (in pages)

The size of the working set of the file system cache, in bytes. See sec. 44.6.1 on p. 428.

In Windows 7, this counter has the same value of the Cache Bytes counter.

50.16   System Code Resident Bytes

Process Explorer name: Kernel WS, in the Physical Memory section (in kB)
Kernel variable: `MmSystemCodePage` (in pages)

The number of currently resident pageable pages used by the kernel, converted in bytes. This is one of the components of the System PTE working set, see sec. 44.8.4 on p. 473. This value does not include physical pages consumed by non-pageable code.

50.17   System Driver Resident Bytes

Process Explorer name: Driver WS, in the Physical Memory section (in kB)
Kernel variable: `MmSystemDriverPage` (in pages)

The number of currently resident pageable pages used by kernel mode driver images, converted in bytes. This is one of the components of the System PTE working set, see sec. 44.8.4 on p. 473. This value does not include physical pages consumed by non-pageable code.

Appendixes

A The !pfn Command Extension

This appendix describes most of the information displayed by the !pfn extension, which formats the content of an _MMPFN.

Below is the output for an active dirty page:

```
0: kd> !pfn 3faec
    PFN 0003FAEC at address FFFFFA8000BF0C40
    flink       00000183  blink / share count 00000001  pteaddress FFFFF68000000600
    reference count 0001     used entry count  0000        Cached     color 0   Priority 5
    restore pte 00000080  containing page      00F369 Active     M
    Modified
```

We are now going to explain the information printed.

at address: after this label, the address of the _MMPFN instance for the page is displayed. We can examine it with dt nt!_MMPFN *address*

flink: the value of _MMPFN.u1. This member has different meanings depending on the page state.

- For an active page like the one above, it stores the index of the WS entry for the page (_MMPFN.u1.WsIndex).

- When the page is on PFN-linked a list, it stores the forward link, expressed as the PFN of the next page on the list (_MMPFN.u1.Flink). For any page, the PFN is also the index of the _MMPFN instance for the page in the PFN database. If the page is the last one of the list, this member is set to 0xFFFFFFFFFFFFFFFF.

- When the page is on a singly linked list, it stores the virtual address of the next _MMPFN instance (_MMPFN.u1.Next).

- When there is a read in progress on the page, it stores the address of the event which is signaled when the operation completes (_MMPFN.u1.Event).

blink / share count: the value of _MMPFN.u2, which also has different meanings depending on the state.

- For an active page, it stores the share count (_MMPFN.u2.ShareCount). For private pages the share count is 0 or 1; for paging structures pages and shared memory it can be greater than 1.

- For a page on a PFN-linked list, it stores the PFN of the previous page on the list, or 0xFFFFFFFFFFFFFFFF if this is the first page (`_MMPFN.u2.Blink`).

`pteaddress`: `_MMPFN.PteAddress`, i.e. the address of the PTE mapping this page, when applicable.

`reference count`: the value of `_MMPFN.u3.ReferenceCount`, which is the page reference count.

`used entry count`: the value of `_MMPFN.UsedPageTableEntries`.

`Cached/NonCached/WriteComb`: to the right of the `used entry count` value, is a label corresponding to the value of `_MMPFN.u3.e1.CacheAttribute` (see sec. 26.6.3 on p. 167). The following table shows the relationship between the member value and the label:

CacheAttribute	Label
00	NonCached
01	Cached
10	WriteComb

`Priority`: the value of `_MMPFN.u3.e1.Priority`, representing the memory priority of the page.

`restore pte`: the content of `_MMPFN.OriginalPte`, i.e. the value to assign to the PTE mapping the page, when the latter is repurposed.

`containing page`: the value of `_MMPFN.u4.PteFrame`, i.e. the PFN of the paging structure storing the PTE mapping this page.

`Zeroed/Free/...`: to the right of the value of `containing page` is a label corresponding to the value of `_MMPFN.u3.e1.PageLocation`, which represents the page state. The following table shows the relationship between the label and the member value:

PageLocation	Label
000	Zeroed
001	Free
010	Standby
011	Modified
100	ModNoWrt
101	Bad
110	Active
111	Trans

Flags: to the right of the page state is a set of one character labels each corresponding to a flag bit in the _MMPFN. If the corresponding bit is set, the label is printed, together with a long, more readable label on the line below. In the example above, we see the short label M and the long label Modified. They are printed because this page has _MMPF.u3.e1.Modified = 1. The following table shows each flag bit together with the short label and the long label.

Bit	Short Label	Long Label
_MMPFN.u3.e1.WriteInProgress	W	WriteInProgress
_MMPFN.u3.e1.Modified	M	Modified[1]
_MMPFN.u3.e1.ReadInProgress	R	ReadInProgress
_MMPFN.u3.e1.Rom	No label printed	No label printed
_MMPFN.u3.e1.InPageError	E	InPageError
_MMPFN.u3.e1.KernelStack	No label printed	No label printed

_MMPFN.u3.e1.RemovalRequested	Y	RemovalRequested
_MMPFN.u3.e1.ParityError	X	ParityError
_MMPFN.u4.PrototypePte	P	Shared

Notes

1. This label should not be confused with the identical one printed when the page is on the Modified list. Below is a sample `!pfn` output showing both labels:

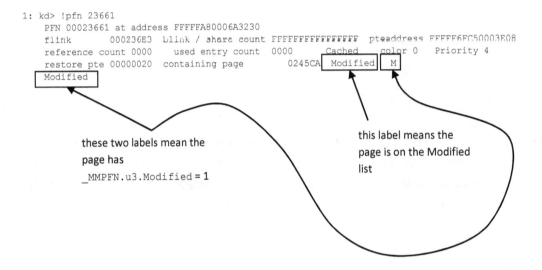

Table of Figures

Acronyms

BSM: Balance Set Manager

CM: Cache Manager

CPL: Current Privilege Level

DDI: Device Driver Interface

IDT: Interrupt Descriptor Table

IRQL: Interrupt Request Level

ISR: Interrupt Service Routine

LFH: Low Fragmentation Heap

LRU: Least Recently Used

MAPW: Mapped Page Writer

MDL: Memory Descriptor List

MPW: Modified Page Writer

MTRR: Memory Type Range Register

NPP: Nonpaged Pool

NUMA: Non Uniform Memory Access

OS: Operating System

PAT: Page Attribute Table

PD: Page Directory

PDE: Page Directory Entry

PDPT: Page Directory Pointer Table

PDPTE: Page Directory Pointer Table Entry

PE32+: Portable Executable 32+

PF: Page Fault

PFN: Page Frame Number

PFNDB: Page Frame Number Database

PFNDBE: Page Frame Number Database Entry

PML4: Page Map Level 4

PML4E: Page Map Level 4 Entry

PP: Paged Pool

PS: Paging Structure

PT: Page Table

PTE: Page Table Entry

PxE: Generic Paging Structure Entry

RVA: Relative Virtual Address

SMP: Symmetric Multiprocessing

TLB: Translation Lookaside Buffer

TSS: Task Status Segment

UC: Uncached Memory

UMAB: User Mode Address Space Bitmap

UMPB: User Mode Page Tables Bitmap

VA: Virtual Address

VPN: Virtual Page Number

WB: Writeback Memory

WC: Write Combining Memory

WS: Working Set

WSL: Working Set List

WSLE: Working Set List Entry

WSM: Working Set Manager

References

[1] -   M. E. Russinovich, D. A. Solomon, A. Ionescu, *Windows Internals*, 5th edition, 2009, Microsoft Press

[2] -   *X64 Kernel* Virtual *Address Space*, CodeMachine

http://www.codemachine.com/article_x64kvas.html

[3] -   D. A. Solomon, M. E. Russinovich, *Inside Microsoft Windows 2000*, 3rd edition, Microsoft Press, 2000

[4] -   B. Dolan-Gavitt, *The VAD tree: A process-eye view of physical memory*, Digital Investigation 4S (2007) S62 – S64, DFRWS, Elsevier Ltd.

http://www.dfrws.org/2007/proceedings/p62-dolan-gavitt.pdf

[5] -   W. Lei, *TRK Case 1: Working Set*, Beihang University, Microsoft Research

http://research.microsoft.com/en-us/collaboration/global/asia-pacific/programs/trk_case1_working_set.pdf

[6] -   *Advances in Memory Management for Windows*, Microsoft Corporation, October 12, 2007

http://msdn.microsoft.com/en-us/windows/hardware/gg463344

[7] -   T. Sneath, *PDC10: Mysteries of Windows Memory Management Revealed*, MSDN Blogs, Tim Sneath, Microsoft Corporation

http://blogs.msdn.com/b/tims/archive/2010/10/28/pdc10-mysteries-of-windows-memory-management-revealed-part-one.aspx

http://blogs.msdn.com/b/tims/archive/2010/10/29/pdc10-mysteries-of-windows-memory-management-revealed-part-two.aspx

[8] -   J. Ross, *Silver's Weblog - Windows' Memory Management*, October 26, 2006

http://james-ross.co.uk/weblog/2006/10/26/01

[9] -   U. Drepper, *What Every Programmer Should Know About Memory*, November 21, 2007, Red Hat, Inc.

http://www.unilim.fr/sci/wiki/_media/cali/cpumemory.pdf

[10] -   *Comparison of 32-bit and 64-bit memory architecture for 64-bit editions of Windows XP and Windows Server 2003*, Article ID: 294418 - Last Review: April 29, 2008 - Revision: 6.1, Microsoft Corporation

http://support.microsoft.com/kb/294418

[11] -   *Intel 64 and IA-32 Architectures Software Developer's Manual*, September 2010, Order Numbers 253665-036US (Vol. 1), 253666-036US (Vol. 2A), 253667-036US (Vol. 2B), 253668-036US (Vol. 3A), 253669-036US (Vol. 3B) , Intel Corporation

[12] -   S. B. Schreiber, *Undocumented Windows 2000 Secrets*, 2001, Addison-Wesley

[13] -   M. Pietrek, *An In-Depth Look into the Win32 Portable Executable File Format*, MSDN Magazine, February, 2002, Microsoft Corporation

[14] -   *MSDN Library for Visual Studio 2008 SP1*, Microsoft Corporation

[15] -   *How To Manage User Privileges Programmatically in Windows NT*, Article ID: 132958 - Last Review: March 1, 2005 - Revision: 3.2, Microsoft Corporation

http://support.microsoft.com/kb/132958/en-us?fr=1

[16] -   *Windows Driver Kit Documentation*, WDK version 7.1.0, Microsoft Corporation

[17] -   M. Justice, *Desktop Heap Overview*, Ntdebugging Blog, January 4, 2007, Microsoft Corporation

http://blogs.msdn.com/b/ntdebugging/archive/2007/01/04/desktop-heap-overview.aspx

[18] -   *Master of the Obvious -- MDLs are Lists that Describe Memory*, The NT Insider, Vol 12, Issue 4, September-October 2005, Open Systems Resources, Inc.

http://www.osronline.com/custom.cfm?name=articlePrint.cfm&id=423

[19] -   M. Russinovich, *Pushing the Limits of Windows: Processes and Threads*, Mark Russinovich's Blog, July 8, 2009, Microsoft Corporation

http://blogs.technet.com/b/markrussinovich/archive/2009/07/08/3261309.aspx

[20] -   *Memory Object*, Windows Server 2003 Deployment Guide, Microsoft Corporation

http://technet.microsoft.com/en-us/library/cc778082(WS.10).aspx

[21] -   M. Russinovich, *Pushing the Limits of Windows: Paged and Nonpaged Pool*, Mark Russinovich's Blog, March 26, 2009, Microsoft Corporation

http://blogs.technet.com/b/markrussinovich/archive/2009/03/26/3211216.aspx

[22] -   E. Martignetti, *Windows Vista APC Internals*, May 2009

http://www.opening-windows.com/techart_windows_vista_apc_internals.htm

Enrico Martignetti

Enrico Martignetti graduated in Electronic Engineering at Politecnico di Torino in 1993. He has been working as a software developer since 1990 and has been cultivating a strong interest on the Windows architecture since the late nineties, when he decided, quite short-sightedly, to study the kernel of Windows 98. He then moved to the Windows NT family kernel in 2001 and has been trying to make sense of it ever since.

www.ingramcontent.com/pod-product-compliance
Lightning Source LLC
Chambersburg PA
CBHW080130060326
40689CB00018B/3735

9781479114290